MW01265474

This publication is designed to provide information and opinions in regard to its subject matter. It is sold with the understanding that the publisher and author (and all those associated with them) are not engaged in rendering legal, accounting, psychological, or other professional service. If legal advice or other expert assistance is required, the services of a competent professional person should be sought.

Derived from a Declaration of Principles Jointly Adopted by a Committee of the American Bar Association and a Committee of Publishers and Associations.

This book is not a substitute for legal advice. *Statement required by the Texas State Bar Association.*

ISBN (print version) 978-0-9716188-1-7

ISBN (ebook version) 978-0-9716188-2-4

Book design and layout by Diane Nolden

Library of Congress Control Number: 2007900670

Blue House Press
322 Walker Loop Road
Huntsville, TX 77342

To the men in my life and especially Glenn,
who helped me understand.

The Laws of Love:

A Legal Guide for Couples

The following icons are used throughout the book to highlight the specified information.

ICON	MEANING
	Questions and answers
	Key points
	Myths and fantasies
	Legal points and cases
	Look out!
	Checklists and important records you may want to keep

Disclaimer and Waiver

This book is intended to provide informative and provocative opinions for people who are curious about the law governing marriage and cohabitation relationships. It is not a substitute either for consultation with an experienced legal professional or for counseling or therapy. No part of this book should be relied on in place of personal advice from an attorney or mental health professional.

Marriage or living together can be one of the most important relationships of one's life, financially and emotionally, for oneself and those one cares about, including children; to rely on a guidebook like this in handling such an important matter could lead to unwanted consequences. The law is complicated and facts that appear insignificant to non-lawyers can change the outcome of a case. Individual psychology is even more complicated and unique to each person and couple.

Some of the cases discussed are hypothetical cases or examples created by combining aspects of several different cases. In every real case, the rules of procedure, state law, evidence, local practice, court orders, and applicable case law should be independently checked by an attorney. Laws, rules, and other matters can change frequently and without notice to the non-lawyer community, and state laws vary from state to state.

If you are troubled by aspects of your relationship, you should consult a reputable therapist, pastor, or other professional who can help you with your particular situation.

If you or your significant other suffers from any mental or emotional illness, including depression, you should consult with a therapist before using this or any other self help book to avoid inadvertently causing additional problems. If you are in therapy, you should discuss the advisability of using this book with your therapist.

Table of Contents

Chapter One

Love, law, and lawyers 1

    Using this book 4

    Families and the law 9

    Nature of American law 10

        A moveable population 19

        Dealing with attorneys – choosing your lawyer 24

        Dealing with lawyers – the basics of consulting an attorney 25

        A special situation — dealing with social workers and psychologists 33

    Conclusions and advice 34

Chapter Two

A brief history of love 35

    Love and marriage in historical context 37

    Our myths about love and marriage in past times 40

        Historical evidence about birth control 51

        Moral and legal opinion on birth control 55

    The history of marriage as a legal institution – common law and ceremonial 69

        The legal status of informal marriage 69

        Society's interests in the marital relationship 72

        Social attitudes and laws about sexual relations 73

        Social attitudes and laws about children and marriage 76

        Social attitudes and laws about marriage and property 77

        Social attitudes and laws about love and marriage 80

        The effect of social migration on marriage laws 82

    Conclusion 83

Chapter Three

Love and marriage today 87

    Cohabitation 87

        Social reality of cohabitation 88

        Emotional reality of cohabitation 89

        Duration of cohabiting relationships 90

Effect on children whose parents cohabit 91
Legal reality of cohabitation 93
Marriage and Divorce 96
Sociological Facts 96
The liberalization of divorce laws 97
Well-being, marriage, and cohabitation 98
Social changes, laws, and values 101
Religion, marriage, and sex 102
Conclusions and advice 103

Chapter Four

Same sex couples and the law 105
Persons of varying sexuality 105
Homosexuality and marriage 106
Domestic Partner Benefits 110
Homosexuality and Other Sexual Variations Conduct as Illegal 114
Marriage and Same Sex Couples — the Goodridge case 121
Cohabitation agreements and same sex couples 126
Discrimination and sexual preference 128
Transgender, bisexuality and other variations 130
Conclusions and advice 134

Chapter Five

Marriage and living together —what's the (legal) difference? 137
Owning things 140
Unmarried Couples 142
Ownership 148
Married Couples 148
Table of state laws on common law marriage and property 150
Management of property during marriage 155
Ownership of different kinds of property — married or not 159
Social security and pension benefits 168
Other legal implications of marriage and cohabitation 169
Medical and financial decisions for incapacitated persons 179
Income and estate taxes 180

Testimonial Privilege 183
Discrimination in housing 183
Other governmental programs 184
Abuse – physical and emotional 185
Contracts 188
Domestic partnerships and other legal connections 188
Polygamy, polyandry, and polyamory — the more the merrier? 191
Lawsuits and living together 194
Ending the relationship – amicably and otherwise 194
Going to court 195
Other differences between marriage and living together 197
Conclusions and advice 198
Table of Differences between marriage and cohabitation 199

Chapter Six

Marriage and Divorce 203
Beginning a marriage 204
Ceremonial marriage 204
Covenant marriage 209
Lawsuits about marriage 210
Common law marriage 211
Ending a marriage 220
Separation 221
Annulment 222
Divorce 227
Conclusions and Advice 229

Chapter Seven

The Rights of Children and Parents 231
Children's rights and parental obligations 232
To be taken care of 234
Medical care – parental duties and rights 234
Medical care – a child's right to decide 244
Support and contracts 246
The unexpected child 247
To inherit 249

To be free from abuse and neglect 251
Cohabitation and children 261
Special issues – gay and lesbian parents 261
Termination and limitation of parental rights 263
The rights of adults with regard to children 268
When children aren't wanted 269
Sterilization and birth control 269
Abortion 271
Biology and the law 275
Married parents 276
Custody after divorce 277
Gender and custody 278
Grandparents – visitation and custody 279
Unmarried parents 280
Establishment of paternity 281
Marriage, biology, and love 282
Contracts and children 285
Responsibility of a parent for a child's actions 286
Inheritance 287
The incapacitated parent — support, abuse, and medical decisions 287
An injured adult family member and lawsuits 291
A disabled family member 292
Different biological relationships — assisted reproduction 293
Proposed clarification of the law on parentage 301
Adoption 304
Conclusions and advice 314

Chapter Eight

Promises, promises 317
What contracts can and can't do for a relationship 317
The real law of contracts (or at least the part of it about couples) 326
Elements of a valid contract 326
Consideration 327
Ascertainable terms – written and oral contracts 328
Unenforceable and unlawful contracts 329
The facts and nothing but the facts – disclosure to each other. 330
Contracts in intimate relationships 334

The law is not charitable to people who do dumb things. 335
    Fairness 338
    Trust 339
Conclusions and advice 347

Chapter Nine

Writing a Contract for Yourself 349
  Basic procedure 350
    The Important Questions 352
    Steps to a Contract 354
    Money – yours, mine and ours 355
    Children – yours, mine, and ours? 357
  Standard Clauses 358
    All the terms and nothing but the terms 358
    Anti-modification clauses 359
    Consideration 359
    Arbitration and mediation clauses. 359
    Choice of law 362
    Prenuptial/marital agreement waiver clauses 362
    Sample agreement 363
    Conclusions and Advice 366

Chapter Ten

Getting clear about your relationship 367
  Expectations about your relationship 368
  Patterns from the past — desires conscious and unconscious 371
  What to do with this information together 379
  Conclusions and advice 381

Chapter Eleven

The Tangled Web — What a Mess We Can Make 383
  Neither fish nor fowl 383
  More Myths about Love and the Law 384
  Effect of a prior entanglement on subsequent relationships 389
    Bigamy 389

    Alimony (spousal support) that you are receiving 390

    Alimony that you are paying 390

    Child support and child custody 391

  Effect of prior relationships on assets you own 391

  Why straighten it out? 392

  The right way 394

  Children 395

  Conclusions and Advice 396

Chapter Twelve

Crafting families 397

  Together, but separate 397

    Guidelines for protecting your assets in a relationship 398

  Legal togetherness — sharing a future 399

  How much financial disclosure do we need? 401

    Financial Information to share 402

    Checking on financial disclosures (and other matters) 403

    What financial matters should a couple consider? 405

  Other questions about the relationship — children 408

  Taking care of each other legally 409

  Other legal documents 411

    Wills and trusts 411

    Durable powers of attorney and advance directives 419

    Designation of guardian 423

  Taking care of each other legally – relationships with other people 425

  Conclusions and Advice 427

Chapter Thirteen

Living Together and Loving Each Other – Older Couples 429

  Financial matters 430

    Governmental benefits 430

  Inheritance rights 432

  Benefit Rights 433

  Kids and grandkids 434

Taking care of each other legally 438

Conclusions and advice 442

Chapter Fourteen

Breaking Up a Long-term Relationship 443

Legal rights and realities at the end 444

Division of assets when a cohabiting couple part company 445

Debts and cohabiting couples 450

Undoing formal entanglements with other people 450

Terminating a cohabitation agreement 451

Terminating moral obligations 451

Division of property when a marriage ends by divorce or annulment 452

Community property states 453

Title to assets 454

Mingled assets and contributions by one spouse to the other 455

The court's discretion in community property states 456

Equitable distribution states (non community property states) 457

Common Issues in all states 458

Spousal misconduct 458

Pensions and other benefits 459

Alimony and spousal support 460

Prenuptial agreements, divorce agreements, and married couples 462

Debts and divorce 463

Finality – getting it all over with 464

Division of property when one of you dies 466

Inheritance 467

Legal Mechanics 467

Will or no will 469

A dead person's debts 473

Life insurance 477

Children 481

Children who were not born in this relationship 481

Children born of this relationship 484

Children born out of wedlock 484

Children born in a marriage 485

Child Custody – the legal mechanics 485
    Courtroom procedures 487
    Factors considered 488
    Division of the child 489
    Custody agreements and court orders 490
    Child support 494
    Enforcement of support orders 501
    Custody struggles – when disagreement becomes crime 502
Disputes over child custody 503
Mechanics of splitting up 504
    Peaceable splits 505
    When things are not (entirely) amicable? 506
Prudent salvage — the paperwork 506
More steps to protect yourself – joint assets 507
When things are really ugly. 508
Dealing with an abusive significant other 520
Enforcing a cohabitation agreement 520
Conclusions and Advice 521

Chapter Fifteen

Truth, proof, and evidence — Lovers and Lawyers 523
    Summary of lawsuits and mediations 524
Going to court 525
    Truth, justice, and reality – both sides now 525
    Settlement – the art of compromise 526
    Be prepared 527
What counts as evidence and proof 531
    Documents 533
    Witnesses' statements 533
Truth, proof, and evidence—common law marriage 535
Truth, proof, and evidence — paternity, maternity, and child custody 536
    Paternity 536
    Unwed mothers 536
    Unwed fathers. 537
    Child custody cases 539
    Child support cases 541

Truth, proof, and evidence — cohabitation and prenuptial agreements 542
    Times have changed 546
    I don't want to 547
    We didn't exactly adhere to the terms of the agreement 547
    I was robbed 548
    We never got around to signing an agreement 549
Truth, proof and evidence – divorce and money 550
Conclusions and advice 551

The Workbook
Places to go for help 556
    Places and people 556
    Useful references — books 557
    Internet resources 558
    Looking up the law 560
Sample Agreements 562
    Suggested Clauses for More Complicated Relationships 563
    Taking Care of Each Other — More Documents 587
    Directive to Physicians (Texas form) 591
    Powers of Attorney — Points to Consider 595
    Last Will and Testament 601
    Writing wills – the details 601
    Other preparations for death or incapacity – funerals, pets, etc. 603
    Sample will — notes 604
    Revocation of Documents 610
Informal Marriage 611
    Common law marriage questions 611
    Here's How To Understand Your Answers 615
Breaking Up 617
    Basic steps to take when you break up with a significant other 617
    What to do if things are acrimonious and may wind up in court 618
    Organizing your case 618
    Basic questions for all relationship disputes 618
    Child Custody and Visitation Questions 620
    Information for Fathers of Children Born Out of Wedlock 621
    You want an active role in a child's life, but baby is not yet born ... 622
    Checklist — what to do after the child is born 624
    Checklist for men (wrongfully) named as a child's father 629

      Agreement for support and custody of a child — considerations 630
   Cohabitation dispute information 633
      Preparation for a child custody dispute 634
      Checklist of steps to take in a cohabitation agreement dispute 640
      Considerations in getting evidence from witnesses 642
      Considerations in your own testimony 643
      Considerations in other people's testimony 644
      Documents in disputes and common law marriage questions 645
      Documents to gather 645
         Coast Guard Requirements to Prove Common-law Marriage 647
         Sample Affidavits 648
  Other family disputes – parents and adult children 654
 Understanding Your Relationship 656
   Questions toward understanding a relationship 658
      Consequences of your answers 662
      Seeing your partner clearly 665
      What to do with this information alone 668
      What to do with this information together 670
      Consequences and conclusions—myself 671
      Consequences and conclusions about my significant other 671
      Using this information 672

Glossary 673

Index 677

The Laws of Love:

The Main Volume

General information
History of the law
Summaries of the law
Guidance for couples

Chapter One

LOVE, LAW, AND LAWYERS

The institution of marriage weaves together many strands of human life. Attitudes toward love, money, sex, affection, dependency, property, morality, religious belief, and social standing interweave in the law of marriage. Those strands also form some of the issues about which people have the most passionate opinions.

This chapter surveys the various ways in which laws and courts affects families, including an introduction to dealing with lawyers and courts. It also includes a synopsis of the structure of the American legal system. To really understand your own rights and obligations, you need to have a basic understanding of the government that enforces them.

In today's United States society, we label heterosexual couples according to the social category of their relationship. Some are married, some are dating, some are just friends, and some are living together but not married. Sometimes, we're not sure exactly what kind of relationship our friends have. Remarkably often, neither are they! Each of these social categories has different, and often unforeseen, legal consequences.

We usually think of married couples as those who have gone through a ceremony. In thirteen states, however, a couple that lives together as husband and wife can be legally married without any formal ceremony. That marriage is a "common law" or "informal" marriage. A common law marriage exists when the couple lives together as husband and wife in one of those states, intend to be married, and tell people that they are married.

The Laws of Love is a guide to some of the legal ramifications of being a couple. Couples who do not wish to be married in a marriage ceremony can use it to explore the legal consequences of their decision. Couples who wish to marry can learn more about the legal consequences of marriage. Married or not, couples may decide that they need a clear agreement about their financial commitment, or lack of commitment, to each other. For engaged couples, that agreement is called a "prenuptial agreement." For unmarried couples, it is called a "cohabitation agreement." For couples who are already married, it is called a "marital agreement."

The best use of this book is as a springboard to consider your own personal situation, including your values and needs. When you understand the legal implications of the various possibilities, you may decide that you and your children will be happiest in a stable marriage based on your faith, culture, and family traditions. If you can marry a person who shares those values and if both of you are willing to work to keep those values in your marriage, then you and your children may perhaps enjoy a rich and happy family life. On the other hand, you may come to realize that you want to avoid emotional or financial commitment to your significant other. In addition to limiting your relationships to persons of like mind, you can take steps to keep your assets separate from those of your lover. Or, you may decide that a committed, but non-marital, arrangement best suits your values and character, in which case you may want to document your financial expectations of each other in a written agreement.

Understanding the law that applies to couples requires understanding the interaction of society and the legal system. Changes in the way people live affect the law. People's beliefs about morality and the law affect the way that they conduct themselves.

This remainder of this chapter explains the framework of the American legal system, into which the laws governing families fit. The next two chapters sketch the evolving perception of marriage in America and the history of the laws governing families. Later chapters provide guidance on the legal mechanics of marriage and cohabitation.

QUESTION: *"We want to get married. Is this book only for people who are living in sin?"*

ANSWER: *No. The information in this book about family law applies to everyone.*

This is a book for couples of all kinds. The legal affairs of unmarried couples, however, can be more uncertain and unstable. That is because the law is unsettled on cohabitation issues. Also, cohabiting couples often are deliberately not making the commitment of marriage. Therefore, that couple may need to take more care to protect their respective interests. On the other hand, many married couples also use written agreements to document their financial expectations and to avoid legal consequences that they don't want.

This book is primarily written in terms of heterosexual couples, because most of the decided cases on couples concern relationships between a man and a woman. At present, no state solidly recognizes the union of two people of the same sex as a legal marriage. Vermont and Massachusetts are in the process of recognizing gay unions, as have several European countries and some Canadian provinces. Other states are passing laws prohibiting such marriages. California's law is in turmoil.

Gay and lesbian couples can use this book to protect their mutual expectations. Given the legal uncertainties surrounding homosexual marriage, a homosexual couple need to take appropriate legal actions, such as having valid wills, to take care of each other financially.

The fact that this book is for all couples makes it difficult to know how to refer to the people who comprise couples. Obviously, terms like "spouse" or "husband and wife" would make all this advice sound like it only applied to married people. On the other hand, terms like "lover" have a pejorative tone to some people. Even though sex is an important part of marriage, "lover" can sound like an illicit relationship. "Significant other" is nice and neutral but cumbersome. The term "partner" is widely used today to refer to the other party in a committed relationship. I don't like that term because it is ambiguous between its social use for romantic relationships and its legal use for business partnerships.

Therefore, I have made some effort to use terms like "spouse" where I intend to discuss married people, "lover" for more informal relationships, and "significant other" or "partner" for committed relationships, whether married or not. However, the use of the term "lover" does not mean that the information is irrelevant to a married couple.

This book does not cover all the important legal topics about families. First, this is a general work. No one book can be a reliable guide for handling any individual case or writing an agreement for any real couple. It's a starting point, not a road map. For life's important financial matters, the best course is to see a competent attorney about your own individual needs. The reasons why people need attorneys, including the times when they may not, are discussed starting at page 25.

Second, this book does not provide guidance on establishing a good relationship or solving the emotional problems in an existing one. Friends and competent therapists can help with your emotional issues. The best source for help on the intricate and delicate matter of relationships is a good therapist. Self-help books can be useful in gathering one's thoughts but, again, a book is inherently a source of general advice, not personal guidance.

Third, this book seeks to remain relatively neutral about some of the crucial legal and moral issues facing our society. It is not my purpose to argue for, or against, cohabitation, or homosexual marriage, or abortion, or reform of the child custody system to give more rights to fathers. The respective merits of these issues belong in a different book.

This book tries to stay within historical, social, and legal reality. The reality is that cohabitation without marriage is now a part of our social fabric.

However, the fact that a living arrangement has become common in society does not mean that it is fully recognized by the legal institutions nor that it is the best living arrangement that a couple might choose. Many sociological studies suggest that a stable marriage benefits both the married couple and their children. On the other hand, some sociologists disagree about the proper interpretation of the statistics and the validity of the scientists' conclusions.

Using this book

The Laws of Love is for people who want to think through the various aspects of their relationship. People who understand the basic law governing families can consider the extent to which the law protects, or does not protect, their expectations of relationships. The best way to use this book is to read it straight through once and then return to the chapters that seem most relevant to your present situation.

If you have a specific question at this very moment, such about common law marriage or child custody, then you can turn now to that particular chapter and to the related material in the Workbook sections.

Reading one chapter in isolation, however, creates a greater risk that you will misunderstand part of your situation. A court may consider rules from different areas of law to reach a final decision.

Even if you already have decided that you want a cohabitation or prenuptial agreement, for example, you should to read at least the chapters on the legal implications of marriage.

Cohabitation agreements and contracts made before a couple marries (prenuptial agreements) change the obligations that a couple would otherwise have to each other. It would be unwise to just glance over the contract chapters and then open the workbook section at a likely-looking form. You run the risk that you will overlook some fact about your relationship or some legal consideration that could be important to your decision.

In other words, if a couple decide to live together and have a written cohabitation agreement, they are foregoing the rights (or avoiding the legal burdens) that marriage would afford them. Such a decision should be made knowingly. Similarly, an engaged couple that decides to arrange their financial obligations to each other before the marriage by a prenuptial agreement would be wise to understand the way that their agreement changes the rights and obligations that the law would otherwise afford.

Here's a chart to help you find responses to some common questions. Remember, there may be additional information in another chapter on a related topic.

Guide to The Laws of Love - a Table of Common Questions and Answers

Question	How to find an answer	Where to look
Are we common law married?	If you intended to be married, told people that you were married, and lived together as husband and wife in one of the 13 states that recognizes common law marriage, you may well be married.	See Chapter Eight
What rights does the father of my child have if we are not married?	Until a court rules differently, both parents theoretically have equal rights to custody of their child and equal obligations to support the child. Usually, a court will award primary custody to the mother and visitation to the father.	See Chapter Seven
My husband and I are getting divorced and his lawyer says that my husband gets all our savings because we signed a prenuptial agreement. Is that possible?	The answer depends on the terms of the prenuptial agreement and whether you were fairly advised and informed when you signed it.	See Chapter Eight and Chapter Fifteen
Does the mother of my child have to pay child support if I have custody?	Normally yes, if the child is biologically hers.	See Chapter Nine
I want to get health insurance for my significant other from my employer. Do we have to get married?	Probably. Some states have domestic partner laws and some employers have voluntarily provided these benefits to domestic partners, regardless of sexual orientation.	Check with your employer's human resources department and with the insurance company itself to be sure. See Chapter Four
My significant other and I adopted a child while we were together. Does she have any rights to the child?	If both of you adopted the child, both are legal parents and have rights. If only one of you did, the issues of your respective rights are complicated. The adoptive parent may have sole right to the child. The standard should be the best interests of the child.	See Chapter Seven
My lover promised to leave me her house when she died, but she didn't change her will. Do I inherit anything?	You are not her heir but you are still entitled to your share of any jointly owned property. You might be able to sue her estate and claim that she promised you an inheritance, but such cases rarely succeed.	See Chapter Fourteen
I lived with a rich man for several years and now he dumped me. Can I collect palimony?	Probably not.	See Chapter Fourteen

QUESTION: *"My partner and I are sure that we want a cohabitation agreement. How can we use this book to write one?"*

ANSWER: *You can use the checklists and questions in this book to gather information about your thoughts and needs. You can use the forms to write a preliminary draft of your agreement, which you should have a competent attorney review.*

Writing a cohabitation or prenuptial agreement depends on how complicated your situation is, how accurate your present beliefs about the law are, and how clear you are about what you (and your partner) want. A good agreement provides a clear memorial of your agreement, both about the present situation and the future. In other words, a good contract covers those possible future events that you can foresee. For example, you and your significant other may both be in good health now and both have good jobs. Those facts may change, however, either by choice or by events over which you have little control.

If you believe that all you need is a form to fill out, you probably bought the wrong book. This book does not provide simple fill-in-the-blank agreements. This book can help you determine whether you want a cohabitation or prenuptial agreement and what its terms need to be. It cannot, and doesn't try to, provide a "one size fits all" formula for all couples. Maybe you only need a simple form agreement, but maybe you have more issues to think through and write down. Filling in the blanks in a simple form, without carefully thinking through your real situation, might lead you to overlook a financial issue that could be very important to you.

Presumably, somewhere in America, there are some couples whose relationships are clear and uncomplicated, who fully understand the legal implications of what they are doing, who know what the future will bring, and who are quite clear about what they want. Those couples don't need this book – they already know it all. They also floss after every meal, eat a perfectly balanced diet, exercise regularly, never squeeze their pimples or pick their nose, and make a fortune in the stock market by their prudent, perfectly rational, investing. There are forms available online and in print that cater to people who believe they know everything, and such couples should use them.

The rest of us recognize that life is complicated and uncertain. Our needs and wants change over time. We find it hard to figure out what relationship is best for us. We struggle to compromise our fantasized "dream lover" with the real people whom we meet. When we are in a relationship, we have to work hard to reach a working compromise between our needs – rational and irrational – and those of our partner.

QUESTION: *"What's the biggest potential problem with having a prenuptial or cohabitation agreement?"*

ANSWER: *The biggest danger is that it might turn out to be a legally binding contract.*

The first problem with having a written agreement about your relationship is that people don't make rational decisions when they are in love. Often, the initial agreement was unfair from the beginning, or times changed and the agreement didn't. Then, one person can be stuck with the results of an imprudent contract made when he or she was deeply in love and not inclined to think clearly about money.

Sometimes, one party is just greedier or more assertive or more dishonest than the other. That can lead to them both signing an agreement that is unfair to the more vulnerable party. There is a risk that one of a couple will sign away important rights or a valuable asset either because he or she doesn't know what rights he or she might otherwise have or because he or she doesn't think through the financial impact of the agreement on possible future circumstances.

The second problem is that many people forget about the agreement once they have written it. Worse, they often don't remember its terms accurately. A change in the couple's situation does not automatically change the agreement; terms that were fair ten years ago may be grossly inequitable now, but still legally in place.

Often, couples are not careful about rewriting the agreement to meet new circumstances or even about reaching a new shared understanding. A typical example of the often silent misery caused by this lapse is when a homemaker takes a job. The previous understanding between the couple may have been that one partner would stay home and take care of the house and yard and the other would go out to work. If one partner works outside the home, it may be quite reasonable for him or her to expect to come home to a tidy home and a home-cooked meal, and the other partner may find those expectations comfortable and fair. That reasonable expectation (and comfortable existence), however, can become unfair and unworkable when both partners come home tired to a messy house and cold pizza for supper. For obvious reasons, the partner who has become accustomed to having little or no responsibility for household duties may be reluctant to accept a changed arrangement in which he or she has to come home tired and frazzled to do his or her share of the laundry and vacuuming.

Clearly, if such a couple did reach a new accord about their relationship, they would need a modified agreement that covered the new financial arrangement also.

One judge put this rather harsh legal rule very clearly in the case of the Simeone family. Dr. Simeone was a 39 year old neurosurgeon when he proposed marriage to the future Mrs. Simeone. She was a 23 year old nurse. She was unemployed but he earned $90,000 plus annually. Sounds like the blissful ending of a second rate medical romance novel, right?

Just before the wedding, his attorney presented a prenuptial agreement to the blushing bride. She signed it without getting any advice, from the doctor's lawyer or her own. The agreement provided that if the couple divorced, the future Mrs. Simeone would receive $200 per week up to a maximum of $25,000. Nine years later, the couple filed for divorce.

Mrs. Simeone tried to get a larger share of her husband's assets or more support, claiming that the agreement was unfair and that she hadn't had any independent advice.

The judge noted that earlier court decisions had protected women from imprudent premarital agreements. Those decisions had rested upon the judges' "belief that spouses are of unequal status and that women are not knowledgeable enough to understand the nature of contracts that they enter." He rejected that paternalistic assumption in favor of a feminist perspective, noting

> *Society has advanced, however, to the point where women are no longer regarded as the 'weaker party' in marriage or in society generally. Nor is there viability in the presumption that women are uniformed, uneducated, and readily subjected to unfair advantage in marital agreements.*

The judge declined to evaluate the reasonableness of the agreement. He believed that the parties to a contract needed to be able to rely on the contract's being valid. He said:

> *"further, everyone who enters a long-term agreement knows that circumstances can change during its term, so that what initially appeared desirable might prove to be an unfavorable bargain. Such are the risks that contracting parties routinely assume. Certainly, the possibility of illness, birth of children, reliance upon a spouse, career change, financial gain or loss, and the numerous other events that can occur in the course of a marriage cannot be regarded as unforeseeable. If the parties choose not to address such matters in their prenuptial agreements, they must be regarded as having contracted to bear the risk of events that alter the value of their bargains."[1]*

In other words, if the engaged couple didn't bother to think through the possible twists and turns of their future life together, the court was not going to write a better agreement for them. The Uniform Premarital Agreement Act provides somewhat more protection for people who enter into imprudent or unfair agreements. Still, every written contract should be regarded as binding as written. More information on contracts is in Chapter Eight and Chapter Nine, starting at page 317.

Families and the law

Our personal relationships take place between individuals in a society. This means that these relationships are both intensely private and partly public. The public interest in couples' relationships is expressed in the law. The judges and juries that administer the law have their own social values and beliefs about relationships.

The Constitution protects private life from government interference to some extent. The Supreme Court has held that the right to live one's family life in accordance with one's own values is a fundamental right in our society. For example, the Constitutional right of privacy shields private sexual conduct between consenting adults from state interference.

However, the government still exercises considerable control over families. Laws against child and spousal abuse, for example, directly control conduct inside the home. The law also influences private relationships by its control of the financial fallout of relationships and by its control over the living arrangements of children.

If there is a dispute between the parties, whether they are married or cohabiting, that dispute will either be worked out by the couple or decided by someone else, usually a judge and possibly a jury. The three most important aspects of the relationship that courts often decide are (1) the rights and obligations relating to children, (2) those relating to money and property, and (3) those relating to contact between the parties, such as requiring that an abusive lover stay away from his or her victim.

Some, but not all, of the legal obligations and rights between a couple can be modified by agreement. That is true whether the two people involved are roommates, lovers, business partners, or husband and wife. The agreement, however, must itself be made according to the laws governing valid contracts, if the parties want the courts to enforce it.

People can act, among themselves, within broad legal parameters. As far as the law is concerned, more or less, they can spend their money as they like, live where they want, and keep their house as they choose. Increasingly, from a legal point of view, they can have sexual relations with any other consenting adult.

Moreover, they can make any promises that they want to each other about these activities. The legal system, however, will not lend its countenance to all of those promises. Some contracts are unlawful and will not be enforced by a court. Some obligations cannot be signed away and some rights cannot be given up.

The law imposes obligations on parents with regard to children, regardless of the wishes of the parents. Although our legal system allows people wide discretion to control their own property, if there is a dispute between two people, the rights to that property will be decided within a context of legal rules, not just by the parties' wishes. Finally, abusive behavior can be controlled or punished, although that part of the system is far from perfect.

Nature of American law

Some legal questions only make sense in the context of our governmental system. If you want to skip the civics lesson, however, you can turn directly to the chapters that are relevant to your particular situation. American law has three distinct components. Part of the law is set out in statutes, which are, of course, rules adopted by state legislatures and the United States Congress. Federal law, including laws passed by Congress, the United States Constitution, and Supreme Court decisions interpreting them, take precedence over state laws. In other words, state laws don't apply where they contradict federal laws.

Another part of our law is set out in decisions by the courts in specific, real-life, cases. This body of law is called the "common law." American common law began with the common law of 18th century England. The common law is a decision-guiding process in which the judges look to earlier decisions for the reasoning to apply to the case before them. They analyze how closely the present case resembles past cases and how it differs from those examples.

Although statutes might seem clearer than case law, real life is such a muddle that it takes careful thought to decide how the rules ought to apply to a particular case.

In deciding cases, judges also look to works by legal scholars. Groups of legal experts, including professors, judges, and practicing lawyers, have formed to try to devise the best rules to fit our modern society and its values. They put forth their ideas in the form of proposed uniform statutes, which the states are free to adopt or not. These include the Uniform Premarital Agreement Act, the Uniform Paternity Act, and other model statutes and analyses of the law. It is important to realize that these uniform acts are not the law unless a state legislature enacts them. Consequently, although I sometimes refer to these acts in this book, because they represent the consensus of legal scholars about what a sensible rule would be, they may or may not be the law in your state.

Similar groups of experts also write summaries of the law called "restatements." Judges and lawyers consult these for the most concise statement of the common law rules. They also consult scholarly articles about the law.

QUESTION: *"Why do the laws vary from one place to another?"*

ANSWER: *People in different parts of the United States have different values and ideas of how couples ought to live.*

The people of the various states have different ideas about how family matters ought to be governed. Some want to encourage traditional family life, while others give more importance to individual happiness. Some people believe that wives who stayed home with their children during a marriage should receive generous alimony from their ex-husbands, while others put more emphasis on women's equal ability to earn their own living. That's why state laws differ on questions of family property, marriage, and cohabitation.

As a rule, the United States Congress does not pass many laws expressly about family matters, which are generally considered to be matters for the individual states to control. Recent concern over various social issues, however, has led to enactment of several federal laws that directly affect families. Most importantly, Congress has passed statutes that require the states to make the establishment of paternity of a child easier, that prohibit one parent's illegally removing a child from the custody of the other parent, and that require the enforcement of child support orders.

Although family matters are largely regulated by state laws, Congress frequently enacts laws that indirectly, but profoundly, affect family life by controlling federal spending and regulating national corporate matters. For example, income tax, pension, welfare, and social security laws affect married and unmarried couples differently.

In addition to cases and statutes, various government agencies promulgate rules and regulations that have an impact on family finances. The tax regulations of the IRS take up two volumes, for example. These rules are a kind of law and often more complicated than statutes. Federal tax law, for example, governs what tax rights and obligations spouses have to each other, but state law controls who is a spouse.

The federal structure of our government, as set forth in the Constitution, requires one state to treat a court decision from another state as a valid decision. However, one state is not constitutionally obligated to follow other states' statutes. Each state may enact its own laws and have its own policies, within limits.[2] In other words, if you get divorced in Alabama, California has to treat you as a divorced person, even if its laws about divorce are different.

One state may, to some extent, refuse to honor another state's laws if those offend an important policy of the first state. To be specific, suppose that State A has adopted a constitutional amendment prohibiting same sex marriage; by doing so, that state has made clear that limiting marriage to heterosexual couples is a very important policy to its citizens. Suppose that State B has passed laws permitting same sex marriages. Is State A required to recognize the marriage of a same sex couple from State B as valid?

So, same sex marriage, domestic partnerships, and other laws about couples create complex legal issues within the fundamental structure of our government.

QUESTION: *"Why do judges make laws about families? I thought that only the legislature made law."*

ANSWER: *The law-making powers of the courts are an integral part of our legal system.*

Remember – in the English and American system, judges have always made law.

Judges make the rules of the common law, and they also interpret statutes when they are applying those statutes to a particular case. The legislature, whether the United States Congress or a state legislature, adopts general rules, i.e. statutes, but it is up to the courts to decide how those rules apply to a specific situation, with all its complexities and ambiguities. Moreover, the judges must often decide which law applies since a particular case may involve the laws of two or more states plus the federal government.

Even children argue over the meaning of the rules of hide and seek or jacks when they are playing a game. Think how much more room for argument there is when a court tries to untangle something as complicated as the intersection of two adult lives.

Let us consider a hypothetical case where a man leaves his family and lives with another woman for a number of years. When he dies, both women make claims to his estate. On the one hand, considerations of social stability and traditional morality might incline the court to be most sympathetic to the abandoned wife and children. Logically, the judge might reason, the first marriage remained valid, so the mistreated wife and children ought to get everything that her straying husband owned. On the other hand, the judge might also feel some sympathy for the other woman. Perhaps she didn't know about the first marriage and thought that she was legally married. The courts evolved the concept of a "putative spouse" to protect people who thought that they were legally married but weren't, especially when they had been deceived by their supposed spouse. Perhaps the wife more or less consented to the arrangement and took a lover of her own. The courts have to apply general rules to mixed-up, complicated lives.

The law is like a logical seesaw. Judges' reasoning oscillates between a main rule and exceptions to that rule.

The question is then, where do judges find out what the law ought to be? They look to the values of society, to the principles embodied in earlier cases, and to their own values.

Over the centuries, judges struggled to compare different cases and reach a just result in each one, depending on the particular facts of each case. A broad rule that the court announced in one case might lead to a manifestly unfair result in another case. So, the judges worked through the facts in the case in front of them, using the broad principles but also drawing on common social understandings to reach a reasoned result.

Change is integral to the common law. As one legal writer expressed it in 1869, the common law rested on "the law of Nature, the law of God, to common sense, to legal reason, justice, and humanity."[3]

The great American judge, Learned Hand, wrote in 1952 that the common law is "a combination of custom and its successive adaptations. The judges receive it and profess to treat it as authoritative, while they gently mould it the better to fit changed ideas."[4]

The Texas Supreme Court in 1975 wrote that "The system and tradition that we call the 'common law' is not a body of law which evolved in historic England or a bygone age to stand immutable ever afterward."[5]

In other words, it is in the nature of the American legal system for changing social ideas to be gradually incorporated into both judges' decisions and statutes.

It can take many years before the courts and legislatures fully integrate changes in social values into the law.

The evolving property rights of married women is a good example of how the law changes. In the 19th century, Texas adopted laws that made clear that women and men had equal rights to own property and to share in property that the couple earned during the marriage. Court cases implemented these policies, protecting women's rights to their share of a family's assets, sometimes even when the couple was not married. Those laws were more progressive than many other states which held that a married woman could not own property and that anything she owned while single became her husband's property when she married. For some decades, however, even

Texas law gave the management of the couple's property to the husband. Then, the legislature changed the law to recognize the woman's equal right to manage the family assets also.

QUESTION: *"Why does the Supreme Court of the United States get involved in family matters?"*

ANSWER: *The Supreme Court has the duty to protect Americans' constitutional rights by deciding when a statute is inconsistent with the United States Constitution.*

Shortly after the United States became a country, the question came up of what branch of government had the responsibility to decide when a law violated the important rights set out in the Constitution. John Marshall, the first Chief Justice of the United States, reasoned that the responsibility had to fall to the Supreme Court. Marshall had was one of the founding fathers and had helped write the Constitution to form the United States government.

The Constitution applies to family life in two important ways. The first is the right of privacy. The right of privacy is the general right that people have to be left alone by the government. That means that the government should not interfere in the intimate aspects of people's lives unless there is a compelling public policy reason to do so. The second is the Court's recognition of family life as among our fundamental rights. Although the states can regulate marriages and the relationships of parents and children, for example, they cannot unduly intrude into the sanctity of the home.

An example of the intersection of moral bias and governmental action came up in the case of Linda Littlejohn. Linda was an elementary school teacher in a public school. She had always received good evaluations. She didn't have tenure, but the school usually rehired teachers without tenure for the next year. The principal recommended Linda, but the school superintendent decided not to rehire her because she and her husband had filed for divorce. The superintendent disapproved of divorce.

Linda sued the school. The federal courts held that the school's refusal to hire a person based on her seeking a divorce violated her fundamental right to a private family life.[6] The court might have decided the Littlejohn case differently if the school had been not been a public school. A public school is a governmental entity, and our Constitutional rights limit the government's power to interfere in our private lives. The school superintendent used his power as a government official to punish another person for not conforming to his personal social values. On the other hand, a private parochial school, for example, might have the right to ensure that the teachers exemplified the religious values of the school.

Many of most hotly debated Supreme Court decisions, such as those dealing with the right to abortion and birth control and the rights of parents, rest on the Court's commitment to the sanctity of private life in one's home. That right is called the right of privacy, which means the right to live one's family life as one chooses. That right is limited by constraints on not hurting other people.

QUESTION: *"Why does the Supreme Court sometimes invalidate a law that has been on the books for years?"*

ANSWER: *In cases about constitutional rights, the justices consider the history of the law to understand the logic and rationale of the law. Sometimes, no one has seriously considered whether a law is consistent with the United States Constitution. Other times, our rights under the Constitution have been reinterpreted.*

The history of the law fits into constitutional reasoning in several ways. First, it is a guide to what the founding fathers may have had in mind when they wrote the Constitution. Second, thinking about our civil rights involves a balance between acknowledging evolving concepts of human liberty and accepting well-established limitations on that liberty.[7]

This tension is well illustrated in America's evolving laws about slavery and racial equality. In the 18th century, slavery was a well-established social institution. The economy of the British Empire flourished in part because of the trade in African slaves and the products, such as sugar and cotton, that slave labor produced. Even then, however, many thoughtful people condemned slavery as immoral and argued that it was philosophically and morally inconsistent to attribute civil liberties to white men only. Others believed that persons of other races were inferior to white men, just as women were, and needed to be governed by white males.

When the American constitution was being written, some of the founding fathers foresaw that the institution of slavery would divide the country. Others believed that slavery was an essential part of the economy of some of the nascent states. The result was an unstable compromise; slavery was impliedly recognized in the Constitution but no racial distinction was expressly embodied in its language.

Slavery was such an accepted social institution that the Texas Constitution expressly protected a married woman's property rights in her slaves and their children. In other words, Texas family law was liberal, for its time, in affording married women the right to own their property, but backward in failing to recognize the most basic rights of African Americans who were held in slavery.

In the 19th century, reform opinion prevailed in England and some American states. Britain outlawed the slave trade and eventually slavery itself in British colonies. British ships patrolled the African coast to interdict shipments of black slaves to the United States and South America. Many states outlawed slavery.

In the case of *Dred Scott v. Sandford*, in 1856, a slave named Dred Scott sued his master, seeking his freedom on the ground that Scott had lived for several years in one of the free states, i.e. where slavery was illegal. The Supreme Court not only ruled against Scott but said:

> *The question is simply this: Can a negro, whose ancestors were imported into this country, and sold as slaves, become a member of the political community formed and brought into existence by the Constitution of the United States, and as such become entitled to all the rights, and privileges, and immunities, guarantied by that instrument to the citizen?*

The Court noted that if people of African American descent could become citizens, then they would have all the rights of white people to travel, to vote, to bear arms, and so on. That result was so clearly unacceptable that the Court answered its own question in these words:

> *The Constitution] guaranties rights to the citizen, and the State cannot withhold them. And these rights are of a character and would lead to consequences which make it absolutely certain that the African race were not included under the name of citizens of a State, and were not in the contemplation of the framers of the Constitution when these privileges and immunities were provided for the protection of the citizen in other States.*

In other words, the Supreme Court held that African Americans could never become citizens of the United States and had no constitutional protection. To the contrary, the Court held that under the Constitution, black people were the property of white people and that the Constitution protected those property rights. To reach that decision, the Court looked at the history of laws that treated black people differently from white people; the Court consciously ignored the changes that had taken place in society's views on the equality of all people.[8]

To our eyes, that decision seems shameful. In fact, the *Dred Scott* case was one of the factors that led to the Civil War and to amendments to the Constitution to make clear that its liberties applied to everyone. Our moral and legal reaction to Mr. Scott's case differs from the reactions of people in 1856 because the overall social concepts of equality and rights have evolved.

Constitutional law is now clear that the government cannot give different rights to different groups of people unless there is a rational, non-racial, basis for the distinction.

Analogously, in matters of family life, including sexual conduct, the Supreme Court carefully considers laws that may have been acceptable in the past to see whether those laws conform to our present concept of liberty. Sometimes, no one has bothered to consider whether those laws ever were consistent with the general principles of freedom that govern our country.

QUESTION: *"Why is there uncertainty about what laws apply to cohabiting couples?"*

ANSWER: *The legislatures have not enacted comprehensive laws governing cohabitation which leaves the questions about cohabiting couples' legal rights up to the courts.*

Over the centuries, the legislatures have enacted comprehensive laws about the rights and obligations of married couples. There are no comparable codes about cohabiting couples. There is no special statute that says "Cohabiting couples have no rights," for example. Some states have laws that provide that a cohabitation agreement must be in writing to be valid. However, there are many laws about marriage and thousands of court decisions applying those laws to individual couples. There have not been many cases about cohabiting couples, so the judges do not have a lot of precedents to look to for guidance.

Therefore, the courts are struggling to figure out what rules should apply to cohabitation arrangements. There are three fundamental choices: the court can treat the relationship as (1) analogous to a marriage; (2) analogous to an ordinary business relationship; or (3) as a deliberately immoral way of life. Plausible reasons support each of these choices.

On the one hand, the parties have deliberately chosen to opt out of the usual social structure for cohabitation, which is marriage. One can argue that it would be inconsistent with that conscious choice for a court to treat them "as if" they were married; after all, married is precisely what they did not want to be.

Moreover, the law embodies social norms in an institutional structure. People who behave in some illegal or immoral ways usually cannot turn to the legal system for help. That's why contracts for the sale of illegal drugs and debts from illegal gambling are not enforceable in court; the legal system deliberately refrains from lending its powers to resolve situations that are criminal or immoral. If cohabitation is more like prostitution than marriage, then it follows that the courts should not protect the parties but should leave them to fend for themselves. Some court decisions are based on this kind of reasoning.

On the other hand, treating the parties to a marriage or cohabitation as if they were just people involved in a business transaction doesn't quite fit the facts either. Millions of couples live together in more or less stable arrangements. Couples who have lived together, married or not, have had feelings of love, lust, trust, and anger for each other that influenced their judgment. The model of two rationally self-interested people entering into a business deal as commercial adversaries does not capture the psychological dynamics of a love affair, at least, we hope, for most couples. Perhaps one might consider lovers as more like two close friends who become partners in a business. Perhaps one might consider them as having more or less the same obligations as married people. But, if courts did that, what would the difference be between marriage and cohabitation? When would the "marriage like" obligations accrue? What if the couple expressly didn't want those obligations and rights?

This uncertainty, which is discussed further at page 138, is one reason why a book like this one can only be a guide; to make important decisions, a person should consult a qualified lawyer. Being better informed, however, can help a person evaluate their lawyer's advice and make better decisions.

QUESTION: *"Why do you make this all sound so complicated?"*

ANSWER: *Because for most of us, it is.*

Relationships are complicated webs of emotion and reason. In our sexual and romantic relationships, we play out both our adult desires and what we learned about relationships from our parents during our childhood. If a woman's experience as the daughter of her father teaches her that men are distant and selfish, she may well unconsciously expect her husband/lover/male friends to be unreliable and cold. If a man experienced his mother as clinging and exploitative, he may well regard his wife/lover/female friends with guarded suspicion whenever one of them makes any sort of financial request, no matter how reasonable it is.

Even when people recognize these tendencies in themselves and try not to follow them blindly, the past continues to affect their day-to-day reactions to people. The woman who had a cold, distant father may consciously realize that not all men are like that. Perhaps she will seek out a warm, sensitive man, but even in consciously seeking out such a guy, she is still responding to her experiences. She may, for example, deeply wish for a caring relationship with him but find it difficult to trust even a thoughtful warm man. Or, she may seek out a cold, unfeeling partner, unconsciously validating her psychological biases.

The law of relationships is complicated because the law tries to deal with human relationships that are capable of almost infinite variation. Psychological factors that shape relationships also warp the legal consequences. Courts and legislatures struggle with their own feelings of moral outrage, fairness, and sympathy. Reading the decisions in divorce cases reveals people's amazing ability to complicate their lives, financially, emotionally, and legally.

The same ambiguities and uncertainties that make judges' decisions difficult also plague a couple trying to work out the terms of their relationship. A couple that decides to forego the traditional structure of marriage has to forge the terms of their relationship out of whole cloth; they cannot rely on society to provide them with a fair arrangement. On the other hand, they don't exist independently of social norms and rules. If they do not consciously adopt the provisions that will govern at least their financial arrangements, then the default provisions afforded by the legal system will be applied if there is a dispute between them.

Similarly, many people find their expectations of marriage rudely shattered when divorce intervenes. In our society, women still typically earn less than men but are regarded as the natural caretakers of children. This can mean that a woman who counted on the pleasant lifestyle supported by her husband's higher salary may see that lifestyle simply evaporate on divorce. A man who regarded himself as an involved and devoted father may find his participation in his children's lives marginalized to "visitation" rather than "parenting" and his commitment reduced to burdensome support payments.

Private agreements between the couple can address some of these problems, at least in principle, but if the dispute goes to court, the final decision is still the province of judges with their own prejudices and social theories.

A moveable population

In a country with 50 states and one federal government, the question of what law applies is a complex one. The states have different social policies, and more importantly, different social values. These values and laws affect child custody questions, the division of property if there is a divorce, and the enforceability of couples' contracts.

 QUESTION: *"You've said that the law varies from state to state. If people move from one state to another, which law applies?"*

ANSWER: *Good question. Usually, the law of the state where the couple married determines whether the marriage was valid or not. The law of the*

state where the couple divorces normally applies to property division, child support and so on. In a lawsuit over a cohabitation or prenuptial agreement, the court would probably apply the law of the state where the agreement was signed.

There are three key situations when it matters what law applies. These are the (1) division of property in a divorce, (2) the question of which court will decide about the custody of a child; and (3) the validity of marriage or other relationships between couples. The latter point is of particular importance to gay and lesbian couples.

Child custody – when parents move

"Jurisdiction" means the legal authority to decide a case. The technical legal question when the parents are in different states is which court has jurisdiction.

QUESTION: *"What state makes decisions about child custody when the parents live in different states?"*

ANSWER: *The state with the most contacts with the child should have jurisdiction to decide issues of custody and support.*

It is not true that both spouses have to be living in the same state to divorce there. On the other hand, there are basic doctrines of fairness and due process that limit a state's power to decide cases about a person who has no contacts with the state.

When a relationship ends, one party will often try to obtain a better result by moving to another state where the law is more favorable or where the prevailing social values are more conservative or liberal. Obviously, for example, a gay parent who was seeking custody of a child from a heterosexual ex-spouse might reasonably hope for more success in San Francisco or Manhattan than in Lubbock or Little Rock.

Until relatively recently, a parent who lost a custody case often moved with the child to another state and reopened the case there. At one time, the courts had jurisdiction over any child that was living in their state.

The law of jurisdiction over child custody cases has changed. Federal and state laws now limit parents' ability to challenge one court's decision in another court. The states and the federal government have adopted a strong policy of stopping such "forum shopping."

The Uniform Child Custody Jurisdiction and Enforcement Act provides that a child's "home state" has continuing jurisdiction over custody questions. The express purpose of that law is to deter parents from abducting their own child and to keep parents from endlessly litigating custody issues. The act prohibits other states from changing a custody order until the home state decides that it has lost all meaningful contact with the family. It specifically provides that one parent's moving a child out of state will not give jurisdiction over custody to the state to which the parent moved.

"Home state" means the state where the child was living when the custody proceedings (usually part of a divorce) began. If a child lived in the state for six months before the case started but has been taken out of state by one parent, the state where the kid lived is still the home state.

Consider the case of Rosemary Greenlaw and Daniel Smith. Rosemary and Daniel lived in the state of Washington.[9] When they divorced, the court awarded Mary the custody of their three year old son, Alexander. Frank and Rosemary continued to bicker over custody for the next twelve years. When Alex was seven, Rosemary got a job with the United States Army which required her to move to Germany for three years. Because she traveled on business, she enrolled Alex in a German boarding school. Alex visited her on holidays and weekends and had little contact with his father. Three years later, Rosemary moved to California. For a while, Alex lived with Rosemary's old boyfriend while she went to law school. While they lived in California, Alex began visiting his father again in Washington. Daniel got Alex into therapy (which by that time the kid no doubt needed).

Daniel asked the Washington court to change the custody order and give custody to him. The counselor testified that Alex would be better with his father. Rosemary objected to the Washington court deciding the case because she hadn't lived there for years and neither had Alex. The court held that the state of Washington still had jurisdiction because it had made the original decision, the child visited his father there, and the father still lived in the state. The mother could not change the court's jurisdiction by moving away. The court said:

> [T]state in which the initial decree was entered has exclusive continuing jurisdiction to modify the initial decree if (1) one of the parents continues to reside in [that] state; and (2) the child continues to have some connection with [that] state, such as visitation.

There are exceptions to the home state having jurisdiction. If the child has been abandoned or is in danger of abuse or neglect, the court where the child physically is can take jurisdiction over his or her custody. Similarly, if the child and one parent have a "significant connection" with the state and there is "substantial evidence concerning the child's present or future care, protection, training, and personal relationships" in the state, then that state can exercise its jurisdiction and decide the case.

Obviously, the questions of what a child's home state is or what "significant connection" means are not entirely clear so that there can still be a dispute between the parents about which court has jurisdiction. What is clear is that mere physical presence in the court is not enough.[10]

As discussed below at page 502, violating a state custody order can be a crime that will get the FBI involved.

Sometimes custody disputes involve more than one country. There is an international treaty that governs these disputes among the countries that have adopted it. The United States is a party to the Hague Convention on the Civil Aspects of International Child Abduction, as are over 70 other countries. Under that treaty the country where the child has his or her "habitual residence" has jurisdiction over child custody questions. United States courts have sent children back to parents in other countries even if one of the child's parents is an American citizen and even if that parent brings the child to this country.[11]

Division of property in a divorce—which state decides?

When couples move from one state to another, the job of sorting out property ownership becomes tricky. Some of their property may be governed by one state's system and some by the others', depending on where they were living when they acquired a particular asset. The courts have evolved rules to decide which set of rules to apply to which asset.

A couple that has acquired substantial assets and has also lived in several states may have complicated property questions to resolve if they decide to divorce. The technical issues may not matter very much if the two can work out an amicable resolution. If, however, they insist on fighting over the division, then they will need sophisticated lawyers to untangle their respective shares.

QUESTION: *"My wife and I lived in Illinois. When we separated, I moved to Arizona. The kids stayed with her and I visited every month or so. She filed for divorce in Illinois. Can she do that even though I don't live there anymore?"*

ANSWER: *Yes. Usually, a person can file for divorce in the state where he or she lives.*

A state has jurisdiction to dissolve a marriage if one of the spouses lives in that state. The states have different requirements for how long you have to live there before you can file for divorce in that state. The other spouse does not have to live in the state.

However, a state does not have the legal power to divide the couple's property unless both spouses have some contact with the state. So, in the question above, for example, the Illinois' courts have jurisdiction both to end the marriage and to divide the couple's property because the husband had many contacts with the state.

If both spouses move to new states when they separate, the question of which court system has jurisdiction to divide the couple's assets can be a thorny one. Obviously, each spouse wants the litigation in his or her local courts. Jurisdiction depends on the circumstances of each case.

The most important point is that once a court with jurisdiction makes a decision, all other courts must honor that decision. In other words, in theory at least, neither spouse can reopen the question somewhere else.

Like many technical legal issues, the question of jurisdiction probably doesn't matter to most divorcing couples.

In some cases, however, the question of jurisdiction can become a critical factor in a lawsuit. One party may be at a substantial disadvantage if he or she has to travel to a distant court for hearings and has to deal with the lawyer "long distance." Sometimes, the hassle and expense become too burdensome, and the distant party more or less gives up. Sometimes, because the social policies and laws of the states differ, one party can have a much better chance of a favorable outcome in one state than another. This jockeying for geographical advantage is why a couple's lawyers will fight over which court has jurisdiction.

Different states and different laws—gay marriage

Few topics have engendered as ferocious debate as that of gay and lesbian relationships. Some states and foreign countries have enacted laws that permit gay and lesbian couples to marry. Others have provided for a third legal option (to marriage and plain cohabitation), which is a domestic partnership. More states have enacted laws prohibiting gay and lesbian relationships from being recognized as marriages.

Controversy over gay marriage has led to Congress' passing the Defense of Marriage Act, which entitles states to disregard homosexual marriages performed legally in other states. It is uncertain whether that law is constitutional or not, because it may conflict with the provision of the Constitution that requires states to honor other state's laws.

Consequently, a homosexual couple cannot rely on their legal status remaining the same as they move from one state to another.

Domestic partnership laws raise another area of uncertainty, which concerns both homosexual couples and heterosexual couples. A relationship formed in one state (or city) that accords a legal status to domestic partnerships may have different legal implications in a locale that doesn't. These topics are discussed further in Chapter Four.

QUESTION: *"But how can I find out exactly what the law is in my state and how it applies to my situation?"*

ANSWER: *You can consult a competent attorney who specializes in family law matters or you can try to find out the answers for yourself, or both.*

The fastest way to understand your situation from a legal standpoint is to consult a qualified attorney. Finding a qualified attorney, however, may not be an easy matter, just as finding the right physician is not easy. You are better prepared to consult an attorney if you are more informed about the law. If nothing else, you can ask more intelligent questions. The following sections discuss dealing with attorneys and learning about the law yourself.

You can begin by reading the relevant topics in this book carefully. There is a section in the Workbook on how to look up the law and a list of some of the more usable legal references; starting at "Places to go for help" on page 556 and the other information contained in that section. Looking up the law takes time and patience. That's why lawyers get paid. On the other hand, a reasonably intelligent, patient person can often acquire a sufficient understanding for his or her needs. If you don't have the time to look up the information yourself, then your only options are to pay an attorney or take your chances.

Dealing with attorneys – choosing your lawyer

The complexity of family law is also why some lawyers are more qualified than others. A good lawyer needs to be experienced in how cases are typically decided in his or her geographic area, as well as informed on trends in the law, which may result in different results being reached in the future.

Some states have adopted a system of board certification, somewhat like that used by the medical establishment. To be certified as specialist in family law matters, an attorney must have a certain amount of experience and have passed an exam, or satisfied other qualifications, depending on the state. Finding a board-certified specialist is always a good place to start.

Also, you can talk to your friends and relatives about attorneys whom they know or have hired in the past. A certain amount of discretion in asking for recommendations is probably a good idea if any sort of dispute is in progress or is looming on the horizon.

You may or may not want to reveal (even indirectly) to your significant other that things have gotten to the point where you believe that you need legal advice.

The local bar association may also operate a referral service. If you live in a large metropolitan area, there is probably a bar association in your city. If you live in a less populous town or rural area, you can contact the state bar association, which is normally located in the state capital.

One source of referrals is a support or advocacy group. For examples, some churches sponsor divorced people's groups, and there are advocacy groups for fathers who are seeking custody of their children. The members of organizations like these may be able to refer you to an attorney whom they have successfully consulted (or warn you against those who have let them down.)

A word of caution is in order. Be careful in hiring an attorney based on any recommendation that did not involve the attorney's work in the exact field where you need him or her. Lawyers today tend to specialize, and the lady who handled your Uncle Fred's auto accident claim may not be the best advisor about your child custody problems. In other words, a lawyer who did a bang up job on a building contract for an architect may be a complete failure in the courtroom and a lawyer who is a gifted and aggressive advocate may lack the skills necessary to carefully craft a prenuptial or cohabitation agreement.

You can also check the yellow pages and research attorneys on line. You should remember, however, that these sources are advertisements, not neutral recommendations.

Dealing with lawyers – the basics of consulting an attorney

When consulting an attorney, you should expect, of course, to pay for his or her time. The time involved will include at least the time spent meeting with you or talking with you on the phone, as well as time reviewing any documents, talking to your significant other's lawyer (if he or she has one), and researching any points of law that the lawyer feels the need to check.

Some attorneys provide a free initial consultation but others do not. You will need to be candid when discussing fees with the attorney prior to your first meeting. The ethical rules of the profession normally prohibit lawyers from taking family law cases on a contingent basis, which is where the lawyer's fee is paid from the money that is won in the case.

It is unfair, and unreasonable, to expect the attorney to answer your questions over the phone for free. Similarly, asking free legal advice at a party or other social occasion is inappropriate and not likely to get you good advice. First, the lawyer's knowledge and experience are his or her stock in trade. Second, the lawyer needs to focus his or her attention on you and the facts of your situation and take the time to get all the important details; an off-the-cuff remark is not the level of attention that your life deserves.

Legal fees today can be outrageous. In major cities, such as Houston or Chicago, you can expect to pay fees ranging from $175 to $400 per hour for a good attorney. On the other hand, in those cities, you may have to pay $90 or $100 per hour for the guy who fixes the software problem in your computer or installs your home theater system.

One frequent complaint is that the lawyer "didn't do anything." Unfortunately, much of the attorney's work is invisible to the client. Talking to the other side's lawyer, drafting papers, and reading your information all count as legal work, even if these things seem like "nothing" to the client.

It's like a doctor or dentist. Even if a treatment doesn't immediately solve the problem, the patient still has to pay the bill because he or she is paying for the work done, not for the result. The client is, however, entitled to a detailed explanation of exactly what the attorney did do in the time expended. The client is also entitled to question any time billed or that seems excessive for the amount accomplished.

Being organized and prepared for any meeting with an attorney will get you the best bang for your buck. Your organization work saves the attorney time and therefore saves you money. Being organized has two basic parts, which are (1) assembling the facts in a coherent manner and (2) having a reasonably clear idea of the questions to which you need answers. This book and the accompanying Workbook can help assemble this information.

The prerequisite to a successful meeting with an attorney is to have the relevant facts of your situation assembled in a clear and logical format. Many people begin their consultation with their attorney with a rambling narrative that progresses from the first time they saw Aunt Ruby's new hat to what their brother-in-law George's cousin who used to work for a hairdresser said about their case. This is natural because all these facts are part of the fabric of our lives and experiences. However, the legal clock is ticking as you talk so reciting your family history is costing you money. No matter how patient and understanding the lawyer is, he or she will probably expect you to pay for all the time that you spent in his or her office, just as a therapist expects you to pay for all your sessions, whether you reach any particular insight or not.

The technical legal word for such ramblings is, of course, "irrelevant." It is difficult, however, to determine in advance what is, or is not, relevant. What seems irrelevant to the nonprofessional may be quite relevant in the context of recent court decisions. Nonetheless, you save money if you write down a chronological account of the events that have led you to consult the attorney before your first meeting with him or her.

Here is a checklist of things to have for the best meeting with an attorney:

✓ *a neat, coherent, chronological narrative of the essential facts;*

✓ *a folder of relevant documents (never give your lawyer your only copy of anything);*

✓ *a list of pertinent questions;*

✓ *a basic understanding of the legal issues.*

To prepare your narrative, think back to the beginning of the relationship and write out a clear chronological history. Try to keep your narrative within 5 to 10 pages in length. Your lawyer may need more information, but he or she can ask for what is needed. The chapters on evidence in this book and the Workbook can help you gather the relevant documents. See Chapter Fifteen and the Workbook sections at starting at page 618.

To prepare a list of pertinent questions, you need to think through what concerns you and then list those concerns in order of importance.

Representing yourself – a fool for a client?

Representing yourself in an important matter is not usually a good idea because emotional factors or inexperience may lead you to mishandle your case or write an ineffective contract. Lawyers quote Abraham Lincoln to the effect that "A person who handles his own case has a fool for a client."

The courts, and most mediators and arbitrators, are not set up to help you protect your own rights. Fairly or not, judges and arbitrators function primarily as an umpire between two adversaries. The usual result of this (usually) unequal contest between a party with a lawyer and one without one is a sore loser who complains bitterly that the system is crooked.

Emotional factors can lead you to decide not to hire an attorney. If your lover has dominated you, you may unconsciously hesitate to call out the big guns to oppose him/her. If you feel unworthy of getting your fair share, you may find it difficult to have someone assert your rights in an effective way. If you are accustomed to the victim's role, you may find it impossible to contemplate being a victor. In other words, representing yourself can be a way of ensuring that you'll lose. Unconsciously, the "poor me" role may be more powerful than rational, financial, self-interest. These factors can be at work even if you are otherwise a sophisticated, shrewd person, such as a lawyer, accountant, or businessperson.

A skilled lawyer's advantages, obviously, are his or her superior knowledge of the law, the procedures, the system, and the quirks of the particular judges, as well as his or her talent in presenting the facts in an appealing manner. On the other hand, some disgruntled clients feel, with some justification, that lawyers become jaded and only seek the usual result that anyone could get on their own. In contract negotiations, the person who has gotten legal advice just has more information than the unrepresented person does; without a lawyer, you may give up entitlements you did not know you had.

The law, and especially the procedural rules that govern court proceedings, are full of traps for the unwary; lawyers fall into them all the time and they spend every working day dealing with them.

To look up the law applicable to a particular case, a good lawyer checks both the general rules set out in statutes and the written case reports, where appellate courts have considered the law as applied to the dispute before them.

He or she also factors in his or her knowledge of the judges in the city or county where the case has arisen. A distinct shift in the rulings of the local courts can be expected when several judges of a particular political view are elected. Family courts in one large Texas city became much more conservative on family law issues after the election of several Republican judges. The election of those judges in turn reflected the substantial power of a conservative local Republican organization, which was in turn allegedly influenced by Southern Baptists who belonged to a particular church.

Representing yourself in a dispute

On the other hand, legal work is not some arcane mystery. Much of the law is commonsense, and some people do quite well in representing themselves.

An energetic, sensible person may get a better result handling his or her own case than he or she would with a lazy or incompetent or dishonest lawyer.

Obviously, it is more reasonable to represent yourself if neither you nor your significant other has a lawyer and if you can resolve the dispute by agreement. You each take the risk that you will inadvertently give up some important right but if you both regard the result as fair, then that may not matter so much to you.

Many states provide excellent help for people who want to handle their own case, especially divorces. A person without an attorney is referred to as "pro se," which means "for himself." (You just knew that it had to be in Latin, if some lawyer wrote it, didn't you?) These resources range from helpful clerks to referrals to legal aid or volunteer lawyers who work with people who cannot afford a private attorney, to online guidance in handling your own divorce.

A great deal of information for pro se litigants is available on line from official state sources. Arizona, New Mexico, New York, New Jersey, and Indiana are among the states that offer online help to pro se parties in divorce actions. These states recognize that a diligent person of normal intelligence can handle their own family matters if the case is not too complicated.

Arizona judges, for example, have adopted a very sensible approach to helping people handle their own case. The Supreme Court has made a self-help center available on line. On that site, you can find forms and information that cover legal topics from a minor who wants to have an abortion without her parents' consent to adoption issues (including confidential intermediaries who will help adopted persons reunite with their birth parents) to a parent assistance hotline.

Some Arizona counties make the forms used in that county available on line or in the county law library. John Marshall, a court administrator in Phoenix, gave me an excellent tour of the forms and explanations that were available on Maricopa County's self service web site and in the library. The courts had prepared forms for people to copy and use to file a case for divorce or to handle other common cases, such as probating a will or solving a dispute with a landlord.

The Utah self-help web site has an interview based program to enable people to draft the legal papers necessary to handle their own divorce or get a protective order against an abusive spouse or lover. The program walks the user through a series of questions, like tax preparation software does. After completion of the questions, the program prepares the documents for filing. Utah's regulations limit the use of this program for divorces in which the family income is less than $10,000 per month and there are no more than six children. (References to helpful web sites are in the Workbook at "Internet resources" on page 558).

The courts' helpfulness however, more or less ends at the courthouse door if the case is hotly contested. Once in the courtroom, the judge is still supposed to be a neutral decision maker, not an advisor. In other words, many judges will let you make a major error without alerting you to it, because it is not fair for a judge to help one side against the other. In fact, it is unethical for a judge to talk to you about your case privately if your opponent is not there.

If you and your spouse don't have a lot of money, you may be able to represent yourself adequately even if the two of you disagree completely, as long as your significant other does not have a good attorney. However, if your whole future hinges on this case and you cannot work out a reasonable resolution, you really should hire an attorney. You may be able to do some of the work yourself, such as drafting the papers, if you can find a lawyer who will work with you on that basis.

If finances are a problem, the county law library also is a good place to start for referrals to various legal aid organizations. Often the librarian will have a printed list of legal organizations that offer referrals to lawyers, legal aid, and reduced fee services. Houston Volunteer Lawyers, for examples, has lawyers available for brief, but free consultations, in a small cubicle at the courthouse. Some bar associations, such as the Houston Young Lawyers, have published helpful guides for people who want to handle their own divorce.

If you decide to handle your own case, you need to be prepared to put enough time and effort so that your preparation, at least in this one case, rivals that of your lover or his or her attorney.

Those who act as their own lawyer and win are typically of a self-confident, even brash or show-off, temperament. If you hesitate to speak your mind, or find it difficult to hold your own in family arguments, you are less likely to present a convincing argument in court or mediation. Similarly, if you can't see the merit in the other person's views, then you are unlikely to make realistic judgments about your case.

The people who have the most success at representing themselves are (1) self-confident; (2) firmly convinced of the rightness of their position; (3) able to control their temper; (4) able to see the merits of the other side's position and respond rationally to it; and (5) willing to work hard to learn the system and its rules.

An alternative to representing yourself alone is to hire a lawyer as a consultant. In that role, the lawyer offers guidance but you do the work. Some people make this work rather well and essentially have a "behind the scenes" lawyer. Most lawyers are unwilling to take this role because their responsibility (and later malpractice liability) to you is not clear. However, some will take on this role, and it is common enough that the county law library in Phoenix, Arizona, for example, offers a list of lawyers who are willing to advise a party without taking on the whole representation.

Representing yourself in writing an agreement

The situation is slightly different when it comes to representing yourself in a prenuptial, marital, or cohabitation agreement. A layperson is more likely to write an adequate contract than to present a brilliant trial. Writing a good contract requires conscientious attention to detail and common sense, as well as some basic legal concepts.

On the other hand, it helps to have an unbiased person review the contract to make sure that it actually covers the situation properly. You may be so worried about one issue now that you overlook a future problem. Even lawyers make mistakes when they write their own agreements.

As an example, two law firms set out to write a fee agreement in a complex case. Both wanted to write an agreement that was fair to the client; because of the number of parties, there was a variety of possible verdicts, some of which could be ruinous for the client. In their care to set out the possible options, the lawyers overlooked an obvious contingency and cut themselves out of several hundred thousand dollars in fees.

You may think that the picture of a bunch of smart lawyers outsmarting themselves is just dandy, but it may not seem so amusing when you act as your own lawyer and make a similar mistake. As the court held in the *Simeone* case, if you forget to provide for some eventuality, you may be stuck with an unfortunate result.

If there is later a dispute between you and your significant other over this agreement, the fairness of the agreement (at the time you made it) may be in question. One criterion for a fair agreement is that both parties had independent advice. Hence, it may be a good idea for both of you to submit a proposed premarital or cohabitation agreement to separate attorneys, at least if a lot of money is involved, and if one of you has a personal attorney. The agreement may not be valid if the negotiations were one-sided.

If you insist

If you want to represent yourself in a dispute that is probably going to court, you will need to inform yourself about the applicable law and then gather the relevant evidence. This book is a good starting point on legal issues but you will need to find out exactly what the law is in your particular state. You will need to organize your presentation of your position in a clear, persuasive way.

Remember, if you are going to court, you will need to master at least the common rules of evidence, filing procedures, and other mechanical matters such as how papers are served on opposing parties. Sometimes clerks of court, especially in small claims court, can be very helpful, but remember that they are not allowed to practice law. There are often paperback books that compile the rules of evidence and the rules of procedure in one helpful place. These can be expensive but well worth the while; lawyers usually have a copy in their briefcase.

Perhaps the best way to learn about court procedure is to hang around the courthouse and watch a few trials and hearings. You may have to rummage around to find out where something like your case is being heard but at least you'll know when to stand up and when to sit down.

If you are writing a cohabitation or marital agreement, you can use this book to get a general idea of the law and to gather the information you can use to make more prudent decision. You can then use the sample agreements as source material for writing your own contract.

After that, it would be a good idea to have someone whom you trust read over the agreement. The person should at least have some business experience and be reasonably sophisticated, if not a lawyer. Then you can ask your consultant whether the contract seems to cover all the eventualities and whether it seems clear and unambiguous.

However, there is still the risk that you will overlook some contingencies or that you may a legal error that can undermine the whole agreement. Having a lawyer read your agreement is the only sensible way to get some assurance that it means what you think it says.

Dealing with government agencies

Dealing with government agencies on your own is some what different than being involved in the court system. At least as important as the written rules are the unwritten mechanisms by which the government accomplishes its business. These include the forms of documents that a bureaucracy will accept, how many copies they require, what has to be notarized, etc. Most of these rules are not written down; some of them aren't even official rules at all but only the way that some doddering old bat has always done it.

Regardless of how stupid or even illegal the paperwork requirements are, however, they are not probably worth fighting over. If you are in a complex and painful personal situation, you really don't need another battle convincing some minion that he or she must accept your document printed by hand in pink ink on flowered wallpaper instead of laser printed on the white 100 per cent cotton bond to which he/she is accustomed. You may win the battle and lose the war; for example, a disgruntled clerk may grudgingly accept your filing and then conveniently lose it, delay its being recorded, or take any number of other petty bureaucratic revenges on you. Some of these can lose your case for you.

On the other hand, if you are polite and very, very patient, many clerks are helpful and will direct you to the right place, help you find the forms, and even check to see that you filled it out "correctly."

If you need to file a document with the government, such as an application for social security benefits, you normally need the correct official form. You can either look up the necessary information online or visit the local government office to see what needs to be done or both. This is one situation where clerks and other officials can be helpful -- or not. If you are stuck and can't figure out what to do, you can try the local law library, usually in the county courthouse and usually open to the public.

Finally, if you are stymied in dealing with a government agency you can contact your state or federal representative (i.e. your Congressperson). Many of these politicians maintain a staff to help constituents and they will sometimes help you through the governmental maze. Moreover, many of them can be found and reached via the Internet. A letter or E-mail requesting assistance is the best way to go, although sometimes a telephone call will work. Your representative in Congress can be helpful in dealing with social security and related matters when the problem is that the agency won't give you a decision.

A special situation — dealing with social workers and psychologists

There is one exception to the above advice about representing yourself. That exception is if you have the misfortune to become entangled either with a social service agency that investigates child abuse and neglect cases or with the experts that evaluate parents and children in custody cases.

Obviously, a good social worker or court investigator is trying to do his or her important job protecting children from abusive or neglectful parents. A conscientious and intelligent worker is in this field does a great deal of good in helping families stay together where possible and in removing children from untenable situations. Court-appointed experts and investigators help family judges reach rational decisions about child custody and other important matters. A good psychologist or child psychiatrist can help a judge decide what custody arrangement will be best for the children.

However, you often don't get to pick your social worker or court-appointed expert. You don't know whether you will be dealing with a conscientious, sensible person or an overbearing jerk enamored of his or her own power. An adverse decision by a mental health professional can result in your losing custody of your child or being prosecuted for child abuse or neglect.

Therefore, treat any social service or court representative with politeness and caution. Be extremely careful what you say and limit your responses to the simplest and clearest factual statements.

If possible, refuse to participate in an interview about suspected child abuse or neglect until you have spoken with a lawyer. **This is one situation where you need**

a good attorney right away. You can lose custody of your child and face spending several years in jail if the situation unwinds unfavorably to you.

Conclusions and advice

The laws that govern the financial implications of marriage and cohabitation change as social values change. Marriage involves explicit financial obligations to each other, although it is no longer a guarantee of lifelong financial security. On the other hand, cohabiting couples can not entirely count on being exempt from obligations to each other.

If you have explicit financial needs and expectations from a relationship, you need to manage the relevant documents and legal structure of your assets carefully. Probably, you will also want to have a premarital or cohabitation agreement. Those actions will give you the best chance of the legal outcome being what you wanted.

Remember -- your best insurance of a reasonable outcome is to check with a good attorney. You are the best judge of your own needs but an attorney is the best judge of whether your actions will achieve the result that you want.

(Endnotes)

[1] *Simeone v. Simeone*, 525 Pa. 392, 581 A. 2d. 162 (1990), discussed in Harry D. Krause and David D. Meyer, *Family Law*, 3rd. Edition, West Publishing Company, 2004. Emphasis supplied.

[2] Mark Strasser, *The Challenge of Same-Sex Marriage Federalist Principles and Constitutional Protections* (Westport, CT: Praeger Publishers, 1999)

[3] Broom, *Commentaries on the Common Law*, (4th Edition, 1869), p. 21, quoted in *Davis v. Davis*, 521 S.W. 2d 603 (Tex. 1975).

[4] Learned Hand, *The Spirit of Liberty* (1952) at page 52, quoted in *Davis v. Davis*, supra.

[5] End note; *Davis v. Davis*, supra, quoted in *Texas Marital Property Rights*, infra.

[6] *Littlejohn v. Rose* 768 F.2d 765 (6th Cir. 1985) cert. den. 475 U.S. 1045 (1986)

[7] For more information about the founding fathers thinking, see *The Ideological Origins of the American Revolution* by...

[8] *Dred Scott v. Sandford*, 60 U.S. 393 (1856)

[9] *Greenlaw v. Smith* 869 P.2d 1024(1994)

[10] See the Washington version of the uniform statute at RCW 26.27.01

[11] *Freidrich v. Freidrich* 983 F.2d 1396 (6th Cir. 1993).

Chapter Two

A BRIEF HISTORY OF LOVE

This chapter contains a brief survey of social attitudes and laws about love and marriage over the past two hundred years. It focuses on differing views of family life and how those opinions have varied over the decades. From 1950 to 2000, the theory and practice of family life in the United States changed dramatically. Social changes such as unmarried couples living together, single parent homes, developments in reproductive technology, and increased openness of gay and lesbian couples, have changed the laws governing couples.

Values, laws, and social conduct change in a synergistic way. Shifts in the moral weight that people ascribe to an action, such as two people living together, occur in tandem with an increase in the conduct itself. In other words, acceptance of unmarried cohabitation as a lifestyle choice has occurred more or less contemporaneously with more couples cohabiting. The figures may differ slightly from one study to another but the overall trends are unmistakable.

In their National Marriage Project, Rutgers University sociologists have been studying people's opinions about relationships for the past twenty years. These social scientists pose questions about marriage and family life to different groups of people and compile the answers. Their work confirms the number of homes comprised of a cohabiting couple has increased from about 400,000 in 1960 to about 4.7 million in 2002.[1]

Moreover, teenagers' attitudes toward living together without marriage, having a child out of wedlock, and the value of marriage reveal changes in American society. Many teenagers now report that having a child out of wedlock is just "doing your own thing."

These opinions parallel social facts. The number of children who are living with a single parent has risen from about 10 per cent in 1960 to 27.4 per cent in 2003. In addition, "more than a third of all births and more than two-thirds of black births in 2002, the latest year for which have complete data were out of wedlock."[2]

In a recent Scientific American article, Rodger Doyle summarized the most recent United States Census data on how couples arrange their lives. From 1950 to the present, the percentage of Americans who are married has declined while the percentages of Americans who have never married, or who are cohabiting with another person, have increased.

In 1950, approximately 65 per cent of adult Americans were married, while slightly less than 25 per cent had never married and less than five per cent were divorced. By 2004, the percentage of married people had declined to about 53 per cent while the percentage of divorced persons had increased to almost ten percent and the percent of those cohabiting to about five per cent. Doyle observed, "In America today, for every 100 married couples, there are 10 couples living together."[3]

These changes, however, have not occurred uniformly throughout society. As Doyle notes, "Cohabitation tends to be most prevalent in New England, Florida and the West and least prevalent in the South, the most conservatively religious region in the U.S."

Drs. David Popenoe and Barbara Defoe Whitehead, the authors of *The State of our Unions 2004*, a research publication sponsored by Rutgers University, note that

> *Most people now live together before they marry for the first time. An even higher percentage of those divorced who subsequently remarry live together first. And a growing number of persons, both young and old, are living together with no plans for eventual marriage.*[4]

They estimate that almost 50 per cent of women between the ages of 25 and 39 are either living with a partner or have lived with one in the past. Today, one in four children "can expect to live in a cohabiting family sometime during childhood."[5] That means, of course, that a far greater percentage of children will have a schoolmate or friend who lives with unmarried adults.

In the face of this reweaving of the fabric of society, some politicians and religious leaders invoke an ideal version of family life that seems to have existed in some other, simpler, time. Values and living arrangements have changed, but many claims that are made about some golden age of morality distort the historical facts. There never was a time when everyone followed the moral rules or when there were no homosexuals or birth control or abortion or divorce.

The history of marriage helps us understand the laws that govern marriage and living together today. The sexual standards, religious beliefs, sociological ideas, and economic considerations that governed marriages in earlier periods still affect our concepts of the relationships between men and women.

Lawmakers have sometimes recognized social changes and sometimes opposed them. Legal rules about marriage have vacillated between rigid standards intended to preserve traditional families and more relaxed standards emphasizing individual freedom and personal happiness.

This brief history is only that — a synopsis of some of the major aspects of marriage and family life in other times. As a very general overview, it necessarily is somewhat inaccurate, and it cannot cover the special issues pertaining to Native American, African-American, or other specific communities.

Love and marriage in historical context

It is difficult to get reliable information about the daily lives of people in past historical periods. The details of family life are often private and unrecorded, if not hidden. People's private conduct can diverge from their public norms. Historians raise many questions about people in other times. How many followed the dictates of the church? Were their sexual lives as inhibited as social norms apparently required? Did working people regard marriage differently than members of the middle class or the aristocracy? If divorce was unobtainable, did people stay together forever or did they sometimes go their separate ways informally?[6]

To research family life, historians consult public sources, including court cases, parish records of births, deaths, and marriages; wills and other legal documents; treatises on marriage; and sermons. They also read private documents such as letters and diaries. However, historians and demographers still disagree about the interpretation of the data. For example, they disagree about the prevalence of contraception in Europe prior to the 19th century.[7]

Often, these sources cast different lights upon the same social institution. In the late 19th century, for example, the prominent reformer Andrew Comstock crusaded against sexual immorality, including pornography and birth control. His crusade persuaded Congress to make mailing information about birth control a crime because he thought that informing people about contraception encouraged fornication. The private letters of two sisters from the same time, however, show them exchanging well-informed advice about birth control methods. Both of these contradictory facts are true but neither presents the complete story.

Love, sexual desire, the role of the family in the community, religion, and other factors intertwine in the institution of marriage. At different times, society has emphasized different aspects of the marital relationship. John Witte, Jr. summarized eloquently four of these factors in his essay on "The Meanings of Marriage."[8]

The Western tradition has, from its beginnings, viewed marriage from at least four perspectives…Marriage is a contract, formed by the mutual consent of the marital couple…Marriage is a spiritual association, subject to the creed of the religious community…Marriage is a social estate, subject to special state

*laws of property, inheritance, and evidence, and to the expectations and
exactions of the local community...and marriage is a natural institution,
subject to the natural laws taught by reason and conscience, nature and
custom.*[8]

Up to the 14th century, Catholic religious concepts dominated the institution of
marriage in England. Marriage was a holy sacrament. Chastity had a high value, and to
some, marriage was only the "remedy for lust."

In the period from the 15th century to the 19th century, Protestant views came
to the fore. These reformers regarded marriage more as a social institution in which
family, church, and state all played a role. They did not value celibacy as a morally
superior way of life. They saw marriage as the natural state of man and woman. Ideally,
each spouse sought their own happiness, including sexual satisfaction and
companionship. Many Protestants also believed that the family formed the foundation
of society. Therefore, the state had a legitimate interest in promoting stable families.

Under that ideology, the requirements for a valid marriage combined family,
state, and church. The law required that a marriage be celebrated by a clergyman in the
presence of two witnesses and recorded in government records. A valid marriage
required the consent of the parents of each party.

Shared interests and companionship outside the home have not always been a
valued goal of marriage. People considered other matters, such as supporting the
extended family's economic interests, more important. Society assumed that men and
women had different spheres of interest and abilities. As a stereotype, women did not
expect to take a direct interest in financial matters nor men in the raising of young
children or household management.

One factor that has varied most over time is the importance assigned to love in
the marital relationship. Obviously, most people have felt that compatibility in the
home is a good thing. Poems and songs celebrated love. In the 18th and early 19th
century, many people regarded romantic love as a dangerous infatuation. It was
dangerous because it might lead a man or woman into an illicit love affair or into a
disadvantageous marriage, to the detriment of the unfortunate lover and his or her
family.

Similarly, from at least the 17th century onward, some people continued to regard
sexual passion as sinful. Decent women engaged in sexual intercourse only to have
children or to gratify their husband's base desires.

From our sexually liberated (or obsessed) perspective, we tend to imagine all
Victorians as sexually inhibited. In fact, some married couples then enjoyed a varied

and satisfying sex life, while others were unhappy. The dominant morality stressed the base nature of male "needs" but many couples still had a happy sexual relationship. In other words, then as now, some people had a satisfying sex life while others didn't.

The Oxford Book of Marriage quotes two very different 19th century letters on the issue of marital sexuality. In 1857, the prominent Anglican clergyman Charles Kingsley wrote to his beloved wife Fanny seven years after they were married. His letter said,

> *Oh, that I were with you or rather you with me here. The beds are so small that we should be forced to lie inside each other, and the weather is so hot that you might walk about naked all day, as well as night — [that goes without saying]. Oh, those naked nights at Chelsea! When will they come again?*

Clearly, this minister and his wife enjoyed their sensual relationship.

On the other hand, in 1843 the French noblewoman Aurore Dudevant wrote to her half-brother on the eve of her niece's marriage. She said,

> *Try to prevent your son-in-law from brutalizing your daughter on their wedding night. Men do not sufficiently understand that their pleasure is our martyrdom. Nothing is more horrible than the terror, the sufferings, and the revulsion of a poor girl, ignorant of the facts of life, who finds herself raped by a brute. As far as possible, we bring them up as saints, and then we hand them over as if they were fillies.*

We know Dudevant under her pseudonym as the flamboyant novelist Georges Sand. She had several famous lovers, including the composer Frederick Chopin. Yet, her letter draws a picture of sexual incompatibility and misery.[9]

For another example, the legal historian Nancy Cott notes that during the debate over slavery in the United States, before the Civil War, abolitionists pointed out the abuse of slave families. A slave owner had the power to "sever relationships between slave couples and families" and to sexually abuse slave women. Supporters of slavery "emphasized its more benign parallels to marriage: wives and slaves; both slaves and wives were dependents, subordinated to the authority of the husband or master and subject to his guidance and protection." Supporters of slavery quoted Biblical passages that enjoined slaves to obey their masters and wives to obey their husbands. They perhaps did not stress the parallel injunctions on masters and husbands to behave with kindness and respect.[11]

These statements are all, of course, stereotypes. At best, they reflect the overall tone of a time. Historical evidence shows us that some people in all times longed for love, enjoyed sex, and valued the companionship of their spouse.

Our myths about love and marriage in past times

One particular difficulty, in understanding how the law interacts with social standards and institutions is that we hold on to myths about past times. We like to think that, in the past, families were stable, divorce was rare, and everyone had the same moral and family values. In fact, the institutions of marriage and the family have been in flux in the United States since the country's founding in the 17th century and even before that, in England, where American law comes from.

Here are some common myths about love and marriage in past times.

MYTH—"*In the past, everyone believed that sexual intercourse outside of marriage was immoral. Women were always virgins when they married.*"

FACT—*While it is generally true that the official values in past times condemned sexual relations outside of marriage, not everyone agreed. In addition, the extent to which people strictly obeyed the rules is a doubtful question.*

Diaries, novels, and sermons, as well as court records, all suggest that sex outside of marriage was common in the 17th, 18th, and 19th centuries, although the frequency varied by gender and social class.[10] Men had more opportunities to indulge their sexual appetites outside of marriage without suffering social condemnation. Similarly, the social restrictions on men and women of the working class were often less rigid than those imposed on the middle and upper classes. It is clear from parish records of marriages and births that women from farming and laboring classes were often pregnant when they married.

"Free love," some like to think, began in the hippie communes of the 1960's, but in fact, social reformers had advocated greater freedom of sexual behavior for well over a century. In the 19th century, various social theorists, such as Robert Owen, and religious groups, such as the Shakers, proposed different ways of organizing society. These proposals were referred to as "utopias" or idealistic visions of perfect societies. Many of the utopian proposals for human society included recognition of women's rights to sexual choice. Idealistic social reformers proposed that unions between men and women should last only so long as both the arrangement made both parties happy. In 1830, for example, one reformer proposed an ideal community where couples cohabited based on their own preferences. In his ideal, the community would own in common and would devote all the assets to the greater good of the community.

Surveys and other historical evidence show that at the turn of the 20th century, women began to experiment openly with sexual freedom. One survey showed that almost 90 per cent of women born before 1890 were virgins when they got married, but only 32 per cent of those born after 1910 were.

In 1910, for example, some commentators deplored the sexual promiscuity of young women.

Just as it is important not to have an unduly idealistic view of the past, it is important not to attribute current mores and customs to other time periods. Small groups may have tried these radical proposals, but the larger society continued to espouse traditional values that condemned sexual relations outside of marriage and regarded marriage as a lifelong commitment. The difficult historical question is how many people actually followed the larger society's values. The rate of hypocrisy is as difficult to determine as the rate of sin.

In addition to people who conscientiously had different values than the larger community, there were also those who simply violated its mores. Even in the Victorian period, which we imagine as a time of straitlaced values, sexual misconduct was common, as is evidenced by the prevalence of prostitution at the time.

Some historians have estimated that there were over 50,000 prostitutes in London in the latter 19th century. Child prostitution in 19th century London was so common that girls as young as 10 or 12 were sold into brothels. To illustrate the problem, one social reformer bought a young girl for five pounds and then wrote an article about the experience. (The article got so much attention that he was prosecuted for kidnapping and spent three months in Newgate Prison.) The age of consent then was 13. Social reformers urged Parliament to raise the age so that sex with young girls became illegal. Parliament reluctantly acted and raised it to 16. In the same law, it increased the penalty for homosexuality.

MYTH—*"In the past, people were married in church or by a judge. Common law marriage is a relatively recent legal invention that the courts developed to deal with the problem of people just shacking up."*

FACT—*Common law marriage is a very old institution. The very term, "common law marriage" reflects the fact that it is a form of marriage recognized by the common law, which is the law established by court decisions.*

What constitutes a legally binding marriage has varied over the centuries. The involvement of the government, the church, and the family differed over time. For example, in 15th century Florence Italy, couples were traditionally married in front of a notary, rather than in church.[12] Oliver Cromwell introduced a legal provision for civil marriage (without a priest) in England in the 17th century.

Since the agreement of the parties has always been the legal core of marriage (at least for the last few centuries), the question was what formalities were required. Legal experts agreed that the marriage occurred when the couple exchanged words of marriage. In several famous cases, couples who wished to marry in spite of family opposition claimed that they had privately exchanged promises of marriage. For example, King Henry II of France planned to marry his daughter to the son of a high official. The young man revealed, however, that he had exchanged words of marriage with a lady-in-waiting at the royal court. A church court determined that the couple in fact had married, although the father later had the "marriage" avoided.[13]

In less exalted cases, a pregnant young woman might claim that she and her lover had married because they exchanged private vows. In other words, she (and her outraged parents) informed the young man's family that he and she were in fact married even though there had not been a church ceremony. Many questions of marriage and morality were decided at times by church courts. If the case went to an ecclesiastical court, the question would be whether the woman was simply immoral, whether the man had used promises of marriage to seduce her, or whether the couple had married each other. Each factual scenario had a different legal outcome; only the exchange of words of marriage meant that a legal marriage had taken place.

Church and government officials at various times tried to insist on different formalities, including a public wedding, a clergyman or government functionary officiating, licenses, witnesses, or the consent of the parents of the young couple.

MYTH—*"In the past, women stayed at home and took care of their home and children. Men went out to work and supported the family."*

FACT—*The degree to which women occupied most of their in hard work, in the home or outside the home, has varied greatly with historical period and social class.*

Both the realities of child care and the ideals of how best to raise a child have varied widely over the last few centuries. It is probably accurate to say that from the 19th century onward, the dominant social ideal was that (white prosperous middle class) women stayed at home and occupied themselves primarily with managing the household. The social ideal held that the care of a husband and home, along with socially approved charitable works, was a woman's "natural" sphere. On that ideology, the ideal home offered the husband a morally pure refuge from the rough and tumble of commercial life.

One factor that influences the lives of children is the economic conditions of their parents. One reality was that the wives of farmers and small businessmen worked hard in the family business, whether their work consisted of helping on the farm or running a small shop or tavern. For most people, before at least the late 19th century, the wife's work (and that of the couple's children) was essential to the survival of the family. Moreover, prior to the Industrial Revolution in the mid-19th century, a typical man's work was also in or near the home, whether the man worked on a farm or ran a small business such as a blacksmith shop or tavern.

After the industrial revolution, most working-class families needed the income from both spouses and their children to provide the essentials of life. Many wives worked in mills and other factories. So did children as young as five years old. Social reformers describe the picture of a father carrying his sleeping child to their work at the factory in the morning and carrying the exhausted child home at night.

Around the turn of the previous century, many changes had taken place in the lives of Americans, especially women. One of these was that the birthrate fell. In 1800, the average white woman had seven children or more, but by 1900, the average was 3.5, and by 1929, it had fallen to slightly over two. The second was that women's lives were made freer by other social changes. Clothing styles changed from pounds of petticoats and long skirts to higher hemlines and simpler clothing. In 1890, only one college-age woman in 50 went to college, but by 1910, that rate had tripled. The number of women in the work force outside their homes doubled between 1880 and 1900.

Third, by the end of the century, the passage of some reform legislation led to improved working conditions. General economic prosperity meant that the lives of the working and middle classes, both men and women, improved. Laws were passed requiring that children receive some education, and the hours that they could work were limited.

Child care

At various times from at least the 17th century onward, farming infants out to wet nurses for the first two or three years of their lives was common among families wealthy enough to afford the custom. Even middle class women often entrusted their infants to other women to nurse and take care of for the first two years.

This custom sometimes had interesting side effects. The 17th century writer Madame de Sévignè noted that a wet nurse in her daughter's family had broken out with a rash resembling syphilis. Her letters also revealed, however, that the baby had oddly shaped teeth, which suggests that the child had congenital syphilis, probably contracted from her diseased, but high-class, father. The nurse might well have contracted the disease from the infected child.

In less wealthy homes, children were often cared for by whoever was handy, whether a maid or an elderly relative. In times when a farm housewife spun her own thread, wove her own cloth, and sewed most, if not all of the family's clothes and linens, as well as cooking, preserving foods, keeping the garden, feeding the chickens and pigs, making butter and cheese, and even brewing beer, the care and education of the young children often took a backseat to the more pressing needs of the household. A city housewife might not have the same garden and livestock chores as the farm wife but she often engaged in other activities in an effort to help the family survive financially, such as working in the family business.

Poor women, especially those without husbands, might be forced to entrust their small children to the notorious "baby farms" where a woman would undertake to care for a group of children, many of whom quickly died of neglect or abuse. According to Gottlieb, "Overlaid and starved at nurse" was often given as a cause of infant deaths in official lists in 17th century London;[40] "overlaid" meant that the nurse had rolled over on the baby in her sleep and suffocated the child. Some suggest that these "nurses" gave unwanted infants a hefty dose of gin to "quiet" them, which it did — often to the point of death.

Older children have been cared for in a variety of ways in different time periods. In wealthy families, nannies, governesses and tutors all played a part in caring for children. In less prosperous families, the parents either sent them to school or put them to work. Even among working-class families, families who could afford it sent their children to school. Many working class children, however, started work when they were five or six years old.

The idea of childhood as a time of play and learning is a relatively recent one. Even in the 19th and early 20th century, society regarded children as economic contributors to the household, whether they worked in the home, on the farm, or in a factory. Interestingly, many men who belonged to labor unions opposed legalized birth control. They believed that available contraception would infringe on their right to have large families. They wanted to have large families so they could have more wages earned by their children. Remember that at the time, children went to work and their wages belonged to the father.

Before child labor laws passed in the 19th century, children as young as five years old went to work, sometimes in coal mines or factories. Under the law, a father had a right to his child's earnings. A girl of 10 or 12 might work as a kitchen maid or in mill working at huge industrial looms, while little boys went to work in mines or factories. Well into the 20th century, children who were 14 or 15 years old left school to work in a variety of jobs, including as office boys, messengers, or household help.

At various times and in different social classes, children were sent away from home for many reasons — to work, to live with wealthy relatives, or to go to school. They might be sent away as young as the age of seven.

Contrary to our current views, many commentators advised that, after the age of five or so, fathers should definitely take over the supervision of their children's upbringing. Too much influence from the mother or other women, such as maids, could be deleterious to the child's intellect and morals.

The ideal of the wife whose attention focused entirely on the care of her children and husband is largely an ideal of the prosperous urban middle class of the late 19th century. For that class, the image of the husband who went out to work and the wife who stayed home reading to her young child reflected both an ideal and, to some extent, a reality for many middle class families. To some extent, that ideal was feasible because of the availability of relatively cheap household labor; the prosperous housewife's work was managing the household, rather than actually doing the work of cleaning and cooking.

Some commentators suggest that the idea that children need hours of intense attention and effort from their parents is a figment of the late 20th century. In fact, some psychologists believe that the current ideal of intense, even intrusive, attention from parents has led to a generation of neurotic, dependent, and essentially dysfunctional young adults.

The idealized image of a woman devoting her loving attention and effort solely to her children had both positive and negative aspects for men and women. For women, the dominant ideology postulated that women were by nature more loving, pious, and pure than men. Therefore, their nature fitted them to provide a tender, morally uplifting home where children could grow into upright citizens and which would be a refuge for men from the temptations and turmoil of the business and industrial world. For men, this ideology held that they were stronger mentally, and physically than women and better able to endure the stress of earning a living. In the family, the ideal father tempered the mother's tenderness with stern discipline.

The negative sides of this ideology, however, contributed to the repression of women and the increasing exclusion of men from family life. In the pernicious version of these views, women are too weak to go out in the workaday world. Even when that position became less socially permissible, some may still regard the woman's natural role as being that of caretaker of the home. It reduced the father's role to that of a distant breadwinner.

One view is that these myths contributed to the current disparity in awards of custody. Giving the mother the larger responsibility of raising the children, represented by primary physical custody, and limiting the father's role to "visitation" and payment of money mirrored these stereotyped roles of mother and father. It was not necessarily in the best interests of the mother, the father, or the children.

As these myths illustrate, we tend to describe American society in the past as having vastly different norms and ways of behaving than are common now. To that extent, we may regard our own behavior as being very different from that of our parents or grandparents.

MYTH— *"In the past, people got married and stayed married for their whole lives."*

FACT— *Prior to about 1920, many marriages ended after a relatively short period, sometimes by the death of one of the spouses or, less frequently, by divorce.*

"Till death do us part" had a different meaning when epidemic disease, lack of effective medical treatment, and the risks of childbirth meant that many adults died relatively young. Although some marriages lasted for the long lifetime of both spouses, it was more common for marriages to end with the death of one of them.

Moreover, during the 18th and 19th centuries, the growth of populous cities and the expansion of colonial empires made it much easier for men to abandon their wives. One historian has noted that turn-of-the-century Yiddish newspapers in American cities carried personal ads placed by Jewish wives who were still in eastern Europe. Their husbands had immigrated to the new world and left their family behind. These women sometimes had not heard from their husband for years, but they could not remarry because he might still be alive. They placed advertisements looking for information on their vanished husbands. Sometimes, the man had died with no one to let his family back home know. Sometimes, he had taken a new wife and conveniently failed to send money for the original wife's passage to America.

That is just one example of how improved transportation made it easier for a man (or less commonly a woman) to simply abandon his or her spouse and family. He could immigrate to the New World, move to the big city, or set out for the frontier. Perhaps the understanding was that he would send for his wife when he established himself. Perhaps both of them understood that their parting was a permanent separation. Prior to that period, it had been more common for people to live in one small geographical area for their entire lives, which made it difficult for an ordinary couple to part company informally.

The availability of divorce is another area in which our stereotypes of past times do not match historical reality. Many people think that until recently it had always been very hard to get a divorce in the United States and that few people were divorced. In fact, the laws of divorce have fluctuated greatly. The percentage of couples who divorced has also varied.

In England, the divorce law had typically been very restrictive, although some reformers like John Milton had argued for more liberal laws. At one time, an act of Parliament was required for a couple to be divorced. Similarly, in the 18th and early

19th centuries, American law provided limited and specific grounds that justified a court in granting a divorce. These grounds included physical cruelty and adultery by the wife. Adultery by the husband did not justify the wife's getting a divorce.

In the mid to late 19th century, some states liberalized the grounds for divorce. Ideals of personal freedom and happiness led some state legislatures to enact laws that made it easier for unhappy couples to separate. During t he 19th century, for a while at least, Illinois became a divorce haven, as Las Vegas would be in the 20th century. Unhappy couples traveled to frontier states where the law afforded them a way out of their unsatisfactory marriage.

By 1889, the United States had the highest divorce rate in the world. Most states allowed divorce on any grounds that the court deemed sufficient, and there were over 400 possible grounds for divorce. From 1870 onward, the divorce rate had risen sharply, and by 1916, in San Francisco, one marriage in four ended in divorce. In Chicago, the rate was one out of seven. In an effort to preserve marriages, at the turn of the century, the state legislatures tightened the restrictions on divorce, making it harder to obtain. New York would only permit divorce on grounds of adultery, while South Carolina did not permit divorce at all. Nonetheless, the divorce rate continued to rise. By 1924, the national rate was that one marriage in seven ended in divorce.

However, from the 1930's until the 1970's, the laws again made divorces relatively hard to get. These restrictive laws were a reaction to the alarmingly high rate of divorce in previous decades.

The proceedings were long and expensive, and the grounds had been limited. Usually, one spouse had to prove that the other had committed adultery or was more abusive than social norms tolerated.

A divorce based on the fault of one party, however, had severe legal consequences. The sinning party sometimes could not legally remarry. Moreover, the ex-husband was not obligated to support an adulterous ex-wife. And, agreements contemplating divorce were illegal. Hence, the parties could not make a valid contract to "give' each other a divorce and therefore had little ability to modify the consequences of the law. At times, the law has permitted agreements governing separations but a separated couple, of course, cannot remarry.

MYTH—*"Because people stayed married in the old days, there were no "blended" families."*

FACT—*The high mortality rate, especially from childbirth, meant that many children grew up in families composed of stepparents, half brothers and sisters, and other stepchildren.*

Death from disease, famine, and war was common enough in prior centuries that a reasonably large proportion of children grew up with a stepparent or as orphans. Sometimes, relatives might raise an orphan in their home. Sometimes, orphaned children ended up in brutal public institutions. Often, the children simply had to try to survive as best they could on the streets. In some foundlings' homes, over 90 per cent of the children died.

Widowers often sought to remarry quickly in order to secure a wife to take care of their motherless children. Widows often needed to remarry in order to obtain a man's support. There were, however, many social advantages to being a wealthy widow. As Beatrice Gottlieb notes, "For the first time in their lives, they had the means to be somewhat independent, with an identity no longer derived from either father or husband."[14]

If nothing else, the prevalence of fairy tales about wicked stepmothers should tell us that people were familiar with the problems of second marriages. In the classic fairy tale of Hansel and Gretel, the stepmother persuades the poor woodman to abandon the children from his first marriage alone in the forest, presumably to die. Similarly, the fairy tale of Cinderella is the story of a daughter abused by her stepmother in favor of the second family.

MYTH—*"In the past, people did not use contracts to describe their familial obligations; love or morality told them what to do."*

FACT—*Marriage has traditionally been regarded as both a social institution, governed by morality, religion, and the law, and a contract in which certain obligations are voluntarily assumed.*

The idea of contract is central to the very idea of marriage. Regardless of the ceremonial trappings and any other requirements imposed by laws or customs, marriage consists of two people agreeing to be married. People used contracts to control various aspects of marriage. Sometimes the spouses entered into a contract about family property before the marriage. Sometimes, they used a contract to formalize the terms of a permanent separation.

In Jewish law and tradition, from the Middle Ages to the present, a couple enters into a marriage contract called a *ketubah*.[15] The *ketubah* sets out the financial terms of the marriage as well as the obligations of each spouse to the other. Part of the contract provides for the husband's financial obligations to his wife in the event of death or divorce and part sets out the terms of the dowry that she is to bring to the marriage. Some contemporary rabbis have added a term that says both parties agree to appear before a rabbinical court if they divorce in order to settle the religious implications of their parting.

Jewish law and rabbinical teaching also set out in some detail the respective marital rights of the parties. Traditionally, the husband acquired ten obligations and four rights. Among his obligations were to furnish his wife with a decent lifestyle and to satisfy her natural sexual needs. He was also obligated to pay his wife's medical bills and the costs of her funeral if she should die. In return, he acquired various financial rights including the right to inherit from her. In addition to bringing him a dowry, a good wife served her husband, cheered and comforted him, and worked hard for their joint success.[16] Each owed the other a duty of marital fidelity. In medieval times, rabbinical law required a couple to divorce if the wife were proven to be unfaithful, even if the husband forgave her.

In other words, obligations derived from contract, tradition, and law have long been mingled in the concept of marriage.

At various times, society considered individual marriage contracts as being "integral to the act of getting married." Gottlieb notes that in 15th century Florence, the marriage contract may have been the most important document in a person's life. In Jewish tradition and law, the marriage contract has been an integral part of marriage for many centuries.[17]

The families of the bride and groom worked out the economic terms of the marriage. The engaged couple often had little to say about the choice of their spouse or the terms. Gottlieb cites the interchange between an aristocratic French father and his son. When the son asked about the girl being considered as his bride, the father responded, "Attend to your own business, sir."

A premarital contract has long been a part of marriage, even for relatively poor people. Gottlieb notes that "Even after the legal requirements for weddings changed in the 16th century, the making of marriage contracts continued, not only as a practical business matter but also because they were still considered integral to the act of getting married." The marriage contract mainly dealt with property matters, including especially the amount of the dowry provided by the bride's family to the husband.

For centuries, the law entrusted most of the power in family relationships to the male. Under the law, "husband and wife were one and that one was the husband," as the legal commentator Blackstone put it. A married woman literally had no legal identity, unless the couple sought a divorce. Married women did not have the right to control the use or disposition of property. They could not sue in their own name. Their husbands controlled all of the family assets, including any money that the wife and children earned.

Some men, however, were well aware of the financial havoc that an improvident son-in-law could cause and took appropriate legal precautions to protect their widows or daughters. They tied up the family assets in various trusts and contracts in an effort to protect them. Sometimes these contracts governed what happened to the family property on the marriages and deaths of the great grandchildren anticipated from the marriage.

Moreover, a couple that could no longer stand to live together could use a contract to set the terms of a permanent separation. During the times when divorces were difficult to obtain, a couple might formally separate, and the terms of the separation could be set out in a written agreement. The couple could not, however, contract for a separation before they actually physically parted because the courts thought that such agreements might tend to encourage couples to separate or divorce.

A permanent separation could be recognized in the courts as a divorce *a mensa et thoro*, which is Latin for "from bed and board." In some states, one can still obtain a legal separation. Under this doctrine a couple that does not believe in divorce can get a declaration that they are officially living apart.

In contemporary America, separation agreements and prenuptial agreements can form the basis for a property division in divorce proceedings. During the divorce, however, the parties may ask the court to modify the terms of the agreement, and the agreement may, or may not, be made part of the formal decree of divorce, depending on the judge's decision.

In general, today, the law holds that prenuptial and separation agreements are valid contracts, provided that the agreement is not grossly unfair and neither party cheated the other. Today, all states have adopted the Uniform Marriage and Divorce Act which provides that separation agreements are valid unless they are so unfair as to be unconscionable or unless one party coerced or defrauded the other. Misrepresenting financial matters, including understating one's assets, constitutes a kind of fraud.

There are some limits on which prenuptial or separation agreements a court will honor, however. Agreements about custody and child support are not binding on a court; the judge can determine these matters in the best interests of the child. The court need not enforce a prenuptial agreement that is unfair, especially if one party didn't have full information or a lawyer.

Agreements that restrict a person's ability to marry, or to remarry following a divorce, are also invalid, and a court will not enforce them, although courts will usually enforce provisions that alimony or spousal support payments end if the former spouse remarries or cohabits.

MYTH—*"In the past, old people lived in the family home; families cherished their wisdom and willingly took care of them."*

FACT—*Aging people have long feared being left with no one to care for them or with insufficient assets to ensure their comfort.*

Older parents have traditionally feared ending up destitute and uncared for. The noted historian and ethicist Thomas Cole in his book *The Journey of Life: A Cultural History of Aging*[18] has documented some of the arrangements that parents made to keep control of their assets and protect themselves from neglect by their children. Marriage contracts also dealt with the support of aged parents.

Older people feared literally ending up in the workhouse, which was a grim and often brutal physical institution where the desperately poor could obtain some minimal shelter and food, paid for by the local government. Certainly, some extended families took loving care of their older relatives but historical records of property settlements and lawsuits reveal that parents often did not trust their grown children to take care of them.

MYTH—*"Before the 1960's, birth control was unknown."*

FACT—*Contraceptive methods have been known for thousands of years. Condoms were in use as early as the 17th century, although primarily to avoid venereal disease. Several effective forms of birth control were known by the mid-19th century, but laws were passed making it illegal to have this knowledge.*

People have sought to avoid unwanted pregnancies for thousands of years. They have used both contraception and abortion.

Historical evidence about birth control

Historical records suggest that people have known about more or less effective contraception and abortion methods for thousands of years. Information about effective methods, however, has sometimes been suppressed or forgotten. In addition, many old beliefs were wrong.

Historians look to different kinds of evidence for the existence and efficacy of birth control methods. They study records of the number of children in families. If fewer children were born than would be biologically expected, the inference is that couples practiced some form of contraception. Old medical textbooks provide information on what was known about preventing conception and inducing miscarriage. Legal and religious writings record social opinions about these practices and can suggest that abortion or contraception took place in that society. If an ancient law, for example, prohibited abortion, then the inference is that the practice existed at that time. Otherwise, the authorities would not have felt the need for a law. In later periods, historians can consult private diaries and letters, as well as popular books, pamphlets, advertisements, and popular lectures.

The historian Helen Lefkowitz Horowitz notes that in 18th and 19th century America, books, advertising literature, and private communication among women spread information about birth control. Several popular home medical guides of the 18th and early 19th centuries candidly discussed sexual anatomy and birth control.[19]

In fact, one book, titled *Aristotle's Masterpiece*, was considered especially appropriate reading for women, as part of their natural sphere as wives and mothers. One pioneer woman in the early 19th century wrote a letter to her sister with accurate information about condoms and "female preventatives" (diaphragms) for limiting the number of children.

In the mid to late 19th century, traveling lecturers, complete with anatomically correct mannequins gave talks about sexuality. Their advertisements reassured their prospective audiences that the tasteful discussion would not offend even the most lady-like woman.

Medical information and technology

Ancient Egyptian papyrus manuscripts give detailed instructions for the prevention and termination of pregnancy. Greek manuscripts from 400 BCE to 100 AD contain equally detailed information. Medieval Arabic sources preserved some of these works, as well as other ancient treatises, such as those of Plato and Aristotle.

However, like other scientific information, a great deal of this knowledge was suppressed or lost in western Europe. Several factors contributed to the loss of knowledge. During the Middle Ages, social turmoil and deliberate destruction by the Catholic Church reduced the availability of ancient manuscripts. Some ancient teachings were recovered during the Renaissance in about 1400 when interest in knowledge of the natural world became acceptable again. Shortly after

Many historians have assumed that ancient herbal remedies were ineffective. Indeed, it seems unlikely that a paste of crocodile feces mixed with beer or the smoke from the burned hoof of a mule would have any significant effect.

However, more recent scientific research suggests that these assumptions were wrong. Some ancient birth control ingredients have now been tested in laboratory animals and found to be effective, either to prevent conception by interfering with ovulation or to induce an early miscarriage. Plants such as rue, juniper, pennyroyal, and pomegranate have been shown to affect fertility. In addition, some ancient birth control suggestions involved substances placed in the vagina or rubbed on the head of the penis prior to intercourse. Some of these suggestions may have been effective as a barrier to the sperm or had a spermicidal effect.

As John Riddle points out, it was somewhat arrogant for modern historians and doctors to assume that discussions of contraception in earlier times were completely rooted in ignorance and fantasy. He notes that observation of farm animals could easily have led ancient people to deduce which herbs caused miscarriage in cows, for example, and to have applied that observation to people.[20]

Medical knowledge prior to the 20th century had significant limitations, however. Neither doctors nor women could reliably determine whether a woman who had ceased to menstruate was in the early stage of pregnancy or suffering from some other condition that interferes with menses, such as depression, anorexia, menopause, or other hormonal issues. Drugs caused a woman to menstruate, therefore, they might or might not be causing a very early abortion.

In other time, physicians also debated whether both the male and female contributed seed to the child or only the male. Some writers felt that the woman simply provided a place for the male seed to grow. Finally, many authorities were confused on the timing of a woman's fertile period, so advice on rhythm methods of birth control was sometimes worse than useless.

Ancient Greek and Roman literature did not mention coitus interruptus (withdrawal by the man before he ejaculates) as a method of birth control. It is possible that the technique was so commonly known that there was no reason to mention it, but it is equally likely that the method was not widely used then.

Historians agree that the *coitus interruptus* method was widely known and practiced in the American colonies at least from the 18th century onward. In one 1742 Massachusetts case, a man was prosecuted for fathering a child out of wedlock; he testified that he could not be the father because, although he admitted to having had sex with the woman, he had "always minded my pullbacks."

The first known form of condom was made from a thin membrane from sheep's intestines (like sausage casings). It came into use in the 17th century primarily to protect men from contracting venereal disease from prostitutes. The invention of vulcanized rubber in the 19th century made the condom more reliable and popular as a birth control method. Condoms were expensive and were reused. Some doctors and other moralists disapproved of the use of condoms by married people because the device was suggestive of a brothel.

The historian Yale notes "By the 1840's, vaginal sponges also became increasingly available, not only from dubious sources like advertisements and traveling salesmen, but also from reputable druggists and physicians." She observes that the diaphragm itself, which had been invented in 1882 in Europe, did not become widely available in the United States until the 1920's, but that a similar device called "The Wife's Protector" had been patented in the US in 1846 and that a wide assortment of vaginal caps was available in the 1860's and 1870's.

By the 1830's and 1840's, several other means of contraception were widely known. In addition to abstinence, barrier methods (such as condoms, vaginal sponges, and early forms of diaphragms), and withdrawal, experts advocated various forms of the rhythm method. Perhaps the most widely recommended method, however, was the vaginal douche. Experts encouraged women to douche immediately before or after sexual intercourse, using a variety of solutions, including plain water, saline, and vinegar and water mixtures.

There is disagreement about the effectiveness of these methods, but the spacing of children in families and surveys of women who used birth control suggest that these methods had some effectiveness, at least in reducing the number of conceptions.

Misogyny and knowledge

Some historians believe that misogynistic attitudes played an important role in social attitudes about pregnancy. Some commentators interpreted Biblical texts, especially the story of Adam and Eve, to mean that women deserved to suffer repeated painful and dangerous pregnancies because that was God's curse on woman for eating the forbidden apple. Another view was that women's sexuality tempted men to sin, and, therefore, women deserved the pains and risks of repeated pregnancies.

Some feminist historians also note that knowledge about the medicinal effects of herbs, including their uses for contraception and abortion, may have been preserved within the community of women, along with other information necessary to running a household, such as recipes and information about caring for babies and treating common ailments. Such knowledge might have been passed down, for example, from mother to daughter, even when it had been lost to the medical literature.

The wisdom possessed by women about the medicinal use of herbs, however, would have been outside accepted "knowledge." Social norms held medical knowledge to be the exclusive province of trained physicians or apothecaries. Those same norms barred women from any such training. When the holder of herbal information was an elderly widow, perhaps one who lived in an isolated cottage with her cat, church authorities (who were also all male) might well have regarded her as a witch and her skills as magical and diabolical. She was a not a man; therefore, she could not have the socially approved (male) training. Therefore, her information was suspect. It is not accidental, perhaps, that some early laws against abortion refer to the use of "maleficium," which was black magic.

Some historians also interpret the suppression of knowledge about birth control by moral reformers in the late 19th and early 20th century as attempts to limit the growing political and economic power of women. If a woman was shackled to the home by repeated childbearing, she could not take any meaningful role in the larger world.

Moral and legal opinion on birth control

In the ancient world, the prevailing opinion was that it was quite proper to limit the number of children in a family, although there were contrary opinions, especially when governmental policies encouraged citizens to have large families to increase the population. Some people disapproved of permitting women to avoid having children because it might deprive husbands of having a legitimate heir. They considered the man's interest in having heirs of greater importance than the woman's desire to avoid childbirth

From the Middle Ages to the present, some religious authorities have condemned contraception. Among other grounds, some interpreted the passage in Genesis that enjoined mankind to "be fruitful and multiply" to mean that a couple should have as many children as occurred naturally.

Many moralists condemned *coitus interruptus* as the sin of Onan. Under ancient Hebrew law, a man whose elder brother died without having children was supposed to father a son with his brother's widow. According to the Bible, Onan had sex with his brother's widow but "spilled his seed on the ground." God punished him for this act. Some moralists interpreted this story as expressing divine condemnation of masturbation, which was therefore called "onanism." Others, however, read it only as condemning *coitus interruptus*. (Incidentally, at the least, the story shows that the ancient Hebrews were well aware of one effective method of birth control.)

Not all religious authorities read the relevant Biblical texts the same way. Jewish tradition contains the story of one eminent rabbi's wife who had a very difficult and painful childbirth. She asked her pious husband if God's command to be fruitful applied to both men and women or only to men. He responded that the divine command applied only to men, as God addressed that command to Adam. Cheerfully, she went off and sought effective contraception. The rabbi later lamented that he wished that they had had one more child. Significantly, there is no suggestion in the story that the rabbi/husband believed that his wife's action was in any way wrong or immoral.

Still many other religious authorities read other texts, especially in Paul's letters in the New Testament, as condemning all sensual pleasure as inherently sinful. They held that celibacy was the morally preferable state. Some writers taught that sexual relations were solely for the procreation of children, not for pleasure, even between married people. They condemned contraception of any form (except abstinence), abortion, masturbation, sex outside marriage, oral sex, anal sex, couples seeing each other nude, and sex between persons who could not produce a child, including sex after the wife's menopause, because none of these practices were intended to produce a child. At best, sexual pleasure was acceptable in marriage because it helped people avoid the sin of fornication. Later protestant writers, such as the poet and essayist John Milton, suggested that sexual pleasure was a desirable part of married life.

Given that historical evidence suggests that people limited the size of their families during all of these periods, it seems likely that many people simply ignored these doctrines and used some form of birth control.

By the 19th century, in the United States, some social reformers urged women to space their children in order to promote a happier, more prosperous family, with a healthier mother. Repeated childbearing endangered the mother's health and strained the family's ability to provide for all the children.

Theories of eugenics also played a role. Insanity and criminal conduct as well as various illnesses were considered hereditary. Some 19th and early 20th century physicians urged persons who had relatives with these problems not to have children.

However, not everyone in the United States believed that even married couples should be able to limit the size of their families. As early as 1845, in some states, publishing information on contraception and abortion constituted the crime of obscenity. In effect, any discussion of sexuality was obscene. New laws also prohibited birth control itself. Some of these laws prohibited the dissemination of any information about contraception by anyone. Laws in other states permitted married couples to obtain contraceptive devices, such as condoms, from a physician or pharmacist, but it was illegal to advertise birth control information or devices.

The social factors that led to opposition to contraception included the economics of medical practice, racism, repression of women, and objections to "vice." The medical establishment was gaining power and physicians wanted to control the practice of medicine by limiting medical procedures to men trained in particular schools and by effacing the roles of pharmacists, midwives, and other practitioners. Obviously, in part, these efforts were intended to protect people from outright quacks.

Racism played a role since some believed that supposedly inferior immigrant groups would overwhelm those of supposedly superior Northern European origin.

Racist views included the opinion that "inferior" groups, such as African Americans, Jews, Italians, and people from Eastern Europe, had stronger sex drives and were more fertile than the "superior races." On these views, white women of Northern European heritage should be encouraged to have larger families.

For many years, many doctors refused to perform the necessary surgery to render a person incapable of producing a child, which is called "sterilization," at least if the reason was simply to avoid having more children. There were a variety of reasons for this opposition, including moral opposition to birth control, a paternalistic attitude toward women (which included a lack of respect for a woman's capacity to make a rational decision), and sometimes the view that a woman "owed" her husband children, whether she wanted them or not.

Interestingly, however, during the 1930's, the medical profession as a group widely supported sterilizing the unfit," which included retarded persons and "habitual" criminals. Some estimates are that as many as 60,000 people may have been involuntarily sterilized during the height of this policy. During this time, the Supreme Court held that a state could constitutionally sterilize "defective" persons, and in a case concerning a supposedly imbecilic woman, Justice Oliver Wendell Holmes famously remarked, "Three generation of imbeciles are enough." (Interestingly, the woman in that case was not mentally disabled and, after being released from the institution, went on to lead a relatively normal life.) These supposed eugenic rationales were often a disguise for punishment of people whose conduct offended the dominant morality and for discrimination against ethnic minorities and the poor. After the revelation of the Nazi atrocities, support for sterilization on the basis of eugenics (improvement of the race) waned. As discussed elsewhere, the right to control one's reproductive life is now constitutionally protected, and supposed concerns about "improvement of the race" do not justify the government in controlling who can reproduce.

In the latter part of the 19th century, advocates of free love and the sellers of contraceptives clashed with those opposed to contraception. Ironically, much of the opposition to abortion and birth control appeared in print in the "sporting press," which were newspapers aimed at single working men. These papers contained news of boxing matches, horse racing and theatrical performances, as well as erotic or pornographic fiction. Some publishers of the sporting press, despite their profiting from some aspects of morally dubious conduct, also believed that, for women, intercourse outside of marriage should be punished by pregnancy.

Comstock believed that pornography led to masturbation which he regarded as immoral and unhealthy. He also believed that contraception and abortion permitted men and women to sin (have sex) without fear of the "natural" consequence, which was pregnancy. The only way to preserve that fear was to keep people in ignorance; if people understood how to avoid having children, they could freely choose whether to have sexual intercourse or not. As postmaster of the United States, Comstock used anti-pornography legislation to suppress the dissemination of information about birth control

By the end of the 19th century, doctors could not legally discuss contraception with their patients. Some doctors so feared the reach of the anti-pornography laws that they hesitated to discuss the biology of contraception among themselves, in letters, or in medical schools, fearing that any mention of the subject would fall afoul of the restrictive laws. Selling condoms, diaphragms, or other birth control devices was also illegal, although these restrictions could be avoided to some extent by claiming that some birth control methods were for "health reasons," such as avoiding venereal disease, rather than for contraception.

Obviously, Comstock's actions closely resemble both those of the medieval church and those who oppose sex education today. The view is essentially this – "if you have too much information, you might do something that I disapprove of. Therefore, I will keep you ignorant."

Advocates of greater rights for women, including the courageous Margaret Sanger who openly taught women about birth control, opposed this official suppression of information.

Beginning in the 1960's, the courts began to strike down these restrictions. In the case of *Griswold vs. Connecticut, the* United States Supreme Court held that medical advice about family planning was a private matter between physician and patient. In effect, the court ruled in favor of the sanctity of the home by restricting the government's right to pry into a married couple's bedroom. In 19th century London, the only possible shelter for illegitimate children whose mother could not (and father would not) support them was the Foundling Home, which was a harsh institution. Unwed mothers had to convince the overseers to take their child by explaining the circumstances of its birth. The pathetic stories of unmarried mothers, who were often servant girls who had been seduced by men in the household where they worked, make clear that many women were not protected from unwanted pregnancies.[21]

MYTH—*"Abortion was uniformly condemned and illegal until the Supreme Court decided the case of Roe v. Wade in the 1970's."*

FACT—*Women have sought abortions, with varying degrees of success, for centuries, and the practice was often legal or quasi-legal.*

Moral and legal opinions on abortion have varied widely over time. Historical evidence reveals that, from the ancient world onward, people have taken the same positions debated in contemporary society. Some have felt that abortion ought to be entirely the decision of the woman or the family, at least in the early stages of pregnancy. Some felt that both were entirely wrong. Some believed that abortion was wrong except to save the mother's life or health.

Many laws and moral writings distinguished between inducing menstruation before the embryo could be felt to move (called "quickening") and causing an abortion after quickening.[22] (Quickening usually occurs around the end of the second trimester (fifth or sixth month) of pregnancy.) Some believed that when the fetus was "formless," it did not have a soul. At that early stage, aborted was morally acceptable. They believed that after fetus had a recognizable human form, i.e. in the later stages of pregnancy, it had been "ensouled" and hence to kill it was to commit homicide.

In ancient Greece and Rome, it appears that prevailing opinion condoned both abortion and infanticide, at least of newborns. A parent might leave an unwanted infant outside in a deserted area to die of exposure. This practice was probably more common if the child were female; one ancient letter records a husband instructing his pregnant wife to preserve the baby if it were male but expose it if it were female. By law, the ancient Greek or Roman father had the right to determine whether the child lived or died. However, a humane addition to that law provided that parent should leave the child in a particular location where families who wanted a child could go and get the baby. The new family, then, was obligated to raise the child as their own.

Many commentators have noted that the Hippocratic Oath for physicians, which originated in ancient Greece, condemned abortion, or more exactly translated, it prohibited giving a woman a potion to induce abortion. That prohibition is inconsistent with medical texts from the same time that give detailed directions on how to induce a miscarriage, both with herbs and by surgical means. These ancient physicians noted that a medicine might induce menstruation and induce expulsion of the product of conception, which indicates that they had carefully observed miscarriages.

Some ancient medical writers were opposed to abortion, except when the procedure was necessary for the mother's health, as when she was too young or her pelvis was too small to give birth safely. These commentators also sometimes noted that certain drugs that caused abortion would also expel a fetus that had died in the womb, which might be necessary for the mother's health.

From the Renaissance through the early 19th century, the legal and moral situation was murkier. At common law in England, abortion before quickening had been more or less legal but abortion after fetal movement was a misdemeanor, at least if the mother died.

In 1803, Parliament passed Lord Ellenborough's Act, which prohibited giving a woman any "noxious substance" to induce an abortion after quickening.

Enforcement of the law appears to have been rare as there are few reported cases. There were two famous cases, however, which may have deterred doctors from performing the procedure. Interestingly, one of these revealed how much ancient information had been lost.

On the other hand, some English doctors wrote veiled instructions about how to induce an abortion to "spare her fame" (protect the reputation of the woman}. Some historian believe that physicians or midwives may have performed abortions secretly. If a woman died from an abortion, the abortionist could be prosecuted for murder.

Parliament later amended Lord Ellenborough's Act to prohibit abortion at any stage of pregnancy except to preserve the mother's health. That addition meant that a woman could obtain an abortion if her physician believed that the continuation of the pregnancy endangered her health. Later amendments permitted the abortion of a defective child.

Abortion was available and more or less legal in much of the United States for two centuries, until roughly the latter part of the 19th century. America followed English common law (which is the law established by the courts prior to Lord Ellenborough's Act) which provided that abortion before quickening was lawful, and that abortion after quickening was a crime if the mother died.

This is not to suggest that abortion was encouraged or openly regarded as desirable. Although some condemned the practice, information about how to induce abortion was available. For instance, 18th century books on women's matters stressed the importance of regularity in her "courses" (menstruation). These texts gave directions on how to remove "blockages" to menstruation, which was, of course, an indirect way of giving directions for abortion.

In colonial times, American women had access to a variety of traditional abortifacients in the form of various more or less toxic herbs. Whether or not the herbs were effective is another matter. Some of these drugs were powerful purgatives and cathartics, i.e. medicines that cause violent diarrhea and vomiting. These herbs included black hellebore, calomel, aloes, extract of juniper berries, and oil of tansy, all of which were commonly available from apothecaries or growing wild. In 1742, in Connecticut, the colloquial term for using these toxic substances was "taking the trade."[25]

In 1736, a book was published in Philadelphia, titled *Every Man His Own Doctor, or The Poor Planter's Physician.* [26] Riddle notes that the author observed that "a common complaint 'by unmarry'd women' was the 'suppression of the Courses.'" 'Suppression of the Courses' meant absence of menstruation, and obviously, as a complaint of an unmarried woman, meant an unwanted pregnancy. The author gave detailed instructions on what herbs to take to bring on menstruation, i.e. cause an early term abortion.

Brodie describes a book published in 1847 in America with the long and explicit title *The Married Woman's Private Medical Companion, embracing the Treatment of Menstruation or Monthly Turns during Their Stoppage, Irregularity, or Entire Suppression, PREGNANCY and how IT MAY BE DETRMINED with the Treatment of Its Various Diseases. Discovery to PREVENT PREGNANCY: Its Great and Important Necessity Where Malformation or Inability Exists to Give Birth. To Prevent Miscarriage or Abortion When Proper and Necessary. TO EFFECT MISCARRIAGE When Attended with Entire Safety. CAUSES AND MODE OF CURE OF BARRENNESS OR STERILITY.*[27] Clearly, by the 19th century, some authors were disseminating information about birth control and abortion to the general public.

If the home remedies did not have the desired effect, a woman might turn to a physician, midwife, or abortionist to "restore her monthly courses."[28] Historical research has revealed that by the early 19th century, both doctors and midwives had the obstetrical knowledge needed to terminate a pregnancy. The methods used involved dilating the cervix to induce contractions, piercing the amniotic sac to induce labor, and other surgical procedures. Midwives may have understood the process for a much longer time than doctors because obstetrical matters had been the concern of midwives for centuries.

In 1830's New York, three well-known women openly advertised their services as abortionists. Horowitz argues that before the growth of cities, when most women lived in the countryside, midwives probably performed abortions.

Some free thinking 19th and 20th century groups endorsed abortion as part of promoting free love; freedom for women to engage in sex outside of traditional marriage turned in part on their being able to avoid the consequences of that activity. In response, as with contraception, moral crusaders condemned abortion precisely because it enabled a woman to avoid the "natural" punishment for what they considered immorality.

By the early 19th century, several states had passed laws regulating abortion. Most retained the traditional distinction between abortion before and after quickening. New York, however, passed a law prohibiting any abortion. The courts struck down some of these laws as too restrictive, particularly the law did not allow abortion even to save the mother's life.

Some of the laws against abortion were intended to protect women's health. The abortifacient concoctions were often highly toxic and an overdose could be fatal. Surgery in the 19th century, whether for abortion or not, was hazardous. Without effective anesthesia, antiseptic methods in surgery, or antibiotics, death from any surgical intervention was common. Women died from abortions for the same reason that women would later die in the 20th century from illegal abortions — lack of clean instruments and the use of crude "procedures" that often perforated the vagina or uterus, resulting in fatal infections or hemorrhage.

The nascent American Medical Association joined forces with the anti-abortion movement, in part on moral and health grounds and in part to stamp out non-medical practitioners who were in economic competition with the newly organized doctors. Doctors wanted to take the profitable business of providing medical care for women away from midwives. Ironically, again, this economic and chauvinist movement resulted in the loss of knowledge about reproduction and childbirth, as well as in the death of many women from infection after childbirth. These physicians believed that they knew more than the "ignorant" midwives, but in fact much of their supposed knowledge was mistaken, including in particular the medical establishment's complete ignorance of the importance of cleanliness. The diary of one 18th century American midwife suggests that she delivered over 200 babies, but that only two of her patients died.[23]

In one 19th century Viennese hospital, the ward where wealthy women went to have their babies sometimes had a death rate of over 50 per cent, because the doctors did not wash their hands before delivering the baby. The ward for poor women, where the babies were delivered by midwives, had a far lower death rate.

Doctors at the time did not understand that microbes caused many diseases and therefore did not wash their hands or change their clothes between patients or between dissection of corpses and treatment of live patients. Some insightful doctors realized that they were spreading the infection from infected mothers to healthy ones. One of these physicians was Sir Arthur Conan Doyle in London, who also wrote the Sherlock Holmes mystery stores. Another was Ignaz Semmelweis in Vienna. Both were ridiculed for their view that a doctor could harm a patient.[24]

It is possible that other information accumulated by generations of midwives was also lost in this transfer of power, including the use of herbs to induce early term abortions.

These facts suggest that the midwives' common sense neatness was safer for her patients. The fact remains, however, that pregnancy and childbirth gradually passed into the hands of doctors, who were all men, and therefore out of the hands of women taking care of other women. The doctors, who were, of course, almost all men since women were not generally allowed to attend medical school, crusaded against the "ignorant" midwives. The transfer of the treatment of women's gynecological and obstetrical issues from women to male doctors was one of the factors leading to abortion becoming unavailable as well as illegal. Medical ethics forbade helping a woman terminate a pregnancy.

For a variety of social and moral reasons, by the 1870's, laws had been passed that prohibited advertising abortion services or outlawed the practice itself, either entirely or by limiting it to circumstances where the mother's life was in danger. Laws prohibiting abortion and the efforts to enforce these laws sprang from more than one moral source. Some sought to protect unborn children, some sought to protect women from the hazards of dangerous drugs and procedures, but many simply wanted to ensure that men and women who had sexual relations were properly punished by having to bear and support the consequence of that sexual act. There was a strong current of moral feeling that if a couple, married or not, had sex, they deserved to be burdened with any resulting child, regardless of the effect of that birth on their own lives or the lives of their other children.

However, the view that abortion before quickening was lawful persisted in the New York courts until the 1880's. Moreover, there is convincing evidence that abortions remained readily available from physicians, at least for those sophisticated and wealthy enough to find the right doctor, even if the procedure was technically illegal. In 1942, The New York Times "estimated between 100,000 and 250,000 criminal abortions within the city annually."[37] On the other hand, the forcefulness of efforts made to prevent women from having abortions, especially during the early 20th century should not be understated. Leslie Reagan, who is a professor of the history of medicine and women's studies, in her book *When Abortion Was A Crime*, describes the collaboration of doctors and the police to find and punish those who performed abortions.[36] Sometimes, these methods included physicians and policemen brutally questioning women who were dying from infections following an abortion. Sometimes physicians refused to treat a woman suffering from the aftereffects of a suspected abortion until she confessed that she had had an abortion, rather than a natural miscarriage, and who had performed the abortion. Even where state law permitted therapeutic abortions to protect a woman's health, some hospitals and medical organizations formed committees and adopted rules designed to limit the use of this option.

Later, however, many doctors joined in the effort to liberalize the laws against abortion, in part on the ground that these laws limited a doctor's discretion in undertaking whatever treatment he or she determined was best for his or her patient. See *When Abortion Was A Crime*, supra.

In 1965, several years before the Supreme Court decided the case of *Roe v. Wade*, an article entitled "One Woman's Abortion" appeared in *The Atlantic Monthly*.[38] The anonymous woman author described the process by which she obtained an abortion at a time when the law forbade it. Mrs. X described herself as a college graduate, aged 43, the mother of three children, and living with her husband and family on the east coast. When she became pregnant for the fourth time, she and her husband decided that they lacked the personal and financial resources to care for a fourth child. Having done some research on the incidence of abortion in the United States, she contacted five women friends, all of different religious faiths, and told them she needed an abortion. All five women provided her with some information about how and where to obtain an abortion.

Two said that they themselves had obtained abortions within the last two years. Each gave her without hesitation the name, address, and telephone number of her physician. The fourth friend did a little detective work and in twenty-four hours came up with the name of another physician, remarkable for the fact that his office was directly across the street from one of the city's police precinct stations. Her fifth contact could only obtain information on procedures in a neighboring state, supposedly supervised by a physician.

Mrs. X had her abortion.

By the 1960's, the pendulum of legal opinion had begun to wing back, and sixteen states had legalized abortion. The Supreme Court decided *Roe v. Wade*, in 1973. The Court held that abortion in the early stage of pregnancy was a private matter for the woman and her doctor to decide but that the states could regulate later abortions.

The number of legal abortions in the United States has ranged from somewhat over 600,000 in 1973 to a high of 1.4 million in 1990 to about 800,000 in 1998. Most of these are performed on married women. Some studies estimate the number of abortions to be about 75 million per year in the world. See Abortion on page 271.

In summary, the historical evidence suggests that people have debated the lawfulness of abortion and birth control, and the question of whether it is a matter for the pregnant woman to decide, in the United States from the early 19th century. Information on early term abortion was available in the 18th century and the most sensible conclusion is that abortion before the fetus "quickened" was regarded as the woman's business. Restrictive laws in the first half of the 20th century, however, greatly limited access to abortion at any stage of pregnancy; these laws and changes in society made abortion a strictly medical matter and access to traditional methods, such as herbs, had been lost or outlawed.

QUESTION: *"Were there national debates about family values, religion, and laws in the United States before our own time?"*

ANSWER: *Yes, during the 19th century, the people of the United States debated questions of divorce and birth control among other issues. One of the hottest issues was that of polygamy.*

As historian Sarah Barringer Gordon put it, "In the mid-19th century, an extraordinary contest over religion and law took shape."[29] That debate was over the right of Mormons to practice polygamy.

The polygamy debate, like today's debates over abortion and same sex marriage, involved arguments about family life, religious values, freedom of religion, and the rights of states as opposed to the power of the federal government. Both sides quoted the Bible, and both maintained that the family was the foundation of civil society.

The question was, of course, what kind of family and on what terms?

In 1830, Joseph Smith published *The Book of Mormon: An Account Written by the Hand of Mormon, upon Plates Taken from the Plates of Nephi,* which he presented as a transcription of revelations made to him on golden tablets. That revelation, he taught, was part of God's plan for "the convincing of the Jew and Gentile that Jesus is the Christ."[30] As the Church of Jesus Christ of Latter Day Saints, popularly called the "Mormons," evolved, church leaders revealed that their doctrine encouraged men to take more than one wife, as part of their sacred duty.

Members of the church came under increasing persecution. They initially believed that their version of Christianity was protected by the First Amendment, which guaranteed freedom of religion and prohibited the government from establishing any religion as a state religion.

However, in the first half of the 19th century, the Bill of Rights (including the First Amendment) applied only to the federal government, not to the individual states. States could adopt laws about many things, including religion, marriage, and slavery, even if those laws were inconsistent with the freedoms established in the Bill of Rights. The federal government, therefore, could not legally protect the new church from state interference.

For that reason among others, after Joseph Smith was murdered by a mob comprised largely of members of the Illinois state militia, his successor Brigham Young led the Mormons to the Utah territory. There, Mormon leaders reasoned, they could form their own state; if the Constitution allowed the citizens of each state to make what laws they wanted about religion, then the Mormons would make laws establishing their religious values in the territory where they were the majority.

In the protracted political and legal battles that followed the open adoption of polygamy in the Utah territory, the debate became a national one. Men and women on both sides of the controversy wrote passionate pamphlets for and against polygamy. One of Brigham Young's wives divorced him and went on a highly successful national lecture tour, describing her miserable life in the "harem." President and Mrs. Ulysses Grant attended one of her presentations.

Traditional Christian leaders condemned polygamy as the grossest sort of immorality and cited passages in the epistles of St. Paul urging that the leaders of the church be husbands of only one wife. Mormon writers argued that traditional monogamy was the cause of the decline of the family as well as other social ills such as prostitution. These leaders relied on Biblical precedent for plural marriage, including especially the story of Sarah and Abraham. In that story, in the book of cite, Sarah and her husband Abraham had no children. Sarah gave her servant girl, Hagar, to Abraham to produce a son for him and God rewarded Sarah.

The Utah territory gave women the vote in 1870, decades before other states or the federal government did. Contrary to expectations, Utah women did not vote against polygamy or polygamists; the Mormon majority rose to 95 per cent in territorial elections and most elected officials in Utah were practicing polygamists.

Congress twice refused to admit the Mormons' proposed state of Deseret into the union. In the mid 19th century, Congress passed the Morrill Anti-Bigamy Act, which outlawed polygamy, and the Poland Act which gave federal judges and officials greater control in the territories owned by the United States. Fearful of the economic power of the Mormon church, Congress passed the Edmunds-Tucker Act in the 1880's which was expressly designed to punish the organization for its support of polygamy by confiscating almost all church property and turning it over to the federal government.[31] Claiming that Mormon women's support of polygamy showed that women shouldn't be allowed to vote, Congress revoked women's suffrage in Utah.

Between 1887 and 1890, 200 Utah women were charged with the crime of fornication for participation in plural marriages. The cases were rarely pursued and the women rarely actually went to jail. Of all these indictments, only one woman was convicted by a jury.[32] Mormon men were charged and convicted of polygamy or unlawful cohabitation or both. Some Mormon leaders went into hiding to avoid criminal prosecution.

These laws were challenged in the courts. If the doctrines of state's rights remained constant during these decades, the Mormons' arguments might have been more successful. However, the law had changed after the Civil War. The Fourteenth Amendment extended the protections of the Bills of Rights to all citizens, so that state governments could not longer pass laws that were inconsistent with federal rights, such as freedom of speech and religion. Federal laws abolishing slavery and guaranteeing rights to African Americans were enforced in the states that had been part of the Confederacy, at least for a time.

In 1946, the United States Supreme Court held that members of the Mormon Church who practiced polygamy were committing a crime. A federal law called the Mann Act (still in force) prohibits transporting a woman across state borders for "prostitution, debauchery, or any other immoral purpose." A man named Cleveland and other members of his church had transported women across state lines in order to marry them. The problem was that Cleveland and his co-religionists were already married to other women. Cleveland and the others were convicted of violating the Mann Act. The Supreme Court clearly considered marrying more than one woman at a time to be an immoral relationship, regardless of its religious motivation. To the Court, that was a "notorious example of promiscuity."[33]

The leading case on polygamy, which was intended by Mormon leaders as a test case, was *Reynolds v. United States*, decided in the United States Supreme Court in 1878.[34] The questions were first, whether the federal government could constitutionally intervene in local affairs against the views of the majority of residents, especially on so delicate a subject as marriage, and second, whether, if the Bill of Rights applied to the states, then the Mormon doctrine of polygamy should be protected by the First Amendment's guarantee of freedom of religion. The Supreme Court ruled that the federal government could constitutionally outlaw polygamy in United States territories and that the federal adoption of an essentially Protestant view of marriage did not violate the Constitution. In a later case, the Supreme Court ruled that the government's confiscation of church property was not unconstitutional.[35] The justices referred to the history of laws against bigamy, noting that in the time of King James I of England, bigamy was a crime punishable by death. In about 1788, the new state of Virginia had already adopted a constitution protecting religious liberty but it had also passed a law against bigamy. The Court concluded that:

> *From that day to this, we think it may safely be said there never has been a time in any State of the Union when polygamy has not been an offence against society, cognizable by the civil courts and punishable with more or less severity.*

 MYTH—*"The United States Supreme Court in Roe v. Wade forced the justices' own new and liberal values on an unwilling public."*

FACT—*In many ways, the decision in Roe v. Wade reflected views on abortion that had previously been part of American society and law.*

Careful historical review of American attitudes toward abortion shows that the justices' reasoning in *Roe v Wade* embodied earlier well-accepted views in American society that had been partly or wholly abandoned or modified.[39] For example, the distinction drawn by the Court between abortions in the first three months of pregnancy as opposed to the latter months parallels the traditional distinction between abortion before "quickening" and after it. Another example would be the justices' conclusion that early stage abortion was a private matter between a woman and her physician, which had been the common law in the American Colonies when founders were writing the Constitution. In fact, the Court looked to the historical legality of abortion in reaching its decision.

It is true that the "official" standards of sexual conduct were different in, for example, the 1950's, than they are now. However, even then, a few people lived together without being married. We can see that from the number of cases that courts have considered where couples lived together for 20 years or more, beginning in the 1950's. From the biographies of bohemian writers and artists, we also know that at least some couples cohabitated relatively openly. One difference is that until the 1980's, an ordinary middle-class unmarried couple who lived together often disguised the relationship by telling people that they were married.

Those situations caused some difficult cases for the courts; the moral values of society condemned such relationships but the financial outcome, especially for the woman involved, was frequently so unfair that even moralistic judges were sympathetic to her situation.

QUESTION: *"So, are you saying that relationships haven't changed in American society?"*

ANSWER: *No, of course not. The radical changes have been the increasing acceptance of cohabitation as an alternative to marriage, the openness with which people engage in sexual relations before marriage, and the growing tolerance of different sexual orientations.*

From 1970 to 2000, American society has radically revised the acceptability of an unmarried couple cohabiting. Cohabitation has moved from something that was socially unacceptable to a social norm, accepted, however reluctantly, by the majority of people. The point is that change, while radical, did not spring up full-blown right after Woodstock. It has roots in the mores and habits of past times.

The following section provides a brief and more or less neutral summary of the laws of marriage and cohabitation over different historical periods relevant to American law over the years. This summary only covers the Western European laws, and particularly the English traditions, that primarily influenced American law. It cannot, and does not, cover the traditions and laws of Native Americans, African Americans under the institution of slavery, or the rich heritage of other cultures and nations whose citizens have become part of America. In particular, this history does not cover Islamic law and custom, because that law is not incorporated into contemporary American legal institutions, however much it may influence the behavior and views of Muslim communities in the United States.

The history of marriage as a legal institution – common law and ceremonial

Under English and American law, marriage has been a mixture of religious morality, contract, legal status, social ideas, and sexuality. The law has been shaped by the judges' and legislatures' views that society has a strong interest in promoting the stability of the family, in upholding established moral values, in providing for the rearing of children, and in keeping track of the property relationships that are affected by marriage.

The legal status of informal marriage

Informal marriage is a legal marriage that came into being without the usually formalities or with a minimum of them. The formal requirements included at various times marriage contracts, a ceremony by a clergyman, witnesses, and a state license.

Over the centuries, society's attitudes toward informal marriages have varied, and so have the rules of law. Social organizations have had differing positions on the desirability of recognizing an informal relationship as a marriage. On the one hand, the dominant churches have wanted the relationships of men and women to be sanctified by church ritual and perhaps to collect the fees that were payable for the ceremony. On the other hand, as a general policy, the government favored characterizing a relationship as a marriage rather than recognizing the existence of openly immoral non-ceremonial relationships; from the standpoint of morality and social stability, an informal, but valid, marriage was preferable to open immorality. In other words, it was sometimes considered better to provide for legal recognition of existing committed relationships between men and women than to demand a formal ceremony that the couple was simply not going to have. Thus, the courts recognized informal marriages; a couple was considered married if they lived together as husband and wife, if they held themselves out as married, and if they intended to be married.

The courts and society, however, drew a clear line between informal marriage and meretricious relationships, such as that between a man and his mistress. Marriage without ceremony was one thing; mere fornication was something else entirely. A wealthy man might provide his lover with a luxurious house and jewels and support her and their children for a number of years, but in the eyes of the law and in the eyes of society, she was a whore, not a wife. A more polite word, like "courtesan" might be used but the social difference in status was rigid. No matter how long the relationship lasted, she never acquired the rights or status of a wife. Moreover, it was important to social values that she not acquire those rights: people felt that there should be a profound moral, religious, and legal different between a wife and a mistress.

Not all states were so rigid, however. For example, in 1859, Thomas Jefferson (not the president) went through a marriage ceremony with Margreth Williams in Pennsylvania. Unfortunately, he was already married to someone else, and Margreth knew this. Margreth and Thomas moved to New Orleans and then, in 1889, to Cooke county, Texas, where Thomas bought a farm. Eventually, Thomas went back to New Orleans but Margreth and their illegitimate children stayed in Texas and worked the farm. During the next quarter century, Thomas came and went. Eventually, he sued Margreth for divorce, but realizing that they were not married, he dismissed that case and sued her to get back the land which was in his name. The court held that if Margreth could prove that she had earned part of the money that was used to buy the farm, then she was entitled to a share in the land. The title might have been in Thomas' name but he held title as a trustee for her interest. The court said,

> *It is not necessary that Margreth Williams should prove that she produced by her labor a part of the very money that was used in purchasing the land. If she and Thomas Jefferson were working together to a common purpose, and the proceeds of labor performed by them became the joint property of the two, then she would occupy the position that a man would occupied in relation to Thomas Jefferson under the same circumstances; each would own the property acquired in proportion to the value of his labor contributed to the acquisition of it.*[41]

In other words, the Texas court, in 1905, treated this couple as economic partners, just as if they had been two men in business together.

However, the recognition of informal marriages created difficult problems of proof, especially where money, such as an inheritance, was involved. Judges thought that there was a great possibility of fraud, since any lover might claim that the couple had entered into a common law marriage.

Moreover, the same fear of fraud and the same desire to draw a bright moral and legal line between cohabiting couples and married couples have led many courts to deny various property rights to cohabiting couples. Thus, the moral values and legal concerns of past centuries continue to shape our present laws.

In the Jewish tradition, marriage was considered the only natural and happy state for men and women. As two scholars noted, "This ancient rabbinical determination that Jews should all marry and raise families was so strong that up to the third century, a man and a woman could wed merely by expressing mutual consent followed by consummation."[42] There was no requirement of living together for any particular period, as there had been under Roman laws. After the religious law was changed, some couples still followed the older tradition and to protect their children, the rabbis decided that those children would have almost the same rights as children born of a formal marriage.[43]

In other words, as with other cultures, the rabbinical tradition in Judaism varied between recognizing informal unions as marriages, because of the spiritual and worldly importance of marriage, to declining to treat those unions as true marriages but recognizing that they occurred and were, in some ways, close to a marriage.

For centuries, the law in Germany, northern France, and England looked almost entirely to the spoken word to determine whether a marriage had taken place.[44] Under that doctrine, if a man and woman exchanged marriage promises, they were married, whether or not there were witnesses and whether or not that marriage took place in church. The traditional form was "I take thee for my wedded [spouse]" but other expressions would suffice to create a valid marriage. The key element was that the words had to be in the present tense, i.e. "I now marry you" and not in the future tense, i.e. "Let's get married someday."

In England, the Anglican Church followed the old religious law. Under English civil law also, if a couple told each other they were married, then they were legally married. English law did not change until the middle of the 18th century. In the 18th century, Parliament passed a law which proclaimed that informal marriages would not be legal. Even then, some objected to the government's imposing formal, secular requirements on a matter that was properly the province of God. One member of Parliament objected that changing the law was one of "the most cruel enterprises against the fair sex," presumably because a woman who had been seduced under promise of marriage could no longer claim that she believed herself to be validly married.

Some states in America followed English common law while others did not. In 1890 in New Jersey, for example, the court held that a couple who told each other that they were married by those words was in fact legally married. The words were an express contract to marry.[45]

71

In America, some of the states adopted that prohibition on common law marriage while others recognized the ancient option. Thus, in some states one can enter into a valid common law marriage while other states only recognize formal marriages as valid.

Society's interests in the marital relationship

People have stressed different aspects of marriage in different historical times. Up until the end of the 18th century, society largely considered marriage an economic matter. In principle, men and women married to solidify or increase the financial stability of their extended families. The legitimacy of children was a vital part of this arrangement since the procreation of children, born of a particular father, kept property in the family. In the 19th century, people began to regard marriage primarily as a source of emotional closeness for the couple. Love, compatibility (including sexual compatibility), and harmony were considered more important.

Consistently over time, church doctrine has held marriage to be a holy union, primarily for procreating children, although also for the legitimate satisfaction of the carnal needs of the spouses. The spouses' expectation that marriage would meet their sexual needs was sometimes called the "marital debt," meaning that husband and wife owed each other this indulgence. The law recognized these values in annulling a marriage if the husband was permanently impotent. In the late 1800's, the wife of famous art critic John Ruskin obtained an annulment by proving that her husband was impotent and that the marriage had never been consummated. When it had become apparent how unhappy she was in the marriage, his family tried to trick her into having an affair. Their reasoning presumably was that if she were not a virgin, she probably could not obtain the annulment because the courts would assume that she had had intercourse with her husband. The young woman was smart enough (or moral enough) however, to remain chaste, and she obtained her annulment.[46]

In the eyes of the law, regardless of any agreement between the husband and wife, being married changed one's legal status. Marriage simply consisted of acquiring a particular legal status. Husband and wife could not tailor the legal relationship to suit their preferences, except that they could put some constraints on the husband's rights to his wife's property.

Once married, of course, one could not legally marry anyone else unless one's first wife or husband had died or one had been divorced. Divorce was rare and usually difficult to obtain. Sexual relationships, if committed by the wife (but not husband), were grounds for divorce; a husband's philandering was considered natural, if not moral, but the wife's, following Biblical injunction, was a gross offence.

Any children born to an unmarried woman were illegitimate; any children born to a married woman, unless the husband was physically so far away that he couldn't possibly have fathered the child, were their legitimate heirs. The wife was entitled to be supported by her husband, as were their children.

Because sex outside of marriage was frowned upon, sexual misconduct by one spouse or the other affected the division of property in a divorce, at those times when divorce was available The grounds for divorce were limited and adultery by the wife (but not by the husband) was one of the few reasons divorce might be granted. For many years, the husband's adultery was not considered such a major moral breach as to entitle the wife to a divorce, but if she did obtain a divorce, his immorality might affect the support he was obligated to pay her and might increase her share of their property. An adulterous wife, therefore, was quite likely to receive very little of the family property in the event of a divorce, while an adulterous husband might be condemned as immoral but was probably somewhat likely to be punished financially.

A couple could change some rights of marriage by a contract, especially property rights, but the contract could not modify all marital rights. Up until the latter part of the 19th century, for example, the husband obtained the right to control all of his wife's property unless he agreed to give up that right. She had no rights to manage or control anything of his or her own, unless their contract gave her that right.

Sexual matters and divorce could not, however, be matters of contract. The husband had a right to his wife's sexual "favors" and, therefore, until recently a husband could not be guilty of the crime of rape against his wife. Similarly, it was unlawful to provide in advance for a divorce in a prenuptial contract, except for limited provision for a separation.

Women's property rights were greatly expanded by the widespread adoption of laws called "married women's property acts" in the 19th century. These laws permitted married women to own property which was their own, i.e. not subject to the husband's management and control. Couples could still use a contract to make clear who would own what, but the contract could not provide terms for a future divorce. Couples could also use contracts to provide for a marital separation.

Social attitudes and laws about sexual relations

For most of 19th and 20th centuries, in the United States, many, if not most, people considered sexual relations outside of marriage immoral. There were laws against open fornication, which consisted in having sex outside of marriage and letting people know about it. As Hotels had detectives on their staff in those days, whose job was to try and keep unmarried couples from sleeping together in the hotel. As late as

1979, for example, the Illinois Criminal Code, Section 11-8, provided that "any person who cohabits or has sexual intercourse with another (who is) not his spouse commits fornication if the behavior is open and notorious." Moreover, these laws were (sometimes) enforced. At least one 19th century couple were sentenced to 90 days imprisonment in the notorious Yuma Territorial Prison in Arizona for the crime of adultery. Interesting, both the man and the woman involved received the same sentence. In another case, a young man was sentenced to two years imprisonment there for the crime of seducing a young woman "under promise of marriage," i.e. for obtaining sexual favors from a respectable woman by promising to marry her.

Of course, many people had ongoing sexual relationships without being married to each other; but because the social norms forbade such relationships, these relationships were largely secret. Even a man as famous as Benjamin Franklin had an illegitimate son and, after several unsuccessful attempts to marry a woman with a substantial dowry, contracted a common law marriage with a less wealthy woman. His fiancée simply moved in with him and took his name, but that arrangement was neither uncommon nor disreputable in mid-18th century. He described his marriage as an arrangement to satisfy his strong sexual desires, but it was apparently a happy and prosperous one in many ways. Later, his romantic exploits when he was in France as the representative of the fledgling United States were legendary.

In the late 19th century, an intellectual young Englishwoman moved in with a married man, who left his wife to live with her. His wife had been having an open affair for a number of years with another man, and the other man had fathered two of her four children. Nonetheless, divorce would have been ruinous for the family, so the couple had stayed married. When he took up residence with the young woman, however, many of their friends shunned the new couple. The psychological stress of the social disapproval was so great that they lived abroad for many years; the young woman would become physically ill when the couple came back to England. The young woman became a famous novelist under the name of George Elliot. Although some of their friends tolerated her relationship with her lover, many more did not, and she was never able to be comfortable at social functions in England so long as her lover's wife was alive.

In other words, it is as simplistic and misleading to believe that people in earlier time periods were just hypocrites (who paid lip service to morality while behaving just as people do now) as it is to believe that in some mythical past, almost everyone obeyed the moral norms of society. The point is that the social prohibitions did embody moral values and that society did impose penalties for flagrant violation of those norms, but society also tolerated a certain amount of discrete misbehavior as well. As part of this century's social changes, most states no longer permit women or their fathers to sue the woman's lover for breach of promise to marry or for seduction. In an era of sexual freedom, suing a man for having sex with a woman, unless he has infected her with a disease such as herpes or AIDS, seems absurd.

If we look at romance novels as embodying our contemporary fantasies about marriage, what do we see? In the typical romance plot, the hero (usually Lord Someone or Another) is irresistibly handsome, wealthy, and self-assured, but emotionally inhibited by some prior trauma involving a hard-hearted woman. The heroine (usually named Priscilla or Amanda) is feisty and beautiful.

Their love begins in intense, instant, sexual attraction. After many hardships and misunderstandings, Priscilla and Lord Darling achieve complete understanding. Lord Darling admits that he cannot resist his desire for Priscilla, and her lust for him overwhelms her. He wants only to protect and cherish her. She wants only to love him. His emotional wounds heal instantly, and they get married. End of story. Any children born along the way are beautiful and capture their father's heart. In these stories, overwhelming lust and intense sexual gratification lead inevitably to lifelong loyalty, cheerful companionship, and a happy home. If you are waiting for this story to take place in your own life, you don't need this book – you need a good shrink.

These romance novels may have their counterpart for men in tales of virile, dauntless heros who simultaneously defend democracy and seduce beautiful women.

These fantasy scenarios are just that - fantasy. They can be unhelpful, however, to the extent that they suggest that a happy home, in real life, begins in overwhelming lust. rather than in mutual commitment, affection, shared interests, and respect, as well as sex.

Until the 18th century, in England both ecclesiastical and civil courts had jurisdiction over marriages, divorces, and sexual offenses. Religious law and state laws paralleled each other, and Biblical proscriptions of sexual conduct of various kinds were crimes. Thus, church courts tried some sexual offenses such as adultery, sodomy, and others. Other sexual offenses, such as rape, could be prosecuted in both systems. An ecclesiastical court might impose penalties of penance and public confession of the sin, while a civil court could impose fines or floggings. Bigamy was a capital offense.

Until recently, adultery, fornication, homosexuality, and other sexual practices were still crimes in many states. Enforcement of these laws was becoming relatively rare by the turn of the century, and the courts have declared that most are unconstitutional. Until recently, many people, including psychiatrists, considered that oral sex was a disgusting sexual perversion. Even Freud said that most people regarded oral sexual contact as the most revolting of the perversions. Today it is a common enough part of sexual conduct to be at least suggested in many mainstream movies.

Some popular novels now contain reasonably explicit references to sodomy (anal sex), at lest between men and women.

Social attitudes and laws about children and marriage

In American society, until quite recently, if a woman became pregnant without being married, her family concealed her condition, if possible, and the baby secretly given up for adoption. Both the birth mother and the adoptive parents wanted to keep the matter one of complete secrecy, so that the birth mother could "get a fresh start on her life."

In the 19th century, her family and friends would often have ostracized a woman who was pregnant out of wedlock. Many such women ended up as prostitutes. A household servant, who became pregnant, even if her employer fathered her child, would be fired without a "character," which was a letter of reference. Without that reference, she could not hope for another good job, because employers wanted "good moral character" in their employees.

Adoption was less common in the 19th century than today. Parents abandoned many illegitimate children at orphanages and foundling homes. A child born out of wedlock was a bastard which was an inferior social and legal status. Illegitimate children did not inherit from their father (unless he expressly mentioned them in his will). They could not enter some professions such as law.

The stigma of having an illegitimate child was so great that it is believed that infanticide was not uncommon, although obviously it is hard, if not impossible, to have accurate figures on a matter that people went to great lengths to conceal. In Scotland, a woman could receive the death penalty if she gave birth without another woman in attendance and the baby died. The assumption was that the mother did not seek help from a midwife because she wanted to conceal the birth and that the baby died because she killed it.

Killing an unwanted infant has been called the "poor man's abortion." The neglectful "baby farms" discussed earlier may have had an unspoken function as a way of disposing of an unwanted child while ostensibly providing for its care.

These tendencies, although we may feel that they are outdated, persist to some extent. Even now, we read in the newspaper about young women giving birth, for example, in the restroom at school and abandoning or killing the infant. The problem is so serious that some states have instituted programs where a woman can safely leave her baby at a fire station or with a law enforcement officer and not be prosecuted for abandoning the child.

Attitudes toward the parenting of children have also changed. In the 19th century, children more or less belonged to the father. When the novelist Charles Dickens left his wife, he had the legal right to take their several children with him and he did; ironically, his wife's sister kept house for him and the kids. Even more ironically, Dickens was an immensely popular novelist and made a great deal of money giving public readings of his books. The public thought of him as an icon of English family values. In fact, however, he was having a torrid affair with the English actress Ellen Terry and went to great lengths to conceal his love life from his fans.

Today, many judges still tend to feel that children, especially young children, belong with the mother. Thus, it is often difficult for the husband in a divorce action to obtain custody, or even extensive visitation. In a non-marital relationship, if the man wants a relationship with his children, he will first have to prove that he is the father of the children; if he does so, he is then liable for child support and normally entitled to visitation.

The emotional devastation on children who are born into an unstable and temporary relationship and who lack the consistent attention and involvement of their father cannot be over-estimated. At best, these youngsters grow up with no experience of loving, responsible, stable relationships between men and women, which makes it unlikely that they themselves can have a stable happy family life.

Social attitudes and laws about marriage and property

For purposes of the law, however, the primary importance of marriage was the way that it affected people's rights to property. The legitimacy or illegitimacy of a child affected property rights as well as morality. Even the question of sexuality in marriage, from the law's point of view, was primarily a matter of setting out the rules of inheritance and other property rights. Families needed heirs; therefore, wives should be sexually available to their husbands. In the 17th and 18th centuries, "courts of equity began to ameliorate the harsh common law disabilities by allowing specific property to be held in trust for the wife's 'sole and separate use.'" [47]

Wealthy people entered into elaborate contracts, called "settlements," to decide what happened to their various properties when they married. If a rich woman's family wanted to try to keep her property on her side of the family or if they wanted to protect her from a husband that they thought was a gambler or otherwise irresponsible, they would have the lawyers put provisions in the contract that controlled the money.

Although the husband controlled all of the couple's property during the marriage, he could not completely disinherit his wife. She had a right to a share in his estate, called her "dower." Likewise, the husband had a continued interest in his wife's estate, called "curtesy."

Most ordinary people didn't enter into formal marriage settlements, and the general law of marriage governed their rights. Therefore, the laws of marriage and property were critically important to the financial status of men and women.

Most states provided that the couple's assets belonged to the husband during the marriage. He was obligated to support his wife. If there were a divorce, moral fault played a large part in the parties' respective rights and obligations. The law referred to an unmarried woman as a "feme sole" and to a married one as a "feme covert." A feme sole could own property and keep her own earnings. A feme covert's earnings and property belonged to her husband. If one of the spouses died, the other had a right to a share of the estate. The man's right was "curtsy" and the woman's was "dower." She had the right, for example, to live in the family home for the rest of her life.

In the late 19th century, as noted earlier, all the states passed "Married Woman's Property" laws which recognized the right of women to own property. After that, a couple's assets legally belonged to the spouse whose name was on the title. This often meant that everything still belonged to the husband because he was still often the breadwinner; since he controlled his earnings, he could put every asset in his own name or he could put them in his and his wife's name jointly.

In separate property states, then, when a couple divorced, each got the property that was in his or her name, **although** a blameless wife was entitled to alimony, since she was not regarded as being able or obligated to support herself. The unequal property division, however, frequently resulted in impoverishing the wife. The common law did not recognize the marriage as creating an economic partnership between the spouses.

One of the harshest illustrations of that doctrine is the 1971 case of *Wirth v. Wirth*. In that case, Mr. and Mrs. Wirth were married for 22 years. Both husband and wife worked. Her salary was used for household expenses, but the husband kept some of his salary and bought investments in his own name. So, when they divorced, the couple had some joint assets, but the family home was in the husband's name. The husband said that he was saving for both of them. The court held that the property in the husband's name belonged to him entirely. His promises and the wife's reliance on him in using her money to pay the bills didn't count.[48]

The injustices of cases like the *Wirth* case and pressures from the feminist movement for greater recognition of women's contribution to the family's economic existence have led to the state's adopting laws that require that marital property be divided equitably. See Chapter Fourteen on page 443.

Several states, however, adopted a system of property ownership called "community property." The community property system derived from Spanish and Mexican law. Under that system, husband and wife owned equal shares of all the assets earned during the marriage. Each also owned separately whatever assets he or she acquired before the marriage or by gift or inheritance. Their assets, therefore, fell into two ownership categories – separate property that belonged to one of them alone and community property in which they both had an equal share.

Traditionally, however, the husband had the right to manage all the property, although the states later changed the law to provide that each spouse had an equal management right. The community property system conceived of the family as an economic partnership; the wife's contribution to the family was equal, but different, from the husband's.

Society's attitudes about the respective natures of men and women influenced (and continue to influence) the laws that govern the ownership and control of the couple's assets. For much of the 19th century, many people regarded women as intellectually inferior to men and as emotionally more fragile. Many people believed that God or Nature intended women to be wives and mothers. Working in business would be too much of a strain for their more delicate or more pure nervous systems. State laws, for example, prohibited women from taking the bar exam, for example, so they could not practice law.

Men, on the other hand, were considered naturally fit to conduct business and work in industry. It made sense to put management of the property in the husband's hands, since, on those views, he was intellectually suited to understand business matters. Equally, it seemed fair to require him to support her, because she was (in theory) not physically or mentally able to gain her own living.

It is important to keep in mind, however, that these attitudes were widespread, but not universal. Some men and some women argued that women had the same capabilities as men, although most people probably believed that a woman's highest calling was to raise her children.

These laws meant that a married woman was effectively financially powerless; she had no realistic legal means to protect herself financially from an imprudent or corrupt husband. Except in the community property states, if she obtained a legal separation, her earnings still belonged to her husband. Separation agreements sometimes protected the wife from her husband's financial failings either by requiring him to support her or at least by allocating a share of the family's assets for her. Until the late 19th century, however, those assets still were owned by a man because a married woman could not own property.

As a widow, however, a woman gained more financial power because she could manage her own property and keep her own earnings. She had become a feme sole again. Moreover, she might actually have some assets because she was entitled to a part of her husband's estate if he died, regardless of what he put in his will. If he died without a will, her children would also inherit from him.

A woman who was living in sin with a man, to whom she was not married, however, had none of these rights or disabilities. By not marrying the man, she had morally forfeited the legal protections offered to a proper wife. She could own property in her own name, however.

Social attitudes and laws about love and marriage

Social ideas about the role of love in marriage have varied widely over time.

In the 18th century, romantic love and sexual desire were widely regarded as dangerous emotions that threatened to cause immoral conduct and that could injure the financial well being of the family. Society held it to be a child's obligation to enter a marriage that was socially and financially advantageous to his or her family. Romantic passion might lead a son or daughter to a disadvantageous liaison.

The ideal marriage was to someone of a slightly higher social level from a well-to-do family. A disastrous marriage was one to a poor person from a significantly lower social class. The purposes of marriage, then, were, in order of importance: first, the financial and social stability of the extended family; second the procreation of children to carry on the family line; and only third, the emotional and sexual satisfaction of the parties. The primary virtues of a wife were chastity, obedience to her husband, and thriftiness.

The law at that time recognized the nature of marriage as a family matter by recognizing lawsuits relating to courtship and seduction. One was breach of promise to marry. A girl, or her father, could sue a young man who promised to marry her and then reneged. The unspoken premise of those suits was that the girl had sex with the boy. The lawsuit was one in tort (an injury case) rather than a contract case. Since she was no longer a virgin, her prospects of a good marriage were impaired and the family was entitled to recover money damages for this loss. The courts recognized that these it would be easy to make false allegations of seduction or a secret engagement, which could amount to blackmail. Eventually, the courts or the legislature abolished these lawsuits.

The importance of family, and the distrust of young people's love for each other, were reinforced by the great importance accorded to the bride's virginity. Her virgin status at marriage not only reflected her morality but ensured the legitimacy of her husband's family's heirs.

In the 18th century, a popular author wrote two immensely popular novels about young women who were seduced or raped. In the first, *Clarissa*, a passionate suitor abducts the heroine, Clarissa Harlow. Her parents, of course, promptly disown her. They write to her, making clear that whether she willingly succumbs to the evil rake's sensuous embraces, or is raped by him, he has ruined her and they never wish to see her again. In the second book, called *Pamela*, the hitherto virtuous Pamela gives in to her lover's sexual desires. Her immoral lust, of course, destroys her life, and when she inevitably dies young and alone, her coffin is decorated with a broken lily, symbolizing the tragic loss of her purity.

The popularity of these books suggests that they captured a widespread fantasy or ideology about the relationship between sexual desire, love, and marriage. That belief was that romantic passion led young women to make foolish choices that ruined their lives. The fact that Fielding wrote a wickedly funny parody of *Pamela*, called *Shamela*, in which the young woman is anything but innocent, tells us that a fair number of people recognized the hypocritical and unrealistic nature of that fantasy. In addition, the still charming romantic comedies of the 18th century which feature complicated, often adulterous affairs show that playwrights and their audiences understood that some blithely ignored the social standards.

To us, these novels seem both foreign and familiar. We have almost lost the concept of seduction as an unsavory act in which a cad persuades a woman to have sex with him against her better judgment and virtue. We do have, however, the amorphous concept of date rape, which may not be that far from what earlier generations called seduction. As *Clarissa* and *Pamela* illustrate, earlier generations considered the woman to be at fault if she was seduced or even raped. Laws against date rape place the blame on the man as the aggressor and give the right of decision about sex to the woman. The irregular and unreliable enforcement of those laws, however, suggest that we are not that clear in our own minds about whether perhaps a woman who goes to a man's apartment late at night is an imprudent victim or "asking for it" or a "tease" who "deserves what she gets." Finally, in today's popular romance novels, the handsome rake's seduction of the impetuous heiress usually leads to wedded bliss. Sexual desire is portrayed as an indication of enduring love, not as a dangerous impulse leading to lifelong ruin.

By the late 19th century, however, people began to look at marriage less as a matter of family ties and property than as a source of emotional warmth and mutual support between husband and wife. Instead of regarding the choice of spouse as a matter of filial obligation to their parents, social mores permitted couples to seek to gratify their individual needs for affection, companionship, love, and sexual pleasure in marriage.

During that century, other individualistic trends blossomed in social values and the law. Women, for example, acquired increased rights to property, and many began to seek an education. Foreign observers noted that young unmarried American women had much more freedom than young women in Western Europe. Marriage, however, still meant that a young woman gave up many of these freedoms, because society still expected her to confine her interests to her home and children. So many women began to postpone or avoid marriage.

The effect of social migration on marriage laws

During the early 19th and 20th centuries, cities and towns were widely scattered and communication was difficult. Until the building of the railroads in the late 1800's, the mail was very slow and somewhat unreliable. Of course, there weren't any telephones. Also, medicine and sanitation were not as advanced as now, and many people died of illnesses such as cholera and small pox. Moreover, the settlers were moving into primitive and hazardous living conditions. Sometimes the man of the family went into new territory ahead of his wife and children. All of these factors meant that families were sometimes separated from each other. Situations of mistaken information or outright abandonment could easily occur.

That historical situation had two consequences for the laws of marriage. First, sometimes on the frontier a man and woman would live together as husband and wife without going through a religious ceremony, because there was no preacher within many miles. They might eventually have a formal ceremony when a minister came around or the community built a church, but sometimes not. Moreover, in sparsely settled areas, people didn't keep well-organized public records, so there might not be any place to record a marriage even if there was a ceremony.

Second, sometimes husbands and wives lived in different places; the husband might go ahead into a new territory to get started while the wife waited back on the East Coast. Since communication was so difficult, sometimes a person would mistakenly hear that his or her spouse had died in a distant place or that he or she had obtained a divorce. In the mid-19th century, President Andrew Jackson and his beloved wife Rachel endured a tumultuous scandal because they married when they thought, mistakenly, that her first husband had gotten a divorce back in her home town.

As discussed earlier, the relative ease of movement and the lack of communication meant that spouses could, by mutual agreement or otherwise, abandon a marriage. Sometimes, a couple just split up and went their separate ways; if someone said that he or she was divorced or widowed, there was no reliable and easy way to check.

In other words, in that particular historical context, common law marriage served as a way of society's extending the legal shelter of marriage to respectable women and their children, whom society had decided to protect. The community had no desire to recognize any rights in women of loose morals and certainly not to give immoral persons the same rights as married people, but judges and legislators did want to protect otherwise morally conventional couples who genuinely thought that they were married, that is, people who believed that they were behaving according to the norms of society.

Men and women who deliberately cohabited without marriage or engaged in illicit sex were not entitled to the legal protections that married people had. Couples who intended to be married, but lacked one of the formalities of a valid marriage, presented vexing questions to the courts and legislatures.

Conclusion

The fact is that the historical truth about family life in the past is complicated, unsettled, and diverse. While conduct that is common and open today might have been infrequent and secret in the past, some aspects of contemporary family life also characterized family life in the 18th and 19th centuries.

A good use of this information would be to take a calmer look at today's conduct and laws. On the one hand, the fact of couples living together without a formal marriage ceremony is not a completely novel invention of irresolute baby boomers. On the other hand, couples today flout moral norms that most people more or less adhered to prior to the social changes of the decades from 1960 to 2000.

Thus, we may conclude that families exist in a continually evolving social framework. As concepts and values associated with love, individual happiness, morality, and the proper roles of men and women change, so do the laws governing cohabitation and marriage.

(Endnotes)

[1] *The State of Our Unions 2004* edited by David Popenoe and Barbara Defoe Whitehead, The National Marriage Project Rutgers University (June 2004) p. 20., downloaded from www.mariage.rutgers.edu. See also *The State of Our Unions 2005* edited by David Popenoe and Barbara Defoe Whitehead, The

National Marriage Project Rutgers University (June 2005) dowloaded from www.mariage.rutgers.edu.

2   *The State of Our Unions 2004*, p 24.

3   Rodger Doyle, "Living Together: In the U.S., Cohabitation Is Here To Stay" *Scientific American*, January 2004, p. 28.

4   *The State of Our Unions 2004*, supra, p. 18.

5   Rodger Doyle, "Living Together: In the U.S., Cohabitation Is Here To Stay" *Scientific American*, January 2004, p. 28.

6   See Stone, *The Family, Sex and Marriage*, infra, pp. 21 et seq.

7   John M. Riddle *Eve's Herbs; A History of Contraception and Abortion in the West*, (Harvard University Press, Cambridge, Mass, 1997), p. 169 et seq. See also John M. Riddle, *Contraception and Abortion from the Ancient World to the Renaissance* (Harvard University Press, Cambridge, Mass, 1992), especially at p. 199 where he discusses the contraceptive advice given by the philosopher Maimonides in his *Treatise on Cohabitation* and his discussion at pp. 160 et. seq. of the position that some physicians took on providing abortions, as well as the availability of supposed abortifacient medicines.

8   John Witte, Jr. "The Meanings of Marriage," 126 First Things 30 — 41, at 31, October 2002.

9   The *Oxford Book of Marriage*, Helge Rubinstein, edt. Oxford University Press, New York, 1990.

10 For more detailed information about changing sexual mores, standards of family life, and related topics, see Lawrence Stone, *The Family, Sex and Marriage in England 1500- 1800*. Harper Torch Books, New York, 1977 and Francoise Barret-Ducroco, *Love in the Time of Victoria: Sexuality and Desire among Working Class Men and Women in Nineteenth Century London*. Penguin Books, New York, 1989.

11 Nancy F. Cott, *Public Vows: A History of Marriage and the Nation*. Harvard University Press, Cambridge, Mass., 2000, reviewed in Ann Laquer Estin "Marriage and Belonging" 100 Mich. Law. Rev. 1690 (2002).

12 *The Family in the Western World*, p. 70.

13 *The Family in the Western World*, p. 84 – 85.

14 Beatrice Gottlieb, *The Family in the Western World from the Black Death to the Industrial Age*, Oxford University Press, 1993. especially, pp. 70—75, 84 – 85, 65-66, 147 and 72.

15 Most of this paragraph is derived from *Under the Marriage Canopy*, by Gross and Gross, supra, at pp.101 to 105.

16 Id at 68 et seq.

17 Beatrice Gottlieb *The Family in the Western World: From the Black Death to the Industrial Age* (Oxford University Press: New York, 1993.) especially pp. 65 - 66, 70 - 74, 84, and 147.

18 Thomas Cole. *The Journey of Life: A Cultural History of Aging.* New York: Cambridge University Press, 1992.

19 Helen Lefkowitz Hororwitz, *Rereading Sex; Battles over Sexual Knowledge and Suppression in Nineteenth-Century America.* Knopf, New York, 2002, especially pp. 200 et seq, 196, 190 et seq and 467 – 468.

20 John Riddle, *Eve's Herbs*, supra.

21 *Love in the Time of Victoria, supra,* at ppg. 148 eq seq.

22 Much of the information on the history of contraception and abortion is from Janet Farrell Brodie, *Contraception and Abortion in 19th Century America*, Cornell University Press, Ithaca, New York, 1994.

23 Laurel Thatcher Ulrich, *A Midwife's Tale: The Life of Martha Ballard, Based on Her Diary, 1785-1812.* New York: Vintage Books, 1990.

24 See Milton Wainwright, "The Semmelweis Myth" Vol. 28 Microbiology Today 1731.

25 Helen Lefkowitz Hororwitz, *Rereading Sex; Battles over Sexual Knowledge and Suppression in Nineteenth-Century America.* Knopf, New York, 2002, pp.96, and 200 et seq.

26 Riddle, p. 201 et seq.

27 Brodie, p. 363.

28 See Horowitz, Brodie, and Riddle, supra.

29 Sarah Barringer Gordon, *The Mormon Question: Polygamy and Constitutional Conflict in Nineteenth Century America* (University of North Carolina Press, Chapel Hill and London, 2002),

30 The *Book of Mormon*, frontispiece, reprinted in *The Mormon Question*, page, 2

31 *The Mormon Question* at 185.

32 *The Mormon Question*, at 181.

33 .*Cleveland v. United States*, 329 U.S. 12 (1946)

34 *Reynolds v. U.S.*, 98 U.S. 145 (1878)

35 *Mormon Church v. United States*, 136 U.S. 1 (1890)

36 Leslie Reagan, *When Abortion Was a Crime: Women, Medicine, and Law in the United States, 1867-1973*, University of California Press (reprint edition), California, 1998.

37 Riddle, p. 4.

38 Mrs. X, "One Woman's Abortion." *The Atlantic Monthly*, August 1965.

39 *Roe v. Wade*, 410 U.S. 113 (1973)

40 *The Family in the Western World*, p. 147

41 *Hayworth v. Williams* 116 S.W. 43 (1909), cited in *Texas Marital Property Rights*, at 500.

42 Gross and Gross, infra, Under the Wedding Canopy, p. 76/

43 Id.

44 *The Family in the Western World*, p. 72.

45 *Voorhees v. Voorhees*, 19 A. 172 (NY 1890)

46 See Phyllis Rose, *Parallel Lives; Five Victorian Marriages*. Alfred A. Knopf, New York, 1984.

47 John De Witt Gregory, Peter N. Swisher, and Sheryl L. Wolf, *Understanding Family Law* (2nd Edt.) Lexis Nexis, New York, 2001, at 67.

48 *Wirth v. Wirth* 326 N.Y.S. 2d 308 (NY App. Div. 1971).

Chapter Three

Love and marriage today

Since the 1960's and 1970's, popular social values (those that people acknowledge openly) about sexuality changed radically from those of the 1950's. In the 1940's, public knowledge of an illicit love affair might have gravely damaged a movie star or politician's career; now it is common for entertainment and sports figures openly to have children with lovers to whom they are not married.

Two primary changes that have taken place in American family life in the last forty years are the increased divorced rate and the growing social acceptance of cohabitation. Both of these have led to an increasing number of children for whom a single parent home or a home with cohabiting adults are a way of life. Changes in attitudes toward same sex couples have also occurred but those changes are better described as being in process, rather than as having become settled social views of family life. For a longer discussion of the legal status of same sex couples, see Chapter Four starting on page 105.

Ordinary people have changed their values and their conduct. Couples live together openly for a while and then split up. Sometimes they have children together without any particular intention of marrying. Statistically, many cohabiting couples regard their living arrangement as a prelude to marriage, but a large percentage do not intend to marry. The following sections summarize some of these social changes.

Cohabitation

"Cohabitation" in this book means, obviously, a couple who live together in a relationship that includes some form of sexual alliance. It doesn't include people who are roommates or married, although, in a literal sense, both of these groups cohabit. The United States Census Bureau coined the acronym "POSSLQ" for "Persons Of The Opposite Sex Sharing Living Quarters." That's one way of describing cohabitation, of course, but it could also refer to roommates of the opposite sex who have no intimate relationship beyond keeping lettuce in the same refrigerator.

The Alternatives to Marriage website uses the term "marriagefree" to refer to couples who "have made a conscious decision not to marry or who are actively opposed to marriage." Marriagefree, they note, is different from the state of those who are living together but intend to marry someone someday.[1]

Social reality of cohabitation

A recent radio broadcast noted that, as of 2006, for the first time, more women were living without a spouse than were married; sociological data suggests that over 50 per cent of American women either live alone or with someone to whom they are not married. In one paper that gathered information on both Americans and Canadians, the authors concluded that approximately half of younger adults have cohabited at some point in their lives.[2] They noted that various reasons for the increase in cohabitation have been given, including "rising individualism," which means an increased emphasis on attainment of individual goals, a decline in adherence to traditional religious values, a lessening of social condemnation of sexual activity outside marriage, and economic factors, such as women's increasing economic independence.

United States Census statistics show that between 1960 and 2000, "the number of unmarried couples in America increased by over 1000 percent." Today, approximately 4.7 million couples cohabit without marriage. That's over 9 million individuals. About a quarter of unmarried women, between the ages of 25 and 39, are living with someone.[3] For every ten couples who marry, statistically there's a couple that cohabit.

Living together is more common among those with a high school education than those with a college degree, although 37 percent of college graduates have cohabited. Cohabiting couples more often have been divorced themselves or have parents who were divorced. People who cohabit tend to be less religious than those who don't.

According to a report prepared by The Marriage Project at Rutgers University, "Since 1960, there has also been an 860 percent increase in the number of cohabiting couples who live with children. An estimated 40 percent of all children today are expected to spend some time in a cohabiting couple household during their growing up years." Sociologists estimate that over a million cohabiting couples have children living with them.[4]

An analysis of the figures by two sociologists reveals that "41% of first births to unmarried women are actually babies born to cohabiting couples, not "single" women." In other words, these children are born into a two-parent home, not to a woman living alone.[5]

The number of unwed parents continues to rise. Both the percentage of births to unwed mothers and the percentage of children living with a single parent increased slightly, reaching record highs in 2003.[6] Financially, these arrangements are not usually beneficial to the children. Statistically, the "majority of children who grow up outside of married families have experienced at least one year of dire poverty."[7]

Studies of teenagers suggest that most of them believe that they will eventually marry but that a large percentage are pessimistic about the chance of their marriage lasting for a lifetime. Well over half believe that living together before marriage is a good idea.[8]

Emotional reality of cohabitation

Why do people live together instead of getting married? There are many reasons.

Some couples genuinely do not believe in the social or religious strictures that underlie the legal structure of marriage. For example, some feminists object to ideals of male domination of women that were included in many of the laws governing marriage.

Some couples recognize that their connection is a temporary or limited one, arising out of passing lust or loneliness. The cohabitation may meet the need for companionship or for a sexual outlet. Such a relationship may last for years. Some people who have been married and divorced find it easier to sustain an informal relationship than one that has been formalized.

Sometimes one of the couple is exploiting the other sexually, financially, or emotionally. A woman who loves a man, for example, may consent to live with him against her better judgment and religious values, if a limited relationship is the only one that he offers. Sometimes the relationship may be mutually exploitative in the sense that each gets something out of the relationship, other than a sincere commitment.

Prior to the widespread acceptance of cohabitation, a woman's desire for commitment, relative permanence, and social recognition of the relationship was reinforced by the force of community values. In those days, in principle at least, decent women did not give out sexual favors without the protection of marriage and men who desired sexual relationships knew that the only officially socially permissible way to obtain such favors, as well as having a wife to care for his home and raise his children, was to marry.

Kay Hymowitz, writing critically about proposals for increased legal recognition of cohabitation relationships, noted:

> *Thirty years ago or so, young people fresh out of college tried every deception in the book to avoid telling their parents they were moving in with their boyfriends or girlfriends. How things have changed. This Thanksgiving, my parents welcomed into their guestroom my niece and her live-in boyfriend as if they were Uncle Joe and Aunt Millie.*[9]

One popular view is that a couple can learn about each other by living together before marriage and therefore have a better chance at a lasting marriage. Statistics tell a different story—couples who live together before marriage are significantly more likely to divorce than those who don't. Some studies suggest that a couple who live together before marriage is 50 per cent more likely to divorce than couples who do not.

However, the meaning of that figure is difficult to evaluate. Are people who are willing to cohabit just the kind of people who attach less importance to a permanent relationship? Or, are they people who have the gumption to craft the kind of relationship that they personally want? Perhaps these couples are people who value individual liberty over stasis. Perhaps one of them is simply unable to make a more formal commitment.

No one knows how many terrible marriages have been avoided by a couple's living together prior to marriage and discovering that they were completely unsuited to each other?

Presumably, people who don't live together before marriage have values that are more traditional or belong to a more conservative religion that prohibits such conduct. If that is the case, then perhaps those values reinforce the marriage. Or, perhaps, those values simply discourage divorce.

In my experience, the reason many couples live together, rather than marry, is that one or both of them are unwilling to make a true commitment to each other. Each seeks the gratification of company, of sex, of some financial contribution to the household, without the soul-searching that ought to accompany marriage. Each knows that the relationship is fundamentally temporary and that he or she is free to leave on a whim or for a better deal or because the relationship becomes inconvenient.

It is also perhaps true that the easy availability of divorce has blurred the line in some people's minds between marriage and living together. While the legal changes that made it easier to obtain a divorce may have freed people from burdensome or abusive relationships, those changes also may have made younger people casual about sexual liaisons. If Mom and Dad have been married two or three times, and have had a string of relationships along the way, can one really expect Sissy or Junior to take their sexual relationships seriously?

Duration of cohabiting relationships

According to sociologists, most cohabitation relationships last about a year. That figure is as difficult to evaluate as the statistic that about 50 percent of marriages end in divorce. Some cohabitation relationships last for decades. Our common experience in society, however, suggests that most cohabitation relationships do not last as long as the typical marriage.

More important than the statistics is the psychological and social fact that a cohabitation relationship is, by its very nature, one in which the parties have declined to make the formal commitment recognized by society. They may have made a profound commitment to each other but they have done so outside the social mechanism for commitment.

MYTH—*"Living together is good preparation for marriage. You can find out whether the relationship will work or not."*

FACT—*Living together may sometimes enable a person to discover that a relationship is not going to work. It doesn't seem to work the other way.*

Statistical studies by social scientists tend to show that couples who live together before marriage are more likely to divorce later. The exact reasons for this phenomenon are not proven. It may be that couples with more liberal values tend to live together and that such couples resort to divorce more readily. It may be that couples who live together are inherently less able to make a stable commitment to each other. It may also be that one member of the couple cannot tolerate the level of commitment reflected by the marriage ceremony.

Whatever the underlying cause, the fact seems to be that living together is not a particularly good test run for marriage. The studies do not, of course, tell us much about the couples who avoided a bad marriage by finding out that they couldn't stand living together.

So, cohabiting may be a good way of exploring a relationship about which you are uncertain before you get married. A pleasant cohabitation is no guarantee, however, that the marriage will work.

Effect on children whose parents cohabit

From the standpoint of moral education, cohabiting parents teach their children by their own example that living together without marrying is morally acceptable.

Depending on their relationship, parents who lightly cohabit without marrying may also indirectly teach their children that commitment is not important. Parents who repeatedly divorce and remarry may teach the same lesson.

These observations are not ironclad, however. The children of parents who were married for many years may themselves have multiple divorces or serial short-term relationships. Conversely, children whose parents cohabit may decide that they want a stable, "official" marital relationship, perhaps in reaction to the unofficial nature of their parents' relationship.

Studies suggest that the children of divorced parents are likely to be divorced themselves, so perhaps the institution of easy divorce, which was intended in part to protect children from hostile and traumatic marriages, may have created a generation incapable of the lasting emotional commitment necessary for a lasting marriage.

Leaving aside question of moral example, there is no direct evidence that the cohabitation of a child's parents in and of itself is harmful to the child in any direct manner. There is, however, statistical evidence that children living in cohabiting households do not do as well as children in the household of married parents.[10] Sociologists look for some objective measure of children's welfare.

Some of the aspects of a child's life that they consider are how often the child is read to, whether the child is more likely to have behavioral problems, and whether the child is likely to go hungry. On all of these measures, children of cohabiting couples are more likely to be worse off than the children of married parents.

However, a child in a household with a cohabiting couple is likely to be better off on these factors than a child in a household with a single mother. The inference is that in some ways a child may be better with two adults in his or her household than with a single parent, regardless of whether the two adults are married or not.

These figures, like most sociological data, are subject to intense debate because they bear on political questions. One of the articles that I referred to in writing this book was published, for example, by the Urban Institute. The Urban Institute is a think tank that endorses the "new federalism," which is a positive sounding term for conservative, largely Republican, social policies. That does not mean that the data was false, of course, but it does mean that the conclusions drawn also supported a conservative agenda.

Similarly, Whitehead and Popenoe who edit the valuable *State of Our Unions* series have distilled the data into suggested guidelines for teenagers; those guidelines make clear that marriage is the preferred option. Are those guidelines simply advice based on objective sociological fact or are the sociological results influenced by the authors' values? Some philosophers of science have argued that all supposedly objective scientific research actually incorporates the researchers' theories and values.

Some researchers conclude that children are adversely affected by cohabitation relationships only to the extent that the relationship is unstable, while others dispute that inference. In other words, some social scientists believe that children have more problems when the relationships of the adults in their lives are unreliable; it is the instability that is harmful to the child, not whether the relationship is the socially recognized one of marriage. Other researchers note that, since many cohabiting couples are poorer and less educated, their children may suffer the adverse consequences of poverty and a lower socioeconomic status, and not by the unmarried status of their parents.

There is some evidence to support the conclusion that children whose parents were cohabiting but unmarried tended to have earlier sexual experiences, to be more likely to have a baby as a teenager, and to be less likely to finish high school. Some researchers have found that these correlations hold true regardless of whether the cohabitation relationship was a stable one or a transitory one.

The inherent difficulty in all such studies is sorting out the cause from the effect. If it is true that children do less well in a cohabiting household, at least on some measurement, then why is that true? Is it due to the character or predispositions of the parents, which may predispose them to less committed relationships, including less committed care of their children? Does the stability of socially recognized marriage provide a better emotional environmental for a child's development? Are parents who are willing to marry in order to have a more traditional family structure more likely to be better parents because they are more stable, well-balanced people? Perhaps the fact that a child's parents are married conveys a message to the child about the best structure for relationships which in turn predisposes the child to postpone sexual relationships and stay in school?

Consider a hypothetical family in which two adults decide to live together and have children. Both parents are college educated and the family income is well above average. The parents remain together throughout the children's childhood. Their relationship is a stable one based on their shared values which include the rejection of traditional male/female social relationships, which they believe to be patriarchal and unjust.

Would the children of such a family be read to less often than the children of a divorced mother who has remarried? Would they be less likely to finish high school or more likely to have a baby out of wedlock in their teen years than the children of an unhappy but nominally Christian family? There are no conclusive scientific studies to answer this question.

Legal reality of cohabitation

The changing social perception of cohabitation relationships has not led to cohabitation being accorded the same legal status as marriage. This makes sense because of the simple fact that heterosexual persons who cohabit have made a decision not to marry. In other words, the relationship may be said to be defined in part by its quality as a not-married relationship. Indeed, the whole point of cohabitation for many couples is that they are not married and do not choose to be married.

Cohabitation has, however, lost much of its earlier stigma as an inherently immoral relationship. Some of the social and legal disabilities of that status have been removed, at least for couples. These legal disabilities included laws that made sexual intercourse outside of marriage unlawful and laws that made contracts between different sex couples in an "immoral" relationship unenforceable.

In the 18th century, most of the criminal cases in puritanical Plymouth Colony were prosecutions for fornication. All of the American colonies had laws against fornication and also against bastardy, which was a crime committed by a woman who gave birth to child out of wedlock. In the late 17th and early 18th century, for example, the government of Virginia prosecuted many women for bastardy.[11] Part of the reason for these prosecutions was to force the mother to reveal the father's name so that he could be made responsible for supporting the child. Then, as now, local governments did not want to be burdened with welfare payments.

As late as 1985, thirteen states still had laws making cohabitation illegal, at least if one of the parties was married.[12] As an American Civil Liberties Union handbook for single people noted in 1985:

> *There is a modest trend against laws forbidding cohabitation. During the last several years, Alaska, Kansas, and Wisconsin have repealed anticohabitation statutes.*[13]

Few states still have these laws or try to enforce them, although they are still on the books in some states.

Interestingly, some states also had laws making fornication a crime. Fornication is sexual intercourse between unmarried people of the opposite sex. So, an unmarried couple could, in principle, be charged with two crimes — cohabitation and fornication.

Today, it is effectively legal for a heterosexual couple to live together. If statutes forbidding fornication (sex outside marriage) are still on the books, they are rarely enforced and would likely be found unconstitutional if a zealous prosecutor tried to enforce them.

Similarly, a cohabiting couple can, in most states, enter a binding contract about their finances, although not about their sex lives.

It is effectively legal for a gay or lesbian couple to live together and to have a contract governing their finances. This area of the law is, however, less well settled, especially in light of new laws prohibiting legal recognition of any "marriage-like" relationship for same sex couples. The laws governing private sexual conduct are discussed further in Chapter Four, starting at page 114 and page 132.

QUESTION: *"Can a person have more than one spouse—polygamy, polyandry, and polyamory —the more the merrier?"*

ANSWER: *No. A person cannot be legally married to more than one person at a time in the United States, regardless of their cultural or religious traditions.*

Many societies have recognized marriage institutions in which more than two individuals are involved. Most of these have recognized polygamous marriage in which one man is married to more than one woman at the same time. Some Islamic countries permit such marriages today. A very few societies have recognized polyandry, in which one woman can be married to more than one man at a time.

In the United States, however, multiple marriages have never been legal, except briefly in the Utah Territory, before Utah became a state. Although changes in social mores have led to changes in the law regarding single parents, gay couples, and couples cohabitating, the law has not changed to recognize an institution of plural marriage.

The United States required Utah to outlaw polygamy as a condition to its becoming a state. Indeed, attempted polygamy can be a crime, although one still occasionally reads about families organized on this basis. Recently a man in Utah was convicted of various crimes for having married several women, at least one of whom was legally a minor at the time.

It is not illegal for a group of people to live together, as in a commune. for example. It is probably not illegal for them to have whatever sexual relationship they want, although this issue has not been addressed by the courts.

It is unclear whether this group could have a valid contract among themselves. A court might decide that the contract rested on an unlawful relationship, i.e. a polygamous one. On the other hand, if there were a business activity involved, the court might decide that the sexual aspects were irrelevant and that the contract was just a regular business deal. For example, a group of people living in a communal relationship might operate an organic truck farm. If they had an agreement that was only about sharing work and proceeds from the farm, a court should treat it as a binding contract. Logically, some might say, a court should regard the sexual arrangement as irrelevant to the financial one, but moral values and prejudices might lead a judge to find a legal basis to invalidate the contract.

While the police might not ordinarily interfere with a group of persons who want to cohabit and have multiple sexual connections among themselves, the government may well take action if that group consists of persons purporting to be married. The government can, and does, prosecute persons in polygamous relationships for bigamy. Usually, however, the relationship also leads to violations of other laws, such as welfare laws. Sometimes, as noted above, one of the purported plural marriages involves an underage girl and therefore constitutes child molestation.

It is possible that a court might someday find that prohibiting plural marriage violates Constitutional guarantees of privacy or religious freedom.[14] On the other hand, rights of privacy and freedom of religion do not shelter all conduct, and such a decision seems unlikely. It is far more likely that the Supreme Court will continue to hold that living and sexual arrangements are a private matter unless the conduct violates some other law.

Marriage and Divorce

The number of people who marry in the United States has fallen over the last few decades, and the number of those marriages that end in divorce has increased, even if the rate has now leveled off. The increase in divorce has paralleled changes in the law that make divorce legally easier.

Sociological Facts

Daniel Goleman, an insightful commentator on relationships gives the following figures: in 1890, 10 per cent of new marriages ended in divorce; in 1920, 18 percent; in 1950, 30 percent; in 1970, 50 percent; and in 1990, 67 percent. Goleman notes that over the course of this century, newlyweds have faced an increasing risk of being divorced. He argues that increasing divorce rates are in part due to a decline in "emotional intelligence" as well as various social pressures.[15] By emotional intelligence, as I understand it, he means the developed ability to function in a relationship.

As noted in Chapter One, one of the most thorough ongoing studies of marriage and the family in the United States is that conducted by The National Marriage Project, sponsored by Rutgers University. In their 2005 study, *The State of Our Unions 2005; The Social Health of Marriage in America*, the authors noted:

The divorce rate, one indicator of marital stability, continued to drop last year, continuing a downward trend that began around 1980 when the rate was 22.6 per 1000 married women. It fell to 17.7 in 2004 from 18.1 in the prior year.

However, the marriage rate, the number of marriages per 1000 unmarried women, has also been dropping—by nearly 50 percent since 1970 when the rate was 76.5. It fell to 39.9 in 2004 from 40.8 the prior year. Overall, except for the drop in divorce, the latest indicators point to little improvement in marital health and wellbeing.[16]

Those figures, of course, only reflect statistical aspects of society and may or may not be predictive for any given couple. Moreover, the last sentence reveals that these sociologists are studying "marital health" which suggests that they regard marriage as a good thing.

The divorce rates however, can at best only reflect the number of couples who sought legal relief in court. The figures do not include the number of miserably unhappy couples who led separate lives under the same roof, either unable to afford the expense of a legal divorce or unable to manufacture the grounds for the divorce or unwilling to face the social and financial consequences of divorce. Nor do they include the number of marriages that ended in death, desertion, or more or less consensual separation.

More importantly, the number of divorces says little or nothing about whether these terminated marriages are a good or bad thing for society or for the individual. Various social commentators have taken different moral, political, and psychological positions on the issue.

Some have argued that the family is the foundation of society and therefore that the law should not allow easy changes in the composition of a family. Others have argued that the ability to have transient relationships that last only as long as the couple desires them is essential to true happiness and that any constraint on the man or the woman to stay in the marriage is "slavery" or "legalized prostitution."

Psychologists have disagreed about the relative advantages and disadvantages for children, of living in the painful household of an unhappy marriage or being subject to the pain of divorce and possible remarriages. Religious writers have stressed the importance of a married couple's making sincere, faith-based efforts to mend their relationship.

The liberalization of divorce laws

For most of American history, divorce was based on fault. Although, as noted above, there were earlier periods when some state laws permitted a couple to obtain a divorce on the grounds that they no longer got along, most of the laws required that one spouse prove that the other had breached the marriage contract in some irretrievable way.

The outcome of a divorce could be ruinous for the spouse who was found to be at fault. If a husband could prove that his wife had committed adultery, then the court would not require him to support her after the divorce. An innocent wife, however, was entitled to be supported by her ex-husband. In the last half of the 20th century, however, all states adopted increasingly liberal divorce laws. In effect, it is not necessary to prove any legal ground for the divorce beyond one spouse telling the court that he or she no longer wishes to be married. There are still some provisions for counseling and some requirements for a period of separation before the divorce but, in general, a marriage can be easily ended by either spouse. Marital fault has become, in many states, virtually irrelevant to questions of child custody, division of property, and alimony.

When "mental cruelty" became an accepted ground for divorce, divorces became easier to obtain because admitting that one had been guilty of this vague offense could be seen by one social acquaintances as simply acceding to the legal ritual necessary to divorce.

Well-being, marriage, and cohabitation

The normative changes of family life have occurred in the context of increasing fractures in the social structure in general. The social isolation and loneliness of individuals in our culture is obvious. This anomie may be seen as the price of increasing respect for the individual or it may be seen as the fallout of a disintegrating society, depending on your point of view.

The price of the legal and social freedom to arrange our relationships as we see fit at the moment is the loss of a stable (or rigid) social structure in which those relationships exist. Cohabitation can promote happiness by permitting a couple to live together and lessen their respective loneliness. But that relationship is inherently temporary and any comfort it provides is contingent. The contingency is not simply the natural contingency of life in which people change and even die but the contingency of a deliberate lack of commitment. By cohabiting, a couple may be telling each other that the relationship is transient.

Some studies of physical and emotional health seem to support the proposition that "stable and satisfactory marriages are crucial for the wellbeing of adults." Married people tend to lead longer, healthier lives, emotionally and physically. The rate of depression, for example, is significantly lower among married men than among single men. On the other hand, other studies suggest that these figures are not true for women, although some studies that suggest that the benefits in terms of physical health and contentment are the same for men and women.

At one time, many commentators decried the idea of unhappy couples staying together. The thought was that everyone was better off if an unhappy marriage ended.

In some sociological studies, however, scientists studied couples who were unhappy at one point but stayed together. When the couples were interviewed ten years later, a large percentage reported that they were now happy. Other commentators have suggested that an intact two parent family benefits the children even if the parents are not happy, assuming of course that physical violence, substance abuse, and similar grave problems are not present.

Financially, married couples clearly prosper compared to single people, at least if the couples stay married. One study of retired people suggested that, compared to a continuously married couple, "those who never married have a reduction in wealth of 75% and those who divorced and didn't remarry have a reduction of 73%."[17] On the average, married men earn more money and married couples more savings than single people.

Common sense implies that these financial advantages accrue from the simple fact that two can live together more cheaply than they can live separately. Obviously, they have only one mortgage, one utility bill, and so on. Ideally, the couple can then invest the savings. However, there is some evidence that marriage serves as a strong incentive for responsible conduct, i.e. a married man and woman who feel obligated to provide for their family work harder and handle their money more prudently.

The reasons why married couples have better physical health and report greater contentment are harder to fathom. Perhaps a committed relationship is simply the natural state of humans. Perhaps the couple's commitment leads them to take care of each other by making sure the significant other leads a healthier life or gets regular checkups.

On the other hand, "serial monogamy" in which a person is married and divorced several times can be financially devastating. As one mentor put it to a young lawyer, "You can't keep dividing the pie and expect to end up with a big slice."

Interpreting the relevance of social statistics to an individual's life decisions is difficult. Clearly, a lifelong marriage will probably benefit the couple financially, emotionally, and in terms of their physical health. Equally clearly, many marriages end in divorce with its attendant financial losses, depression, and grief.

On average, most cohabitation relationships last about a year. It is hard to know what that means. Did those couples discover that they shouldn't be together and part without the hassle and expense of a divorce? Did they stay together as long as the relationship was mutually agreeable and part amicably when they wanted to move on? Did they lose the chance of a lifelong relationship because it was too easy to part after a quarrel?

Perhaps the reason that many divorced people later cohabit with a significant other instead of marrying is that they have learned that the marriage relationship does not suit their temperament and needs. Or, perhaps, they have not learned how to make the compromises and adjustments necessary in a long-term relationship.

Over the long term, a couple has a greater chance at happiness if their interpersonal relationship exists in a stable web of other relationships. A family flourishes when it functions within a larger social and familial framework. When a larger context supports the family, its structure can be more stable than when it rests solely on the relatively ephemeral relationship of love.

A cohabitation relationship is likely to be something of a do-it-yourself project. By its nature, the relationship lacks some of the socially defined expectations of marriage, whether those expectations are positive or negative. The good thing about this is that the couple is freer to work out a healthy partnership without the possibly crippling hangovers from the bad marriages of parents and others. The bad thing is that do-it-yourself relationships are hard to craft and harder to maintain because every problem that arises is a novel one that the couple must solve on their own.

A shared spiritual life can be one solid foundation for a relationship. Religious precepts can guide a spiritually motivated couple when times are tough. The Bible offers many valuable teachings for married persons from the celebration of sensual love in the Song of Songs to the praise of the good wife in Proverbs to the injunction of mutual respect and affection in the New Testament. A sincere belief that God created the institution of marriage can lead some couples to work harder to make the relationship last.

Many people find Biblical teachings on sexuality and marriage to be old-fashioned or chauvinistic. Some verses endorse the authority of men over women. These passages can make a man feel entitled to abuse his wife and can lead a woman to feel obligated to suffer such abuse.

Other passages condemn homosexuality, adultery, sexual relations during a woman's menstrual period, and sex outside marriage. Obviously, in contemporary American society, some of these commandments are observed by some religious groups and some are not. Some Orthodox Jews, for example, still obey the prohibition on sexual relations when the woman is ritually unclean due to her menstruation. Few, if any, mainstream evangelical Christian churches urge their congregations to follow those rules, but they continue to condemn adultery and especially homosexuality. The Biblical limitations on sex outside marriage applied more to women than to men. One of the most challenging Biblical issues for conservative religious groups is the many passages in the Old Testament that speak approvingly of plural marriages for men and their keeping of concubines. There have been many different interpretations of these writings in an effort to reconcile them with other teachings, such as the New Testament's emphasis on the desirability of one lifetime marriage.

Many couples, however, find comfort in a mutually acceptable congregation where the teachings and the spiritual community, as well as the clergyman's guidance, help to support a lasting relationship.

Religious values can affect the beginning and ending of a marriage, both in the secular courts and in the church's view of a couple's status. With regard to beginning a marriage, some conservative Christian pastors encourage their parishioners to enter covenant marriages, which are sanctified by specific vows by the couple to not divorce. Some states provide for legal recognition of these covenant marriages. See page 209. Religious matters may also affect the grounds for an annulment. See page 224.

Conversely, in some religions, a civil marriage (one performed by a judge or other official) may not be considered a true marriage; the marriage has all the secular legal incidents of marriage, but not the religious ones. These religions may, therefore, not condemn a divorce between such a couple.

Within churches, such as the Catholic Church which has continued to support traditional prohibitions on divorce and remarriage, there is controversy over the meaning and applicability of even traditional values.

In the case of a troubled marriage, some clergy may guide a couple in deciding that divorce is permissible in accordance with their interpretation of the relevant scriptures.

Social changes, laws, and values

Not all social values have changed for all people. Many people still consciously reject the proposition that cohabitation is morally acceptable or that same sex couples are merely a variation in lifestyle. For these people, cohabitation without marriage is immoral, whether the couple is heterosexual or homosexual, although the homosexual relationship may also be regarded as abnormal or as more sinful. On the other hand, many of these same people are living together without marriage.

Moreover, consciously and unconsciously, many people carry forward the conflicting views of past time periods into their own actions today. Many unmarried couples have signed a hotel register as "Mr. and Mrs.," out of embarrassment or shyness. Sometimes, they tell their employers that they are married, so that one of them can qualify for the health insurance benefits that may only be available to married people. Sometimes they tell their parents that they are engaged and will get married later. If one of them owns the house, the other may call his or her share of the expenses "rent." (Husbands and wives don't generally charge each other rent.) All of these variations often make it difficult to determine whether a couple is common law married or not, or whether they had an agreement about their finances, or not, which, of course, keeps lawyers in business.

Even though many marriages end in divorce and many married people have affairs (or fight like cats and dogs) and even though a couple living together may be more truly devoted to each other than many other married couples, the law does not turn on love or affection or devotion. A married couple still has a different legal status from a cohabiting couple.

In addition, the law is administered by judges and juries who may carry a variety of stereotypes based on their individual values and psychology. For example, a judge in a cohabitation case may know that married people are sometimes unfaithful to each other but still frown on a woman who is living with one man and has affairs with others. The fact that she has other lovers will be considered when deciding whether she and the man she is living with are common law married or just casual lovers. Her conduct may be considered in awarding or denying her alimony. Some jurors might not find her a very believable witness. The woman's personal values, i.e. whether she regards herself as a tramp or a liberated woman, don't necessarily govern the legal system's decisions.

Religion, marriage, and sex

QUESTION: *"Why don't you explain more about the religious precepts that underlie marriage?"*

ANSWER: *Religious beliefs vary widely, and debate over them is usually acrimonious. Also, I'm a lawyer, not a preacher.*

That said, the fact remains that religion influences both conduct and laws in the area of marriage and families. At present, the influence of various conservative Christian groups affects political and social opposition to same sex marriage and parallel efforts to reinforce an ideal of lifelong heterosexual marriage. One of the latter efforts is the new institution of covenant marriage, which embodies traditional religious concepts of marriage in a legal format slightly different from ordinary marriages. See page 209 for further information.

Moreover, different sects have different concepts of marriage and its obligations. Those variations are far beyond the scope of this book. If the religious dimension of marriage (or cohabitation) is important to you, you would be better to advised to seek guidance from a clergyman of the relevant institution.

As stated elsewhere, however, religious law does not negate state law. See page 229 for more information on this topic.

Conclusions and advice

The purpose of this book is neither to endorse nor to condemn any of these views, but to try to help people understand how the new relationships fit into the old legal molds.

The fact is that the law has adapted to such social changes as children being born out of wedlock, couples living together without marriage, marriages dissolving, and people frequently moving from one place to another. Whether these changes are beneficial for society or for the individuals, or not, they and the attendant shifts in the law are the facts of life.

Cohabitation has become a widespread and accepted part of American social life. Clearly, many couples believe that a living arrangement outside the legal structure of matrimony meets their needs. Cohabitation can provide some of the same economic benefits as marriage if the couple properly arrange their affairs. It can also avoid some of the economically disastrous consequences of divorce. However, it does not provide either the legal incidents of marriage nor the benefits.

(Endnotes)

[1] See Alternatives to Marriage Project, at www.unmarried.org/marriagefree.php, downloaded July, 2006.

[2] Pamela J. Smock, and Sanjeev Gupta, "4 Cohabitation in Contemporary North America," Just Living Together: Implications of Cohabitation on Families, Children, and Social Policy, ed. Alan Booth and Ann C. Crouter (Mahwah, NJ: Lawrence Erlbaum Associates, 2002) 56, Questia, 13 Feb. 2006 <http://www.questia.com/PM.qst?a=o&d=104628344>.

[3] Rodger Doyle, "Living Together: In the U.S., Cohabitation Is Here To Stay" *Scientific American*, January 2004, p. 28. See also *The State of Our Unions* reports cited below for 2003, 2004, and 2005.

[4] *The State of Our Unions 2004* edited by David Popenoe and Barbara Defoe Whitehead, The National Marriage Project Rutgers University (June 2004) p. 20., available at www.mariage.rutgers.edu. See also the United States Census figures summarized by The Alternatives to Marriage Project, at www.unmarried.org/statistics.html.

[5] Bumpass, Larry and Lu, Hsien-Hen(2000). "Trends in Cohabitation and Implications for Children's Family Contexts in the United States." *Population Studies*, 54: 29-41, quoted at www.unmarried.org/statistics.html.

[6] Barbara Dafoe Whitehead and David Popenoe, *The State of Our Unions 2005; The Social Health of Marriage in America* (The National Marriage Project, Rutgers University, New Jersey, 2005), p. 1, downloaded from www.marriage.rutgers.edu.

7   Mark A. Rank and Thomas A. Hirschl, "The Economic Risk of Childhood in America: Estimating the Probability of Poverty Across the Formative Years," Journal of Marriage and the Family, 61:1058-1067, 1999, cited in The State of our Unions 2004, at p. 17.

8   See the statistics gathered in Barbara Dafoe Whitehead and David Popenoe, "Changes in Teen Attitudes Toward Marriage, Cohabitation, and Children 1975 to 1995," a publication of the National Marriage Project, Rutgers University, downloaded from www.marriage.rutgers.edu.

9   Kay S. Hymowitz, "The Cohabitation Blues," Commentary Mar. 2003.

10 The information in this section is taken in part from Gregory Acs and Sandi Nelson, "The Kids are Alright? Children's Well-Being and the Rise in Cohabitation" The Urban Institute, Series B, Number b-48, July, 2002, and Wendy D. Manning and Ronald E. Bulanda "Parental Cohabitation Experience and Adolescent Behavioral Outcomes" Bowling Green State University Working Paper Series 03-0, downloaded from www.bgsu.edu/organizations/cfdr/main.html.

11 John Watkins, "Insolent And Contemptuous Carriages": Re-Conceptualizing Illegitimacy In Colonial British America, Thesis Department of History, University of South Florida, (2003)

12 Those states were Alabama, Arizona, Florida, Idaho, Illinois, Massachusetts, Michigan, Mississippi, New Mexico, North Dakota, South Carolina, Virginia, and West Virginia.

13 Mitchell Bernard, The Rights of Single People (Toronto: Bantam Books, 1985). This book is one of several handbooks promulgated by the American Civil Liberties Union.

14 For more information on this lifestyle, see the website "Loving More: New Models for Relationships" at www.lovemore.com/.

15 Daniel Goleman, *Emotional Intelligence.* (Bantam Books, New York, 1995.)

16 *The State of Our Unions 2004* edited by David Popenoe and Barbara Defoe Whitehead, The National Marriage Project Rutgers University (June 2004) p. 20., available at www.mariage.rutgers.edu. See also the United States Census figures summarized by The Alternatives to Marriage Project, at www.unmarried.org/statistics.html.

17 Janet Winmoth and Gregor Koso, "Does Marital History Matter? Martial Status and Wealth Outcomes Among Preretirement Adults, "Journal of Marriage and the Family, 64:254-68, 2002, cited in *The State of Our Unions, 2004*, p. 17.

Chapter Four

SAME SEX COUPLES AND THE LAW

There are two primary difficulties when writing about same sex couples (or transgender couples) and the law. First, a full history of discrimination against persons of differing sexual orientations is beyond the scope of this book. Second, the effect of sexual orientation on legal decisions involving family life is a hotly debated area of law that is in constant flux. Therefore, definite answers cannot be given to many questions.

While some same sex couples aspire to the legal status of marriage, others do not. Regardless of that preference, however, the passionate dispute over what the law ought to be means that prudent same sex couples in long-term, committed, relationships need to consider establishing their legal obligations to each other by contract. The cohabitation agreements in the Workbook can be used by same sex couples as well as by heterosexual couples. The reason is that more liberal court decisions or other changes in the law that favor the rights of gay couples may subsequently be undone. The exact legal status of gay couples in many states may not be resolved for several years.

Persons of varying sexuality

For economy of space, this book focuses on the legal issues relating to same sex couples, rather than trying to cover all the permutations in human sexual experience.

A common expression used to refer to all persons whose sexual preferences are other than wholly heterosexual is "GLBT," which is an abbreviation for "gay, lesbian, bisexual, and transgender." In that usage, the term "gay" is used to refer to male homosexuals. In this book, I use "gay" to refer to both male and female homosexual persons and intend by it to refer to persons whose sexual preference is largely or exclusively toward persons of their own gender.

In general, transgender, and bisexual persons face similar problems in the legal aspects of their relationships to those experienced by homosexual people.

Legally, a transgender or bisexual person has the gender assigned by society to persons of his or her genital configuration.

Although many laws controlling gender expression, such as those prohibiting people from dressing in the clothing usually associated with the opposite sex, are no longer in force, some laws about gender identity, such as using rest rooms remain in effect. These laws are probably valid to the extent that they apply to public, rather than private, conduct.

Homosexuality and marriage

In almost all states, the laws of marriage apply only to heterosexual couples. However, this aspect of the law is changing. Unfortunately, the changes teeter on a seesaw of liberalization and reaction. Most state legislatures have taken a conservative line, passing statutes that preclude homosexual couples from claiming the legal rights of heterosexual married couples. Some state courts have taken a more liberal stance and found protection for same sex couples in the provisions of state constitutions.

It is important to remember in this context the difference between state supreme courts, which interpret state constitutions, and the United States Supreme Court, which interprets the federal constitution. State constitutions often contain provisions that are analogous to those in the United States Constitution; all state governments must comply with the provisions of the federal constitution but states are free to be more liberal or more conservative when interpreting their own constitution.

A state court can take a more liberal stance in interpreting the equal protection provisions of its state constitution than the federal Supreme Court does in interpreting the federal constitution. In other words, the states may grant their citizens more rights than the federal government does but may not take away the rights guaranteed on a national level.

As of the date of writing this book, 37 states have passed laws that define marriage as existing only between a man and a woman. In those states, obviously, a same sex couple cannot legally marry.

The state of Vermont has effectively recognized same sex marriages, as have several Canadian provinces. Several foreign countries, including Spain and South Africa, have also granted legal recognition to same sex unions. The legal status, however, of a union recognized in one state (or country) and not in another is unsettled.

The Supreme Court of Vermont has ruled that the state cannot constitutionally discriminate between gay couples and heterosexual couples. To be more exact, in the case of *Baker v. State of Vermont*, the court ruled that, under the Vermont constitution, same-sex partners are entitled to the same benefits as married couples. The case was brought by three same-sex couples who were seeking marriage licenses.

The court ordered that the marriage licenses be issued in "recognition of our common humanity." Chief Justice Jeffrey L. Amestoy wrote that "We hold that the state is constitutionally required to extend to same-sex couples the common benefits and protections that flow from marriage under Vermont law."[1] In other words, although the court left the question of whether gay couples could marry to the state legislature, it gave gay couples the same rights that married couples have, which would mean presumably that a gay partner would, for example, have the same right to inherit from his or her partner as a spouse would from his or her spouse.

That ruling means that gay marriages will soon be legal in Vermont, at least for a time. The legislature passed a law recognizing homosexual marriage in response to the court's decision. That decision can only be overridden by an amendment to the state constitution, which will take several years. If an amendment to the state constitution is adopted, however, future gay marriages will be unlawful, and the legal status of gay marriages that took place in the interim will be dubious.

Just before publication of this book, the city of San Francisco began issuing marriage licenses for gay couples. Many marriage ceremonies have been performed by volunteer city workers and clergymen in that city. The city's action was a deliberate challenge to state law that limits marriage to heterosexuals. The status of those marriages is, therefore, in a sort of legal limbo.

Hawaii also was in the process of recognizing gay marriage but the state legislature passed a quick constitution amendment defining marriage as the union of a man and a woman. Massachusetts has adopted a law that same sex couples can enter into a marriage-like status, called a "civil union." Colorado has consider a law called a preferred beneficiary arrangement, which would afford some of the legal incidents of marriage to same sex couples who chose that status.

Under conservative pressure, 30 states have also adopted laws stating that marriages between persons of the same sex will not be recognized even if the marriage is legal in another state. These are called "defense of marriage acts." The United States Congress has passed a Defense of Marriage Act also. Since, the United States Constitution provides that each state must give "full faith and credit" to the legal actions of other states, it is likely that the Supreme Court will find that these laws violate Constitution. But, several years will elapse before a suit can be filed, appealed, and finally decided.

In Europe, some countries such as Lithuania, Poland, and Estonia have outlawed same sex marriage. The European Union, however, has ruled that discrimination against homosexual people violates human rights. As this book goes to press, the European Union is considering what action to take against member countries that adopt laws prejudicial to same sex couples. On the other hand, South Africa has recently recognized same sex marriage. One compromise that has been proposed in the United States is for the states to create a status for gay couples, usually called a "civil union," which would afford the legal protections of marriage but not be called a "marriage." Such a compromise might satisfy those who support legal rights for gay couples while not overly offending those who oppose homosexual marriages. The distinction would, however, perpetuate the rule that gay couples are legally different from heterosexual couples. The court, interestingly, ruled that the state could not properly establish a "civil union" for gay couples and restrict marriage to heterosexuals because that would unfairly discriminate between the different sexual orientations.

It is also possible that homosexual couples could eventually have the same rights, such as inheritance rights, as married couples, even if their relationship does not have the label "marriage" attached to it.

In other words, there have been recent efforts to change discriminatory laws and countervailing efforts to undo those changes. It is possible that the Supreme Court will eventually rule that states may not afford the legal benefits of marriage to heterosexual couples without making a comparable legal status available to homosexual couples as well. It seems reasonable to predict that some form of legal status analogous to marriage will be made available to homosexual couples within the next decade, if not sooner.

Suffice it to say, however – the laws of common law marriage do not apply to same sex couples. Only a man and woman can be common law married. So far as I know, no court has yet considered whether a couple in which one partner has undergone a sex change operation can be common law married.

Some same sex couples have sought religious ceremonies commemorating their relationship, even if the ceremony does not confer legal rights. Many of these couples have been active in their congregations for many years, and some have met through religious organizations. For these couples, the primary motive for the marriage ceremony is to sanctify their relationship in the eyes of God.

Some United Church of Christ clergy and some Episcopalian clergy will openly perform modified marriage ceremonies for gay couples. Some Roman Catholic clergy have been performing blessing rituals for gay couples more or less secretly. Some urban denominations minster especially to the gay community.

A couple who participates in one of these ceremonies should be aware that even if homosexual marriages are later legalized in their state, the religious ceremony may or may not be a legal marriage. For one reason, the ceremony may not be a legal marriage because it took place before the legalization of gay marriage.

Hence, gay couples who want to legalize their relationship will need both to use contracts (and other legal documents) and also to keep watch on the legal developments in their state.

Philosophically, and logically, the question of gay marriage presents several thorny issues. On the one hand, the institution of marriage in this country undeniably has its conceptual roots in Biblical injunctions. The institution has always involved moral concepts, and indeed, in its nature, it designates some sexual conduct (that within marriage) as morally acceptable and conveying certain legal rights and other sexual conduct (that outside marriage or with certain partners) as immoral and not conveying those rights. That's why there's a legal difference between having a one-night stand and being married.

Moral concepts of marriage also are the basis of restrictions on marriage, such as the non-recognition of plural marriages and the limitations on the age at which people can legally marry. The traditional values of the larger society mean that the law does not permit a traditional Moslem father to force his thirteen-year-old daughter into a marriage to an older man selected by her parents, regardless of the father's belief that his rights are based on God's law.

On the other hand, some restrictions on the marital relationship are no longer regarded as the government's business, regardless of their moral weight. Laws against particular sexual conduct within the marriage relationship, such as laws against birth control and laws prohibiting the marriage of persons of different races, have been declared unconstitutional. Although interracial marriage was once thought to be both against God's laws and a threat to the genetic integrity of the nation, contemporary concepts of equal rights forbid the government to distinguish between mixed race couples and same race couples. Similarly, the nature of sexual conduct within the marriage, such as whether a couple engages in oral sex or sodomy, is no longer within the reach of the law, although laws prohibiting such supposed perversions were once universal.

Although most consensual sexual conduct is constitutionally protected from state interference, non-consensual conduct such as rape is still illegal. Yet, the relevance of consent to whether conduct is legal or illegal is a moral notion.

Similarly, the extent to which marriage created a particular legal status based on Biblical teachings about the right of men to govern their wives has been eroded by the recognition of equal rights for women.

The other side of the social coin is that marriage is today a matter of civil legal status and entitlements that have little to do with morality and much to do with money. Questions of who receives a pension benefit or health insurance are economic and contractual questions, and it is hard to see why such decisions should turn on who is in bed with whom under what rubric. If two people have a long-standing relationship in which both contribute to the financial well-being of themselves as a couple, why should the allocation of those financial rewards depend on the sex of the parties?

One answer would be that financial benefits should only go to those who observe Biblical moral imperatives, but if that were the standard, few corporate executives would ever collect their stock options.

Domestic Partner Benefits

The term "domestic partner" can apply to unmarried, but committed, heterosexual or homosexual partners. There is no accepted standard for distinguishing a committed relationship from an uncommitted one. Usually, the standards involve a requirement that the relationship has lasted for a set time period and that the parties declare that the relationship exists.

One of the most liberal laws about domestic partnerships is that of California. That state created a domestic partnership status that extends the rights and obligations of spouses to registered domestic partners. The statute, Section 297.5 of the Family Code, actually reads as follows:

(a) Registered domestic partners shall have the same rights, protections, and benefits, and shall be subject to the same responsibilities, obligations, and duties under law, whether they derive from statutes, administrative regulations, court rules, government policies, common law, or any other provisions or sources of law, as are granted to and imposed upon spouses.

(b) Former registered domestic partners shall have the same rights, protections, and benefits, and shall be subject to the same responsibilities, obligations, and duties under law, whether they derive from statutes, administrative regulations, court rules, government policies, common law, or any other provisions or sources of law, as are granted to and imposed upon former spouses.

(c) A surviving registered domestic partner, following the death of the other partner, shall have the same rights, protections, and benefits, and shall be subject to the same responsibilities, obligations, and duties under law, whether they derive from statutes, administrative regulations, court rules, government

policies, common law, or any other provisions or sources of law, as are granted to and imposed upon a widow or a widower.

(d) The rights and obligations of registered domestic partners with respect to a child of either of them shall be the same as those of spouses. The rights and obligations of former or surviving registered domestic partners with respect to a child of either of them shall be the same as those of former or surviving spouses.

(e) To the extent that provisions of California law adopt, refer to, or rely upon, provisions of federal law in a way that otherwise would cause registered domestic partners to be treated differently than spouses, registered domestic partners shall be treated by California law as if federal law recognized a domestic partnership in the same manner as California law.

(f) Registered domestic partners shall have the same rights regarding nondiscrimination as those provided to spouses.

In other words, registered domestic partners have the same child custody and visitation rights, inheritance rights, marital property share rights, support obligations, and so on as married couples do. If the couple splits up, then they are treated as if they were a divorced couple.

The California statute gives domestic partners virtually every right possible under state law, but it cannot change federal law. Section (e) above implicitly recognizes that California law cannot change federal laws, such as social security laws, that don't recognize relationships other than marriage. In other words, being domestic partners under this law, does not entitle the partners to benefits that are provided to spouses by federal laws. Federal laws, do not extend to significant others, whether the relationship is heterosexual or homosexual. However, some laws, including especially the Defense of Marriage Act, preclude federal benefits from being available to same sex partners, even if they are married in a state which recognizes same sex marriages.

The fact that the statute is limited to same sex couples and those over 62 suggests that the legislature wanted to over legal benefits both to gay people and to older couples who don't want to marry because of social security benefits that they are receiving as the widow or widower of a previous spouse. Many older couples, as discussed in Chapter Thirteen, want a recognized relationship with the incidents of marriage but cannot, for financial reasons, marry.

A domestic partnership is created in California by filing the appropriate form with the state. The California Secretary of State has an informative web site where persons wishing to register as domestic partners can download the forms to do so, along with instructions on how and where to file them.

The requirements for being domestic partners in California are these:

✓ *that the couple live in the same residence;*

✓ *that they either be of the same sex or that one of them be over 62;*

✓ *that they would, in other respects, be eligible to marry in California,*
   i.e. that they are not too closely related or married to someone else.

✓ *that both are over age 18.*

Since the domestic partnership law expressly includes same sex couples, obviously, the fact that California does not recognize gay marriage does not apply. It is important to note that people who married to another person cannot enter into a valid domestic partnership. In other words, if you are married, you must divorce before you can register a new relationship as a domestic partnership in California. That may, or may not be true of domestic partnerships that are recognized elsewhere or by corporations.

Interestingly, the California statute does not require that the couple live in California, so in theory, couples from outside the state could register. However, it is unknown what their rights would be in other states that do not have comparable laws. A court in another state might treat the domestic partnership status as valid, just as a contract signed in California would be valid or a legal business partnership in California could be a legal partnership in another state. The court could, however, refuse to recognize it based on the absence of any such entity in its state's laws.

A couple that registers as domestic partners in California has to take legal action to dissolve the partnership if the relationship ends. Some couples can simply file a notice of dissolution with the state, just as they filed a form to create the partnership. Others, however, need to file a court proceeding somewhat like a divorce. It is not clear when a couple must do one or both of these[1].

The information provided by the California Secretary of State's office explains their law as follows: It is important to register if you want your relationship to have legal standing. While registration isn't the same as marriage, it does secure many important rights and responsibilities. Under current law, registration can protect your rights in times of family crisis, protect your children, and give your access to family benefits at work.

Obviously, the California domestic partner law comes close to establishing a sort of civil union, however, it is still unclear how those rights would be interpreted if the couple moved to another state. It is possible that a court in another state might find that the domestic partnership status continued in that state, like a valid contract made in another state or a business partnership formed in another state. Equally, a court might say that the domestic partnership was an entity unknown to its laws.[2]

"Domestic partner benefits" often refers to the extension of contractual benefits, usually associated with employment, to the unmarried significant other of an employee.

The company Ben & Jerry's Homemade Inc., which makes ice cream, was one of the first companies to extend benefits such as health insurance to same-sex couples. The company changed insurers in 1989 and the new insurance company offered domestic partner policies. Voila. Steve Anderson, writing in *Corporate Times Magazine* in 2000, said "Ben & Jerry's also provide benefits for opposite sex domestic partners and defines a domestic partner as anyone who is not a blood relative who has been in a relationship and living with a partner for more than six months."

According to John D. Canoni, chairman of the labor and employee benefits practice at a law firm in New York "Today, almost all major carriers offer coverage [for same sex couples]. An employer who wants to get that coverage can, and it's relatively inexpensive." Canoni notes:

There are three reasons that participation is low. The first is that most same-sex partners work for different employers. Therefore, they have their own coverage. Second, many same-sex partners prefer to keep their relationship confidential and wouldn't come forward even if the opportunity presented itself for more benefits. The third and most important reason is that the Internal Revenue Code makes this taxable.

It is important to realize that corporate domestic partner benefits may, or may not, depending on the company involved, be extended to unmarried heterosexual couples. At least one court has ruled that a company may lawfully limit benefits to homosexual domestic partners and heterosexual married persons, i.e. excluding unmarried heterosexual couples.

About 65 cities have domestic partner registries. The effect of these provisions outside the particular city is unclear, but it may be assumed that registering as domestic partners at least makes clear that some commitment was intended. A list of these cities can be found at www.hrc.org or through the Alternatives to Marriage website. See page 189 for more information.

Homosexuality and Other Sexual Variations Conduct as Illegal

The opposition to rights for gay people is based on the belief that sexual conduct between persons of the same sex is immoral. The Old Testament contains express prohibitions of homosexual practices between men, although lesbianism is not specifically mentioned. Homosexual conduct between men is termed an abomination and the prescribed punishment is death. The Apostle Paul's letters list degrading and immoral conduct between men as a sin, along with undue greed, uncontrolled anger, and so on. In our current society, obviously, the sexual misconduct that he decried gets a lot more political attention than the sin of undue attention to making money.

There may also be psychological factors at work in the opposition to homosexuality. Sometimes the fear or disgust experienced at the thought of homosexual conduct arises from a person's distrust of their own sexuality. The urge to control others' sexual practices can arise from a fear that one's own impulses might be out of control.

The general tendency in American law has been to protect people's right to live their private lives as they see fit, regardless of the moral beliefs of others. This right to privacy is one of the rights that prohibit the police from searching your home, or eavesdropping on phone calls without a warrant. However, for many years, the courts drew a clear line between the rights of heterosexual couples and those of homosexual people. In their excellent book, *Courting Justice; Gay Men and Lesbians v. The Supreme Court*, Joyce Murdock and Deb Price chronicle in detail the legal struggles of homosexual people. The judges, naturally, continued to reflect the dominant views of American society. Homosexuality was a moral perversion or a mental illness; it was disgusting and abhorrent to all right-thinking people. Also, of course, the justices continued the ignorance and fear of that society. Justice Lewis Powell, for example, was kind, gentlemanly man who struggled with the questions of the rights of gay people. He wondered aloud if he had ever met a homosexual; in fact, several of his legal aides (called "clerks") were gay. [3]

Birth control, adultery, fornication, oral sex, and anal intercourse (sodomy) have been against the law in all states, although the dates of enactment of these laws have varied and they were relatively seldom enforced in the last thirty years. These sexual acts were prohibited whether the acts were performed by heterosexual or homosexual couples.

Patricia Anderson, in *When Passion Reigned: Sex and the Victorians*,[4] notes that during the last half of the 19th century, attitudes toward "normal" and "abnormal" sexual behavior changed. Increasingly, sexual conduct other than that between a man and a woman designed for procreation became designated as abnormal. The word "heterosexual" entered the English language in 1892 and "homosexuality" in 1897, as part of the effort to distinguish normal and abnormal conduct. Until the 1920's, legislators and the public had little notion of a lesbian identity. Earlier laws and concepts had focused on particular sexual acts between individuals; now, the focus could shift to groups of persons as well as particular sexual conduct. In the 1890's, there were several notorious prosecutions, including that of Oscar Wilde, for homosexual conduct, and new laws were passed against pornography, prostitution, and sex between men. It is worth noting that the laws against prostitution tended to be addressed most to the women who were prostitutes and not to their customers.

Some feminist historians regard this as a continuation of the medieval Christian view of woman as the temptress Eve who leads men into sexual sin; it may also be related, however, to the view that men had stronger, "baser" drives than women and it was a pure woman's duty to help men control these urges.

Today, although the sexual privacy of heterosexual couples has greater protection, these laws have still been recently applied to gay couples. The United States Supreme Court has ruled that the United States Constitution forbids the government to intervene in private, intimate matters. The Supreme Court has held that part of freedom in this country is the right to conduct our family life (including private sexual conduct, educating our children, and using birth control) without government interference, unless that private conduct hurts someone else or is done in public.

Under this right of privacy, the police have no legitimate role in policing our bedrooms, unless some other compelling government interest is at stake. This protection is analogous to that afforded by the Constitution to our private thoughts and political opinions. Consensual adult sexual conduct in the home is shielded from the government just as our private books and papers and conversations in the home are shielded. The Court applied these guarantees of liberty to heterosexual sexual conduct in *Griswold v. Connecticut* (which held that the state could not prohibit the use of birth control) and *Roe v. Wade* (which held that the government could not prohibit a woman from having an abortion in the first three months of pregnancy).

The Supreme Court recently declared that guarantees of privacy that protect heterosexual conduct also prohibit government intrusion into private consensual homosexual conduct, which effectively cancelled the laws against sodomy and, by implication, laws prohibiting other private consensual sexual acts.

Two important court decisions concerning homosexual relationships are *Lawrence v. Texas*, which was decided by the United States Supreme Court, and *Goodridge v. Department of Public Health*, which was decided by the Massachusetts Supreme Court. These cases affect the rights of both homosexual and heterosexual couples because they continue the courts' delineation of the government's right to control the private lives of citizens.

One of the first of the privacy cases was the *Griswold* case. The *Griswold* case concerned the right of married people to get birth control information from their doctors. Many states, starting in the 19th century, had outlawed information about birth control in an effort to control sexual conduct regarded by some as sinful.

In the *Bodde* case, which was one of the first cases on homosexual conduct, the Court considered a case where two men were prosecuted for engaging in consensual sexual conduct in a private house. Georgia had a statute that made anal intercourse (sodomy) illegal, regardless of whether the sex was between a man and a woman or two men. The Court reasoned that there had been laws against that form of sexual intercourse for many centuries. The law did not discriminate between homosexuals and heterosexual people. Therefore, the Court held that such laws did not violate people's liberty in their private lives.

Several years later, however, a case came before the Court concerning a Texas statute that made oral sex and anal sex illegal but only between same sex couples. In that case, the Court reconsidered its earlier reasoning in *Bodde*.

In *Lawrence v. Texas*, the police "were dispatched to a private resident in response to a reported weapons disturbance." When the officers entered Lawrence's apartment, they saw him and another man engaging in sex. They arrested them for "deviate sexual intercourse, namely anal sex, with a member of the same sex." Lawrence and his companion were convicted and they appealed on the ground that the law was unconstitutional.

There was no arrest for any illegal weapon, and some have suggested that the disturbance call was a set-up.

MYTH—*"Once, again the Supreme Court changes ancient and well-established moral law. Homosexuality has always been illegal. The justices are imposing their views on the rest of us."*

FACT—*Historical review shows that anal intercourse (sodomy) has been against the law for several centuries. However, those laws prohibited both heterosexual and homosexual conduct of this sort and were primarily applied to cases of rape or abuse of a child. Moreover, 37 states had already repealed their laws against sodomy when the Court ruled.*

As in the *Roe v. Wade* abortion case, the Supreme Court in *Lawrence v. Texas* carefully reviewed the history of laws governing sexual conduct.

Interestingly, the concept of people as being either heterosexual or homosexual was developed in the late 19th century. Prior to that time, obviously, people distinguished different kinds of sexual conduct, including oral sex, anal sex, and vaginal intercourse, but some historians suggest that people did not make a clear distinction between groups of people based on sexual orientation.

For several centuries, any form of sexual conduct that was not designed for procreation was condemned as immoral or perverted. In other words, anal sex was considered immoral whether the partners were two men or a man and a woman.

People knew, obviously, that some people preferred one or the other of these forms and that some preferred partners of the same sex or the opposite sex. In Western Europe in modern times, oral or anal sex between same sex persons was condemned; however, the same conduct between a man and a woman was also considered illegal, immoral, and perverted, although the fact that people engaged in these forms of sexual expression was, obviously, widely known. Masturbation was also considered immoral and unhealthy. The only morally acceptable form of intercourse was intercourse intended or likely to produce children. That's why, at various times, there were legal prohibitions against both birth control and sexual variations such as oral sex or anal sex.

The Supreme Court described the history of laws against homosexuality this way:

At the outset it should be noted that there is no long standing history in this country of laws directed at homosexual conduct as a distinct matter. Beginning in colonial times there were prohibitions of sodomy derived from the English criminal laws passed in the first instance by the Reformation Parliament of 1533.

117

The English prohibition was understood to include relations between men and women as well as relations between men and men. Nineteenth-century commentators similarly read American sodomy, buggery, and crime-against-mature statutes as criminalizing certain relations between men and women and between men and men.[5]

The Court went on to note that

Laws prohibiting sodomy do not seem to have been enforced against consenting adults acting in private. A substantial number of sodomy prosecutions and convictions for which there are surviving records were for predatory acts against those who could not or did not consent, as in the case of a minor or the victim of an assault. As to these, one purpose for the prohibitions was to ensure there would be no lack of coverage if a predator committed a sexual assault that did not constitute rape as defined by the criminal law. Instead of targeting relations between consenting adults in private, 19th century sodomy prosecutions typically involved relations between men and minor girls or minor boys, relations between adults involving force, relations between adults implicating disparity in status, or relations between and animals.[6]

The Court then turned to modern law and observed that

It was not until the 1970's that any State singled out same-sex relations for criminal prosecution, and only nine states have done so. Over the course of the last decades, States with same-sex prohibitions have moved toward abolishing them.

The justices also observed that laws against sodomy were seldom enforced. Even Georgia had not had a prosecution for the crime of anal intercourse for decades.

In other words, there was no long standing history of laws against homosexuality being enforced. (Despite the Court's view of history, some well-known examples of prosecutions for sodomy (or "crimes against nature") such as that of Oscar Wilde in the 19th century suggest that these laws were enforced sometimes, at least when the conduct was so open as to be flagrantly offensive to social mores.) Moreover, the modern trend was against such laws.

In 1980, the scholars who drafted the Model Penal Code had deliberately omitted any prohibition against private consensual sexual conduct between adults. Those scholars gave three reasons for their decision. First, such laws undermined respect for the law because many people engaged in these sex acts. Second, the laws prohibited private conduct that did not harm another person, and third, because the laws were so irregularly enforced, they created opportunities for blackmail. Many state legislatures agreed with those reasons and abolished their laws against homosexual conduct. At the time of the *Lawrence* case, only 13 states still had laws against sodomy and of those, four enforced the law only against homosexuals.

The Supreme Court noted that the European Court of Human Rights had held that laws proscribing homosexual conduct violated the European Convention on Human Rights. That decision applied to 45 European countries.

In *Lawrence*, the Court considered the widespread moral condemnation of homosexuality. The justices said

> *The condemnation has been shaped by religious beliefs, conceptions of right and acceptable behavior, and respect for the traditional family. For many persons these are not trivial concerns but profound and deep convictions accepted as ethical and moral principles to which they aspire and which thus determine the course of their lives. These considerations do not answer the question before us, however. The issue is whether the majority may use the power of the State to enforce these views on the whole society through operation of the criminal law.*

The Court cited earlier decisions on the privacy of the home, saying "our laws and tradition afford constitutional protection to personal decisions relating to marriage, procreation, contraception, family relationships, child rearing and education." The Court quoted an earlier decision on birth control, repeating that "These matters, involving the most intimate and personal choice a person may make in a lifetime, choices central to personal dignity and autonomy, are central to the liberty" protected by the Constitution.

Therefore, the Court ruled that private, consensual homosexual conduct between adults could not constitutionally be outlawed. This decision also protects the rights of heterosexual married couples to engage in anal or oral intercourse in the privacy of their home.

QUESTION: *"What is the legal status of same sex partners in regard to children of the relationship?"*

ANSWER: *Their legal status is uncertain and depends on evolving decisions in the various states.*

A number of cases and statutes have addressed the possible legal relationships of same sex partners to children involved the relationship. Several states have adopted laws prohibiting same sex couples from adopting or from serving as foster parents. When same sex couples want to adopt a child, some attorneys avoid these prohibitions by having two separate adoption proceedings – one for each of the prospective parents.

It is not clear whether these laws violate the United States or state constitutions, such as the guarantees of equal protection of the law for all citizens. In some cases, the courts have held those statutes unconstitutional, while other courts have disagreed and found that the laws were permissible. The issue is whether there is a rational social purpose for a state to discriminate among its citizens in regard to adoption based on the prospective parents' sexual orientation. Obviously, the answer depends on one's moral and political views.

On the other hand, some states permit both partners to adopt the same child so that both become the legal parents of the child.

More difficult questions arise when one partner has a biological relationship to the child and the other does not. Here are some sample situations:

Case 1

George and Mary are married. They have three children. George comes out of the closet, revealing that he is gay. When they divorce, George gets custody of the children. He moves in with his significant other, Fred. Fred and George live together for ten years and Fred becomes very involved in the children's lives. They love him and he loves them. Then, Fred and George split. What legal rights does Fred have?

There is no certain answer to that question. Some courts look entirely to the biological connection of George and his children. Others look to the psychological relationship of the adults and children and try to decide in the best interests of the child. Some states have statues that permit any adult who has a significant relationship with a child to petition for visitation rights with the child. In those more liberal jurisdictions, Fred may have the right to visitation with the children, just as Mary would have when she and George divorced.

Case 2

Cecile and Jane are long time lovers. They decide that they want children and Cecile has a baby. Cecile and Jane continue to live together for ten years and Jane acts in all respects as a parent to their son, Elmer. Then Cecile and Jane part after a bitter argument. What rights does Jane have?

Some states permit Jane to adopt Elmer, in which case she would be his legal parent and have the same rights as any other parent in a divorce-type split.

If Jane did not adopt Elmer, her rights depend on the same factors as in Case 1, i.e. whether her state (a) recognizes the concept of a psychological parent and (b) applies that concept to same sex relationships.

Other countries are not bound by American law or mores. Many couples now seek to adopt children from foreign countries. In many of those countries, religious and moral standards condemn same sex relationships. Officials in these countries will not permit an adoption if it becomes apparent that a same sex couple is involved. For example, even if one prospective parent applies to adopt a child alone, the officials may inquire as to whether the prospective parent lives with another person. If that person is of the same sex, the adoption may be denied

Marriage and Same Sex Couples — the Goodridge case

In the *Goodridge* case, the Supreme Court of Massachusetts considered whether the state could legally "deny the protections, benefits, and obligations conferred by civil marriage to two individuals of the same sex who wish to marry."[7] The court concluded "it may not." Those justices reasoned that the Massachusetts Constitution "affirms the dignity and equality of all individuals. It forbids the creation of second-class citizens." They concluded that the state had failed to give any adequate reason for denying the legal status of marriage to same-sex couples.

The court acknowledged that many people "hold deep-seated religious, moral, and ethical convictions that marriage should be limited to the union of one man and one woman, and that homosexual conduct is immoral. Many hold equally strong religious, moral, and ethical convictions that same-sex couples are entitled to be married, and that homosexual persons should be treated no differently than their heterosexual neighbors." However, the justices noted, the strength of different moral views didn't decide the question; the question was how the state constitution should apply to "every person properly within its reach."

The justices noted that civil marriage is a governmental institution, as opposed to marriage as a religious covenant. Civil marriage is regulated by the state government;

the couple decides whether to marry or divorce but the government sets the terms.

> *In a real sense, there are three partners to every civil marriage: two willing spouses and an approving State. While only the parties can mutually assent to marriage, the terms of the marriage — who may marry and what obligations, benefits, and liabilities attach to civil marriage — are set by the Commonwealth. Conversely, while only the parties can agree to end the marriage (absent the death of one of them or a marriage void ab initio), The Commonwealth defines the exit terms.*[8]

The Court acknowledged the benefits to society of the marriage institution, both to the individual and to society.

However, the justices also noted that the legal status of marriage conferred many governmental benefits on the couple, including property rights and inheritance rights. As they said, "The benefits accessible only by way of a marriage license are enormous, touching nearly every aspect of life and death." Literally, hundreds of statutes relate to marriage.

The attorneys who were arguing against same sex marriage argued that restricting marriage to heterosexual promoted better homes for children. The justices noted that might be true, but that in fact, good child care wasn't a policy that was actually tied to marriage by the law. State law didn't require that couples be fertile in order to marry nor provide that infertility was a ground for divorce. Unmarried couples could freely have children, while married couples could, if they chose, decide not to.

Moreover, as a matter of social fact, the traditional two parent family supposedly facilitated by restricting marriage no longer represents a typical household in our current society. Other laws about family matters reflect the changing demographics of our society.

Moreover, there was no evidence that prohibiting same sex marriages would encourage couples to form heterosexual marriages and procreate. In other words, the ostensible justification for the law didn't make any sense. In other words, in reality, society had already separated marriage from the ideology that ostensibly underlay it. Although society might pay lip service to improving the home life of children and so on, in fact, social policies were not consistently directed to those ends.

Therefore, the Massachusetts Supreme Court concluded that

The marriage ban works a deep and scarring hardship on a very real segment of the community for no rational reason. The absence of any reasonable relationship between, on the one hand, an absolute disqualification of same-sex couples who wish to enter into civil marriage and, on the other, protection of public health, safety, or general welfare, suggests that the marriage restriction is rooted in persistent prejudices against persons who are (or who are believed to be homosexual.

One way of putting the more liberal reasoning, exemplified in the court's analysis, is the following. Laws can only discriminate against one group of people if there is a rational basis for the government to do so. The government cannot prohibit marriages between people of different races or different religions because there is no acceptable social goal that would be advanced by such a policy.

The conduct of our society strongly suggests that we no longer regard it as the government's business to control consensual sexual conduct. In fact, it appears that, as a society, we don't express much disapproval of conduct that violates traditional morality, at least unless a politician is concerned.

Moreover, from the governmental point of view, marriage is a legal institution that relates more to financial matters, such as pensions, than to procreation. From one point of view, there is no particular reason to link those financial consequences to any particular religious tradition.

Christian and Jewish religious law condemns sex relations between men, among other sexual crimes such as incest, sodomy, and sex with animals (bestiality). The Old Testament declares that homosexual conduct (sex between men) is an abomination. Some conservative Christians extend that prohibition to sex between women, sometimes on the ground that it supposedly was one of the forms of sexual immorality practiced in Egypt or in Sodom and Gomorrah.

Under rabbinical interpretations, "Lesbianism was not mentioned in the Bible but is prohibited in Talmudic law."

More liberal religious scholars and clergymen have reinterpreted Biblical texts to permit a more tolerant and accepting approach to gay and lesbian people.

The Bible prescribes the death penalty, usually by stoning, for some sexual crimes, including a man who has intercourse with another man. In the Talmudic tradition, sex between women was punishable by flogging.

Even very conservative religious people today, at least in the United States, do not advocate the death penalty for sexual misconduct; however, they do oppose any social or governmental condonation of homosexual conduct, especially any effort to create a recognized "marriage like" status for homosexual couples.

(In some Muslin countries, however, the death penalty can still be imposed for sexual offenses, especially adultery by a wife. Chastity in a daughter is so valued that some fathers commit "honor killings" in which they murder their daughters for real or rumored sexual transgressions. Women's rights groups complain that these murders, even if technically illegal, are effectively tolerated.)

Significantly, most Biblical prohibitions focus on sexual conduct, as opposed to homosexuality in the sense of sexual identity. Desire to commit a sexual offense is described as sinful principally because daydreaming about improper sexual acts is regarded as likely to lead to the act itself or at least to an alienation from right thinking and conduct.[9]

In my view, imposing various penalties on persons who practice homosexuality runs the risk of being hypocritical. It is at least an attempt to continue one particular Biblical proscription in a society which, in the secular domain, no longer gives much weight to any of the others. After all, adultery violates one of the Ten Commandments but it is no longer an important factor in divorces. Sex with children is regarded as a grave crime in today's society but isn't subject to nearly the same condemnation in the Bible.

As a matter of practice and law, however, we do not condition many government benefits on compliance with traditional Biblical morality. Society has become more secular in the sense that the governmental aspects of family life have been divorced from some moral considerations. Alimony and child custody no longer turn entirely on sexual propriety. We don't deny Social Security benefits to a widow because she had an affair or used birth control, although current law conditions some benefits on the existence of a continuing marriage. We no longer recognize a husband's right to force himself sexually upon his wife or to control all of her money, although some Biblical traditions endorse those positions.

The law does not restrict marriage to couples who want to have children. The institution of marriage is separate from the Biblical injunction to "be fruitful and multiply." In other words, although some may say that command is the underlying purpose of marriage, in fact, we don't design social institutions along those lines.

Another way to look at the issue of same sex marriage is that secular law no longer concerns itself with many aspects of sexual behavior between consenting adults. The police haven't been arrested many adulterers or fornicators for decades. Few people believe that the government should control what sexual positions are legal or that it would be a good idea for the police to check out people's bedrooms to make sure that no one was engaging in oral sex or masturbating. Those who believe that the government should enforce morality usually believe that it is their personal moral code that should be enforced on others, not that of others on them. Relatively few who would happily see those of whom they disapprove prosecuted would endorse prosecution of themselves for some other violation of Biblical morality, such as gossiping or greed for material goods or adultery.

These considerations lead some people to reconsider the question of whether civil marriage, i.e. marriage as a governmental status, should be restricted to heterosexuals. If child-bearing is not the purpose of marriage (as seen by the law) and heterosexual moral strictures are no longer determinative, then why should one particular moral injunction be critical?

One response to this line of reasoning is that marriage *should* be focused on procreation as part of an increased emphasis on the importance of family life, where a family is considered to be comprised of a male husband/father, a female wife/mother, and their biological children. On this view, increased tolerance of sexual variation is the sign of a decadent society. No doubt, some would support having the police arrest those who had sexual relations outside of marriage. Some believe that contraception, or at least those methods (such as the IUD) that prevent implantation of a fertilized ovum, should be illegal. Some also believe that young adults should not be informed about how to avoid sexually transmitted diseases. It seems unlikely, however, that even the most fundamentalist Christian really wants the vice squad to be checking his or her bedroom for signs of sexual misconduct.

QUESTION: *"What happens (legally) when a person has a sex change operation?"*

ANSWER: *That person legally becomes a person of the new sex for most purposes.*

In many respects, a person who has a sex change operation becomes, legally, a person of the new sex. He or she may apply for a name change from, for example, "John" to "Jane" and courts usually recognize the gender reassignment and legally change the person's name to one reflecting his or her new gender. In some states, the person's birth certificate can be changed to reflect his or her new gender, and other documents, such as driver's licenses, can be appropriately, legally, altered. Many states permit persons who have had such surgery to assume the legal status of their new gender. Such persons can, for example, now use the restrooms designated for their (new) sex. This can matter in states where it is unlawful to enter the restroom designated for the opposite sex. Many, if not most states, permit persons who have undergone gender reassignment to marry a person of the (new) opposite sex. However, some courts have held that such marriages are invalid. Courts are particularly puzzled by situations in which a person previously, legally, male marries a woman and then undergoes gender reassignment surgery. He then takes all legal steps to change his legal identity to that of a woman, such as getting a new driver's license and so on. The situation raises many questions. If the state has prohibited same sex marriages, is the marriage now void? If the couple divorces, can the former husband (now a woman) marry a man? The answer varies from state to state.

Cohabitation agreements and same sex couples

Just as the courts traditionally refused to enforce contracts between heterosexual couples, some might refuse to enforce a contract between same sex couples on the ground that the underlying relationship was immoral.

It is likely, but not certain, that the courts in most states will now recognize agreements between cohabiting same sex couples as valid contracts. Some states might require that the agreement be in writing, while others might enforce an oral or implied agreement, if the evidence of the couple's intentions was sufficiently persuasive.

California courts, for example, have ruled that agreements between same sex couples are as valid as agreements between heterosexual couples[10]

Some states, however, have adopted laws to prohibit cohabitation agreements between same sex couples. Montana's law, for example, prohibits a marriage between persons of the same sex and declares, "A contractual relationship entered into for the purpose of achieving a civil relationship that is prohibited under subsection (1) is void as against public policy."[11] In other words, a cohabitation agreement that creates a marriage-like relationship for a same sex couple is not a valid agreement in Montana.

It is not clear what kind of contract gay partners could make with each other in states with laws like these. Presumably ordinary business transactions would be legal, but the boundaries are not obvious. It is clear, however, that any such contract should not refer to marriage laws or marital property laws, such as stating that the couple "regard ourselves as married" or "intend to have the same rights as married people."

Some of the sample contracts in this book have language such as that; those clauses may be appropriate for heterosexual couples in some states but would be inadvisable for same sex couples.

Even if the laws are not that specific, a similar potential difficulty arises because many states have adopted constitutional amendments prohibiting the recognition of "marriage-like" relationships other than traditional heterosexual marriages. These new provisions cast doubt on whether gay couples (or even, possibly, unmarried heterosexual couples) can enter a valid cohabitation agreement. A conservative court could interpret such an agreement as creating a marriage-like relationship, especially if the agreement contains a description of the relationship that refers to love or life partnership or other terms of endearment.

The problem is that these constitutional amendments seem inconsistent with other laws, such as those that make written cohabitation agreements valid or those that recognize a "marriage-like" relationship for innocent spouses in an invalid marriage (putative spouses). Because of this theoretical doubt, in the present political climate, some expert lawyers now try to avoid the issue by describing the couple in documents as "friends who respect each other" or other romantically and sexually neutral language.[12]

If there are family members who object to the couple's relationship on moral or religious grounds, the couple needs to be especially careful in making legal provision for each other. If one of the couple dies, for example, family members may challenge the will.

In particular, because a cohabitation agreement may or may not be valid, the same sex couple should consider using other legal means to achieve their goals. Deeds and wills should be carefully prepared to reflect the couple's intentions. Some lawyers suggest that the couple might enter into a partnership agreement, like a business, rather than a cohabitation agreement.

Also, same sex couples need to have documents that clearly provide for health care decisions, including making clear that you want your partner to receive health care information. Federal privacy laws might preclude a doctor or hospital from sharing information with a non-relative unless the patient has clearly given permission for such disclosure. Similarly, if family members object, a morally conservative hospital may exclude a same sex partner from a patient's hospital room. Your health care documents should clearly state that you want your partner to receive medical information about you and to have the right to visit you in your hospital room. If it matters to you, you should also have documents that provide for possible bad situations, including who will be your guardian if you are disabled, your health care decisions, and your funeral arrangements.

Some expert lawyers recommend that the formalities of signing a will or other agreement be followed with elaborate care. Because a family member may claim that a partner "made him homosexual," they may challenge a will or cohabitation agreement on the grounds of undue influence or duress. To avoid these claims, some lawyers videotape the signing of the agreement and have it signed by each person separately without the other present. The point is to have a record that there wasn't any obvious duress being exercised by one person on the other. (Ideally, some lawyers would want both of the couple to have his or her own attorney, but that is too expensive and complicated for most couples.)

Discrimination and sexual preference

In most states, it is legal for a private person or organization to discriminate against people based on their sexual preferences, but not on their gender. In other words, in many places, it is legal for landlords, employers, clubs, and others to treat gay, lesbian, bisexual and transgender people differently from heterosexual people. Private organizations, for example, can discriminate on the basis of sexual orientation. Thus, for example, the Boy Scouts of America can lawfully exclude openly gay men and boys (as well as all girls and women) from membership and from serving as troop leaders. Some cities, however, have revoked the tax exemptions previously granted to that organization, however, on the ground that its discriminatory practice violated city policies.

Although it is largely legal to discriminate on the basis of sexual orientation (in many places), discrimination on the basis of gender is largely unlawful. Large organizations, such as most "private" clubs, employers, and large apartment complexes, are not permitted to discriminate between men and women. An employer cannot refuse to hire a qualified woman, even if the manager thinks that women should not work outside the home. The manager of an apartment house cannot refuse to rent to a single woman if the manager is willing to rent to a single man.

As a matter of constitutional law, and the employment laws of many places, a person can often be denied employment because he or she is cohabiting with another person, whether the relationship is heterosexual or homosexual. However, any such policy or decision must be applied in accordance with other employment laws and cannot be a pretext for discriminating against women, for example.

Even the government can, sometimes, refuse or terminate a public employee's employment, based on his or her living with another, at least if the government can show that the policy serves a necessary state interest and doesn't unduly interfere with the person's privacy rights. Two police officers (a man and a woman) were fired for living together, for example, and a lesbian woman who openly planned to go through a Jewish marriage ceremony with her partner was denied employment by the state attorney general's office. In the attorney general's case, he successfully argued that a lesbian employee would cast doubt on his office's enforcement of various laws relating to morality.

This area of the law is in flux, however, and if you have lost a job because of your sexual preference or private life, you should consult a local attorney who is familiar with employment laws of your area.

Some cities, for example, prohibit such discrimination. Moreover, sometimes it is unconstitutional for a governmental entity, such as a school district, to take action against someone based on some official's own moral view of people's private lives. In general, the government must have a rational basis to discriminate among its citizens, and unless a person's private conduct affects their work, for example, the government should not take it into account.

Your rights to your private life in the context of your employment depend on the circumstances.[13]

However, there are two important limitations on a person's right to discriminate against homosexual people. First, some states and cities have local statutes or ordinances that prohibit discrimination based on sexual orientation in hiring and in housing. Second, the government cannot legally discriminate between citizens unless there is some rational social purpose for the distinction. The extent to which this protect homosexual persons is unclear.

The basic requirement of equal treatment for all citizens does not mean, however, that the laws must be exactly the same for all. The law need not permit a person who is (legally) a male to use the ladies' dressing room in a store or the women's locker room at a country club, just because he/she feels more at home there. The state may, to some extent, act to protect the ordinary sensibilities of the average citizen, at least in public places.

Theoretically, in the eyes of the law, heterosexuals and everyone else must be treated equally, as far as government matters like court cases, voting, police protection, and other rights are concerned, unless the government has a legitimate reason to discriminate. The question, obviously, is what a legitimate reason is. For example, the United States military can lawfully discharge an openly gay person and can also properly exclude women from some positions, such as submarine service. The reasoning is that these policies, in the judgment of armed forces officials, are necessary to a functioning wartime military. In principle, the military also prohibits other moral infractions and may, for example, court-martial an officer who commits adultery.

Recently, more importantly, several states have adopted laws prohibiting same sex couples from adopting or from serving as foster parents. When same sex couples want to adopt a child, some attorneys avoid these prohibitions by having two separate adoption proceedings – one for each of the prospective parents.

It is not clear whether these laws violate the United States or state constitutions, such as the guarantees of equal protection of the law for all citizens. The issue is whether there is a rational social purpose for a state to discriminate among its citizens in regard to adoption based on the prospective parents' sexual orientation. Obviously, the answer depends on one's moral and political views.

Other countries are not bound by American law or mores. Many couples now seek to adopt children from foreign countries. In many of those countries, religious and moral standards condemn same sex relationships. Officials in these countries will not permit an adoption if it becomes apparent that a same sex couple is involved. For example, even if one prospective parent applies to adopt a child alone, the officials may inquire as to whether the prospective parent lives with another person. If that person is of the same sex, the adoption may be denied.

Transgender, bisexuality and other variations

One of the more complex questions in the law at present is the effect of medical interventions for transgender persons.

The legal status of marriage for persons who have undergone sex reassignment surgery is somewhat unclear.

A person who has a feminine perception of self but a male body remains, legally, a male unless and until he/she undergoes a sex change operation, after which she is, in some states, legally a woman.

During the transitional period, transgender people must exercise discretion as to their appearance, use of gender-designated rest rooms, and so on.

A person who has had gender reassignment surgery can have his or her legal identity modified in most states. This includes legal name changes, driver's license changes, and even passport changes. Some states permit birth certificates to be modified. Other states limit these options. The staff of a physician who performs such surgeries, such as a social worker or psychologist, can be an excellent resource for sources of information on the exact legal consequences of the surgery in any given state.

In some states, a person who has had sex reassignment surgery can marry a person of the (new) opposite sex. (He or she cannot marry a person of the (new) same sex in any state that prohibits same sex marriages.) However, the issue is not settled. Some states have refused to recognize these marriages on the theory that one's gender is established by the genitalia that one has at birth. Others have considered whether it would be grounds for annulment if a person who had had such surgery married someone who didn't know the facts. Finally, a marriage may be annulled if one party is incapable of sexual intercourse, which means male penetration of the female's vagina.[14]

Bisexual persons can only legally marry (in most states) persons of the opposite sex. It is not illegal to be attracted to persons of both sexes, nor, as discussed below, are private sexual acts between consenting adults illegal.

Persons who have genetic or physiological anomalies, such as hermaphrodites (persons with some of the sexual characteristics of both sexes) are usually considered to have the (legal) gender of the sex to which their appearance most conforms, i.e. a man if they have stereotypical masculine characteristics or a woman if they have feminine characteristics. In effect, the doctor who delivers the baby usually decides. Once their sexual identity is assigned, they can only legally marry someone of the opposite sex. If the person later decides that he or she is actually of the other gender, it is possible, but uncommon, to have his or her gender legally changed by changing his or her birth certificate, driver's license, name, etc. The legal process involves demonstrating to a court that the medical facts support assigning the person to the other gender and that the legal assignment of gender should match the medical reality.

QUESTION: *"What about the rest of human sexual variations? You don't have much to say about bisexual and transgendered people or those in sadomasochistic relationships."*

ANSWER: *No book can cover every possible scenario. The same basic rules apply to these persons as to others in analogous situations. The legal consequences of one's actions depend on who is involved, where the action takes place, and the surrounding circumstances.*

Bisexual persons are likely to have the same legal protections and hassles as those who are exclusively homosexual, with the added complexity of possibly also being the biological parent of a child from a traditional marriage.

Regardless of its form, private, consensual, adult sexual conduct is generally protected from government intrusion. Bisexual, fetishist, and sadomasochistic conduct is not usually criminal. The private possession of pornography or sexual gadgets is largely protected by constitutional rights of privacy.

Cross-dressing is technically still illegal in many states but these laws are seldom enforced, even if the person appears in public, unless some other law is violated. Cross-dressers must, however, use the restroom of their anatomical sex, not that of their attire.

QUESTION: *"What are some of the legal limitations on sexuality?"*

ANSWER: *Sexuality can be regulated when it directly involves others or society*

There are limits on liberty. Paying for sex is illegal, regardless of its form. Sex with underage persons is unlawful, as are the possession of pornography involving minors and soliciting sex with a child. (Internet pedophiles should be aware that their obscene exchanges with supposed children may actually be with undercover FBI officers.)

Most forms of forcing one's indulgences on others are unlawful. In other words, a homosexual voyeur who is caught masturbating in a man's backyard commits a crime just as does a heterosexual voyeur caught in a woman's yard. A fetishist who strokes people's feet in the subway commits an offense whether the unwilling recipient of his (or her) attentions is male or female.

In addition, while it may be lawful to possess adult pornography or sex toys in one's home, it is not necessarily legal to sell these items. Some cities, for example, have ordinances prohibiting the sale or public display of "lewd" objects. Some stores refer coyly to "adult novelties" rather than explicitly to sex toys. In 2005, for example, a respectable housewife was prosecuted in a mid-sized Texas city for selling sex toys at private parties.

Pornography is defined as an obscene depiction that is intended to appeal to a person's prurient interest and that has no redeeming social value. Sexually explicit pictures in a medical journal are not likely to be considered pornographic because they are for the useful social purpose of educating doctors. Generally, whether an image is obscene or not depends on the standards of the community where any prosecution is brought.

Overall, social mores have become both more national and more lax so that widely distributed and popular mainstream films contain language and images that would have clearly been considered pornographic only a few decades ago. Consequently, prosecutions for sale of pornography are now relatively uncommon. However, cities may still enforce ordinances against the sale of obscene materials in certain places, such as near a church or school, or in a certain manner, such as requiring that the materials not be available to minors.

The complexity and cultural variability of these issues can be seen in the case of a small town Texas teacher who was disciplined by school officials (in 2006!) because she took her students on a field trip to an art museum where one of the kids saw a nude statue. The child told his parents, who complained to school officials. Many parents would have been delighted to find that at least one teacher was trying to compensate for the lack of funds for art education in the schools. The teacher lost her job but later won a financial settlement from the school district.

Analogously, offended shoppers compelled a shopping center in Houston (in 2004) to move a nude statue (a copy of Michelangelo's David) to the top of a building so that customers wouldn't be able to see the anatomical details. In Florence, Italy, the original statue is a treasure of a world famous art museum, which is visited each year by thousands of American tourists, and a reproduction is proudly displayed on the street.

Again, however, private individuals have more freedom to disapprove of others' conduct than the government does. A company may, for example, prohibit its employees from surfing pornographic websites using a company-owned computer. Similarly, a company may refuse to reimburse an employee for "business entertainment expenses" incurred at establishments, such as nude bars, of which management disapproves, at least if the company has a clear policy about which expenses are legitimate and which are not.

These policies are subject to some limitations; for example, a large company may have a policy against supervisors dating subordinates but that policy should apply to all romantic approaches, gay or straight.

In most states, however, it is still lawful for a company to fire an employee on the ground that he or she is homosexual. Also, as noted earlier, more or less private organizations such as the Boy Scouts, may lawfully discriminate against homosexual persons.

The power of a large company to refuse to hire someone or to fire an employee on the ground that his or her private conduct is immoral has lessened, as a practical matter if not by law. A national enterprise does not want the hassle of adjusting its policies to each state's and city's standards, since an action that might be legal in one place could easily give rise to a lawsuit in another. Even if it were technically legal for them to take action based on a manager's personal moral values, most companies stay well out of their employees' personal affairs unless those activities have a significant potential to involve the company, as where the company prohibits all office romances in order to avoid any claims of sexual harassment. The days when employers required their employees to attend church every Sunday or to avoid "women of ill repute" are gone unless there is some economic connection between the employee's conduct and the employer's business.

However, a private person, such as a mother who is hiring a housekeeper or a small businessperson who is hiring a bookkeeper, has more latitude to exercise his or her moral judgments as to the employee's behavior and values.

Usually, sadomasochistic behavior, whether bondage, whipping, or other activity, is not the crime of assault or battery, even though physical pain or even harm is inflicted. This is because one is not liable for assault or battery where the other person consented. That's why football players aren't liable for battery even though they tackle one another, as long as the conduct takes place within the context of the game.

However, a person can be liable either criminally or civilly if the activity becomes significantly more violent or dangerous than the other expected or takes place in another context than that agreed on. Spanking a sexual companion in the bedroom as part of mutually agreeable sex play is lawful, but surprising the same companion with a hearty swat on the behind at a fancy cocktail party may not be. Finally, of course, conduct that results in a death or serious injury can give rise to criminal charges, such as manslaughter, regardless of the exact variation that the couple was involved in and regardless of whether it was consensual.

The effect of sexual conduct on the outcome of a divorce or child custody dispute is uncertain and depends on the values of the community and the judge. To some people, a man who frequents topless bars behaves immorally, even if the establishment is a lawful one, and they would sympathize with his wife in a divorce. Similarly, if a judge regards a particular sex act as perverted, then he or she is likely to regard a spouse's objections to it as natural and understandable.

The parents' sexual proclivities may or may not affect the outcome of a child custody suit. If explicit sexual conduct is carefully screened from the children, the court may regard it as not having any bearing on the child's welfare. If, however, the conduct takes place in a manner that exposes the child to an unhealthy environment, psychologically or morally, the court may be influenced to grant primary custody to the other parent.

As with all private behavior, discretion is usually well advised. If you feel an overwhelming urge to parade your sexual proclivities at work, get a therapist, not a lawyer.

Conclusions and advice

In the changing legal landscape, same sex couples cannot count on the government providing them with the legal protections and burdens of marriage. At present, only Massachusetts expressly recognizes same sex marriages, while Vermont affords a civil union status analogous to marriage and California permits registration of a domestic partnership which affords many of the rights of marriage. The status of these legal arrangements in other states is uncertain. On the other hand, a same sex couple cannot count on being entirely free of legal obligations to each other either.

Therefore, to an even greater extent than other couples, same sex couples need to take appropriate action to delineate the terms of their relationship by written agreements and other appropriate documents. It is especially important for same sex couples to use every legally available means to clarify their legal status with any children of the relationship. If at all possible, the partner who is not biologically related to the child should adopt the child. If that is not possible, at the least, the couple should enter into a written contract about custody, visitation and so on. The contract may not be technically binding but a court may be influenced by their agreement.

(Endnotes)

[1] California Secretary of State Website, www.ss.ca.gov/dpregistry.

[2] See the form promulgated by the California Secretary of State, pursuant to Section 298 of the California Family Code, available on line at www.ss.ca.gov/dpregistry.

[3] Joyce Murdock and Deb Price, *Courting Justice; Gay Men and Lesbians v. The Supreme Court*. Basic Books, New York, 2001.

[4] Patricia Rose, *When Passion Reigned: Sex and the Victorians*, Basic Books, New York, 1995, at 22 et seq.

[5] *Lawrence v. Texas* 539 U.S. 558 (2003)

[6] *Lawrence v. Texas* 539 U.S. 558 (2003)

[7] *Goodridge v. Department of Public Health*, 798 N.E.2d 941 (Masss. 2003)

[8] *Goodridge v. Department of Public Health*, 798 N.E. 2d 941 (Masss. 2003)

[9] David C. Gross and Esther R. Gross, *Under the Wedding Canopy; Love and Marriage in Judaism*. Hippocrene Books, New York, 1996, at 113.

[10] *Whorton v. Dillingham*, 202 Cal. App. 3d 447 (1988)

[11] Montana Code Annotated 40-1-401

[12] "Representing Nontraditional Families," Texas State Bar Association Continuing Legal Education, April 26, 2006, panel discussion and accompanying materials, Jerry W. Simoneaux, Jr., "Rightpracticing Law in the Grey Shadow of the Texas Marriage Amendment."

[13] See *Kukla v. Village of Antioch*, 647 F. Supp. 799 (N.D.Ill. 1986); *Shahar v. Bowers* 70 F.3d 1218 (11th Cir. 1995).

[14] One of the best articles on these issues is William H. Hohengarten, "Same-sex marriage and the right of privacy," The Yale Law Journal, Volume 103, Issue g (1984), pp. 1495 – 1531. The article was written before the Defense of Marriage Act but it clearly sets out the legal reasoning involved in these issues.

Chapter Five

MARRIAGE AND LIVING TOGETHER —WHAT'S THE (LEGAL) DIFFERENCE?

Marriage has a number of financial and legal consequences whether it is common law or ceremonial. More importantly, for many of these consequences, it is an all-or-nothing proposition: if the couple is married, then each of them has various financial rights — if they are not married, then they have none of these rights.

This chapter covers the basic legal differences between being married and living together. It is organized around basic topics of everyday life — and death — such as owning things and paying for them; life insurance and inheritance; and miscellaneous other legal rights.

 Some writers have argued that the courts should recognize a "marriage-like" relationship between couples who have lived together for a long time. Any legal tendency in this direction has been cast into more doubt by the passage of constitutional amendments in many states that expressly prohibit courts from recognizing any marriage-like relationship other than a marriage between a man and woman. Although these laws were aimed at prohibiting same-sex marriage, they may also have the effect of prohibiting an unmarried couple from being considered to have been in a marriage-like relationship. These laws are new and their scope is unknown because courts have not been asked to decide any cases involving the new amendments yet.

Once again, if you think that the custody of a child or the right to any substantial amount of money – any amount that really matters to you or your children – may turn on a point of law, consult a lawyer. If your health or that of your child were at stake, would you just read a book and treat the disease yourself? No? You'd consult a good doctor? Well, then, use the same good sense here and get an attorney's advice.

QUESTION: *"Why can't you just give me a simple answer? Can't you just look up the law in a book and tell me what it is?"*

ANSWER: *A simple answer to questions about cohabitation, marriage, and money is difficult to give because (1) the law is presently uncertain; (2) each case presents some different facts; and (3) even where the law is clear, it is applied by human judges and juries with their own beliefs and values.*

As social values change, the law changes also. However, the changes in the law may reflect either acceptance of new social norms or attempts to preserve a different culture. Sometimes this book sounds like an advertisement for lawyers, but the fact is that the law is both simple and complex. The basic rules are fairly straightforward, but the application of them to our tangled lives is complicated.

QUESTION: *"What is the largest area of uncertainty when comparing cohabitation and marriage?"*

ANSWER: *The central unsettled question is whether the courts will consider cohabitation to be an uncommitted, immoral, and essentially temporary arrangement or whether they will consider cohabitation as a committed, albeit informal, relationship. The primary consequence is whether judges will imply an agreement between the couple to share the assets gained during the relationship.*

The usual legal view of cohabiting couples is that the relationship was the opposite of marriage and therefore did not confer the legal obligations and rights that marriage did. This rule affected both the property rights and the contract rights of unmarried couples.

First, most courts did not treat cohabiting couples as economic partners or honor any implied agreement between them to share the fruits of their labors. There were more progressive exceptions such as the *Hayworth* case in early 20th century Texas, where a court honored an implied agreement between a couple to work together to earn money to buy a farm.

The traditional rule of law has been that agreements between cohabiting persons were unenforceable. In other words, the courts would not see that a person received his or her rights under an agreement between the couple whether it was in writing or not. A contract between cohabiting lovers was considered to be like a contract between a man and a concubine. Such contracts were unlawful because they embodied an immoral transaction.

Similarly, for many decades, courts would not enforce an agreement that a married couple made in anticipation of a divorce, especially if they made the agreement before the marriage. The reason was that enforcing such agreements would tend to encourage divorce or separation, which was morally undesirable.

For some people, those values persist. If a man and woman live together, his parents may still scornfully refer to her as his "shack up" or his "whore." Her parents may try to keep their daughter's living arrangement a secret from their friends.

Many other people, probably a significant majority, have accepted the idea that it is permissible for unmarried couples to live together. However, the result in a dispute between the couple may turn on the judge's views of such relationships.

If a judge regards cohabitation as an acceptable life style alternative, he or she may be more inclined to regard the couple as having some obligations to each other. He or she may find it plausible, for example, that the couple had an implied agreement to share in the fruits of their relationship. If, on the other hand, a judge regards cohabitation as an irresponsible and immoral sexual arrangement, then he or she may be less likely to find that the couple intended to act responsibly toward each other.

Today, prenuptial agreements are valid contracts, at least if the agreement is not grossly unfair to either party. An engaged couple can sign an agreement that provides for the division of their assets if they later divorce. The courts also honor an agreement that a divorcing couple makes to divide their property, if it is fair and in the best interests of the children.

Similarly, all but two states now honor written cohabitation agreements. Georgia and Illinois do not recognize those agreements as valid. Some states have been willing to honor an oral agreement, but others require that the agreement be in writing. Some courts also use various legal doctrines to reach an equitable result between the couple.

The following sections consider various specific aspects of the law of marriage and living together in more detail. The law governing prenuptial and cohabitation agreements is discussed in Chapter Eight and Chapter Nine.

The main legal issues in a relationship concern money or, to put it more tactfully, assets. Over time, a couple may acquire various assets and debts together; if they separate, or one of them dies, the questions of who owns what must be answered.

Since sex outside of marriage was traditionally considered immoral and was, at times, illegal, the traditional law gave very few rights to illicit lovers. The technical word for such relationships was "meretricious" which essentially means "immoral." The legal doctrine of common law marriage can be described as a kind of "assumption of morality" for couples who intended to be married and who behaved in the community as if they were in fact married. Under the doctrine of common law marriage, their financial obligations to each other were the same as if they had been formally married in a ceremony.

Owning things

The structure of the law about the possessions that a couple acquires is straightforward, at least in principle.

Nowhere is the disparity between married couples and cohabiting couples more dramatic than in the ownership of tangible things. Here are the three basic principles:

✓ *1. In a marriage, both spouses usually and automatically acquire some rights to the tangible assets acquired during the marriage. These rights affect ownership, inheritance, and entitlements to support during and after the marriage.*

✓ *2. In a cohabitation relationship, the lovers do not usually or automatically acquire any rights to the tangible assets earned during the relationship.*

✓ *3. Both married and cohabiting couples can change these basic rules by their conduct. They can make changes by having an agreement among themselves, by changing the title on an asset, or by giving each other gifts.*

In all states, the names that a couple put on a deed or the papers for a bank or brokerage account have drastic legal consequences. Even in a community property state, if there is only one name on the title, the court may decide that the asset belongs solely to that spouse. The title on the document may (or may not) trump the marital property laws of the state and any cohabitation agreement.

In a marriage, the law provides the basic rules for who owns what during the marriage and who gets what if the marriage ends. By itself, the fact of marriage usually alters the property rights that each has. Although state laws have differed more in the past, most states now are moving toward a view of marriage as an economic partnership so that the spouses share to some extent in the proceeds of their life together. The application of that philosophy varies, however, in different circumstances, as seen by the judge. And, of course, a married couple can change the application of state law by a private agreement.

The general rules for living together are the opposite. By itself, living together does not usually change their rights to property. Unless they have an agreement to the contrary, each of them owns everything that he or she has legal title to; that means gifts, inheritances, wages, investment proceeds, and so on. For example, in a 1977 case, a couple lived together for 18 years. When they parted, the woman sued the man for her share of a house which they had supposedly bought together and for compensation for the services that she had provided. The Georgia courts ruled against her on the ground that the cohabitation relationship was immoral. One judge dissented, noting that "[c]ourts normally do not deny judicial relief to sinners. If that were the rule, the caseload in all courts would be drastically reduced."[1]

However, some courts have been willing to find an implied or oral agreement between a cohabiting couple to be partners in their property. For example, Brian and Gay Harrington lived together from 1971 until they married in 1977. They rented apartments in both their names until 1975 when they decided to buy a house together. Brian had an MBA in finance while Gay had a degree in journalism. Brian told Gay that they should buy the house in his name alone because he made more money and had better credit. In 1985, the couple divorced and Brian claimed that the house was his alone, as his separate property. The court found, however, that they intended that they would live in the house together and own it jointly. Because it was bought before the marriage, they owned it as tenants in common, meaning that each owned one-half, as opposed to it being their community property.[2]

The clearest expression of this more liberal rule was in the case of Michelle Marvin against Lee Marvin. The California court there held that the financial relationship of a cohabiting couple could be decided according to the rules of law that applied in other relationships. It said, "The courts may inquire into the conduct of the parties to determine whether that conduct demonstrates an implied contract or implied agreement of partnership or joint."[3]

A judge could also consider whether it would be fair to imply that one of the couple held property in trust for the other or whether one should compensate the other for his or her contribute to their finances. Other state courts, however, have expressly rejected this broad rule.

In summary, the application of state laws of marriage may vary from case to case, but the basic principle that some financial entitlements flow from the status of marriage is relatively clear. It is equally clear that those entitlements don't flow from the status of living together, although some judges may find some degree of entitlement under some factual situations.

Things get complicated, however, for both married and unmarried couples because the ownership of many things is represented by paperwork, such as the account agreement with a bank or the deed to a house. Couples can, and do, put various names on these papers. Some assets may be in both names, some in only one name. The legal effect of the paperwork depends on the intersection (or collision) between the laws of property rights and the laws of marriage.

Things get even more complicated when a couple lives together and then marry.

Consider the sad case of Viki and Andy Lee. The court set out the facts as follows:

When Viki and Andy met in early 1992, Viki owned title to seven lots and a town home. After they began living together, Viki transferred these pieces of property to Andy in May 1992, apparently in accordance with Taiwanese custom. Viki and Andy were ceremonially married in December 1993. Viki filed for divorce in April 1994, alleging that she and Andy had ceased living together as husband and wife in January 1994. Viki's petition alleged that the marriage had become insupportable because of discord and conflict of personalities, and accused Andy of treating her cruelly. Viki requested a just and right division of the marital estate.[4]

Viki's claim sounds only reasonable, right? In the complicated divorce proceedings that followed, Viki tried to get her lots and townhouse, or at least part of them, back. The problem was that she had deeded this property to Andy before they were married, so Andy claimed that the lots were his separate property and not subject to being divided by the court as part of the property of the marriage. Viki claimed that she and Andy had been common law married before the ceremonial marriage, but she couldn't prove that a marriage had taken place. Viki lost her property even though the court found that Andy had physically abused her. Andy got to keep the property because Viki voluntarily "gave" the real estate to him. The facts that she looked forward to marriage and that she acted in accordance with Chinese traditions were irrelevant. She lost her assets to an abusive guy with whom she had lived for less than a year.

Unmarried Couples

Remember, if an unmarried couple does not have a legally valid agreement about sharing the fruits of their relationship, then each owns the assets that they own, which is everything that each of them is given, inherits, or earns, whether before the relationship or afterwards.

A case in point is that of *Hewitt v. Hewitt*.[5] In that case, a couple lived together in Illinois for 15 years. They had three children and lived an outwardly ordinary, respectable, middle-class life. They were never legally married but presented themselves to their acquaintances as married. They did not have an express agreement about sharing the assets that were being earned.

Dr. Hewitt became a successful dentist, specializing in the care of children. His companion, Victoria, called herself "Mrs. Hewitt." She behaved as a traditional housewife, giving parties and entertaining his business acquaintances to further his career. Their house and investments were all in the "husband's" name.

Eventually, Dr. Hewitt tired of Victoria and the relationship ended.

Mrs. Hewitt expected and demanded, of course, to be treated as the long-suffering spouse that she thought she was. She sued for an equal share of the assets that they had accumulated during their relationship. She claimed that she and her lover had an implied agreement to share their assets as well as their life together.

Illinois does not recognize common law marriage, so under that state law, the Hewitts were not married. The Supreme Court of Illinois held that recognizing mutual property rights, based on an implied agreement, would be contrary to the state's express policy favoring marriage. The court did not want to make cohabitation an acceptable alternative to marriage. Result? Everything to the non-hubby and nothing to the supposed wife. Mrs. Hewitt got nothing for herself.

The *Hewitt* case happened in 1979. Some states have adopted a more liberal policy since then, but most have not.

For example, in the 1998 Tennessee case of *Roach v. Renfro*, a woman and a man lived together. While they were together, he bought a house where they resided. The court held that she had no rights at all in the home.[6] If they had been married, the result would most likely have been different. She would have had better claim to a share in the home because it was acquired during the marriage.

A few courts have been willing to find that a couple had an agreement to share some of the money earned during the relationship, even if the agreement was not in writing. The publicized cases involve wealthy celebrities where a lover claims that he or she gave up a career to serve as companion or "assistant" to the more famous person.

The best known case is probably the one involving the actor Lee Marvin and his lover, Michelle, which was mentioned earlier. Michelle persuaded a California court that Lee owed her something for her contribution to the relationship. However, the amount she eventually received was small compared to his income. The court awarded her $104,000 for "rehabilitation," and that amount was later overturned.[7]

For another example, Ruth Tyrangiel sued Bob Dylan for a share of his earnings. The claims in that case can be considered typical of those made in palimony cases. Ms. Tyrangiel's attorney cast her claims of entitlement from the relationship under several legal rubrics.

First, she claimed that the relationship included an express contract that they would share their assets and earnings. (In the following quotation, "Defendant" is Dylan and "Plaintiff" is Ms. Tyrangiel.) Specifically, she alleged in her court papers that:

Defendant would then and thereafter provide for all Plaintiff's financial support and need for the rest of her life in the same style and manner that was established during the parties' relationship consistent with Defendant's annual earnings and accumulations.

That defendant would provide finances for the benefit of Plaintiff.

That Plaintiff and Defendant would be married.

That pursuant to, in confirmation of, and in reliance upon the said agreement, Plaintiff and Defendant maintained relationship from in or about February 1974 through in or about November, 1993. Throughout said relationship, said agreement between Plaintiff and Defendant was reaffirmed and ratified by the parties.

In other words, Ms. Tyrangiel alleged that she lived with Mr. Dylan for almost 20 years and that they had an express, but unwritten, agreement. She said that he promised to share everything that he earned with her and to provide for her for the rest of her life in the style to which she had become accustomed. She in turn promised that she would be "a nurse, confidante, companion, homemaker, housekeeper, cook, social-companion and advisor to Defendant."[8] She alleged that she kept her end of the bargain and that she relied on his promises. Her list of services performed for Dylan included co-writing songs with him, acting as his confidante, and entertaining his friends and business associates. She stated that they had discussed business ventures as if they were partners.

Her second and third legal assertions were variations on the themes that she trusted and relied on Dylan to provide for her. In legal terms, that is a claim that they had a "confidential relationship" and that she justifiably relied on Dylan to take care of her so that he should be considered a trustee for her.

Finally, she accused Dylan of defrauding her by making promises that he didn't keep.

In the court papers in the case between Bob Dylan and Ruth Tyrangiel, one can see the ambiguity and the heartache of a long term relationship between a poorer person and a wealthier one. Entertaining Bob Dylan's friends and being his companion might not seem like tough duty to many people and not exactly the sort of thing that one expects to be paid for. During the period of their relationship, presumably, he was writing songs, performing, and doing the other things that are a performer's work while her efforts were, perhaps, not exactly an arduous job. On the other hand, if the couple had married, his companion of twenty years would have been entitled to a share of the assets accumulated during the marriage, if not to lifelong support in the style of a rock musician's friend.

Certainly, at one time, if they had married, her alleged contributions would have been considered those of a traditional wife. That role itself no longer necessarily carries with it an entitlement to lifelong support. However, after a twenty year marriage to a wealthy and successful person, the courts would quite likely award lifelong alimony to the homemaker spouse.

When a couple live together and do not have a written agreement, then the courts have three choices. The first is to apportion the property according to the title to it, as happened in the *Hewitt* case. The logic is that giving shared property rights to cohabiting couples would amount to treating cohabitation like marriage. Thus, the courts carry forward the reasoning that began in the 18th century: a married person acquires certain rights precisely because of having that legally recognized status, while people in non-marital relationships simply don't have the status or its rights. Traditionally, courts referred to cohabitation relationships as "meretricious," which is a fancy word for "sinful" or "immoral."

Other bases for that position are the prevention of fraud, the difficulty of having reliable proof of what a particular couple had in mind, and the promotion of sexual morality. The courts have reasoned that it would be too easy for a rejected lover to claim that the relationship involved more than a temporary love affair. If nothing else, this legal reasoning establishes a clear line; if you want the financial protection of marriage, get married.

Even on this strict view, the courts usually honor a division of property made by the couple themselves, whether they are married or not. Illinois and Georgia do not honor cohabitation agreements but they do respect changes in the title to property.

In other words, if a couple buys a house with the deed in both their names, then they own it jointly. Their exact shares depend on the circumstances and on any agreement that they signed. Similarly, if a bank account is in both names, then each party has a share in the account and each can withdraw the funds. The exception is that the courts sometimes refuse to countenance a property division that is grossly unfair to one party, especially where it appears that a more sophisticated person took advantage of the relationship.

A second option is for the judge to see if the couple had an implied agreement between themselves. Sometimes it is clear from people's conduct that they have a deal with each other. This legal reasoning is called "implied contract" and it takes effect when the facts make clear that two people intended to exchange one thing for another. This is the usual claim in palimony cases, i.e. that there was some form of agreement, either an explicit oral agreement or an implicit understanding.

The third option is for the court to use a general doctrine of fairness. One of these doctrines is called "quantum meruit," which means in Latin (of course) "how much was it worth." On that view, the court can see if one party to a relationship has contributed significantly to the other's assets so that it would be fairer to equalize their shares. Courts can use these rules to prevent unjust enrichment of one person at the expense of another.

Although there are legal rules that a court can use to redress unfair results from relationships, the use of these rules turns on the court's perception of the facts, as well as state law. A person who falls in love with a cad and foolishly supports him or her cannot count on help from the court. Although our society no longer condemns cohabitation as a gross moral lapse, living together is not marriage, and the legal relationship of the cohabiting couple remains essentially a blank. Maybe they had an implied agreement, maybe they didn't. Maybe it would be unfair to let one walk away with most of the assets that they acquired during their time together, maybe it wouldn't.

The American Law Institute, which is another group of legal scholars who formulate recommended laws, has proposed that long-term cohabiting couples with children who end their relationship be treated, legally, like a married couple who divorce. In other words, the couple's property would be divided as if they had been married and, if appropriate, spousal support could be awarded. This scholarly association concluded that basing a cohabiting couple's financial relationship on contract law did not reflect the reality of living together. These scholars believed that cohabitation was more like marriage and not like a contractual arrangement. The Canadian Bar Association has made a similar proposal.[9]

Other legal experts have objected to this reasoning on the ground that marriage and cohabitation are fundamentally different.[10]

If you and your significant other have specific ideas about who should own what during your relationship, then you should seriously consider having a written agreement, whether you are married or not. For more information on the law of contracts, see Chapter Eight and Chapter Nine.

QUESTION: *"My significant other and I had a beautiful commitment ceremony with all of our friends and family there. We didn't have a marriage license or minister. Does this change our legal status?"*

ANSWER: *Maybe. A commitment ceremony can have different legal consequences ranging from none at all to establishing a cohabitation contract to creating a common law marriage.*

A commitment ceremony is a ceremony in which the couple declare their relationship in a more or less formal way. There have been very few lawsuits involving commitment ceremonies. The Alternatives to Marriage Project web page describes such ceremonies as follows:

A commitment ceremony can look just like a wedding, complete with church, wedding gown, and hundreds of guests — but no marriage license. Or, a commitment ceremony can be the most alternative event imaginable: a ritual to bless your relationship, or just a big party to celebrate your love.

You can call it a commitment ceremony, a wedding, a ceremony of union, or anything else you like![1]

A word of mild caution is in order. Pledges of love in poetic language could still have legal effect. I have not found a case specifically discussing a particular commitment ceremony so the legal interpretation of the ceremony in a later dispute between the couple would be a new area for a court to explore. Since most lawsuits between cohabiting couples turn on disputes about what exactly they promised each other, it seems likely that a court would look to the commitment ceremony as a statement of those promises.

In a state that recognizes common law marriage, a commitment ceremony might be evidence that the couple intended to marry or that they expressly didn't intend to be married. The evidentiary effect of the ceremony would depend largely on the language that they used or didn't use. If the ceremony included phrases expressing their undying love but nothing directly referring to "marriage," a jury might well later decide that the couple was deliberately not marrying each other but celebrating a different kind of relationship.

The vows that the couple made to each other could also be evidence of their intentions, if they later had a dispute over their assets and obligations to each other. For example, if a couple pledged to "care for each other faithfully and honestly," a jury could see that as a promise to be fiduciaries for each other in handling their finances. Fiduciaries have special legal obligations to be fair. Or, if a couple promised "to share all the good things in life," a court could see that as a promise to share earnings and assets acquired during the relationship.

If the commitment vows were written down, they might satisfy the requirement that a cohabitation agreement be in writing.

Think about it – a commitment ceremony is a public celebration of the obligations that the couple have voluntarily undertaken toward each other. Why shouldn't a cold-eyed judge see it just that way?

In other words, don't make flowery promises that you don't intend to keep. If you want to have a poetic commitment ceremony, you would be wise to also have a written, explicit, cohabitation agreement that makes your respective financial commitments to each other clear. That cohabitation agreement should have a clause that says "If any phrase in our commitment ceremony seems to contradict this agreement, this agreement controls." Otherwise, you may someday find a court trying to figure out whether your exquisite quotations from Rumi or John Donne have any legal significance.

Ownership

This section sets out the basic rules governing which spouse owns what property during a marriage. The division of property between the couple if they divorce is discussed in Chapter Fourteen.

Married Couples

The states have two different types of legal structure about the property rights of married couples. These laws govern who controls assets during the marriage and who owns what if the marriage ends, whether by death or divorce. The technicalities of ownership matter during the marriage if the couple disagrees about what to do with a particular asset, such as whether to sell a stock or a house. The legal rules matter even more, however, if the couple divorce.

The primary difference is between the eight community property states such as Texas, Arizona, and California, and the other 32 states, such as Ohio and New York. The marital property system of these 32 states is called, confusingly, "separate property" or "common law property" states.

However, the states are moving to a more uniform treatment of the assets owned by married people. Under the Uniform Marital Property Act, the law looks at marriage as a financial partnership in which each spouse makes an equal contribution.[12] Under that system, all of the property is presumed to be marital property, including all income that is received during the marriage. The spouses can have individual property which is like the separate property in community property states, i.e. assets that were owned before the marriage, were inherited from someone else, or were a gift from someone else. If the individual property increases in value, the increase belongs to the spouse who owned it, unless the other spouse had worked on the property.

With that philosophy, the net result when a couple splits up often comes out much the same, regardless of the names of the rules that the court uses. In community property states, each spouse usually receives more or less one-half of what they acquired during the marriage and in common law states, each gets an equitable share, often more or less one-half. See Chapter Fourteen.

One legal tradition still applies to married couples. When a married couple buys property jointly, the deed often says "John Brown et ux." "Et ux" is Latin for "and wife." It is more modern to use terminology like "John and Mary Brown, husband and wife." If you and your spouse do not share the same last name, it is probably a good idea for the deed to say "John Brown and Mary Smith, husband and wife," in order to make clear that whatever rights your state's law give to married couples apply to this transaction. When a couple refers to themselves as husband and wife on a deed, the language may create a special form of ownership called "tenancy by the entirety" which affords more protection from creditors (see page 155 below), but at least the terminology makes clear that the property is held jointly as a married couple.

Similarly, when a married person wishes to buy an important asset such as real estate or open a brokerage account and the couple intend that the asset be one spouse's separate property (i.e. that the other spouse has no legal interest in the property, now or later), the deed should identify the owner in words like "Mary Brown, as her separate property." If one wants to be sure that the other does not ever have any rights to that asset, it is safer to have a prenuptial agreement (or one made during the marriage) in which the other says some thing to the effect of "I waive any interest that I might have or later be entitled to in _____, including any interest that I might be awarded in a divorce." See the sections on cohabitation and prenuptial agreements on page 568 and page 572 in the Workbook.

The following table summarizes which states have community property or common law marriage and which don't. Remember that these laws change. In this table, "no" to community property means that the state has the common law or separate property tradition. Also remember, if a state is not a community property state, then it is an equitable distribution (separate property) state. Finally, keep in mind that some states are abolishing common law marriage, in whole or in part.

Table of state laws on common law marriage and property

STATE	COMMON-LAW MARRIAGE?	COMMUNITY PROPERTY?
Alabama	Yes	No
Arizona	No	Yes
California	No	Yes
Colorado	No	No
Connecticut	No	No
District of Columbia	Yes	No
Florida	No	No
Idaho	Yes	Yes
Illinois	No	No
Indiana	No	No
Iowa	Yes	No
Kansas	Yes	No
Kentucky	No	No
Louisiana	No	Yes
Maine	No	No
Michigan	No	No
Minnesota	No	No
Mississippi	No	No
Missouri	No	No
Montana	Yes	No
Nebraska	No	No
Nevada	No	Yes
New Hampshire	No and Yes (common0law marriage is not recognized except for purposes of inheritance)	No
New Mexico	No	Yes
New York	No	No
North Carolina	No	No

Table of state laws on common law marriage and property (continued)

STATE	COMMON-LAW MARRIAGE?	COMMUNITY PROPERTY?
North Dakota	No	No
Ohio	Yes and No (law changed to abolish common-law marriage, but a marriage contracted under the old law may still be valid)	No
Oklahoma	Yes	No
Oregon	No	No
Pennsylvania	Yes	No
Rhode Island	Yes	No
South Carolina	Yes	No
South Dakota	No	No
Texas	Yes	Yes
Utah	No	No
Virginia	No	No
Washington	No	Yes
Wisconsin	No	Yes

Marital property in community property states

Eight states follow a community property system. These are Arizona, California, Idaho, Louisiana, New Mexico, Nevada, Texas, and Washington. Most of the community property states are in the west because that area of the country was most influenced by Spanish law during the colonial period. (Don't forget that Louisiana was a Spanish possession for some decades in the 18th century.). The law of Spain and Mexico provided that each spouse owns one-half of the property acquired during marriage.

In community property states the basic presupposition is that everything that a couple earns *during their marriage* belongs one-half to each of them. The principle of community property is that marriage an economic partnership in which each spouse's contribution, although possibly different, is equal.

Community property states divide a couple's assets into two types: community property and separate property. Separate property is the assets that a spouse had before the marriage, assets that he or she inherits (whether before or during the marriage) and assets that he or she is given (whether before or during the marriage). Community property is everything that the couple acquires during the marriage, except for things that are inherited or received as a gift.

The two most important features of community property are (1) that each spouse automatically owns one half of the community property; and (2) that law presumes that everything owned during the marriage is community property.

In other words, the law assumes that everything that the couple has during the marriage belongs to both of them, unless there is clear and convincing evidence to the contrary. If a spouse wants to claim a particular asset as his or her separate property, he or she has to prove that it is not community property.

Property earned during the marriage is regarded as belonging to the community of husband and wife and resulting from their joint efforts. Therefore, inherited property (which is not earned) and property owned before the marriage (which is not the fruit of the couple's joint efforts) remain separate property, i.e. these things belong solely to the spouse who inherited them or who owned them before the marriage. Similarly, gifts to one spouse remain that spouse's separate property.

In other words, what the spouses had when they got married and what they inherit or are given during the marriage is their separate property.

As you can foresee, things often get complicated as time goes by. A common problem is that a couple commingles their funds, mixing together separate and community. Most couples don't keep careful accounts for their money and assets. If they mix separate and community property together, then the court has to sort things out later. The frequent result is that the separate property becomes community property. Remember that all property owned during a marriage is presumed to be community property – a spouse who claims that the property is separate has to prove it and that can be hard. The states disagree about whether they permit a spouse to trace separate money through various accounts in order to prove that it was his or her separate property.

There are other possible variations. Sometimes, a couple put community funds into improving one party's separate property. Sometimes, one spouse works to improve the other's separate property.

If one spouse works on the other's separate property and increases its value, he or she may be entitled to some recompense for the effort. So, if a husband adds a room to a house the wife owned before they got married (her separate property), he doesn't own any part of it by virtue of marrying her. He might be entitled to some reimbursement for his work, but if he lived there, probably not, because he already got the benefit of the work. If one spouse pays a community debt (such as the mortgage on the house) with his or her separate property, he or she may also be entitled to be reimbursed for that contribution.

During a marriage, a spouse's separate property might increase in value. There might also be income from that property, such as interest on a separate bank account.

Community property states differ on the question of what interest the other spouse acquires in the appreciation of the other's separate property. The ownership of profits from separate property, like interest, depends on the state. In Texas, proceeds of separate property become community property. In other states, the proceeds of separate property remain separate.

However, an increase in value that is not realized belongs to the spouse that owns the property. In other words, if one of a couple owns an asset that has increased in value, but where he or she has not sold it, then the appreciation belongs to that spouse alone.

The determination of whether property is separate or community is vital in divorce disputes and may also affect the ability of creditors to seize an asset. In a divorce proceeding, the judge does not have the power to make one spouse share his or her separate property with the other, but has considerable discretion in how to divide the community property. See Chapter Fourteen, "Community property states" on page 453.

Marital property in common law (non-community) property states

The rest of the states have a different system of marital property law. This alternate system is sometimes called "common law property" or "separate property;" the current term is "equitable distribution theory." Robert Oliphant and Nancy Ver Steegh note that "the separate property theory has been rejected in all jurisdictions and replaced in 43 states with the equitable distribution theory." [13]

In other words, the courts almost all states no longer hold that the assets of a married couple belong to the person whose name is on the title. Those states distinguish between the property of the marriage, called "marital property" and property that belongs to each spouse alone.

These states previously had a true separate property system. Under that system, each spouse owned the assets that were in his or her name. When the couple divorced, each got to keep his or her assets, although long term alimony obligations were often imposed.

In a traditional family, where the husband was the wage earner, the previous separate property system meant that almost all the family's assets belonged to him.[14]

On that view of the family, the wife's work in the household was considered to be her duty to her family and did not entitle her to any share in the tangible financial assets earned by the husband.

Under modern law, the courts presume that any property acquired during a marriage belongs to both spouses equally. This presumption applies regardless of what the title documents say. Property acquired during the marriage is called "marital property." A spouse can rebut the presumption by proving that the assets belongs to him or her alone. The marriage is regarded as an economic partnership. A homemaker's contributions are regarded as equal in value to those of a working spouse.

As with community property, gifts, inheritances, and property owned before marriage are not generally considered marital property but are separate property. Income from separate property is usually considered marital property but an increase in the value of the separate property is not.[15]

The family can modify the ownership by an agreement. For example, in *McGehee v. McGehee*, a Mississippi court held that a married couple could also be partners in a business.[16] A Florida court, however, refused to recognize a separate business partnership between a married couple. The couple was in business together but didn't have a written partnership agreement about the business. In that case, the court held that any business relationship that the couple might have had "became merged into their larger partnership of marriage."[17] The business partnership then didn't give either spouse any property rights in the business, apart from those they had as a married couple.

Sixteen states also recognize a special form of ownership called "tenancy by the entirety" that applies only to married couples. When a married couple acquires property as tenants by the entirety, special rights apply. In most of these states, during the marriage, neither spouse can sell his or her share to anyone else without the spouse's consent. The surviving spouse has inheritance rights in the property. Usually, creditors of one spouse cannot seize the property to pay the debt. When property is owned this way, the deed may say something like "John and Mary Brown, husband and wife, as tenants by the entirety."

As discussed further in Chapter Fourteen in the section on ending marriage, when the marriage ends, spouses may have claims to the accumulated assets, regardless of whose name they are in. In a divorce, the court has the power to make an equitable division of the couples' assets; the court is not limited by rules about community and separate property because those rules don't apply in non-community property states. However, the court usually limits any division to marital property, i.e. to assets earned during the marriage.

Management of property during marriage

The term "management" of property refers to which spouse has the right to deal with the asset, i.e. to buy and sell, to improve it or to not maintain it, and so on. The states differ in which spouse gets to control what during the marriage.

Community property states vary in how they assign the right to manage community property. In some, each spouse is entitled to manage his or her separate property and to make decisions about part of the community property, at least up to a certain value.

Texas permits both spouses to manage their separate property and their share of the community assets. Neither needs the consent of the other to make decisions about the property. This is like separate property states. In other states, both spouses have to consent to community property transactions over a certain amount. The rights to manage property are complicated. In real life, again, some title companies want both husband and wife to sign any deeds to real estate unless it is clear that the property is separate.

For example, in *Brown v. Boeing Co.*, a wife sued her deceased husband's employer when she found out that she was not going to continue to receive his pension benefits after his death. She claimed that her husband had cheated her by choosing an option under his pension plan that did not include any pension rights for her. The court decided that the husband had the right to manage his own pension plan during the marriage, even though it was community property. He had not done something to cheat his wife, as by transferring some property to another person. He had just made a decision about how he wanted to receive his pension it turned out badly for her but the choice was one that he was entitled to make. Other states might have reached a different decision.[18]

In separate property states, each spouse is entitled to manage his or her own property which is everything in his or her name. Income from each spouse's property belongs to him or her.

The Uniform Marital Property Act allows each spouse to manage and control the property that is in his or her name, but each spouse has an obligation to act in good faith.[19]

The power that one spouse has to deal with property has both legal and practical implications. On the practical side, the spouse that controls the asset may do something foolish or ill-advised with it. He or she may make a bad investment or even give the property away. For example, in a second marriage, one spouse may give property to his or her children from a previous marriage. Consequently, regardless of the property laws of the state, it is often advisable for a couple to put both their names on the title to any asset that is important to both of them.

If property is in one spouse's name, his or her creditors can seize the property to pay a debt more easily. See "Ownership of different kinds of property — married or not" on page 159.

In real life, however, many transactions involving real estate require both spouses to sign the documents. A person buying a house, for example, or a bank lending money secured by a mortgage, wants to be sure that they have good title to the real estate. They don't want to take the risk that the other spouse might later claim that he or she had a community interest in the land. However, this fact of economic life is not sufficient to protect assets on which both spouses are counting.

QUESTION: *"What happens if one spouse takes advantage of the other one?"*

ANSWER: *It depends on the form that the cheating takes.*

Marrying a trusting wealthy spouse puts a domineering or dishonest person in a good position to take advantage. Sometimes, the dishonesty takes the form of putting most of the couple's assets into his or her separate name. Sometimes, he or she may hide assets or give them to relatives.

These situations present a difficult problem for the courts. Angry spouses may change their version of what happened to the property when they are no longer together.

For example, suppose Loving Husband gives the family farm in Overshoe, Nebraska to his favorite nephew when he and Doting Wife move to Florida. From one perspective, it's reasonable to assume that both spouses agreed to make a gift to a Favorite Nephew for example, because that assumption accords with a benign view of how families ought to work. If Loving Husband and Doting Wife divorce, however, she may take a jaundiced view of that generous gift and claim that she didn't know anything about it or that Hubby told her Favorite Nephew was renting the place or looking after it for them or whatever.

The law tries to deal with these complex situations by beginning with assumptions about human nature. A legal assumption about the world is called a "presumption." It controls how the court will decide a case unless one party rebuts it with convincing evidence.

In community property states, the law assumes that if a couple buys an asset in one spouse's name alone, the couple intended for that spouse to own the property separately. After all, sometimes there are good reasons for a couple to decide that one spouse should have something that is his or hers alone. Most of the time, a transaction like that would only take place if both spouses thought it was a good idea to divide things up that way.

On the other hand, judges are well aware that some people cheat those who trust them. Some spouses are more domineering while some are naïve or malleable. The courts look to all the circumstances to decide what happened.

Community property states have a doctrine called "fraud on the community," which refers to one spouse unfairly plundering what should have belonged to both. Fraud on the community can include giving away community property.

In common law property states, the law makes similar assumptions. For example, in the case of *Butler v. Butler*, Mr. and Mrs. Butler bought some land in both their names. Mrs. Butler put up more of the money for the purchase. The court held that the law assumes that when a couple bought land in a joint tenancy, they intended their respective contributions to be a kind of gift to each other. The court said that it would change their equal joint ownership only if

> *[T]he parties are in fact in a confidential relationship with one party enjoying an advantage over the other because of superior knowledge or influence [and]... That it would be manifestly unjust to allow one party to thereby profit at the expense of the other.*[20]

Similarly, common law property states have rules against one spouse dissipating marital assets to the detriment of the other. Some of the law's presumptions rest on social values that have changed. Judges used to assume that the husband was the dominant party and that if the wife gave him a valuable asset, it was likely that he had taken advantage of her. When the law and society put greater financial power and education in the hands of men, that assumption was reasonable. As women have gained more rights and greater financial equality, the basis for the assumption weakened, and the courts began to regard spouses as more equal.

Unfortunately, the modern assumption of equality doesn't always match the facts either. A grasping, domineering spouse of either sex can browbeat the other into making foolish financial sacrifices.

Many couples leave the financial management of their assets to one spouse. The trusting one may be lazy about finances or uninterested or may recognize his or her partner's greater skill and sophistication. Later, it can be difficult to tell chicanery from bad judgment.

For these reasons, the spouse in charge is not responsible for mistakes or bad investments. If he or she has not deliberately benefited himself or herself to the detriment of the other spouse, the court will not penalize him or her for doing a poor job of managing things.

QUESTION: *"What happens if one lover takes advantage of the other one?"*

ANSWER: *It depends on the form that the cheating takes.*

The law is less settled with regard to cohabiting lovers than with regard to married couples. There have been fewer cases, and the courts have not established underlying presumptions like those in marital cases. Usually, when a gift is completed, it is final.

If one lover puts property in the other's name, the situation is even more ambiguous than it is with married couples, minus the law's assumptions about marriage.

If an older man falls in love with a young honey bunch, is she exploiting him when she asks him for a diamond necklace? A ranch? An oil well? If a small town school teacher marries a big city lawyer, is he taking advantage of her when he invests her small savings in a speculative venture and loses it all?

The courts can use the same doctrine of constructive trust to redress exploitation of one lover by another. A constructive trust case is where a court rules that one person holds property in trust for another, regardless of the names on the title. Courts use this doctrine to readjust ownership where one person has exploited another. Sometimes, reliance on a rat can lead to a court imposing a constructive trust to redress the rat's having taken advantage.

It's hard to predict, however, when the judge and jury will find that one party took such advantage as to amount to an abuse of trust and when they will find that the losing lover was just foolishly in love with a ratfink. People who are in love sometimes squander their money on a faithless lover. A court may or may not feel that the infatuated lover should get legal redress for his or her foolishness.

In other words, constructive trust is an equitable and discretionary doctrine. It is not a matter of entitlement or rights. It depends on the court's perception of the relationship of the parties.

QUESTION: *"What happens if one significant other lies to his or her partner?"*

ANSWER: *The partner has a chance of getting back some of the assets taken.*

Fraud is a different matter from merely taking advantage. Legally, fraud consists in making a false statement about something important that the other person relies on to his or her detriment. If that happens, the defrauded person is entitled to get his or her property back and other recompense.

Again, what the law entitles you to and what you can actually collect from Rat Lover differ depending on whether you can prove your case and whether Rat has anything left for you to collect.

In an intimate couple, it can be hard to tell whether the situation is one of fraud or just a bad love affair. For example, a sleazy spouse who says "I love you" even if he doesn't mean it, probably has not committed fraud. It is hard to prove whether that kind statement true or false, and even if it is a lie, it is so common to misrepresent feelings that you can't sue for a broken heart.

If Sleazy Husband says, "Give me all your money to invest. I know about a great diamond deal in Nigeria," he commits fraud if his lover trustingly hands over all her money and he knows that there is no diamond deal. If there is a diamond mine project, but it just turns out badly, it is harder to prove that her significant other committed fraud unless it is clear that he knew that the deal was a scam.

Ownership of different kinds of property — married or not

Legally, the term "property" means things "that are owned." In legal terms, property is divided into real property (land and houses) and personal property (everything else). Your house is real property. Your furniture is personal property.

Property rights can be tangible (objects) or intangible (legal rights). The cash in your wallet is tangible property. Your right to a pension is intangible property.

The following section sets out the basic rules. Most of these rules apply to both married and unmarried couples, but all of these rules can vary depending on the intersection of title documents, agreements, and marital status.

Cash

Let's start this discussion with money. Money is personal property. Money can be kept in three basic ways; in cash, in instruments (like traveler's checks, not like in your guitar case); and in bank accounts.

Cash belongs to whoever lawfully owns it. Brilliant, right? The problem with cash is determining who that is and then, if the wrong person has it, getting it back. Cash doesn't have an ownership label or a place to register ownership, unlike traveler's checks where there are records of purchases or land titles that are recorded by the government. Unless you can prove that a particular pile of $100 bills is yours, money tends to belong to whoever has possession of it.

Whether a couple is married or not, the chance of getting your cash back from a defaulting lover or spouse is next to zero. First, it is hard to prove whose it is. Even if you can show that the cash came directly from cashing your paycheck, your lover can simply say that you gave it to him or her. Second, it's probably been spent by the time you chase down the rat and try to empty his or her pockets.

In other words, whether you trust your lover or not, keeping your life savings in cash in the house or any other place that he or she (or anyone else) can get to is a bad idea.

Some people keep money in the form of traveler's checks, cashier's checks, or money orders. This method has disadvantages. First, you have to pay a charge to change money into one of these documents. Second, you don't earn any interest. Third, it can be hard to turn the instrument back into cash if you need it in a hurry. Contrary to popular opinion, many banks refuse to cash money orders, and some won't cash traveler's checks or cashier's checks unless you are a customer of the bank.

Traveler's checks, for example, are safer than cash in terms of protection from theft. You have to have valid identification to cash them. If someone steals them, the company that issued them (e.g. American Express) is supposed to refund your money. In order to get the refund, you have to have the numbers of the checks. Therefore, you need to keep a careful record of your purchases; otherwise you can't identify the checks you bought. Obviously, you should keep that record in a separate place from the checks themselves. If the thief takes the record with the checks, you will have a harder time getting any kind of refund.

Forging the owner's signature to such instruments is a crime, although it might be hard to prove that you didn't give permission for your lover or spouse to sign your name. Obviously, though, to keep your lover from cashing your stash of traveler's checks, you cannot use those handy traveler's checks which are designed to be used by two people—those can be cashed by either party and therefore offer no protection from a defaulting lover. Traveler's checks issuers (like American Express) will not stop payment on a traveler's check.

If you want to keep some emergency funds around the house and the amount is more than you feel comfortable keeping in cash, then traveler's checks are an option. You can buy them at many banks and at some organizations like the American Automobile Association.

Bank accounts

Most people, however, keep their spare cash in a bank. Accounts take several forms. The two basic types are checking and savings accounts.

Checking accounts usually don't pay much interest. You spend the money with a debit card or by writing a paper check or by paying bills on the computer.

Savings accounts and other investment accounts, such as certificates of deposit, money market funds, etc., pay interest but usually afford you less access to the money.

All of these accounts can be owned in two different ways. Ownership can be single or joint. If you have your own bank account, for yourself alone, then you are the only one who can legally withdraw money from it. If there is only one name on the account, only that person has legal access to the money. As far as the bank is concerned, that person owns the money and has the right to it. Those rights can only be changed by a court decision or comparable legal action. In some circumstances, a creditor can grab your account, which is called a garnishment. The bank also has the right to limit access to the funds, which is called "freezing" the account. The bank can take the money if you owe it any.

The bank has a legal obligation to see that only the rightful owner draws money out of that account. That is why the clerk asks for your identification when you cash a check. Sometimes, the teller will also check your signature against a copy in the bank's records to make sure that your name has not been forged.

If your spouse or lover forges your name to a check, it is a crime. If you can show that your check was signed by someone other than you, the bank is supposed to refund the money. However, proving this takes a while, and it can be difficult to prove.

If your significant other signs one of your checks, he or she is going to say that you gave him/her permission to do so. If you are in the habit of letting your lover sign your checks, then the bank is not being careless in cashing a check for him or her. The bank does not have to refund your money if the check was not forged but was signed with your permission. In other words, it may be considered your fault if your significant other empties the account. Therefore, it is not a good idea to let your significant other sign your checks with your name.

If things get rocky, you should keep your checkbook in a safe place. The safest thing is to inform the bank in writing of the problem and close your account. You may still owe lots of money in returned check charges, if your lover continues to write checks on your account. You will be spending a lot of time writing "not my signature" letters to local merchants. It is true that stores are supposed to ask for identification, but it's going to be a mess if the local liquor store has become accustomed to cashing your checks for your lover. You cannot blame the bank if you've been letting Rat sign your name and now change your mind. It's worth noting that the banks can, and will, hit you with bounced check charges if your lover pilfers or overdraws your account. So will the businesses to which you trustingly wrote checks when you naively thought that you had plenty of money in your account.

Joint account

If there are two names on an account, it is called a joint account. A joint account has two owners. Joint accounts can be set up in importantly different ways.

One signature or two

When you set up the account, you can specify whether it takes one signature or two to get at the money.

If two signatures are required, both owners have to sign the checks. (Obviously, if two signatures are required, then you can't have an ATM or check card because then one person could access the money without the other's consent or knowledge.) The bank is not supposed to cash a check that only has one signature, and if it does, then it should refund the money.

A two-signature account gives each of you control over how the money is spent. It is designed to prevent either owner from taking the money without the other's permission.

The disadvantage of this account is that it is cumbersome. You can't pay the bills unless both of you sign the checks. This is OK if you are paying bills by mail, but almost impossible at the grocery store. Many businesses may hesitate to take these checks.

If you open a joint checking account with two names on the account, and don't require both signatures on checks, then things are simpler, but there is a greater risk of being taken advantage of.

Regardless of whether the two people are married or not, both of them have equal access to the funds in a joint account unless both signatures are required for a withdrawal. That means that, as far as the bank is concerned, either one can take out all of the money, without the permission or knowledge of the other. That liberty can be changed by agreeing with the bank that both of you must sign any checks or other withdrawals.

Moreover, the bank does not usually have to pay any attention to any agreement between the two of you. The bank follows (or is supposed to follow) the terms of the account agreement with it. If you open a joint account with your spouse or lover, he or she can take out every dime any time he or she wants. It doesn't matter to the bank that you and your significant other privately agreed between the two of you not to withdraw money without the other's permission. It doesn't matter to the bank that the money is community property or the savings for your honeymoon or anything else.

Banks usually refuse to make variations in the terms of their accounts. They have form documents that create different accounts, and those are the only documents that the bank uses or permits.

Here it is important to be clear about the difference between legal rights and real-life outcomes. If you have an agreement with your significant other about the ownership of money or the use of it or whatever, and he or she takes all the money out of your joint account, the bank has probably done nothing wrong in giving it to him or her. Your significant other does not have a legal right to the money (as between the two of you), but as between the two of you and the bank, he or she has a perfect right to withdraw it.

If you and your significant other have an agreement about the money and he or she breaks that agreement, that dispute is between the two of you. You can sue your significant other for violating the agreement. If you win, your significant other is liable to you and has to give you the money back. In the meantime, however, the money is in his or her hands and is probably spent. You have attorneys' fees; he or she has the money.

Right of survivorship

It is possible to provide that an account will be paid to another person if you die. This is called "right of survivorship." During your lifetime, the person has no rights to the account. The owner has the right to spend the money or to change the person who is named as the survivor. When the owner dies, however, the person with right of survivorship owns the account immediately, regardless of what the owner's will says. The assets do not go through the probate (inheritance) court process.

Therefore, in addition to the convenience of paying joint bills, joint accounts have one big advantage for responsible unmarried couples. A joint account can be set up so that it is payable to the survivor if one of you dies. That way, the survivor should have immediate access to the funds, although he or she may have to produce a death certificate to get to the money. It is still a good idea for each person to have some money in a separate account, however, in case there is a problem with other heirs or there is a delay in satisfying the formalities on the joint account.

It is also possible to designate a survivor on an account without creating a joint account. That can be a good way to ensure that your significant other receives those funds when you die without giving him or her any right to them while you are alive.

If you change your mind about your lover's receiving the money, you can change the survivorship designation, empty the account, or close it, all without any notice to him or her. If the two of you part company, obviously, it is vital to change the designation, as otherwise the person named will get the funds, regardless of your will.

Other issues

Internet access to bank accounts and ATM cards open a completely new set of problems. Anyone who knows the account ID and password (or has the card and PIN) can access the funds; no further identification or signature is required. Obviously, a significant other who has your access information and uses it to take money is likely to claim that you authorized him or her to do so. You should not give your lover or spouse access to your account unless you totally trust each other. If you give someone access to your account, it is not the bank's fault if he or she takes all of your money.

QUESTION: *"What happens if I put my significant other's name on my account but all the money in the account is mine?"*

ANSWER: *You have probably made a gift to your significant other of one-half of the account.*

Technically speaking, people can share ownership of an asset in two legal ways. One is as "tenants in common" meaning each owns an undivided portion of the asset. The other is as "joint tenants," in which case each owns an equal share. "Tenants" here doesn't mean renting; it refers to possession. In both situations, both owners have rights to access and use the property, unless they have agreed otherwise.

For married couples, the law assumes that if one spouse puts his or her separate property in joint ownership with the other spouse, he or she intends to make a gift. In other words, a change in title between spouses is presumed to be a gift of one's property to the other.

A court can undo a transfer between spouses if the court is convinced that a dominant spouse took undue advantage of the other. This involves proving two facts. The first requirement is that "the parties are in fact in a confidential relationship with one party enjoying an advantage over the other because of superior knowledge or influence and that this domination caused a gift." The second is that "it would be manifestly unjust to allow one party to thereby profit at the expense of the other."[21]

There is no comparable established law for cohabiting couples. Usually, two people who own an asset together own it in proportion to the amount that each has contributed, so technically if both names were on the account, but one person put in 80 percent of the money and the other only contributed 20 percent, then one owns 80 percent and the other 20. However, this does not affect the power of either to withdraw funds from the account; again, the bank treats joint owners as both having the right to withdraw money. It is possible that a court could use similar reasoning to keep an exploitive person from profiting at your expense.

Regardless of these rules, however, the only safe assumption is that if you put your significant other's name on your account, you have given him or her the money. In other words, don't do this unless you have clearly decided that you want to share your assets with your lover.

Stocks, bonds, and other investments

The same basic rules apply to brokerage accounts (which are the usual way of owning stocks and bonds) as apply to bank accounts. Brokerage accounts are investment accounts at firms such as Merrill Lynch, Prudential Securities, Fidelity Investments, or many other firms. Stocks and bonds are individual investments in different companies, such as AT&T and Microsoft. Technically, you can get tangible stock certificates which represent your investment. These are impressive engraved pieces of paper showing that you are the owner of a tiny chip of IBM, for example. Most shares today, however, are held by brokerage firms for their customers. The brokerage firms don't usually actually have physical stock certificates in your name; your ownership is represented by a computer accounting entry.

If the bond, stock, or brokerage account is in your name alone, only you have legal access to it. Your significant other breaks the law if he or she fraudulently gets access to your money. If that happens, the firm has an obligation to use due care to protect your assets and should pay you back. However, you have to prove that he or she wrongfully took it and, perhaps, that you were not negligent in allowing him or her the opportunity to steal from you.

There is an additional advantage to investment accounts, such as Individual Retirement Accounts ("IRA's"), which is that you can designate a beneficiary of these accounts. The beneficiary is the person to whom the account is paid if you die. That means that if you die, the account will be given to the person whom you named, regardless of what your will says and without going through the probate (inheritance) court system. This is, therefore, one more way to try to ensure that a significant other receives an asset.

Real estate

Real estate presents the same issues as other assets, only more complex. Title to real estate can be in many different forms. One person can own the property alone. Or, the deed can have two names on it.

The title to real estate can be divided several ways. One person can own the minerals (such as oil or gold) under the surface while someone else has the right to the surface (such as for a home or ranch). One person can have the right to use the property during his or her lifetime while someone else owns the right to have the property after the other dies. These various divisions create differing obligations of the owners to each other. For example, a person who has the property for his or her lifetime only is not supposed to destroy its value, such as by clear cutting all the marketable timber.

Two people can own the property as tenants in common or as joint tenants. If they are tenants in common, each usually owns one-half. If they are joint tenants, they may own different shares. All owners normally have equal access to the property and equal rights to use it, including living there.

If the property has both names on the deed, then both people have to join in any transfer of the property.

If the deed provides that they are tenants in common, then, if one person dies, the other does not automatically inherit the whole piece; he or she just keeps his or her share and the other part goes to the heirs of the dead person.

If the property is in the names of two people as joint tenants with right of survivorship, then if one dies, the other inherits the whole thing. Unlike a bank account, one joint tenant of real estate cannot sell the property without the other joining in the sale, but there are ways of ending a joint tenancy, sometimes by a simple deed and sometimes by a court proceeding to divide the property.

A person who owns a share of a piece of property can normally sell his or her interest, unless the owners have a written agreement prohibiting such a sale. His or her creditors can also seize his or her share.

Real estate law has another twist. An oral promise to give or sell someone real estate is not valid in court.

Real estate is a big investment. A mistake can cost you tons of money and heartache. Therefore, consult a lawyer in any real estate transaction unless you are absolutely sure that you understand what you are doing.

Other assets

For many people, their furniture and their car are really their only assets.

Fortunately, car titles are recorded by the state government. The title to a car pretty much determines who owns it unless you can prove that there was an agreement to the contrary.

The person whose name is on the title has the legal power to sell the car. You may be able to get part of the money from him or her if you can prove that you really owned it. The buyer, however, probably has good title to the car unless he or she knew that it was really yours.

For example, Fred and Tom were a gay couple. Fred had a good job and good credit. Tom worked hard but had a bad credit rating. When Tom needed a new car, Fred bought one in his own name, but both of them intended that it be Tom's car. Tom made the payments to Fred who paid the finance company. When Fred died unexpectedly, his family claimed that they inherited "his" car. Tom was able to prove that he and Fred intended that the car was really Tom's. However, the case could have gone either way, and Tom could easily have lost. If the dispute had been between Fred and Tom, it would have been hard to tell who should get the car. Was Tom paying for the car as a gift to Fred? Did Fred sign for the car as a gift to Tom?

The ownership of furniture and appliances is harder to sort out. There's no legal title system for washing machines or big screen TV's. See Chapter Fourteen for what happens if you break up with your significant other.

QUESTION: *"Does a widow or widower have any rights after the other spouse dies?"*

ANSWER: *In most states, the spouse has a right to inherit a share of the deceased's estate, regardless of the terms of the will.*

This right is called the spouse's right of "election," which means that the widow or widower has the right to take a share of his or her dead spouse's assets. That share is usually one-third. The survivor gets his or her share, regardless of whether the property is separate or community property and regardless of what the will says. In other words, the spouse usually has a right to inherit.

Lovers, obviously, don't have that right.

This means that if a couple marry late in life, especially when they have grown children, those children's inheritance rights may be changed by the mere fact of the marriage. Just writing a will does not necessarily cut off the new spouse's rights. Consequently, if it matters to you that your children inherit most of your assets from you, as opposed to your new significant other inheriting, then you need to carefully consider whether to marry and, if you want to marry, how to ensure the financial outcome that you want.

Inheritance is discussed more completely in Chapter Fourteen on the end of relationships.

Social security and pension benefits

Federal law governs many aspects of pension, retirement, and social security benefits. Federal law prevails over state law if there is a conflict. Usually, federal law provides that the named beneficiary will receive a person's pension.

There are two key issues here for couples. The first is whether any arrangement can be made for a significant other who is not a spouse. The second is what happens when one of a couple dies.

Social security and other governmental benefits are only payable to spouses. In other words, lovers are usually out of luck under these programs. Social security pays survivor's benefits to the surviving spouse of someone who was collecting social security. Many social security benefits cannot be changed by an individual. In other words, you can't provide that your social security benefits will be paid to your lover after your death.

Pension benefits, on the other hand, tend to be a combination of choice on the part of the worker and the complex provisions of an elaborate company plan that federal laws govern. This is a hugely complicated area of law. Some pension programs have a domestic partner provision which permits the worker to name his or her lover to receive some benefit. Most, however, only provide for spouses. You can only determine this by talking to the human resources department where you work.

All of these programs can provide some benefit to the survivor of a married couple. Under many pensions, for example, the employee can elect to take a higher benefit during his or her life and have the payments end with his or her death. Alternatively, he or she can elect to receive a smaller payment for his or her lifetime so that his or her surviving spouse receives some payments after his or her death.

As a general rule, a spouse has a right to make this decision as he or she chooses, but if there is a divorce, a court may order that a particular choice be made as part of the division of the couple's assets.

Domestic partners generally do not have property rights when they separate, except in California. Therefore, it appears that each partner controls his or her own retirement benefits. It is possible that if the couple had promised each other a particular benefit, that a court might require a particular election of benefits under the plan. There is no definite law on this point, however, and a court cannot vary the terms of the plan. In other words, if the employer does not offer domestic partner benefits, a court probably cannot change the plan to provide them, regardless of what the couple agreed. A court could require one partner to make a payment to the other when the first received his or her pension, however. That is different that requiring the company to split the payments between the ex-partners.

Again, pension benefits tend to be an all-or-nothing proposition: either you were married and you can receive part of your spouse's benefits or you weren't and you aren't. The only exception is where there is a domestic partner arrangement.

When a couple divorces, often the pension benefits are still in the future. It is hard to know how to divide this "asset" fairly. If the employed spouse gets fired, the benefit may vanish. On the other hand, the benefit was earned, partially, during the marriage. Courts disagree about how to apportion the value of a pension between the husband and wife. Moreover, complex federal rules govern exactly what can and cannot be done.

Other legal implications of marriage and cohabitation

The marriage relationship also carries with it several other important rights and obligations. Some of these can also apply to cohabitation relationships. One of the most important rights is that of inheritance, which is discussed in Chapter Fourteen.

Debt, credit and contracts

Being stuck with a sorry ex-lover's debts can make a temporary heartache into a long-term pain. A couple who are just living together are not generally liable for their partner's debts. A spouse, however, may well have to pay the other's spouses obligations.

Debts come in a variety of forms. (How well we know!) The legal obligation to pay them usually turns on who has promised the lender in writing to make the payment. However, sometimes circumstances make it necessary to pay your significant other's debts.

Sorting out the respective liabilities of the couple is a vitally important task at the end of a relationship. See Chapter Fourteen on ending relationships. In a marriage, the divorce decree should address every outstanding debt that the couple has. In the end of a cohabitation relationship, the couple needs to be sure that every debt is covered. Then, regardless of whether the couple were married or not, they need to take care of all the paperwork to make sure that the final arrangement is followed.

Here again, the couple's private arrangement doesn't necessarily affect the rights of their creditors. Even if a court orders your significant other to pay your credit card bill, you are probably still liable for the debt.

QUESTION: *"Am I liable for my spouse's debts?"*

ANSWER: *Sometimes, to some extent, depending on what kind of debt it is.*

QUESTION: *"Am I liable for my lover's debts?"*

ANSWER: *Usually not, unless you agreed to pay them.*

The question of who owes what to whom is different from who ends up paying the bill. If your significant other's creditors have a lien on your house, you may end paying his or her bills, regardless of whether you are technically liable for them or not.

Avoiding entanglement with a lover's financial problems is at least as important as reaching agreement on how to share your future assets.

The complexity of marriage debt cases arises from the complexity of modern financial arrangements, including the propensity of couples to mingle their assets. For example, Mr. and Mrs. Cockerham married in Texas.[22] E.A. Cockerham ran a dairy farm, and Dorothy Cockerham had a dress shop. They had borrowed money to buy half of the acreage for his farm and invested some of their earnings in her dress shop.

Their divorce was bitter and complicated. Mr. Cockerham claimed that his wife had made improper gifts to a Mr. DeRay Houston; the implication was that DeRay was Dorothy's lover. However, the jury decided differently, finding that Dorothy's gifts to DeRay were not improper. The judge thought that they were, however, and awarded custody of the children to E.A.

The case involved two trials, a bankruptcy, and two appeals.

Mrs. Cockerham filed for bankruptcy and the trustee in her bankruptcy case claimed that the community property of the couple should be used to pay her debts. The Supreme Court of Texas needed several pages of legal writing to winnow through the complicated facts of who owned what and who had managed what. During the marriage, E.A. and Dorothy had shared in each other's business ventures. They had used the property of the marriage (community property) in both the farm and the shop.

Eventually, the decision was that Dorothy's creditors should be paid before E.A. and Dorothy got their respective shares of the marital property. So, even though E.A. wasn't technically liable for the dress shop's liabilities, those debts had to be paid out of the couple's assets, which of course reduced E.A.'s share.

In the case of *Nelson v. Citizens Bank & Trust Co. of Baytown*, the court stated the rule this way:

> *The main issue in this case is whether a spouse can be held personally liable for a corporate debt guaranteed only by the other spouse based solely on the marriage relationship and community property laws. Out answer is: No. However, a non-signing spouse's interest in joint management and control community property is subject to execution to satisfy the debt.*[23]

Mr. and Mrs. Nelson owned hundreds of acres of real estate. Wesley Nelson was president of a storage company. The company borrowed about $500,000, and Wesley personally guaranteed the note. Marcella Nelson didn't sign that note or guarantee it. However, she and Wesley had borrowed money to buy their ranch and the mortgage referred to the loan for the ranch and to the storage company loan. The bank tried to collect the storage company loan from both Mr. and Mrs. Nelson. Marcella claimed that she couldn't be liable for that loan because she hadn't signed the papers and that her share of the community property shouldn't be used to pay it.

Under Texas law, which is reasonably like that of other states, the basic rule is that a person is not liable for a loan unless he or she signs the loan documents.[24]

There are exceptions, of course. The first one is that a spouse can be liable for a debt (that he or she didn't personally sign for) if the other spouse acted as his or her agent. Merely being married, however, doesn't make the spouses legal agents for each other. The legal relationship requires something more, such as where the couple is in business together.

Second, since married people are required to provide the necessities of life for each other, both must pay the bills for these items, such as food, rent, and medical care, regardless of who bought the item.

One spouse's property cannot be taken by creditors to pay the other spouse's debts. Sometimes, if one spouse has complete control of his or her share of the community property, the other spouse's creditors can't get that property. Technically, also, one spouse's assets should not be used to pay the other's debts. In other words, if the couple scrupulously divide their assets and don't share in the management of them, they may be able to insulate part of their assets from each other's creditors.

Third, however, the bottom line is that one spouse's creditors can usually seize the assets that the couple acquired during the marriage. Creditors tend to be rapacious and try to seize whatever assets are available to satisfy the debts.

In real life, the net result often is that the assets of the marriage (assets acquired by the spouses' efforts during the marriage) usually must be used to pay either spouse's debts. For example, in the Cockerham case, E.A. claimed that he never took any part in running the dress shop and Dorothy said that she had no interest in running the dairy farm. However, the couple did not keep their businesses separate. Dorothy wrote checks on E.A.'s account to pay for family expenses and for the dress shop's expenses. They both took income tax deductions for the shop's losses. Consequently, the net result was that E.A. had to pay part of the shop's debts from his share of the community property. Similarly, Mrs. Nelson was technically liable for the warehouse company's debts but a large part of the community property went to pay that loan.

The moral of the story is that a couple with substantial debts should take care that their respective responsibilities are clearly defined and that the assets that can be taken to satisfy the debt are equally clearly identified. A married couple need to exercise considerable care to protect part of their assets from each other's creditors. Usually, this involves keeping each person's assets completely separate and not owning anything jointly.

Credit cards

Credit cards are a lot like bank accounts. If two people have a joint account, both can charge on the card and both are responsible *for all of* the charges on that account.

If one person has a credit account and obtains a card on that account for his or her significant other, then the original cardholder remains completely liable for the amounts that both of them charge. The second cardholder's liability depends on the agreement with the card company.

 Like a bank, a credit card company is usually not required to pay any attention to people's private arrangements. So, if you get a credit card for your significant other (or let him or her use your card), he or she can charge right up to the limit on the card. It doesn't matter to the credit card issuer what your lover promised you. You are liable for the full amount. You're not off the hook even if your significant other promised to pay his or her share or promised not to use the card except in emergencies or even if he or she blew thousands on a tutu for the cat. The credit card company does not even have to try to collect the money from your significant other, no matter what promises the rat made to you.

In other words, whether you're married or not, if you share a credit card with your significant other, you are probably liable for all the charges on the card.

Joint and separate obligations

If two people sign a loan agreement or a mortgage (or a credit card application), both are responsible for the debt. Both or either can be sued by the lender. The creditor is not required to pursue both people and usually chooses to go after the more accessible and prosperous person.

If you and your significant other both sign a loan agreement, then you both are liable for that debt, whether you are married or not.

Unfortunately, ownership and debt can be legally separate. The person whose name is on the deed or title owns the thing. The person who signed the note is liable for the payments. If only one person's name is on the title or deed, then only that person owns the property, even if both names are on the note.

Therefore, if you sign a car note with your live-in lover and put the car in his or her name alone, you can find yourself without a car but with a big monthly payment. When both names are on the note and the title, both parties are entitled to possession of the object and both are liable for the payments.

This worst of all possible worlds is where a couple buys something together and then split up. Suppose George and Maggie buy a wide-screen TV. They promise one another that each will pay half the bill. Both of them sign the finance agreement. George loses his job and takes off with the television. Result—Maggie gets the bills, George gets the TV. George has not stolen the TV from Maggie, because he owns it, too. George still owes the finance company the full amount of the loan for the TV, but so does Maggie. The fact that she doesn't even have the TV anymore is irrelevant to the finance company.

It is important to keep in mind that the rights of third parties, such as banks or finance companies, are not lessened by a private contract between the couple. Therefore, if John and Joan buy a car together with financing from a bank, and John promises Joan that he will make all the payments, Joan is still obligated to the bank. If John skips out with the car, Joan is legally obligated to keep up the payments. The bank may go after John or it may not. It is not obligated to.

Even if John did not sign the loan agreement, his promise to Joan may give the bank the right to sue him too, but it is not required to. In other words, if someone promises (in writing) to pay another person's bills, the lender may be able to enforce that promise, i.e. to collect. However, the lender is not required to sue the person who made the promise. In other words, the bank or other lender does not have to consider your personal problems, unless of course it agreed to (in writing). Creditors usually sue the person who seems most likely to make the payments.

Special liabilities of married couples

A married couple can incur liability for each other's debts, whether or not they both signed the loan application.

Usually, a spouse is not liable for the debts the other spouse had before the marriage. However, that spouse's creditor may collect the debt from property acquired during the marriage. In other words, the net effect may be that the couple's savings go to pay premarital debts, whether or not both spouses are technically liable.

In community property states, both spouses are liable for debts incurred during the marriage. Just as assets become the property of the marriage, so to speak, so do the liabilities.

In all states, a married couple is responsible, to some extent, for each other. Either can incur a debt for necessities for the marriage, such as food, and both are responsible for it.

Moreover, one spouse can often pledge the couple's joint assets as security for a loan. Most lenders prefer that both husband and wife agree to repay the loan and that both sign any mortgage. But it is not safe to rely on this. Both spouses have the right to manage assets in the marriage so, sometimes; one can mortgage property without the other's consenting.

In some states, if one spouse borrows money for his or her business, both spouses can be liable on the debt. It becomes a marital debt.

Other transactions with other people

A person who is outside a given relationship is called in the law a "third party." So, for a couple, there would be the two people in the relationship and everyone else with whom they have dealings, such as creditors. "Third parties" include people to whom the couple might sell something.

Here is where the documentation that a couple uses can totally change the outcome of their situation. The names on deeds and other documents about ownership often control who has the legal power to sell an asset.

A third party who buys property has a right to rely on the apparent ownership. If a person's name is on the title documents, then he or she appears to own it, unless the third party knows that someone else also owns an interest. In other words, for example, if a deed shows the husband as the owner, then he can sell the property, even if his wife owns a share in it. The purchaser gets good title to the property if he or she acted in good faith without any notice of the wife's interest.

Sometimes the legal documents don't accurately reflect family realities. Ownership of family assets can be very complicated where there are deaths, divorces, remarriages, and adoptions in the family.[25] For example, the deed to a house might list only the wife as the owner when she and her husband intended that both of them own it. In most of these situations, someone who buys the property has the right to rely on the official documents unless he or she has notice that they are incomplete or incorrect.

For example, in *Sanburn v. Schuler*, a man bought a piece of property. It was his separate property but he was married. When he died, his widow sold the property. His sister sued the purchaser, trying to get the real estate for herself. She claimed that she should have inherited it because it belonged to the deceased man alone. The court held that the sale was valid, because under the facts, it appeared that the widow had proper title.[26]

These rules usually apply to other transactions, such as mortgaging a piece of property or giving it away.

There are exceptions to this rule, where the recipient knows enough to realize that he or she ought to make further inquiries. For example, if someone buys property from a person who claims to have inherited it, the purchaser may have a responsibility to check and see if the apparent heir really did inherit the property. However, a person is not required to undertake a major investigation in the community to make sure that the apparent owner really owns the property.

The net result is that the person whose name is on the documents has the power to deal with that asset, even if his or her significant other is entitled to part of it.

Today, title companies do most of this work in real estate sales. People buy title insurance to be sure that the person who sold them the real estate really owns it.

Similarly, possession of a more portable item, such as an antique piece of furniture, may justify a purchaser in believing that the person in possession owns that item. A good faith purchaser usually has the right to keep what he or she bought. "Good faith" here means that the purchaser didn't have any reason to suspect that the seller didn't really own the item being sold.

QUESTION: *"My wife had a flower shop. She borrowed a lot of money to start it. The business went bust. She wants to take bankruptcy to get rid of that debt. Do I have to take bankruptcy too?"*

ANSWER: *Very likely you do, unless the flower shop was a separate corporation and its finances were completely separate from yours.*

Bankruptcy is a legal procedure to mange debt that you can't pay. There are various versions available, and the appropriate one depends on your specific financial situation. Some debts are completely wiped out (discharged). Sometimes a payment plan is worked out. A business may be able to force its creditors to restructure the loans so that it's possible to make the payments. Debts that are secured by a lien or mortgage, however, still probably have to be paid.

Although it is possible for one spouse to file for bankruptcy without the other, it is more usual for the couple to file. The reason is that both spouses are usually liable for major debts incurred during the marriage. At least, their joint assets may be at risk. Consequently, it is often prudent for both to file.

To sum up, don't put your name on the dotted line on any loan unless you are willing to make the payments all by yourself. It is usually a bad idea for an unmarried couple to buy portable consumer goods together because of the painful possibility that one of them could skip out with all the stuff and leave the other with all the bills.

If the relationship is going to be a long-term one, you need to make careful disclosure to each other of your financial status, including debts, income and assets, whether you are planning to marry or live together.

If you are getting involved with a person who has substantial financial obligations, you need to consider carefully the respective implications of marriage and cohabitation. In a community property state, some of the community property may be liable for your significant other's obligations. For example, everything that you earn becomes community property, and your spouse owns one-half. His creditors might try to collect from money that you earned during the marriage.

In these situations, it is necessary to be prudent. It may be advisable to keep your earnings and assets carefully separate from those of your spouse. Similarly, you may wish to divide any community or marital property into separate property as it is acquired in order to protect one spouse's share from the other's liabilities. A cohabitation or prenuptial agreement may be essential in these situations.

In any relationship, at the first hint of serious financial instability on the part of your significant other, you need to take appropriate action to protect your own assets. This can include terminating joint accounts, changing title to property and so on. Sometimes, lawyers advise couples to divorce in order to insulate one spouse from the other's liabilities.

Duty to provide the necessities of life to each other

As noted earlier, spouses have a duty to support each other, which means to provide such necessities as food, clothing, shelter, and medical care. Lovers do not have such a duty, unless they enter into a contract. The difference reflects society's reasonable view that people who want to take care of each other in the time-honored way get married, while those who desire a less committed relationship don't.

Traditionally, this duty of support fell only on the husband. The law gave the husband charge over all of the wife's property and in return required that he support her. Society assumed (and ensured) that women were in general unable to support themselves as well as men could. Since at least the 18th century, the law provided that if a wife (or child) purchased food or clothing, the husband was liable for the bill.

Today, such discrimination is considered unconstitutional and, as a result, most states impose the duty to support a spouse on both spouses. That is, both husband and wife have a duty to provide the necessities of life to each other. If one spouse is working and the other is not, in principle, the working spouse must provide food, housing, and some medical care to the other.

The duty of support can be enforced by bringing a lawsuit against the other spouse. Under the *Uniform Reciprocal Enforcement of Support Act*, which all states have adopted, a spouse can enforce the duty of spouse in any state.

Businesses that supply the necessities of life to an impoverished wife could traditionally sue the husband for the costs. Some courts have abolished this doctrine because it is unequal, but others have made the wife equally responsible for her husband's necessary expenses, such as medical costs. About 20 states have "family expense acts," which make the expenses of the family chargeable to both husband and wife. That means that if one spouse buys food on credit, the other spouse can be liable for the debt.

One of the rationales behind requiring spouses to pay the living expenses of the other spouse is to lessen the financial burden on the welfare system. Therefore, even when the husband or wife does not want to seek money for living expenses from the spouse, the government may step in to enforce the obligation.

The obligation continues during the marriage, even if one spouse abandons the household. In the marriage of the Campas family, for example, Mr. and Mrs. Campas were married for 16 years. Then, Mrs. Campas asked Mr. Campas to move out of "her" apartment, which he did. Mrs. Campas, however, later sued Mr. Campas for support, which the court granted. The court said that the statute about support, which said that spouses were obligated to support each (primarily that husbands were obligated to support wives) applied whether or not the couple was living together. There was no exception for defaulting spouses, especially as Mrs. Campas was on welfare.

The expenses that must be paid by one spouse for another vary from state to state, usually based on what a spouse can reasonably provide. However, in a suit for support, the court will not determine what should be provided; in other words, if one spouse is providing the bare necessities according to his or her values, the court will not step in to make him or her provide what the judge might consider a better standard of living.

Lovers and lawsuits

The marriage relationship is sometimes idealized in the law, including especially the duties of financial support. When one spouse is hurt or killed by another person's negligence, the surviving spouse has a right to be compensated for the loss to him or her caused by the injury to the spouse. In other words, when a person is injured or killed in an accident, there is usually a lawsuit to recover damages. The injured person, his or her spouse, and his or her children all have suffered losses and all can bring a lawsuit for the losses each has incurred.

The spouse has lost both the financial support and the companionship of the injured spouse. He or she will naturally portray the injured spouse as a loyal, loving person who provided financial support, help around the house, and companionship. All of these have a financial value in the courts. The children (legitimate or illegitimate) can make similar claims that they have lost the love, guidance, and financial support of their injured or deceased parent.

The reality that the deceased was an indifferent parent and a philandering husband (or shrewish wife) does not necessarily change the claims for damages. Lovers, however, do not have these rights.

When one party to the relationship is hurt or killed in an accident, the other party may try to establish that a common law marriage existed so that he or she can sue for damages.

Recently, however, a California court held that the domestic partner of a woman could sue. The woman was killed by a neighbor's dogs, and her lover sued the neighbors for her loss.

The widow or widower may be awarded a sum of money equal to the value of the amount of support that his or her deceased or disabled spouse would have contributed to the household if the accident hadn't happened, including such contributions as housework that the spouse might have done. The survivor may also be entitled to the intangible, emotional losses he or she has suffered from the loss of companionship and sexual relations. The polite legal term for the loss of the sexual satisfactions of marriage is "loss of consortium." (Incidentally, of course, the injured person can also sue. Usually, damages in a lawsuit or money gotten in a settlement belong as separate property to the person who was injured, but that is not true of money that is compensation for lost wages. Lost wages become community property.)

You can see that being married (or not) can affect a lawsuit in many ways. A man who is injured and has the prospect of a large settlement may feel that he no longer wants his girlfriend or wife around. The wife, on the other hand, may want part of any settlement allocated to her. His lawyers may structure the settlement so that the money is labeled compensation for pain and suffering so that it all belongs to him.

If he is permanently disabled mentally, a guardian may be appointed to manage his money for him; if the couple are married, the wife is a likely choice to be his guardian, but if the couple are not married, then one of his parents is likely to be put in charge.

On the other hand, traditionally, a husband and wife could not sue each other for personal injuries. For example, if the wife was injured in a car accident caused by her husband's negligence, she could not sue him for her injuries. In most states, that rule has been abolished, in part because even state judges recognize that most lawsuits concern insurance coverage more than fault. Some states, however, retain the rule in an effort to protect the family unit from the divisive effect of litigation within the family.

Couples who live together are not bound by this rule, obviously. They can freely sue each other, which may not be the greatest boon in the world.

Medical and financial decisions for incapacitated persons

If a person becomes ill or injured and is unable to make medical decisions for him or herself, the doctors will generally look to the nearest relative to make those decisions. The person consulted will usually be the spouse, but if the injured person is single, then the doctors may look to a parent or adult sibling. That decision-making power can be changed by executing a durable power of attorney, which is discussed on page 419.

A lover, even of many years, may find him or herself excluded from any meaningful role in the medical care of someone about whom they care very deeply. Medical technology has created many difficult issues with regard to the sustaining of life and the nature of treatments that are undertaken. It can be exceptionally painful to find that one has no voice in the care of someone whom one loves greatly. In fact, when unexpected illness strikes, some people suddenly inform the doctor that they were common law married in order to gain some foothold in the decision-making process. A bitter fight at such a time between the injured or ill lover's parents and the significant other can make a tragic situation much more painful.

In addition, if a person is disabled, someone must manage his or her financial affairs. This management can range from simply paying the bills for a few weeks to taking care of investments for many years. If a person becomes disabled to the extent that he or she cannot manage his or her separate business, whether temporarily or permanently, no one else has the inherent authority to do so, although a spouse has the right to manage the marital estate (i.e. assets acquired during the marriage).

The authority to manage another's person's property can only come from two sources: a court decision or a legal document called a power of attorney. A court can appoint a guardian for an incapacitated person. All too often, the guardian is not who the incapacitated person would have chosen. Not uncommonly, if a lot of money is involved, a judge may choose one of his or her buddies to be the guardian, who will then make a fortune in fees. Alternatively, a competent person can execute a document called a durable power of attorney (before he or she is incapacitated, obviously), which sets out who will handle his or her financial matters if he or she should become unable to do so.

If there is no durable power of attorney, courts usually look to family members as the most likely candidates to be the guardians of an incapacitated person as it is assumed, often wrongly, that family members will act in the best interest of their beloved relative. A lover, unless the relationship is one of long standing, is unlikely to be appointed in place of a family member.

Income and estate taxes

Taxation is a legal field of its own. Most people are aware that being married can affect the amount of income tax that a couple pays. It also affects estate (inheritance) taxes. One's marital status may also affect one's state income tax liability.

The implications of marriage for income tax purposes change frequently as Congress tinkers with the law.

Income tax

For a number of years, marriage tended to increase the amount of income tax paid, which is referred to as the "marriage penalty." Congress has attempted to lessen the adverse impact of marriage and some persons have advocated the adoption of a tax benefit for traditional families.

At the time of writing this book, however, there is still a "marriage penalty," which means that married people have lower standard deductions than two single people do.

Married people have the option of filing joint returns or separate returns, if they indicate that they are married, filing separately. In addition, a spouse is responsible for seeing that the proper amount of tax is paid. One cannot share someone's income and not be responsible for the taxes. This can come as quite a painful surprise if one spouse has been counting on the other to pay the income tax. Congress is modifying the liability of the innocent spouse and at present there is a procedure for one spouse to establish his or her innocence, if the other has failed to pay the taxes.

In addition, marital status also affects some other tax issues, such as the amount that can be contributed by a nonworking spouse to an IRA. Some employment benefits, like health insurance, may be taxable if afforded to a domestic partner, but not taxable if afforded to a spouse. These matters require the advice of a tax accountant.

The tax code does not care whether one is common law married or ceremonially married, provided that the marriage is valid.

People who are living together do not have the option of filing a joint return and are not, usually, liable for each other's taxes.

At present, domestic partner benefits offered by an employer are taxable income, although the comparable benefits afforded to a spouse are not. A bill has been introduced in the 2005 Congress to make the tax treatment of employee benefits equal. The bill is called the Domestic Partner Health Benefits Equity Act (S. 1702 in the 108th Congress). It is a bipartisan effort but Congress had not decided as of the publication of this book. See page 110 for more information on domestic partnerships.

Estate tax

Marital status has an even more serious impact, however, on estate taxes. Estate tax is the tax paid on the assets a person leaves in this world when he or she moves on to the next. If you have significant assets, then you need to consider how much your heirs will have to pay the government for the privilege of being related to you when you die.

Inheritance taxes are as much for social policy as for raising money for the government. These taxes were intended to prevent the accumulation of wealth over generations. However, increases in the value of real estate and stocks have led to the tax weighing heavily on the American middle-class family, especially those with family farms and family businesses. Many businesses and farms have had to be sold to pay the estate tax.

Moreover, although you may think that you will never have a million dollars worth of assets, you should consider realistically how much your savings, house and other assets might be worth, particularly if property values are appreciating in your city or if you participate in a stock option plan at work. An increasingly large percentage of Americans are technically millionaires. One accountant who practiced in Baytown Texas, which is a blue-collar city on the Gulf Coast where oil refineries abound, said that many of her clients were working men and women employed in the petrochemical industry and that a surprising number of them would leave estates valued at well over $1 million. The reason was that these working people had often joined one company and worked at that plant for 30 years or more, during which time they had accumulated various stock options and pension benefits. As the oil industry prospered, so did these assets.

Although Congress has considered abolishing the estate tax, and the amount that a middle-class family is likely to have to pay has been reduced considerably, a sizable percentage is still due to the government. Many people consider this to be grossly unfair; after all, working people have already paid taxes on the money they earned and put in their savings account or used to pay for their house or invested in the stock market – why should their heirs have to pay the government again?

Be that as it may, current law provides for a huge penalty for those who live together as opposed to those who are married. A married person can leave an unlimited amount to his or her spouse without any tax being due. Leaving any amount of over $1 million to someone other than a spouse (including children, a lover, or your best friend) subjects the bequest to various tax rates. The tax rate is theoretically applied to almost everything that the deceased owned when he or she died, from aspidistras to zebras, including tax-sheltered investments such as annuities, IRA's, and 401(k) plans. The total can be reduced by bequests to spouses, charities, and payment of various debts.

Therefore, if you are among the fortunate group of working Americans who have significant assets to leave, especially if those assets include a family business or a family farm, you should consider the impact of estate taxes on your decision as to whether to marry your significant other or not. If your relationship involves planning to leave any significant asset to your significant other, he or she will pay a high price for not being married. The maximum percentage charged as tax has been as high as 55 per cent, although 20 to 30 per cent is perhaps more common.

Being married, or not, can also have an impact on the tax consequences of substantial gifts and other transfers, such as the establishment of trusts. If your planning for each other involves setting up trusts, you need to consult a tax professional on the best strategy to adopt.

Testimonial Privilege

Traditionally, a husband or wife cannot be forced to testify against his or her spouse. There are two versions of this privilege.

The first is that a spouse cannot be forced to reveal their confidential communications. Private conversations between husband and wife are confidential, somewhat like communications between attorney and client. Second, a spouse need not testify against his or her spouse. In other words, the government cannot force a husband to be a witness in a case where his wife is accused of a crime.

These privileges only apply while the couple is still married. Moreover, they don't apply in cases of child abuse or lawsuits between the couple themselves. Finally, there is a question about who gets to decide whether the privilege applies or not; often, one spouse may voluntarily decide to rat out his or her spouse.

None of these protections apply to a cohabiting couple.

Discrimination in housing

Federal law prohibits landlords from discriminating against families, at least where the family consists of a married couple with children. That prohibition includes disguised discrimination such as setting occupancy limits so low that couples with children cannot qualify. For example, a landlord might disguise his or her prejudices by limiting occupancy of a two-bedroom apartment to two people, i.e. so that a husband and wife with one child cannot qualify.

Similarly, a landlord cannot legally refuse to rent to a single woman with a child or to a married couple where the wife is pregnant, where the refusal is based on the landlord's dislike of having children in the apartment.

A landlord may, however, refuse to rent to anyone who does not meet objective criteria such as good credit history, financial ability to pay the rent, good references from previous landlords, etc., provided that those standards are applied to everyone equally. For these reasons, if nothing else, you should be careful how you and any lover relate to the landlord; if you default on the rent because a love affair went bad, you may have trouble renting another apartment later, even if you are living alone.

Federal law, however, does not prohibit discrimination based on the landlord's moral disapproval of your relationship. Consequently, in most states and cities, landlords can refuse to rent to unmarried couples or to same sex couples.

Some states, however, have passed laws prohibiting discrimination on the ground of marital status. In five states (Alaska, California, Massachusetts, Michigan and New Jersey), landlords cannot legally refuse to rent to unmarried couples.

In most states, landlords can also legally refuse to rent to homosexual couples. In ten states (California, Connecticut, the District of Columbia, Vermont, Rhode Island, Wisconsin, Massachusetts, Minnesota and New Jersey), landlords cannot legally discriminate against gay couples. Some cities have more liberal ordinances than the state laws, and these ordinances may prohibit discrimination on grounds of marital status or sexual orientation.

You may find questions about the exact nature of your relationship offensive, especially if they are of the "Hey, are you two like roommates or what?" but in most places, these questions are legal. The landlord is not required to allow his or her property to be used for living arrangements that offend his or her values. On the other hand, who wants to live in an apartment where the landlord disapproves of your relationship?

Other governmental programs

Marital status also affects the availability and amount of other governmental benefits. Basically, there are two sorts of impacts to consider; entitlement and amount. The structure and requirements of governmental programs are extremely complex.

As a general rule, being married may lessen your chance of qualifying for such benefits as subsidized health care because your spouse's income may be added to yours to determine the household income or assets. This can only be stated as a very general rule because these programs change frequently and recent political shifts have meant that politicians have begun to try to change these programs to keep the family from being impoverished by one spouse's illness. To date, these efforts do not provide much relief. Similarly, you may find that being married makes it more difficult to negotiate, for example, for reduced hospital charges because again your spouse's income is also counted.

On the other hand, marriage is a precondition for some benefits, such as social security and various pension and survivor's programs.

If you are an older person and concerned about qualifying for Medicaid to pay your nursing home costs, you should consult an elder law attorney. If you marry, your assets may be combined with those of your spouse so that the two of you have to spend a substantial amount of your joint assets before receiving significant benefits. Careful planning is required here and the subject is far too complex, and changeable, to discuss in a print book. Research at the public library or on the Internet may help you understand this particular quagmire.

Abuse – physical and emotional

To the extent that it works, the law protects people from abuse whether the abuse is meted out by a spouse, a significant other, or a stranger.

Domestic violence cases receive much more attention from the courts and the police today than in earlier years. In well-trained police and sheriff's departments, officers are alert for signs of physical abuse even if the victim is not complaining. In one case, a police officer in a small town stopped a suburban woman driving her Volvo late one night to tell her that the license plate light was out. He noticed that she had a black eye and politely but firmly asked whether she was in any difficulty. When she replied that the injury was the result of a horseback riding accident, which obviously sounded like a not very plausible excuse, the conscientious officer told her that, if she was having any problem at home or elsewhere, she did not have to tolerate it. She explained that she trained horses and told him where the farm was, and he accepted her story, but gave her his card so she could call for help if she needed it.

Sanctions against abusive behavior exist in both civil and criminal law, although the criminal primarily deals with physical conduct.

On the criminal side, physical abuse is battery, and physical threats, such as a raised fist, can be assault. Forced sexual contact is rape or sexual battery.

MYTH—*"A man cannot be guilty of raping his wife because the law gives him the right to sexual intercourse with her."*
FACT—*That is no longer the law. A husband can be prosecuted for raping his wife.*

MYTH—*"A man has the right to maintain order in his own home, by physical force if necessary."*
FACT—*No person has the right to use physical violence against another, except in self defense. No adult has the right to "discipline" another.*

Police response to a report of domestic violence can range from arresting the alleged perpetrator to telling him (or her) to pack his/her stuff and get out of the house. In many states, the district attorney can prosecute these crimes whether or not the victim wants to proceed.

In prior years, many frightened women would drop the charges of assault against their husbands or lovers, for a variety of reasons. Sometimes, it was because they could not imagine living without the battering lover or because they were too beaten down to resist or because they needed the financial support of an employed husband and could not afford for him to lose his job. Sometimes, it may have been because they had used the threat of a criminal charge to manipulate the lover. Sometimes, perhaps, the relationship was a sadomasochistic one in which pain and the infliction of pain were central components of the relationship. Regardless of the reasons in the past, the authorities now can and sometimes will proceed with the charges if there is evidence of physical abuse.

In addition, there are now shelters available for battered women, and a few for battered men. Experts suspect that the incidence of battered men is under reported because men are more ashamed to admit that a woman has struck them.

In addition to criminal remedies, there are civil actions that can also be taken. These take two forms. One is a temporary restraining order, i.e. a court order that sets limits on contact between the two people involved. A typical order would prohibit the aggressor from coming within 100 yards of the victim, from telephoning the victim, or from otherwise harassing or threatening her. These orders can be made permanent by the court after a hearing.

Temporary restraining orders have several virtues. First, they can usually be obtained *ex parte*, which means that you can go to court and get the order by swearing to the facts of the situation, without notifying the aggressor of what you plan to do in advance.

Second, and most importantly, a temporary restraining order serves to clarify the situation immediately for any police officer. If the order says that your significant other is not allowed to come within a quarter mile of your house, you can call the police when his car enters the driveway. Any competent police officer will enforce the terms of the order. It doesn't matter that your significant other says that he wanted to apologize or just wanted to get his clothes or whatever. Either he complies with the terms of the order or he will be arrested. For these reasons, you should make copies of any order and keep them handy. Keep one in your kitchen drawer, one in your purse, and one in the glove compartment of your care, for example.

Third, violation of such an order is punishable by being held in contempt. That means your significant other can end up paying a fine or going to jail, just for not obeying the order, regardless of whether he has assaulted you again or not.

In addition to restraining orders, violent conduct can have other civil consequences. Although most marital misconduct, such as adultery, no longer plays a significant role in divorce actions, domestic violence can affect such decisions as child custody and, to a lesser degree, property divisions.

If you have been physically injured by a significant other, you can sue him or her for damages, including the emotional distress that you suffered as a result of living in fear, etc.

The term "emotional abuse" is often used today. Emotional abuse can include shouting, belittling, excessive teasing, and similar behavior. Although therapists recognize that verbal abuse can be very damaging, there are fewer legal remedies for this conduct. As a general rule, your only remedy for this behavior is to leave the relationship, although you can obtain a temporary restraining order, if necessary, to prevent your abuser from contacting you.

If the behavior comprises substantially more than just heated arguments, and if you produce an expert witness, such as a child psychologist, to testify that it is damaging to your children, emotional abuse can be considered by the court in awarding custody and in setting the terms of any visitation by the abuser.

There is a civil remedy in some states called "intentional infliction of emotional distress" or "outrage," but verbal behavior must be truly extreme to fall under this category.

The laws against stalking are an exception to the above remarks. It is illegal in most states to follow or telephone a person who has indicated that he or she does not wish to be contacted. Basically, stalking occurs when one person forces his or her unwanted presence into the life of another whose has made his or her objections clear. There are criminal penalties for doing so, and if your abuser follows you or frightens you in this way, you can talk to the police or the district attorney about whether his or her conduct constitutes stalking.

Remember, the basic rule is that no one has a right to strike another person, even in the family, except in defense of himself or herself or in defense of another person from an immediate threat. Revenge and preemptive strikes are not generally allowed. (Reasonable chastisement of a child, such as a swat on a toddler's diapered bottom, *may* be an exception.)

For example, during a family gathering, a woman, her husband, and her father were all playing a friendly, but competitive, game of pool. The couple's little girl interrupted the husband during a critical shot. Infuriated, he wheeled around and punched his daughter in the face with his fist. The mother later described the result as "I picked up my Daddy's pool cue and gave my husband a lesson in why it's not nice to hit people." Some judges would have given the woman a medal, but the judge in her case gave her two years in prison for assault. While she served her sentence, the little girl remained with her father.

Contracts

The uses of contracts in intimate relationships is discussed below in Chapter Eight and Chapter Nine. This section only mentions the difference between contracts for an engaged or married couple and contracts for a cohabiting couple.

Most states require both antenuptial agreements and cohabitation agreements to be in writing, although, as always, there can be exceptions.

The Uniform Premarital Agreement Act, which has been adopted in some states, provides two specific rules for antenuptial agreements. The first is that the contract takes effect only if the couple marries. The second rule, in summary, is that the contract must not be "unconscionable when entered" and that the parties must have made honest disclosure of their finances to each other.

There is no comparable rule for unmarried couples.

Domestic partnerships and other legal connections

Some legislatures have considered enacting laws providing for different legal structures for couples. Sometimes these laws are called "domestic partner" laws and sometimes "civil union" laws. Other names have also been tried. The primary discussion of these arrangements is in Chapter Four, starting on page 110.

QUESTION: *"What are domestic partner laws about?"*

ANSWER: *Some of these provisions provide a sort of marital status to gay and lesbian couples, while others confer legal benefits on all unmarried couples who comply with the rules.*

In France, a couple can register their relationship with a state office; such a recorded relationship entitles them to the various social and legal benefits afforded to married couples. That relationship is called, in French, *concubinage*. Although the word is the same as the English word "concubinage" which refers to the arrangement by which a man keeps a mistress (or a harem), the legal use of the term does not carry the denigrating implications. Recently, the French government made a similar legal registration available to homosexual couples for the same purpose of enabling the partners to have the various legal rights afforded to married persons.

California offers such a statute. This statute is discussed further on page 110.

Some cities have ordinances that provide for registration of couples as domestic partners. These cities include Tucson, Arizona, Washington, D.C, and Santa Barbara, California. Most cities require that the people registering be residents of the city, and most make the registry available to same sex and different sex couples. However, Seattle does not require that the registrants be residents of that city and will accept applications by mail. A list of these cities is available on line at www.hrc.org.

However, some cities expressly prohibit recognition of such an arrangement, at least as it might be applied to same sex couples.

There has been debate about whether such a system is necessary for different sex couples; heterosexual couples who want the benefits of marriage can simply marry. The Alternatives to Marriage Project has advocated for such a legal arrangement to accommodate couples who do not want to marry but want to obtain the legal benefits of marriage for their partners. Its website offers extensive advice on these arrangements.

One ongoing question is what meaningful differences there would be between a civil marriage ceremony and a domestic partner registration or civil union arrangement. One usual consequence is that a domestic partner relationship could be terminated by simply giving notice, as under California law.

At present, the most common recognition of domestic partner relationships is in corporate employee benefit programs. About 45 per cent of the Fortune 500 companies (the largest companies in the United States) make these benefits available. Nike and Ben & Jerry's Ice Cream are two that do, for example. Most of these companies extend benefits to couples who have been together for a certain period of time. Most afford these benefits whether the couple is heterosexual or homosexual, but some domestic partner laws and corporate policies apply only to gay couples.

Remember that corporate policies, although very valuable where they exist, are limited in scope. They make various employment benefits such as insurance, available to couples who are in a stable, long standing relationship or prohibit discrimination based on the sexual orientation of the couple. Even when they are adopted by a governmental entity, they do not create a legal status entirely comparable to marriage.

For example, in August, 2005, the mayor and a city councilwoman of Salt Lake City, Utah, announced that the city would try to extend employee benefits "to the domestic partners of city employees, including those siblings and parents with whom employees share a home." That effort would not mean that everyone in Salt Lake City would be able to get benefits for his or her significant other but only that the employees of the city itself would have such benefits.

The value of such programs, and their symbolic importance should not be underestimated, but they do not resolve all of the legal problems of unmarried couples.

Some of these laws and programs require the domestic partners to take some action to make their relationship known or official. If you are relying on these benefits, you need to be sure that you or your partner has taken the appropriate action to qualify your relationship.

Perhaps the most important question is what legal effect the registration of a domestic partnership will have in other places that don't have a law recognizing that status.

Moreover, there has been a backlash against some of these (pro traditional marriage or anti gay, depending on how you look at it) city ordinances. A prominent computer company, for example, is reported to have decided not to move part of its business to Austin, Texas, because that city had a policy against extending equal benefits to gay couples.

This area of the law changes frequently. Persons who wish to utilize such an official, but non-marital, arrangement need to check the law in their state, any ordinances in their city, and their employers' benefit programs.

QUESTION: *"Can lovers be in other legal relationships with each other?"*

ANSWER: *Yes, lovers can also be in a variety of legal relationships with each other. A couple can be partners in a business or investment. They can be co-owners of real estate or other assets.*

In addition to the palimony question, you may wish to give some thought to the question of whether you have another, non-marital, legal relationship with your significant other. Other legal relationships can exist together with or apart from a marital or cohabitation relationship.

For example, if two people start a business together and then start a romance, they may be partners in the legal, as well as the sexual, sense. More importantly, if one significant other works in the other's business, he or she may later claim that they entered into a legal partnership. If there were promises made, such as "If you'll help me out at the shop, I'll split the profits with you," then a court may decide that the two jointly own the business or that there was a profit-sharing agreement. The use of the word "partner" can become ambiguous in a context in which the parties share both romantic and business activities. In a lawsuit, the question might be raised as to whether calling each other "my partner" had the usual business and legal meaning or the current relationship meaning.

Similarly, one of a couple may later claim that they entered into an agreement to split the stock of a corporation started by one of them or split the profits from an invention that one of them is working on.

It is worth noting that oral agreements can be binding, especially if they are partially carried out. For example, if a couple agrees to work together in a business and split the profits later, that agreement may be enforceable if in fact they have both worked in the business or contributed to it. So, an agreement about a business can create various legal business arrangements. A court might decide that there is a contract about profit-sharing or a partnership or a joint venture. Each of these legal relationships creates obligations and rights of its own. Partners, for example, are legally obligated to treat each other fairly and in good faith. **Obviously, this is one of those times when you need a good lawyer**.

One of the more interesting variations on this idea is that of deliberately embodying a personal relationship in the form of a legal entity, such as a limited liability company, which is a form of corporation.

A company, called Relationship LLC, has been formed to promote the concept of using the legal structure of the limited liability company to create the legal structure for a relationship. They say,

> *It is our position that limited liability companies or "LLC's" may prove to be the new marriage model. Marriage is presently available only to one man and one woman. LLC's are available to everyone, couples (of any sexual mix) who wish to pursue life together, a single parent family, and groups of friends. Marriage is based on family law, while limited liability companies are based on partnership law and the legal arrangement its "members" agree to.*[27]

The legal and practical effectiveness of these arrangements has not been tested in the courts. It is possible that they would provide a workable solution to nontraditional couples who had significant assets for which they wanted to arrange the ownership in a fairly sophisticated and complicated way. However, great care must be taken that the structure is set up to allow for a fair dissolution of the LLC, if necessary, if the relationship ends. It would be a special kind of hell to be tied to an ex-lover in your on-going business and financial dealings.

Polygamy, polyandry, and polyamory — the more the merrier?

The most common form of plural marriage is polygamy in which one man has several wives. A rare form is polyandry in which one woman takes more than one husband.

Some historians have suggested that at times, in impoverished rural areas of Western Europe, women "married" more than one man at a time. Two brothers, for example, might share a single "wife." In this way, both men had access to sexual satisfaction and household help even if the family farm would not support two couples. Sometimes a son might "marry" his widowed mother. Under that arrangement, he and she obtained sexual gratification and they did not have to share the limited resources of their farm with another woman. These "marriages" were not, of course, legally recognized and the larger society deplored them from a moral standpoint.

Neither polygamy nor polyandry has been legal in the United States, except for a brief period in the Utah territory, which is discussed in more detail in Chapter One. Today, bigamy (and hence polygamy) is a crime.

Today, some advocates for free form sexual unions use the term "polyamorous" to describe relationships comprised of more than two people. The term derives from Greek words meaning "many loves."

In the current climate of sex *à la carte*, it is perhaps inevitable that some people would create their own free form multiple partner relationships. "Swingers" may be described as people who engage in sex with a number of partners, but these encounters are not usually long-term relationships. Unlike mere promiscuity, the participants in polyamorous relationships intend for their multi-faceted relationship to be a relatively lasting one.

Some people have crafted multiple-party, stable, marriage-like relationships. Some of the participants in such relationships describe themselves as pagan and believe that the pagan or Celtic religions of Europe fostered freer lifestyles. Some are bisexual people who find that a three person household/relationship best meets their emotional and sexual desires.

As journalist Jennifer Mathieu describes it

[I]f you cannot tame your jealousy, polyamory simply cannot work for you. And that is because even though there are several ways of 'doing polyamory,' the bottom-line is that if you are a polyamorist, someone you love and adore is sometimes going to be sleeping with somebody else. And you are going to know about it.[28]

The couples whom she interviewed had structured their lives in different ways to suit their different desires and needs from the quite domestic to the rather more sexually adventurous. Sometimes, one couple in the group was married—to each other, that is.

In another article, a man described his household of two women and one man, all of whom were sexually involved with each other.

> *Now the three of us have been together about 13 years… We had to figure out how each of us could spend time as couples, as a family, and alone… We worked this all out ourselves because we were pretty much in the closet and didn't know anyone else who lived like us until we met you guys… our close friends know we're a triad, and we went to see a couple of shrinks for advice, but none of them had any experience with our kind of lifestyle.*[29]

Whatever the emotional or religious ties of the people involved however, only one couple of the group can be legally married. If a man lives with two women and refers to them both as "wives," he is legally married only to the first one whom he married, whether by common law or by ceremony. The second woman is not even a putative spouse, because she is aware of the circumstances and is, therefore, not an innocent, deceived party.

It is important to remember that such a group could be a legal mess if any substantial amount of money were to be at issue. Sorting out who owns what after a many-year relationship of this sort could be a giant hassle, to say nothing of the likelihood that courts would not recognize any child visitation rights for anyone except the child's biological parents (or their respective married partner).

A formal agreement in such a situation would require careful thought. It might be more practical to have a formal contract for each substantial financial transaction, like buying a house. For example, all participants could own the house jointly, although that structure presents its own problems. For example, if the group splits up or one member leaves, the only workable choice might be to sell the house.

A conservative court might refuse to enforce a contract among the parties to such a multiple relationship, unless the contract strictly concerned financial matters and looked more or less like an ordinary business relationship. If the contract dealt expressly with the living arrangements, a court might find the multiple sexual relationships to be so profoundly in violation of customary mores that the agreement was invalid. On the other hand, a more liberal court might take a more neutral moral stance and simply examine the contractual issues.

One legal right of multiple party relationships has been recognized. Federal law affords limited protection from discrimination in housing based on family composition. Although a city, for example, can legally limit the number of persons residing in a single-family house, the city cannot constitutionally require that the persons living there stand in any particular biological or marital relationship to each other.

These cases first arose with the communal living arrangements of the 1960's when the Supreme Court decided that the right of privacy protected the living arrangements of unconventional families of hippies. In other words, a city or county cannot legally prohibit unmarried adults from living together.

However, in most states, a private landlord can refuse to rent his or her property to persons whose living arrangement is immoral by the landlord's standards. Some states and cities have ordinances that prohibit landlords from discriminating against couples based on their sexual preference, so that a landlord cannot refuse to rent to a gay couple, for example.

Lawsuits and living together

The differences between marriage and living together continue in the area of disputes between couples.

This section summarizes some of the legal mechanics involved in taking a dispute to court. More information is in "Chapter Fourteen" on page 443 as well as in The Workbook.

Ending the relationship – amicably and otherwise

From the legal point of view, marriages and cohabitations end very differently. A marriage can only end by death, divorce or annulment. The last two are court proceedings. A cohabitation can just end. Each party takes his or her things and they split. A married couple can informally separate, but they remain married until they divorce or one of them dies.

Remember that a separation does not legally end a marriage, whether the marriage is a common law one or a ceremonial marriage. Living apart, however, constituted one of the traditional grounds for divorce, as abandonment and it remains one of the grounds for dissolving a covenant marriage. Also, an informal separation does not settle legal questions of property and other rights.

Obviously, ending a cohabitation arrangement can be done informally. A cohabiting couple can end their relationship by just walking away from it. Walking away does not end legal entanglements incidental to the relationship, such as jointly owned property, joint debts, or a shared business partnership. These legal connections remain, but can be severed by the couple with the agreement of any third parties such as creditors.

In other words, the cohabiting couple can end their relationship without going to court, if they can agree on everything, but a married couple must take legal action to end their relationship. Some people regard this as a major advantage of cohabitation arrangements.

A cohabiting couple only need a court, or other decision maker, such as an arbitrator, if they are unable to work things out amicably. However, their agreement is only a contract and does not have the force of a court order.

Even if a married couple are on the best of terms and even if they have a prenuptial agreement, one of them needs to sue the other for divorce in order to end their relationship. The final division of their assets and debts must be memorialized in a court order. Similarly, matters of child custody and support are resolved in a court order.

Usually, but not always, the judge will go along with any reasonable agreement that the couple make about property and about their children.

Regardless of their agreement and regardless of whether they are married or not, a couple cannot deprive the courts of the power to decide child custody and support issues. In other words, if one party wants the court to decide child custody questions, then the dispute will end up in court.

Going to court

The differences between marriages and cohabitations continue into the court system if the couple has to go to court.

Remember that there are federal trial courts and state trial courts. Traditionally, the federal courts refused to hear domestic relations cases. Family cases were left exclusively to the state courts because states have a particular interest in family matters. This doctrine presented an interesting question when unmarried couples began to sue each other, because ordinarily federal courts could have jurisdiction of a contract dispute for example.

Today, the rule probably is that a pure contract dispute between an unmarried couple could be heard in federal court if the other requirements for its jurisdiction are met, such as residency, amount in dispute and so on.[30]

In most states, different courts have jurisdiction of different kinds of cases. In rural counties and small towns, one court may handle nearly all lawsuits. More populous counties have separate courts for family-related lawsuits, including divorces and child custody cases. In those counties (which include most big cities), other courts handle other kinds of lawsuits, such as accident and contract cases. The states use a variety of names for their courts.

For simplicity, I call the courts that hear most cases "trial courts." I call the courts with jurisdiction over divorces, child custody, and paternity cases "family courts" and those with jurisdiction over inheritance questions "probate courts."

Disputes between a cohabiting couple and disputes between a married couple may be heard in different courts, depending on what's at stake. Nearly all family related cases are heard in state courts, rather than the federal court system. However, divorces and child custody cases might be decided in a different branch of the state court system from a lawsuit over a contract.

When a married couple divorces, all of their disputes will be heard in the family court. Family courts decide matters of divorce, child custody, adoption, and property division. The family court will usually decide questions about the couple's prenuptial agreement, if there is one. Usually, in family courts, the judge (not a jury) decides nearly all of the issues. He or she will rule on the legal issues and determine the facts.

To the contrary, if a cohabiting couple have a financial disagreement, a regular trial court would probably have jurisdiction over it. It is just like any other lawsuit over a contract.

But, if the cohabiting couple also disagrees about custody of their children, then the family courts probably have jurisdiction over that issue. As with a married couple, the judge would decide what the best interests of the child were. The cohabiting couple might end up with two lawsuits over the end of their relationship, one about the kids and one about money.

In other words, different courts may have jurisdiction over various disagreements between a cohabiting couple. (It's worth noting here that deciding where to file a case can be a complex decision that can affect the outcome of the case. Filing in the wrong court can delay things substantially. A person who is handling his or her own case needs to sort out which court in his or her area is the appropriate one.)

There are three significant differences between family court proceedings and ordinary lawsuits.

One difference between divorces and other law suits is that there is usually a waiting period between the time the petition is filed and the time a divorce can be granted. Even if the couple agree on everything, the judge cannot sign the final decree until that time period has passed. Ninety days is a common time period.

A second difference is that a family court judge can often require the couple to go to counseling. Both trial courts and family courts can require the parties to try mediation.

A third difference is that a family court often has various staff members who help the judge. The judge may have an assistant judge to decide some questions, for example. He or she may also have an investigator who looks into allegations of abuse. Some courts can appoint an advocate for the children in a divorce case. Often, these are volunteers who keep an eye on the proceedings to make sure that the children's interests are considered. Sometimes, an attorney may be formally appointed by the court to represent the children. See Chapter Seven and Chapter Fourteen for more information.

Other differences between marriage and living together

It is perhaps superfluous to note that people who attach traditional moral values to sexual conduct regard living together without benefit of matrimony as immoral or sinful, and marriage as a morally better state of affairs.

The emotional support and comfort that comes from mutual commitment on a permanent basis are also important. Many sociological studies have asked partners in various relationships to rate their happiness and satisfaction with life. In general, married people report greater contentment and happiness. Specifically, a greater percentage of married report that they are happy or moderately happy than single men. Some studies suggest that the figures may be less for women. Statistically, married men live longer than single or cohabiting men.

The economic benefits of marriage are substantial. According to the Rutgers University report *State of Our Unions 2004*, "Married couples create more economic assets on average than do otherwise similar singles or cohabiting couples. Compared to those who are continuously married, those never married have a reduction in wealth of 75% and those who divorced and didn't remarry have a reduction of 73%." Typically, married men earn more than single men. These economic effects may be due to the simple fact that two together can live more cheaply than two separately.[31] Social norms that encourage responsible financial behavior in married couples may also play a part, especially to those men who feel a genuine sense of responsibility to "provide for my family."

Last but certainly not least, a parent should consider what sort of lessons living with different lovers conveys to his or her children. Leaving aside the moral issues for the moment, such relationships can cause great distress to a child if the lovers separate.

The child loses the essential sense of the stability and reliability of adults that children need for healthy emotional growth. As a result, the child may not be able to form lasting attachments when he or she grows up or may come to believe that no other person is trustworthy. A child from such an environment may grow up to be promiscuous because he or she simply hasn't learned what a stable, mutually supportive, adult relationship is like.

Children grow best – emotionally and otherwise – in a stable two-parent home. The adults involved owe it to their children to try their best to provide such a healthy environment for the child, even if staying together, for example, does not happen to suit the parents' convenience or sexual urges at the moment. Statistically, children from cohabiting homes do less well in life than children of married couples, at least in terms of such factors as their likelihood to finish high school, to have a child out of wedlock, and so on. There are, of course, many exceptions to any statistical study, and the experts disagree about the effects, good and bad, of cohabitation on the children involved.

Conclusions and advice

From a legal point of view, marriage can simplify some financial aspects of shared lives. The law spells out the rights of both parties to a marriage. The problem is that the application of those rights to any particular situation can produce widely varying results. A married couple can make many changes in the financial arrangement specified by the law to suit their own situation, but the law provides a sort of default sharing. It may or may not be fair or what they wanted, but usually spouses have some share in the fruits of the marriage.

The law does not spell out the rights of those in informal relationships. If anything, the law provides that informal couples have no financial rights with regard to each other. Therefore, an informal couple must either create their own legal relationship or accept that, financially, each of them is on his or her own. They can create a legal relationship of sharing by three basic means: changing the title to property; writing an agreement about their property; and writing a will.

On the other hand, the law provides for how questions relating to all children will be decided. Those laws are more or less the same for married and unmarried couples, except that an unmarried father has fewer rights than a married father.

Marriage does not guarantee a particular economic outcome of a relationship. Cohabitation offers even less legal security. In either relationship, the parties can entangle themselves in a financial mess.

Anyone who has important financial expectations from a relationship, whether it's a marriage or a cohabitation, should memorialize those expectations in a written agreement. If your partner will not put his or her promises in writing, then you cannot rely on your expectations being fulfilled.

The following table summarizes some of the usual legal and financial differences between marriage and living together.

Table of Differences between marriage and cohabitation

TOPIC	MARRIED	UNMARRIED
Joint credit cards?	Both can use, both are liable for entire amount.	Both can use, both are liable for entire amount.
Separate credit cards?	Only named person can use (except with permission) but both may be liable for debts, especially if used for household expenses.	Only named person can use (except with permission) and only that person is liable to the credit card company.
Separate credit card in name of one party but with other party given a card by the credit company?	Both can use; original party is liable to credit card company for debts and spouse may be also, depending on state law. Liability of person who is issued an extra card depends in part on terms of agreement with issuing company.	Both can use; original party is liable to credit card company for all debts – i.e. for all amounts that either run up. Liability of person who is issued an extra card depends on terms of agreement with issuing company.
Joint checking account (requiring only one signature on checks)?	Both can withdraw part or all of the money. The bank is not responsible for parties' private agreements.	Both can withdraw part or all of the money. The bank is not responsible for parties' private agreements.
Separate checking account?	Only named person can withdraw funds but spouse may have some rights to the money if they divorce.	Only named party can withdraw funds, but significant other may acquire an interest in the money by agreement.
Rights in property earned during the relationship?	Depends on state law but each spouse is usually entitled to some share in all assets earned during marriage by both.	No rights to assets earned by the other unless there is an agreement or another legal relationship such as a partnership.
Inheritance rights?	Specified by state law; spouse usually inherits unless there is a will to the contrary.	None, unless there is a will or joint account, etc.
Duty to support each other?	Usually.	No, unless there is a contract.
Duty to support children?	Yes.	Yes.

Table of Differences between marriage and cohabitation (continued)

TOPIC	MARRIED	UNMARRIED
Alimony or support paid when the parties are separated or divorced?	Depends on state law and parties' circumstances.	No, unless there is an agreement to the contrary.
Responsible for taxes owed by couple?	Yes, spouse may share responsibility, although innocent spouses have some protection.	No liability for the other's problems, unless participate in scheme to cheat IRS.
Testimonial privilege?	Yes.	No.
Right to sue each other for injuries?	Yes, in most states, no in others.	Yes.
Right to sue a wrongdoer who injures the significant other?	Yes.	Almost never.
Liability for debts of the other person incurred during this relationship?	Yes to some extent, depending on state law.	No, unless both signed the loan papers or otherwise agreed to pay.
Joint accounts with right of survivorship?	Survivor gets the money.	Survivor gets the money.
New relationship changes alimony rights from previous marriage?	Remarriage usually ends alimony from the previous marriage.	Change depends on divorce decree's terms.
New relationship changes child support from previous relationship?	Probably no change.	Probably no change, but possible changes in custody or visitation.

(Endnotes)

1   *Rehak v. Mathis*, 238 S.E. 81 (GA. 1977), cited in *Texas Marital Property* at 498

2   *Harrington v. Harrington*, 742 S.W.2d 722 (Tex. App. -- Houston [1st Dist.] 1987, no writ)

3   *Marvin v. Marvin*, 557 P.2d 106 (Cal. 1976).

4   *Viki Lee v. An Tai Lee*, 44 S.W.3d 151 (Tex.App.-Houston [1st Dist.] 2001) at 153

5   *Hewitt v. Hewitt*, 394 N.E.2d 1204 (Il. Sup. Ct. 1979)

6   *Roach v. Renfro* 989 SW2d 335 (Tenn. Ct. App. 1998)

7   *Marvin v. Marvin* 557 P.2d 106 (Cal Sup. Ct. 1976)

8   *Tyrangiel v. Zimmerman*, Complaint, Case No. BC 115656, Superior Court for the County of Los Angeles (1994)

9   Daniel Cere, "Courtship Today: The View from Academia," Public Interest Spring 2001: 53,

10   Kay S. Hymowitz, "The Cohabitation Blues," Commentary Mar. 2003.

11   "Commitment Ceremonies," The Alternatives to Marriage Project, http://www.unmarried.org/ceremonies.html, downloaded August 8, 2005.

12   Uniform Marital Property Act §4. See *Understanding Family Law*, at 75

13   Robert Oliphant and Nancy Van Steegh, *Family Law: Examples and Explanations*. Aspen Publishers, New York, 2004, at 228.

14   *Understanding Family Law*, at 66.

15   *Family Law, Examples and Explanations*, supra

16   *McGehee v. McGehee*, 85 So. 799 (Miss. 1956), cited in *Understanding Family Law*, at 6, n.11.

17   *Choachou v. Choachou*, 135 So. 2d 206, 214.(Fla. 1961), cited in *Understanding Family Law*, at 66, n. 11

18   *Brown v. Boeing Co.* 622 P.2d 1313 (Wash. Ct. App. 1980)

19   Uniform Marital Property Act §4. See *Understanding Family Law*, at 75.

20   *Butler v. Butler* 347 A.2d 477 (1975).

21   *Butler v. Butler* 347 A.2d 477 (1975).

22 *Cockerham v. Cockerham* 527 S.W.2d 162 (Tex. 1975), discussed in Pamela E. George, *Texas Marital Property Rights; Cases and Materials* (Imprimatur Press, Dallas, Texas, 2004), at 275 et seq.

23 *Nelson v. Citizens Bank & Trust Co. of Baytown*, 881 S.W.2d 128 (Tex. App. – Houston [1st Dist.] 1994, no writ), cited in George, supra, at 287.

24 Tex. Bus. & Com. Code Ann. 3.401(a) "No person is liable on an instrument unless his signature appears thereon."

25 See, for example, *Moran v. Adler* 570 S.W.2d 883 (Tex. 1978) where two children unsuccessfully asserted their rights to inherit from their stepmother on the ground that she had informally adopted them.

26 *Sanburn v. Schuler*, 23 S.W. 61 (Texas, 1893.

27 Quoted from website of Relationship LLC, www.relattionshipllc.com, 1999.

28 Jennifer Mathieu, "Meet Mr. and Mrs. And Mrs. Jones," Vol. 12, No. 48, Houston Press, November-December 6, 2000, p. 28 et seq.

29 "Threesome Makes It Last" at the Love More website, http://lovemore.com/articles/threesome, downloaded August 8, 2005. (Reprinted on the site from *Loving More Magazine*, 1996)

30 See *Anastasi v. Anastasi*, 544 F. Supp. 866 (D.N.J. 1982) and *Ankenbrandt v. Richards*, 504 U.S. 689 (1992).

31 *State of Our Unions 2004*, p. 17.

Chapter Six

MARRIAGE AND DIVORCE

From the law's point of view, marriage is more than a lifestyle arrangement between two people. Unlike cohabitation, marriage changes a couple's legal status. Although a couple can change some of the legal incidents of marriage by a contract between themselves, their relationship still has different legal consequences than living together.

Moreover, marriage is an all or nothing legal proposition. Either you are married or you are not. No matter how devoted a cohabiting couple may be to each other, they do not acquire the automatic legal rights and obligations of a married couple. The couple can give each other some of these rights by a private contract between themselves but they cannot confer all the legal rights of marriage on each other, except by getting married.

There are two ways to get married in the United States. The most usual way is for a couple to obtain any required license and to have a legally proper ceremony before a person (such as a minister or justice of the peace) who is licensed by the state to marry people. The other way is to satisfy the requirements of a common law marriage.

There are only two ways to end a valid marriage – death of one spouse or divorce.

Some apparent marriages, however, suffer from a legal flaw that makes them invalid. Some of these apparent marriages are simply void. There is not, and cannot be a valid marriage, no matter what the couple wants. If the flaw is less serious, the couple can simply continue to live together and the marriage may become valid. In either case, a court can declare the apparent marriage to be invalid. A court can declare these marriages invalid.

The idea of marriage as a status, rather than a contractual relationship between two people, derives from the Biblical concept of a married couple as joined together in the eyes of God. The status of marriage has been so important that the law presumes that an apparent marriage is valid. If a man and woman have been in previous relationships, the courts assume that the last marriage is a valid one. This assumption is one of the strongest in the law because legally, marriage has so many important consequences. In other words, a person who wants to challenge the validity of a current marriage has a heavy burden.

The right to marry is a fundamental right. It is part of our constitutional rights to a private family life. The Supreme Court has held that the states cannot unreasonably burden people's right to marry, although the states can regulate marriage. One state, for example, passed a law that people who were paying child support could not marry again without court permission. They had to prove to the court that they were supporting the children from their previous relationships. The Supreme Court held that law excessively interfered with the right to marry. The states could enforce child support by other legal means, but not by precluding a person from marrying.[1]

This chapter covers the legal rules governing marriage and divorce. Chapter Fourteen and Chapter Fifteen cover the mechanics of family litigation.

Beginning a marriage

Remember that marriage begins with the consent of the couple, but state laws set the conditions under which that consent becomes a valid marriage.

Ceremonial marriage

In this book, the term "ceremonial marriage" means a marriage celebrated according to the laws of the state where the marriage takes place. It includes marriages performed by justices of the peace and other judges, as well as marriages performed by ministers.

All states set limits on who can marry. These include age limits, limits on how close the couple can be related, and how many persons one can be married to at a time.

Age limits

All states set age limits on those who can marry. In almost every state, the age at which one can marry without one's parents' permission is 18. In Mississippi, boys can marry at 17 and girls at 15.

In every state, people can marry when they are younger than 18 if their parents consent; the ages for marriage with parental consent vary among the states. Girls as young as 12 and boys as young as 14 in Massachusetts and Kansas can legally marry. The typical age limit is 16 for both boys and girls.

A purported marriage by someone below the legal age is not a valid marriage. A child of 10 cannot marry in any state, regardless of his or her parents' consent.

These laws impinge on the desires of parents from cultures and religions in which arranged child marriages are common. The religious predilections of the parents, however, do not make such arrangements valid in this country.

Consanguinity and gender

All states prohibit the marriage of person who are closely related. Fathers cannot marry their daughters nor mothers their sons. All states prohibit marriages between uncles and nieces, grandparents and grandchildren, and so on. Only one state permits first cousins to marry. The California statute is typical. It says simply

No man may marry his mother, grandmother, daughter, granddaughter, sister, aunt, niece, stepmother or stepdaughter, and no woman may marry her father, grandfather, son, grandson, brother, uncle, nephew, stepfather or stepson. Any marriage within these degrees is void.

The courts held that that statute included half-siblings, so that it prohibited a marriage between half-brother and half-sister.

These laws rest on moral considerations and eugenics. Some people believe that it is natural for incest to seem repugnant. The exact prohibitions, however, derive largely from Old Testament injunctions on who could marry whom. The other social concern is that marriages of close relatives would increase the chance of birth defects in any children.

In fact, this fear is largely unfounded. In the ordinary course of events, it would take several generations of incestuous marriages before an increased number of genetic flaws appeared, unless of course the initial couple were both carriers of a gene linked to an inheritable problem.[2]

Some states also prohibit marriages between persons who have been members of the same family even if they are not genetically connected. In some states, today, a stepfather cannot marry his stepdaughter. This prohibition reflects a sense that certain new marriages would likely corrupt family relationships, rather than a concern about biological incest. Prohibitions like these occur in some Biblical restrictions and continue to today. For example, in England, in the 19th century, a young woman fell in love at first sight with her elder sister's fiancé. When the sister died after a short marriage, her widower fell in love with his former sister-in-law (the young woman who had fallen in love with him at first sight). English law, however, regarded their marriage as incestuous and prohibited the union. The couple married happily in another country. He was a prominent artist, but English society ostracized the couple and they had to spend much of their time outside England.

Marriage to a close relative may also constitute the crime of incest. Prosecutors rarely bring charges against adults in incestuous relationships, partly because often no one is complaining and hence there are no witnesses. Occasionally, there are cases in which accusations against fathers in polygamous, fundamentalist, Mormon families include both polygamy and incest. For example, John Daniel Kingston was accused of child abuse for whipping his daughter with a belt to punish her for running away from her arranged polygamous marriage to his brother, who was, obviously, her uncle. She alleged that her father and mother were half-brother and sister who had had 10 children together. The county prosecutor said that he didn't "have any qualms about prosecuting" couples who were closely related. Such cases are rarely brought, however, in part because of the lack of witnesses and in part because police resources are usually spent on other investigations.[3]

An incestuous marriage is void. Marriages of first cousins are legal in a few states and prohibited in others. If the marriage was legal where it was performed, then it is probably valid in all other states. However, technically, the couple are still committing the crime of incest. Prosecutions in these situations are virtually unknown.

Free to marry — bigamy

Getting married to someone while still married to someone else (without getting divorced first) is bigamy, which is a crime.[4] Prosecutions are relatively rare.

Leaving aside the criminal implications of bigamy, the second marriage is void. The second couple is simply not married. However, if the previous marriage ends (e.g. by death or divorce) and the common law couple continue to cohabit and hold themselves out as married, a common law marriage can be created at that time.[5]

When the purported but bigamous marriage is void, it has no legal standing at all as a marriage. The bigamous spouses do not have to go through a divorce to end their purported marriage, although one spouse may seek an annulment to make the legal matters absolutely clear.

The importance of a marriage's being void is that the spouses do not have any of the rights of married people toward each other. Laws of community property, inheritance, and so on that afford rights to married people simply do not apply. The couple may or may not have acquired some property rights toward each other by agreement or otherwise, like cohabiting couples.

QUESTION: *"What if one member of a couple lies about whether he or she is married to someone else?"*

ANSWER: *The deceived person is out of luck as far as being married goes, although he or she may have some rights to assets acquired during the time when he or she thought there was a valid marriage.*

The law regards people as either married or not. But, sometimes, one party to a relationship profoundly deceives the other. Sometimes people get involved in a marriage-like relationship even when they are already married to others.

Perhaps the most famous example is in the novel *Jane Eyre* when the infatuated Mr. Rochester attempts to enter into a bigamous marriage with the plain but pure Jane Eyre by not telling her about his insane wife, whom he has locked up in the attic. A real life example is that of a California doctor who was "married" to three different women. He managed to keep up three households, with children in each, and to practice medicine, all without any of his fellow doctors (or spouses!) discovering the charade. His spouses reported that he never "slipped" – he never forgot a birthday or a special family event. It was only when he died that the three families discovered that only the first wife was legally married to him.

Sometimes, people are simply mistaken about their marital status. They may have been told that a Mexican or Caribbean divorce is valid or believe that a long separation dissolved a common law marriage. They may have conveniently forgotten that they lived with another partner in a common law marriage state.

At any rate, sometimes one party to the "marriage" believes that he or she is legally married when in fact the marriage is not valid because the other party is still married to someone else. In these situations, the innocent party may be entitled to some financial protection. The deceived person, who is a "putative spouse," gets some of the legal protections of marriage, but not all of them. The putative spouse has some property rights in assets acquired during the apparent marriage.[6]

A situation similar to that of the California doctor occurred in the case of the *Estate of Vargas.* Mr. Vargas lived a double life for over 20 years. He married his first wife, Mildred, in 1929.[7] Mildred and Mr. Vargas had three children together and they lived together continuously, except when he "had to be away on business." Vargas married his second wife, Josephine, in 1945. He assured her that he was divorced. They lived on the west side of Los Angeles and had four children together. He had dinner (and sex) with Josephine every night but didn't sleep at their home – he also had to be away from her "on business." Ironically, Mildred and Vargas did not have any substantial savings until after he "married" Josephine. Vargas died in a car accident in 1969 without a will.

The question then was – who inherits from hubby Vargas? The California court divided his estate equally between the two women. The judges held that Josephine was a putative spouse, because she had married Mr. Vargas in good faith. Unfortunately, the law didn't provide any clear guidelines for who got what, even if Josephine and Mildred were both innocent parties. California is a community property state, so a spouse should get one-half but one-half of what? The court noted that the laws governing inheritance were not designed to deal with the innocent heirs of bigamists. Ultimately, the court looked to the basic fairness of the situation, in which neither "wife" was to blame, and divided the estate equally.

It is important to realize, however, that a putative spouse situation can exist only where one party is innocent, i.e. where he or she believes that there is a valid marriage and doesn't know about the other spouse. A person who knows that his or her significant other never got divorced is not a putative spouse. A couple that go through a marriage ceremony while knowing that one or both of them remain married to someone else might still have some rights toward the property acquired during the relationship, like other cohabiting couples, but courts might be less sympathetic because the relationship was not only informal but inconsistent with the existing marital relationship with other people.

Other impediments and requirements

All states have various administrative tasks for a couple to marry. These include a requirement that the couple obtain a marriage license and that the marriage be performed by a person authorized by the state government to perform marriages. Ministers and justices of the peace are authorized to perform marriages, for example. Obviously, also, the marriage must actually be celebrated. It is not sufficient for a couple to be engaged and get a license; they must go through an appropriate ceremony with a licensed official.

States also impose various health requirements. The most common requirements are that a couple must not have syphilis and that a woman of child bearing age must be immune to rubella (German measles). That disease can cause birth defects if a pregnant woman contracts it. She may be immune either by having had the disease or by vaccination. A couple must furnish proof that they meet these health requirements before the clerk will issue a marriage license.

In addition, people are not free to marry if they are under any legal disability. A legal disability is where a court has determined that the person is legally incompetent to conduct their own affairs. "Incompetent" in this sense doesn't mean dumb or foolish. It refers to a person who is mentally disabled or impaired to such an extent that he or she cannot rationally handle his or her financial and personal matters. For example, a person who is brain damaged in an accident may be adjudged incompetent, as may a person who is addicted to cocaine or alcohol. Courts appoint someone, usually called a "guardian" or a "conservator," to handle the incompetent person's finances. See Chapter Twelve and Chapter Thirteen for more information on guardianships

An incompetent person can marry with the permission of his or her guardian. If someone marries such a person without the guardian's consent, the marriage can be annulled, and the new spouse does not acquire any interest in the incompetent person's property. In other words, if a court has determined that a person cannot run his or her own affairs, then an unscrupulous person cannot marry the disabled person and gain control of his or her assets.

The legal impact of failing to comply with these administrative requirements varies among the states. In some states, failure to have a proper license, for example, invalidates the marriage; in those states, the requirements are mandatory. Other states are not so strict; in those states, the requirements are "directory," meaning that the marriage can be valid even if there was some technical flaw in the wedding.

Covenant marriage

QUESTION: *"Why don't you explain more about the religious precepts that underlie marriage?"*

ANSWER: *Religious beliefs vary widely, and debate over them is usually acrimonious. Also, I'm a lawyer, not a preacher.*

The influence of conservative religious groups includes efforts to reinforce an ideal of lifelong heterosexual marriage. One of these efforts is the new institution of covenant marriage.

Three states (Arkansas, Louisiana, and Arizona) have adopted an alternative form of marriage, called "covenant marriage." Other states have considered such legislation in recent years

The legal effect of a covenant marriage in states that don't have such a law is not settled yet. In other words, if a couple agrees to restrict their right to divorce under the law of Louisiana, would another state with less restrictive divorce laws be obligated to honor Louisiana's restrictions? Probably not, but the question is not settled yet.

QUESTION: *"What is covenant marriage?"*

ANSWER: *Covenant marriage is a legal variation on the marriage law in a few states. The couple agrees to limit their rights to divorce.*

In a covenant marriage, the couple voluntarily agrees to limit their rights to divorce. The Louisiana statute, for example, limits the grounds for divorce in a covenant marriage more or less to the traditional grounds plus requiring that the parties get counseling before they file for divorce. It provides that a spouse to a covenant marriage may obtain a judgment of divorce only upon proof of any of the following:

(1) The other spouse has committed adultery.

(2) The other spouse has committed a felony and has been sentenced to death or imprisonment at hard labor.

(3) The other spouse has abandoned the matrimonial domicile for a period of one year and constantly refuses to return.

(4) The other spouse has physically or sexually abused the spouse seeking the divorce or a child of one of the spouses.

(5) The spouses have been living separate and apart continuously without reconciliation for a period of two years.

Louisiana law also provides grounds for a couple to obtain a divorce from bed and board (legal separation) and to divorce if they have remained separated under that decree.

These grounds differ from Louisiana's ordinary divorce law which provides that a couple get obtain a no-fault divorce after they have lived apart for six months.

There are also organizations that encourage couples to consider their marriage in terms of traditional religious values as set out in the Bible. These groups regard marriage as a covenant in the sense of an important commitment, but their beliefs do not change the laws of marriage.

The question about the legal effect of such promises, such as whether a formal promise not to divorce would affect a property division in a divorce, for example, have not been decided. These promises might be a valid prenuptial agreement, as to financial matters, but the contract will not prevent a divorce.

Lawsuits about marriage

In the days when marriage was a woman's only assured way to financial stability, breaking an engagement had serious consequences. Like other contracts, it could be the ground for a lawsuit.

Today, most states have abolished these lawsuits. Some still permit them, however. Either the bride or groom can sue.

The jilted person can recover damages for financial losses (such as the cost of the canceled wedding plans), mental anguish, and any injury to his or her reputation. However, the disappointed fiancé cannot sue for the loss of a better financial or social situation. In other words, if you get engaged to a wealthy person and he or she leaves you at the altar, you may be able to get some money for your hurt feelings but you're not entitled to the pot of gold that you thought you had snagged.

In addition, at one time, adultery was referred to in the law as "criminal conversation." A man who had sexual relations with another man's wife was considered to have done harm to the husband. The injured husband could sue for damages. Some states still permit these lawsuits although they are rare. In the absence of some specific harm, such as the transmission of a venereal disease to the husband, it is unlikely that an aggrieved husband today could recover much in damages from his wife's lover. To the extent that such lawsuits are still permitted, an aggrieved wife would have equal rights, of course.

Common law marriage

A couple is common law married when four basic conditions are satisfied: (1) both of the parties are free to marry; (2) they agree to be married to each other; (3) they hold themselves out as married; and (4) they live together as husband and wife.

Common law marriage is a valid, legally binding marriage established without an official ceremony. Another name for common law marriage is "informal marriage."

The most important aspect of common law marriage is that it is a real marriage in the eyes of the law; it is not a second-class relationship or one that doesn't have all the legal bells and whistles of a ceremonial marriage. Once the requirements of common law marriage are satisfied, you are just as much married as if you had said "I do" in front of the bishop and your assembled families for three generations on both sides of the aisle.

However, not all states permit people to get common law married in their state. In those 27 states, you either get legally married in a formal ceremony or you have not been legally married in that state.

Under the United States constitution, however, states have to give "full faith and credit" to the laws of the other states. Just to make things a little more complicated, therefore, states must recognize marriages as valid if the marriage was valid in the state where the couple got married. In other words, California, for example, does not permit informal marriages (you can't get common law married there) but must consider a couple married if they either got married in California or got married in some other state. If that other state happens to be a common law marriage state, then California will consider the couple legally married, even if the legal marriage happens to be by the common law marriage standards of another state, such as Texas. However, a state can refuse to recognize a marriage from another state as valid if the marriage violates an important state policy, such as the policy against incest.

QUESTION: *"We want to be sure that we are common law married. What should we do?"*

ANSWER: *It would a lot easier to just get a marriage license and get married. If, however, you really want an informal marriage, you need to be able to prove that you fulfilled all the requirements.*

Some states, like Texas, have a registry for common law marriages. If your state or county has a registry for common law marriages, then, obviously filing the appropriate form is the best solution. You can go to the county records office and record your common law marriage officially. To find out if your state has such a system, check with the county records office or the secretary of state.

Two basic documents might also help, which are (1) an agreement to be married and (2) a sworn statement from a friend or neighbor that you lived as husband and wife and held yourselves out as married. You can sign an agreement to be married and stating that you have lived together. It may not be necessary to have the agreement notarized, but it's a nice touch.

Another useful thing would be to have friends sign a statement that evidences the elements of common law marriage. There are examples of these documents in the Workbook.

QUESTION: *"My boyfriend claims that we are common law married. I say we're not. I want to get married in church."*

ANSWER: *Even if you are common law married, you can go through the formalities of marriage, and, assuming that you want to be married, that's the clearest legal course.*

QUESTION: *"My old girlfriend claims that we are common law married. I say we're not. I want to marry my new girlfriend."*

ANSWER: *If you and your old girlfriend met the requirements for common law marriage, then you are married. If there is any significant doubt about the facts, you probably should file for a divorce or annulment from your old girlfriend. Otherwise, your marriage to your new girlfriend might not be a valid marriage.*

If you have lived with someone in a common law marriage state and told people that you were married, there is some risk that you did informally marry each other. The risk may be small, depending on the circumstances, but it could wreck havoc on your later relationships.

To evaluate the situation, you can gather all the evidence about the relationship. Maybe you have letters or emails that make clear that you never intended to marry each other. If there is any serious dispute about whether you were informally married or not, you need to keep all these records in a safe place for future use.

There are examples of witness statements, checklists, and a questionnaire in the Workbook section to help you gather information and documentation on either side of these questions. See page 645 and related materials.

The fact remains, however, that if you did informally marry, you remain married to that person until he or she dies or you divorce each other. Remember that long term separation doesn't end the marriage. Sometimes a person who is in a situation where there might be a common law marriage will file for an annulment, i.e. for a court declaration that there was no marriage.

Free to marry — legal requirements

Because a common law marriage is a real marriage, people can only get informally married if they are legally free to marry. That means that they have to meet all the other legal requirements to marry. In other words, you can't get informally married if you're married to someone else at the time or if you're only joking and so on.

One quasi-exception is that the courts sometimes recognize a valid common law marriage where the couple was below the legal age limit to marry. In Texas, for example, a person who is under the legal age to marry without parental consent can avoid the age limit by entering into a common law marriage, although the marriage can be set aside by a court

Agreeing to be married

The first requirement is that the parties agree to be married. Agreement is a state of mind, and like all psychological issues, it can be a complicated thing. The core element is that both people involved have to mean to be married to the other. That means that they don't think they are "just living together" or "are going to get married someday if things work out" or anything else; they think of each other as husband and wife right now.

In some states, the agreement to be married can be inferred from the fact that the couple are living together and presenting themselves out as married. In others, such as Texas, the legislature has required that the agreement be separately proved, although it can be established by circumstantial evidence, such as letters referring to "my darling wife."[8] Under Texas law, the parties must have intended to have a "present, immediate and permanent marital relationship."

Let's consider three parallel hypothetical situations.

Case 1

Mary Traditional and George Straightlaced go through all the traditional rituals of dating, getting engaged, and getting married. They meet at a church picnic. They do not have sexual relations or live together before they are married. Even though George has a lot of doubts about being married at all and especially about whether he wants to marry Mary, once the wedding planning gets started, he goes along. George and Mary go through a big church wedding. George is thinking "No, no, let me out of here" to himself even while he's saying "I do" to the preacher. George and Mary go on a traditional honeymoon in the Bahamas.

Are George and Mary married? Yes. With very few exceptions (that are seldom heard of, like someone being forced to go through a ceremony at gun point), people's secret reservations don't invalidate their marriage. If they did, a lot of married men would be single to this very day!

Case 2

Mary Hippie and George Freespirit don't believe in traditional religion or the legal system. They decide to get married "in spirit." They invite all their friends to a big party and announce that they have decided to take each other as husband and wife. They recite love poetry that they have written, pledging to be each other's spouse forever. Mary Hippie and George Freespirit live together and have great sex. They tell their parents and new people they meet that they are married. They introduce each other as "my husband" or "my wife." They buy a cabin in the woods together, and the deed lists them as husband and wife.

In Texas and 12 other states, Mary Hippie and George Freespirit have gotten common law married, but in other states, the ceremony is just a party and the couple is not married.

Case 3

Mary Modern and George Swinger meet in a bar. They date for a few weeks and soon are sharing George's apartment. When they go out with friends, they introduce each other as "my partner" or "the person that I'm living with." At that point, Mary Modern and George Swinger are not married. After a few years, though, Mary Modern gets a great new job in Oklahoma, and she and George move to Tulsa together. She wants to appear more respectable, and she and George want him to have health insurance under her company's policy. So, when Mary fills out the insurance forms at work, she lists George as her husband. When George needs surgery to have his appendix taken out, he files a claim form with the health insurance company as Mary's husband. When they go to parties at her company, Mary introduces George as her husband and George refers to Mary as his wife.

Are Mary Modern and George Swinger common law married?
The answer is—probably.

The reason for the "probably" is that it's not clear what Mary and George intended. Oklahoma recognizes common law marriage. Did Mary and George intend to be married? Well, sort of. On the one hand, they told people they were married, but on the other hand it was more a matter of social and financial convenience. Did they commit a fraud on the insurance company if they were not married?

One element of "agreeing to be married" is whether the couple gives the impression that they intend to stay together "until death do us part." Even with the high rate of divorce in the United States, one difference between a one-night stand and a marriage is just that both participants (hopefully) regard the one night stand as a fling. When people live together casually, both regard themselves as relatively free to leave when the mood strikes them. Married people on the other hand are supposed to feel a commitment to the relationship; in theory at least, they don't just walk out blithely when they meet someone better looking at the El Rodeo Bar and Grill.

Holding oneself out as married

To hold oneself out as married is, simply, to tell people that one is married. That is, in our society, there are many opportunities to introduce the significant people in our lives and to describe them. Let us consider some of these opportunities:

One of the most important situations is with regard to our parents. For adults, parental consent to marry has not been required by law for almost 200 years, but (at least in the minds of jurors) if a couple are married, they usually (but not always) tell their parents. If a woman calls her significant other her "boyfriend" when she is gossiping with her mother on the telephone, she probably doesn't really think of him as her husband.

At parties, for another example, people introduce their significant other to other guests. If people regard themselves as married, they customarily introduce their significant other as "my husband" or at least "my old man." If they don't regard themselves as married, they may call each other "my boyfriend" or "my girlfriend" or "my partner" or even "my roommate." In case you hadn't noticed, married people do not generally call each other their "roommate."

Another time when we have to identify people by their relationship to us is on legal papers of various kinds, ranging from job applications to the lease on the apartment to income tax forms. Married people check the box marked "married" when they apply for a job. If they can afford it, they usually arrange for health insurance benefits for their spouse and list their spouse as the beneficiary on their life insurance policy. When they rent an apartment, they do so as "Mr. and Mrs." or at least "husband and wife."

The law does not specify what degree of "holding out" is required to demonstrate that a marriage exists. In the case of the *Estate of Claveria v. Claveria*, the Texas Supreme Court held that a single public act, such as signing a mortgage, could support a finding that the couple was common law married.[9] On the other hand, the same court has held that a weekend in a motel is not sufficient to establish that the couple has held themselves out as married.

In one Texas case, which could be straight out of a sentimental country ballad, a young woman and man were very much in love. His mother, a strong-willed woman, disapproved of the relationship because the girl was from a poor background while the boy's family was well-to-do and socially prominent in their town. The boy and girl sneaked off together for a short time. They went to Mexico and went through a wedding ceremony. The mother retrieved the boy and took him with her to another city. The girl went back to living with her parents. Soon after all this the boy died. Since he had already inherited a lot of money, his heirs would inherit a lot from him. If he was married, the girl, his wife, inherited.

The question was whether he and his true love had been married. The girl pointed out that they had gone through the marriage ceremony in Mexico. At the time of the ceremony, however, the boy was underage under Mexico's law and could not legally marry. The girl then claimed that she and the boy were common law married. The boy's mother proved, however, that the boy and girl had never "held themselves out as married," i.e. had not told their families that they were married. The girl lost the case and the mother inherited all of her son's money. (Whether this case had a happy or a sad ending depends on your view of the facts and where your sympathies lie.)

A sadder case is that of Ms. Pipkin and Mr. Dallman.[10] Like so many disputes about common law marriages, it came up in a fight over his estate. Ms. Pipkin moved into Mr. Dallman's home in 1945. She was 21 and he was 37. He was a widower, and she became his housekeeper. He had four children and she had one son. He asked her to marry him and, at first, she refused. A year later, she agreed, but his grown children objected. So, Ms. Pipkin and Mr. Dallman agreed to live together as husband and wife without a formal ceremony. They went to church together and traveled together, staying in the same hotel rooms. But, they filed separate income tax returns, indicating on the returns that they were single. Ms. Pipkin used her own name, and they referred to themselves as single in various social situations. When Mr. Dallman died in 1972, after the couple had lived together for 33 years, he left Ms. Pipkin $1000 and a car. She brought suit to claim the share of his estate that a wife would have. The court held that she could prove that they agreed to be married and that they lived together as husband and wife, but not that they held themselves out as married. The court looked for a general or substantial holding out or an open declaration to the public.

The judge said "To hold that a common law marriage is established without public acknowledgement of the marriage status of the contracting parties where there is an unwitnessed oral agreement, would open the door to perjury and fraud, deny the parties themselves the protection to which they are each entitled, and jeopardize the sanctity of the basic institution of all civilized society, the home." In other words, the judge felt that if a couple didn't publicly tell people they were married, anyone could claim that they had a secret agreement between themselves, especially when the other party was dead. So, the children who had opposed the marriage thirty years before won out in the end.

Living together as husband and wife

As noted above, living together as husband and wife usually includes having sexual intercourse. Sex is considered an important aspect of the marriage relationship in general. In some states, even a ceremonial marriage may be annulled if one party to the marriage was permanently impotent at the time of the marriage and the other did not know about the impotency.

Sex alone, however, is not enough to convert a relationship into a marriage, as many a marriage counselor knows. In the eyes of the law, sex doesn't make a marriage either, unless it takes place in the context of a couple who believe that they are married and who intend to be in a permanent relationship.

Often, when trying to decide whether a couple is married, the judge and jurors will be looking to see if the couple behaves in ways that he or she thinks are the ways in which married people behave. Things like dating other people, keeping completely separate finances, not taking joint title to a house or car, may make a couple look more like temporary lovers than like married people. On the other hand, a man who does household errands, works around the house, and generally acts like a typical suburban husband, looks more like a husband and less like a live-in lover. None of these facts is determinative, but any of them might influence a judge or jury.

Other requirements

Even if the legal requirements for a common law marriage are satisfied, there are sometimes other legal conditions that must be fulfilled in order to establish the existence of the relationship. For example, in Texas at one time, a person claiming to be common law married had to bring a lawsuit to establish that fact within one year after the relationship ended. For example, if one party to a relationship died and the other person wanted to be considered to have been common law married to the deceased, he or she had to bring an action, such as a claim in the probate court where estates are distributed, within one year of the person's death. That law was repealed, but other conditions have been imposed by statute in various states.

Proving it

Cases about common law marriage come to the courthouse when a substantial amount of money turns on the question of whether someone is, or is not, married to another person. Often these cases involve inheritances, but sometimes they involve lawsuits over accidents or over the division of property. Because people who live together don't generally acquire any rights in each other's property, the dispute can be fierce and the evidence ambiguous.

The ambiguity of a relationship can be seen in the mixed-up lives of Voula and Don.[11] Voula and Don met at a nightclub and began to date. Don had just been divorced and Voula was a single mother of three children. According to Don, they quickly became intimate and Voula moved in with him, bringing her cosmetics, clothes, and other personal items. Voula said that she spent the night with Don and traveled with him but did not move in. She claimed that two other men lived in Don's house with him and that she lived with her children in her own house. Both Voula and Don agreed that they had sexual relations. They also agreed that Don asked Voula to marry him.

Voula said she flatly refused.

Don said that Voula replied, "Baby, we don't have to get married to be married. You've had problems with your credit since your heart trouble. Let's get your debts straight and then we'll do it right." To Don, this meant that they were married, just not ceremonially.

The couple opened a joint bank account, but Voula said that was just to keep the IRS from seizing Don's money. Voula let Don use her American Express card in his business, and she claimed that she loaned him $20,000. Eventually, Voula, Don, Voula's daughter, Don's lawyer, and a bank went through a complicated deal in which

Voula ended up buying Don's house. The net result was that Don's debts got paid, including an IRS lien and legal bills owing to his former divorce lawyer.

Don, however, later claimed that Voula had promised that he would still have an interest in the house. He tried to make the payments but she wouldn't let him. Finally, he told her to move out and she did.

Voula and Don split up. Don sued for divorce and wanted his house back, claiming that Voula had defrauded him of it. Voula responded that the house was hers and that they were never married.

The court noted that the evidence was divided, to say the least. "Several of [Don's} friends and employees testified that they thought, for various reasons, the two were married." An employee of the bank testified that none of the paperwork suggested that the couple were married and that the deed identified Voula as a single person.

The jury believed Don. The appellate court, however, decided in favor of Voula on the marriage question. The court held that there was evidence that the couple had agreed to be married and had lived together as husband and wife. But, the court found that there was insufficient evidence that the couple held themselves out to the community as married. The judges noted that "occasional introductions as husband and wife do not establish the element of holding out." The court held that, for example, two introductions would not be enough, but having the reputation in the community would be, even if some family members don't know about the marriage.

The law is clear — either you are married and have the rights and obligations of married people or you aren't and you don't. The facts, however, can be messily ambiguous.

QUESTION: *"How can we tell whether we are just living together or informally married?"*

ANSWER: *Assuming that you live in a state that recognizes informal marriage, a common law married couple act like they are married. A cohabiting couple acts like they are living together. Merely cohabiting does not turn into marriage.*

Many people wonder if they could "accidentally" get common law married if they are living together. There's a longer discussion of that issue in the answer to the next question.

A couple does not automatically become married by living together for a certain period. To marry, they must agree to be married, live together as husband and wife (with all the social conventions that implies) and tell people that they are married.

Some judges, for example, find that the most telling piece of evidence is whether the couple filed a joint tax return as married. This act may be persuasive evidence because it shows that the couple accepted the economic consequences of marriage or because many people hesitate to lie to the IRS.

QUESTION: *"What if a couple are ambivalent about their relationship?"*

ANSWER: *It doesn't really matter until something important turns on the question of whether they are married or not.*

Sometimes a couple simply can't make up their minds as to what they want from their relationship. In that situation, they may vacillate from one version of what's going on to another. Sometimes, the different versions that they tell different people are not consistent. For example, a couple may sometimes refer to their relationship as being engaged and sometimes as being married. In that situation, if there were ever a court case, it would be a question of who and what the jury believed.

Things can get even more complicated when a couple gets divorced and then gets back together. Often after the reunion, the couple refers to themselves as "husband and wife," naturally enough. If they live together as husband and wife and agree to be married, then in a common law marriage state, they may in fact have remarried.

But, as often happens in such a tumultuous relationship, the couple may split up again. What happens if the wife goes back to the divorce court to enforce her rights to child support payments under the divorce decree? Well, you can't be divorced and married at the same time. Her enforcement of the divorce decree is, logically and legally, inconsistent with claiming that she and her husband had gotten back together as husband and wife. In fact, it legally bars her from claiming a common law marriage with her former husband.

Socially, a couple may be neither fish nor fowl, sometimes acting like they are married and sometimes acting like they are not. Legally, however, a court is going to decide one way or the other.

Ending a marriage

This section discusses the legal mechanics of divorce. Discussions of the property implications are in Chapter Fourteen on ending relationships and Chapter Fifteen on court disputes.

In legal terms, a marriage can end by the death of one spouse, by annulment, or by divorce. Divorce, separation, and annulment all legally affect marriage. Only death, divorce, and annulment legally end a marriage.

Separation

A legal separation is a court proceeding that is sometimes called a "limited divorce." In the days when a woman was legally obligated to live with her husband, it gave her official permission to live apart. Today, a legal separation often involves a married couple who want to live apart and want to divide their assets, arrange for child custody, and so. It does not legally end the marriage and the couple are not free to remarry.

However, we often say that a couple has "separated" when they simply decided to live apart. Often, there is no legal process involved. Sometimes, the separation is a prelude to divorce. Sometimes it becomes a permanent, agreeable, living arrangement, where a couple who still love each other find that their lives are more pleasant if they don't live in the same house. An informal separation like this can have legal consequences in those states where it is one ground for divorce.

Sometimes, the situation is ambiguous. For example, one spouse may move to another state to take a job while the other remains in the family home, perhaps so that the children can stay in their accustomed school. In that case, we would not usually refer to the couple as having separated. They are not living apart because the marriage is troubled but for financial reasons.

QUESTION: *"What's the difference between a legal separation and a divorce?"*

ANSWER: *A legal separation is a court declaration that a couple may legally live apart but remain married. The court can order support payments.*

Some states recognize two forms of legal separation, but many states have abolished these doctrines. Legal separations, in which a court is involved, are different from a couple that just separates, i.e. live in different places.

Before divorce was legally available, couples could only seek a legal separation. In law language, that separation was called a divorce *a mensa and thoro*, which means more or less, a divorce "from bed and board." The most important part of this procedure was that the decree entitled a wife to live apart from her husband; absent a legal separation, she was required to live with him. Keeping in mind that legally, at that time, a husband could not rape his wife because she was obligated to provide him with sexual access to her body, one can see the importance of the legal permission to separate. Traditionally, legal separations often were sought by women to protect themselves from marriages that were simply more than the woman could stand. Today, most couples simply divorce if they are not getting along; those who seek a legal separation usually do so because they are not ready to divorce but don't want to live together.

Traditionally, public policy opposed separation almost as much as divorce. A couple could enter into an agreement to separate only when the marriage was already insupportable. They could not provide for a separation, for example, in any prenuptial agreement.

Today, legal separation provides as a way for couples who are morally opposed to divorce to arrange their financial affairs. Sometimes, legal separation is called a "limited divorce," because the court divides the couple's property between them and can order spousal support. Prenuptial agreements can legally contain clauses about any later separation.

Sometimes, a couple will seek a legal separation when they want to divide their assets and live separately but do not yet want to divorce. Usually, this occurs when one spouse still hopes for reconciliation.

The grounds for a legal separation are the same as for divorce — basically, that the couple can no longer live together. The decree will state that they remain married but may live apart. A legal separation obviously does not permit either party to marry someone else.

There is also a more limited legal separation in some states. In that case, a spouse seeks support from the other spouse when they are living apart. Usually, this proceeding is brought by the spouse who has fewer assets and income earning ability. Since the proceeding only concerns support, the court does not divide family's assets.

All forms of legal separation proceedings are much rarer because divorce is easy to obtain. A legal separation can be easily converted to a divorce in those states that still recognize separations apart from divorce. Some caution is needed, however, because the legal separation could have financial consequences that would affect the court's decision in any later divorce proceedings.

Annulment

Before the law permitted divorce, the only legal way to end a marriage was through annulment. An annulment was a declaration that an apparent marriage had never been a valid marriage.

The consequences of annulment could be harsh. The wife was not entitled to support from her apparent husband and any children of the relationship became, legally, bastards. At the time, that status barred the children from inheriting from the father (unless he specially named them in a will) and from certain professions.

However, for some religious people, an annulment has religious significance; because it is a determination that a marriage never existed, the ex-spouses may be permitted to remarry according to the rites of their religion. Sometimes, however, the annulment must be one obtained according to the laws of the church and within church procedures.

QUESTION: *"What's the difference between an annulment and a divorce?"*

ANSWER: *An annulment is a court declaration that an apparent marriage was not a legal marriage. The grounds for an annulment rest on legal flaws in the marriage. Because the couple was never married, marital property doctrines do not usually apply.*

An annulment is a court decision that a serious legal defect made an apparent marriage invalid. The defect has to be one that existed at the time of the marriage, not a problem that came up later. The difference between a divorce and an annulment is that divorce ends a valid marriage while annulment is a legal proclamation that an apparent marriage wasn't ever valid.

The Uniform Marriage and Divorce Act refers to annulment as "declaration of invalidity."[12] In most states, a specific statute describes the grounds for an annulment. Even in states that don't have a specific statute, a court can still grant an annulment if it is equitable for it to do so.

People seek an annulment, rather than a divorce for several reasons.

One reason is religion. If a person belongs to a church that forbids divorce, an annulment can free the person to remarry in the church. However, the actual legal effect is a matter of church doctrine, which is governed by the laws of the church. In the Catholic church, a canon law proceeding within the church itself may be required for a person to be allowed to remarry under church law.

An apparent spouse may want an annulment for social or financial reasons. If a marriage becomes insupportable immediately after the ceremony, he or she can avoid any embarrassment at having been so quickly divorced.

An annulment, however, often involves the parents of the married couple, if one of the purported spouses being under the legal age to marry.

Technically, lawyers distinguish between marriages that are completely void (meaning that the marriage simply wasn't a marriage at all) and those that are voidable (meaning that there is a technical flaw in the marriage and the couple can have it legally set aside if one of them wants to).

Annulment usually avoids the financial consequences of marriage. Community property rules and alimony laws do not apply because the couple was never married. However, if one party to the apparent marriage didn't know about the fatal flaw in the marriage, the court can divide the property to avoid unfair result. The innocent spouse is called a putative spouse. See discussion on page 207.

An annulment probably also keeps any prenuptial agreement from ever becoming valid. Prenuptial agreements become effective, usually, only when the couple marry. If an annulment is granted, it probably has the legal effect of making the prenuptial agreement unenforceable, but unwinding the couple's financial affairs could be complicated if one or the other had relied on the agreement.

QUESTION: *"What are the grounds for an annulment?"*

ANSWER: *The grounds are those which raise a serious flaw in the marriage proceedings, including fraud about an important matter, incest, duress, bigamy, and being underage.*

Annulment is the court proceeding to declare that an apparent marriage is not valid.

Marriages are void when the facts of the marriage violate important social policies integral to the institution of marriage. An incestuous marriage offends strong moral considerations, as does a bigamous marriage. These couples simply cannot legally marry. If they have gone through a marriage ceremony, they are still not married.

Technically, a void marriage has no legal effect and it is not necessary for a couple to go through any court proceeding to have it declared void. It simply is not a marriage. However, an annulment establishes a clear legal record that the marriage was not valid. Therefore, a "spouse" who believes that his or her apparent marriage is void should get a formal annulment to avoid legal complications and hassles that might arise decades later.

A voidable marriage is one that has a legal flaw. These legal flaws invalidate one of the elements of a valid marriage but do not involve the foundations of the social institution of marriage. The marriage is called "voidable" because a court can declare that the marriage was invalid if someone brings a suit to have it annulled. If the marriage is not annulled, however, it becomes effectively a valid marriage. In other words, the parties can stay married if no one sues to annul the marriage.

Some of these legal flaws include mental incompetency, impotence, fraud, and duress.

A valid marriage requires the consent of both parties, and a mentally incompetent person cannot give his or her valid consent. A person can be mentally incompetent because of mental retardation or serious mental illness. A person who is so intoxicated during the ceremony that he or she doesn't understand what is happening is also sufficiently incompetent that he or she may be able to get the marriage annulled. Sometimes the family of an insane person will bring an action to have his or her marriage annulled.

The issue of annulment sometimes is raised by the children of an elderly person who has made a marriage that the kids don't like. In one sad case, an old man had become mentally confused and partially paralyzed. He didn't dress himself neatly any more. A nurse, however, helped him regain his strength and health. He married her. One of his children tried to have the marriage annulled on the ground that the old man was insane at the time of the marriage. The court refused on the ground that, given the man's improvement, the kid didn't prove that the father didn't understand what he was doing.[17]

For example, in *Patey v. Peaslee*, several family members of a sick woman sued to have her marriage to her "husband" annulled. They claimed that she was both mentally incompetent and near death when she married him. Obviously, they thought that her husband married her only to inherit from her. The court refused to annul the marriage because the would-be heirs waited until after the apparent wife was dead when it was too late to annul a marriage.[13]

A marriage that is just a joke is also not a valid marriage. That means literally that the parties didn't intend to really marry at all; it doesn't apply to marriages that turned out so badly as to be a joke. A mock marriage is a ceremony that the parties had "as the result of jest, exuberance, hilarity or dare and harbor no intention to be bound thereby," as one court said.[14] An annulment proceeding may be necessary if the couple disagree about whether the ceremony was serious or not or if they want to be sure that it doesn't have any legal effect.

Since sex and children are an important part of marriage, some lies about these matters will entitle the unhappy party to an annulment. If a husband is permanently impotent before the marriage, the wife is entitled to have the marriage annulled. If a spouse conceals a serious venereal disease or sterility, the other spouse may be able to obtain an annulment. Similarly, misrepresentations about pregnancy are sometimes grounds for an annulment. Suppose for example that a woman becomes pregnant and the child's father vanishes. She meets a nice young man. Desperate, she tells the young man that she is a virgin. In some circumstances, deceit of this magnitude may entitle the young "husband" to an annulment, provided at least that he takes action reasonably promptly after he learns the truth. Similarly, a pregnant woman who falsely tells a man that he is the father of her child commits fraud on him, and the marriage can usually be annulled. However, if the woman simply lies about being pregnant in order to persuade her lover to marry her, he usually cannot get an annulment.

Complete and permanent impotence (the inability to have sexual intercourse) is grounds for an annulment, but sterility (inability to father children) is usually not. However, both of these conditions can be grounds for annulment if a person lies about them.

Serious misrepresentations about other important matters can be grounds for annulment also. The falsehood has to be about something so important that the other person would not have gotten married if he or she had known the truth. One court said that the lie must be of "an extreme nature, going to one of the essentials of marriage."[15] For example, in the case of *Kober v. Kober*, Herr Kober concealed the fact that he had been a Nazi during WWII and was still violently anti-Semitic.[16] He demanded that the new Mrs. Kober cease associating with her Jewish friends. She had the marriage annulled on the ground that she would never have married Kober if she had known about his background.

In the *Bilowit* case, a man was dating a girl who was an Orthodox Jew. He told her that he was Orthodox also, which was a lie. When she found out, she got the marriage annulled because she would not knowingly have married outside her faith.

Lies about other serious problems, like drug addiction, alcoholism, and mental illness can also invalidate a marriage. Lies about love, however, are not usually sufficient unless they are part of a larger scheme.

A marriage must be freely entered into. A person who is coerced into marriage can have the marriage set aside later. The coercion has to be such that the person was forced into the marriage, although it doesn't necessarily have to involve a shotgun.

Unlike divorce today, annulment is not a unilateral matter. In other words, the other spouse can oppose the annulment. An annulment will not be granted if the couple continue to live together as married after the deceived person learns about a misrepresentation or after the duress is removed. Similarly, if a person knows about a flaw in the other before marriage (such as impotency), he or she may not be able to obtain an annulment later. There are also time limits, which vary from state to state, within which an annulment must be sought.

Divorce

Every state today permits a couple to divorce on the ground that the marriage is emotionally over. It is not necessary to prove any form of marital misconduct, such as adultery or abuse.

MYTH—*"You can't get a divorce on grounds of incompatibility unless both spouses agree."*
FACT—*One spouse can obtain a divorce regardless of the other's wishes.*

For many years, a divorce was only available if there was a major breach in the marriage contract. Some of these grounds for divorce included habitual drunkenness or drug addiction, insanity, conviction of a serious crime, abandonment, adultery, and failure to support the spouse. Other grounds, which actually made divorce more liberally available, were cruelty or gross neglect.

In the days when one spouse had to prove that the other had breached the marriage contract, a person who didn't want a divorce could contest the lawsuit, just as in other lawsuits. There were various defenses to divorce actions. For example, a wife whose husband sued her for divorce on the ground of her adultery could offer the defense that he had condoned her lapse and taken her back into the home.

Today, however, these maneuvers rarely occur. The old grounds for divorce, such as adultery and cruelty, are still on the books but it is no longer necessary to prove one of them. All states now provide for a divorce when one of the couple wants out. Usually, the statutes refer to these grounds as "incompatibility" or "irreconcilable differences." The Uniform Marriage and Divorce Act refers to "serious marital discord adversely affecting the attitude of one or both of the parties."[18]

Sometimes a couple disagrees about whether a marriage can be saved or not. In other words, one claims that the marriage is irretrievably broken and the other tells the court that if they got counseling, they could stay together. The courts still grant the divorce because a marriage requires the consent of both spouses. If one thinks that the marriage is over, legally, it will be.

Some states encourage a divorcing couple to go through counseling. Some have required that the couple have lived separately for a period before they can divorce. None of these laws, however, significantly limit the ability to get a divorce.

The division of property and child custody can be complicated and hotly contested legal issues in a divorce. But, the question of whether the couple will in fact be divorced is no longer a legal issue. In other words, couples can fight over who gets what and who the children will live with, but they can no longer effectively litigate the question of whether they will be divorced. If one of them wants a legal end to the marriage, he or she will get that result.

Interestingly, statistics suggest that unhappy couples who stay together eventually become happier. At least, when interviewed by sociologists, couples who were once contemplating divorce but stayed married usually report that they are happier now than they were. Studies such as these, and the high divorce rate, have led some commentators to suggest that it should be legally harder to get a divorce.

However, there is no convincing evidence that lengthening a waiting period for divorce, for example, would encourage couples to stay together. They would simply live separately longer.

QUESTION: *"What if divorce is against my religion? Can my spouse still get a legal divorce?"*

ANSWER: *Yes. State law trumps religious doctrine on this point.*

As noted above, religion can influence a couple's decisions and sometimes enters into the law, as a conscious or unconscious factor in a court's decision or as the underpinning of a statute, such as the laws against homosexual marriage. However, the government's secular laws govern secular matters, including property. Regardless of Biblical prohibitions, all states permit divorce and permit remarriage of divorced persons.

Even if the couple have entered into a religious marriage contract that prohibits divorce, either spouse can still get a legal divorce.

However, religious law and secular law can intersect. As part of divorce proceedings, a court may, if requested, require the couple to fulfill the requirements for a religious divorce as well as the secular one. For example, in the divorce of a religiously observant Jewish couple, the judge can order one spouse to provide a *get*, which is a religious decree of divorce.

Many divorced Catholics who wish to remarry in a religious service go through the formal proceedings, within the canon (religious) law to have their previous marriage annulled.

If the (religious) legal requirements for a divorce are not met, the parties cannot remarry in a (religious) ceremony, at least if the priest, rabbi, or minister adheres strictly to their faith's laws. For example, under Jewish law, a divorcee can remarry but "she may not marry a *kohen*, a member of the priestly tribe."[19] Orthodox Jews and some Conservative Jews may observe this law but most Reform rabbis ignore it.[20]

Similarly, some conservative Christian churches hold that divorce is against Church law and may regard a second marriage as adulterous and hence, sinful. Even these churches, however, may have formulated sufficient exceptions to permit the second marriage, impliedly or explicitly recognizing the divorce as having ended the first marriage.

However, in the United States, the decision of church authorities does not affect the legality of a divorce or a remarriage. The legal status of a couple is determined by secular law.

Conclusions and Advice

The advent of no-fault divorce has eroded the distinction between marriage and living together. When one spouse can unilaterally end a marriage, marriage can seem like just a variation on living together. Getting a divorce no longer necessarily involves a court battle, although it can still be expensive and painful. However, the legal status of being married is still different from that of living together. Ending a marriage still takes some legal action, even if the grounds have been liberalized.

Marriage, whether common law or ceremonial, brings with it both rights and obligations. In particular, marriage gives rise to substantial property rights. More importantly, marriage is still a different status than not being married. For many people, marriage involves commitment and living together involves a denial of that commitment.

(Endnotes)

[1] *Zablocki v. Redhail*, 434 U.S. 374 (1978).

[2] Richard Connif. "Go Ahead, Kiss Your Cousin. Heck, Marry Her If You Want To" Discover, August 2003, Vol. 24, Issue 8, p. 60.

[3] Greg Burton, "Officers Say They're Willing to Pursue Incest, Polygamy Cases" The Salt Lake Tribune

[4] *Bodde v. State*, 568 S.W.2d 344 (Tex. Crim. App. 1978)

[5] *Garduno v. Garduno*, 760 S.W.2d 735 (Tex. App. 1988)

[6] Hon. Russell Austin and Darlene Payne Smith, "Putative Spouses in the Probate Process," Unpublished Handout, Probate Court Number One, Harris County Texas (1998).

[7] *In re Estate of Vargas*, 36 Cal. App. 3d (Cal. Sup. Ct. 1974).

[8] Austin and Snith, supra, at p. 3.

[9] *Estate of Claveria v. Claveria*, 615 S.W.2d 164 (Tex. 1981).

[10] *In re Estate of Dallman*, 228 N.W.2d 187 (Iowa, 1975).

11 *Eris v. Phares*, 39 SW 3d 708 (Tex. App.-Houston [1st. Dist.] 2001)

12 UMDA §208.

13 *Patey v. Peasless*, 111 A.2d 194 (1955)

14 *Mypilliris v. Hellenic Lines*, Ltd. 323 F. Supp. 865 (S.D.Tex. 1969)

15 *Biolwitt v. Dolitsky* 304 A.2d 774 (N.J.Super. 1973).

16 *Kober v. Kober*, 2111 N.E.2d 817 (N.Y. 1965)

17 *Fischer v. Adams*, 38 N.W.2d 337 9nebraska, 194()

18 Uniform Marriage and Divorce Act, § 302.

19 Gross, *Love and Marriage in Judaism*, supra, at 109.

20 Id.

Chapter Seven

THE RIGHTS OF CHILDREN AND PARENTS

This chapter describes the legal rights of parents and their children. Most of the information is equally applicable to children born of married parents or out of wedlock. This equality reflects profound changes in society and in the law. These changes include recognition of family life as a fundamental right, increased sexual freedom, and increased gender equality.

The right to raise one's family as one chooses is a fundamental Constitutional right in this country. For example, the Supreme Court has held that the government could not compel Amish parents to send their children to public schools after the eighth grade. In that community, the parents educated their children at home in the practical skills of farming and housework after they had learned to read, write, and do basic math. The parents had a fundamental right to the lifestyle that they chose within wide standards. In other words, the parents' rights had limits but their right to live as they chose in their own home was very important.

The number of children born out of wedlock has increased substantially. Approximately, one-third of American children each year are born to unmarried women.

The law concerning the status of children of informal relationships has changed more than the laws that concern the adults in those relationships. First, the rights of children born to unmarried parents have been expanded. In over 30 cases since 1900, the Supreme Court of the United States has ruled that the law cannot discriminate between legitimate and illegitimate children. Prior to those rulings, many laws embodied society's disapproval of the parents' unmarried sexual conduct. That disapproval took the form of imposing special restrictions on the offspring of the relationship. For example, bastards did not inherit from their father unless he specially provided for then in his will. Now that discrimination based on illegitimacy has been legally abolished, in some ways the children of informal relationships may have more rights than the lovers.

A substantial percentage of American teenagers now believe that having a child out of wedlock is just "doing your own thing." Their view is reinforced by the number of famous people who have openly had children outside of marriage. In addition to young movie stars and sports figures, a number of older prominent people have acknowledged their out-of-wedlock kids. These include not just young starlets but also older, prominent people. Violinist Zubin Mehta acknowledged that he sired a child out of wedlock in Israel, Jesse Jackson acknowledged a love child in the United States, and after many decades of secrecy to protect his political career, the illegitimate, mixed race daughter of segregationist Congressman Strom Thurmond acknowledged that he was her father.

The rights of fathers have been given greater recognition in custody decisions. With regard to children born out of wedlock, earlier laws assumed that the father of an illegitimate child had no particular desire to take a role in the child's life and that even if he did want to, he had little moral standing to be involved with the child'. Gradually, the courts are recognizing that at least some fathers of children out of wedlock love and cherish those children. These fathers now have more say in whether the child is placed or adoption or not.

The courts have also given more recognition to the parenting role of fathers in custody decisions in divorce cases. Although mothers still receive primary custody in most cases, a determined and diligent father now has a chance of gaining primary custody.

Perhaps the hardest questions facing courts today concern the rights of adults who have had the role of a parent in a child's life but are not biologically related to the child. The courts are struggling with the question of what legal recognition to give to non-traditional families, including those comprising unmarried persons and those comprising gay people.

In addition to the complicated and bitter questions that can arise around the custody of children conceived in the ordinary way by a married couple, the new technologies of in-vitro fertilization, artificial insemination, and surrogacy now pose their own legal and moral complexities. These technologies are called, collectively, "assisted reproduction." The legal question is "Who are the (legal) parents of this child?"

The following discussion is divided into two primary sections. The first deals with parental obligations toward children and the second deals with parental rights to their children.

Children's rights and parental obligations

The three primary legal rights that children have vis-a-vis their parents are the right to support and care, the right to inherit from a parent unless deliberately disinherited by the parent, and the right to be free from abuse or neglect. The child has the right to support from its parents and to be free from abuse by any person.

These rights continue until the child reaches age 18 or is emancipated. A child is emancipated when he or she legally marries or becomes self-supporting and independent of the family. If a child is disabled, the duty to support him or her continues after he or she reaches 18.

State law imposes some procedural requirements on children born out of wedlock who want to establish their paternity in order to have the same rights as a child born of married parents. For example, New York requires that a child born out of wedlock must legally establish his or her paternity before the alleged father dies. Even if the father has acknowledged the child, the child is not entitled to inherit from the father unless either paternity was formally established in accord with state procedures or unless the father named the child in his will.

Some states require that a child born out of wedlock sue for child support within a certain number of years after his or her birth. If the suit is not brought in a timely fashion, then the courts will not require the parent to pay child support for all the missed years.

Under typical state statutes, once the parentage of a child is established, the same rules apply to a child born out of wedlock as to a child born of married parents. Arkansas statutes, for example, apply the same standard to an out of wedlock child as to one born to married parents; after paternity is established by DNA testing, the father is obligated to support the child until he or she turns 18. In some states, the father can be obligated to continue support payments to help with the costs of the child's college education.

Parentage can be established by filing a formal acknowledgement of paternity or by a court case; the court case is started by an interested person filing a petition. It is important to note that sometimes weird procedural limits govern who can make the legal claim of having fathered a particular child. "Standing" is the legal term for those who can invoke various laws. The Arkansas statute, for example, limits those with standing to the biological mother, the putative father (i.e. her husband), any man who is not presumed by law to be the father (i.e. anyone but the husband), and a state agency.

For example, if the child's parent is killed in an industrial accident, the illegitimate child has the same right to receive worker's compensation benefits as children born in a marriage, provided that parentage can be established.

One significant difference in the rights of cohabiting couples with children as opposed to married couples is in the area of welfare reform. The Supreme Court has held that a state may decide to provide public assistance only to "households of married adults and their children."[1]

To be taken care of

Both of a child's biological parents are obligated to support the child. There are two exceptions to this general obligation. The first is where the parental relationship has been severed by law (as when a child is legally adopted by others). The second is where the parentage of the child has not been proven in accordance with legal requirements. In that situation, however, the duty of support may be said to accrue, and if the parentage of the child is later established, the parents may be liable for the support that was not paid during the previous years.

So, if a couple who are living together produce a child, then that child is entitled to be supported by both parents, regardless of whether the couple is married or not.

Within broad limits, parents in an intact family decide the child's lifestyle. This rule applies whether the parents are married or not. They are not required to maintain the kid in accordance with their own standard of living or to send the little nipper to college or to provide him or her with anything else beyond the necessities of life, such as food, clothing, education as prescribed by state law, and adequate medical care. For example, the rights of parents to educate their children at home, which is called "home schooling" rather than send them to state approved public or private schools is now recognized. The parents must, however, provide an education that meets state standards, including the attainment of various basic skills, such as reading, and levels of knowledge. In some communities, public facilities, such as a city gymnasium, afford home schooled children opportunities to engage in organized sports and other group activities.

That parental discretion changes when the government gets involved. In a divorce or custody suit, for example, the court will set the amount of support that will be paid from one parent to the other. In cases of abuse or neglect, the court may impose various kinds of supervision on the family, such as visits from social workers, and may also require the parents to attend classes in parenting or anger management. The court or a social service agency may remove the children from the parents' home and arrange for care of the children in a temporary foster home with a family or in an institution. If necessary, the rights of the birth parents may be permanently severed and their legal relationship with the child ended. In that case, the child may be adopted or may remain in state care, such as foster homes or other institutions.

Medical care – parental duties and rights

In general, parents decide what medical care a child needs. So long as a couple lives together in more or less harmony and the decision is not so extreme as to be a denial of clearly necessary care, the government doesn't get involved. Thus, for example, the parents can decide whether a child has plastic surgery to correct a minor deformity or not. The fact that other parents or doctors might think that such care was a good idea is not the controlling factor.

Parents cannot, however, deny the child clearly necessary care or care, such as inoculations, that is required by state law. The parents have a legal obligation to provide the level of medical care that accords with widely accepted social values. So, for example, if the parents fail to have the child's broken arm properly set, they may be guilty of neglect. The question of how sick a child has to be before the parents are legally obligated to take the child to a doctor is an ambiguous one. Some parents may rush to the pediatrician every time their son or daughter has a slight fever, while others may wait until their child's temperature is higher or lasts longer. With wide boundaries, these decisions are matters for the parents to decide.

Treatment of disease — who decides?

Sometimes, physicians disagree with parents as to what medical treatment is best for a child. Usually, if the choice is between two medically recognized options, then the parents' decision governs. If, however, the parents opt for a markedly unorthodox treatment or if their values differ radically from those of the doctors, the doctors or hospital may ask a court to take the decision away from the parents. The legal ground is that the parents are neglecting the child, even though they may be behaving according to their own sincere views about religion or the child's welfare.

In some cases, the courts have taken custody of the child away from the parents and given the decision-making power to the doctors or to a social service agency. For example, the parents of a child with leukemia refused to continue some of the child's chemotherapy treatments. The parents loved the child but for their own reasons elected to discontinue the treatment. The doctors believed that the child needed the treatment and that without it, the child would die. The court removed the child from the parents' custody so that the chemotherapy and radiation could continue.[2] Interestingly, in this situation, the child was 14 years old, who agreed with her parents' views. She resisted all efforts to treat her, and her condition deteriorated, despite the social workers' intervention. Finally, her parents regained custody and the form of treatment that they preferred was begun.

Similarly, the parents do not have the right to consent to medical procedures that are not in the child's best interests. In one tragic case, Jean Pierre, a twelve year old boy, had a virulent form of leukemia. The boy's only hope for survival was a bone marrow transplant. His father had five children. Neither Jean Pierre's father, mother, or 23 year old brother could be donors. Two of the children were three year old twins who had a different mother than Jean Pierre did. The mother had custody of the twins

235

who did not know that Jean Pierre was their half-brother. She refused to consent to the twins' being tested as possible bone marrow donors. The transplant procedure was painful but not dangerous. The father asked a court to overrule the mother's decision. The court upheld the mother's choice. The twins' best interest was the standard that the court considered. If the children had a close emotional connection to Jean Pierre, it might have been appropriate to subject them to the transplant procedure but in these circumstances, the court did not think so. Jean Pierre died.[3]

In other cases, courts have authorized a medical procedure on one child to benefit another child in the family. The factors include the emotional connection of the children, the dangers to each child, and the child's own preferences, if he or she is old enough to express them.

Cases of disagreement between parents and doctors are particularly difficult where the parents base their decision on their religious beliefs and those beliefs fall outside mainstream views. In many cases, the parents may legally refuse medical treatment for the child in accordance with religious tenets. Generally, Christian Scientists (who rely on faith and prayer in preference to medical intervention) may legally choose to consult a Christian Science practitioner in place of a physician, and Jehovah's Witnesses (who believe that the Bible forbids consumption of blood) may refuse to permit their child to have a blood transfusion.

However the courts sometimes intervene where the child's life or quality of life is at stake. For example, a young boy had a facial deformity that made him so grotesque that he could not attend school. His mother was willing for him to have plastic surgery to correct his appearance but not to have a blood transfusion. The surgeons knew that a transfusion might be necessary during the surgery. The court gave the surgeons permission to do the transfusion if necessary because without the surgery, the boy's "chances for a normal, useful life are virtually nil."[4]

Moreover, prosecutors sometimes file charges against parents for criminal neglect of a child when the parents provide only prayer for a critically ill child and refuse to get medical care.[5] Criminal charges are perhaps more likely where the parents' beliefs are idiosyncratic, rather than part of an established church.

The right of parents to refuse treatment for their child based on their own value judgments is hotly debated, particularly where the parents simply don't want a defective child to survive. For many years, parents sometimes refused lifesaving surgery for newborn babies whom the parents did not want to raise. Some babies with Down's syndrome, for example, are also born with a defect in the esophagus that makes it impossible for the child to swallow. Without corrective surgery, the child would die. Many parents declined the surgery and allowed the child to die.

The law now somewhat limits the rights of parents to make such decisions, but the rules are unclear. Federal law prohibits a hospital from withholding treatment from a disabled child solely based on the child's disability; however, it doesn't expressly require that severely deformed children be treated if the parents object. The Supreme Court has ruled that the government cannot adopt broad regulations that completely preempt the parents' rights to decide.[6]

Other courts, however, have required that a child be treated. For example, a mother gave birth to a child with multiple deformities, including a missing eye, a missing ear, and a deformed thumb. The parents ordered the doctors not to perform a life-saving operation on the child. The court held that the parents could not deny necessary medical care to a child just because they didn't want a less than perfect child to survive.

However, when a child is terminally ill or so severely deformed as to be unlikely to survive very long, the parents usually have the right to decide when continued treatment would be unkind. As a rule, people can refuse medical care, especially if it would be futile or would just prolong their suffering; parents can exercise that right on behalf of their children.

In this context, "futile" means that the treatment would not effect a cure or a significant prolongation of meaningful life. Obviously, the application of "meaningful" varies with one's values.

Many hospitals now offer help to parents in caring for a dying child. When it is determined that the child's condition is terminal and that continued aggressive treatment will neither cure the child nor meaningfully prolong his or her life, hospital staff can design a program of palliative care to keep the child as comfortable as possible. "Palliative care" refers to medical treatment that makes a person more comfortable, including relief from pain, but does not treat the underlying illness.

Sometimes, arrangements can be made for the child to leave the hospital and die peacefully at home. These arrangements can be a great comfort to some families because the child has a last opportunity to be with pets and siblings in a familiar loving environment, away from the high technology world of the hospital with its visiting hours, rules, and other distractions. Not all parents, however, can tolerate the thought of their child dying at home, and the decision must necessarily be one tailored to each family with the guidance of compassionate physicians and other health care providers.

The question of whether parents can decide to discontinue care of a child who is permanently comatose but not terminally ill is undecided and hotly debated. Usually, such care consists in artificially administering water and food, as well as caring for the child's bodily functions and preventing infections.

The most likely reasoning of the courts is that a young child, like an adult, has a right not to be kept alive where life is of no benefit to the child. In the case of a severely brain damaged young child, who could not have an opinion, the parents probably have the right to ask that life support be terminated. In the case of an older child, however, such a teenager, the government can require that there be clear evidence of the child's wishes. If there is no evidence about the older child's values, the parents do not have an absolute right to discontinue the care.[7]

In some states, a hospital has the right to discontinue medical treatment of a child or other person where the treatment is futile. In this context, "futile" means that the child is close to death regardless of what is done. The hospital can stop life-sustaining treatment regardless of the family's wishes, after giving the family time to try to move the patient to another facility.

There are special restrictions on parents' rights to agree to experimental treatment of a child. Researchers must follow special guidelines before a child is enrolled in a clinical trial of a drug, for example, to make sure that the child is not subjected to undue risk or suffering.

Mental health care

Parents can consent to mental health treatment of their child on the same basis as they consent to other treatment, but there are some limitations.

The right of parents to have a child committed to a mental hospital is broad, but not unlimited. The law does not require that there be a court hearing (as is required for an adult) but some independent person must be involved in the decision. That person must carefully evaluate whether the child really needs hospitalization.[8]

Despite these supposed protections, there have been recent scandals in which it is alleged that salespeople for mental health facilities persuaded worried parents to unnecessarily institutionalize their children for weeks or months of care. Sometimes, the salespeople masqueraded as a "troubled child" hotline but their "advice" was, if the parent had insurance, to take the child to the hospital. Sometimes the parent was instructed in ways to trick the child into going to the facility, such as by telling the child that they were going on a weekend trip. The doctors at these hospitals then allegedly certified that the children were mentally ill when in fact the children either were simply normal, if rambunctious, children or at most suffered from relatively ordinary, treatable mental illnesses, such as depression, that are usually treated on an outpatient basis. The courts did not adequately monitor these situations but relied too much on the doctors' assessments.

Reputable psychiatrists consult with the parents and the child and normally choose the least invasive treatment that will ameliorate the child's condition. They do not lightly recommend hospitalization.

In particular, if a mentally ill child needs a particularly invasive treatment, such as electroconvulsive therapy or antipsychotic medication, the parents and doctors may have to petition a court to approve the treatment.

There are a number of expensive mental health facilities for children in isolated rural locations that specialize in treating "uncontrollable children." Often the treatment involves a relatively Spartan lifestyle in a disciplined environment with compulsory group and individual therapy. These facilities are sometimes called "behavior modification" facilities.

Sometimes the treatment begins with the unsuspecting child being rousted out of bed in the middle of the night by large, authoritative men. They hustle the child out of the home and onto a plane to a distant state. The representatives of the institution are sometimes ex-police officers or ex-military. Unless the kid is unusually self-possessed, he or she has no opportunity to protest. Surprise, fear, and helplessness, as well as the imposition of adult authority, are part of the process. In one sense, the purpose is to break down the child's self-centered behavior and replace it with a healthier attitude. The resemblance to KGB methods is not accidental, although hopefully the goals are more benign.

Once at the facility, the child may be deprived of any contact with his or her former friends (who may have been a bad influence or a source of illegal drugs) or even his or her family. The school imposes a rigid daily schedule of chores, exercise, therapy, and study. Some of these programs stress taking the child off any psychoactive medication that has been prescribed.

The theory is to take a child out of the self-indulgent, irresponsible, culture of our society and put him or her in a structured environment that teaches self-respect, self-confidence, and respect for the rights of others. The lifestyle complements the therapy; group therapy coordinates with group living. Ideally, the children assume responsibility for chores with their housemates and participate in challenging outdoor activities. At their best, these programs can change a child's life for the better. They can also change the family dynamics by confronting the parents with their role in the child's behavior.

However, some state laws provide that an older adolescent, usually age 16, has the right to refuse to stay at a mental health facility. In all states, a child has a constitutional right to have his or her condition evaluated by an independent fact finder before he or she is confined for treatment. The program might provide an examination by one of the staff but it is unclear whether such an exam is sufficiently independent. Therefore, the practice of transporting an unwilling adolescent over 16 for inpatient treatment is of dubious legality, at best.

Some reputable mental health facilities make clear that any child over 16 has the right to leave the facility and that his or her continued participation must be voluntary. Sometimes, however, there is an informal arrangement with local police that runaways will be returned to the facility without formal legal process. Some question might be raised as to how voluntary a child's choice is in these circumstances.

The best of these programs involve the parents in mandatory therapy also, (although the parents are not imprisoned in the snowy outback). Some get excellent results, and a child whose life might have been ruined by his or her conduct goes on to lead a happy, normal existence. Success often depends on the willingness of the family to change, including the parents, although some children are helped by being removed from an emotionally dysfunctional environment. Unfortunately, if the child returns to ineffective parents who unconsciously enabled or caused the child's problems, any gains made at the facility may be quickly undone.

Education, therapy, and abuse

Parents have the right to determine where their child gets an education, spends his or her vacations, and so on. So, for example, parents can send their children to boarding school, regardless of the child's wishes, provided that the school meets state requirements. Similarly, the parents decide what summer camp their child will attend, whether the kid likes the place or not. (The school or camp may or may not succeed in preventing a rebellious child from simply running away.) There are a variety of facilities for children offering various combinations of education, therapy, discipline, and outdoor experiences. Within wide limits, parents have the legal authority to decide which of these will best suit their children.

The remote mental health facilities described above are not the same as the so-called boot camps. There are a number of facilities for children, especially boys, which impose a life style modeled after a military boot camp. Discipline is rigorous and the program stresses physical challenge and personal responsibility. Often, however, the promoters of these programs have neither psychological nor medical training. The purpose is to change a child's behavior through instilling new values rather than through therapy.

At their worst, these camps legitimize sadism in the name of discipline. Excessive physical discipline, such as requiring a child to stand in the hot desert sun without water, has resulted in children's deaths and criminal prosecution of the organizers. Sick children have been ridiculed for being "whiners" and been refused medical care. Some of these children have died from treatable illnesses.

At their best, these camps give an otherwise normal, if spoiled, child a genuine chance to develop the healthy sense of self-respect that comes from mastering a challenging physical and mental situation.

At one time, boot camps were popular as an alternative to incarceration for juvenile offenders. However, the hopes that rigorous discipline would straighten out teens has not been borne out.

The National Mental Health Association concludes:

Most correctional and military experts agree that a confrontational model, employing tactics of intimidation and humiliation, is counterproductive for most youth in the juvenile justice system. The use of this kind of model has led to disturbing incidents of abuse. For youth of color (who represent the vast majority of the juveniles sentenced to boot camps)-as well as for youth with emotional, behavioral, or learning problems-degrading tactics may be particularly inappropriate and potentially damaging.[9]

A variation on the boot camp theme is residential programs, often located in remote or rural areas where the child lives in a highly structured environment from which he or she cannot easily leave. These schools also stress outdoor activities that build physical confidence and teamwork. These schools may or may not offer formal therapy. The idea usually is to provide a healthy environment with reasonable rules and penalties to accustom the child to conforming to socially accepted values.

All these programs should in turn be distinguished both from established outdoor adventure programs, such as Outward Bound, and from homes for troubled children. These well-established programs may also offer physical challenges and teach responsibility but in a less punitive and restrictive manner. These programs are voluntary on the part of both parents and child.

For example, the Boys Ranch of West Texas has provided a home for many "good boys in bad situations." Boys are admitted to the program only after extensive interviews with the child's family and the boy himself. The program is not for severely troubled boys nor for those who have already committed serious crimes. The boys live in cottages occupied by a husband and wife and their children. This environment provides a model for the child of a family in which everyone has responsibilities and in which the boy's daily life is well-ordered, with parental figures who supervise his schoolwork and his home environment. The ranch also provides the boys with outdoor recreation opportunities, including riding, fishing, and working with cattle.[10]

Alternative living programs like these make the valid point that our current social norms encourage children to be self-indulgent, lazy, and irresponsible. To some extent, parents enable these behaviors also. They may be uncertain of their authority or unwilling to take the time from their jobs to impose a structured daily life on their children. It is hard for a parent who doesn't get home from work until after 9 pm to make sure that the after school hours his or her child spends alone are not spent with video games, drugs, and general indolence. Sending the child to a rigorous boarding school, rural residential program, or boot camp removes the child (to an extent) not only from the corrupting influence of the larger society but also from a home in which the parents have been unable to establish healthy standards of behavior. Such programs, therefore, can be a responsible choice.

It is hard for desperate, angry, frustrated parents to choose a good option for a wayward, obnoxious child, particularly where the child's misconduct is destroying any semblance of normal family life for the rest of the family. A parent who is considering a camp or remote mental health facility should get advice from more than one source.

If the "school" or "camp" is not recommended by a reputable child psychiatrist in your home community, you need to exercise great caution. You should examine your own motives carefully, including considering whether your own rage at the child makes you want to find someone else to treat the child harshly.

A parent who has a rude, defiant, unruly child may feel like a failure as a mother or father. He or she may take out that anger by putting the child in a harsh environment, rather than by taking the responsibility of becoming a better parent. On the other hand, a parent may be at his or her wit's end and utterly unable to cope with a child who is truly out of the parent's control. Ideally, the parents would, if necessary, both provide a more disciplined environment for their child and also devote themselves to being better parents. However, that may not be possible and an alternative living arrangement, even if it is only a strict boarding or military school, may be the only workable solution to a painful family situation.

A degree from a good university and a current state license are no guarantee of good care but they are some protection against outright quackery. At a minimum, any residential mental health treatment of a child should include the following:

- ✓ *Mandatory parental involvement, including therapy;*
- ✓ *Adequate medical professionals at the camp or within easy reach;*
- ✓ *Trained therapists with standard credentials, such as psychologists, psychiatric social workers, and so.*

The staff of a camp, residential school, or home in distinction to a therapeutic facility, should be able to answer responsible questions about the aims and methods of their facility, including clear standards for getting medical care for the campers and the training of the staff.

Any camp or school should satisfy you that both the physical activities and punishments are within reasonable bounds. Many of these programs refer to deprivation of "privileges" for infractions of the camp rules. Forfeiting the camp movie obviously is a reasonable loss of a privilege; deprivation of water in the hot summer is not. It should be clear that the staff understand the limits of their approach and that appropriate precautions for the children's health are taken. You should feel that the lifestyle imposed is in fact a healthy one. Obviously, the camp or school should have the licenses required in your state for such a facility.

You should be aware that many of these facilities require payment of the tuition in advance and make no refunds if the child drops out of the program. Drop out rates can be as high as 50 per cent of the children enrolled.

The legality of boot camps and outdoor schools is not entirely clear. A parent has a right to determine where a child will live. Consequently, the parent can send the child to Bible school, boarding school, summer camp, or boot camp regardless of the child's wishes. In reality, the parents can "commit" a child because the child normally lacks the resources to complain legally or to lodge an effective protest with the appropriate court.

On the other hand, as noted above, a child over the age of 16 has the right to leave a treatment facility unless committed by a court, and every child has the right to an independent determination of whether inpatient psychiatric treatment is medically necessary. In addition, there are legal requirements for attending school and so on. Other relatives may take legal action on the child's behalf if they believe that the situation is abusive or otherwise unlawful. If a camp or school advertises that it changes children's behavior but does not claim to be therapy, these limitations about commitment might not apply, but the camp must still afford an education in accordance with state law. On the other hand, neither a parent nor anyone else has the right to hold an adolescent as a prisoner, at least after the age at which the child would be entitled to be emancipated, which is usually 16. See the discussion below on delinquent and incorrigible children.

Moreover, a parent does not have the right to consent to abuse of his or her child.

The question of abuse is an elastic one. The promoters of one boot camp argue that their program shouldn't be considered abusive because it is modeled after military boot camps. They say, in effect, "If our techniques are unacceptably harsh, then so are those of military training." Well, yes, actually. Military training does involve psychological and physical abuse, but the harsh treatment is, in principle, for a recognized social purpose. The differences are that military recruits are young adults, that the conduct of the instructors is subject to oversight and control by other officers, and that the purpose of the indoctrination is to produce a soldier who will be able to fulfill his or her duties in combat and have some chance of surviving. These points don't apply to an ordinary suburban eleven year old child.

Medical care – a child's right to decide

As a general rule, a doctor or hospital cannot legally provide medical care to a child without the consent of a parent or other authorized person. This is why it is essential that, when a child is cared for another person, the parent provides written authorization for that person to consent to medical care for the child. Otherwise, in an emergency, valuable time might be lost while the parents are located.

In many states, however, an older child has some rights in regard to medical procedures. Ideally, the child should be informed about his or her illness in a manner appropriate to his or her age and involved in care decisions. However, of course, a young child cannot be casually allowed to refuse frightening or even painful procedures; in some situations, however, a child who is terminally ill may have a voice in declining further futile and painful treatment. Doctors are more willingly to forcibly treat small children than an adolescent. If an older child disagrees radically with the treatment course proposed by his or her parents and physicians, the doctors and hospital will usually simply go ahead, regardless of the child's protests. Sometimes, however, the physician or hospital involved may want a court to approve their actions in advance, particularly if other relatives intervene on the child's behalf.

In cases where the parents and doctors disagree, the doctors and court will ideally consult the child as to his or her values and preferences, at least if he or she is old enough to understand what is happening.

A young person's right to consent to medical care is at issue in abortion and birth control cases. Many states have enacted statutes requiring that the parents consent to their daughter's abortion or to any child's receiving birth control. The law is in flux on these points, but in general, an adolescent has the right to obtain information about birth control, including birth control devices such as condoms, without his or her parents' consent and an adolescent girl has some rights to obtain an abortion without notifying her parents (if there is danger of the parents' reactions involving physical abuse), and also to have the procedure, over her parents' objections.

The Supreme Court has held that it is constitutional for a state to require that a doctor notify a minor's parents before performing an abortion on her, unless there is danger of physical abuse. The Court has also held, however, that these statutes must provide a way for the minor to obtain the abortion over her parents' objections. Usually, the statutes provide that the young woman may ask a court to authorize the procedure. The standard is whether (1) "the young woman is mature and capable of giving her informed consent," and (2) she "has in fact given her informed consent" or (3) "the abortion would be in her best interests."[11]

In other words, a minor child does not have the same right to an abortion than an adult woman does. However, her parents do not have the final decision either. The Court recognized that just being old enough to get pregnant did not automatically mean that a child was old enough to make this medical decision but, also, that a young woman who became pregnant had the right to control her own reproductive function.

As noted above, parents do not have an unlimited right to have a child confined in a mental health facility. At a minimum, an independent expert must confirm the need for that treatment; in some circumstances, a formal commitment proceeding may be required, in which case the child will have the opportunity to express his or her wishes. A court may appoint a lawyer or other representative to protect the child's interests and to ascertain whether the proposed confinement is really necessary

Food, clothing, education etc.

As noted above, children in an intact family do not have a right to any particular lifestyle. The parents are free to provide luxuries or to afford only a Spartan lifestyle for their child, so long as his or her basic needs are met. If the parents are vegetarians, they can raise their children on a vegetarian diet, provided that the kids are well-nourished.

Parents can also condition various goodies on the child's compliance with the parents' reasonable wishes, again so long as basic needs are met. In one case, a wealthy lawyer agreed to send his daughter to college but only if she lived in a dormitory. The kid moved into an apartment and sued her father to force him to provide appropriate support for her, meaning, "Pay my bills, Pops." (You have to wonder if the judges didn't get a little chuckle at the spectacle of a rich attorney being sued by his own kid.) The court ruled that the father had the right to require that his daughter follow his rules as a condition of her receiving support from him, at least when the child was over 18 and capable of getting a job.[12]

However, in a divorce, child support payments normally end when the child reaches 18, but some courts have required the parents to pay for college education or even graduate school.[13] See Chapter Fourteen and the relevant Workbook sections (e.g., "Agreement for support and custody of a child — considerations" on page 630) for more information on child support payments.

Support and contracts

One of the most important laws about children is that their right to support cannot usually be waived by a contract between their biological parents. For example, a man may agree to father a child with his lover, provided that she agrees never to ask him to support the child. If she changes her mind about not needing support, or if they split up and she is angry, the rules of the game can change.

Although the law is still somewhat undecided on these issues, a court would probably not honor that agreement, and the father may well end up paying child support anyway. When children are concerned, the courts generally take the position that they act in the "best interests" of the child, and that the parents cannot "sign away" the child's rights. Similarly, the mother cannot agree that the child will not inherit from the father. Likewise, a father who wants a child cannot preclude the child from someday seeking out the mother, even if the father promised the mother that would never happen.

There are, of course, many apparent exceptions to this rule. For example, courts will generally go along with an agreement about custody and support reached by the parents in a divorce. The custodial parent may not want any ongoing contract with the other parent and may be able to provide for the children without his or her financial assistance. The point is, however, that the judge doesn't have to go along with any agreement that the parents make. Usually, he or she will accept any reasonable arrangement that the parents make, but the judge always has the right to change the arrangement in the best interests of the child. Sometimes, especially where the father agreed to father a child for a woman who promised not to ask for support and where the mother waited many years to ask for child support, the courts may be reluctant to require him to make any significant payment

On the other hand, however, a contract that provides that a person will support a child can be enforceable, regardless of whether the child is the biological offspring of that person. In other words, a child may be entitled to support from a person, whether or not that person is a biological parent of the child, if the adult has agreed to support the child.

For example, Helen already had a daughter by another man when she married Michael. Helen and Michael had a son together. When they divorced, neither had a lawyer. Michael agreed to support Helen's daughter, although he had not adopted the child nor was he her biological parent. Later, Michael tried to get out of his child support obligations. The court held that where a stepfather agrees to support a child, that contractual obligation continues after a divorce. The agreement might be oral or written in those states that permit oral agreements; the court might imply an agreement on principles of fairness.[14]

Presumably the same rules would apply whether the couple was married or not. This is an important and difficult point. If a woman lies to a man and tells him falsely that he is the father of her child, the man may believe her and take on the role of a father toward the child. He may take the child into his own home to raise or may agree to a court ruling that declares that he is the father and requires him to pay child support. At some point in the future, the man may discover that the mother lied or was mistaken.

If the man has acted as a father to the child, it would be cruel and damaging to the child for him to abandon that role. On the other hand, he has been cheated; he is making payments that he had no legal obligation to make.

The law is divided on this point. Some courts have held that the man's contract can be set aside because the mother committed fraud when she lied to him. A few courts have even reversed court orders of support when the true facts of paternity were revealed.

Other courts have reasoned that a person who has taken on a parental role toward a child should not be permitted to abandon that child. The child, after all, did not cheat the supposed father.

Uncertainty on this point is why no man should agree to support a child unless either the paternity of the child has been scientifically established or he loves the child and wants to take of him or her regardless of whether he is the father or not.

The obligations of a stepparent to support a child differ from one state to another. Generally, the stepparent must provide support for the child during the marriage but not afterwards. In some states, the stepparent has no obligation toward his or her stepchildren.

The unexpected child

Many men think that they shouldn't have to support a child whom they didn't intend to father. That is not true. For more information on disputes over paternity and support obligations, see Chapter Fifteen and the relevant Workbook sections. Any man who believes that he may have fathered a child, or has been accused of fathering a child, needs to act promptly and on an informed basis to protect his rights. As discussed later, it is my view that no man should allow himself to be identified as the child's father until DNA testing has established the genetic reality of the relationship or not. The exception is where the man loves the child, regardless of his or her parentage, and wishes to take on the role of father to the child.

Here are some claims that will not insulate a man from his obligation to pay child support:

- ✓ *"She told me that she was on the Pill."*
- ✓ *"The condom broke."*
- ✓ *"She told me that she couldn't get pregnant."*
- ✓ *"She promised me that if she got pregnant, she would have an abortion."*
- ✓ *"She is only trying to make me marry her and I don't want to."*

The mother's misconduct does not relieve the father of his obligations to his child. It may seem unfair to some men who expected to have their fun without consequences, but that's the way it is. The child, after all, didn't deceive the man.

Some hypothetical cases may help make these rules more clear.

Case 1

Amy and George are dating. On her 35th birthday, Amy tells George that she is not getting any younger and that she wants to have a child. George shrinks from any kind of commitment but he likes Amy. He agrees to have sexual relations with her without using any kind of contraceptive, and she agrees that if she gets pregnant, she will never ask him to support the baby. She even puts her promise in writing. Sure enough, Amy conceives. George isn't interested in the pregnancy gig and stops calling. After the requisite nine months, Amy gives birth to Georgiana. Amy quickly discovers that single parenthood is not only tiring, but expensive. She goes to court to make George pay her medical bills and child support. George admits he is Georgiana's father but shows the judge the contract saying that Amy won't ask him to pay child support.

Result: George may not have to pay Amy's personal medical bills but he will likely have to pay child support for Georgiana at least until she is 18. Amy could not legally sign away Georgiana's rights to support from her father. George also has a right to visitation with Georgiana, unless he is shown to be abusive or otherwise unfit.

Case 2

Mary and Fred want to have children, but Fred had a vasectomy many years ago. Fred agrees that if Mary has sex with their mutual friend George and gets pregnant, he (Fred) will support the child, just as if it were "his own." George fathers a child with Mary. Fred becomes insanely jealous and reneges on his agreement. Mary sues Fred for child support.

Result: Fred may well have to support the child based on his contract, but the law on this is uncertain. In some informal surrogate parenting cases, the non-biological father has been excused from his obligation. George, however, is probably responsible for this kid too.

Case 3

After he breaks up with Amy and in between trysts with Mary, George moves in with Liz. George is sick of paying child support, and he gets Liz to agree that if she gets pregnant, she will have an abortion. She promises that if she doesn't have an abortion, he will have no obligation to support the child. Liz, of course, gets pregnant by George. She refuses to have an abortion. George goes to court, asking the judge to either order Liz to have an abortion or rule that George has no obligation to the child.

Result: George, the cad, loses again.

A woman's right to choose whether or not to have an abortion cannot be signed away by a contract; no judge in his or her right mind is going to force a healthy woman to abort a healthy baby, just because the father wants the abortion.

To inherit

At one time, a child's right to inherit from his or her father (and consequent social status as an heir) were largely determined by whether the child's parents were legally married at the time of the child's birth. The Supreme Court of the United States has ruled that states cannot discriminate against acknowledged illegitimate children in inheritance matters, because, in effect, it was not the kid's fault that his parents led an immoral life. Therefore, if a parent dies without a will, then the children inherit from that parent, whether they were born in wedlock or not. State law sets out the shares that each child receives from a deceased parent who dies without a valid will. The shares vary depending on the number of children and whether there is a surviving spouse or not.

However, the legal requirements for establishing the paternity of an out of wedlock child must have been fulfilled.

By will

If a parent writes a will, he or she is not required to leave a child any share of his or her estate. The sole exception is Louisiana where a child cannot be disinherited unless he or she has attempted to murder the parent.

Moreover, a parent is free to pick and choose among his or her children as to who will inherit and who will not, provided that the parent executes a valid will. A person can leave his or her property to legitimate descendants or illegitimate descendants or those who are born of a marriage (as opposed to those who are adopted), etc. Since testamentary dispositions (gifts by will) often apply to more than one generation, the effect can be far-reaching. Many wills and trusts still limit inheritance to legitimate biological descendants.

For example, consider the family of wealthy Grandpa Frederick, his son Fred, and his grandson Little Freddy. Suppose that Grandpa Frederick executes a will leaving everything to "my son Fred or if he should die before me, then to the legitimate heirs of his body." That language refers to Fred's legitimate biological children and to their descendants. It excludes children born out of wedlock and adopted children. If Fred died before Grandpa Frederick and Little Freddy was the biological child of Fred and his wife, then Little Freddy would inherit Grandpa's millions when Grandpa finally died. If, however, Fred had not married Little Freddy's mother or if the child had been adopted, then Little Freddy would not inherit.

Although it may be a crass reason to marry, limitations on inheritance may be worth considering if you or your significant other stand to inherit from a wealthy relative or if either of you is the beneficiary of a family trust. Many, if not most, trust documents and wills limit inheritance to the legitimate, biological children of a married couple. Deciding to have children without getting married may deprive your children of their share of the family fortune.

By intestacy – when a parent dies without a will

A person who dies without having written a valid will is said to die "intestate." (A will is a "testamentary" document and an intestate person is one without a testament.) There is more information in Chapter Fifteen on inheritance. This section only discusses the rights of children to inherit from their parents.

If there is no will, state law determines who inherits. In every state, a person's children are his or her heirs if there is no will. If the deceased was not married at the time of death, then usually his or her entire estate will be divided among his children. If he or she was married, their shares depend on state law, which divides the person's property between the surviving spouse and the children.

Moreover, children inherit whether they were born in wedlock or out of wedlock, provided that the legal requirements for proving their parentage have been satisfied. States have varying time limits, for example, within which a child must establish that he or she is the child of a particular man.

Adopted children inherit equally with biological children, from a parent who dies intestate. It is important to realize, however, that this rule only applies to legally adopted children. No matter how close you are to your significant other's children, they will not inherit from you unless you have either adopted them or named them in your will. If you and your lover (or spouse) have a blended family, and if you want all of the children to inherit from both of you, it is critically important that either you both adopt each other's children or, if that is not possible, that you both have valid wills that set out exactly who inherits what from whom.

If a parent's rights are terminated by a court, as where someone else legally adopts the child, then the child no longer has the right to inherit from his or her biological parents.

To be free from abuse and neglect

The right of a child to be free from physical abuse has been recognized for many years. Now our society is coming to recognize that children may also have a right to be free from emotional abuse. The notion of abuse is highly ambiguous, however, and varies with social and religious standards.

Parents can be guilty of great cruelty toward their children, ranging from physical beatings to years of starvation and neglect. No one can remain unmoved at the sight of children whose psychopathic parents have kept them locked in closets or attics for years at a time, causing profound psychological and physical damage. In one case, a mother locked her three children away in her house and starved them; when the children were discovered, the oldest girl was 15 but her growth had been so stunted that she was the size of a normal ten-year old.

Moreover, there is now convincing evidence that many instances of sexual abuse were concealed or ignored by those who could and should have helped the children. Prudish teachers and clergy not only denied children's allegations of sexual abuse, including incest and sexual exploitation by clergymen, but punished the children for making up such scandalous "lies." Even Sigmund Freud, who helped create the science of psychology, vacillated about whether his patients' accounts of incest in "respectable" families were true memories of actual events or childish sexual fantasies.

On the other hand, the so-called helping professions have also been guilty of infringing on the right of conscientious parents to raise their children as they believe best. Driven by rigid and unproven psychological theories, such as the premise that children are incapable of lying about sexual matters, some social workers have torn families apart and deprived children of loving parents.

A parent has a duty not only to refrain from abusing a child but also to protect the child from abuse at the hands of others. It is a crime for a parent to stand by while a child is abused physically or sexually by another person. If the parent cannot prevent the abuse, he or she has a legal duty to report it to the appropriate authorities. Constitutional rights of privacy do not protect physical or sexual abuse of children.

Similarly, the right to free exercise of religion does not protect sexual conduct with children, such as arranged marriages of young girls. See page 266 below for more information on the legal consequences of abuse and neglect of children.

Moreover, in many states, doctors, nurses, teachers, and others who are know that a child is being abused have a legal duty to report the abuse. **This can put psychologists an**d other therapists in an untenable ethical position; their duty of confidentiality protects their patients' secrets and revealing hidden conduct can be the only way to get help, but, on the other hand, reporting laws require that the therapist reveal child abuse to the authorities to protect the child.

Failing to report abuse can result in an accusation of participation in the abuse. In theory, a man who lived with a woman and who knew that she was physically abusing or neglecting her children could be prosecuted for failing to report the abuse to the authorities.

Discipline and physical abuse

The law permits a parent to exercise reasonable discipline over his or her children.

There was a time in the United States when cultural norms extended the right to discipline children to any responsible adult acquainted with the child. My father, who was born in 1915 and grew up in Columbus, Ohio, remembered well the time when some boys through stones at a passing car. The driver pursued them in righteous indignation. There was no question that the man would have thrashed the boys if he had caught one of them and no question that they would have felt that he was entitled. In the 1920's, neighbors felt free to chastise misbehaving children, at least verbally, and to physically take them home to outraged parents.

Those days are gone. Even teachers are limited in the physical discipline that they can impose, at least without the parents' written consent. School administrators cannot suspend a child from school for a significant period without affording some form of fair process.

The notion of "reasonable" is an elastic one that varies with one's cultural background. Some people consider any physical correction of a child beyond a mild slap on the bottom as physical abuse (and some experts regard even a mild spanking as harmful to the child's development). Some people believe that a whipping with a belt on the bottom is reasonable and salutary, while many would regard it as excessive or even child abuse.

For example, a father was convicted of child abuse when he whipped his daughter with a belt. His 15 year old daughter skipped school. When she came home, he hit her on her legs, arms, neck, and back over 20 times. He did not inflict any lasting physical injury. The court found that beating exceed any proper discipline.[15]

Some conservative religious groups encourage parents to physically discipline their children. Child development experts disagree over the desirability of these practices; at least one has offered substantial evidence that conservative Christian parents who physically disciplined their children also offered them more expressions of love than less conservative parents. Frequent expressions of love and affection are widely considered to be an indication of good parenting.

Any significant deprivation of food or shelter or clothing beyond being sent to bed without supper (and even that may be criticized) is likely to be considered abusive.

The critical fact for cohabiting lovers is that permission does not extend to people unrelated to the child. In other words, a spanking that *might* be lawful if administered by a father could legally be abuse if administered by the mother's live in boyfriend. The boyfriend does not have the natural relationship of a parent to a child. Most people assume that most parents love their children and want the best for them. There is no such assumption for the parent's lover.

To be prudent, therefore, an unmarried adult should refrain entirely from physically chastising his or her lover's children.

Of course, if you are thinking of moving in with a lover who has children, you should discuss the subject of discipline for the children before you move in together. Like married parents, a cohabiting couple should agree on the rules for the children.

But, even if your lover encourages you to whip a misbehaving child, it is legally imprudent for you to do so. The parent should be the one who metes out discipline for breaches of whatever rules have been agreed on, at least physical discipline. The parent's consent does not legalize a lover's conduct because a parent cannot legally agree to let a child be abused. In fact, the parent has a legal obligation to prevent abuse of the child.

Finally, there is the obvious risk that a parent may condone his or her lover's actions when the relationship is going well and condemn them when the relationship has soured. For example, a mother may tolerate, or even appreciate, her boyfriend disciplining her rowdy son when Mom and Boyfriend are getting along. If the boyfriend moves out, however, a malicious Mom and an angry child can claim that the lover's actions went beyond proper correction to abuse.

Similarly, a vengeful ex-spouse, who has lost a battle over custody of his or her children, may seek a change in custody by accusing the custodial parent's lover (or even new spouse) of mistreating the children.

A lover is not legally a parent. The courts will not judge your conduct with whatever indulgence they grant to a (supposedly) loving parent. Depending on the values of the authorities involved, at best, you are the parent's boyfriend or girlfriend; at worst, you are a person living a deliberately immoral life who slapped his lover's kid around. Not an attractive picture.

Sexual abuse

The sad fact is that any man in today's society who spends time alone with a little girl or boy in private, especially if the girl is not his daughter, runs some risk of being accused of sexually molesting the child. The more tragic fact is that some men do take advantage of innocent occasions to sexually molest children.

It may be unfair but a woman's actions with children are less likely to be interpreted as sexual in nature, perhaps because our society presumes that women are caretakers of children, not exploiters. When sexual conduct between an adult woman and an underage boy comes to light, it usually involves an adolescent child who is physically capable of the sexual act, rather than a small boy. The number of cases of sexual abuse brought against women is extremely small in comparison to the number brought against men.

Sexual abuse can take a variety of forms, ranging from an adult exposing himself or herself to a child to perverted intercourse. Sexual abuse by heterosexual men of little girls is far more common than abuse of a little boy by a homosexual man. Some male sexual predators abuse both little girls and little boys.

The sexual dynamics in a family are complicated. Children learn their sexual roles in part by acting out their impulses toward their parents and other important adults in their life.

Little girls can be sexy and can flirt charmingly with the man in Mother's life. Little boys can offer their manly protection to Dad's girlfriend. These behaviors are normal. Current fashions encourage parents to dress little girls in styles that imitate those worn by sexy adult celebrities, which can set the stage for precocious sexual behavior.

It is the responsibility of adults to restrain their own conscious or unconscious temptation to be drawn into inappropriate participation in the children's actions and to set clear limits on their response to the child's behavior. Even if a child is seductive, it is the adult's responsibility to refuse any inappropriate contact.

Many experts now believe that overzealous therapists inadvertently create false memories of child abuse in their patients' minds. A therapist can inadvertently coach a young child to describe sexual conduct, particularly when the therapist uses an anatomically correct doll in interviewing the child and asks leading questions such as "Did Uncle Billy touch you here?" If the therapist believes that the child has been abused, his or her body language may convey to the child that a "yes" answer is the only correct one. Moreover, a young child may not be capable of distinguishing between innocent touching, such as bathing, and erotic contact.

On the other hand, many sexual predators tell the child to keep the behavior secret, sometimes by threatening to harm the child's family if he or she tells anyone. A skilled investigator needs to work with the child with great care to uncover these secrets while not inadvertently coaching the child in an inaccurate account.

An older, intelligent child can make a false accusation, perhaps out of jealousy or dislike of the new man in Mom's life or perhaps to side with a non-custodial father. If the child has been sexually active with anyone, then a medical examination may support the allegation, at least to the extent of possibly establishing whether he or she has been sexually active. In other words, for example, if your fourteen year old step daughter has had intercourse with her boy friend, a gynecological examination will reveal that she has had intercourse, but unless a scientific examination of any trace evidence, such as a DNA examination of any semen that is present, is done, there will not be any medical evidence of the identity of her lover.

Some clear boundaries can be set, while others are a matter of judgment and context. Here are some suggestions as to some relatively clear, prudent, boundaries:

- ✓ *An adult should not have manual contact with a young child's genitals except for normal, routine care such as changing diapers and bathing. (It goes without saying that any contact between the mouth of an adult and the genitals of a child is sexual in nature and clearly unacceptable.)*
- ✓ *There is never a legitimate occasion for a child to have contact with an adult's genitals.*

There are few legitimate reasons for an adult to have physical contact with the genitals of a child old enough to dress himself or herself. The exceptions would be where the child has a physical problem, in which case the treatment would normally be overseen by a physician. For example, a child with the flu might need to have medicine administered by suppository.

✓ *Experts disagree about when the age at which it is no longer healthy for a parent of the opposite sex to bathe a child. Clearly, this is a matter of judgment. For safety reasons, the adult may want to be present or close by while the child is bathing. As a matter of prudence, however, an unrelated partner of the parent should refrain from physical contact with a nude child who is old enough to bathe himself or herself.*

✓ *Some adults disguise their unconscious desire to have sexual contact with children by an imagined or exaggerated medical need, such as the "need" to examine the child's backside for "worms" or the child's "need" for frequent enemas.*

Except on a doctor's direction, parents who find themselves frequently "needing" to apply ointment to their children's genitals (after the children are out of diapers) or to take an apparently healthy child's temperature with a rectal thermometer may need to consider whether their actions have an erotic component and should seek psychiatric help.

✓ *As a matter of prudence and good sense, casual nudity by adults in front of children should be avoided.*

Sex education does not include live-on-stage show and tell. Occasionally glimpsing Mom or Dad in the shower is not going to damage a child for life, but an adult's repeatedly exposing him or herself to a child can be harmful. A child of the same sex as the parent may be intimidated by the appearance of the adult's body; a child of the opposite sex may be unduly stimulated by it. In other words, a little boy who sees an adult man in the nude may wonder why his own penis is so much smaller. A little girl in the same situation may be sexually stimulated in a way that she is not ready to understand. That said, families differ widely in their comfort with nudity in the home. Many people believe in a relatively open attitude toward their bodies and want their children to accept their bodies as something healthy, not something to be concealed as shameful. An unrelated person living in the household should keep in mind, however, that a judge may not have the same elastic values.

✓ *Sexual conduct with your lover in front of the child is harmful to the children and can be a form of sexual abuse. Exposing the children to sexual scenes can be the grounds for a court taking custody away from the parent involved.*

The following guidelines are primarily for male live-in lovers, but some of them also apply to parents. All of them, again, are a matter of judgment and personal values. These are prudent suggestions, not statements of the law.

✔ *Do not bathe or shower with children. Adults should stay out of the bathroom when an older child or adolescent is bathing or dressing or using the toilet. An exception would be to accompany a child to a public rest room.*

✔ *If you are in the child's bedroom with him or her for any reason, leave the door open and the lights on.*

✔ *Do not permit the child to be nude in your presence, unless you are performing some ordinary task at the mother's request like dressing a toddler or helping him or her put on a swimsuit.*

✔ *Do not sleep in the child's bed or allow him or her to sleep in yours.*

✔ *Keep your clothes on in the child's presence. Do not allow him or her to be in the bathroom with you when you are using the toilet or bathing.*

✔ *If you want to go camping or on any overnight trip with the child, take advantage of group excursions. Go with another guy and his kids or with a scout troop, for instance.*

✔ *Put a lock or bolt on your bedroom door and make sure the door is locked when you and your partner wish to be intimate. Better yet, limit your overnight stays to the weekends or nights when the child is with his or her other parent.*

✔ *Do not move in with the child's parent unless you intend the relationship to be a lasting one.*

✔ *Gay men should keep in mind that many people believe that all homosexual men desire sex with little boys. Their conduct needs to be especially circumspect.*

When his partner's children are between the ages of two and puberty, a man must use his own judgment as to his conduct with them. It would be a shame to deprive a little boy or girl of having a loving stepfather read a bedtime story to him or her every night, particularly if the biological father is not taking an active role in the child's life. Similarly, it would be unfortunate if a kindly man could not take a lonely boy on a "guys only" fishing trip. Regrettably, these innocent occasions have been used by sexual predators as a cover for sexual conduct with the children.

Different behavior is appropriate with adolescent children. It is prudent for an unrelated man to stay out of the bedroom of an adolescent girl (who is not his daughter) when she is in bed or undressed. A gay man should observe the same precautions with an adolescent boy.

Allegations of sexual abuse are all too easy to make and all too difficult to refute, but, on the other hand, it is easy to slip from innocent play to erotic involvement. For example, a nude photograph of a little girl in the tub may seem charming and innocent to some people but to others may appear uncomfortably erotic in nature (and may actually involve a conscious or unconscious erotic element). Possession of such a picture could be considered the possession of child pornography. A jury is much more likely to regard such a picture as innocent in the hands of a doting father than in the hands of Mom's live-in lover.

One of the most important things to remember is that a mother's consent to her significant other's conduct is no defense to a prosecution for child abuse. In a custody proceeding, a mother's consent may actually be the basis for a judge's changing custody from her to the father. Her consent could be the basis of charges of child neglect or abuse against her as well as her lover. The reason is that the custodial parent has an obligation to protect the children; if she consents to behavior by her significant other that is later determined to be abusive or inappropriate, the court may find that her consent was a form of neglect or at least inadequate parenting.

In any court proceeding, therefore, the mother may well decide to deny that she ever consented to her lover's conduct. Regardless, her personal feeling that it would be OK, for example, for her lover to swim in the nude with her young daughters will carry very little weight with an outraged family court judge who has very different notions of propriety.

Obviously, this advice applies to fathers, too. For example, a father cannot legally consent to his underage daughter having sexual intercourse with a man. Therefore, a father does not have the authority to marry his daughter off in an arranged marriage, regardless of his religious or cultural background. In some states, the "husband" in this situation can be prosecuted for statutory rape even if he and the girl have gone through some form of marriage ceremony. See below at page 259 for more information about the age of consent.

For example, there is the case of Adam and his friends. Adam's old friend Bob married Mabel, who had a 13-year-old daughter, Eve. Mabel and Bob believed in their own version of an ancient pagan religion and followed its rites as they imagined them to have been. Therefore, they enlisted Adam's "help" to give Eve her first sexual experience on one of their holidays because they wanted that experience to be a "good"

one, in their home, etc. Adam had some form of intimate contact with Eve, who seemed more than willing. Adam later denied that they had sexual intercourse. Bob took some nude photos of Eve and Mabel and emailed them to Adam.

Eve told her school counselor that she had sexual contact with Adam. In the ensuring prosecution, the family's unorthodox ideas about sexual initiation carried no weight at all. All of the adults were charged with child abuse — Mabel for permitting Adam's and Bob's conduct, Adam for the sexual conduct, and Bob for the pornographic pictures. Mabel persuaded the jury that she didn't know what was happening, so she escaped being convicted for child abuse but lost custody of Eve to her ex-husband. Adam and Bob were convicted, served time in jail, and must register as sex offenders for the rest of their lives. Their friends, family, and prospective employers can check out their mug shots on the state's sex offender web site. Both men are barred from contact with children and prohibited from visiting any place such as a school where there are likely to be children. Neither Eve's consent nor Mabel's complicity nor the family's religious beliefs formed any legal defense to the adults' conduct.

QUESTION: *"What is the age of consent?"*

ANSWER: *The age of consent is the age at which a person can lawfully give consent to sexual relations. Sexual relations with a person less than that age are a crime.*

The age of consent in the United States varies from 16 to 18. These laws are a tangle of exceptions that vary from state to state. The basic rule is that sex with a person under the age of consent is a crime. This conduct and its criminal consequences go by various names including "statutory rape," "indecency with a minor," "felony child seduction," and others.

The key point here is that the underage person cannot lawfully give consent to any form of sexual contact, whether vaginal intercourse, sodomy, oral intercourse, or other forms of intimate touching. The limits on what constitutes the prohibited sexual contact can be somewhat vague. Usually, the prohibited conduct involves some genital contact by one or the other. In some states, statutory rape only consists in actual sexual penetration. But, the sexual conduct may violate some other law, such as indecency with a minor or contributing to the delinquency of a minor.

In other words, a hug is not (usually) legally sexual abuse, although it may be psychologically abusive if it is unwelcome or unduly intimate.

In a few states, the age of consent for homosexual conduct is higher, than that for heterosexual intercourse: for example, the relevant age of consent may be 18 when the age for heterosexual conduct is 16. Sometimes the higher age expressly applies only to male homosexual conduct, so the inference is that lesbian conduct is governed by the lower age. The statutes don't say this explicitly, however.

There are other variations. In Massachusetts, for example, the age of consent is 16 unless the person is 16 or 17 years old and also a virgin, in which case the conduct is a crime. In some states, the age of consent varies depending on the age of the other partner. In still others, it depends on whether the couple is married or not.

There are also additional restrictions on teachers and other people in a position of authority over a child. In those cases, the age of consent is higher, usually 18. In some states, a minor cannot legally consent even to "French kissing" a teacher.

MYTH—*"I can't get in trouble for having sex with my boyfriend even if he is less than 16 because I'm not that much older than he is."*

FACT—*In most states, sex with an underage person is illegal, regardless of the age of the other lover. Some states have limited exceptions for people approximately the same age.*

The purpose of laws prohibiting sexual conduct with minors is to protect children from sexual involvement that they are not mature enough to make a sensible decision about or to refuse.

Most of these laws, however, aim at preventing sexual exploitation of young people by older adults, especially young girls or boys by older men. The laws are not necessarily intended to prevent young people from having sex. Therefore, some states have "Romeo and Juliet" laws. Under those laws, sexual conduct with a minor is not statutory rape if the older person is close to the minor in age. For example, in Kansas, if both lovers are under 18 and no more than five years apart in age, then the penalty for their sexual conduct is only 15 months in jail. In other words, the conduct is still a crime, but the penalties are not as severe as for an adult who engages in sex with a minor. In Tennessee, for example, the conduct is legal if the couple are between 13 and 18 and are no more than four years apart in age. In other words, two fourteen year-olds can lawfully have sex in that state, as can a 17 year old and a 13 year old.

MYTH—*"I can't get in trouble for having sex with my girlfriend even if she is less than 16 because if she gets pregnant, we'll just get married."*

FACT—*Sex with an underage girl before marriage is illegal, even if the couple later marries. Some states (but not all) permit a married couple to have sex even if one of them is underage.*

In 2005, the state of Nebraska prosecuted a 22 year old man for sexual misconduct with a minor because he had sex with a 13 year old girl. When she got pregnant, her mother agreed to let them get married. The couple went to Kansas to marry, because Kansas permits minors to marry with parental consent and Nebraska does not. They then returned to Nebraska to live. The Nebraska prosecutor filed charges against the man for sexual abuse of a child (statutory rape).

The possible punishment was 50 years in prison. The child bride was seven months pregnant at the time. The fact that the couple had legally married in another state was not considered a defense. Other states have varying exceptions for sexual conduct between married persons, even if one of them is underage. Obviously, this exception depends the marriage being a valid one, i.e. both people must at least have been old enough to legally marry. In some states, a girl as young as 13 can marry if her parents agree.

Cohabitation and children

Anyone who is contemplating living with a lover who has children should consider seriously the effect of the living arrangement on those children. This is so whether the living arrangement is to be a marriage or not.

The children's potential relationship with their parent's lover deserves as much, if not more, thoughtful consideration as the relationship of the lovers. The presence of another adult in the household necessarily affects the children. The behavior of the significant adults in their life models adult relationships for children. If the parents have a series of casual live in arrangements, the child can absorb the lesson that adult relationships do not last. That lesson can make it difficult for the child to have a lasting marriage when he or she grows up.

Even more importantly, if the child forms a meaningful attachment to the parent's lover, he or she suffers a grievous loss when that adult moves out.

A parent having uncommitted live-in relationships may impair his or her child's emotional development. The child may stifle his or her desire to form attachments for fear of being hurt when the adults' relationship ends.

Special issues – gay and lesbian parents

In most states, the sexual orientation of the respective parents should not determine which parent gets primary custody in a divorce. See Chapter Fifteen on ending a relationship and Chapter Four for more information on these issues.

The American Psychological Association has adopted a strong resolution in favor of non-discrimination against homosexual people in child custody, adoption, and other child related issues. That resolution includes the following:

Research has shown that the adjustment, development, and psychological well-being of children is unrelated to parental sexual orientation and that the children of lesbian and gay parents are as likely as those of heterosexual parents.

The association cited census data to the effect that at least half a million households the United States are comprised of gay or lesbian couples; the figures are estimated to be slightly more than 300,000 male couples and about 293,000 female couples.[16]

In the present political climate, however, gay and lesbian lovers and parents may need to adjust their conduct to the social expectations of the community in which they live. Conduct that is seen as ordinary and harmless in San Francisco or Chicago may be perceived as suspicious or immoral in Fort Worth.

Some people in the United States believe that there is a "homosexual agenda" to convert others to "a homosexual lifestyle." The gay rights movement is not seen as a civil liberties movement but as an effort to proselytize for homosexual conduct. Homosexuality is not seen as a sexual orientation that is an inherent part of a person, but as a deliberate choice of an immoral lifestyle, one that the Bible condemns as an "abomination." On that viewpoint, it is believed that homosexual parents or lovers will try to convert children in their home to homosexuality and that children are vulnerable to being convinced to "choose" homosexuality.

Many supporters of gay rights disagree with such a characterization of the gay rights movement and homosexuality in general. However, some of the rhetoric calling for change in the laws and social conventions about families is frankly radical. Some groups have called for the "deconstruction of the American family." Many people might agree with social and legal changes to recognize that the traditional nuclear family is no longer typical of American society, but radical language about the end of the traditional family can and does make even some moderately liberal people uncomfortable.

Also, as noted earlier, many people believe that all homosexual men desire sex with young boys. The fact that by far the greatest number of sexual predators are heterosexual men who seek intercourse with young girls has not changed this perception.

The falsity of these perceptions does not mean that gay and lesbian people can ignore them. The social and scientific facts about the actual composition of American families are not irrelevant, but they may not keep a gay couple from legal hassles.

In conservative states with a large fundamentalist population or if there is an ongoing custody dispute in any state, gay and lesbian parents and their lovers would be well advised to be careful of the appearances they create. For example, if a couple of good ol' boys from the local Baptist church take their sons deer hunting and they all go skinny dipping in Grandpa's swimming hole, a family judge in a rural county might not see anything objectionable. If, however, a father and his homosexual partner do the same thing, the reaction might be very different.

Courts are particularly sensitive to homosexual or lesbian conduct seen by the children. Gay and lesbian lovers should exercise particularly conservative judgment in their conduct toward each in front of the children if there has been any dispute over custody.

Termination and limitation of parental rights

The legal relationship of parent and child changes when the child reaches eighteen, is adopted, or is emancipated. Parental rights can also be terminated or limited in cases of abuse.

The grown up child

When a child legally becomes a legal adult, the parents no longer have the duty to support the child. A child becomes an adult when he or she reaches the age of 18 or is emancipated.

An emancipated child is one who has assumed the social role of an adult. Usually, this means that the child has moved out of his or her parents' home and become economically self-supporting. In most cases, the child has voluntarily left home. An indifferent parent who kicks the kid out cannot usually then claim that the child is emancipated. He or she remains obligated to support the child. A court proceeding is sometimes brought to formally establish that the child is emancipated. Sometimes this is necessary in order for a young person to apply for financial aid at a school, for example, because he or she needs to prove that his or her parents are not legally obligated to provide support.

The delinquent or uncontrollable child

Sometimes, the parent of an uncontrollable child will exclude the child from the family home, either to end intolerable family turmoil or to protect themselves and other children from violence or from exposure to drugs and criminal behavior. In that situation, the courts and social service agencies may become involved. The uncontrollable child may still be considered legally dependent on the parents, but in a legal status usually called "dependent and in need of assistance." Ideally, in these situations, less emphasis on blaming the parent, as compared to abuse and neglect cases, and more emphasis on the family's situation. In an abuse case, the parent has little excuse; in some dependency cases, the parents' conduct is understandable.

Social workers may make an effort to reunite the family or they may place the child in foster care. If the child is truly delinquent or unmanageable, the child may be placed in an institution, either a mental hospital or a juvenile detention center. The parents' obligations to continue to pay for the support of the child vary in these circumstances, depending on the child's conduct and mental health, the parents' resources, and so on. A judge can decide that an older child is so out of control that he or she should be committed to the care of an institution. The court may also determine that the parents' normal role is impossible and that the child should be considered emancipated or the parental relationship otherwise terminated.

Frequently, a difficult or uncontrollable child may also be breaking the law, ranging from truancy (not attending school) to use of illegal drugs to serious crimes. The subject of the juvenile justice system is beyond the scope of this book. however, it affects the rights of parents and children so some discussion is in order.

A person who commits a crime while under the age of 18 is treated differently by the legal system than an adult who commits the same crime. Usually, the case against the child is handled in a separate court system. The penalties are milder and the child, if necessary, is sent to a special facility for children who have committed crimes, rather than to prison. Usually, these arrangements are intended, theoretically, to reform the kid, and any confinement ends when the child reaches 18. Like prisons, juvenile facilities are often schools for criminals, and abuse by guards and other juveniles is common.

If the child's offense is relatively minor, the court may send the child to a foster home, for example, to remove the child from a bad environment. He or she may agree that the child be sent to a boarding school, especially if the parents can pay for a military school or boarding school oriented toward reform of the child's behavior.

In principle, records of crimes committed by juveniles are sealed, meaning that almost no one can gain access to them.

If, however, the person is old enough and the crime serious enough, such as murder, the prosecutor may seek to handle the case as if the perpetrator were an adult.

In that situation, the "child" goes to prison if convicted. The state cannot execute a person who commits a capital offense while under the age of 17, however.

Parents can petition to be relieved of any further responsibility for an adolescent that is truly out of control, especially if criminal conduct is involved. Such a child may be called "incorrigible." A court or social service agency may then try to place the child in a facility for troubled children, ranging from a foster home to a mental hospital. A court can also effectively commit a child to a residential school or other facility.

As noted above, in these situations, the parents may be encouraged or required to seek therapy or to attend classes on effective parenting. The policy is to try to preserve a functioning family, if possible. If the family simply does not work, then the legal parent/child relationship can be terminated by a court.

There are some situations in which a child poses a danger to the rest of the family. As with any dangerous person, families have tried to use the legal system for protection, by getting restraining orders and so on. Tragically, these measures are often not effective if the child is truly out of control and vicious. Sometimes, the family simply moves away, leaving no forwarding address, while the child is out of the house. While technically, this may be abandonment of a child and the parents may still legally be liable to support the child (if their obligation has not been terminated by a court), sometimes it seems to be the family's only recourse.

In these situations, the rights of children and parents are changed by the state's involvement. The parents' rights to decide about their child's life may be limited or overruled by court decisions, while the child's preferences may also be overruled by the decisions of others. If the parents, for example, have their parental responsibility terminated, the child no longer has the right to look to them for support, medical care, etc. He or she must either fend for himself or herself or, more likely, be cared for by some facility chosen by a social worker or court.

The impaired child

Parents can petition a court to commit a mentally ill child to a mental hospital or similar facility for treatment. In that case, as with any effort to compel a person to get treatment for mental illness, the child's wishes are simply overruled. As a general rule, the parents of a severely handicapped child have considerable latitude in deciding to place the child in an institution. Although many parents choose to provide their handicapped children with as normal a home life as possible, others believe that institutional care is better for the family. If the child is severely disabled, institutional care may be the only feasible alternative. Legally speaking, most courts are inclined to follow the parents' decision. Sometimes, matters are arranged without formal legal proceedings, especially if the child's physician encourages institutional placement.

The parental obligation to support a child continues after the child becomes 18 if the child is mentally or physically disabled. A disabled child may be eligible for various governmental benefits, such as supplemental social security income. Sometimes, these payments can be made to the parents, if they are responsible in handling the funds for the child's benefit. If control of the money is given to the parents, they need not spend it directly for the child. Using the money to repair the family home, for example, may be considered a proper use because it benefits the child who lives there.

The adopted child

Adoption ends the legal relationship of the child to his or her birth parents. The birth parents legal status as parents is terminated in the adoption proceeding. They no longer have obligations of support to the child. The child does not have a right to inherit from his or her birth parents unless mentioned in their will. The adopted child, however, acquires the right to inherit from his or her adoptive parents unless disinherited by their will. In other words, in an adoption, the adoptive parents acquire the legal status of parent and the birth parents lose that status. Adoption is discussed further at page 304 below.

The abused or neglected child

The law distinguishes between children who are not receiving proper care and those whose parents are abusing them. Different states have different terms for a neglected child. Some refer to "dependent children" and others to a child "in need of assistance." The legal consequences to the parents and children are not much different whether the determination is that the children were abused or merely neglected. In either case, the legal relationship of parent and child can be changed

The Pennsylvania standard for a dependent child is where the child is not receiving "proper parental care or control necessary for his physical, mental, or emotional health, or morals." In Maryland, a court described the standard as where" the child's heal or welfare is harmed or placed at substantial risk of harm or the child has suffered mental injury to been placed at substantial risk of mental injury,"[17]

When a social service agency determines that a child is dependent or abused, the courts can change the legal relationship of parent and child. An agency can place the child temporarily in foster care. The agency can petition a court to terminate the parents' rights permanently or can seek various intermediary solutions, such as leaving the child in foster care while the parents seek counseling or substance abuse treatment. It can also include putting limits on the parent child relationship, such as having a social worker check up on the children.

As one court put it:

the trial court, in making a best-interests determination, is charged with the daunting task of weighing and balancing the following statutory factors, all in light of the child's age and developmental needs:

> *(a) the physical safety and welfare of the child;*
>
> *(b) the development of the child's identity;*
>
> *(c) the child's background and ties;*
>
> *(d) the child's sense of attachments, including:*
>
>> *(i) where the child actually feels love, attachment, and a sense of being valued;*
>>
>> *(ii) the child's sense of security;*
>>
>> *(iii) the child's sense of familiarity;*
>
> *(iv) continuity of affection for the child;*
>
> *(v) the least disruptive placement alternative for the child;*
>
> *(e) the child's wishes and long-term goals;*
>
> *(f) the child's community ties, including church, school, and friends;*
>
> *(g) the child's need for permanence;*
>
> *(h) the uniqueness of every family and child;*
>
> *(i) the risks attendant to entering and being in substitute care; and*
>
> *(j) the preferences of the persons available to care for the child.*[18]

In that case, a child had been savagely abused by the mother's boyfriend; despite her successful completion of extensive therapy and parental training, the trial court ruled that the mother was an unfit parent because of her pervasive failure to protect her child. The decision of the appellate court, however, required the lower court to reconsider that ruling in light of the high importance placed on a parent's rights.

Under applicable Supreme Court decisions, a parent's right to be with his or her child is so important that the state must show by clear and convincing evidence that the parent neglects or abuses his or her child and that the best interests of the child would be served by terminating the parental relationship.[19]

Terminating a parent's connection with his or her child requires a court to determine both whether the parent's misconduct justifies severing the relationship and whether the best interests of the child will be served by doing so. The standard of proof required from state agencies is higher than in ordinary lawsuits, although not as strict as the "beyond a reasonable doubt" standard applicable to criminal cases.

In principle, the fact that a child has been in foster care because of a parent's neglect or abuse does not justify automatically terminating the parents' rights.

As an Illinois court interpreted the Supreme Court's rulings, "the liberty interest of parents in the care, custody and management of their child 'does not evaporate simply because they have not been model parents or have lost temporary custody of their child to the State.'" [20]

When the parental relationship has been terminated, the parent no longer has any legal connection with his or her child, whether the child is adopted or remains in care provided by the state, such as a foster home or a group home.

When a parent abuses or neglects a child, even if his or her parental rights are not completely terminated, a court may give primary custody of the children to another family member, such as a grandparent or other relative. In those situations, the parents may have to pay child support. Federal laws now require that social service agencies make every effort to resolve these ambiguous situations in as short a time as reasonably possible. See the section on adoption below at page 304 et seq for more information. Sadly, many children remain in an administrative limbo, often living in a series of foster families for many years.

The rights of adults with regard to children

The United States Supreme Court has held that the Constitution protects people's rights to procreate and to participate in family life. The Court has said that enjoyment of family life is among the most fundamental rights in our legal system. Over the past 200 years, the Court protected family rights in a variety of situations, from protecting people's rights not to be involuntarily sterilized to ensuring that, within wide limits, parents may educate their children as they see fit.

Among other important decisions, the Court has also held that the father of a child born out of wedlock has some right to be involved in the child's life and that the child cannot be adopted by other people without his consent, at least where the father's paternity has been established and where he has shown some interest in the child.

Courts and legislatures today, however, struggle with the intertwined and competing demands of various ideologies in deciding questions about the relationship between children and adults. These differing imperatives include the traditional rules based on the marriage relationship, viz. the disapproval of non-marital relationships; the social norm that the mother (or the father) is the more important parent in the child's life; and the belief that gay or lesbian persons are inherently unfit to be parents. Today, different moral views and social imperatives, such as the trend to give equal rights to men and women and the view that gays and lesbians can be good parents, challenge the older views.

The rights of adults in regard to children have always been determined by intertwined legal and moral rules and beliefs about what factors produce healthy children. When sex outside of marriage was deemed immoral, the courts and legislatures gave very short shrift to the legal claims of unwed mothers or fathers. As discussed in the section on adoption, some social service agencies, hospitals, doctors, and courts believed that the unwed mother was an immoral person who had few rights and whose feelings could, and should, be ignored. It was assumed that the father of a child out of wedlock had no emotional interest in the child and certainly no rights to the child, who was better off away from such a person.

When children aren't wanted

The issue of whether and when to have children is one of the most important, and sometimes most painful, questions in any relationship.

Since it is no longer necessary to have legal grounds for a divorce, the inability or unwillingness to have children is not, legally, a major question in most divorces, although the judge's opinion of one spouse's decision may affect the property division.

In general, each person has the constitutional right to control his or her own reproductive life. For both men and women, this includes decisions about voluntary infertility through birth control or sterilization, while, for women, it also includes the right to end a pregnancy.

Sterilization and birth control

Under the right to privacy doctrine, both married and unmarried people have a right to obtain and use birth control. Earlier statutes that made it a crime to dispense birth control devices or advice have been struck down as unconstitutional.[21] The Supreme Court has held that the rationale for outlawing birth control (which was to discourage sex outside of marriage by punishing the couple with an illegitimate child) was "plainly unreasonable."

A person can elect to use birth control regardless of the wishes of his or her significant other. A husband is not entitled to any notice that his wife has obtained a birth control device or drug from her physician and, indeed, it would illegal for the doctor to reveal such information without his patient's (the woman's) permission.

Consequently, a person cannot legally force another to use birth control. If a person promises in a contract to use birth control but does not, there may be financial consequences but he or she will not be physically forced to so by a court.

The usual procedure for permanently ensuring infertility involves severing the tubes that carry the sperm or egg, which are the fallopian tubes in women and the vas deferens in men. The procedures are called a "tubal ligation" or "vasectomy," respectively. These procedures are more or less permanent although they can sometimes be reversed and, although they are not infallible, are generally effective. Naturally, the complete removal of reproductive organs also results in sterility. Today, vasectomies and tubal ligations are widely available to adults and are a permanent form of birth control. Few doctors now refuse to perform these surgeries, and even if one particular physician is reluctant, many others are available.

Under current law, a disabled person or minor cannot be sterilized without his or her consent or a court order that it is in the person's best interest. Legally, a parent, in other words, cannot have an adolescent child sterilized or forcibly provided with birth control (such as an intrauterine device) against the child's wishes. Doctors may or may not follow the law, depending on their own moral values.

Sometimes, the guardian of a mentally disabled woman will ask a court to authorize sterilization in order to protect her from unwanted pregnancies; the question is whether the pregnancy is unwanted by the guardian (or institution) or by the woman herself. A developmentally disabled person has the same reproductive rights as other persons, unless he or she is so impaired as to be unable to understand the decision or where other factors put him or her at risk. The availability of reversible means of birth control, such as intrauterine devices, means that sterilization is less necessary as a means of protecting the developmentally disabled.

Under the law, no one has the legal right to force another person to produce a child. A man, married or not, can obtain a vasectomy, although some doctors will discourage him having the surgery if his wife objects. A woman can elect to have her fallopian tubes tied with or without her husband's permission.

Some states have tried to force men to have vasectomies where they are delinquent in paying child support for the children that they already have. These efforts have largely been determined to be unconstitutional as an undue infringement of the right of privacy in sexual and reproductive matters. However, sometimes, indirect coercion such as conditioning release from jail on having a vasectomy has occurred and is probably legal.

Although a person cannot be forced to use birth control, lying about it can be the basis for a lawsuit. In one case, Roni told her lover Stephen that she was using contraception, which was a lie. When she became pregnant, she sued him for child support and he sued her for fraud. He lost because the court reasoned that he could have used birth control himself if he wanted to avoid being responsible for a child. The mother's lies do not deprive the child of his or her right to support from both parents.

In another case, however, John assured his lover Barbara that he was sterile. He lied. When she became pregnant with an ectopic pregnancy, which is a life-threatening abnormal pregnancy, she sued him. She won, because she was suing for her physical harm, not because she gave birth to an unwanted baby.[22]

Abortion

In general, a woman has the right to have an abortion regardless of the wishes of the father of the child or anyone else. The sole exceptions to these rules are1) limitations on abortion late in the term of the pregnancy, (2) limitations on some abortion methods, and (3) restrictions on minor girls' access to abortion.

Under *Roe v. Wade* and subsequent decisions, American law regulates abortion based on the stage of the pregnancy. In the first three months (called the "first trimester"), the decision as to whether to continue the pregnancy or not is entirely up to the woman.

In an effort to discourage abortion, some states adopted laws requiring that the woman's husband be notified or even that he consent. These laws have been held unconstitutional. The father of the child has no right to be notified of the woman's decision or to interfere with her actions at any stage of the pregnancy. Similarly, the fact that other persons (such as prospective grandparents or adoptive parents) might be willing to raise the child is not legally relevant and these people have no right to interfere with the woman's decision.

During the first two trimesters, the government has a limited right to regulate the circumstances of abortions however, including requiring reasonable waiting periods (24 hours, for example), provision of information to the woman, and informed consent, as well as safety and health related regulation of clinics and hospitals. The government cannot impose regulations that unduly burden the right of abortion, such as requiring an expensive hospital procedure rather than a simple outpatient clinical one.

The government is not constitutionally required to provide abortion care even if it elects to provide medical care for pregnant women who elect to carry their baby to term.

During the second trimester (months 3 to 6 of the pregnancy), the woman still has the right to terminate the pregnancy. However, the government can probably impose more regulations, provided that those regulations are justified by some legitimate state policy other than discouraging abortion by making it too burdensome on the woman. A state can require that a later term fetus be tested for viability, for example, because such a test furthers the state's legitimate interest in life, even life before birth.

Some physicians are morally opposed to later term abortions and refuse to perform them; they have the constitutional right to act on their own moral beliefs and cannot legally be compelled to perform such a surgery.

Although abortions in the first three months are relatively easy to obtain, those in the next three months may be more difficult. The procedure is medically more complicated as the pregnancy advances and some physicians are unwilling to abort a later term infant. Legally, however the woman may decide to have a later term abortion (from the third to the sixth month) for any reason that seems adequate to her. As a general rule, she and her physician may use any method that seems right to them, even if it results in the death of the fetus. In some procedures, the woman delivers a fetus which is moving and clearly alive but is allowed to die. Usually, a method is used which kills the fetus in the womb.

However, there are efforts to change the law to require the physician to try to preserve the life of the fetus if it is viable.

After the sixth month, however, the woman's right is much more limited. She no longer has the right to abort a viable fetus simply because she doesn't want the child. The state's interest in fetal life at this stage outweighs the mother's right to control her own body, at least to an extent. The state can prohibit abortion of a viable fetus except to save the mother's life. What this means is that the woman must carry the fetus to term unless doing so would endanger her own life or cause her grave physical harm.

One of the more hotly debated issues is the relevance of knowledge that a woman is carrying a fetus that will be gravely deformed, severely mentally impaired, or nonviable (unable to live).

With regard to viability, the question is one of definition. If a fetus could survive outside the mother's body with extensive, state of the art, care, is it viable? Or, does "viable" mean "able to live on its own or with minimal, ordinary, medical care"? If a fetus might be born alive but is certainly doomed to die (such as an anencephalic child, which is one without a functioning brain), what protection is the fetus entitled to?

The mother does not have the right to ensure that a viable fetus is killed after it is born; no one has the right to directly take the life of a living child that has been born, although there are circumstances in which indirectly bringing about the death of the infant is permitted, such as not providing essential medical care to a severely deformed child. (Obviously, abortion in its nature takes the life of a living (potential) child before birth.)

A woman who is carrying a fetus that has died may have the dead fetus removed, regardless of the stage of pregnancy. Removal of a dead or dying fetus is not an abortion.

Medical tests can reveal likely or certain problems with the baby. The presence of such problems, however, does not entitle the woman to an abortion late in the pregnancy if state law otherwise forbids it. The birth of severely impaired children may be considered a waste of resources by some, but the law does not permit the killing of such children.

A variation on that social issue is a medical procedure in which a later term abortion is performed by inducing labor and then, when the fetus has moved partially into the birth canal, removing it in pieces. This operation is usually used to terminate a later term pregnancy in which the fetus, while perhaps still technically alive, is ultimately nonviable, such as one in which no functioning brain is developing. The operation protects the mother's reproductive and emotional health by not requiring her to go through a full labor and delivery of a doomed child. Anti-abortion activist have coined the term "partial birth abortion" for this operation, but that is not the medical term for it.

Many people find the thought of such a procedure repulsive; however, many operations are repulsive and gory to people other than surgeons. All abortions end fetal life, and the manner of ending it is not appealing if graphically described, whether the fetus is extracted by a vacuum method (whole or in pieces) or killed by an injection of saline solution prior to being removed.

Regardless, some states have outlawed the "partial birth" procedure, and the federal government has passed a law against it. In general, these laws are unconstitutional if they inhibit the right to abortion early in the pregnancy or if they don't contain an exception for protecting the mother's health. If the state permits other medical procedures to end a pregnancy and if it permits the partial birth procedure if medically necessary to protect the mother's health, then the state may legally prohibit the procedure in other circumstances.

The rights of women under age 18 to obtain an abortion is a thorny one. The Supreme Court and the state legislatures have tried to balance the rights of parents to be involved in their daughters' lives with the right of a young woman not to carry an unwanted child to term. The problem is particularly difficult because some of these pregnancies are the result of sexual abuse by a family member and because a daughter of a fundamentalist family may legitimately fear abuse or other retaliation for her conduct if it is regarded as sinful by her parents. Remember that a parent does not have an unlimited right to force his or her moral values on his or her children. Just as a parent cannot legally force an unwilling daughter into an arranged marriage or sell her sexual services to his or her friends, he or she cannot force her to bear a child. See page 244 for more information

States have tried either to prohibit young women from obtaining an abortion or to require the consent of one or both parents. In general, these restrictions are unconstitutional. A state may require that a minor child's parents be notified of her pregnancy and intent to have an abortion, but the law must provide an alternative means for the young woman to obtain an abortion without such notification. For example, she may be afforded an opportunity to go before a judge and explain the circumstances, in which case the court may permit the abortion without parental involvement.

A woman has some obligations to her unborn child, however. Some women have been prosecuted for child abuse or even homicide where they damaged or killed their unborn child by using illegal drugs during pregnancy. Some efforts have been made to force women who were abusing various substances to be confined in a hospital or forced to receive prenatal care. Most of these efforts violate the woman's rights. In particular, a doctor or hospital cannot secretly test a pregnant woman for unlawful drug use.

Generally, a pregnant woman has the same right to control her medical care as any other patient. For example, a pregnant woman who has cancer may elect to receive treatment that may harm or even kill her unborn child and she can refuse a procedure, such as a Caesarean, that would endanger her own health.

However, where a woman's decision is based on her personal values (such as a refusal to have a Cesarean operation because of her religious beliefs), the courts have reached different decisions. Most have held that the woman has the right to make medical decisions about her own body, regardless of their impact on the unborn child; the courts should not try to balance the fetus' interests against those of the mother. A few courts, however, have ordered the woman to receive medical treatment against her will where the life of an unborn child was at stake.[23] The names of these cases, such as *In re Baby Boy Doe v. Doe* (which translates as "the case of baby boy against his mother") or *In re Fetus Brown* ("the case of the unborn Brown") show the inherent and tragic conflict. In one case, a court required a woman to have a Caesarean section to deliver her child where the fetus was viable (could survive) if she had the surgery but would likely die if she did not, but other courts have refused to force a person to have medical care against her wishes even if her decision may result in harm to her unborn child.

Despite the right to abortion, some recent laws make it a crime to injure an unborn child, at least where the injury occurs in the course of another crime. A bank robber who shoots a pregnant woman and kills her unborn child, for example, may be guilty of a form of homicide as well as bank robbery, even if the mother survives. The federal law on this subject is called the Unborn Victims of Violence Act, and many states have similar laws.

Biology and the law

The rights of an adult in regard to a child still rest largely upon their biological relationship. The biological connection of parentage determines the legal relationship until legal steps have been taken to alter it. For example, a biological father has the legal status of a parent until his legal connection with the child is severed, as where the child is legally adopted by someone else. Conversely, a man who has raised a child who is not biologically his has few, if any, legal rights unless he adopts the child.

Here again technology has affected the legal implications of biological connection. The courts have struggled with the questions of whether genetic connection alone makes someone a parent. For example, if a man donates sperm so that a woman can have a baby, is he the legal father of the baby? Does the fact that he has never met the woman or had sexual intercourse with her change his legal status?

Historically, the motherhood of a child was considered an obvious fact. Unless outright deception was practiced, maternity was clear from the fact that she gave birth to the child. Gestation and genetics were usually inseparable. Deceptions may have occurred when a midwife, a mother, and a childless woman collaborated to simultaneously conceal an out-of-wedlock birth and provide a child to a woman who was unable to have one of her own. If everyone agreed, the midwife might simply have taken the newborn of one woman and given it to another. Although less common than questions of paternity, today the legal status of mother can be difficult to decide when the technologies of egg donation or surrogate motherhood are employed. Is the woman who donates an ovum the legal mother of the resulting child? If a woman gives birth to a child that is genetically unrelated to her, is she still the child's legal mother?

Among the most influential social changes that have affected the law is the development of scientific methods of determining the parentage of a child.

For centuries, the courts protected the family structure by holding that a child born of a married couple was the legitimate child of the husband if he had sexual access to his wife during the time when the child was conceived. That is, the husband was deemed to be the father of the child if he was not physically out of the country when the child was conceived. It didn't matter if he claimed that he and his wife had not had sexual relations during that time or if the child looked more like the wife's lover than like her husband.

That substantive rule was reinforced by procedural rules that precluded anyone from challenging the paternity of the child. In other words, there was no court procedure for the mother's lover to legally claim the child as his own.

By these rules, the law prevented anyone from challenging the child's rights as a legitimate member of his or her father's family. When social and legal status, including the right to inherit, depended on legitimacy, this rule provided important protection to children and their mothers and prevented subjective contests about whether a wife was faithful or not or whether the child resembled someone other than the husband. The rule made sense when there was no sound scientific method for deciding who the father of the child really was.

Today, these rules are changing, but gradually. If you are involved in such a situation, it is essential to check the current law in your state.

Married parents

The law has always had to deal with the painful situation of a wife who has been unfaithful to her husband and conceived a child during the adulterous affair.

Today, when adulterous affairs are often openly revealed, the biological father's desire to raise his biological child may conflict with the claims of the husband of the child's mother, who may have come to love the child. The law still favors the presumption that a child born to a married woman is the child of her husband.

The traditional rule, however, conflicts with modern scientific reality, as well as with changing social norms about parentage, inheritance, and sexual conduct. For example, in the case of *Espree v. Guillory*, a wife sued her husband for divorce. In the divorce case, she alleged that her lover was the father of her child, and her lover filed a paternity case claiming to be the father. She and her husband reached a compromise in the divorce case, however, and the court entered a decree that the child was legitimate (i.e. the child of the husband) because the child was born during the marriage. In the paternity case, the lover proved that he was the child's father. The biological parent contradicted the legal finding. An appellate court decided that the lover/biological father didn't have any legal right to claim that he was the father. Legal doctrine trumped biological reality; the fact that the divorce court had declared the child legitimate meant that legally the husband was the father. In the logic of the law, if the husband was the father, then no one else could claim to be the father of the child. The court said that "The presumption of legitimacy of a child born during marriage is one of the strongest presumptions known to law."[24] Under Texas law, once the divorce decree was entered, the question had been settled; the child was legally that of the husband, even though neither the husband, the mother, nor the biological father really intended that result.

Gradually, the law is moving toward both permitting a husband to deny that a child is his and allowing the wife's lover to claim her child as his, i.e. to make legal status consistent with biological and social fact. In fact, in the highly publicized divorce case of Neil Bush (the brother of President George W. Bush) and his wife, the latter demanded that the child of her husband's supposed lover be tested to see if he was the father, even though the supposed lover was married to another man at the time.

Custody after divorce

In a divorce, the court divides the children between the parents. The court decides how much time each child will spend with each parent. The court also decides who will have primary authority to make decisions about the child. Usually, one parent is required to make payments to the other parent to support the child.

The standard for all of these decisions is the best interest of the child. Courts consider the stability of the environment provided to the child, the quality of the care and attention provided to the child, and other factors.

Judges often look to mental health experts in making these decisions. For example, in the case of *Greenlaw v. Smith*, a father asked the court to give him custody of his son. The mother had custody. When the she lived in Germany, she put her son in boarding school. When she lived in California, she left the child with an ex-boyfriend while she went to law school. The court changed the custody of the child from the mother to the father when a counselor who had been seeing the child testified:

> *In summary, the emotional and mental needs of Alex, including needs of warmth, love, nurturing, caring and involvement in the social, cultural and family development have not been met or provided by his mother in the years that she has been charged with the custodial relationship of Alex. Similarly, these needs have not been met by the surrogate caretakers which Alex's mother has placed him with during several of these years. Alex has inappropriately been put in the position of self-parenting as a result of the neglect and virtual*

parental abandonment by his mother, his custodial parent. This situation is injurious to Alex and in my opinion there is an immediate need for corrective intervention to avoid additional injury and to assist Alex in a program of normal childhood development.[25]

The counselor's testimony contains a good laundry list of what good parents should provide for a child in addition to meeting mere physical needs – "warmth, love, nurturing, caring and involvement in social, cultural, and family development." Some courts include religious and moral training and fostering the child receiving a good education in their criteria.

Gender and custody

The rights of a parent toward a child should legally be the same whether the parent is male or female. Historically, that was not the case. At one time, the father was legally entitled to the possession of his children; it was presumed that the father was the better parent. Women were thought to be incapable of raising children because they were believed to be too tenderhearted to provide proper discipline, and it was believed that children needed the firm guidance of the father. That rule was changed in 1813 in the United States, and thereafter, courts awarded custody to the mother almost automatically under the theory that women were intended by nature to nurture small children. In recent years, that presupposition has also been rejected.[26]

Today, courts struggle to craft gender-neutral guidelines for awarding custody of children, when the biological parents disagree. Although there is no longer an explicit presumption that women are better caregivers, some preference tends to be given to the mother, at least if she has in fact been taking care of the child or if the child is very young. It is difficult for courts to balance the respective interests of father and mother in light of changing assumptions about the roles of men and women; the law, however, gives both parents a shot at custody.

In the case of *Burchard v. Garay*, for example, Garay and Burchard were lovers and produced a child.[27] Garay initially denied that he was the father; when a blood test proved his paternity, Garay began to visit the child and to pay child support. Eventually, Garay sought custody of the child, and Burchard denied him any visitation at all. Garay argued that he was better fitted to take care of his son because he made a lot of money and his new wife was a full time homemaker, while Burchard was a working mom. The lower court awarded custody to Garay, but the appellate court disagreed, in part because the mother had already been the caregiver.

Today, it is generally acknowledged that a father who is involved in the life of his child, whether or not he and the mother were ever married, has certain rights to the child, including the right to see him or her.

In the Massachusetts case of *Whallon v. Lynn*, Ms. Whallon and Mr. Lynn had lived together in Cabo San Lucas, Mexico, although they were both American citizens. They had a daughter, Micheli. Even after Lynn and he split up, Whallon spent time with his daughter and was involved in her life, driving her to nursery school, buying her clothes, and playing with her. When Lynn decided to take the little girl to Massachusetts to live, however, an ugly custody battle ensued. The court held that under an international treaty on custody, Whallon had a sufficient relationship with his daughter to give rise to various legal rights, including the right to require that she not leave Mexico.

Grandparents – visitation and custody

Several states have adopted laws granting the grandparents rights to visitation with their grandchildren and to be considered for custody of the children. The problem is that several of these statutes about grandparents' rights to visitation have been held to be unconstitutional as interfering with the rights of parents to make decisions about family life. Some of the custody statutes, however, were modified to meet the constitutional limitations.[28]

The visitation rights statutes afforded grandparents the right to visit their grandchildren when the family situation changed, as when the parents divorced or separated or one parent died. Usually, these rights came into play when the grandparents' child died and the remaining parent (of the grandchildren) no longer wanted his or her deceased spouse's parents involved in the grandchildren's lives.

One recent case concerned two daughters born to a cohabiting couple. The father of the children eventually committed suicide. The mother continued to raise the girls herself. No one claimed that she was an unfit mother, and she allowed the children to visit their grandparents occasionally. However, the parents of the deceased father wanted more time with their grandchildren, which the mother refused. They sued under the law in their state that gave grandparents visitation rights. The Supreme Court decided that the law unconstitutionally infringed the mother's rights to raise her own children as she saw fit.

Under some modified "grandparents' rights" statutes, the grandparents can ask a court to grant them access to their grandchildren over the parents' objections, but the grandparents have a heavy burden of proving to a court that the parents' decision is clearly not in the child's best interests. In other words, these statutes don't give grandparents a clear right to visit their grandchildren. The decision of the child's parents still receives considerable deference and can only be overridden if it doesn't serve the child's best interests.

Some of these laws also provide that grandparents have a right to be considered for custody of the children when the parents are not fit parents, as where both parents have a drug problem. These statutes have not been overturned because they do not interfere to the same extent with the parents' rights, and therefore, grandparents have a chance at getting custody of a grandchild if the parents' are to be terminated. Some grandparents have formed an alliance to promote the rights of grandparents to have a role in their grandchildrens' lives. They have a website at www.grandparentsforchildren.org.

Unmarried parents

Until recently, if the mother was not married to the child's father, the biological father had few rights but was obligated to support the child. For many years, the assumption was that the father of a bastard child had no interest in the child.

The legal right of an adult to be involved in the life of a child begins with the adult's biological relationship to the child. Unless a court terminates the biological parent's rights, as where there has been a lawful adoption or other proceeding, both biological parents have various rights and obligations concerning their child.

In most states, today, both biological parents have equal obligations to support the child and equal rights to spend time with the child. The implementation of these rights, however, still varies between mothers and fathers.

If the biological father has established at least some connection with the child, as where he has visited the child or provided support for the child, he has the right to be notified of any adoption proceedings. Similarly, he has the right to seek custody of the child.

However, the fact remains that an unmarried father needs to be vigilant and well-informed if he wishes to remain involved in his child's life. An advocate for fathers' rights says bluntly "A father who is not married to his child's mother must act swiftly and decisively to assert and protect his parental rights."[29]

The father has the obligation to support his children whether or not he has ever visited them or expressed any interest in them at all, at least until his parental rights are terminated, as when the children are adopted by another family.

MYTH—*The biological mother of a child born out of wedlock automatically has legal custody of the child.*

FACT—*Both biological parents of a child born out of wedlock have rights to the child.*

Many people assume that the biological mother of a child has custody of the child automatically and that the father needs her permission to visit the child. Strictly speaking this is not the legal rule, although it is such a widespread assumption that it is effectively the rule.

Technically, both biological parents of a child born out of wedlock have equal rights to the child. Legally, the mother does not control the father's rights to visit the child or even to have possession of the child. If the parents do not agree, then a court needs to decide the issues of custody and visitation.

However, a man who believes that he is the father of a child should not seize the child from the mother, especially if his paternity has not been confirmed by genetic testing. Grabbing the child will clearly violate criminal laws, including kidnapping, if the man turns out not to be the biological father. Even if the mother has told the man that he is the father, he does not have a legal right to the child if he is not in fact the father.

Moreover, the father does not have the right to force his way in to see his child; any violence will probably be a criminal offense. His paternity does not give him the right, for example, to force his way into another person's house. If he needs to compel the mother (or other relatives) to afford him time with his child, he must go to court, prove that he is the biological father, and get a court order setting the terms of custody and visitation. As in divorce cases, courts still usually give primary custody of very young children to the mother, unless the father can demonstrate that the child's best interests will be served by granting primary custody to the father.

If you want clear legal custody of your child, whether you are the mother or the father, you need to get a court order establishing both parents' rights. Otherwise, you may find that the other parent has taken the kid to a distant state and that he or she has a perfect right to do so.

The laws governing parental kidnapping apply equally to married parents and unmarried parents if there is a court order on custody.

Establishment of paternity

The legal relationship of fatherhood rests on the biological fact of having sired the child.

281

There are several legal mechanisms to establish that fact. If the parents marry after the child is born, then the child's parentage is established. The father may also acknowledge the child as his own, but the acknowledgement must be in the legally prescribed form. Finally, the child's parentage can be established in a paternity suit. Either the father or the mother may file such a lawsuit to have the question of paternity settled. In that suit, the court will determine who the father of the child is and what custody and support arrangement should be.

Today, the courts primarily rely on genetic testing to determine paternity. These tests are relatively inexpensive and provide near medical certainty. The test requires only a few cells, which are sometimes collected with a swab from the inside of the mouth or by a blood test. The laboratory compares the child's genetic makeup with that of the possible father. The test can rule out a man as the father and can establish who is the father with a reasonable degree of certainty.

In 1996, as discussed elsewhere, Congress adopted a statute designed to increase the amount of child support collected. That law required the states to adopt policies encouraging the identification of fathers in order to promote the goal of securing support for children. Part of that process was to require the states to provide for nonjudicial means for legal paternity to be established, i.e. ways for paternity to be legally recognized that were less cumbersome and expensive that going to court. Under federal law, therefore, if a mother and father formally acknowledge that the man is the father of their child, then the states must treat that as legally establishing the child's parentage.[30]

Marriage, biology, and love

The intertwined issues of marriage, morality, biology, and love can be seen in the range of cases that have been decided on these complex and painful issues.

Love of a child has not always been given a high priority by the courts. A person who is not biologically related to a child, even if that person has cohabited with the biological parent of a child, may have no rights at all in regard to the child, no matter how close their relationship has become.

In the case of *Alison v. Virginia*, two lesbian women lived together and planned the birth of a child, which Virginia conceived by artificial insemination. [31] When the couple split, the court ruled that someone who is a biological stranger to the child had no right to seek visitation with him or her, so Alison had no legal right to be with the child. One judge disagreed and suggested that the courts should develop a more modern understanding of what a family is and should look to the relationship between the child and the person who has been "like a parent" to that child.

In a recent case with similar facts, the state courts reached the opposite result, holding that the mother's partner had the right to try to prove that she had been a de facto parent. "De facto" is Latin for "in fact" or "in reality;" in other words, the court ruled that the partner, who was not biologically related to the child, should have a chance to gain some parental rights by showing that she had in fact been a parent. On that ruling, a person's legal relationship to a child could reflect their emotional connection.

On the other hand, sometimes if the biological parents have emotionally abandoned the child, someone else that has taken the child into his or her home may have the right to custody. In one heartrending case, the parents of a retarded child put him child in an institution. They rarely, if ever, visited the child who was essentially warehoused. A loving couple who worked at the institution became fond of him and had him visit at their house as a member of their family.

The parents sued to put a stop to the visits, apparently feeling that if they didn't want the child, no one else should either. The court held that the biological parents had emotionally abandoned the child by placing him in an institution and not visiting. In that situation, people who had taken on the role of parents were entitled to custody.

Although the case of *Alison v. Virginia* involved two women, many courts would reach the same result with regard to a man and a woman who lived together and participated in raising a child who was biologically related only to one of them. Unless a legal relationship was established, the non-biological "parent" might have a difficult time persuading a court to recognize any relationship between the child and that "parent" once the couple had split up, unless the biological parents died, abandoned the child, or were clearly unfit to be parents.

The importance that courts still attach to marriage in family matters can be seen by comparing *Ray v. Ray* with *Alison v. Virginia*. In *Ray v. Ray*, an Ohio case, Mrs. Ray had a child, Scott, from a previous relationship.[32] When Mr. and Mrs. Ray divorced, Mr. Ray wanted custody of Scott. Scott had no contact with his biological father and had been supported and raised by Mr. Ray. The court gave custody of Scott to Mr. Ray because the judge found that would be in Scott's best interest.

Except in unusual circumstances, when a biological parent and his or her lover split, both the child and the adult who has become a parent to him or her suffer painful losses. Similarly, the rights of foster parents, no matter how close they have become to the child, are subordinate to the rights of the child's biological parents.

Four states have specific statutes that allow a court to give any person the right to visit the child if the visitation would be in the child's best interest. These states are Alaska, California, Connecticut, and Maine. Other states are moving toward recognition that a biologically or legally unrelated person can still be an important figure in a child's life. As people in our society engage in more and more unstructured relationships, some judges are willing to step in and protect the child's emotional attachment to a responsible adult.

However, these efforts have to be balanced against the fundamental rights of parents to structure their family life as they see fit. The rights of legal parents usually trump the needs of their children.

Although a parent cannot sign away the child's rights, good arguments can be made that courts should enforce an agreement permitting a biologically unrelated person access to the child, at least if the person had previously been involved in the child's life and there was no evidence of abuse or other misconduct. In other words, if you are cohabiting with a person and his or her children *and* you want to be involved in the children's' lives even after you and your sweetheart split up, it is worth adding a provision to that effect in your cohabitation agreement.

There are four basic legal strategies that a person who is not biologically a parent and who has not adopted a child can use to try to maintain some contact with the child. All of them involve going to court and proving that the adult's presence in the child's life would be in the best interests of the child and that the adult has already established an on-going parent-like relationship with the child.

First, a few states have adopted statutes that permit the courts to award visitation rights to any person who "has an interest in the welfare of the child." These rights normally apply only when the child's parents are divorced or separated. As with the grandparents' rights statutes, it is not clear if these laws are constitutional.

Second, a few other states have adopted statutes that provide that a person who has acted as a child's parent for a substantial period of time, usually a year, has the legal right to seek custody of the child. These statutes are often invoked by relatives on whom a child has been more or less dumped.

Third, rarely, the courts have used an obscure common law doctrine called "putative adoption" to achieve this result. Under that doctrine, in cases where a person intended to adopt a child but the legal technicalities were not complied with, the court will find that the child had in fact been adopted and that the would-be parent is the child's legal parent.

Fourth, when those close to a child want to make sure that a biologically unrelated person has legal rights with regard to the child, it is sometimes possible to have that person named as the child's guardian. Technically, being a guardian is not the same as having custody of the child. The guardian has the same rights and responsibilities to the child as a custodial parent does, except that the guardian does not have a legal obligation to support the child and does not usually have the same obligations to other people whom the child might injure. The guardian can consent to medical care for the child and so on. A guardianship is frequently used as an arrangement to permit an unrelated person to care for a child if the parents both die. For example, many parents have a provision in their wills that if they both die, a family friend will become the guardian of their children. In that situation, the friend does not adopt the child nor does he or she become the child's legal parent.

Sometimes, a guardianship may be established if the parents are temporarily unable to care for a child. If the parents change their minds, the judge that appointed the guardian has the power to alter the arrangement. Again, the best interest of the child should be the guide, but the wishes of parents will usually govern, except in circumstances where the parents have effectively abandoned the child or are so impaired that they cannot or will not properly care for him or her.

Contracts and children

Parents can enter some contracts on behalf of their children. For example, a parent can sign a release of liability to permit a child to participate in sporting events. Such releases are usually valid contracts, as least so long as the parent was reasonably well informed of the risks and the risk to the child was not unreasonably great.

There are special limitations on a parent's right to contract for a child in certain circumstances, however. These include the gifted child who can earn a lot of money and the child who has been injured in an accident.

The parents of a talented young athlete or actor can sign contracts on behalf of the child for the child to appear in a play or a tennis tournament. However, there have been many cases in which the parents have squandered the child's earnings. The laws in some states, such as New York, try to provide some protection for the child by requiring that the parents put aside some of the money and so on. Some children, when they realize that their manager/parent is spending all the money, have asked a court to appoint a guardian for them for the purpose of handling their earnings.

A child who is injured in an accident often needs expensive medical and rehabilitation. A severely injured child may need care for the rest of his or her life. Usually, when there is a lawsuit over these accidents, the court appoints a guardian ad litem for the child. A guardian ad litem is an attorney who doesn't present the child's case in court but watches over the proceedings to make sure that they are fair to the child.

Sometimes, a court will require that the proceeds of a lawsuit for an injured child be placed in a trust or deposited with the court until the child becomes an adult. All too often, however, the proceeds are turned over to the parents who cheerfully spend the money on a new house, car, and boat, rather than on physical therapy and devoted nurses. After all, sometimes they might take poor crippled little Johnny for a ride in the boat. Once the case is over, the child's attorneys have little or no duty to see that the money is properly spent, since the care of the injured child is left to the parent's discretion.

In one egregious case, a young man suffered brain damage in a car accident. He could not live on his own because he did not have good control of his temper and was impulsive. He was normally intelligent and was not dangerous but needed supervision. For example, he could have lived quite happily on a farm if he had a caretaker to watch over him. His father settled the lawsuit for the boy's injuries for millions of dollars based on his son's need for caregivers and therapy. Immediately after he got his hands on the money, the father had the boy committed to the state hospital for the insane.

While his son languished in locked wards with seriously mentally ill people, the father lived with his new mistress on their lovely new farm. A crusading lawyer brought suit to force the father to account for the money and succeeded in gaining a more pleasant life for this disabled young man. In that case, the decent attorney also proved that the child's original lawyer should be held responsible because that lawyer helped the father steal the money from his disabled child.

Responsibility of a parent for a child's actions

In some states, parents are financially responsible for damage caused by their child. This includes accidents that the child has while driving the parent's car.

There is a doctrine called "negligent entrustment." That refers to the situation where one person foolishly allows a child to use something that is dangerous. Guns, ATV's, and motorboats are examples of things that can be dangerous when the person using them is inexperienced or has poor judgment. A parent who negligently lets his or her child ride an ATV, for example, can be liable if someone else is hurt.

Many jurisdictions have specific laws that impose responsibility on parents when a child has access to the parent's firearm.

In addition, some states have laws that make a parent responsible for malicious damage caused by his or her children. This includes vandalism and similar misconduct. A parent is not legally responsible for the actions of a grown child or an emancipated child.

Inheritance

Parents inherit from their children unless the child marries or leaves his or her property to another person by will. A minor child cannot make a valid will so a wealthy child's parents (married or not) stand to inherit if the kid dies.

Parents remain their child's heirs, regardless of the child's age. In other words, if an adult child dies without a will (and without a spouse or children of his or her own), his or her parents inherit at least part of his or her assets.

The incapacitated parent — support, abuse, and medical decisions

The obligations of support in a family are reciprocal. When an adult becomes incapable of caring for himself or herself, his or children have obligations toward their parent.

Legally, grown children have the duty to support their parents if the parents are aged or incapacitated. This obligation is rarely enforced. That is, it is unusual for a court to get involved in requiring an adult child to pay for his or her parent's nursing home, for example.

Periodically there are political movements toward greater enforcement of this legal obligation, sometimes as part of efforts to reform the welfare system.

An adult child does not have the right to discipline his or her incapacitated parent. Physical restraint, such as tying up the elder person, is probably abusive unless supervised by a health care provider. Obviously, striking the disabled parent is also abuse.

As the police and social service agencies have become more alert to spousal abuse, so they are now more aware of the problem of elder abuse. Tragically, the frustrations of daily care for an incapacitated parent, combined perhaps with old angers left over from childhood, can lead to physical abuse or gross neglect of an elderly person.

Elderly people are often unwilling to complain about abuse or neglect. Sometimes, they are ashamed of being dependent or embarrassed to be a victim. Sometimes they fear losing whatever home they have, no matter how dismal. More and more health care providers and law enforcement people are being trained to recognize signs of elder abuse. However, most experts believe that it is underreported.

There are analogous criminal penalties for abusing an elderly dependent person as for abusing a child. Striking an elderly person is the crime of battery. In some states, financial exploitation of an endangered adult is a crime. Financial exploitation includes taking the person's property or work for one's own benefit.[33]

Leaving aside abuse, in most situations, the children are recognized as the natural representative or caregiver for an incapacitated parent. For example, if a parent is mentally incapacitated, doctors look to the person's spouse, or if there is no competent spouse, then to his or her grown children for consent to medical procedures.

If, however, the parent has executed a valid durable power of attorney, then the person named in that document has the legal power to make decisions for the parent. That person's decisions should prevail over the preferences of the parent's spouse, children, or other relatives.

If family members disagree among themselves about an incapacitated parent's medical care, then the family or the doctors can go to court and ask a judge to decide. The court will take into account the parent's values and expressed wishes (if any are known), the doctors' medical opinion about the best course of treatment, and the children's wishes. The incapacitated person's best interest is the guide, allowing for his or her values. For example, if a person has clearly said "I wouldn't want to be kept alive if I didn't any chance of ever having a normal life," the court will consider that in deciding between alternative treatments or whether to continue treatment at all.

As with children, in some states, hospitals have the right to discontinue care that is futile i.e. where there is no hope of the patient recovering.

Perhaps the most difficult situation arises when an adult is becoming incapacitated but is still, legally, a competent person. In those situations, as with Alzheimer's disease, where the outcome can be foreseen, the only prudent course of conduct is to take legal action while the person is still competent. Wills, durable powers of attorney, and information about assets are essential at this time.

Another difficult situation can arise when an elderly parent takes a lover. Many adult children resent Mom or Dad's involvement with a new lover or spouse. These children may fear that their parent will squander his or her resources on a new amour. Sometimes, these fears are justified, but sometimes the anxiety is more over inheritance than over a parent's happiness. Remember that an adult person has the right to manage his or her financial affairs until a court takes that right away.

In one case, Norbert was a little old man who lived in a pleasant older neighborhood near a university in Atlanta. His house was smaller than many in the gentrifying neighborhood but had appreciated dramatically. Norbert was a retired engineer of conservative habits who had taken advantage of every stock option that his company offered. Although he lived modestly, Norbert actually had a lot of money.

Norbert's children more or less ignored him. They sent cards on his birthday and called on Christmas. They found his stories boring and didn't like to listen to his rambling reminiscences.

Norbert had a housekeeper for many years, Beulah. Beulah gradually started spending more time with Norbert. Eventually, she was living with him, although she kept her own house. They had a nice routine. Every morning while she fixed his breakfast, he read *The Wall Street Journal*. He bought an RV so they could travel together and gave her relatively small gifts, like a new washer and dryer. She helped him run errands. Once or twice, she cashed a CD for him at the bank, putting the money in his account.

One day, Beulah came home from some errands and Norbert was gone. She got a pitiful call that night from him — "Baby, come get me. I don't like it here."

Norbert's son had arrived for a visit while Beulah was out and invited his father to go for a drive. The drive was to a distant nursing home where the son, without benefit of any legal authority, had decided that his father ought to live. Beulah promptly drove over and took Norbert back to his house.

After Norbert died, his children inherited millions, but they still sued Beulah and Norbert's bank, claiming that she had taken advantage of him and that the bank had been negligent. Beulah and the bank won. There was no real evidence that Norbert wasn't able to make sensible decisions or that Beulah took undue advantage of him. Yes, she did cash $100,000 CD's for him but the children could not prove that she got any improper amount of the money, since the proceeds were deposited in Norbert's account.

On the other hand, unfortunately, sometimes an older person can be the victim of an unscrupulous scam artist. Many elderly people are so lonely after the death of a spouse that they are easily victimized by a caregiver or even a pushy neighbor. In her article "For Love or Money," Gail Bensinger described how a younger woman took advantage of her ailing father. Ms. Bensinger and her brothers lived a long ways from their father.[34] A lonely widower, he began spending time with a younger woman. As he became mentally more incapacitated, the woman acquired more and more influence over him. Eventually, she moved him out of reach of his children, so that they had to hire a detective to find him. The 80 year old man paid his "friend's" extravagant bills, for a luxury lifestyle. Ms. Bensinger notes that "The victims can be people with dementia who don't realize anything bad has happened, or fully competent seniors who picked the wrong people to trust." Even after an expensive suit, the man's children had to settle for retrieving a fraction of his assets.

In another case, a lonely wealthy woman (whose children lived in distant states) formed a new friendship with a neighbor lady in her Tucson condominium development. They ate out together, watched TV, and so on. The wealthy woman gave her new friend a key to her lavishly decorated condo. When the older woman had a fatal heart attack one evening, the new friend used her key to help herself to the furs, art work, and sterling that "she promised me I could have."

Situations like this are ambiguous. Did the neighbor/friend take advantage? Was the wealthy woman simply lonely because her daughter only visited on the infrequent occasions when the daughter could spare time from her career?

An adult has the legal right to handle his or her assets until a legal change is made. That change can be made by a durable power of attorney taking effect or by a court's finding the person incompetent and appointing a guardian for him or her. See Chapter Twelve, Chapter Thirteen, and the Workbook (page 595) for more information on these topics.

One of the most dramatic, and expensive, cases of this sort, was the legal war between some of the heirs of the Johnson & Johnson health care company fortune and the widow of one family member. J. Seward Johnson, Sr., an extremely wealthy man, married his housekeeper, a Polish refugee named Basia Piasecka. In the later litigation, the dysfunctional family battled for years. His children and other relatives claimed that Basia had isolated and abused him. Basia persuasively claimed that she had cared for him and that they loved each other. Basia ended up with much of the vast fortune at stake.[35]

If you suspect that your parent is being abused or taken advantage of, the first step is communication directly with him or her. If he or she denies that there is a problem, your options may be limited. You can contact the local social service agency, often called "adult protective services." If your parent has a durable power of attorney that provides for a doctor's examination to determine competency, you can contact the doctor named in the power of attorney to find out whether he or she considers your parent to be sufficiently impaired for the power of attorney to take effect. You can try visiting your parent's doctor regardless of whether there is a power of attorney, but under federal privacy laws, the physician should be unwilling to discuss a patient with you without the patient's permission. Finally, you can file a petition with a local court to have your parent declared legally unable to manage his or her affairs and to have a guardian appointed for him or her.

QUESTION: *"Are there special legal considerations for family members with special needs?"*

ANSWER: *Absolutely. Planning for the care of a mentally or physically challenged loved one requires legal work, financial planning, and good advice.*

Mentally and physically challenged persons may be eligible for a variety of governmental and private programs. The availability of these benefits depends on the exact circumstances of the person and family involved.

Planning to maximize governmental and pension benefits can be critical to the family's financial health. For example, the federal health benefits for the elderly (Medicare) do not cover most prolonged nursing home care unless the recipient is impoverished. There are limits on a person's legal right to give away his or her assets in order to become poor enough to qualify for the additional federal assistance (Medicaid). Basically, these are time limits; in other words, a person can give away his or her assets (and become legally poor) if the gifts are made sufficiently in advance of him or her needing financial assistance to pay for nursing home care. Similarly, some assets, like the family home, have special protection.

These regulations are very complex and change frequently. It is vital to gather as much information as possible from different sources so that the right decisions can be made in as timely a manner as possible. Hospital social workers often know the regulations well. Attorneys, unless they specialize in elder law, may not be the best sources of information.

An injured adult family member and lawsuits

An adult who suffers a catastrophic injury may be entitled to compensation from the person who caused his or her injury. Such a person might be an adult injured in an industrial accident for example. If there is a large settlement in a lawsuit, those proceeds need to be managed so as to conserve them for the lifetime of the injured person.

These matters are both complicated and vital. Sorry, but once again, you need a lawyer who has extensive experience in the intertwined areas of liability law, social security law, special education benefits, etc. Even lawyers who handle injury cases may not be experienced or knowledgeable in managing the proceeds of those lawsuits and in maximizing an injured person's rights to various government programs.

Often, when a person suffers a catastrophic injury, the payments from the person who caused the injury may be made over a period of years. These arrangements are called a "structured settlement." They can be a very useful device for ensuring long term access to funds. Unfortunately, like other investment programs, they are also a product that is sold by sales representatives operating on commission, whose advice, therefore, may not be unbiased or even correct.

A disabled family member

Many tragic disabilities, however, are no one's fault. In those situations, the family's entire financial planning may have to be adjusted to provide as far as possible for the disabled person. These situations can range from an adult who suffers from a progressive disorder such as amyotrophic later sclerosis (Lou Gehrig's disease) or Alzheimer's disease to a child with a chronic disorder such as muscular dystrophy or mental retardation.

As an example of planning, life insurance and mortgage insurance may become much more important because of the critical need to assure that funds will be available if the family's main source of income should be disabled or injured. Mortgage insurance, which pays off the mortgage if the breadwinner dies or is disabled, may or may not be desirable for a young healthy couple, if both of whom can pay the mortgage out of his or her salary. However, if they have a disabled child, then mortgage insurance can help assure that a surviving spouse or the child have a place to live.

In all such cases, one member of the family needs to make it his or her job to learn about and maximize the various sources of financial support. These may include social security disability income, workmen's compensation, unemployment benefits, welfare, special education, rehabilitative facilities, special medical care facilities such as the Shriner's Hospital for burn patients, and so on.

Both the disabled person and the family can also benefit from emotional and practical help from various support groups that exist. Other people who have family members with similar problems can offer emotional support, practical hints, and leads for information. In particular, these groups can be great sources of referrals to social service agencies and, if necessary, an attorney experienced in providing for the care of such persons.

The key to providing for the care of a disabled or chronically ill family member is to coordinate the various resources. For example, it may or may not be a good idea to set up a trust for the benefit of the disabled person because the availability of those assets may disqualify him or her from public benefits.

One of the hardest tasks facing families in these difficult circumstances is planning for the care of the disabled person in the event of the death of the original caregiver, who is often the spouse. Sometimes a surviving child can take over this task, but it can be burdensome and frustrating.[36] Sometimes a family can work out an arrangement of shared responsibilities among various siblings and other relatives. Sometimes, public or private care is the only solution.

In addition to a good attorney, there are excellent private consulting services that help families coordinate care and benefits. Some of these services are social workers connected with a hospital or care facility while others are in private practice. Hiring a care coordinator can be one of the best uses of family money. A good care coordinator can handle everyday matters for the disabled person, ranging from making sure that he or she keeps doctor visits to seeing that he or she receives the funds to which he or she is qualified, and so on.[37] These coordinators can also help decide what sort of facility will best meet the patient's and family's needs.

Sometimes these consultants are called "care managers." They may be social workers or nurses. A good specialist lawyer may be able to refer the family to such a coordinator.[38]

Different biological relationships — assisted reproduction

The courts and legislatures have not yet sorted out the respective rights and responsibilities of persons who enter into the complex biological relationships made possible by modern reproductive technology. In particular, the rights and obligations of persons who arrange for a surrogate mother to carry a child have not been determined.

It appears likely, however, that some of these difficulties will be resolved by contract, in which the person who is not biologically related to the child can assume responsibility for that child. The widely publicized and unsavory lawsuits in which such a "parent" refuses to have anything to do with the resulting child illustrate how legally uncertain matters are and how slimy people can be.

Sperm and ova donors

Medical technology now permits the reproductive cells of one person to be transferred to another. In other words, the gestation of the child can be separated from the genetic makeup of the child. A woman's egg cell can be fertilized outside her body, either by her husband's semen or by the semen from a donor. The embryo can then be implanted in her womb, or the womb of another woman, for the child to be carried to term.

Many legal issues in this area are still undecided. One of the most painful, and unsettled, questions is the legal consequences when the technology does not produce a perfect child. Unfortunately, but perhaps understandably, the would be parents usually expect a normal child from the expense and pain of these procedures. Sometimes, however, the child has a birth defect. In those cases, tragically, no one wants the child, and the question of parenthood becomes a question of financial responsibility because no court can force an unwilling or selfish adult to become a loving parent.

Semen and egg donors must be carefully screened. A donor who is HIV positive, for example, could transmit the virus in his semen. Any genetic abnormality in the donor will possibly be carried forward in the donated ovum or sperm.

Most courts have held that the donor's contract (which normally provides for relinquishment of parental rights to any resulting child) is a binding contract. In other words, the donor (like a biological parent whose rights have been terminated) is not the legal father of the child.

However, sometimes couples have used infertility treatments involving donation of sperm or eggs. Sometimes, the wife may be inseminated with her husband's sperm after his death; in those cases, the donor/husband is the legal father of the resulting child. The same legal result obtains when a man dies while his wife is pregnant. Ancient law provides that a child born within nine months of the husband's death is his legal child and hence, his heir.

Artificial insemination of a married woman

The courts have also tended to look to the biological and marital relationships as a starting point in deciding who are the (legal) parents of a child born as a result of artificial insemination. In an English case early in the technological revolution in reproduction, a husband sued his wife for divorce on the ground of adultery, arguing that she had been inseminated with another man's sperm and that the insemination constituted adultery. The court agreed, reasoning that preventing the procreation of children who are not the biological children of the husband is the reason that adultery is prohibited. The fact that no sexual act was involved was less important than that a child was produced.

That case illustrates how the courts struggle to apply traditional legal concepts and social values to a new situation. Historically, one of the reasons for the insistence on chastity in a wife was to protect the family inheritance, i.e. to make sure that the family assets descended only to someone of the desired paternal bloodline. On that reasoning, the fact of the biological non-relationship of the husband to the wife's child sufficed for the court to determine that such a conception was adulterous even though no stranger's penis penetrated the wife; the physical act of sexual intercourse was less important to the judges than the genetic infidelity.

Today, some states (about 20 at the time of writing this book) have statutes dealing with the paternity of a child conceived by artificial insemination. If the semen used is that of the husband, then he is the father; the fact that the sexual mechanism was not ordinary intercourse does not change his status as the legal father of the child.

If the semen used is that of a donor (i.e. not the husband), these laws provide that the husband is the legal father of the child, provided that certain conditions are met. The statutes vary but the usual conditions include at least two requirements which are (1) that a doctor perform the insemination and (2) that the husband has consented to the procedure, usually in writing.

If the husband is the legal father of the child, then the biological father logically should not have any rights to the child, nor any obligation to support the child. If the statute does not expressly deny the biological father's rights, the result should still follow from the older rules that prohibited anyone from challenging the parentage of a legitimate child born in a marriage. Similarly, the child should not have any rights vis a vis the biological father, such as the right to inherit from him.

As a general rule, the sperm donor (biological father) is not the legal father of the child provided that various legal conditions are met. These conditions usually include a requirement that the insemination be performed by a doctor and that the donor is anonymous. In other words, these statutes do not apply to cases where a man and woman informally arrange for him to father her child, even if sexual intercourse is not the means involved.

The social purpose of such laws is to protect men who are willing to donate sperm so that infertile men or single women can have children. Not being the legal father means that the donor has no obligation to support the child nor any right to visit the child. The child does not inherit from the donor, unless especially mentioned in his will. In other words, the legal relationship of father does not exist between the genetic father and the resulting child.

Usually, the identity of the donor is kept strictly confidential by the clinic that handles the procedure. The question of whether the resulting child can find out the identify of his or her father is undecided. Sometimes, there is a medical reason for the child to have the information as where the medical history of the parents becomes relevant in treating the child. Other times, the child simply wants to know who his or her genetic father is.

In an informal arrangement, however, the genetic father can be the legal father of the resulting child. Where there has been a lawsuit, most courts have held that the man is the legal father and has the rights and obligations inherent in that role. In other words, the sperm donor in an informal arrangement can be the legal father.

In one case, two gay couples agreed to produce children. One couple consisted in two gay men and the other in two lesbians. One of the gay men donated sperm and one of the lesbians had two children. The couples agreed that the gay men would have visitation rights, and the biological father's name was entered on the children's birth certificates. When the lesbian couple parted, the father wanted to spend more time with the children. The mother refused, and he sued. She claimed that he was just a sperm donor who had no rights, but she conceded that the children loved him as their father. The court held that the man was entitled to be treated legally as a parent and that the visitation rights that had been agreed on would be applied by the court only if the arrangement was in the best interest of the children. In other words, the father was not limited to the exact arrangement that the couples had originally agreed to.

It is worth noting that even if the written agreement didn't control the court's decision, it may well have been important evidence of the father's intentions and the mother's promises.[39]

For example, in the case of *Jhordan C. v. Mary K*, the donor wanted to be the child's legal father.[40] California had a statute that provided that a sperm donor would not be the legal father if the legal requirements were complied with, but Jhordan and Mary had not complied with the requirements. The insemination had not been done by a doctor. Jhordan had also spent some time with the child. The court held that in those circumstances, he had a right to be considered as the child's father.

A genetic father's parental rights can be terminated, however, by a court in an adoption. In other words, if a couple wanted to have a child and arranged informally for artificial insemination of one partner, the other partner could then later petition to adopt the child. The genetic father could either consent to the adoption or simply not comply with the statutory requirements to assert his parental rights. An infertile heterosexual couple or a lesbian couple who wanted to have a child fathered by a male friend might use this strategy. The risks are obvious; the biological father might assert his rights to his child or the mother might seek child support from him.

For another example of the possible uncertainties, consider this Alaska case. The parties were only identified by their initials to protect their privacy. The man, JW, could not have children because he had had a vasectomy. His significant other, KE, had one child by another man. She and JW wanted to get married but she wanted another child. After much discussion of their options and over JW's protests, KE decided to have another child fathered by her previous lover, the father of her existing child. She got pregnant and she and JW married before the baby was born. JW never adopted the baby but he and KE told the child that he was the father, although their friends knew that he was not. Three years later, KE filed for divorce and asked for child support from JW. She argued that he had promised to support the baby, that he had consented to her getting pregnant, and that in all fairness, he should not be allowed to deny that he was the legal father of the child after this length of time.

The court held that under Alaska law a man who tells a child that he is the child's father cannot change his mind and deny his paternity later if four conditions were met. These conditions are: (1) that the supposed father told the child that he was his or her father; (2) that he intended the child to rely on those statements; (3) that the child established a parent/child relationship with the man; and (4) the child did not know the actual facts. The court reasoned that the purpose of that rule was to protect a child who had relied on what he or she had been told; for example, it might be too late for the child to find his or her actual biological father or to get child support. In the case of JW and KE, however, the baby had not had time to develop a close relationship with JW, according to the judges, and KE could seek child support from her former lover who had fathered the child. The child was not lose "the status of legitimacy" because JW and KE did not represent to their friends that the child was his. Also, the court observed that JW never expressly promised to support the child; he had objected to the way in which KE got pregnant. It is noteworthy that the court did not rely on the ancient rule that a husband is presumed to be the legal father of a child born during the marriage.[41]

In other words, where a woman has a child by a man other than her husband, the legal responsibilities of the parties can be very unclear. Her husband may, or may not, be legally obligated to support the child, depending on whether he agreed to do so. If he has claimed the child as his, he may later be precluded from changing his mind if his change would hurt the child. The biological father of the child still has the obligation to support the child unless the baby is adopted by the husband.

Artificial insemination of a single woman

Many women are now deciding to have children out of wedlock where the father of the child is a person with whom the mother does not have an ongoing relationship.

As with artificial insemination of a married woman, the procedure can be performed by a doctor in a clinic using sperm from an anonymous donor. In that case, the donor is not the legal father. If the woman is not married, the child does not have a legal father, unless a man adopts the child.

The procedure may also be done informally by the man and woman themselves. In that case, the genetic father of the child is also the child's legal father.

Informal, or privately arranged, artificial insemination of a single woman for the purpose of producing a child has somewhat murky legal boundaries. There have been relatively few reported cases, to date, where the mother of the resulting child has brought suit for support of the child, perhaps because mothers who bear children under those circumstances are independent-minded to start with. However, the most likely outcome is that the biological father remains liable for support of the resulting child, unless another man assumes that responsibility by adopting the child. Similarly, the biological father presumably has the ordinary rights to visitation or custody.

The question of whether one man, such as the mother's husband, could stand in a paternal role to the baby while another man had to pay child support is unclear. If the husband were supporting the baby, it is possible that the biological father might be relieved of that obligation by termination of his parental rights. A more difficult situation will present itself if the mother dies and the guardianship of the child passes to someone else, at least if the identity of the father is known or ascertainable.

Some lesbian couples have had children by artificial insemination of one of them. In that case, the woman who bears the child is the child's legal mother. The other partner often has no legal connection with the child, unless she adopts him or her. Some states are changing this rule to recognize the parental rights of persons in a committed relationship who stand in a parental role to a child.

This legal separation of biology and love can produce sad consequences for the child and the other parent if the partners separate. She may have little or no right to visitation with a child to whom she may have served as a parent. Some statutes that afford rights to persons with an interest in the child have been used by lesbian partners to assert some claim to the child. Also, some states permit one partner in such a relationship to adopt the other's child. In that case, both partners are the child's legal parents.

Ova donors

The above rules should also apply to a woman who donates an ovum to be implanted in another woman. The donation of ova and the subsequent implantation into a woman of a biologically unrelated embryo conceived in a laboratory, necessarily involves more technology and skilled assistance, including doctors and technicians, than artificial insemination does. Consequently, such arrangements are more likely to be accompanied by contracts and institutional guidelines. There remains the risk, however, that the biological donor of the egg could later assert her right to be involved in the child's life.

Again, some states have expressly addressed this issue and others have not. The Uniform Status of Children of Assisted Conception Act provides that the egg donor has no legal rights to the child and is not his or her legal mother.

Surrogate motherhood – contracts and conception

Surrogate motherhood involves a further division of parenthood into its component parts. A surrogate mother (now called a "gestational mother") carries a child to term with the express intention, decided in advance, of relinquishing the child to another woman. There are several possible biological combinations.

In one California case, a woman who had a hysterectomy wanted to have a child with her husband. She could not, obviously, carry a child. So, one of her eggs was fertilized with her husband's sperm and implanted in another woman. They all agreed that the gestational mother would give birth to the baby and then relinquish the child to the genetic parents. The married couple agreed to pay the other woman to carry the child. The other woman refused to give up the baby. The California courts found that the statutes were conflicting on the issue. One statute provided that a woman who gives birth is the legal mother and the other provided for genetic testing to establish parenthood. The court ruled that the genetic parents were the legal parents of the child, primarily because that was the parties' intention.[42]

In a New Jersey case, a married couple wanted children but decided that it would not be wise for the wife to have the child because she had multiple sclerosis. Another woman was inseminated with the husband's sperm. They all agreed that the gestational mother, who was also the genetic mother would give up the child for the wife to adopt. The gestational mother refused. The court held such a contract was illegal. It amounted to circumventing the state's adoption laws by allowing a couple to pay for a baby. The genetic father was the legal father but the surrogate mother was the legal mother.[43]

The scholars who drafted the first proposed uniform laws could not agree on what the result ought to be in surrogate mother situations. Some states have expressly adopted laws that forbid such contracts, on the ground that they will not take a child away from the woman who has given birth to the child. Arizona, Indiana and North Dakota decided that these contracts were unenforceable. In Michigan, surrogacy arrangements are illegal and in fact a crime. In most states, the contracts cannot be enforced against the will of the birth mother. Several states have prohibited the payment of money to the surrogate mother, just as paying for a baby to adopt in other circumstances is unlawful.

Virginia and New Hampshire, for example, expressly permit the contracts. Virginia has adopted a system under which the contract can be pre-approved by a court before the embryo is implanted. If the contract is pre-approved, then the baby may be taken from the birth mother even if she changes her mind.

By the year 2000, six states declared gestational agreements void (unenforceable), eight states didn't outright ban these agreements but prohibited paying the surrogate mother, and eleven states recognized the agreement as valid. The law was undecided in the rest.[44]

Basically, the law and social regulation of technologically-based biological, familial, and emotional relationships are still in such flux that it is difficult to predict how a particular case will come out or a particular situation be resolved. The courts are struggling to fit these new connections into the old frameworks of inheritance, parental responsibility for children, social responsibility for the upbringing of children, and the theoretical commitment to the honoring of private contracts about private family matters.

In all such situations, a written agreement at least has the merit of making clear what the parties thought they were doing. There is no consensus about when such a contract should be honored and no clear guarantee of the result of a dispute.

Embryos

Technology and medical science have also created the ability to produce viable embryos in the laboratory by combining eggs and sperm. This technology is called "in vitro fertilization;" "vitro" is the Latin word for "glass."

The embryos can be frozen for future use. They later could be destroyed. They could be kept frozen for some period of time, until no longer viable. They could be implanted in another woman or used for research. In particular, the embryos can be allowed to develop for a few days so that they become a source of stem cells, which are the basis for promising medical treatments of several diseases. The moral and ethical questions of what to do with these embryos are a matter of heated debate. At present, federal law prohibits using federal government funds for this research. Some states, such as California, support this research.

The existence of the embryos makes it theoretically possible for a person to become a parent of more children after he or she has decided not to have more children. Presumably, the genetic donors are not the legal parents of any resulting offspring if their embryo was implanted in a stranger.

When a couple makes use of assisted reproduction, there are often extra embryos produced, i.e. there are more viable embryos than are needed to produce children for the original couple. The clinics that perform assisted reproduction require that the couple sign an agreement about what will happen to the extra embryos. Sometimes, these agreements provide that the clinic may use the "leftover" embryos to produce a child for other couples, where husband wife are both infertile. The embryo can be implanted in the wife if she can carry a child or in a surrogate mother. However, it is not clear that courts would enforce these contracts against the biological parents.

At present, the "ownership" of these frozen embryos, in the sense of who controls their destiny, is unclear. In one case, Mary Sue and Junior Davis, a married couple, donated eggs and sperm that produced seven viable embryos which were frozen. Then, the couple divorced. Mary Sue wanted to donate the embryos to other couples who wanted children. Junior didn't want to be a father of an unknown child. The court gave each parent the right to veto the other's disposition of the embryos.[45]

Obviously, that conclusion protects the genetic parents' right *not* to become parents, but it doesn't protect their right *to become* parents. Other courts have considered that an infertile person who has managed to produce a viable embryo might have the right to have that child carried to term or at least that the donors' respective rights should be balanced.

Proposed clarification of the law on parentage

The National Conference of Commissioners on Uniform State Laws (the group of law professors, judges, and lawyers that formulate proposed statutes to resolve complex issues) prepared a new proposed Uniform Parentage Act in 2000. The American Bar Association approved this draft in 2003. This draft code would clarify many of the unsettled legal questions about unmarried fathers, assisted reproduction, and so on, but it remains to be seen how many states will adopt the proposed laws. Even if the legislatures don't pass these laws, courts may be influenced by the reasoning of the eminent writers who have carefully considered the issues.

That code proposes to clarify the legalities of parental status in the following ways. Remember that it may or may not have become the law in your state yet.

Paternity

A man will be presumed to be the father of a child in five circumstances. These are:

1. The child is born during the parents' marriage;

2. The child is born within 300 days after the parents' marriage ends, whether by court action or the death of one of the parents;

3. The first two provisions apply even if the parents' marriage has some legal flaw.

4. The parents go through a marriage ceremony after the child's birth and the father acknowledges that he is the father, provided that his acknowledgement consists in (a) a written record of some sort, or (b) his agreeing to be named on the birth certificate, or (c) his promising in writing to support the child as his own.

5. The man lives with the child for the first two years of the child's life and openly holds the child out as his (publicly says that the child is his).[46]

The first two provisions continue the traditional rule; the latter three codify aspects of contemporaneous couples.

The mother and father may sign an acknowledgement of the child's paternity if they want to clearly establish the child's parentage. That acknowledgement must be in some form of written record and must clearly state that no other man is the presumed father. In other words, if some other man would legally be presumed to be the father, another man and the mother cannot change that presumption unilaterally. For example, if a married woman gives birth to a child by a man other than her husband, she and her lover cannot (under this proposed law) declare that the lover, not the husband, is the father.

The proposed code, however, also provides a mechanism for a man to deny to he is the father. If the presumed father (e.g. the mother's husband in the above hypothetical situation) files a denial of paternity and the mother and her lover file an acknowledgement of the lover's paternity, then legally the lover is the father and the husband is not. In other words, the proposed code continues the ancient assumption that the husband is the father of his wife's child but provides a way for everyone involved to change the legal facts to match the biological ones.

An important aspect of this proposal is that once the presumed paternity conditions are met, the man is the legal father unless there is a court proceeding to change his status. In other words, some form of legal proceeding is required for a man to rescind his status as the child's father once he is presumed to be the father. If, for example, a man discovers that he is not the biological father of a child that he has acknowledged, he must take prompt action to correct the legal record. There are time limits within which he must act, but those time limits are extended if he can prove that he did not have sex with the mother during the time when the baby was conceived and he never held the baby out as his.

The proposed code also provides for a registry for men who believe that they are the father of a child and protects their rights to the child, including their right to oppose the adoption of the baby.

The Uniform Parentage Act tries to address some of the complex issues presented by the many variations of assisted reproduction. It does not address the ownership or control of embryos produced by reproductive technology.

Artificial insemination

A more modern term is "intrauterine insemination." The proposed code covers several aspects of this technology. Its focus is on the consent of the parties involved.

First, the Act provides that if the baby is the genetic offspring of married parents, regardless of whether there was medical intervention, then they are the legal parents of the child, just as if the child resulted from ordinary marital intercourse.

Second, the Act proposes that a man is the legal parent of a child resulting from assisted reproduction if he and the mother sign a consent form to her being inseminated by another man's sperm. This is intended to cover the situation where a couple wants a baby but where one parent's infertility makes him or her unable to create a baby. For example, if husband and wife want a child but he is sterile, then if they both consent to her becoming pregnant by use of another man's semen, then the husband is the legal father of the resulting child. The sperm donor is not the legal father but remains, of course, the genetic father. The key to this proposal is that there must be a record that the would-be parents both consented to creating a child through use of another person's sperm or egg, or both, and that both intended to be the parents of the resulting baby. This proposal would whether the assistance consists in use of donated sperm or ovum or both.

Third, even if there is no written consent, a man can become the legal father of a child conceived by assisted reproduction if he and the mother live together for the first two years of the child's life and he holds the child out as his.

A married man whose wife gives birth to a child using assisted reproduction, however, can repudiate his legal status as the child's father if he can prove that he did not consent to her becoming pregnant in this manner.

Fourth, in general, the draft code makes clear that donors of ova or sperm are not the legal parents of the resulting child unless one of the above conditions applies. In other words, if a husband provides sperm with which his wife is inseminated, producing a baby, he is the legal father of the resulting child. An unrelated donor is not.

Surrogate motherhood

The modern term for a woman who bears a child for another couple is "gestational mother."

There can be as many as eight people involved in this procedure, not counting medical personnel and grandparents. These are (1) the genetic mother, (2) the genetic father, (3) the woman who will carry the baby in her womb, (4) her husband (if any), (5) the proposed mother of the baby, (6) the proposed father of the baby, and of course (7) the baby. Some of these people may be the same, or all may be different individuals.

The proposed uniform code refers to a contract by which one woman agrees to bear a child for another couple as a "gestational agreement." Basically, the proposed code treats gestational agreements as analogous to adoptions.[47] The proposed parents of the resulting baby and the mother enter into an agreement about the baby but their agreement must be approved by a court. This is analogous to a birth mother agreeing to relinquish a baby for adoption; the prospective parents and the birth parents can agree to the arrangement but a court must approve it.

Before the gestational mother actually becomes pregnant, any of the people involved can withdraw their consent to the agreement or a court can terminate the agreement for "good cause." "Good cause" is not defined.

After the baby is born, the proposed parents are supposed to file a notice with the court which declares that they are the legal parents of the resulting child. In other words, they inform the judge that the approved agreement has led to the birth of the intended baby and that they are now to become his or her legal parents. The court can order the gestational mother to turn over the child to the new legal parents. If the parents don't file the notice, a state agency can file it; the proposed parents, who agreed to be the resulting child's parents, are then declared financially responsible for the child.

The draft code thus tries to cover the situation where the proposed parents change their mind after the child is born, as where the child is born with some form of defect. The proposed parents are the legal parents, just as if they had produced the child in the ordinary way.

It also covers the situation where the gestational mother does not want to relinquish the child, as the tragic case of Baby M where the couple who wanted a baby and the gestational mother battled over custody of the child.[48]

If sperm or ovum donors are involved in a surrogacy situation, they are not the legal parents of the resulting child.

If the parents of the child do not follow the rules provided, the gestational mother (neither the donors nor the proposed parents) is the mother of the child. The proposed parents, however, may be liable for support of the child if they agreed to support him or her.

Adoption

Adoption of a child consists in the termination of the biological parents' legal status and the creation of the legal status of parent in a new couple. Sometimes, this only involves one parent, as where the biological father's rights are severed so that a stepfather can adopt the child. In other words, legally, a child has only one father and one mother, and the adoptive parents' step into those roles when the biological parents' role has been legally ended. A court may terminate the biological parents' rights when the parent consents to the termination (as when a mother gives up her child for adoption) or when the parent has abandoned or neglected the child to such a degree that the parent is deemed to be unfit.

Emotionally, the ties are complicated. Some parents want to find the children that they relinquished for adoption; others do not. Some adopted children passionately want to establish a relationship with their biological parents; others do not. For example, country music star Tim McGraw worked hard to make a connection with his biological father, who was the professional baseball player, Tug McGraw.[49]

There are many excellent, touching memoirs by birth mothers who relinquished children for adoption, adopted children who searched for and found their birth parents, adoptive parents who journeyed back to the foreign country of their child's birth, and so on. Two that I found particularly moving are the following. In her book, *Waiting to Forget; A Mother Opens the Door to her Secret Past*, Margaret Moorman describes her experience as a unmarried pregnant teenager forty years ago when a secret birth and closed adoption were the only accepted solutions to a girl who decided against marriage to her child's father.[50]

The title refers to the assurances that she received at the time of the birth that she would quickly forget all about her child and go on with her life. Instead, she thought about the baby for the rest of her life. She also describes their successful reunion. A similar book is *A Man and His Mother* by Tim Green, in which Green describes his search for his biological mother and his feelings about her and his adoptive parents, whom he loved.[51]

Placing a baby for adoption

Society's treatment of unwed mothers has often been emotionally brutal, whether or not the woman wished to keep her baby or to give it up for adoption.

The traditional assumption was that a baby was better off in a home with two parents and that the mother, to the extent that anyone gave a thought to her welfare, should go on with her life and try to forget (and conceal) her lapse from grace. These views sometimes justified cold or even cruel behavior of doctors, social workers, and others towards the expectant mother.

Many people believed that the birth mother should not be allowed to see her baby. Doctors, for example, would frequently order a nurse to cover the woman's face immediately before delivery of the baby. The mother would not be allowed even to know the sex of her child.

For similar reasons, well-meaning social workers representing adoption agencies would browbeat a mother into consenting to adoption. Sometimes, there was outright, perhaps well-meaning, deception of the mother. For example, an agency representative might tell the mother that the baby would be temporarily taken care of at the agency and that she could reclaim the kid when she left the hospital and recovered from the delivery. When she returned for her baby, the child had already been adopted. In the absence of laws providing for waiting periods during which the mother could change her mind, there were instances when a mother tried and failed to stop the adoption.

It may be argued that these doctrines had more appeal when the incidence of child abuse and neglect in families that seemed otherwise respectable was either less known or less acknowledged.

Today, ironically, some medical and other personnel espouse the opposite values, i.e. that a mother should always keep her child. Thus, even when the woman wants to give the baby up for adoption, and even when she does not want to see the child she is relinquishing, nurses and social workers can behave harshly toward her. Stories are told of tearful mothers being forced to dress, feed, and care for a baby while the adoptive parents are outside the room waiting for the longed-for baby.

Even now, doctors are not above trying to impose their personal views on their patients. One obstetrician, who opposed adoption, told the expectant mother that he would report her for child neglect before the baby left the hospital. In other words, he threatened to claim that she was neglecting her baby even while the kid was still under the care of hospital staff and even though he knew that an adoptive family awaited the baby.

Young women have always been, and still are, vulnerable to pressure from their parents, either to keep the child or to relinquish him or her or to abort the pregnancy. There are still instances, for example, where a young unwed mother relinquishes her baby for adoption by her own parents. If the true relationships are concealed, the child grows up believing that his mother is his sister and that his grandparents are his parents, which can lead to great heartache when the truth is uncovered.

Social worker, nurse, and physician solicitude, however, usually did not extend to protection of an unmarried father's interest in his child when the mother was willing to have the child adopted. If the mother said that the father was unknown or uninterested, relatively little attention has been paid to the father's possible desire to be involved with his child. If the child was the result of a casual liaison, the father may have had no particular interest in a relationship or even affirmatively wished for someone else to take responsibility for him or her. Social policy assumed that these were the fathers' attitudes, which were based on stereotypes of ne'er do well fathers or perhaps upon a view that the child would be better off with "more responsible" parents.

With the growth of cohabitation relationships in which the identity of the father is clearly known and in which the father may well be aware of the impending birth, matters are changing to some degree.

The law now requires that the father be notified of any petition for adoption of the child and given some opportunity to assert his rights, at least if he has had any meaningful contact with the baby. States differ, however, in what constitutes sufficient notice to the father and how much time he has to assert his rights to his child. The father's rights in this situation have a constitutional dimension and an adoption carried through in violation of his rights to notice and participation may be set aside later, even years afterwards.

Unwed fathers in most states now have the right to be notified of the birth of a child whom they believe may be theirs, regardless of the mother's wishes. Thirty-nine states have "putative father" registries where a man who thinks that he may be the father of an expected baby can register; if he does so, then legally he must be given notice of the child's birth. These registries are intended to protect a man's right to be involved in the life of his child. By registering, the man can, in theory, prevent the mother from giving up the baby for adoption.

The mother can attempt to defeat the father's rights by failing to identify him as the father on the birth certificate and by failing to tell him about her pregnancy or the birth. Practically speaking, the mother has substantial control over the situation. If she wishes to the child up for adoption, she can quietly move to another state, have the baby, lie to the adoption agency by saying that she had sex with several men and that she doesn't know who the father is, and relinquish the child for adoption. If she wishes to raise the child herself, and has not told the father that she is pregnant, she can simply move away and never tell the man that he is a father.

Moreover, the time periods for a father to assert his rights can be very short indeed, sometimes only a few days. Some states limit the father's right to object to the adoption in other ways, although these limitations may be subject to constitutional challenge.

Maneuvers by the mother to defeat the father's rights may not be legal (and may result in substantial heartache for everyone) but some women still practice them, whether out of fear or desperation or malice. It is important to realize that these subterfuges may not defeat the father's rights; if he is sufficiently determined to find his child, and does so, he may be able to regain custody of the child even if an apparently legal adoption has taken place.

There may be situations in which such conduct on the mother's part is perhaps morally justified, as where the child is the product of rape or the father is a confirmed criminal or seriously mentally ill. It is not justified, however, for the mother's convenience and certainly not as a spiteful act toward the father. Even if the mother does not want to raise the child herself, she owes it to the child and to the father to treat the latter honestly and fairly.

If the father opposes the adoption, then it generally will not take place. The exceptions are where the father has shown no interest in the child for a period of years or has been abusive of other children. In the eyes of the law, however, again biological relationships tend to trump emotional commitments, so that a couple who have adopted a child and had him or her in their family for several years may find that they have to turn the child over to a stranger.

Adopting a child - introduction to the process

In the past, some informal adoptions took place. That is, another couple would simply take a child into their home to raise as their own when the birth parents could not care for the child. Today, such arrangements are difficult because of legal requirements for birth certificates and other forms of identification.

A form of informal adoption may be considered to have taken place when grandparents or other relatives raise a child whose birth parents cannot provide adequate care. However, these arrangements do not have any clear legal status. For the reasons set out above, a couple that plans to adopt a child needs to be certain that all legal requirements are complied with.

Most prospective adoptive couples would prefer to adopt a newborn baby that looks like them, i.e. that could be their biological child. However, the availability of abortion and birth control, as well as increasing social acceptance of unwed motherhood, has reduced the number of "perfect" newborns available for adoption. "Perfect" in this context usually meant a white baby with no discernible physical or emotional problems whose birth mother was a "nice girl from a good family who got in trouble." Therefore, some prospective parents have adopted children of other races, older children who have been removed from abusive or neglectful homes, children with physical or mental challenges, or children from other countries. Each of these alternatives presents its own challenges.

A couple desiring to adopt a baby can work through an adoption agency, either in this country or abroad, or can work with an attorney to arrange a private adoption. People pursuing the latter course usually place a standardized advertisement in the personal columns of national newspapers in the hope of finding a young, healthy woman who has decided to give up her baby for adoption.

Frequently, these parents pay for the legal expenses and the birth mother's medical expenses. It is illegal to pay any amount of money that looks like "buying" the baby. Desperate would be parents sometimes try to circumvent the legal restriction by offering secret cash payments, but this strategy can result in losing a chance to adopt.

Many times these negotiations can be heartbreaking, as the birth mother retains the right to change her mind at the last moment, either to keep the baby or to choose another couple.

Many times, the mother (and rarely the birth father) want to have some ongoing contact with their offspring. These relationships can be difficult for all concerned or the basis for a rewarding and healthy extended family for the adopted child.

Regardless of whether the adoption is through an agency or not, however, a social agency will check out the prospective parents. These evaluations usually include interviews, some background checks, and at least one or more home visits.

Adoption is one of those areas of family law where expert advice is absolutely essential. It is advisable to retain an attorney who specializes in adoption and also to join a local support group, as well as doing research on the Internet. Foreign adoptions, in particular, involve not only the laws and customs of the other country but American law governing immigration. The rules and regulations, particularly in countries with unsettled political situations, can change dramatically and overnight. There are some excellent organizations devoted to helping prospective parents navigate the complexities of adopting in another country. Perhaps the best way to locate a helpful agency is to join one of the support groups for people who have adopted a child from abroad; as in any family matter, you need to be cautious as some organizations are less scrupulous or less competent than others.

In addition, in foreign adoptions, the advice of a good pediatrician who is familiar with the process is also desirable. Some parents have found it necessary to carry antibiotics and other medicines with them when they travel to pick out the child, since conditions in orphanages in poor countries are frequently inadequate by American standards.

Anyone contemplating a foreign adoption from a war-torn country needs to consider the possible long term damage to the child's mental health that can be caused by abuse, neglect, and trauma. In some societies, such as China, there have been periodic scandals about orphanages buying unwanted children, especially baby girls, who are still widely considered less desirable than boys in that culture.

An often over-looked aspect of common law marriage and cohabitation is the difficulty that such relationships pose for couples if they decide that they want to adopt a child. Needless to say, some social workers and social agencies do not regard cohabitation arrangements with favor when it comes to placing a child, whether for moral reasons or for reasons of the emotional stability and reliability of the relationship of the adoptive parents.

Even if the couple quickly marries to satisfy the preferences of the adoption agency in question, the marriage naturally appears to be of short duration. More than one couple, when they decide to adopt, have abruptly announced that they have been common law married for several years, in order to satisfy the adoption agency. The logical problem that a common law marriage cannot be a secret one is conveniently glossed over by all involved.

There may still be a difficulty, however, in producing a sufficiently official-looking document to satisfy the agency in question, especially if a foreign country is involved, since such countries can be more bureaucratically oriented and accustomed to formal documentation of such matters as marriage. Some states, such as Texas, offer a registration arrangement for informal marriages, where the arrangement can be recorded at the county courthouse, but the certificate involved may or may not be sufficiently official for the adoption officials.

Regardless of the mechanics, an adoption is not an instantaneous legal process. Different states impose different time periods before the adoption is legally final. The uncertainty can be misery for the adopting parents, particularly if the biological father (or his parents) assert a right to the child. The emotional bonding process to a baby can often take place almost immediately but the legal bond does not.

Foreign adoptions also involve inevitable delays in finalizing the child's right to remain in this country.

It is also worth noting that the law is changing with regard to the final separation of biological parents from the adopted baby. For many years, adoption agencies and state laws guaranteed that the child could not find out who his or her biological parents were and the biological parents could not find out where the child had gone. Those laws are either being changed or being circumvented. A biological parent can no longer rely on never being contacted by the child. Similarly, an adoptive parent is no longer able to absolutely guarantee that the biological parents will never contact them. Some mothers who give up children for adoption are insisting on meeting the prospective adoptive parents and on staying in touch with the child over the years.

Various organizations offer to help adopted children find and contact their biological parents and vice versa. These organizations can be located on the Internet, so it is unwise to expect that if you give up a child for adoption, he or she will never be able to find you. There are services, including online services, that allow parents who wish to find their biological children and children seeking their biological parents to register. There are also private detectives who specialize in trying to find the parent or child. Obviously, before spending money on such a quest, you should carefully check the references and reputation of anyone that you hire.

Adoption — the legal mechanics

Adoption requires two legal actions – the termination of the birth parents' status as legal parent and the substitution of the adoptive parents.[52]

Birth parents

In all states, only the biological parents have the power to determine voluntarily whether a child is placed for adoption or not. They may voluntarily place the child for adoption or their parental rights may be involuntarily terminated by state action, such as for abuse or neglect of the child.

The mechanics by which a birth mother relinquishes her child for adoption vary from state to state. All of these involve the mother signing a document indicating that she wishes to relinquish her parental rights. In some states, she can sign this document before the baby's birth, while others require a waiting period after the child arrives.

The point at which that relinquishment becomes final and irrevocable also varies considerably. For humane reasons, courts are reluctant to remove a baby from an adoptive home where parents and baby have bonded, even if the birth mother changes her mind. In some states, the mother may change her mind within a relatively short time period, such as 30 days, if she has a good reason for doing so. In others, she needs to show that she was deceived or under duress when she signed the relevant papers.

Some states require the birth mother to appear in court to finalize the adoption while others do not.

Adoptive parents who suspect that the birth mother may have lied about the baby's paternity are well advised to proceed very carefully. No matter how much they may want a baby of their own, only heartache results if the adoptive parents more or less conspire with the birth mother to deprive the birth father of his rights in his own child.

The mechanics for termination of the father's rights are considerably more abbreviated than those for the birth mother. He may choose to sign a document formally relinquishing his rights. He may simply not assert any interest that he has in the child. His parental status may be terminated by a court, even if he wants the child, for a variety of reasons. The basis for termination of the father's rights can include any of the following: (1) his inability to provide a home for the child; (2) his failure to assert his rights in a timely manner; and (3) his failure to take any role in the child's life when he became aware of his or her birth.

The birth father, of course, may attempt to avoid his responsibilities and negate his rights by denying his paternity. It is easy for a birth father to allow an adoption since only his inaction is usually required.

For many years, thousands of children lived in a kind of bureaucratic no man's land. Their birth parents had so abused or neglected them that the children had been placed in foster care. However, the prevailing ideology focused on preserving the family. Even though the parents did not show any significant signs of improvement, the children could not be adopted.

Concern over this situation led Congress to adopt a statute that requires the states to make a decision about the children's futures. If a child has been in foster care and is not returned to his or her family, for a period of 15 out of 22 months, the state must move to terminate his or her parents' rights or return the child to the birth parents. There has been a significant increase in the number of adoptions in the United States since that law was passed.

Adoptive parents

Adoptions may be arranged by either a state licensed agency or, in come states, by a private person such as an attorney. Usually, prospective adoptive parents contact either an agency or a well-known attorney who handles adoptions.

In every state, the adoptive parents are subject to some screening process. The cost and depth of this process varies from a simple home visit after the new parents have possession of the child to extensive background checks, home visits, and psychological testing. In some states, the costs of this process can run as high as $10,000 while in others it may be as little as $300.

The prospective adoptive parents can advertise their desire to adopt, and a really good adoption attorney has many contacts among obstetricians and others who may know of a woman who is contemplating arranging for an adoption of her expected child.

All states prohibit paying for a baby, although the birth mother may be paid for her expenses.

The practice of open adoption is growing. Open adoption is where the biological parents meet, or even choose, the adoptive parents. Usually, the biological mother is the one primarily involved, although sometimes biological fathers also participate in this process. All the parties reach an agreement about their future contact. Some biological parents just want to receive an occasional note or photo letting them know that their child is flourishing. Others arrange for regular visits.

Current studies suggest that open adoption avoids, or lessens, the psychological trauma suffered by a child who is adopted. Many such children feel that their birth parents did not love them or that they are defective in some way, which caused the birth parents to reject them. If the birth parents remain involved in the child's life, the child can see that these parents loved him or her and still care about their child.

Some adoptive parents fear that the birth parents may try to kidnap or reclaim the child or that they will compete for the child's affection. In fact, these unfortunate events almost never occur. Most birth parents in open adoptions remain comfortable with their decision; although there may be lingering sadness, the birth mother rarely wants to interfere in her baby's new family.

One difficulty about open adoption is that the legal enforceability of the visitation agreement is uncertain. Some experts believe that these agreements are not legally binding, and the issue is not settled. In other words, the court order establishing the adoption ends the birth parents' rights. Unless the order itself spells out that the birth parents have a right to visitation or information about the baby, their only rights rest in the adoptive parents' agreement. If the agreement is in writing, then it may be an enforceable contract but the law remains unsettled. If it is an oral agreement, the courts may not enforce it.

Undoing an adoption

In some tragic situations, adoptive parents have sought to undo the adoption. Sometimes, the agency placing the child for adoption has the right to remove the child from the family before the adoption is final. One prominent adoption agency, for example, retained the right to remove a baby from the adoptive home if, within the first six months, the child turned out to be mentally retarded. That agency believed that the perspective parents would not want, and should be burdened with, a less than "perfect" child.

Some of these sad situations involve adopted children who develop severe mental problems. These problems may have a neurological basis, as where the child's biological mother drank alcohol or abused drugs during the pregnancy, which can result in severe learning disabilities and behavioral problems. Excessive drinking during pregnancy can result in a complex of physical and mental abnormalities known as "fetal alcohol syndrome."

Sometimes a child that has been neglected or subjected to extreme abuse suffers lifelong damage. It was previously thought that a child who had been abused as an infant or toddler would have no memory of the abuse. Experts now believe, however, that whether or not the child consciously recalls the events, severe abuse or neglect can cause lifelong mental problems.

Regrettably, some adoption agencies deliberately concealed the facts of the children's past from adoptive parents. Their motives may have been laudable in that the agency was trying to find a home for a child. The result, however, was that unsuspecting parents found themselves saddled with a gravely impaired child. Sometimes, the child's behavioral problems could not be helped with therapy. Family life became a misery.

In these circumstances, some parents have had the adoption legally rescinded and the child returned to institutional care. Some parents (whether they kept the child or not) have sued for damages for the failure of the agency to disclose the magnitude of the child's potential problems.

Finally, an adoptive parent's rights can be terminated like any other parent's, as for abuse or neglect.

Conclusions and advice

It is almost always better if matters concerning children can be resolved by agreement of the adults involved. If you do need to go to court, remember that the best interests of the child are supposed to be the primary concern of everyone. Try to appear, and be, a conscientious, reasonable, loving parent.

(Endnotes)

[1] *New Jersey Welfare Rights Organization v. Cahill*, 411 U.S. 619 (1974), discussed in Hill and Emanuel, at p. 210.

[2] *In re Custody of a minor* 379 N.E.2d 1053 (1979).

[3] *Curzon v. Bosze*, 566 N.E.2d 1319 (1990).

[4] *In re Sampson*, 317 N.Y.S.2d 641(1970).

[5] *Walker v. Superior Court* 763 P2d 852 (1988).

[6] *Bowen v. American Hospital Association*, 476 U.S. 610 (1986).

[7] See *Cruzan v. Missouri Department of Health*, 110 S. Crt. 2341 (1990).

[8] *Parham v. J.R.* 442 U.S. 584 (1979).

[9] National Mental Health Association, fact sheet on boot camps, downloaded from www.nmha.org/children/justjuv/bootcamp.cfm

[10] Lorie Woodward Cantu, "West Texas Boy's Ranch," *The Cattleman*, Volume XCII, No. 9, pp. 96-97, 98, 100, 102, 104, February 2006; See also the West Texas Boys Ranch website, www.wtbr.org.

[11] *Planned Parenthood v. Casey* 505 U.S. 833 (1992).

[12] *Roe v. Roe* 272 N.W.2d 567 (N.Y. 1971).

[13] *Ross v. Ross*, 400 A.2d 1233 (N.J.Super 1979).

[14] *Dewey v. Dewey*, 866 P.2d 623 (Alaska, 1994).

[15] *Bowers v. State* 389 A. 2d 341 (1978).

[16] *"Resolution on Sexual Orientation, Parents, and Children," adopted by American Psychological Association, 2004, available online.*

[17] *In re Andrew A*, 815 A.2d 931 (2203).

[18] *In re D.T., A Minor (The People of the State of Illinois et al., Appellants, v. Brenda T., Appellee)*, Opinion filed October 21, 2004, interpreting Illinois law at 705 ILCS 405/1-3(4.05) (West 2000).

[19] *Santosky v. Kramer*, 455 U.S. 745, 71 L. Ed. 2d 599, 102 S. Ct. 1388 (1982).

[20] *In re D*, supra, quoting *Santosky*, 455 U.S. at 753, 71 L. Ed. 2d at 606, 102 S. Ct. at 1394-95.

[21] *Eisenstadt v. Baird*, 405 U.S. 438 (1972).

[22] *Stephen K. v. Roni L.*, 164 Cal Rptr. 618 (Ct. App. 1980); *Barbara A. vs. John G.* 193 Cal Rptr. 422 (Ct. App. 1983).

[23] See *Jefferson v. Griffin-Spaulding City Hospital Authority*, 274 S.E.2d 457 (Ga. 1981), *In re Baby Boy Doe v. Doe*, 632 N.e.2D 326 (Ill. App. Ct. 1994); *In re Fetus Brown*, 689 N.E.2d 397 (Ill. App. Ct. 1997).

[24] *Espree v. Guillory*, 753 SW 2d 722 (Tex.Civ. App {Houston 1st Dist} 1988.

[25] *Greenlaw v. Smith*, supra.

[26] *Commonwealth v. Addicks*, 5 Binn 520 (Pa. 1813); *Pusey v. Pusey* 728 P.2d 117 (Utah 1986).

[27] *Burchard v. Garay*, 42 Cal. 3d 5312, 724 P.2d 486 (1986).

[28] See John B. Doe, *Grandparents' Rights*, 3d ed. Reading, MA: Smith Jones, 1996.

[29] Leving, infra, at 199.

[30] Uniform Parentage Act (200), Section 102, Comment; 48 U.S.C. Section 666.

[31] *Alison D. v. Virginia M.*, 552 N.Y.S.2d 321 (N.Y. App. Div. 1990).

[32] *Ray v. Ray* 1989 Ohio App. LEXIS 4696.

33   See, for example, Indiana Code 35-46-I-12.

34   Gail Bensinger, "For Love or Money" Reader's Digest, November 2004, p. 149.

35   David Margolick, *Undue Influence: the Epic Battle for the Johnson & Johnson Fortune* (William Morrow & Company, New York, 1993).

36   *My Sister's Keeper.*

37   "The Aftermath of Catastrophic Medical Events" State Bar of Texas 29th Annual Advanced Estate Planning and Probate Course, presented June, 2005.

38   "Keeping the Focus on Quality of Care" State Bar of Texas 29th Annual Advanced Estate Planning and Probate Course, presented June, 2005;

39   *Tripp v. Hinckley*, 736 N.Y.S.2d 506 (App. Div. 2002).

40   *Jhordan C. v. Mary K.*, 224 Cal. Rptr. 530 (Super. Ct. Cal, 1986).

41   *KE v. JW*, 899 P.2d 133 (1995).

42   *Johnson v. Calvert*, 851 P.2d 776 (Cal. 1993).

43   *In re Baby M.*537 A. 2d 1227 (N.J. 1988).

44   Uniform Parentage Act (2000), Article 8, Gestational Agreement, Comment.

45   *Davis v. Davis*, (Tenn. Ct. App. 1990).

46   Uniform Parentage Act, Section 204.

47   Uniform Parentage Act (2000), Article 8, Gestational Agreement, Comment.

48   *In re Baby M*, 537 A.2d 1227 (N.J. 1988)

49   Alana Nash, "Ties that Bind" Reader's Digest, November 2004, pp. 158 et seq.

50   Margaret Moorman, *Waiting to Forget; A Mother Opens the Door to her Secret Past.* (W. W. Norton & Co. New York, 1996)

51   Tim Green, *A Man and His Mother.* Harper Collins, New York, 1997).

52   Useful references are Hill and Emanuel, at pp.158 et seq., Leslie Forge and Gail Mosconi, *The Third Choice: A Woman's Guide to Placing a Child for Adoption.* Creative Arts Book Company, Berkeley, CA, 1999. and Raymond Godwin and Laura Beauvais Godwin, *Complete Adoption; Everything You Need to Know to Adopt a Child*, Adams Media Corporation, Massachusetts, 2000.

Chapter Eight

Promises, promises

Before you can intelligently enter into a prenuptial or cohabitation agreement, you need to understand the structure of contract law. Contracts between couples are still contracts, governed by the general laws. This chapter sets out the basic rules of contracts.

What contracts can and can't do for a relationship

The most important thing to remember about a contract is that having a written agreement can help alleviate disputes, but it is not a panacea for all relationship problems.

There are myths about contracts and contract law just as there are about marriages and marriage law. Some self-help books suggest that a written contract will avoid all future disputes; it won't, but it will, hopefully, simplify the resolution of those disputes.

Myth—*"I don't have to worry about my relationship with my live-in lover because we have a written agreement."*

Fact—*A written contract is just a record of promises made at a particular time. It doesn't magically make a person keep those promises, and a court may, or may not, enforce the contract later.*

Many people, including many first year law students, believe that if someone signs an agreement, then they have to do what it says. Not necessarily. Dishonest or desperate people are perfectly capable of walking away from the most solemn promises. Contracts are not magic—they don't physically make a person do something. A written agreement is just a written record of promises.

Even those who realize that a written contract has no magical power to make the parties obey its terms may still believe that, if someone doesn't do what they promised to do, then the courts will require him or her to do the right thing. Not necessarily.

First, the law of contracts provides various defenses in lawsuits over contracts. The contract might not be a legally valid one or there might be a good reason why the defaulting person was not obligated to follow the terms of the contract. Second, in civil cases, courts usually are reluctant to try to make a person follow a particular course of conduct over a long period of time. Basically, judges prefer to enter decisions that resolve the dispute in short order. A single payment or a single change in the title to stock or real estate can be done immediately and if the loser does not do as he or she has been ordered, then the court can enforce its order relatively quickly.

QUESTION: *"All right then, what kind of relationship warrants a cohabitation or prenuptial agreement?"*

ANSWER: *If the couple, together or separately, has any significant assets or any important financial expectations from the relationship, then, usually, they should have a written contract that memorializes the financial aspects of the relationship.*

A written cohabitation, or prenuptial, agreement is a good idea when one partner has important financial expectations of the other. Those expectations can range from believing that no commitment is involved — "I don't owe you anything but a good time for the moment" — to offering lifetime support — "I will take care of you for the rest of your life."

Unfortunately, the act of making these expectations explicit often reveals that one party has no real intention of making such a commitment. The image of yearly trips to Paris and a beautiful condo in downtown San Francisco may just be one person's fantasy.

Promises of "sharing a life together" that may have been made in the heat of romance (or lust) often appear unacceptable in the cold light of a beady-eyed lawyer's office. Realizing this can be a painful, but vitally important, experience. At least, it's better to discover the "misunderstanding" before the hopeful party invests years in an illusory commitment.

Various common psychological obstacles keep lovers from working out an honest written cohabitation agreement. I call this group of psychological issues the "secret dream problem."

The secret dream problem occurs where one lover has a rosy view of the relationship that is not shared by the other. It is often easier to leave the exact basis of the relationship unexpressed, especially if unconsciously we know that the other party doesn't share our views. For example, *she* may believe that her lover will eventually get a divorce and marry her; *he* may be quite comfortable with the way things are now. If the two of them were to honestly write down their respective views of the relationship, they would be painfully confronted with their divergent dreams. Silence and secret beliefs open the door to disappointment and broken promises later.

One version of the secret dream problem occurs where the parties' expectations differ markedly about the consequences of a big decision in their lives. One partner may believe that acquiescing in the other's desires on an important matter carries a certain obligation with it. In other words, one partner feels that he or she is owed something in exchange for having gone along with a particular decision. A difficult situation arises where one partner sacrifices his or her financial situation in order to secure advantages for the other partner.

These situations have occurred in real life in the disputes between celebrities and their less famous lovers. But these unspoken sacrifice situations occur in the lives of ordinary mortals too. For example, to many couples, if the man is offered a promotion, it still seems natural for the woman to quit her job and move to another city so that he can advance his career.

That decision may be beneficial for both of them, but it may mean a big loss for her in her career. What is hard is for both of them to think through their mutual expectations before that move. She may well assume that her actions justify her in regarding the relationship as more permanent, while her lover may assume that the old arrangement of "as long as we both feel like it" will still govern. What if he meets a new honey at his new office shortly after the move? What if she can't get a comparable job in the new city? Will he continue to contribute to her support if they split up? How long?

Remember that no agreement, not even marriage vows, can guarantee that the relationship will endure. In a marriage, a woman in the above situation may assume that the relationship is ongoing and that the promotion benefits the family, rather than just the husband.

Certainly, the image of the long-suffering wife who repeatedly packed up and moved as her husband accepted one promotion after another is part of our image of the 1950's and 1960's in America. The expectation was that the inconvenience that she and the children suffered would be compensated for by the greater financial comforts of the family. Similarly, her efforts to entertain his business associations and advance his career indirectly through volunteer work with approved social organizations may also have been part of a mutually understood package of expectations.

These expectations may have been justified when women had fewer career opportunities and the divorce rate was lower, particularly when it was socially frowned on for a partner in a major law firm or a corporate executive to divorce. Ideally, the husband recognized that his wife's work advanced his career and that his earnings (and retirement benefits) properly belonged to both of them. Not so ideally, permanent alimony may have somewhat compensated the wife if the couple divorced; often, however, her financial position radically deteriorated and his remained more or less the same.

As the stigma of divorce has lessened, the number of divorces sought by middle-aged executives from their helpmate wives increased. Sometimes, the wife may have been simply enjoying the good life around the country club pool; sometimes her diligent efforts enabled her spouse to advance his career free of worries about household management, child care, and having a nice house to which he could invite his boss. A more liberated (or feminist) view of women led to some judges assuming that such a wife could go back to work, sometimes ignoring the earning power that she had lost by being a homemaker.

Many middle-aged former wives found themselves relatively poor, disillusioned and bitter as the corporate rewards for years of work were shared with a younger trophy wife. Some women who could prove that they devoted their efforts to their husbands' careers have been awarded generous portions of the husband's otherwise separate corporate assets.

A variation on this theme is where one partner supports the other's education. There is an old joke about what the new medical school graduate's first words were to his long suffering wife – "well, my dear, I guess this is goodbye." If you are putting your lover through school out of affection, fine, but if you expect that the relationship will lead to marriage or that she will pay you back after she graduates, then you need to have those expectations clear and, in the case of a loan, in writing.

A common variant of the secret dream problem could be called "the shy lover problem." It arises when one party to the relationship simply cannot express his or her actual financial expectations. If you are too shy to state what you feel entitled to, then you are quite likely to be disappointed or even cheated. Your lover may be perfectly trustworthy and honorable, but his or her understanding may still differ radically from yours; no matter how plain it seems to you that your lover "just owes me," he or she may reasonably feel that, after all, you're an adult too and shouldn't have relied on some unspoken idea about obligations if they were that important.

It is very important to remember that a court will quite likely regard one partner's sacrifices on behalf of the other as made out of love, rather than out of expectation of being repaid. Remember too that most courts do not regard a professional degree as part of the marital property, so whether you are married or not, if you are putting your significant other through school, a written agreement of your expectations is necessary.

The reason for this common disillusionment is that love, sex, money, and companionship entangle in our intimate relationships. For example, a woman says that she dreams of finding her soul mate. Simultaneously, she expends time, effort, and money at the gym, at the makeup counter at Neiman Marcus, and at the snootiest tennis club or the "right" high society church or the hottest country western bar. Her actions show that, regardless of her statements, she wants a soul mate who is also wealthy and successful. A man who says that he is looking for a woman who is "sincere, honest, and warm" may reject out of hand a woman who works as a coffee shop waitress, instead of as a corporate lawyer, or who doesn't have a Barbie doll figure.

A written agreement, whether prenuptial or cohabitation, can't solve these ambivalent and inconsistent desires, but it can make the financial aspects more clear. Lawsuits usually happen when the claimed expectations and promises of the couple are uneven. These cases often involve a situation where one partner is wealthy and the other later claims that he or she is entitled to be paid for his or her "sacrifices" made to provide "companionship" to the other or to "take care of the home."

These disputes can occur whether the couple is married or not. A written cohabitation or prenuptial agreement helps make any such expectation (or lack of it) explicit.

A prenuptial or cohabitation agreement is particularly relevant in these situations:

- ✔ *One partner is making a significant sacrifice for the relationship, as where one partner is putting the other through school and expects to reap the reward of the luxurious lifestyle to be earned later by the other. An agreement can provide for a share of future earnings or transform the contribution into a loan if the couple split up.*
- ✔ *One partner is counting on financial benefits from this relationship, even if the "sacrifice" is less obvious.*

For example, a woman who quits work to raise a couple's children may lead quite a pleasant lifestyle in the suburbs. She may feel "entitled" to that lifestyle for the rest of her life because she "gave up her career," even if in reality she was only working as a secretary when she married the boss' son. Regardless of the morality of her expectations, or the sincerity of the couple's intentions when they married, in a divorce, she may well find that her rosy suburban future is not guaranteed by the law of alimony and child support. On the other hand, her husband may find be surprised to find that the judge doesn't expect her to immediately go back to work as a receptionist and live on her modest salary.

✓ *If the financial situation of the partners differs substantially, whether in earnings or inherited money, an agreement can make clear how financial affairs will be managed in the relationship (who pays for what) and what, if any, financial benefit the poorer partner will take away from the relationship.*

One of the most common uses of a prenuptial agreement is where a wealthy man marries a younger trophy wife and wants to limit her claims on his assets in case she later decides that she prefers the handsome young golf pro to the aging duffer that she married.

✓ *If one partner is solvent and the other is in debt, the better off partner's assets need protection from the other's (financial) problems. For example, having separate financial arrangements is essential if one partner has a substance abuse problem, a gambling addiction, overwhelming debts (especially tax obligations), or just permanent fiscal imprudence.*

Realistic consideration of his or her financial arrangements for the future can lead a person to take different steps to secure his or her own hopes. A woman who realizes that she is not guaranteed a country club lifestyle for the rest of her life, no matter what the marriage vows say, may decide that she won't let her work skills get too rusty or that she will go back to work when her youngest kid starts school.

The plain fact is that many couples unconsciously regard their relationship, whether a marriage or living together, as inherently temporary or conditional. Both (or, tragically, only one of them) may feel that "if things don't work out, we can always get a divorce." The high divorce rate and the number of couples who are cohabiting (which is often an inherently provisional arrangement) mean that a couple cannot rely solely on passionate courtship promises, or vague legal expectations, to secure the financial aspects of their future.

Only someone who understands his or her present expectations, desires, and promises can determine what the terms of a cohabitation or prenuptial agreement ought to be. This book tries to provide guidance in reaching that understanding and in converting that understanding into a written agreement. More concrete guides to ascertaining your status and then reaching a written agreement are in the Workbook

However, none of the agreements in this book or the Workbook will completely match any real life couple's situation. In other words, the sample agreements are samples or suggestions, not forms to be mechanically filled out.

There are more form agreements available on line and in law books. Be careful of rushing into any agreement – in this book or any other one. You must figure out for yourself what you want and make sure that any written agreement reflects your decision and nothing else. The same caution applies to an agreement drafted by a lawyer. It's your life and your agreement, and you are the one who will be stuck with the result if the contract doesn't say what you meant.

Finally, remember that no agreement can ensure that the future turns out as you wish; like any promise, an agreement can be broken. Economic reverses, emotional betrayal, and courtroom disasters can undo any arrangement. The best use of a written agreement may be to provide a memorial of what a couple intended at the beginning and what they promised each other.

QUESTION: *"Wait a minute. What about things like who does the dishes? I thought that cohabitation agreements divided chores and stuff."*

ANSWER: *As a legal concept, contracts are primarily used to record agreements about financial matters. It can be very useful for a couple to write down their understandings about other aspects of a relationship, but these other promises may not be legally enforceable.*

QUESTION: *"I thought that a contract was a contract. If he promises to do the laundry, the judge should make him do it."*

ANSWER: *The more aspects of their relationship that a couple agrees on, the more harmonious the relationship is likely to be. However, money matters can be decided by a court but who cleans the toilet probably won't be.*

Being able to discuss the details of living together usually leads to a couple's shared life being more pleasant for both of them. Even arguing about these details can be useful if it leads to mutual appreciation of the other's point of view and to a workable compromise.

Writing down the shared understanding about who keeps the apartment tidy and who does whose laundry can be helpful because the writing serves as a record of the couple's promises. Later discussions, even if heated, have a staring point, which is the shared understanding that once existed. Writing an agreement about the ordinary issues of living together can act as a catalyst to expose hidden divergent expectations. Ideally, it also provides an opportunity to work through them. Expressly working out the terms of daily life provides an opportunity for the couple to discuss the issues expressly instead of relying on unspoken assumptions or vague hopes. In many couples, one partner is more forceful in expressing his or her opinion and demanding consideration of his or her needs and desires. Sometimes, the act of writing an agreement can give the more compliant partner a chance to state his or her needs.

From a legal perspective, agreement about details such as who does the dishes, however, has a different importance than promises about joint bank accounts. A court could theoretically order someone to vacuum the rug once a week but there is no mechanism for the judge to see that his or her order is carried out. What's she going to do? Send the sheriff out every Monday to check the rug?

Courts have historically been unwilling to intervene in people's day-to-day lives. Courts can enter an injunction (an order requiring or forbidding future conduct) in some cases. The most common examples are orders prohibiting an abusive partner from harassing his or her family and orders controlling visitation with children. It is unlikely that a judge will order someone to do the dishes, although he or she might consider persistent failure to fulfill one's obligations in deciding how to interpret the agreement later.

Also, some aspects of living together are hard to describe unambiguously because the words have different meanings to the two partners. For example, to one person, a "tidy" house may be one in which the week's newspapers are more or less neatly piled on the coffee table. To someone else, a "tidy" house has the previous day's paper neatly stacked in the recycling bin after all the coupons have been cut out and filed alphabetically and cross-indexed by expiration date. Ambiguities like these make cohabitation agreements about everyday life hard to enforce in court.

QUESTION: *"Are there any aspects of a relationship that can't legally be governed by a written contract?"*

ANSWER: *Yes. Contractual provisions about sex, abortion, custody of children, and limitations on marriage or divorce are generally invalid.*

Oddly enough, some of the most important aspects of a couple's joint life – sex, children, and marriage cannot be controlled by a contract.

In general, a couple cannot impose limitations on their rights to divorce or to remarry. For example, a couple might want to ensure the stability of a marriage by promising not to file for divorce. A court will not enforce such clauses; the couple still has all their rights under state law to end the marriage. Similarly, a cohabitation agreement that provided that neither would ever marry anyone else would not prevent either of them from legally marrying another person. Under the law, our rights to arrange our family life as we see fit are too fundamental to be entirely given up in a contract.

However, courts allow some financial penalties for people's conduct, even if the court will not enforce a complete prohibition on that conduct. In other words, a court will not prohibit a woman from remarrying after her divorce but the judge will probably enforce an agreement that her alimony from her first marriage ends if she remarries.

The law is not clear on the extent to which a couple can agree to penalize each other for exercising a legal right. In divorce matters, state law sets the terms of property division, child support, and alimony and the judge retains considerable discretion. Although a couple can alter their personal property arrangements under those laws, there are probably some limits on how far their agreement can go. An agreement that a married person forfeits all of his or her property rights under state law if he or she files for divorce might well not be binding. See the discussion at page 392 about prenuptial agreements and religion.

Similarly, the law is not clear on whether a couple can try to control each other's conduct by financial penalties. For example, suppose a couple agree that if either of them commits adultery, the guilty party forfeits all of his or her marital property rights. On the one hand, a judge might reason that this clause was not very far from old laws about marriage. On the other hand, he or she might reason that such a penalty was far too harsh to be justly enforced by a court because the law does not favor extreme penalties in contracts.

It is likely that an agreement that imposed some reasonable financial penalty for particular conduct, such as providing that if one of the couple is sexually unfaithful, the other is excused from an obligation of support under the agreement, would be valid. Some clauses are clearly not enforceable. These are discussed elsewhere in this book. Here is a brief recapitulation.

First, a court will not enforce any provision that conditions a financial benefit on sex. These clauses are considered to offend morality, and anyway, courts do not want to be in the business of regulating people's sex lives. See page 327 for a discussion of sexual activity and contracts.

Second, a woman cannot sign away her right to control of her reproductive life. A judge will not force her to have an abortion, no matter what she promised.

However, again, it might be lawful to condition financial benefits on whether she did not have a child; for example, a man might agree to pay his significant other some money as long as they had no children, and she might agree to give up some financial benefit if she had a baby. It is possible that a court would enforce a contract like this, but the question is unsettled, especially given the strong opposition to abortion. A judge might find a contract that encouraged abortion repugnant.

Alternatively, a couple might agree that the man would provide generously for his significant other if she had his child. This sort of clause seems more appealing, at least if the couple is married or if the payments clearly also benefit the child. However, there are some legal limitations on the payments that can be made for surrogate parenting and adoption; any contract providing for a financial windfall to a woman for having a baby might fall afoul of these laws.

Third, a court need not follow a couple's agreement about child custody or child support. The child has a right to be supported, and any decision about custody depends on the best interests of the child, although the parents' wishes carry considerable weight. For example, a prior agreement that one parent will get primary custody of any child of the marriage is not binding on the court, but the parents' reasons for making that agreement might well be relevant to the judge's decision. For example, the parents might have agreed that one of them is a more responsible person than the other or that one of them doesn't really want the hassle of taking care of a child. Here is another reason to write down some of the background facts in any cohabitation or prenuptial agreement; the particular clause might not be binding on the court but the rationale behind it might be very important.

The real law of contracts (or at least the part of it about couples)

Here's a basic introduction to law contracts. My contract course in law school lasted a full year, so believe me when I tell you that I didn't manage to condense all that of it into these few pages, no matter how boring they are.

QUESTION: *"What is a contract?"*

ANSWER: *A contract is a legally recognized exchange of one thing for another.*

A contract can consist of the exchange of money for property, for example. Or, a contract might consist of one promise being given in exchange for a reciprocal promise. An employment contract is a promise that money will be paid in the future. For example, I might sell you my faithful steed, Old Dobbin, for $100. Or, one neighbor promise not to mow his lawn before 6.00 a.m. If the other neighbor will turn off her stereo before 11.00 p.m. In these contracts, both sides are obligated to do certain things.

Elements of a valid contract

A valid contract is one that a court will enforce. In other words, if a contract is legally binding, the court will either require both parties to perform their obligations or will require one party to pay compensation to the other.

The elements of a legally valid contract are (1) that both parties receive consideration for their commitment; (2) that the terms of the agreement are reasonably ascertainable; and (3) that the contract does not violate some other law.

Consideration

The items exchanged by the parties to the contracts – whether these are promises or tangible things– are called the consideration for the contract. A contract is not valid unless both parties receive something of value or give up something of value.

There is an important distinction between prenuptial agreements and cohabitation agreements on the question of consideration. The Uniform Prenuptial Agreement Act provides that no specific consideration is required for an antenuptial agreement to be enforceable. That is because the mutual promises of marriage are sufficient consideration. It also means that the agreement never comes into force unless the parties marry. In other words, a prenuptial agreement is only a valid agreement if the couple actually gets married. A court can, however, give some relief if one of the parties has acted in reliance on the contract.

There is no comparable statute for cohabitation agreements, so those agreements are only valid if the couple exchanges something of value between them. Usually, this is only a formality because their mutual promises are sufficient consideration, even if it is only "Jane promises to do the dishes and Dick promises to do the laundry." Sometimes, however, consideration becomes an important issue in cohabitation agreements, especially if the agreement is not in writing. This is because consideration must be something lawful.

Sex is not a valid consideration for a contract. Sexual activity is lawful, but paying for it is not. Any contract where one party promises to provide sexual favors in exchange for something else is unlawful. It is in fact commonly known as prostitution. (No, we are not going to get into the debate about whether traditional marriage is just socially recognized prostitution. Persons with a religious view of marriage regard it as a complex relationship between a man and a woman, sanctioned by God and including sexual love—those who don't have those beliefs, conceive the institution in some other way, as an intimate partnership or a socially sanctioned sexual relationship.)

The point is that the courts will not enforce a contract where one person promises to pay another for sex. This is the issue in palimony suits where one lover sues his or her wealthier former companion. Typically, when the relationship ends, Poor Lover is no longer able to afford the lifestyle that he or she had when the couple were together.

Annoyed, Poor Lover sues Wealthy Lover for "palimony," claiming that
Wealthy Lover promised to support Poor Lover in the style to which Poor Lover had
become accustomed. If the couple were "only" lovers, then the alleged promises of
financial compensation are not valid. If, on the other hand, Poor Lover furnished
Wealthy with some service, other than sex, or made some financial sacrifice for the
relationship, such as abandoning his or her own career plans, then the contract may
be a valid one.

It is worth noting that in some societies where forms of sexual relationship other
than marriage were informally recognized, a contract might have governed the financial
aspects of the relationship. For example, in 19th century New Orleans, England, and
France, a wealthy man who took a mistress for a long-term relationship could enter
into a contract to provide for her. The sexual terms of the relationship were not
expressly part of the contract, of course. Often her mother or another older woman
(sometimes a procuress) would handle the negotiations for the young girl. Legend says
that in New Orleans, wealthy white men attended the famous, but discrete, Octoroon
Balls to meet lovely young women of color.

For moral reasons, courts officially disapproved of these arrangements, and the
law imposed limits on what a man could do for his mistress. Louisiana law derives
from French 19th century law, which is called the Napoleonic Code. Under that Code,
a father could not disinherit his legitimate children and he could not leave the family
plantation to his lover.

Ascertainable terms – written and oral contracts

A court cannot enforce a contract if the judge and jury cannot determine what
the parties agreed to. This is one reason that lawyers recommend that contracts be in
writing. The court needs to be satisfied that the parties intended to make binding
promises to each other and needs to know what those promises were.

In most situations, a valid contract can be in writing or just in spoken words. A
contract can even be unspoken if the intended terms are sufficiently clear from the
parties' actions. The key is whether the terms of the agreement can be proven with
sufficient clarity. However, as discussed in the next section, some states have enacted
laws that require that contracts between lovers be in writing.

Some situations are so familiar in our society that the law implies a contract. For
example, suppose that one Saturday, a kid in the neighborhood offers to mow your
lawn for $25. You agree, he mows the grass, and you pay him. Each Saturday, for the
next six weeks, he asks, you agree, he mows, and you pay. Eventually, he just yells,
"Hey, mister, you want I should do the grass?" and you nod. Even though the

transaction has been abbreviated and no payment was expressly promised, the common understanding in our society is that most people don't do chores for others without an expectation of being paid. You owe the kid the $25.

Lawmakers have always had mixed feelings about oral contracts and have declared some of them unenforceable. On the one hand, making oral contracts legally effective protects people who relied on a spoken promise. On the other hand, without a written document, people can lie (or be mistaken) about what was said. Recording a promise in writing makes it easier to prove later that the promise was actually made. It keeps a later lawsuit from being just a swearing contest about who said what to whom.

To avoid endless lawsuits, state legislatures have adopted laws called the "statute of frauds" which provide that some oral contracts are not valid agreements. These include contracts to transfer title to real estate, agreements to pay someone else's bills, and contracts for employment, if the employment is for more than a year.

In some states, there are specific statutes that require that cohabitation agreements be in writing. In those states, oral agreements based on cohabitation are probably not valid contracts.

Almost all states require prenuptial agreements to be in writing. Missouri requires the prenuptial agreement to be notarized. In the past, courts have disagreed about whether they would enforce oral business agreements between spouses. Some courts believed that the business relationship was subsumed in the "larger" marital one. If you are counting on an unwritten financial arrangement with your lover or spouse, you may not have any legal rights.

Psychologically, a written contract also tends to make people stop and think before they sign it. Sometimes, it can help to make a person do what he or she promised because the contract serves as a reminder of the promise. Finally, the act of writing down the terms of a relationship may encourage one party to admit that he or she doesn't really want the obligations being discussed. A lover may be comfortable promising vaguely to "take care of" the other person but not willing to sign a written agreement to that effect. Sometimes, making the terms of the relationship explicit reveals that the couple doesn't understand the situation in the same way.

Unenforceable and unlawful contracts

Some contracts are flatly illegal, such as contracts to provide sex or contracts to commit a crime. Some contracts are simply unenforceable. "Unenforceable" means that the court will not make the parties fulfill their promises. Verbal promises are hard to enforce; some states do not recognize contracts between cohabiting people if the contract is not in writing. The agreement is not against the law, but the courts will not make the parties follow it.

Many conservative lawmakers feel that cohabitation arrangements are fundamentally immoral and that the courts should not enforce promises made in that context. Others believe that in such an emotionally charged situation, the parties may not be making rational decisions and that one may take advantage of the other.

Lawsuits between lovers are different than a dispute between two corporations. A lawsuit that ostensibly concerns mutual investments between two lovers may actually be a vengeful act by a jilted ex-lover. Finally, there is the risk of fraud; one lover may simply make up a financial claim against a wealthier significant other. In a contract dispute between two former lovers (or spouses), the facts are murky and ambiguous; often, it is simply a swearing contest. One lover claims that the other made a promise and the other denies it.

For all of these reasons, almost all states will require the parties to honor a written cohabitation agreement. A court might or might not enforce unwritten expectations. At best, you might be able to make your lover do what he or she promised, at least if the promises are clear and if not enforcing them would be very unfair.

Consequently, if you are relying on any financial arrangement with your significant other, the agreement needs to be clear, in writing, and based on express mutual promises. It should be notarized. To be safe, each of you should have independent advice or be equally sophisticated.

The facts and nothing but the facts – disclosure to each other.

A written contract is, basically, a record of promises that are being made at a given time. Usually, it is wise to record both parties' understanding about the facts on which the promises are based. This ensures that both parties to the contract have the same information when they make their decisions. If there is litigation later, the court can see the contract in context. Providing information to each other is called "disclosure" and the law requires some financial disclosures.

Factual statements in a contract are "representations" or "warranties." Here, "warranty" does not mean a guarantee that your washer will work for two years. It means that the statements are true. Representations are promises themselves; they are in effect, a promise that the facts are the way they are set out in the contract. So, if I tell you that my horse is healthy, it's no big deal whether he is or isn't, but if I sell you Old Dobbin and I promise you that he is sound, then I have warranted that he really is.

One aspect of representations is that they have to be reasonably complete. If I start telling you about Old Dobbin's health problems, I can't be selective in what I disclose. If I tell you that he's allergic to hay, I can't stop there and not tell you that he also breaks out in a rash around oats.

What does all this stuff about Old Dobbin have to do with you? When a couple starts deciding how to manage their money, they need to be both clear and honest. Either they should agree not to tell each other anything or they should be straightforward with each other. It is both unfair and dishonest to admit that you have a few debts but fail to mention that the IRS has a lien on everything that you own.

Here again, there are differences in the law between cohabitation agreements and premarital agreements. The Uniform Prenuptial Agreement Act provides that an agreement is not valid if it is unfair (see below) and if each person" was not provided fair and reasonable disclosure of the property or financial obligations of the other party. and did not have, or reasonably could not have had, an adequate knowledge of the property or financial obligations of the other party."[1] Notice that the required disclosure includes both assets and debts.

The effect of this provision is that a prenuptial agreement is not valid if one party didn't know about the other's assets or debts.

The couple can agree to waive such disclosure but they have to do so in writing. Not all states have adopted the uniform act. Some have comparable protections for couples signing prenuptial agreements.

There is no comparable law for cohabitation agreements. Presumably, then, ordinary contract law would apply. A cohabiting couple can make any disclosure of their finances or none. However, any significant statements that are made must be true.

Lying, or even making a substantially misleading "disclosure" of your finances, can invalidate your cohabitation agreement and conceivably make you liable for fraud if your significant other suffers a financial loss because of your dishonesty. To say nothing of it being a slimy thing to do to your lover.

 QUESTION: *"Can I put a clause in the contract that it's void if I don't get enough sex?"*

ANSWER: *No. Such a clause is neither practically nor legally enforceable.*

As noted earlier, contracts for sex are illegal. More importantly, a written contract cannot make someone love you. Sound obvious? Well, think about it – the traditional marriage vows in the Christian religion contain such words as "love" and "cherish."

But, we all know that those vows often come to seem an empty mockery when the marriage deteriorates to a relationship characterized by spite, jealousy, and indifference.

So, trust me, if vows before God don't ensure a lasting love, a written contract is not going to do any better. On the other hand, love and caring are two of the most important emotions in this life and talking about them is a good idea. The written record can help you remember how you once felt.

Although sexual considerations cannot form a legal basis for a contract, sexual matters, such as impotence or infidelity, do enter into divorce cases and presumably can be a factor in a cohabitation or prenuptial agreement. Permanent impotence can be grounds for an annulment, although inability to have children generally is not. Deceit about these matters, especially if it involves a sexually transmitted disease, might invalidate a contract or even give rise to a suit for damages. If you are counting on having children, for example, it would seem proper to state in your agreement that both of you believe that you are capable of having a child, and intend to have children. Such statements would be false and a form of fraud, obviously, if one of you had been surgically sterilized.

So, the question is whether it is worth writing down how you feel about each other. And, in my view, the answer is "yes." Not because it gives rise to a binding legal agreement, but because figuring out what to say gives you a chance to really talk about the relationship and about what the importance (or non-importance) of sex, companionship, and love have to that relationship. I'm not suggesting that you set out explicitly what your sexual desires are. ("Honeybunch agrees to ___ my ___ at least ___ times per ___" will only embarrass you later.)

QUESTION: *"But, she promised! She said that we would share everything. Now, she says that it's all in her name. Can she get away with that?"*

ANSWER: *Often, yes. Good luck.*

Remember that oral cohabitation and prenuptial agreements are not valid in some states. Even if they are valid, oral contracts are notoriously hard to prove, and the official title to the property is persuasive evidence and may be legally conclusive. Persuading a court that you didn't really mean that the stock and the cars and the house and the savings account should belong to your significant other, just because you let her put everything in her name, would be difficult and expensive.

The law provides for various assumptions about relationships. In a marriage, for example, suppose that a valuable piece of property is bought by a couple during the marriage. Ordinarily, in their state, the property would be marital property and would be divided more or less equally if they divorced. However, this couple deliberately put the property in the woman's name alone. In many states, the presumption would be that the husband intended to give her his interest in the property.

It is likely that courts would apply similar reasoning to a cohabitation relationship. There have not been enough cases to entirely settle the matter, but where a couple have not married, the law does not provide default provisions for dividing up the assets accumulated during the relationship. It seems that it would be even harder to convince a judge and jury that the paperwork doesn't reflect what the couple intended. A jury might, or might not, believe that a cohabiting couple trusted each other or intended a long term financial commitment when they did not make the formal commitment of marriage.

Finally, remember, some oral contracts about real estate (houses, ranches, and some condos), other people's bills, and jobs (more than one year) are not valid. In some states, oral contracts based on cohabitation are not legally enforceable either.

 QUESTION: *"He promised to marry me! I would never have slept with him if we weren't engaged. Now, he's called off the wedding and moved in with some slut. He's broken my heart. Can't I sue him?"*

ANSWER: *Probably not.*

In the days when respectable marriage was a woman's only available course in life, seduction was a serious wrong to her. Illicit sex jeopardized, if not ruined, her future. Therefore, in those days, the law afforded her (or her father) a remedy. She (or her father) could sue the man for breach of his promise to marry her or for seduction. Sometimes, her father brought the lawsuit. Lawyers called these lawsuits "heart balm actions" because they sought compensation for a broken heart. In effect, those lawsuits compensated the seduced woman and her family for the fact that she would now be unlikely to make a good marriage because she was no longer a virgin. Most states have abolished lawsuits for seduction and similar claims that really are just to compensate someone for hurt feelings; these antiquated lawsuits were called "heart balm actions."

In these days, seduction does not have the same lifelong economic implications, although the emotional pain remains the same. Public policy has changed, and courts and legislatures are more unwilling to permit lawsuits over a broken heart. About half of the states still permit a jilted fiancé to sue for being left at the altar. The unhappy lover, however, cannot recover damages for his or her loss of the economic benefits of marrying a wealthy person. He or she can sue for the mental distress of being jilted and for any injury to his or her reputation.

The other half of the states have discontinued allowing lawsuits for breach of promise to marry. The damage just doesn't seem so socially important any more, and the idea of an engagement as a contract has lost some of its force. Some courts have hesitated to enforce cohabitation agreements because the judge felt that the lawsuit was just a disguised "heart balm" action.

Contracts in intimate relationships

Psychologists and family therapists have long advocated the value of openness in relationships. It is widely assumed that keeping secrets or not expressing one's feelings is psychologically harmful. Analogously, many people assume that getting clear about the parameters of a relationship will strengthen the relationship. Some therapists have advocated "family contracts" in which parents and children write down their mutual expectations and agreements. There is no real scientific evidence for any of these views, although clinical experience and common sense seem to offer some support for their truth.

A corollary of these widespread psychological assumptions is the belief that writing down the terms of a relationship can be helpful. Many books on cohabitation treat a living together agreement as a panacea for all possible future woes. Lawyers have the same reflexive attachment to written agreements as psychologists do to open communication.

As noted in Chapter One, the primary danger of a contract, or any written document (such as a trust), is that it might actually be binding. That may sound paradoxical — after all, the whole purpose of a written agreement is to create a legally stable arrangement. However, a contract or other arrangement that is ill-advised or is entered into under the influence of love or lust or just the overbearing personality of another person can be the source of heartache and regret later.

Because the law sets out the basic rights and obligations of married people, the couple doesn't have to set out their obligations for themselves, at least if they more or less like the default arrangement created by the law. For many couples, therefore, the respective obligations and rights are set by statute; in some circumstances, this prearrangement can protect the more vulnerable party. In others, the result can be unexpected and unfair.

Too often, however, a written agreement, whether it is a prenuptial agreement or a cohabitation agreement, favors the stronger and more cold-blooded person.

In other words, neither a written agreement, nor the strictures of matrimony, offer complete protection from greed or pathology. In the marriage of Susanna and Joe, for example, Joe was a wealthy middle-aged businessman with a wife and children when he met, and fell head over heels in love with, Susanna. Susanna threatened to kill herself if he didn't marry her. Unable to bear her dramatic scenes (which included running her motorcycle off a bridge) and unable to resist his passionate desire for her, Joe complied. Her histrionic demands, which may well have been rooted in a psychological disorder as well as in her greed and selfishness, did not stop with marriage. She emotionally tormented him, their children, and his family to maintain her control of the relationship and to gain greater control of his finances.

QUESTION: *"My lover and I had a serious relationship that lasted 10 years. We both worked and we bought a lot of stuff. He took me to a meeting with his lawyer and I signed a cohabitation agreement. I didn't read the agreement carefully because it was in legalese and I trusted my lover. When we split up, he told me that I wasn't entitled to anything except my clothes and my checking account, which was almost empty. Everything else was in his name. I read the agreement and that's what it said. What can I do?"*

ANSWER: *Probably, not much. You might be able to try to set aside the agreement and claim part of the assets that were earned by both of you, but the likelihood of success is not very high.*

The law is not charitable to people who do dumb things.

One of the most common, and most foolish, decisions is failing to read a legal document. People refuse to read legal papers because the documents are often boring and complicated, although a person of ordinary intelligence can usually figure out enough to know if the documents say approximately what has been agreed to. Sometimes, people don't read a contract because the other party assures them that the terms are what they agreed on. Sometimes, people are so in love (or so in lust) that they can't take their eyes off the other party long enough to read anything. None of these count as excuses if you sign a bad deal.

For a sad example, consider the case of Perry and Mary. Perry lived for several years with Mary. He was a sophisticated and successful business executive. They got involved when she was at a low point in her life, financially and emotionally. He supported her and her children, paying many of the bills and helping to raise the kids, who had their own problems.

One of the big payments that he made was Mary's mortgage on the large and expensive home where they lived. She promised that she would pay him back someday. Not being totally stupid, Perry asked Mary to give him a mortgage on her house, to ensure that she would actually pay him back if she sold the house. She agreed. Mary had a good job and gradually was able to get back on her feet. When she did, she told Perry that she wanted to refinance the house but that his interest would be protected. On a busy day, Perry went to the mortgage company and signed all the papers in a hurry without reading them. One of them was a release of Mary's debt to him and release of his interest in the house.

When Perry confronted Mary (with the "how could you do this to me when I have done so much for you and your kids?" speech), she calmly explained that she had planned the entire scam from the beginning. Mary knew that Perry took better care of his company and his friends than he did of himself and she knew that he probably wouldn't read the documents. She also understood that Perry thought he was smarter and more sophisticated about business than she was and that he probably wouldn't be very careful about the "refinancing." Even when she needed him, secretly she resented the way he "took over" her life. Mary told the officer at the mortgage company to just slip the release of Perry's interest into the pile of legalese, which the officer did. Perry didn't notice the additional document, didn't read it, and signed it.

Perry consulted a lawyer who told him that an intelligent businessman had no chance with a claim of "but I trusted her," and no excuse for not reading the documents.

Unless someone outright lies to you about what kind of document you are signing, (i.e. tells you that it's a change of address form when it's really the deed to your house) the law usually holds a person responsible for a document that he or she signs. If your lover asks you to sign a form and tells you that it is just for the personnel office at work, when in fact, it is a deed turning over your house to him, you may be able to persuade a court to give you your house back: If your lover (or business associate) says "You don't need to read this, it's just what we agreed on," you need to read it.

Dishonest lovers (married or not) use the same lines to get property that seductive sleazes use to get sex. These include "If you loved me, you wouldn't ask me to wear a condom," which has its economic parallel in "If you loved me, you wouldn't want your own lawyer to read this agreement." "If you trusted me, you wouldn't ask me where I was on Saturday night," ranks up there with "If you trusted me, you wouldn't ask whose name the stocks are in."

I hate to say it but think of your lawyer as a condom – if everything is fine, it may have been an unnecessary precaution and somewhat inhibits the experience. If everything is not fine, at least you won't have a venereal disease or an empty bank account, as the case may be.

QUESTION: *"My lover's lawyer advised us to put our assets in a trust in the Cayman Islands in my lover's name to protect our savings from my creditors. We did what he said and we both understood that everything still belonged to both of us. When we split up, my lover said that all of his assets were his and that the trust was irrevocable. What can I do?"*

ANSWER: *Probably not much.*

First, lawyers only represent their clients, i.e. if you are not the official client, the lawyer may well feel no obligation to you at all. Therefore, if your lover has a lawyer, you need a lawyer of your own. At least, you need to make clear to your supposedly joint attorney *in writing* that you are relying on the lawyer's advice and that he or she represents both of you.

Second, when you sign away your assets, whether to an irrevocable trust or by a deed, the assets are usually legally gone. They are no longer yours but belong to the trust (which is a separate legal entity) or to the person named in the deed. Any private oral side agreements mean little or nothing (unless they amount to a fraud on you).

A key rule of contract law is that a written agreement is presumed to contain all the terms of the agreement between the parties. Frequently contracts contain a clause that makes that presumption explicit. This clause usually says something like "This agreement contains the full and final agreement of the parties."

Jane was an orthopedic surgeon and orthopedic surgeons get sued a lot by unhappy patients. Her husband Bill was a landscape architect and much less likely to have legal problems. A clever lawyer suggested that the family put all of their assets in Bill's name so that if Jane were sued by a patient, she could swear that she had no assets except her minimal malpractice insurance. (This faintly fraudulent maneuver has been quite popular among panicked doctors who want to avoid responsibility for their mistakes.)

In the lawyer's office, Jane and Bill both said, "Of course, this arrangement is just a legal formality," and that they both knew that everything still belonged to both of them. Several years later, however, when Jane and Bill were in the middle of a bitter divorce, Bill didn't remember it quite that way. He pointed out that Jane, an intelligent woman with legal counsel at her side, had voluntarily put everything in his name. Surely, she meant to give it to him; after all, that's what the papers said. Result: Bill was legally entitled to everything.

QUESTION: *"Doesn't the law protect people who trust each other? What if the contract is unfair?"*

ANSWER: *Not much, and too bad.*

The basic premise of American common law is that most people deal with others as commercial adversaries. The law treats the parties to a contract as two independent persons, each of whom is looking out for his or her best interest.

Judges are not supposed to write contracts for the parties. The court's role is to determine whether a contract is legal and, if so, to decide whether and how to enforce its terms. Therefore, a court will usually decide only whether a contract is enforceable or not. Usually, the judge will not substitute new terms for the ones on which the parties agreed; to do so would be for the judge to substitute his or her views for those of the couple. That would interfere with their freedom to arrange their lives as they see fit.

On the other hand, judges are not supposed to be indifferent to injustice nor are they blind to the fact that people sometimes trust the wrong person. In balancing these ideological commitments, the courts have evolved some rules that sometimes justify a court in redressing unfairness in an agreement.

Fairness

Obviously, a contract between people in love should be fair to both. Generally, the law, however, does not require that contracts be fair and it does not contain standards for fairness in contracts. Part of our freedom is the right to make our own decisions.

In the United States, as a rule, most parties to contracts deal with each other at "arm's length," meaning that the law assumes that both people have their wits about them and each is looking out for his or her self-interest. The actual situation, where one party is more knowledgeable or more ruthless than the other, doesn't matter legally unless there is fraud or gross imposition.

As a rule, the mere fact that a contract is unfair is virtually irrelevant to a court. This rule doesn't reflect social callousness, but rather it reflects a view that it is not for some judge to tell a person that he or she shouldn't have agreed to something or that the judge had a better idea of what was a couple should have done.

Usually, therefore, judges will not refuse to enforce an unfair agreement unless there is a compelling reason. If one party was victimized in some way, even if not actually defrauded in a legal sense, then a court may give that party some relief.

There are, however, some minimal standards, and once again, there are different rules for cohabitation agreements and prenuptial agreements. Twenty six states have adopted the Uniform Prenuptial Agreement Act. That statute says that a premarital contract is not enforceable if "the agreement was unconscionable when it was executed" and there was not proper disclosure. In other words, a court can decide that the agreement was so inequitable that the court will not honor it. "Unconscionable" means more than merely unfair or a bad deal. It means "a contract which no man in his senses, not under delusion, would make, on the one hand, and which no fair and honest man would accept, on the other."[2]

Other states have different laws. California requires a seven day waiting period between the time that a bride or bridegroom first sees a written copy of a proposed premarital contract and the time when he or she signs it. This helps to prevent one prospective spouse from confronting the other with a prenuptial agreement on the day of the wedding ceremony. Some states permit prenuptial agreements but don't provide any standards for them. Alaska, Wyoming, South Carolina and Vermont don't have any special laws governing prenuptial or marital agreements.

There is no comparable law for cohabitation agreements which would presumably fall under the general law of contracts. In every state (except Texas), every contract contains, automatically, a covenant of good faith and fair dealing. That means that the parties to the contract must exhibit a minimum level of honesty and fairness toward each other. And guess who determines what that minimum level in fact is? The judge or jury, of course – that very same judge or jury with their own views about love and marriage.

Good faith usually is limited more or less to not outright cheating each other and to being "honest in fact," meaning that you don't lie about concrete matters of fact. So, a couple writing a cohabitation agreement probably have some obligations of good faith and fair dealing to each other. At least, they are as obligated, legally, to refrain from dishonesty and sharp dealing as two businesspeople would be. Whether they have a greater duty of fairness to each other is an unsettled legal question in most states.

Trust

Despite all the above cynicism, the law does recognize that sometimes people are in relationships that involve trust and confidence in each other, as well as emotional influence.

In some legally recognized relationships, the parties have a higher obligation to be fair to each other and not to take advantage. These relationships include business partners and people in a joint business venture. Under these rules, for example, business partners cannot legally exploit the other partner. Legally, partners have to treat each fairly and honestly and cannot take advantage. Legally, trustees have to be honest and fair to the beneficiaries of the trust, although they are not responsible for honest, sensible mistakes. Often, of course, people don't live up to their legal obligations.

The law, to some extent, recognizes marriages and, to a lesser extent, cohabitation as relationships in which one person has opportunities to exploit the other. The law, however, does not impose a general duty of fairness on spouses or lovers. Married people are not legally obligated to be fair to each other. A married couple can divide their property in ways that are grossly inequitable if they want to, within the broad limits of a judge's sense of fairness. A cohabiting couple is even freer to do as they like.

The fact that a person makes a foolish decision because he or she was in love is mostly irrelevant to the court. Remember the case of Viki Lee? (see page 142 supra.) The Simeones? (see page 8 supra.) The Hewitts? (see page 142 supra.) In all of those cases, one lover trusted another, and the other took ruthless advantage. Whether the couple married or didn't, the courts didn't protect the imprudent lover.

Sometimes, however, trusting the other person can create a legal duty on his or her part to be honest and fair. These duties arise when one person expressly entrusts the other with his or her assets. It is not enough that one person likes the other and thinks that he or she is honest. The relationship of trust has to be explicit, although not necessarily in writing.

There is a legal relationship of trust, called a fiduciary relationship. Usually, a fiduciary relationship is established where one person explicitly entrusts money to another person. Therefore, an exception to the rule that the law does not protect trusting souls very much (you knew there had to be one, didn't you?) is where one person justifiably and expressly reposes trust and confidence in the other person to, for example, handle the finances. In that case, the court might impose a "constructive trust" on the couple's assets. If one party has abused the trust reposed in him or her, the court can reallocate the money to a more fair distribution. If there is a legal trust relationship, the person trusted has a high level of obligation to the person who trusts him or her.

Usually, in our society, the rule is pretty much that everyone should paddle his or her own canoe. If, however, two people are in a relationship where it would be natural for a less sophisticated person to trust the other, more sophisticated, person, and where the other person knows that he or she is being relied on to be fair and do what is right, then a court may find that a trust relationship has been established.

In law, a relationship of trust means more than just that one person trusted another; it is a legal relationship with duties and responsibilities, like being partners. "Trust me darling" probably won't establish a fiduciary relationship but a long pattern of one spouse turning over all the money to the other to handle might suffice.

Consider the case of Louis and Louisa. Louisa pursued a career as a professor while Louis became a highly paid engineer. They lived happily together for 20 years. Louisa accepted their pleasant lifestyle (with trips to Europe, dining out at good restaurants etc.) as her right. She let Louis handle everything and didn't trouble herself about what was being invested or where.

Louis handled matters to his advantage, although he didn't outright steal from Louisa. He urged her to trust him and ridiculed her questions. When Louis fell in love with a young lady engineer at his company, however, Louisa found her lifestyle reduced to what she could afford on a professor's salary, not what she could afford in the combined union of an engineer and a professor. Her future financial picture had drastically altered. In the divorce negotiations, she got around 65 per cent of their savings but her rosy retirement was going to be much less comfortable.

Judges are probably more inclined to find that one spouse justifiably trusted the other because, ideally, the marriage relationship involves love and trust. Most states prohibit one spouse from cheating the other, such as by diverting money that would otherwise be marital property. However, in general, the law does not require that spouses look out for each other's best interests. The unanswered question is whether and when courts will be willing to find a relationship of trust in a cohabitation relationship. Humane and enlightened judges might well do so, but conservative judges might well decline.

The uncertainty comes from the fact that few cohabitation cases have ever been taken to court. Consequently, although the lines of reasoning that a court might follow can be deduced from analogous cases, such as premarital contracts, the law has not been determined.

QUESTION: *"My fiancée and I are devout Christians. We want our prenuptial agreement to reflect a wife's duty to honor and obey her husband, and his to love and guard her. How do we do that?"*

ANSWER: *This is a difficult question. The woman in such a situation should realize that she might be creating a legal structure that changes her rights in a way that could later cost her dearly. The husband should realize that he might be taking on more legal responsibility than the law imposes.*

Conservative branches of Judaism, Christianity, and Islam teach that the authority, and responsibility, for a married couple's home life rest with the husband. A woman who adheres to these tenets may voluntarily conform her conduct to them, just as she may voluntarily dress in the manner prescribed by her faith. She and her husband may, however, want to incorporate them in a prenuptial agreement, so that the (secular) legal structure of their marriage conforms to their religious beliefs. If her husband proves unworthy of the trust she has reposed in him, then her contract may still have given him control of their finances. On the other hand, the man might be assuming a greater responsibility than he had under the law.

Some organizations that advocate a return to a more Christian view of marriage as a sacred covenant also offer forms for a marriage agreement or ceremony based on those values. The legal force of these agreements as a prenuptial contract is unknown because they may, or may not, conform to state laws governing premarital agreements or may contain terms that are not legally enforceable.

If I wanted to put such a clause in a prenuptial agreement, I would probably include the Biblical passage that most mattered to me in a general statement of intention something like the following:

> *We intend to live our marriage by Christian principles. St. Paul said in the Letter to the Ephesians, "Wives, submit yourselves to your husbands, as to the Lord. For a husband has authority over his wife in the same way that Christ has authority over the church. Husbands love your wives in the same way that Christ loved the church and gave his life for it. Men ought to love their wives as they love their own bodies. Every husband must love his wife as himself, and every wife must respect her husband." We agree to try to treat each other according to those precepts and the others contained in the Bible.*

That paragraph sets out the couple's intent but does not specifically address financial matters or directly change the parties' legal rights. If one party failed significantly to live up to those principles, it might influence how the court enforced the terms of the contract. That language, however, does not expressly change the couple's legal rights, although a court might feel that it imposed a higher duty of fairness on the husband.

The bride could also formally give the prospective husband all power over financial decisions, for example, or provide that she would obey her husband in the household or any other provision that the couple wanted. Some of these might or might not have legal effect. In my view, it is so unwise to completely abdicate the right to control your own financial destiny that I have not included any sample provisions where one spouse completely turns everything over to the other.

If the husband were to be given legal charge of all financial decisions in the family, then it would be prudent to put that decision in the form of an express trust. In other words, if the husband takes on the responsibility of handling the couple's assets, then he should have the legal status of a fiduciary, i.e. one who is responsible for the property of another. See page 339 et seq. Any woman who consciously entrusts her husband with the right to make all of their financial decisions should understand that she will have to live with the result — good, bad, or indifferent.

One wise pastor (and his wife) have offered important advice about the wife's duty of submission to her husband. That advice is that the husband must remember that he is answerable to God for his conduct in the marriage and that he is enjoined to love his wife and to care for her as God cared for his church. That means that the husband has a high responsibility to provide for his family and is not free to make decisions to satisfy his own needs or desires.[3] A woman who enters a marriage with the intention of obeying these Biblical commands (or the comparable standards set out in the Koran) should make sure that she is marrying a man who intends sincerely to fulfil his duties under those same religious texts.

A woman who has any doubts (or realistic perceptions) of her prospective husband's ability to handle the family finances, for example, should seek counsel from her clergyman as her responsibilities in the marriage. In my personal opinion, these Biblical injunctions do not require a wife to allow her husband to gamble away the family home, for example, or to invest all the family's saving in a single speculative venture. Personally, therefore, I would not recommend that a religious woman sign away her legal rights. She can retain her legal rights to own and manage property. Then, if during the marriage, she wishes to follow her husband's decisions, she can, but if she becomes convinced that he is not trustworthy, she can exercise her legal rights as she deems best at that time.

QUESTION: *"Is there a way to keep my money out of my lover's hands for sure?"*

ANSWER: *Maybe. You can try to hide assets, in the United States or in an offshore trust or bank account.*

If you are absolutely secretive, careful, and dishonest, you can hide money or property from your significant other by simply not telling him or her about it. You have to keep all records in a place where he or she can't find them. Or, you can go a little farther and put the property in another name, bury the cash under the floorboards at your weekend cottage, keep a stash of gold coins in a locked trunk in the attic, etc. Obviously, all of these strategies have vulnerabilities, such as a thief finding your hoard, as well as being somewhat sleazy.

Remember, too, that you may later need to commit perjury to keep these assets hidden. Judges are so used to people lying about their assets that many divorce decrees contain a clause that says, in effect, "If it ever turns out that one of the spouses lied about his or her assets, then the other spouse gets that asset." In other words, if you get caught, your ex gets whatever you hid.

The primary problem is that you can't maintain absolute secrecy. If you want someone else to get the property when you die or if you are disabled, you have to leave some trail of breadcrumbs so that people can find it after you are gone. Equally clearly, that revelation needs to be hidden itself or placed with someone you trust. Your lawyer is not a good choice to confide in because he or she should not be willing to help you lie to a court, i.e. in a divorce. In other words, if you pick a crooked lawyer to help with your dishonest scheme, you have every reason to think that he or she will cheat you later, given half a chance.

Regardless of the problems, there are many stories of families who discovered that a trusted husband and father had hidden many thousands of dollars in bank accounts under various names. Buyers of antiques occasionally find cash or securities or jewelry hidden in old furniture. Each year, many unclaimed bank accounts pass into the coffers of the state; presumably, some of these unclaimed funds were squirreled away by people who later died (without telling anyone about the account) or forgot where the account was or the fake name that it was in. (Using a fake name is almost impossible now because of banking regulations that require a person to produce identification before opening an account.)

More formally, a trust or a bank account can be established in an offshore jurisdiction, such as the Cayman Islands. "Offshore" here means "out of the jurisdiction of the United States." Wealthy people use these trusts and accounts to insulate some of their assets from liabilities imposed by courts in the United States. A local lawyer in Panama, for example, becomes the trustee of a trust which owns the stock in a foreign corporation which in turn owns various assets. The person who wants to shelter his or her assets transfers them to the foreign corporation. It is difficult, if not impossible, for a United States court to seize these assets because of the international formalities involved. Obviously, setting up such an arrangement is not cheap, and you have to trust the stability of the foreign jurisdiction. Various property, whether land, stock, or money, are then owned by the company or trust and not by the individual who created it. Money and stocks are usually kept in a foreign bank.

The laws of some other countries such as Switzerland, the Cayman Islands, Lichtenstein, and Panama impose strict rules of confidentiality about banking and trust records. The laws of these countries may limit the rights of creditors trying to get the trust assets; if nothing else, it is difficult and expensive to try to get the assets back to this country because, at best, the outraged spouse or creditor has to bring a lawsuit overseas. In effect, these trusts and bank accounts either put assets out of the legal reach of the United States court system or simply hide the money.

These trusts and accounts have both honest and dishonest purposes. On the one hand, a person may legitimately feel that liability lawsuits in the United States are out of control and want to put money where his or her creditors cannot get it. Or, he or she may want to invest in a foreign country, such as buying a vacation home in the Caymans. On the other hand, a person may want to cheat his or her spouse or the IRS.

Even in countries that afford the protections of banking privacy, there are limits on what make these trusts legitimate. If the transfers are made prior to a marriage, then the new spouse probably doesn't acquire any right at all in those assets.

However, some of these countries will not shelter money that is transferred during a marriage or after a debt is incurred. Obviously, also, these governments are less willing to protect your privacy if the money came from an illegal source, such as drug trafficking or an allegedly terrorist organization.

Finally, sometimes a court in the United States will put considerable pressure on you to bring the assets back to this country; sometimes a person with an offshore account has to decide between protecting the money and perjury. Think about it – the point of the secrecy can be to enable a person to lie. Leaving aside the moral objections and the fact that being dishonest from the start is not a good omen for a relationship, are you willing to take the risk of going to jail for perjury?

At the very least, these devices work only if you keep their existence to yourself, i.e. if you are trying to cheat your significant other, don't tell him or her where you hid the goodies.

Obviously, as with any trust, you need to pick your trustee carefully and you need an attorney experienced with these strategies to help you set up the arrangement. American lawyers familiar with these arrangements can refer you to an attorney in another country if you want a foreign trust.

Opening a foreign bank account is easier; all you need is a little vacation time, a passport, and some cash. Remember, however, that there are legal limits on how much cash you can carry out of the United States. If you really want to protect your assets, the transfers have to be done in a way that does not leave an obvious trail but that does not create legal problems of its own.

QUESTION: *"Short of lying to each other, what legal strategies can we adopt to keep our respective assets separate?"*

ANSWER: *Limited partnerships and trusts can be set up to own assets and make clear that these assets are not part of the marital property.*

A properly designed structure of limited partnerships and trusts can protect a family's assets. The family business or ranch, for example, can be sheltered to some extent from the claims of future spouses and creditors.

As with any legal structure, these arrangements require careful planning and ongoing attention to working within the legal parameters for the structure. In other words, you can't set up a legal structure of limited partnerships and family trusts and then ignore the legal entities. First, the outcome will be messy and expensive, especially with regard to adverse tax implications. Second, the legal protections will likely by lost because when you ignored the legal entities, with their attendant formalities, you may have nullified their legal existence.

For example, suppose Farmer Brown has built a prosperous organic dairy business. She inherited a couple of rent houses, which produce income but need maintenance. She bought a dairy farm, with cows, tractors, milking equipment and so on. She runs the farm. She also has on-line business selling artisanal farm products, such as hand-woven shawls, organic cheeses, and so on. Farmer Brown has three grown children from her first marriage. Her daughter helps her run Farmer Brown's On-Line Organic Farm. Then Farmer Brown falls in love with Hired Hand. She wants to be sure that he has a place to live for the rest of his life on the farm. Then, she wants the farm to go to a charity that works to preserve family farms and sustainable agriculture. She wants her children to inherit the rent houses and the on-line business. But, she wants to keep control of all of the assets until she dies or is incapacitated. If she and Hired split up later, she doesn't want to divide her hard-earned assets with him.

A good lawyer might recommend that Farmer Brown transfer ownership of her rental properties to a limited partnership or a limited liability company, depending on the tax consequences. That partnership would be owned by a family trust. Similarly, ownership of the farm, cattle, and so on would be placed in another company, which would also be owned by the trust. The trust would provide for a home and support for Hired for his lifetime. Upon his death (or remarriage or cohabitation) and that of Farmer Brown, the assets of the trust would be distributed to her children and the charity. Hired and Farmer Brown would also sign a premarital agreement stating that he didn't have any interest in these assets and companies. He also would waive his surviving spouse election.

In addition, a new legal device to protect family properties has been established by some states. This is called a "domestic asset protection trust." Because these are new, no one knows exactly how they will be interpreted by the courts.[4]

These are trusts that a few states, including Florida, Nevada, and Alaska, have created which are expressly designed to keep your assets out of the hands of various claimants. They resemble offshore asset protection trusts but they are subject to United States laws and courts. The laws creating these entities changed traditional rules which prohibited people from putting their assets out of reach of their creditors.

These trusts need careful legal work because their effectiveness depends on compliance with the new state laws creating them. Because they only exist in a few states, no one yet knows what effect other states will give to these trusts.

A reasonable prediction would be that the trust will protect assets (1) if the trust was created before a debt existed, (2) if it was created before a marriage, or (3) if it was expressly permitted under a prenuptial agreement. Likewise, it is likely, in my opinion of future court rulings, that the trust may be set aside by a court if it was, for example, created by one spouse after a marriage in an effort to deprive the other spouse of his or her lawful share.

Conclusions and advice

If you and your lover have any significant financial expectations of each other or if your financial affairs are (or may become) intertwined to any degree, you need to have a written agreement. Keep in mind that, unless you are scrupulously careful, over time, couples tend to obscure the exact lines between "mine and thine."

That agreement needs to be clear and to cover all the important aspects of your relationship. You also need to take appropriate steps to make sure that your economic interest is protected.

That protection can range from making sure that everything is in both names to making sure that nothing is, depending on the relationship. In other words, you have a responsibility to yourself to check periodically to make sure that all the money really is being handled as your partner promised it would be.

However, whether you're contemplating marriage or an informal relationship, you should face the fact that you cannot guarantee that your version of the future will be fulfilled. Unless you snare a millionaire who outright gives you enough money to last the rest of your life, you may be financially disappointed when the relationship ends.

(Endnotes)

1   UPAA § 6(a).

2   "Unconscionable" in *Black's Law Dictionary* 4th Edt. (West's Publishing Co. St. Paul, Minn. 1968), p. 1694, citing *Hume v. United States*, 132 U.S. 406.

3   Pastor Randy and Darla Weaver, Bible Studies Class, Lone Star Cowboy Church, February 1, 2006

4   "Premarital Planning without a Premarital Agreement" presented at State Bar of Texas 31st th Annual Advanced Family Law Course, presented August, 2005.

Chapter Nine

Writing a Contract for Yourself

This chapter can help you write a contract (if you insist on the do-it-yourself approach) or assemble your ideas to go to a lawyer for review (the recommended procedure.)

Writing a worthwhile contract that actually reflects what two people have agreed on is not easy. That's why lawyers get paid to do it. I once helped write a contract for a bunch of banks that went through over 50 separate drafts. When the team of lawyers was finished, the contract was only 20 pages long. Seems like a ridiculous waste of time? That contract governed the relationship among several law firms and six financial institutions for several years and eventually controlled the distribution of many millions of dollars.

Writing a contract about a relationship can be even harder than one about any commercial deal (no matter how complicated it is) because the issues have more emotional freight. Before you can even begin figuring the financial implications of your relationship, you need to decide what the nature of the relationship is, including whether it is a long-term one or a relatively uncommitted one.

This chapter is about procedures that you can use to write a contract, but you may find that you have a lot of work to do on the nature of your relationship before you can even think about what kind of agreement you want. In other words, if you are engaged, you and your significant other have made many decisions about your connection already — that you are committed to each other, that you want the relationship to be a legally recognized, lasting one, and so on. Therefore, you may not need to agonize over analyzing your relationship. Even if you are not engaged, the terms of the emotional commitment may be relatively clear to each of you.

Drafting a contract for a relationship has four basic phases. The first is deciding what you want to agree to and what you want to put in writing in the contract. The second is finding out what your significant other wants. The third is reaching a compromise on any items that the two of you disagree on. The fourth is making sure that the written agreement coincides with what you want.

It might seem natural to wait until you have finished working out all the details before you write down the terms. But, in fact, putting your ideas in writing will help you work through the issues. Writing down your thoughts as clearly and fairly as possible clarifies them.

Basic procedure

The ideal way to use the substantive information in this chapter and the sample forms in the Workbook is to work through them with your significant other. If both of you want to make the terms of the relationship as clear as possible, then you can work together to write a mutually agreeable contract.

To use the Workbook together, you can follow these steps:

✓ *First, read the relevant materials;*

✓ *Second, discuss each topic and decide on what you both want;*

✓ *Third, write down the terms of your agreements; and*

✓ *Fourth, have an attorney check it over.*

In many relationships, however, this tidy scenario simply isn't going to happen. One party or the other is far more motivated to formalize the relationship. Often, but not always, the woman is more interested in talking about it. Sometimes, one party has a greater stake in being sure of the financial arrangements.

In these situations, the burden falls on the motivated person to come up with a first draft of any agreement. A decent person would try to write up a draft that fairly reflects both parties' interests and desires. To do so, first write down what you personally want out of the relationship. Then, try to put yourself in your lover's shoes – what does he or she want or need or deserve? In other words, try to answer the questions in the Workbook from both points of view. Then, using the Workbook as a guide, try to write up an agreement that fairly reflects both of your interests.

QUESTION: *"My significant other and I just can't agree on how to handle our money. He makes a lot more than me and I think that we should pool our income expenses and savings. He wants each of us to contribute an equal amount to an account for expenses and keep the rest of what we earn. I think that he is being selfish. What should we do?"*

ANSWER: *Beats me. You can keep discussing the issue as calmly as both of you can, but in the end, each of you only controls your own money. Since any agreement has to be mutually acceptable (both to be legal and to actually work), one of you will have to give in. Since you can't force him to contribute more than he wants (I hope), you will probably have to concede or leave the relationship. You should be aware that he apparently does not want to share his success with you.*

The best that can come out of an impasse in a couple is a clear understanding of where each of you stands. There is no magical way to transform a relationship into everything that you want.

Here are some strategies you can try:

- ✓ *First, explain your position as clearly and logically as you can, including how your significant other's stance makes you feel.*
- ✓ *Second, try to understand the other's position and feelings.*
- ✓ *Third, put forth the effort to try to come up with a solution that addresses his or her real concerns. For example, perhaps your lover wants to be sure that he has enough to contribute to his IRA; a solution would be for him to make that contribution and then put the rest of his funds into the common pot. Think about whether there is a compromise that would help. Perhaps the wealthier party could contribute somewhat more than the poorer one but not all of his or her income.*

QUESTION: *"My girlfriend and I tried to work out a written agreement so we could move in together. I am starting a new software business with some buddies from school. She says that she ought to get a share in that business. When I refused, she took an overdose of tranquilizers. What should I do?"*

ANSWER: *Leave the relationship, and the faster the better.*

Trying to get clear about the financial terms of a relationship may end the relationship. That happens because one (or both) parties discover that they just weren't in the relationship they thought they were in. Unfortunately, this is especially true where money is concerned.

Threatening to leave because your lover won't give you what you want can be a manipulative ploy or a perfectly legitimate response to an unreasonable situation, depending on the facts. However, threatening physical harm to yourself or another in order to get your way is always and forever a completely unacceptable maneuver. A person who would threaten suicide to control the other person is either pathologically selfish or mentally disturbed. In either case, being in an intimate relationship with such a person is ill-advised, if not impossible. It is unlikely to lead to the happiness of either party.

The Important Questions

Here are the important topics that a couple should address in any cohabitation agreement. The key element to all of these questions is trying to think about where you are now and what you want from the relationship. There is more information in Chapter Ten about getting clearer about your relationship. The Workbook also includes a more detailed list of questions and sample agreements at page 562 and subsequent sections.

- ✔ *What do we expect from each other?*
- ✔ *What will we do with our money? Who pays for what? Who owns what?*
- ✔ *How long is this relationship going to last? What happens when we split up?*
- ✔ *What about children? His? Hers? Ours?*
- ✔ *How shall we conduct our lives together? Where shall we live?*
- ✔ *How does this agreement relate to the rights that we might otherwise have? If we get married, is this agreement supposed to replace the rights that the law gives married couples?*

The various answers to these questions can be manifold. One person may value romantic love above all else while another looks for companionship or a gorgeous date or a more lavish lifestyle.

The most painful question to answer is about the ending of the relationship. All relationships end, at least for this world. Some end after a few weeks in a passionate blaze of bad temper. Some end when the parties become increasingly cold toward each other and finally manage to disentangle their frost-bitten lives. Some only end in the death of one or the other.

You may not be able to foresee the ending of the relationship. Sometimes, however, as where one party has a terminal disease, the likely end is clear. However, regardless of how solid the connection seems now, you need to ask yourself – what is the most important thing that can happen to me when this relationship ends?

Two sample cases can make these ideas clearer.

Case 1

Alexandra and Maximillian, both 20-somethings, moved in together after a few months of passionate dating in Milwaukee. Sex was great and they had a lot of fun together. Alexandra was an interior designer and collected antique china. Maximillian was an aspiring writer who longed to move to New York.

When they both listened to what they were actually saying to each other, Alexandra realized that she really couldn't see herself trying to compete in the intense New York market. Max realized that he was only marking time until he could support himself in the literary center of the United States.

The most important thing to Max was not being tied down. The most important thing to Alexandra was her antique collection. Any written agreement between them needed to make clear that the antiques belonged to Alexandra and that there was no ongoing obligation of support between them. (Needless to say, Max also needed to take his own precautions about birth control.)

Case 2

Mabel and Homer met at a pool party in an RV park in British Columbia. Both were retired, in their seventies, and enjoyed traveling around North America in their respective vehicles. They got along well. Both were on a fixed income, and they quickly figured out that it would be a lot cheaper to sell one RV and live in the other. At their ages, however, they realized that death or illness could strike either of them at any time or that they could both live for a number of years.

The proceeds of the sold RV and the remaining vehicle would be their primary assets. If Mabel sold her RV and kept the money, then she would have a nice nest egg to take care of herself if she became ill or wanted to stop traveling around. She could also contribute to the upkeep and expenses of Homer's RV from her savings and her social security. On the other hand, if Homer became ill, he wouldn't have that nest egg. His RV would probably have to be sold to cover his expenses, and it would be worth less because they would have used it more. Also, if his RV were sold, where would Mabel live? If he died, he could leave the RV to Mabel in his will, but a will wouldn't save the situation if he were to be incapacitated.

Mabel and Homer decided that the fairest arrangement would be to divide everything 50/50. Mabel sold her RV and transferred one-half of the proceeds to Homer, and Homer in turn made Mabel a joint owner of his RV with the right of survivorship. Each of them then had a smaller nest egg. They wrote an agreement that specified that if one of them were incapacitated, the other could continue to own and operate the RV without the interference of the other's relatives.

Mabel and Homer also executed other necessary documents to implement their decisions. They changed the title on the RV. They signed wills that contained the same terms. They explained their decision to their children and gave them copies of the documents.

Steps to a Contract

When you have sketched out your answers to the key questions, then three steps remain – setting out the background, crafting the major terms of the agreement, and putting these two components into the formal language of a contract.

Here are the basic steps to write a contract, after you've worked out an agreement.

✔ *Write down the facts, financial, and emotional.*

The first step is to write down in plain language the facts about your relationship. You don't need to write a romance novel here, "just the facts, ma'am." You may have seen a formal contract with a bunch of "whereas" clauses at the beginning; these are lawyer's renditions of the background facts about a transaction. A contract is usually easier for a court to interpret correctly (i.e. the way you meant it) if the basic background is stated in the beginning.

The facts include statements that you two have made to each other. These statements (called "representations" or "warranties") can be an important part of the agreement. If your lover has told you that he or she has a steady job at the Munchkin Factory and if that is important to you in deciding to live together, then put that statement in your list of facts.

Again, if you are relying on something your lover said, you should put that in the agreement. Some important statements include: "I'm divorced;" "I make enough for both of us so you can quit your job if you want;" and "My kids live in Mongolia with their mother and she has custody, and I don't have any child support payments to make."

✔ *Write down the terms*

The second step is to write down the terms of your agreement about the relationship. There are some sample clauses in the Workbook and in the sample agreement at the end of this chapter that may help you. However, you can't meaningfully write down the facts or decide on the terms of your agreement until you actually know some things about each other, in particular about each other's finances.

Money – yours, mine and ours

Psychoanalyst David Krueger has accurately called money "the last taboo" in our society.[1] Money is one of the hardest things for couples (or people in therapy) to even discuss, leave alone come to an agreement on.

There are many reasons for this. One of the first is that we learn our styles of handling money from our childhood. If you didn't know where your father and mother worked or why they couldn't afford a new car or braces for your sister, then you probably will have a hard time being open with your significant other. And, after all, complete financial openness is not for everyone, since some people just prefer to feel that their money is their own, to spend as they see fit. That's fine – just don't share a bank account with them.

Another reason for not being straight about money can be the fear of revealing one's real interest in the relationship – you've got it! – money. A guy who thinks that his girlfriend is a dog but enjoys free rent at her apartment and gourmet meals every night is unlikely to put that in writing. A gal who enjoys an older man's attentions so long as they include frequent skiing weekends in Aspen is probably not going to sign on the dotted line that says she agrees to pay half the expenses.

Before you begin telling your significant other everything about your finances, it behooves you to think seriously about exactly how significant this other is. If you are living with someone whom you don't know very well and whom you don't even pretend that you might want to marry, why tell him or her how much you make or what bank your savings are in? In particular, if you have to hog tie your lover to get him or her to talk about financial planning, you should consider that it is probably inappropriate, not to say stupid, to share anything financial with this person.

Some experts believe that sharing financial management is essential to the success of a marriage. In the opinion of some advisors, separate bank accounts mean that the couple are leading separate lives, rather than joining in the sharing that is an important part of marriage. This may be true, but it still seems to me that it depends on the character of the couple; if their values, or their financial self-control, vary widely, then separate financial lives may be necessary. To paraphrase the ancient fable, if a frivolous grasshopper marries a prudent, hardworking ant, it behooves the ant to make sure that the grasshopper doesn't dissipate all their savings.

Assuming that you can talk about money at all with your significant other, here are the four basic questions:

✓ *Should we share the intimate details of our financial lives?*

✓ *Are we going to keep our finances separate or commingle them?*

✓ *If we live together, who pays for what?*

✓ *What does each of us expect to leave the relationship with?*

In my view, there are two primary times when financial disclosure is necessary to a relationship. The first is when one party is counting on the other's financial contribution; he or she is entitled to enough information to know whether or not that reliance is misplaced. The second is when the couple is trying to decide what each should contribute; fairness usually involves considering each other's financial ability to contribute to the shared household.

If you opt for financial intimacy, you could tell each other the following:

✓ *How much do you make?*

✓ *How much to do you owe and to who? Credit cards, tuition loans, taxes, child support, car notes, mortgages, etc., etc.*

✓ *Do you expect me to help pay those debts?*

✓ *How much do you want to save?*

✓ *What are we going to do about a place to live?*

The following questions are only pertinent if you're really nosy or contemplating a long-term relationship.

✓ *How much do you have in savings and investments?*

✓ *Do you have any of the following:*
  ◆ *Pension plan? 401(k)? IRA's? If so, how much is in them? Who are the beneficiaries?*
  ◆ *Insurance policies?*
  ◆ *Stock option plans?*

✓ *Do I get a share of these now or in the future? Will you make me a beneficiary under your will? If not, why not?*

Children – yours, mine, and ours?

If you are in a casual relationship, you probably don't need to discuss the issue of children. What you absolutely must do is use birth control. Notice the pronoun – *you* need to use birth control. Trusting a not-so-significant other (with whom you are unwilling to make a commitment) in this regard would be crazy.

A child is at least an eighteen-year legal, moral, and emotional responsibility no matter what you or your lover agreed on. If you don't believe that this relationship will lead to a healthy, happy family, then take the appropriate precautions to avoid creating a child who will necessarily suffer for your irresponsibility.

If you are considering having a child, the responsible, loving action is to consider a child's need and desire to have both parents in his or her life. *Yes*, it is possible for a child to flourish in a one parent home; *No*, it is not optimal.

✓ *Write down as clearly as you can the terms on which you and your lover have agreed.*

Try to imagine different future events and how you would like the contract to apply to them. This is one of the tasks that lawyers do for their clients. You don't need to think about what would happen if aliens abducted your lover, but you do need to think about what happens if your lover decides to leave or if a child is born.

Many people think that lawyers only make things complicated. That perception has a basis in fact because lawyers are trained to think about the different possibilities for a situation, most of which are unpleasant. Because some of the possible outcomes are unhappy, lawyers tend to bring up things that people don't want to think about.

Remember – if some financial aspect of the relationship is important to you, be sure it gets in the agreement.

✓ *Put your own facts and your own terms in the framework of the basic agreement structure.*

The key to writing the best contract for your situation is use simple language but also to take advantage of the traditional legal structure. That way your agreement has the best chance of being interpreted as you intended.

✓ *Take the agreement to a lawyer to be reviewed.*

Standard Clauses

One of the reasons that people hate dealing with lawyers is that the lawyer makes them feel ignorant and awkward. One of the reasons that people get in trouble with contracts that don't say what the parties intended is that people don't read the contract and ask questions about it. Your contract should not contain any sentence, or even phrase, that you aren't confident that you clearly understand.

MYTH—*"We don't need all that legalese. Lawyers just use that so the rest of us feel stupid."*

FACT—*Leaving aside an individual lawyer's being a jerk, the standard clauses for a contract have specific legal meaning.*

Most contracts contain various standard provisions. These are often called "boilerplate" as if they were useless or unimportant. In fact, they apply to situations that often come up in court cases about contracts and consequently can be very important. Here are some of the common clauses and an explanation of their meanings.

All the terms and nothing but the terms

A completeness clause is frequently found in contracts. These clauses typically read something like this:

This contract contains the only agreement between the parties. We have not made any promises to each other that are not contained herein.

It means what it literally says: that the contract contains all of the agreements of the parties.

This language can be both powerful and problematic. It is powerful because it keeps people from later saying that there were other terms to the contract that just didn't get written down. It is problematic because if you are relying on some other promise that is not in the agreement, you are likely to be out of luck later if there is a court dispute over the agreement. If you use this clause in your contract, you must be sure that the contract really does contain all of the terms that are important to you. A court will probably not allow you later to say "but my lover made other promises to me that aren't in this document."

Anti-modification clauses

The phrase above is not a real legal term, but it describes the function of these clauses. It is common to provide in a contract that the contract cannot be modified except in writing. This clause has the same purpose as the completeness clause. The completeness clause is designed to prevent claims that there were promises made *before the contract was signed* and a "no modifications clause" is designed to keep people from later claiming that the contract was modified *after it was signed.*

The difficulty with this contractual provision is that in ordinary life, working relationships often evolve away from the terms of the original agreement. An agreement that accurately and fairly reflects the relationship of a young couple in college may be completely unfair later when one has graduated and the other is in medical school. The couple, however, may be behaving according to changed understandings that have not been written down.

Don't use a "no changes" (or completeness) clause unless you plan to diligently modify the contract whenever your actual relationship with your lover changes.

Consideration

Remember, to a lawyer, consideration is not just a desirable character trait but an aspect of commercial transactions. In law, contracts rest on the idea of an exchange of items of value. A mere promise by itself is not usually an enforceable contract.

Lawyers often put a sentence in a contract that clarifies what the consideration was, such as "The mutual promises herein are the consideration for this contract." In a cohabitation agreement, it may be prudent to make clear that sex is not the (official) reason for the agreement, such as by saying "Our promises to each other are the consideration for this agreement. Sexual matters are not part of the consideration."

Arbitration and mediation clauses.

Mediation and arbitration are fundamentally different. Both involve an impartial third party, but a mediator tries to persuade the parties to reach an agreement. The mediator does not have the power to make a decision. An arbitrator decides who wins, like a judge. Arbitrators' decisions cannot be appealed to a court, unless the arbitrator was bribed or there was some other gross irregularity.

It has become increasingly popular to put arbitration or mediation clauses in contracts. These clauses mean that instead of going to court, the parties will take any disputes to an impartial, fair person. These provisions seem like a good idea because in theory any dispute resolved more quickly, more cheaply, and perhaps according to common sense.

In reality, however, this hope may or may not be true, because arbitrators and mediators often charge fees as high as lawyers, and you probably need a lawyer to prepare for a mediation or arbitration. In particular, it is common to see contracts that provide that any dispute will be resolved under the rules of the American Arbitration Association. That language looks benign but in fact it requires the parties to use an arbitrator (or three arbitrators) who is a member of that association and to follow their procedures. Those procedures are standard and may help ensure predictability. Some feel that these formalities increase the costs. Remember that you now have to pay for the "judge" as well as for an attorney.

Some people tout the mediation process as benign and peace-making. At its best, which is rare, it can be. Usually, it is emotionally draining, expensive, and ends with both parties feeling cheated.

Many responsible lawyers hate mediation because they know that the mediator's job is to encourage the parties into settling that very day, regardless of the merits of the case and regardless of the fairness of the settlement. At the end of a long day of emotionally draining negotiation, people often agree to anything, just to escape the stress.

Some mediators play on people's fears and vulnerabilities to persuade them to accept a deal. They will suggest that the parties cannot leave the mediator's office or "don't have time for lunch" so that fatigue makes the participants more likely to settle. Often, judges like these mediators because they reduce the judges' workloads. Conscientious lawyers regard them as unscrupulous bastards. A good mediator genuinely tries to help the parties find a mutually acceptable common ground. He or she may pressure each of them to realistically consider the costs of a lawsuit, the chance of losing, and the emotional burden of continued battling.

The counterpart to the sleazy mediator who tries to browbeat the weaker party into a settlement, however, is the unscrupulous lawyer who wants to prolong a court case so that he or she makes more money.

Some trial lawyers love confrontation and struggle so they, consciously or unconsciously, encourage their clients to be adversarial and vicious. Even a conscientious lawyer may focus more on legal rights and entitlements, than on the desirability of a family beginning to heal.

Some mediators will try to move the parties to a reasonable and just result. There are good reasons to seek mediation, especially if the dispute involves children. It can reduce the legal expenses. It spares the children a public confrontation in court between their parents. Sometimes, a less than desirable, but immediate, resolution is preferable to a long, drawn out, struggle.

Litigation is a bitter, miserable process, at best. It is doubly agonizing when the contest is with a former lover. In the process, the feelings of love are forgotten or distorted. There is no place where the saying "hell hath no fury like a woman scorned" is more true than in court. Litigants often display the worst traits of human nature – greed, dishonesty, and malice, among them.

However, in a court case, the judge should follow the rules of law. If he or she does not, then you can go to an appeals court to have the legal ruling corrected. Moreover, except in some family disputes, a jury decides how the law applies to the facts. If there is a question of fraud, for example, the judge defines what fraud is and the jury decides if it actually happened. There is a lot to be said for having your case considered by 12 ordinary people.

The value of jury trials is disputed. Some feel that they want a group of people more or less like themselves to apply common sense to their case; that's the basic reason for having juries instead of just letting pompous judges decide the case. Some feel that it is too hard to predict what sort of people will be on your particular jury. Will they be like you or from a completely different socioeconomic background? Will they agree with your lifestyle or regard it as degenerate?

Ending the dispute process quickly, even if one doesn't get everything that one might win, is often the best choice. The legal process itself can harden people's position and generate new grievances. The parties may continue the bitter struggle of the end of the relationship in the court proceedings.

Mediation and arbitration shorten the confrontation process and put an end to the legal maneuvering. If you want arbitration, instead of litigation, then personally, I believe that it is preferable to say something like

Any dispute that we have will be decided by arbitration. We will select an arbitrator on whom we both agree at the time of any dispute. If we cannot agree on an arbitrator, then we agree to let our friend _____ choose an arbitrator for us. If _____ does not choose an arbitrator, then we will proceed under the rules of the American Arbitration Association.

Some families might want to provide that some trusted person like a minister will be the arbitrator. In that case, presumably, you have some idea what you are getting in the way of values and beliefs. Be sure to get the prospective arbitrator's or mediator's consent first and remember, if you have chosen unwisely, his or her decision will still be just as final.

In a very simple contract between two ordinary people, there probably isn't any real need for an arbitration clause because it is unlikely that either one wants to go to court or to a formal arbitration. If you are worried about future disputes, however, you could put in a provision that any dispute will be decided by a trusted friend (who both of you will then end up hating).

Choice of law

Ordinarily, the law of the state where the parties made the contract will govern a contract. As discussed in Chapter One, the question of what law to apply is a complicated one.

A couple can provide that the laws of a particular state will apply to their contract. They can't choose just any state but must choose one that they have some contact with.

A provision specifying what law applies is a good idea if the couple knows that they are going to be moving around. That provision helps to make the contract clear because it determines what rules a court should apply in interpreting the contract.

However, you can't intelligently specify what state law should apply unless if you know what law you are choosing. In other words, why say "Colorado law will apply to this contract" if you haven't got a clue what that entails?

Another common clause in contracts is one that specifies where any litigation will take place. You can have an analogous clause about mediation or arbitration. This requires some careful thought because if one party moves away, the other can file suit in the specified place. That can mean lots of expensive travel and distant legal fees. On the other hand, if there is a dispute, it has to be resolved some place.

Prenuptial/marital agreement waiver clauses

Often, a couple wants a prenuptial or marital agreement precisely because they don't like the property rights created for married couples by state law. Sadly, divorce is often uppermost in each lover's mind when he or she thinks of the need for a prenuptial agreement. Each may want to avoid any liability for supporting the other if the marriage ends or may want to be sure that he or she leaves the marriage with everything that he or she brings into it.

Therefore, many of these agreements contain a broad, general clause that waives any rights that the spouses might have under state property law. These waiver clauses may be essential to the meaning of the document since the whole point may be to replace the statutory arrangement with a handcrafted one. On the other hand, the couple needs to be sure that this is what they mean.

For example, married people have the right to inherit from each other. Is that being waived? What about pensions? Life insurance? There are several cases on the books when a court had to decide how an agreement (or even a divorce decree) applied to forgotten items like these.

While a waiver of marital rights may be the whole purpose of a prenuptial agreement, the couple needs to keep in mind that if they make a mistake, then their beloved spouse may be out of luck. For example, suppose Mr. and Mrs. Smith agree to waive their rights to inherit from each other. Their plan is to make wills that replace their rights to inherit with a different proposition. They intend to take care of each other carefully. However, if Mr. Smith loses the only copy of his will so that he dies intestate, Mrs. Smith will probably not inherit. Mr. Smith's children from his first marriage may well claim that the second Mrs. Smith waived her right to inherit and therefore that they get everything.

Sample agreement

Let's take a sample case to explain a simple agreement for our imaginary couple, Jane and James.

Jane and James decide to move in together. They like each other and get along well. Both of them are in graduate school, and they are not sure that the relationship will last past school.

Sample Cohabitation Agreement – Jane Smith and James Jones

The parties to this Agreement are Jane Smith and James Jones.

The consideration for this Agreement consists in our mutual promises to each other set out herein. Sexual matters form no part of the consideration for this Agreement.

We agree as follows:

(1) We are not presently married and we do not intend to be married. We agree that any reference, now or in the future, to each other as "husband" or "wife" or any other such language is a matter of social convenience only and does not indicate an intention to marry.

(2) Both of us are entering this agreement freely, as self-sufficient adults. Neither of us has coerced or imposed on the other, and each of us has had ample time to reflect on the terms of this Agreement and to get such advice as he or she felt was appropriate.

(3) Neither of us is carrying a sexually transmitted disease.

(4) We have not disclosed our finances to each other because we are not looking to each other for on-going financial support and our relationship would not justify such disclosure. We regard each other's finances as our private business except that each of us has a teaching assistantship that pays enough to support us.

(5) Jane has leased the apartment at 111 Elm Street. James agrees to move out of the apartment within seven days of being asked by Jane. He agrees that he is not a tenant and has no right to stay in the apartment.

(6) Each of us will keep his or her own property. Anything that we buy during this relationship belongs to the person who pays for it, unless it is clearly given as a gift to the other.

(7) If we loan each other any amount of money over $500, we will memorialize that loan by some form of writing, even if it is only a check marked "loan."

(8) Any loan between us that is not indicated by some writing is not intended by us to be an enforceable obligation, and we agree not to sue to collect it in the future.

(9) Unless we agree in writing to other terms, any loans between us shall be free of interest and shall be repayable on demand. Any such loan will be repaid immediately if one of us moves out.

(10) We agree that expenses will be shared as follows:

(11) Both of us will pay for our own cars, health insurance, and other expenses. Max will pay Jane $600 per month as his part of the rent and utilities on Jane's apartment.

(12) Each Saturday we will go grocery shopping together. Each of us will pay half the bill. Any other groceries that we don't agree on together, the one that wants it will pay for it.

(13) We aren't making any other provision for each other.

(14) This is the only Agreement that we have made with each other. We have not made each other any other promises or representations inconsistent with this Agreement to induce each other to sign this Agreement. Any personal understandings of love or affection, or

agreements about daily household management, are not part of this Agreement, nor are they intended to be legally enforceable.

(15) This agreement may only be modified in writing. The only exception is that we may enter into informal agreements between ourselves with regard to the details of loans, household chores, and expenses. Those agreements will be considered to supplement, not to replace, this Agreement.

(16) This Agreement will last so long as we live together. If either of us moves out of our common household, this Agreement is terminated, except that we agree to divide up the stuff in the apartment amicably.

(17) If there is any dispute over the terms of our relationship or this Agreement, then we will submit the dispute, within 20 days of our splitting up, for binding arbitration, to our mutual friend Mabel Goodfriend, whose decision will be final. The arbitration will take place in Chicago, Illinois.

(18) Any legal question about this agreement will be decided by the law of Illinois and the courts of that state will have jurisdiction over any dispute. Venue will be in Chicago.

[Insert signature lines, dates, and notary form]

There are several points that you will notice about this couple's sample agreement.

✔ *Jane and James are making clear that they have very few obligations to each other.*

✔ *They have included standard clauses so that the agreement is most likely a binding one that can only be changed in writing. If the relationship turns into a long-term one and their expectations of each other change, then the Agreement may well no longer match their situation but it will probably still be in force.*

✔ *The termination provisions mean that James can find himself suddenly without a place to live and Jane without someone to share the rent. If Jane cannot afford the apartment on her own, she could find herself quickly in a financial bind.*

✔ *The binding arbitration clause means that their friend's decision will be final, which puts a lot of responsibility on her.*

✔ *They have waived almost all financial disclosures to each other which means that neither one is counting on the other's resources beyond the teaching assistantship. Obviously, that provision is only a good idea if it matches the reality of their situation.*

✔ *The jurisdiction and venue clauses means that if party moves away, he or she will have to come back to Chicago if there is any dispute. There is no good reason to specify Illinois law unless they know what that law is.*

✔ *Finally, the usefulness of this agreement depends on the parties following it. That means that they should not make any major purchases together during the relationship, such as a car or an expensive stereo, without making clear who owns what and who owes what; any new agreement along those lines needs to be in writing.*

✔ *Their obligations to each other are limited to the terms of this Agreement, unless they make another, separate arrangement, like going into business together.*

✔ *The provisions about James' living in the apartment may be inconsistent with state laws on landlord/tenant relationships. A court might, or might not, force James to move.*

There are more sample agreements in the Workbook section (at page 562 et seq.).

Conclusions and Advice

A simple "what mine is mine, what's yours is yours" agreement can be enticing in its repudiation of commitment, but it may, or may not, reflect the reality of your relationship and needs.

In writing a contract, you should assume that you are to be stuck with whatever you agreed to. Be careful, therefore.

The laws that govern the financial implications of marriage and cohabitation change as social values change. Women can no longer regard marriage as a guarantee of lifelong support and dependency. Marriage still, however, involves financial entanglements. On the other hand, cohabiting couples can not entirely count on being exempt from obligations to each other.

If you have explicit financial needs and expectations from a relationship, you need to manage the relevant documents and legal structure of your assets carefully. Probably, you will want to have a marital or cohabitation agreement. Those two actions will give you the best chance of the legal outcome being what you wanted.

(Endnotes)

[1]   David W. Krueger, *The Last Taboo: Money as Symbol and Reality in Psychoanalysis and Psychotherapy.* Brunner/Mazel, New York, 1986.

Chapter Ten

Getting clear about your relationship

This chapter offers some guidance about how to gain more understanding into your relationship so that you can arrange the legal consequences of that relationship in a rational manner. The settled institution of marriage and the ad hoc relationship of living together interweave many strands of human life. Love, money, sex, affection, dependency, property, morality, religious belief, and social standing are only a few of those strands that weave together the concept and law of marriage. Those strands also form some of the issues that people, as a society and individually, have the most passionate opinions about. Keeping your financial affairs in order requires a clear head about your relationship but the very nature of intimate relationships makes it almost impossible to be clear about them. In other words, the best prenuptial agreement in the world will not achieve the legal result that you want if it is founded on an unrealistic view of your fiancee.

Opting for the less institutional arrangement of living together does not avoid all of those complexities, although it can limit some of the legal hassles. Unfortunately, just as there are myths about society in the past and about the law, there are myths about how relationships can work or should work. The Workbook contains a section with detailed questions to help you gather information about your relationship. See "Understanding Your Relationship" on page 656.

MYTH—*"To have a satisfactory relationship, all you have to do is be clear and rational about what you want and look for a relationship that satisfies those needs."*

FACT—*Many factors, conscious and unconscious, shape our relationships. If you work through this book and think carefully about your relationships, you may be able to act more rationally on the financial side of things, but you (and your significant other) will still be influenced by unconscious feelings and by family history.*

For most people in contemporary America, getting clear about their expectations in a relationship is difficult because our desires are only partly conscious and are only partly realistic. Moreover, contemporary society provides a confusing variety of images of relationships, from the idealized "soul mate" descriptions in romance novels to the bitter and mutually cruel relationships portrayed in more serious fiction such as the play *Who's Afraid of Virginia Woolf* by Edward Albee.

This is not to say that a person cannot profitably work on becoming clearer about what is important in an intimate relationship. Moreover, being able to rank one's values and desires means that a person is better able to make the compromises that an ongoing relationship requires.

One of the most important questions that should be settled in thinking about living together is whether one expects the relationship to lead to marriage or not. Living together can be a prelude to marriage, although approximately 25 per cent of cohabiting couples see their relationship only as an alternative to being alone or on the dating scene, rather than as a prelude to marriage.[1]

Expectations about your relationship

Expectations define what people think a good marriage or relationship should be like. The different types of expectations may be described as falling into three basic categories: "soul mate," "companionate" and "partnership." The following discussion is in terms of marriage but it applies also to cohabitation relationships.[2]

A soul mate relationship is one where the couple shares an intimate connection profoundly different from any other emotional connection with any other person. In romance novels, the couple identifies each other as a potential soul mate based primarily on overwhelming lust.

A companionate relationship is one where each primarily seeks the congenial person who shares his or her values and interests. A partnership relationship is one where each primarily regards the other as a practical helpmate in the business of life, such as careers, raising children, and so on.

In the United States, for many decades, the dominant ideal of marriage has been that of the "soul mate" marriage. In a recent study by Rutgers University, a large percentage of young people said that they believed that somewhere there was one special person with whom they could fall in love and be happy.

This image of marriage stresses the importance of love and sexual passion in the marriage. If each member of the couple expects to find a soul mate in the spouse, then relatively small divergences in interests, values, and goals may be damaging to the relationship. Similarly, if sexual passion wanes, as is common in relationships, the couple may feel that the significant other is not, after all, the soul mate and may end the relationship.

Despite the view that marriage should be to one's soul mate, many young people in 1999 reported that they felt that sustaining a marriage required hard work on the part of both parties. This answer suggests that even teenagers understand that marrying one's soul mate is not the end of the effort required to sustain a relationship.

Historically, as discussed in Chapter Two, marriage was regarded as primarily a family matter; that is, a good marriage strengthened family ties, conserved family resources within a small group, and produced grandchildren to inherit those resources. Feelings of love between the young couple and their sexual desire for one another were far less important.

Moreover, their mutual interests were assumed to be parallel; she wanted a prosperous home and so did he. Shared intellectual interests or shared amusements were not expected, although their presence might be greatly welcomed.

To some extent, it was believed that compatibility and sufficient sexual gratification would follow in a marriage of a man and a woman from the same social background and the same community who had probably known each other for years.

Those expectations persist in some communities. Even in the United States and Western Europe, many arranged marriages last for the lifetime of the couple and are reported to be reasonably happy. This may be because the couple does not expect a passionate romance or shared emotional intimacy. Rather, perhaps, they expect a union that will produce children, that will be mutually supportive according to the social norms of their culture, and that will continue their role in their respective families.

For example, a large group of Pakistani people emigrated from their village in Pakistan to the town of Bradford in England. In the culture and religion of Pakistan, arranged marriage between first cousins was customary. The transplanted villagers continued that custom in Britain; over 85 percent of the marriages among Pakistanis in Bradford were among first cousins. There is no reason to think that those marriages produced any more or less contentment than the happenstance alliances of their non-Pakistani neighbors.

(Incidentally, the belief that first cousin marriages result in defective children is largely a myth. The incidence of birth defects increases noticeably only after a number of generations of such marriages. In Bradford, where an increase of a particular genetic defect was noted, families continued the custom of arranging marriages between cousins but consulted geneticists first to ensure that deleterious genes were not being allied.)

Many arranged marriages defy contemporary stereotypes of "falling in love" and "individual choice." One young woman graduate student from India, for example, described her contentment in her arranged marriage. Her family came from a well-educated professional level of society and found her husband from a similar family. Her family supported her obtaining a doctorate, as did her husband's family. She explained that she trusted her father and mother to choose someone appropriate for her with whom she would get along. They did. She liked and respected her husband and he liked and respected her.

Some people, however, even outside ethnic groups where arranged marriages are the norm, seem to select their spouse by using a checklist of desirable and undesirable qualities. In other words, they arrange the marriage as rationally as an old-fashioned matchmaker. The stereotypical example of this approach is the young woman who sets out to marry for money. The more rational she is, the more she arranges her life around this goal. She dresses and exercises in order to be sexually attractive. She chooses where she works, lives, and vacations based on the population of eligible prosperous men.

The people who are best able to happily accept a rationally chosen mate (especially one chosen by someone else) are probably those who have down-to-earth expectations of the marriage and who are willing to compromise, or forego, other possibilities. In other words, for example, a woman who has low expectations of the companionship that a man can offer will be satisfied if her husband brings home his paycheck regularly, takes care of the exterior of the house, and doesn't beat her up too often.

If she doesn't expect meaningful conversation, or companionship in her hobbies, or help with the housework, or emotional support when she is ill, then a relationship without those aspects will suffice provided that her husband satisfies the expectations that she does have, such as, perhaps, earning a good living, securing a particular social status for her in their social group, and fathering healthy children. Similarly, a person for whom the material delights of life are the important aspects may be satisfied with a wealthy spouse who spends generously.

Persons whose expectations of marriage are more in terms of a working partnership may also be able to be content in a marriage that enables both spouses to obtain the desired benefits of the partnership. For example, a couple that regards marriage as a pleasurable working arrangement that provides companionship and mutual assistance with life's various projects, such as building a business, raising a family, and saving for retirement, along with perhaps some sexual gratification, will not be overwhelmingly disappointed by an absence of romantic evenings.

In different periods of American history, a rational approach to selecting a spouse has been regarded alternately as "the only sensible way to be" or "cold-hearted," or even "gold digging." To some extent, a woman who sets out to marry a wealthy man, more or less regardless of their compatibility, is regarded as mercenary at best and a whore at worst. (On the other hand, it is unlikely that she'll be excluded from the country club.)

The above paragraphs should not be interpreted as saying that everyone with limited expectations is happy or fulfilled or leading a rich and worthwhile life; it is only to say that some people are willing to forego aspects of relationships that others find important.

The type of relationship that you are in determines how much effort is going to be needed to make the relationship legally clear. In a simple living together arrangement, you may want nothing more than a simple contract that specifies that the relationship isn't any big deal and isn't intended to have any legal consequences. But if you are in a long-term, serious relationship, then things like insurance policies, pension plans, and deeds need to be changed.

Many times, however, the nature of the relationship is never really discussed, or, even if there is a discussion, the couple still comes away with differing expectations. Often, the years simply slip away, and a relationship becomes a long-term one without either party really making a decision. Some people regard this flexibility as the strength of cohabitation relationships. The potential legal consequences, however, can be heartbreakingly disappointing.

Patterns from the past — desires conscious and unconscious

All of us are affected unconsciously and consciously by our experiences in relationships, beginning with our experiences with our mothers and fathers. Little girls learn about their relationship with men first from their relationship with their father, and little boys about women from their mother.

If Daddy is harsh and critical, to some extent, the little girl is likely to always expect similar attitudes from the men in her life. The blandest remark from her husband makes her feel demeaned and hurt.

It's hard to know what we want in other words, because so many of our motives and desires are hidden from ourselves. Some desires and feelings make us ashamed and it is almost impossible to acknowledge them to ourselves. Sometimes, a person's behavior is completely inconsistent with the values that he/she would ascribe to him/herself. Moreover, that inconsistency may be almost invisible to the person involved who may deny that it exists or rationalize it away.

If Mom whined, demanded that Junior help her in the house, and made his life a misery, Junior may always feel uncomfortable and resentful of any request for help with household chores. In later life, Junior may consciously believe that household chores should be shared. He may sincerely want to make his wife or roommate happy by keeping the place neat. But in his heart, even the most reasonable request for help with tidying up comes to him in the whining voice of his mother. He doesn't really hear "Hey, there's nothing on TV, could you please help me with the laundry." What he hears is his mother's shrewish voice saying, "I don't care that you want to be out playing ball with your friends. I want you in here doing laundry all day Saturday."

Jim's mother, for example, was a pathologically selfish woman and a hypochondriac. Often, she wore a scarf over her nose and mouth to "protect against bronchitis." When Jim was a child, his mother insisted that he help her in the garden. He hated this gardening, particularly because it forced him to be in constant company with his shrewish mother. Jim's father, however, had grown up on a farm, and visiting his uncle's farm were some of Jim's happiest childhood memories. He longed to live in the country when he grew up. So, on one level, Jim consciously believed that he liked farm-type activities but on the other hand, some "country" activities, like gardening, had very unpleasant associations for him.

When he grew up and married a woman who had horses and liked country life, he couldn't stand to eat the vegetables that his wife grew. He told her that he didn't "know what might be in them." Consciously, he knew that remark was nuts, especially because his wife was an organic gardener. But, unconsciously, to Jim, vegetables from a woman's garden were, literally, poison.

Similarly, when he went to visit a horse farm with his wife, he felt compelled to cover his nose and mouth with a handkerchief to "protect my lungs from the dust." Consciously, he knew he was in good health and that other visitors to the stable didn't need this "protection" but, unconsciously, he still needed to act like his mother. It took years of in-depth therapy, and a divorce, before Jim recognized the controlling elements in himself that were like those in his mother's character and consciously decided to give up some of them.

For another example, Jane could not enjoy sex when she was in a stable relationship. When she was dating, however, Jane came on like a real sexpot. Her flirting and teasing were genuine — that's how she really felt — on a date. What she couldn't acknowledge, though, was that as soon she settled down with a man, she hated the very thought of sex with him. His touch repulsed her. Because she regarded herself as a passionate person, however, Jane ended up running around with guys she met in a bar or at a party.

Even as she pursued sexual relationships with other men, Jane persistently criticized her husband or steady boyfriend for "not wanting anything but sex" or for having "perverted" desires. Jane's long-term relationships were doomed for reasons that she could not see. One after another, her boyfriends and husbands felt betrayed and cheated —feelings that she truly could not understand. Understandably, perhaps, Jane ended up despising the male sex and resolving to just get what she could financially from the series of men in her life.

Talking over things with a significant other and with a good therapist or psychoanalyst can help us recognize these unconscious patterns from the past and can help us avoid repeating them. That self-discovery, however, takes a lot of honesty and effort, and not everyone is willing or able to face these kinds of facts about themselves. It is easier to say "You're always nagging me about something" instead of "It makes me feel angry to be asked to do anything around the house." For one thing, if we understood ourselves better, we might have to give up some of our excuses or even stop blaming others for our problems.

Some bad relationships arise from solvable personal quirks but others are caused by serious psychopathology on the part of one or both of the couple. It is not uncommon for therapists to discover that two people with complementary emotional problems have managed to find one another; although they make each other unhappy, their very misery fits into their respective psychological patterns. These relationships can be very resistant to change; understandably, if one of the parties does get healthier, the relationship often ends because, ironically, the couple are now mismatched.

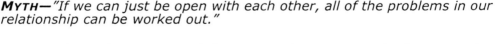

MYTH—"If we can just be open with each other, all of the problems in our relationship can be worked out."

FACT—Talking things over with honesty and tact in a spirit of compromise does help a couple to reach acceptable solutions. But, some people are simply unable or unwilling to carry on a serious conversation; they employ many devices to avoid talking. And, to be honest, sometimes it is better to keep some things to your self in a given relationship.

One of the most persistent ideas in counseling sessions, in women's magazines, and in the minds and hearts of millions of people, is that if we just sit down and talk things over sincerely, we can work everything out. Unfortunately, this is simply not so.

I call this the "talk therapy" myth. I have seen it expressed by individuals and families in therapy, by parties to lawsuits and mediations, and in dozens of hopeful articles on everything from getting along with your neighbors to international peace.

Let's look again at the examples above. A woman like Jane may well say to her new partner that she just loves sex. And, as she bats her eyes at him in a bar, she really means it. What she can't say (because she doesn't understand that part of herself) is that as soon as the relationship becomes a settled one, she will loathe the very idea of sex with him. A man like Jim may tell his fiancé that he looks forward to living in the country and growing their own fruits and vegetables. He sincerely believes that country life appeals to him, because of his happy memories of vacations on his uncle's farm; what he can't tell his fiancée (because this aspect of his character is outside his awareness of himself) is that he really hated his mother's selfishness and will be a complete jerk about his wife's gardening and cooking.

Jane and Jim's problems are the kind of ordinary neurotic issues that many people have. These problems are what make even good relationships so aggravating at times. Other people, however, present issues that are more serious.

The sad fact is that some people are, to put it simply, so flawed that they are incapable of being in any reasonable sort of mutual relationship. We can label these people in moral terms as "selfish" or in psychological terms as "narcissistic" or in everyday language as "only being interested in him or herself," but the label doesn't really matter. Likewise, we can explain their attitude as being caused by a lack of moral education or being raised by a cold, selfish mother or by being influenced by popular culture that stresses "what's in it for me?," but the explanation doesn't change the reality of the harm that they can do to others.

The plain fact is that these individuals simply cannot meaningfully participate in a relationship. Hence, they cannot really participate in a discussion about a relationship. Notice that I say "meaningfully." Many individuals, up to and including some sociopathic predators, can act as if they are participating in a serious discussion; that's how some convicted criminals con naïve social workers and prison reformers. In fact, however, their apparent participation is only apparent; their responses do not reflect their own feelings but their answer to what they believe (often correctly) the other person wants to hear.

Psychologists call pathological selfishness "narcissism." That term refers to a fundamental belief that one simply is the center of the universe. A highly narcissistic person can talk quite sincerely about what *he* needs in the relationship or how *he* feels. What such a person cannot do to any significant extent is genuinely understand or care about his significant other's needs, wants, feelings, etc.

Such a person finds it very difficult to see why he or she should have to compromise any of his or her desires for the greater good of the relationship or for the good of the partner.

Finally, unfortunately, not every participant in a relationship is there for the comfort and closeness that relationships can provide. Sometimes, people do deliberately exploit each other – sexually, emotionally, and financially.

Before you embark on a "let's tell each other everything about our finances, etc." session, it behooves you to think seriously about the person you are involved with and how the relationship has worked so far. Talking things over with an exploitative person will only result in him/her using the information to take further advantage of you, whether that advantage is emotional, sexual, or financial.

QUESTION: *"You sound so pessimistic. Are you saying that there is no way to have a decent relationship and nothing we can do to make things better?"*

ANSWER: *No, all is not lost. There is hope but the process is not an easy or obvious one.*

The process consists of taking a hard look at yourself – flaws, desires, and hopes – and a hard look at your significant other, and then acting on the information that you have gathered. The first step is to look at your actions, not your thoughts. The ancient proverb says that "actions speak louder than words," and it is completely true. Regardless of whether you think you are an honest person, if you consistently take advantage of others, you are not. Regardless of whether you regard yourself as basically loving, if you consistently belittle your significant other, then you are not. Finally, regardless of whether you say that you are just waiting for the right man to come along to settle down, if you hop from one bed to another, you probably are flighty and unable to make a commitment.

The second step consists of acting consistently with the facts, not with half-formed wishes and rationalizations.

Neither step is easy.

QUESTION: *"What are my options when living with someone else? How separate, or how close, can we be?"*

ANSWER: *Emotionally, and practically speaking, there are several basic variations along the lines of commitment and trust.*

We can imagine a graph of a relationship that charts the degree of trust against the degree of commitment. Although these two factors might seem to vary proportionately to each other, in reality, a person can express commitment to a relationship, but not be inclined to trust the other person, especially about money. A simple example would be that of a man married to a woman who was a compulsive gambler or a compulsive shopper; he might be committed to the marriage (and value her for other traits, such as her loving nature and her intelligence) but know that he cannot not trust her with money.

Let's consider the commitment axis first. In my experience, cohabitation relationships that include sex (as opposed to just being roommates) can be roughly divided into four types on the issue of commitment: (1) "We're just living together until something better comes along," aka "More commitment than a one night stand and better sex than being roommates;" (2) "We don't want to commit to anything permanent but we really care about each other and want to be fair to each other as long as this relationship lasts;" (3) "We are planning on a long-term commitment but we don't believe in the religious and moral trappings of marriage;" and (4) "We plan to get married but we are living together first to try things out."

The second axis is trust. Unfortunately romantic love can lead us to trust people who are deceptive and dishonest. Romantic love (and lust) tend to cast an idealizing net over the beloved. We just don't want to notice the signs that he or she is a basically dishonest or irresponsible person.

To be prudent, trust about financial matters should be an evolving aspect of a relationship. It would be foolish to give a new girlfriend your debit card; it might be quite sensible to trust your wife of 25 years with it. Or, it might not, if you have learnt in those 25 years that she is a lovable spendthrift.

Trust about sexual matters, however, is of critical importance from the beginning. Misplaced reliance on a spouse's honesty or fidelity can lead to tragic consequences ranging from an unwanted child to permanent infertility to death.

(By the way, if you really are just roommates who happen to be of the opposite sex, i.e. without any sexual involvement, you might want to make that clear in writing. People have a remarkable ability to change their recollection of the "facts" when a lot of money is involved.)

QUESTION: *"Is there really any emotional difference between getting married and deciding to live together?"*

ANSWER: *That depends entirely on the couple. For some people, there isn't any significant difference, but for most Americans, marriage still carries significant emotional freight.*

The symbolic difference between marriage and living together is the obvious one—marriage represents an official conscious commitment and living together represents an open refusal to enter into a commitment.

Divorce is easy to obtain in every state in America. The easy availability of divorce has blurred the legal distinction between living together and marriage; it is almost as easy to get out of an unwanted marriage as it is to get out of an unwanted cohabitation relationship. "Almost as easy," however, is not the same thing as "just as easy." Ending a marriage still requires official government action. A person cannot end a marriage just by moving out of the house. Moreover, a person cannot (legally) escape any obligations that he or she may have incurred because of being married by just moving away.

QUESTION: *"How do I figure out what I want?"*

ANSWER: *First examine your actions and then examine your expressed values and desires. Then consider how best to reconcile these with your present situation.*

Sure, it sounds simple. Just decide what you want from a relationship and then work out the details with your partner. Unfortunately, for many of us, the hardest part of the equation is figuring out what we ourselves want; leave alone what the significant other wants.

It would be nice to be able to draw up a complicated table that would predict, accurately, whether a particular combination of traits would work in a relationship.

Unfortunately, such a prediction is seldom achievable. The possible variations are too great. Sometimes, opposites attract and balance one another in unexpected ways. Sometimes, people modify their behavior and their beliefs over time. More often, perhaps, a couple can achieve a stable equilibrium despite their differences and even despite the misery that they periodically cause one another.

There are, however, some guidelines, or at least precautions, for relationships that can be drawn from this information. The Workbook contains detailed lists of questions to help you gather this information about yourself and about your significant other. See "Understanding Your Relationship" on page 656.et seq.

These questionnaires cover four basic topics:

- ✓ *Conduct of past relationships, including jobs, lovers, spouses, and pets.*
- ✓ *Dreams and wishes, including finances, houses, relationships, and children.*
- ✓ *Moral values, including honesty and sexual fidelity.*
- ✓ *Character traits, including frugality, reliability, and honesty.*

Gathering this information has several uses. On the broadest level, patterns and themes may emerge that alert you to specific aspects of yourself, your partner, or the relationship. Then, you can act appropriately in light of those themes. On a narrower level, your answers may reveal important values that should be included in your understanding of your relationship. Specifically, your knowledge of yourself and of your significant other may greatly influence the terms of your prenuptial or cohabitation agreement.

If you don't want to fill out the detailed questionnaires, you might try just writing down a careful description of yourself (past and present) and what you know about your lover (past and present). The difficulty is that such self-descriptions tend to be brief and full of unhelpful generalizations. However, even such generalizations may alert you to aspects of the relationship that need attention.

People find it immensely difficult to change. A tremendous effort of will and commitment, as well as therapy, is usually needed to effect any change. Therefore, you may assume that the way you or your significant other acted in the past is the way you or he/she will continue to act in the present relationship.

In other words, you may safely assume that your partner will act toward you as he or she has acted in the past toward others. You should consider whether you would feel well-treated if your partner behaves to you as he or she has behaved to others.

Put another way, ask yourself, "If he treated me like he treated his ex-wife, would I feel good about the relationship?" Or, "Will it make me happy if she is unfaithful to me the way she was to her former husband?"

If, therefore, your significant other has behaved dishonestly in other contexts or other relationships, then you should not trust him or her with any of your money or possessions. A better bit of advice would be that you should skip this relationship and look for a person with more integrity.

If your and your partner's values differ markedly, the relationship is unlikely to succeed. It may be possible to compromise on some things but many values cannot and should not be compromised. If, for example, your partner's ideal vacation is sailing in Aruba and you prefer scuba diving in Belize, some compromise can be reached. If, however, your perfect vacation is visiting gothic cathedrals in rural France and his is drinking pina coladas by the pool at the country club, compromise may be hard, if not impossible, to reach.

While it is possible that you could, for example, alternate vacation destinations (or go on separate trips), it is more likely that the difference in dreams reflects a profound and more irreconcilable difference in interests and values. You'll be bored by his description of getting plastered by the pool and he'll yawn through your slide show of gothic arches. You may secretly despise his indolence and he may secretly resent your intellectual pretensions.

Obviously, however, if your values differ in more fundamental respects, the relationship is likely to be a troubled one. If you're a vegetarian animal rights activist and she fox hunts every weekend with the Snooty Oaks Fox Hounds, the two of you may find yourselves on opposite sides of the fence, literally, too often to be comfortable.

If your values about money and those of your partner differ significantly, the relationship is even more likely to be troubled, if not doomed. The view one takes of money influences a multitude of actions and decisions. Someone, for example, who strongly believes that financial success is the only kind that matters will not be comfortable with a spouse who believes that family life and love are the most important things. When she wants to work overtime or travel six days a week on business, he will feel deprived of her company and support at his family reunion. If honesty, kindness, and time with friends are more important to you than money, you will not likely prosper in a relationship with someone who values financial success more highly.

What to do with this information together

If you can bring yourself to sit down with your partner and exchange the Workbook questionnaires (both the answers that you gave about yourself and those about the other), then you have a wonderful opportunity to work through any differences.

The great Scottish poet Robert Burns, wrote more or less as follows: "Oh, what some gift the good Lord give us/ to see ourselves as others see us." You may be surprised (and hurt or pleased) to learn what your partner believes your values to be.

The process provides you an opportunity to correct any misunderstanding that your lover may have. Perhaps you are not as focused on getting ahead at the firm as he thought.

On the other hand, the process affords you an opportunity to look hard at yourself from another's point of view. You may not like what you see and decide to change it.

Every therapist knows that therapy, including especially in-depth therapies such as psychoanalysis, often means the end of the patient's marriage. Sometimes the increased self-knowledge leads the patient to recognize that he or she is unhappy in the present arrangement. Sometimes, the spouse cannot tolerate the healthier person that the patient has become.

It follows that any process of exploration and change can bring about the end of a relationship. When you look clearly at your present relationship, whether or not your significant other participates, you may well be confronted by a relationship that you do not want. If you look past the excuses and rationalizations, you may see a person whose actions are simply not acceptable.

QUESTION: *"Are you saying that people can't change? What if we are really in love?"*

ANSWER: *No, people can change and sometimes they make terrific changes in themselves because they are in love.*

The difficulty is that there is a vast difference between actual changes and promises to change. However, if there is a clear commitment to a relationship and an unambiguous requirement for change, people can alter their conduct.

For example, Bubba and Jeanine met in a bar. He was a tall, handsome man and she was more than a little overweight. He was a hard working, kindhearted man but the kind of guy who spent most of what he made on whiskey, cigarettes, and fast horses. She was feisty, hardworking, and prudent about money. They both liked a good time.

Within a year after they met, they were living together and looking forward to getting married. Bubba had a long standing health problem fixed. For the first time in his life, he had some money saved. He cut radically back on his drinking and she didn't allow smoking in their house. As he would proudly tell his buddies, "She straightened my ass out."

QUESTION: *"What if my lover just won't talk about the relationship?"*

ANSWER: *You have three choices. The first is to trust that everything will be OK. The second is to write up a cohabitation agreement that reflects your understanding and present it to him or her for signature. The third is to leave.*

The only safe assumption is that anything that your partner won't expressly say is probably not really part of the relationship.

Here are some of the signs that your lover will not (or emotionally cannot) address the main issues in your relationship: always being "too tired;" making jokes (especially dirty jokes) whenever you bring the subject up; "forgetting" that you had set a particular time to talk or that he or she had promised to bring home some records for the two of you to go over; getting unreasonably angry at any of your suggestions; or belittling your thoughts.

These actions, at least if repeated over time, can have a variety of meanings. Not all of these meanings are fatal to a good relationship. Some people feel threatened and uncertain when they try to talk about their feelings. Many people find it hard to say that they expect a certain amount of money or financial stability out of a relationship. Some find it hard to expect anything at all for fear of being hurt when they find out the "truth" about the other person's feelings. Sometimes, the truth is that your partner is not as committed to the relationship as you are. He or she may be seeking to avoid facing up to this fact (and maybe hurting your feelings.)

One way to address these issues is simply to ask, as gently, politely, and firmly as you can – "I notice that we keep putting off these discussions. Is there some problem with us talking about our relationship?" This strategy is a conversational judo throw – you're asking your partner to talk about what he or she can't talk about.

Sometimes, however, regardless of how you approach the issue, you may find that your lover simply doesn't want to be all that specific; perhaps, if he or she wanted specificity and commitment, marriage would be the commitment of choice. In that case, silence is the clearest message – he or she is trying to tell you that there just isn't that much of a relationship there. Or, that whatever his or her idea of the relationship is, you probably don't want to know about it.

Conclusions and advice

A clearer of view of your relationship may show you things that you did not want to see. Refusing to see the true state of affairs may lead to heartbreak and financial ruin.

Some couples, however, do manage to go through life fairly contentedly without ever openly talking about their shared lives. There are a variety of adaptations that couples can make to each other over a lifetime, sometimes without any discussion. Only you can decide whether you would rather suffer in silence or seek another solution.

(Endnotes)

[1] *State of Our Unions*, supra.

[2] See the various *State of Our Union* reports cited herein.

Chapter Eleven

THE TANGLED WEB — WHAT A MESS WE CAN MAKE

In most cases, bringing your relationship within some accepted legal form is an act of love and trust. Leaving matters a legal mess may be convenient now but can result in heartache later.

This chapter deals with some of the most common legal messes that people who live together find themselves in. Some of these problems arise from common misconceptions that people have about the laws of marriage and living together. If one of these situations describes your current relationship, then you should consider straightening out the legal issues.

Neither fish nor fowl

Sometimes a couple simply can't make up their mind about what they want from their relationship. In that situation, they may vacillate from one version of what's going on to another. Sometimes, the different versions that they tell different people are not consistent. For example, a couple may sometimes refer to their relationship as being engaged and sometimes as being married.

Things can get even more complicated when a couple get divorced and then get back together. Often in that case, the couple refers to each other as husband and wife, naturally enough. If they live together as "husband" and "wife" and agree to be married, then in a common law marriage state, they may in fact have remarried (In other states, they remain divorced, no matter how long they stay together.).

But, as may happen in such a tumultuous relationship, the couple may split up again. What happens if the wife goes back to the divorce court to enforce her rights to child support payments under the divorce decree? Well, you can't be divorced and married at the same time. Her enforcement of the divorce decree is, logically and legally, inconsistent with claiming that she and her husband had gotten back together as husband and wife. In fact, it legally bars her from claiming a common law marriage with her former husband.

Many times, the legal ambiguity makes no practical difference. If, however, there is ever any money at stake (as when one partner dies), one person's financial future can turn on whether the couple was or was not married. In that case, it would be a question of who and what the jury believed.

More Myths about Love and the Law

Some of the legal messes that people find themselves in stem from mistaken beliefs about the law and marriage. Myths lead to bad decisions because these beliefs are often unconscious premises on which we take actions, i.e. they are hidden assumptions about the way the world is.

MYTH—*"I don't need to get any promises in writing because my lover is rich, and if we split up, he'll owe me palimony."*

FACT—*The courts have been very reluctant to give one party to a live-in relationship any share in the other party's money.*

After the much-publicized lawsuit between the actor Lee Marvin and his live-in girlfriend, Michele Marvin (the identical last names were a coincidence, not a result of marriage), many people assume that there is a legal right to some compensation if you live with someone who's a lot richer than you and then split up. Well, think again.

First, the case of *Marvin v. Marvin* was a special one and not just because he was a sexy movie star and they lived in Hollywood.[1] Michelle Marvin proved that she and Lee had an express agreement that they would live together, share all their earnings, and hold themselves out as husband and wife. (California does not recognize common law marriage so these circumstances would not create a legal marriage.) Michelle also proved that she gave up her career to devote herself full-time to Lee and his career for six years.

Now, a contract to pay for sex is illegal. So, if Michelle's contract with Lee consisted of his promising to pay her to be a live-in sex toy, then she could not enforce it. In other words, it wouldn't give her any rights because the agreement was illegal. Michelle convinced the court, however, that she and Lee agreed to pool their earnings and that, in effect, the relationship was not just based on sex.

The California Supreme Court held that a cohabiting couple could make a legal agreement about the financial consequences of the relationship and even said that courts could divide the property of cohabiting couples in a fair way, depending on their relationship and the trust that they had in each other.

However, after all the high-powered legal wrangling, the trial court only awarded Michelle $118,000 for "rehabilitation" and the appellate court struck that down. Hundreds of thousands of dollars in legal fees and the net result to Michelle was zip, regardless of the high-sounding principles of law established in her case.

Other states have expressly declined to be so generous to ex-cohabitants and have refused to imply any obligation between them. Remember *Hewitt v. Hewitt*, where the kiddy dentist did his long-time lover and mother of his children out of any share of the property that they had acquired together?

Some courts have gone part way, and in those states, courts will enforce an express contract between two people who live together but won't grant one party any right in the other's earnings unless they have an agreement. In *Morone v. Morone*, for example, Mr. and Mrs. Morone lived together as husband and wife for 23 years, starting in 1952, but were never married. Mrs. Morone said that Mr. Morone promised to support her and give her one-half of the proceeds from his business in exchange for her providing domestic services. When he stopped supporting her, she sued. She lost.[2]

The highest court in New York held that unless there was an express agreement (more than just her saying that they had an oral agreement), the property accumulated during a relationship belongs to the one who accumulated it and will not be divided by the courts when the couple splits up. The court held that the possibility of fraud was too great because one party might just make up an agreement. The court also felt that it was too hard to sort out what services were provided out of affection and what were provided under the contract.

In a way, as unfair as these cases may sound, the courts are actually protecting a sort of freedom for people. People who want to be committed to each other and to share their worldly goods can get married. If they don't want to get married, they can sign a contract to arrange their affairs (pun intended). If they just want to live together, then they are free to do so, no strings attached. But if the relationship lasts longer than they may have expected, the courts will not step in to change the relationship from cohabitation to a quasi-marriage, when the parties did not care to do so from the beginning. In a way, the courts are honoring the couple's freedom not to be committed to each other.

The point is that if you want the freedom to live together without obligation, don't look to the courts to give you a share of your live-in lover's riches. If you want to be responsible to each other, get married, or at least, write up an agreement between the two of you. If you don't take the steps to clarify your relationship, don't whine about the results when a court decides that it wasn't much of a relationship.

MYTH—*"I don't need to worry about clarifying my relationship because my state has enacted a domestic partner law."*

FACT—*Domestic partner laws are in a process of change; these laws sometimes apply only to gay couples and often are limited to specific issues such as employee benefits.*

Some states have enacted statutes called "domestic partner" laws. Some cities have enacted ordinances on this subject, which obviously are more limited in reach, since these ordinances don't apply outside the city, and some companies have adopted corporate policies on the subject. See "Domestic Partner Benefits" on page 110 for more information on domestic partnerships.

Many people assume that these laws will straighten out the legal issues in living together. So far, that is not the case. Sometimes, these provisions are not laws but are only policies adopted by corporations based on a particular company's view of equal treatment of its employees.

MYTH—*"I don't have to worry about being common law married because if we split up, it's a common law divorce."*

FACT—*There is no such thing as common law divorce.*

One of the most persistent myths about common law marriage is that if you can get married informally, you can get divorced the same way. There is no such thing as common law divorce. Once you are married, ceremonially or otherwise, the only way to end the legal relationship is to go through a formal divorce.

The matter can be a little more complicated, however. There have been a few laws that cover how one proves that a common law marriage existed. These laws can present the appearance of a common law divorce. In Texas, for example, a law provided that a couple was presumed *not* to have been married if neither of them took any action to prove the marriage within two years after they separated. The legislature had in mind that if two people really thought they were married, then one or the other would seek a divorce when the relationship ended.

The purpose of law was to prevent one member of a couple from claiming a common law marriage many years after the relationship ended. After many years, evidence is hard to find and unreliable. Neighbors have moved away and friends' memories may be clouded. Couples sometimes separate and get back together, even if only for a few weeks, or they may separate and stay in friendly contact. These mixed-up situations may make it difficult to say whether a couple has really "separated" within the meaning of the law.

The difficulty is that the statute only created a presumption that there was no marriage. A presumption can be refuted by good evidence, such as written documents in which the couple refer to each other as husband and wife. The presumption doesn't mean that the couple never married; it just makes it harder for the one claiming the marriage to prove it.

The myth of common law divorce can create serious hardship for an unsuspecting spouse. If one of a couple has been married before and not divorced, then subsequent marriages are invalid, because, of course, the person was not free to marry, ceremonially or by common law. Therefore, if one party to a ceremonial marriage was common law married at some time in the past, the second apparent "marriage", even if performed in church in front of 300 of the new couple's closest friends, is not valid.

All three people (the first spouse, the "bigamist," and the unlucky second "spouse') may have an interest in the same property, including land, houses, checking accounts, and so on. In a community property state, the first spouse may own part of everything his or her spouse earned over the years. Pension plans, insurance benefits (including health insurance), savings accounts, and investments can all be subject to the claims of the legal spouse. Even if the first spouse dies, if there were children from the previous marriage, it can be very complex and painful to sort out who is entitled to what.

MYTH—_"My common law husband ran off and left me, but he can't ever marry anyone else because that would be bigamy and I'll put his sorry self in jail if he tries it."_

FACT—_People have left marriages without bothering to get a divorce for hundreds of years. The legal consequences may be a mess if he is caught and if he actually goes through a second marriage, but people still do it._

This myth confuses the law with reality. Yes, technically, a man who is common law married and who goes through a form of ceremony with another woman is committing bigamy, but prosecution of that crime is uncommon especially in a common law marriage situation. It's even rarer for a married woman to be prosecuted for entering into a bigamous relationship.

Second, remember that you have to prove that you were common law married. Memories have a way of changing when circumstances change.

MYTH—*"I don't have to worry about any financial entanglements with my lover because I live in a state that doesn't recognize common law marriage."*

FACT—*Other binding legal relationships can exist between two people besides marriage. Moreover, you may have spent sufficient time in a state that does recognize common law marriages to have entered into one.*

MYTH—*"I don't have to worry about financial entanglements with my lover because we never put anything in writing. Besides, our relationship was just for sex and it's not legal to pay someone for sex."*

FACT—*(1) Some oral agreements are valid contracts. (2) You may be surprised to find that you and your lover will later tell very different versions of your relationship.*

Regardless of questions of palimony and implied or oral cohabitation agreements, if you are in business and your lover has been involved in the business in any way, you should give some thought to the question of whether you have another, non-marital, legal relationship with your significant other. Other legal relationships can exist together with, or apart from, a marital or cohabitation relationship.

For example, if two people start a business together and then start a romance, they may be partners in the legal, as well as the sexual, sense. That is, if one significant other works in the other's business, he or she may later claim that they entered into a legal partnership. If there were promises made, such as "If you'll help me out at the shop, I'll split the profits with you," then a court may decide that the two jointly own the business or, at least, that there was a valid contract to split the profits of the business.

Similarly, one of a couple may later claim that they entered into an agreement to jointly own the stock of a corporation started by one of them or to jointly own an invention that one of them is working on.

So, an agreement about business can create various legal business arrangements. A court might decide that there was a valid contract about profit-sharing or a partnership or a joint venture. Each of these legal relationships creates obligations and rights of its own. Partners, for example, are legally obligated to treat each other fairly and in good faith. Obviously, once again this is one of those times when you need a good lawyer.

MYTH—*"I don't have to worry about all those musty old laws and repressive old Bible rules. It's a new world out there and nobody pays any attention to that ancient history any more."*

FACT—*If you ever seek any legal benefit from your relationship, the judge and jury who decide your case may well still be influenced by those "old-fashioned" values that you don't agree with.*

If you look up "common law marriage" on the Internet, your search will lead you both to a web site advocating and explaining alternatives to marriage and to one advocating equally vigorously for traditional heterosexual marriage. Popular American magazines may give the impression that everyone on the planet believes in free and unrestrained sexual expression, but the fact is that a large percentage of the population does not.

Many people in the United States believe that sexual relations outside of marriage are immoral and that a woman who lives with a man to whom she is not married is a whore, especially if she wants any financial benefit from the relationship. When I was marketing this book before its publication, one store manager in an affluent suburb of Houston declined to carry it on the ground that she didn't approve of people living together. On the other hand, the number of young women voluntarily becoming single mothers without giving serious thought to marrying the father of their child has undoubtedly greatly increased.

Despite the fact that millions of couples live together without marriage, a judge in New Mexico recently ruled that one factor in determining the sentence of a young man for a minor criminal matter was that the defendant was living with a woman in an "immoral" relationship.

Effect of a prior entanglement on subsequent relationships

Your prior relationships can have a legal, as well as emotional, effect on your present relationship.

Bigamy

If your prior relationship was a legal marriage and you have not been divorced or widowed, then you cannot legally marry again. In other words, if your previous spouse is still alive, then your present relationship is not a legal marriage, whether common law or otherwise. Actually, bigamy (attempting to marry a second spouse while still married to the first) is still a crime, although, as noted above, prosecutions are rare. To straighten out this mess, you need to divorce your previous spouse and remarry your current spouse.

Alimony (spousal support) that you are receiving

If you are receiving alimony from a previous spouse, remarriage automatically terminates the payments in most states. This is generally true whether your new marriage is a ceremonial one or a common law one.

Living together, however, may or may not affect your right to alimony from a previous relationship. In many states, a long-term or "significant marriage-like" cohabitation arrangement ends your previous spouse's obligation to pay alimony. Even if your new relationship doesn't end the obligation, it may entitle your previous spouse to a reduction in the amount paid. The reasoning is that you don't need as much support if you are living in a two-person household.

The exact effect will depend on the terms of your divorce decree and the law of the state where you were divorced. Many lawyers now put a clause in divorce decrees that says, in effect, "The obligation to pay alimony ends if [the spouse receiving alimony] remarries or cohabits with a person of the opposite sex."

In appropriate cases, the lawyers might also include an analogous clause that terminated the payment of alimony if the spouse receiving the alimony cohabited with a person of the same sex in a lesbian or gay relationship.

Alimony that you are paying

If you owe an ex-spouse alimony, you are still obligated to make the payments even if you marry someone else.

In some states, the court might reduce your payments; if you can show that you have new financial responsibilities in your new household. For example, if you have formally agreed to support your new spouse's children, the court can consider your new financial obligations as a reason to reduce your payments to your previous spouse.

However, courts are usually reluctant to penalize your previous spouse for your lifestyle changes. The court may refuse to reduce your responsibility to your first spouse just because you now have a new one. Cohabiting with a new lover will not entitle you to a reduction.

Child support and child custody

Neither living together nor subsequent marriages necessarily change the obligation to pay child support or the right to receive child support. The living arrangements of the parents do not affect the financial needs of the children. Similarly, your remarriage will not affect your custody of the children, unless the new marriage exposes children to an unhealthy environment or other potential harm. Sometimes, a court will reduce child support payments if a parent has more children in a new relationship. The court's decision depends on the parent's income and other factors.

The legal rule is that cohabitation should not be grounds for a change in custody. Changing social mores mean that fewer judges openly express their moral disapproval of people living together, even with same sex couples. However, the judge may indirectly express his or her disapproval by finding that the new living environment is deleterious to the children. Remember that unless he or she voluntarily agrees to be responsible, a stepparent is usually not legally obligated to support a stepchild. In some states, he or she has a duty to support the child during the second marriage but not after it ends. In other words, if a woman with children marries a man with children, both from previous marriages, and then that new couple divorces, they usually have no duty to support the other's children from their first marriages. These topics are discussed in more detail on page 261 et seq.

Effect of prior relationships on assets you own

If either of you has been married to someone else before your present relationship, your rights to the property acquired during this relationship could be affected, legally, by the rights of the various spouses. Practically speaking, however, the actual result may, or may not, be changed by these prior marriages.

The possible financial and legal permutations are too complex to consider in all their sordid detail but a hypothetical example may help clarify a murky situation.

George and Mary have been living together for ten years. George has never been divorced from his wife, Marlene. Marlene and George haven't spoken to each other in years. George and Mary accumulate large IRA accounts for each of them. They have bought a house together. The house is in both their names, and George and Mary have both made payments. George and Mary start a barbecue business together which is a great success.

Result: If George and Mary split up more or less amicably, and Marlene continues to be uninvolved, George and Mary can probably divide the property any way they want. But, if Marlene gets greedy, she may file for divorce and claim a legal interest in the house, the barbecue business, and at least George's IRA. Even if she doesn't file for divorce, her claims can clutter up the title to the house, for example. It would be hard for George and Mary to sell "their" house because the buyer couldn't get clear title to the property.

Clearly, the outcome in any case like this depends on the particular facts. If Mary didn't know that George was married, she may receive a fairer division of "their" property. If Marlene knew that George was living with Mary, she might have consented to the arrangements. An additional complexity in this situation would be where George owed Marlene child support or spousal support. She might be entitled to collect those debts out of George's assets, including possibly his share of the house or the business.

Speaking cynically, the offstage presence of a possibly vindictive spouse gives prudent lovers a powerful reason to be very careful how they take title to their assets and, in the event of a split, to divide their common assets quietly and amicably.

Why straighten it out?

Whatever kind of legal complexity your affairs are in, the first question is whether you can or should straighten things out. As an attorney, my automatic answer is "Of course – legal uncertainties end up hurting people." And, in truth, they often do. Loyal companions of many years end up with nothing from their companions' estates when a long lost (and ignored) spouse shows up and successfully claim all. A hardworking spouse gets cheated when his wife leaves him for one of the men that she works with.

There are so many possible problems. You could theoretically find out that you didn't have health insurance just when you need it most, if the insurance company discovers that you aren't really the spouse of your lover. In principle, it may be an unlawful misrepresentation to call someone your spouse for insurance purposes when you know perfectly well that you just living together. Later in life, you may find it impossible to claim retirement benefits or social security that would otherwise be available to you from your spouse's lifelong work and savings.

The real life answer is more difficult. In our current society, a remarkable number of people move from one relationship to another, casually referring to a succession of partners by various names. I was once consulted by a hard working policeman who had a wife and a girlfriend who thought that she was a wife, both "common law" and both policewomen and both at the same time! I had very little to do with the ultimate solution since everything that I suggested involved the various parties' making decisions about the relationships and the man involved was unwilling to confront either of the ladies concerned. They (all) worked it out – for the moment, although it ran into quite a bit of money for him since, to keep the peace, he had to pay for two apartments, two refrigerators, etc.

Although technically, it may be some form of fraud to collect health insurance for your current live-in as your wife when you haven't ever been divorced from a previous wife, it may be somewhat unlikely that anyone is going to complain, unless the insurance company discovers the misrepresentation just as your present love is about to undergo extremely expensive cancer treatment, since some health insurance companies will seize any excuse to avoid paying a claim.

Many such entanglements get worked out. A previous spouse from whom you never were divorced may truly vanish from your life, marry someone else, and never give you a second thought, especially if the marriage was a common law one. A boyfriend who might have been a common law husband may leave you and move on with his life and never interfere in yours.

Even if there is a later possible dispute, many people end up with more debts than assets and therefore there may not be a lot of tangible assets to fight over. Things like whose name goes on the tombstone and who is buried next to whom as "beloved spouse" can cause a lot of bitter heartaches, but many people come to terms with the disappointment and betrayal of finding that a longtime companion is in fact married to somebody else.

Some reasons to regularize your relationship in the eyes of the law are the following:

- ✔ *You love and respect the partner you are now with and wish to take care of him or her.*

- ✔ *You have put a lot into the relationship that you are now in, and you want to be sure that you get something (financial) out of it.*

- ✔ *You want to ensure that your (present or former) partner does not end up with any kind of claim to the assets that you are working so hard to accumulate now.*

- ✔ *You think that you and your partner understand the nature of your present relationship (the same way) and you want to make sure that things work out the way that you intend. You may intend to take care of your partner financially or to exclude him or her from any interest in your assets and vice versa.*

- ✔ *You're splitting up from the miserable twit that you've been living with and want to be sure that he or she doesn't get a dime.*

Obviously, some of these reasons are crasser than others. The financial aspect of things can change people's perceptions in a hurry and in painful and disappointing ways, especially when the distribution of money changes over time.

The right way

If a couple desire a mutually supportive, long-term relationship, then the easiest and most straightforward way for them to regularize things has three steps. First, both of them resolve any previous relationships, including getting divorced from previous spouses if necessary. Second, they get married to each other. Third, they execute all the appropriate documents including wills, powers of attorney, insurance changes etc. If they have substantial assets, they may enter into a prenuptial agreement setting out each other's rights and financial responsibilities.

There are at least three major difficulties with this simple solution. First, a couple who are living together may not be emotionally able or willing to make a true commitment to one another. That may be the reason that they are living together instead of being married already.

Second, straightening out previous relationships can be expensive, especially if substantial time has elapsed. Since it is possible that some part of whatever one spouse has earned during the intervening years may well belong to the other spouse, many people prefer to "lie low" and hope that the subject never comes up.

On the other hand, both former partners may have an incentive to clarify their legal status so that they are free to marry their current partner or so that they can have clear title to their own assets. Difficulties can arise in particular when one ex-partner has done significantly better financially than the other.

Finally, some people have religious scruples about divorce. They may have tried diligently to resolve the issues in their marriage and simply have been unable to do so. Or, they may simply be unwilling to make the effort for which their religion calls. For these people, an informal relationship seems preferable to a divorce and remarriage.

The plain fact is that, especially if you got married in a community property state, there are no sure-fire ways to cut your spouse out of some share in your future assets, short of divorce. Therefore, if you want to clear up your legal status and your property rights, you need to get a divorce from your spouse. This is so whether you want to provide financially for your present significant other or simply be certain that you have clear title to your own assets.

No matter how painful or expensive or inconvenient it is now, things will probably only get more painful, expensive, and inconvenient in the future.

If you have determined that you are probably common law married to a person with whom you no longer wish to be involved, then the only legally clear way to straighten things out is to get a divorce or an annulment. Otherwise, matters remain uncertain.

Children

If you have children from a prior relationship, then you have obligations both to those children and to your present partner. Those obligations have legal, financial, emotional, and moral dimensions. Legally, you have obligations to support those children. You also owe it to them to provide a healthy and supportive emotional environment, if at all possible. Morally, you owe them the relationship of a parent.

Moreover, you have those obligations even if the other parent of the child is not presently demanding that you act as a parent. See the discussion of children's rights beginning on page 232.

The psychological facts are plain. First, children do best with the reliable and loving attention of two parents in a stable home. Second, loss of an adult who has been a part of the child's life is painful and potentially damaging to the child. Whether you are the father or the mother, the child will benefit from your responsible involvement in his or her life.

Morally, you also absolutely owe your present partner full disclosure of the existence of your children and your relationship with their mother or father, including any financial obligations that have been formalized. A divorce decree that obligates you to pay child support clearly affects your ability to contribute to the relationship that you are now in, including supporting any children that result from this new relationship.

Consequently, if you have children from a prior relationship, you cannot fully put the present relationship on a sound footing without dealing with your obligations to those children. If you owe past child support, you may jeopardize the financial future of your present partner.

Your children do not need, nor will they benefit from, seeing Mom or Dad move through a series of uncommitted, temporary, more or less tempestuous relationships. Think about the various complexities before you involve your children in your love life — how will kids think or feel about and toward other kids that are "Daddy's new girlfriend's stepchildren"?

If you are married to someone else and simply won't get a divorce, you can try using the agreements in the following chapters, but their legal effect (if your spouse intervenes) is anyone's guess. The legal right of one spouse to transfer property, the rights of an "abandoned" or separated spouse, the right of a spouse to community property, the rights of a deceived lover, and so on, all vary so much from state to state and from circumstance to circumstance that there is no way that a general guide like this can predict what will happen if you try to take care of your present lover without getting divorced from your spouse.

If you elect not to bother with a written agreement, then you should carefully keep all of your assets separate, with the possible exception of a joint account for bill paying or some other individual arrangement.

Conclusions and Advice

Assuming that you want to make the terms of your present relationship clear, there are three steps involved. The first step is to figure out what the situation is now. Are you still married to someone else? Do you have unfulfilled obligations to others, such as alimony or child support? The second is to think through what it is that you want from this relationship. The third is to learn what your significant other wants or will go along with. The last step is to put things in some kind of legal order, usually by resolving your previous commitments and incorporating new ones in legal documents.

(Endnotes)

[1]   *Marvin v. Marvin* 557 P.2d 106 (Cal Sup. Ct. 1976)

[2]   *Morone v. Morone*, 413 N.E.2d 1154 (N.Y.Ct.App. 1980)

Chapter Twelve

CRAFTING FAMILIES

This chapter is primarily for people who are in a committed relationship but who do not want to be married, by common law or otherwise. The chapter has suggestions about how to craft the financial side of a relationship so that it meets your needs and goals.

The advice, however, also applies to people who are considering marriage. If the legal consequences of marriage are not acceptable to you, or if you want to be sure of a particular outcome, then you should consider a prenuptial agreement. The materials in this chapter can help a couple to set the parameters of the legal and financial embodiment of their relationship.

Together, but separate

A long term relationship can be based on emotional closeness but financial separateness. In many cohabitation relationships, the couple want the freedom to leave at any time; to ensure that result, they need to take appropriate care not to create legal entanglements. This is particularly so if one of the couple has a heavy debt load.

A financially separate, but emotionally close, relationship is theoretically possible even in a marriage. However, the couple needs a carefully thought-out prenuptial agreement and diligent attention to paperwork during the marriage. This takes much more care with the paperwork, however. Remember that state laws set the framework for property ownership in marriage. Changing them by contract and conduct requires careful attention to detail and sometimes doesn't fully work as the parties intended.

 QUESTION: *"I'm living with my boyfriend. He moved into my place. I have some nice stuff. I found out that he shoplifts at stores and steals from the petty cash at work. What should I do to protect myself?"*

ANSWER: *When a couple lives together, married or unmarried, the outcome depends on the character of the two cohabitants. So, if one of them is dishonest, the other needs to keep clearly in mind that she is living with a thief. That means keeping all valuables out of the house, not sharing any significant possessions, and not letting your lover anywhere near your money.*

By the way, if you don't trust your significant other, why are you sharing your apartment with him/her, leave alone your bed?

The financial problems with cohabitation arise from the informality of the relationship and the fact that it can be too expensive to go to court to recover any property of yours that your former lover has taken with him or her. Even if the value of the property were enough to make it worthwhile to hire an attorney, the case would still mostly come down to your word against that of your ex-amour.

Perhaps the most important thing in an unpromising relationship like this one is to avoid getting common law married. Remember the basic guidelines — don't tell people that you are married.

The second aspect of a financially independent relationship is to keep your respective financial affairs completely separate. In a limited, casual relationship, it is imprudent to buy any substantial asset together, such as a car or even a stereo. Would you really want to share a car with someone you aren't living with anymore? How would the practicalities be arranged? If you are the one driving it, is there any reason to think that your ex-lover is going to keep up the payments? Most importantly, don't buy anything with your lover that you cannot afford to pay for by yourself.

If you are going to be working together in a business or if one of you has substantially more money than the other, then draw up and sign a cohabitation agreement that expressly provides for the financial arrangement. A separate partnership agreement, or other business arrangement, is the only way to be as secure and clear as you can legally.

Guidelines for protecting your assets in a relationship

Here are the basic ways to protect your possessions in a relationship. By "protect," I mean to increase your chances of having all of your stuff when the relationship falls apart.

- ✓ *Establish and maintain records. The first step in keeping track of your stuff is to know and document what you have. You can buy a simple old-fashioned ledger notebook at the office supply store or use a computer program. Financial programs and database programs often have ready-made templates for keeping an inventory. Don't keep this inventory at your house or apartment.*

- ✓ *Label your stuff. Obviously, this should be a permanent style label. Indelible pens work well on most items but remember that the ink may bleed through to the surface of photographs and prints. Many police departments will loan you an engraving tool for free to put your social security number or other identifying information on things like stereos and cameras.*

✓ *Don't give your lover the PIN number for your ATM card.*

✓ *Don't get a second copy of your credit card for your lover and don't allow him/her to sign checks on your account.*

✓ *Don't keep treasured items, such as heirloom jewelry, around the house. In particular, if you have family photographs don't keep your only copies in the apartment. This advice may be impracticable if you want to have these items out on display but at least consider putting them away for safekeeping if the relationship begins to seem troubled.*

✓ *Don't buy anything significant in both your names, like a house, unless you have a written agreement about that asset, including what will happen when you split up.*

✓ *Don't co-sign a note for your lover or loan him or her any significant amount of money, at least without a written IOU. Remember if you sign the finance agreement for his car, you are liable to the finance company for the payments, regardless of what your lover does with the car.*

Legal togetherness — sharing a future

Setting up the paperwork for a sharing long-term non-marital relationship is more work than setting it up for together, but separate lives.

In a marriage, the law provides at least some guidelines for sharing property and so on, if the relationship ends, although those standards may not reflect the parties' expectations. In a cohabitation relationship, the law's guidelines emphasize separateness, not sharing, so the result may have little or no resemblance to what you intended.

Legally establishing the terms of a long-term relationship requires three steps; deciding on the specific terms of the relationship; writing and signing a cohabitation agreement; and executing the other needed documents, such as wills and powers of attorney. Once you have thought through the basic parameters of your relationship and decided that the two of you want to act responsibly toward each other, you need to decide on the financial and other specifics.

If the couple intends the relationship to a long-term one and they want to share their financial successes (and reverses), then a written agreement is essential to memorialize their understanding and to make clear the legal ownership of various assets.

The point is that whether you are married or not, if you expect your efforts for your significant other to be rewarded financially, then you should have a written cohabitation agreement that spells those expectations out. Moreover, you should be sure that the agreement is updated to reflect significant changes or contributions that the two of you make.

In addition to being a record of promises made, a written agreement can protect one partner from the other's (financial) problems. For example, having completely separate financial arrangements is essential if one partner has a substance abuse problem, a gambling addiction, or just permanent imprudence.

Here it is important to understand the difference between subjective good faith and actual actions. Some people make promises that they sincerely mean to keep but that they cannot or will not fulfill. The disparity between apparent sincerity and conduct can be so severe that it amounts to a kind of psychopathology, such as the sociopaths who can defraud their victims without remorse but with great persuasiveness. More often, however, a lying lover simply wants to please the partner by making the promises that the other wants to hear.

The classic example of this sort of misrepresentation is the married lover who keeps promising his mistress that he will leave his wife. He may sincerely mean to get a divorce someday but be weak willed. He may be outright lying in order to keep the cozy arrangement that he enjoys. He may say whatever the person he is with wants to hear: when he is with his wife, he promises tearfully to give up his lover and when he is with his lover, he promises passionately to leave his cold-hearted wife. Nevertheless, he does neither.

For the wife and lover, the question of whether the straying husband or careless lover is sincere or not is completely academic. His actions affect their lives, regardless of his motives or his sincerity. If the lover wants a husband, then it is irrelevant whether her married lover "sincerely" means to get a divorce or not; what changes her life that he in fact remains married to another woman. If the wife is hurt by his infidelity, his empty promises to reform simply keep her clinging to a painful relationship. Their opinions of his sincerity may make them like him better but it does not change the legal and emotional reality of their situations.

A financial parallel would be the wealthy lover who keeps promising to arrange for the financial security of his or her partner but never "finds the time" to take care of the details.

How much financial disclosure do we need?

A remarkable number of married couples have no real information about their spouse's income. Money is one of the most difficult things to talk about frankly in our society today. Couples who can be open about the details of their sexuality may find it difficult or impossible to be equally open about their finances. Candid disclosure of one's income and debts can require more intimacy and trust than the sexual act.

The reasons for this are many. First, money carries connotations of status and success. A man or woman who dresses well and has a good job may be deeply attached to the appearance of wealth and success even if in fact the appearance rests on a deep mire of credit card bills. In particular, a man's sense of self-worth may hinge on his ability to provide for his family in a certain style; revealing his real income may make apparent the fact that he cannot do so.

Second, financial disclosures create vulnerability. A significant other who does not know how much one makes is less able or likely to demand a share of the wealth. Conversely, a significant other who knows exactly what the household income is may be less impressed by the new car or designer suit and less willing to help pay for it. (It is perhaps worth noting that financial disclosure may also make you vulnerable to a completely dishonest lover who may simply steal from you.)

Third, people tend to repeat in their own intimate relationships the patterns that characterized their families. Many parents keep money matters a deep dark secret from their children; when those children grow up, they may have difficulty shifting to a more appropriate degree of openness with a partner.

If privacy about money is very important to you, then you may wish to consider how much sharing you are really capable of. That is, if you want to truly be a partner with your significant, then some degree of openness about money is required; if you are not comfortable with that openness, you should reexamine the degree of trust that you are willing to repose in another person. It might also be that intuitively you recognize that your significant other is not being open or honest with you.

Fourth, sometimes the foremost expectations are unspoken; frank discussion might reveal that you and your significant other have incompatible ideas about savings, obligations, or almost anything else important.

The basic guideline is simple: if you have any financial expectations from this relationship, the two of you need to make substantial financial disclosure to each other and make clear promises that reflect your mutual expectations. The more you are relying on financial aspects of the relationship in making decisions about your future, the more you need to know about your partner's finances.

The mere fact that you plan to be together for a significant period suggests that you need some information about your partner's finances. Even a simple decision like renting an apartment can become ruinous if the two of you agree to split the rent but your partner can't realistically afford to pay his or her half.

You need financial disclosure because you need to assure yourself that your partner has the financial capacity to fulfill the obligations that he or she is undertaking. Financial disclosure serves the purpose of helping you decide whether your reliance on your partner is well founded or not. More bluntly, it will help to protect you from lying lovers.

(If you have only short-term or limited expectations from each other, such as sharing everyday expenses, then you probably only need minimal disclosure such as where your lover works and how much he or she makes. You can even do without that much disclosure, although doing so is risky. Moreover, in a short-term relationship, it is probably prudent to keep the details of your financial situation to yourself.)

The simplest and best way to make clear financial disclosure is to provide each other with financial statements. These accounting documents list your assets and your debts; a couple could also include their salaries, stock options, and other financial expectations, such as a pending inheritance.

Financial Information to share

The primary questions that you probably need to answer about finances in any relationship are these:

- ✓ *Who is going to pay for what in the relationship?*
- ✓ *What financial aspects of this relationship are each of you relying on?*

The basic financial information to share is each party's income and expenses, so that a fair allocation of shared household expenses can be agreed upon.

The minimum questions, then, are the following:

- ✓ *What are your debts and what are the monthly payments?*
- ✓ *What significant obligations do you have, such as child support and college loans that will come due at a later date?*
- ✓ *How much do you make?*
- ✓ *What do you own now?*

✔ *How shall we divide what we acquire during this relationship?*

When you have the basic information, you can decide who will pay for what and who will own what in your shared household. While it is probably unwise and unworkable to try to split expenses in minute detail, some understanding of who will pay what is necessary.

If both of you are working and earning approximately equal amounts, then an even split probably makes the most sense. If, however, your incomes are substantially disproportionate, then perhaps it makes more sense for each of you to contribute a set percentage of your income toward household costs, with the costs of vacations and so on being decided as the occasion arises.

If one of you is heavily in debt and the other is not, then you have to decide how you feel about paying for someone's obligations.

It is almost never a good idea to assume another's debt, i.e. to make a formal arrangement with the bank or finance company so that you are jointly liable with your lover. The reason this is unwise is that you then become equally liable with your lover just as if you had borrowed the money yourself. Assuming a debt is like co-signing for a loan, except that co-signing usually refers to agreeing to be responsible for the loan at the beginning. Assuming someone else's obligations is a legal obligation that will continue after the end of the relationship; if things don't work out with you and your significant other, you will still be responsible for his or her obligations. If you want to help your significant other get of debt, give him or her the money to pay the bills. Don't get into any relationship with his or her creditors.

Checking on financial disclosures (and other matters)

Financial statements can, to put it bluntly, be false or at least misleadingly incomplete. Think Enron here.

It may seem tacky but a little investigative work may save a lot of heartache. If you are counting on your lover's salary to pay for a new house, you can and should ask to see a pay stub. More than this, you should perhaps keep an eye out for unexplained expenditures or surprising gaps between your lover's stated income and the amount of money that he or she seems to have on hand. You might want to ask for a credit report, which is a record of whether a person has paid his or her debts on time. Credit reporting agencies will, however, only provide these to the individual or to a business that has a contract with the agency. It is hard to ask for these items of proof tactfully and you should of course be willing to reciprocate.

The reason for checking things out is that creating an appearance of being richer than we are is virtually an art form in this country. As a society, we feel that it is important to "keep up with the Joneses," and many people go to great lengths to support a façade of success and high income. Consequently, and again perhaps without conscious intent to deceive, many people lead others to believe that they are wealthier than they are.

Investigative services, which will review various public and private records, such as credit reports, can provide a fairly comprehensive check on key facts about your significant other. There are online services easily available and inexpensive, or you could hire a licensed private investigator to do a background check. If you are making a commitment that will affect the rest of your life, it might be prudent to invest a few dollars in a basic background check on your significant other. The results may break your heart when you learn that he or she has actually been married six times, instead of living the lonely celibate life that he or she represented to you. On the other hand, better a broken heart now than a broken heart and an empty pocketbook later.

Online services can perform a basic background check for a very reasonable fee. This will not protect you from a major scam, as where you lover has been given a new identity in the witness protection program or has fled prosecution and adopted an informal new identity, but it will protect you from modest lies.

A competent private investigator has access to more comprehensive sources and can check employment history and so on for a relatively modest fee, often around $60 an hour. He or she can also personally verify elements of your potential spouse's past, including interviewing former spouses and business associates, if you are willing to invest the money and risk any possible embarrassment.

The hardest lies to protect yourself from are what I call "sincere lies." These are the untruths that people tell when they have convinced themselves that the past is as they choose to remember it. In other words, they draw their significant others into their self-deceptions.

An example would be a man who describes himself as having established a successful internet business during the internet boom and having been cheated out of it by unscrupulous partners. It may be that he did in fact build a small online company but that it never really got off the ground and in fact failed because of his misjudgment of a market trend.

Another example is a woman who portrays herself as having been unfairly fired from her partnership in a law firm because of office politics when in fact she was such an unspeakable witch that the firm couldn't stand having her any longer.

What financial matters should a couple consider?

This section contains a more detailed consideration of financial issues to address in a long-term relationship.

✓ *What ownership will each of you have in the things that the two of you acquire during the relationship?*

One structure that appeals to many people as a fair one in a committed relationship, marital, or cohabitation is that each person keeps everything that he or she had before the relationship began and that they share equally everything acquired during the relationship. However, a couple may need to vary this basic scenario in order to take account of home ownership, pension plans, and so on.

✓ *If one of you owns the house where you plan to live together, will the other acquire any interest in it?*

Mortgage payments and ownership shares are one of the most difficult issues to resolve in a relationship. On the one hand, the house belongs to the one who owned it when the relationship began; that person made the down payment, qualified for the loan, and is the responsible person on the mortgage.

On the other hand, if you live together for a long time, the other spouse may feel that he or she has paid for a big chunk of the house and may well think that he or she is entitled to some ownership interest. Therefore, mortgage payment issues are one that can change over time. If the relationship is short-term, it is inappropriate and cumbersome to give the live-in lover a share in the ownership of the house; if the relationship lasts for 20 years and both contribute to the upkeep and payments, it is probably unfair to not give the lover a share.

Moreover, the house can come to represent a degree of separateness in the relationship: in every fight over cleaning the rug, the couple can scream at each other that "It's my house, I'll keep it as I want," or "It's your house, if you want it so squeaky clean, you can clean it."

✓ *Do the two of you have a joint savings plan for the future or do each of you prefer to keep long-term financial arrangements separate?*

Some people adhere to the "paddle your own canoe" view of life in which it is up to every individual to take care of him or herself, regardless of matters of the heart. The results can be painful, not to say financially ruinous, if you and your significant other disagree on this point of fiscal philosophy.

Here again, the age of the couple makes a big difference. It may be perfectly reasonable and fair for a couple in their sixties who decide to live together to agree to take care of each other for life. They may make decisions about, for example, early retirement based on the commitment of the other person. On the other hand, it may be absurd for two young professionals to promise to support each other for life, whether they marry or not.

In a real life case, two young artists decided that each of them would support the other for one year. During the year, one would work and one would paint, and in the next year they would reverse roles. A nice idea except that the young woman went to work first. When her year of office work was up, the young man announced that his artistic genius precluded him taking a regular job. (It is worth noting that a written contract might not have provided much real life help to the young woman because his "artistic temperament" meant that he was usually broke.)

✓ *If you acquire a major asset in the future, do the two of you intend to own one-half each? Who will pay for it? What happens if you split up?*

It may seem only fair to own a major purchase jointly but you need to give some thought to who gets what if the relationship ends. A house may increase in value, but most major consumer purchases, such as boats, recreational vehicles, and appliances, lose substantial value immediately after purchase.

It's not easy to sell most ordinary assets for as much as you paid for them. Sharing anything with an ex-lover can be a disaster. Think about it -- if you and your ex own a boat together, you have to communicate and agree about using it, paying for repairs, and where to keep it. If you can't sell the boat for enough money to pay off any loan that you took out for it, then the two of you can have ongoing hassles about who paid his or her share or not.

Obviously, it is probably impracticable to share a washing machine or home theater system when the two of you don't live together anymore. The only sensible course may be to divide up what you can and have one party buy the other's share of things that you can't divide.

Investments such as stocks are somewhat easier to handle. You can establish a joint account in both your names and relatively simply divide the investments if you split. Remember, however, that you may take a substantial loss if you have to sell the stock at the time of the split.

✔ *To what extent do you feel that the two of you should have any responsibility to each other after the relationship ends?*

People differ in their concern for the future. If one of you is making plans for retirement and the other is not, how do you plan to deal with this? Perhaps the most obvious solution is to set aside a certain amount for savings and allocate one-half to each party. Then each can invest or spend his or her share as desired. The difficulty with this solution is that it may lead to hard feelings later when the grasshopper envies the ant's storehouse.

Another option would be to set aside a given amount each month or year for savings and then to deposit one-half into each other's IRA.

✔ *What about stock options that each of you get at work? What about pensions and 401(k) plans?*

✔ *If one of you works in a small business without benefits and the other for an established company with lots of benefits, do you plan to equalize things? For now or for the future too?*

✔ *What about other things that you might acquire or improve during the relationship? What if one of you restores antique cars or trains horses or raise purebred sheep? Does the other one get to share in the profit when the car, horse, or sheep is later sold?*

Equalizing each other's retirement assets might include establishing an IRA or other investment account for the person without a corporate plan. The tax consequences are somewhat complicated here. It is also important to consider the risk that big corporation jobs (and their benefits) can be lost on very short notice, although the law provides for some portability.

Other questions about the relationship — children

It may seem cynical that the question of children occupies less space in this chapter than the question of money. The reason is that the questions with regard to children cannot be firmly answered in a contract. The decision to have a child and decisions about how a relationship affects a child are among the most important in life. However, a written contract can record the intentions of the parties to a relationship but it cannot control how they actually behave. Clearly, if you and your lover disagree violently on the subject of having children or the proper care of them, then you should look elsewhere for a long-term relationship.

Ask yourself:

- ✓ *Do you want children?*
- ✓ *Do you enjoy having them around and taking part in activities with them?*
- ✓ *Do you plan to have children in this relationship?*
- ✓ *Do you have children from a previous relationship? If so, what will the role of your significant other be toward these children?*
- ✓ *Who's going to discipline the children? What standards of behavior are you going to set?*

Children prosper best in a stable two-parent home. They do best when their parents are in a stable and affectionate marriage where the parents genuinely enjoy the time and activities shared by the family.

You owe it to any children that you have now, as well to any that you may have in the future, to consider the impact of your present relationship on those children. If you desperately want to have a child and your lover loathes them, then obviously this relationship is a bad idea. If you have children and your lover dislikes every moment spent in the company of a small child, then equally you should discontinue the relationship.

Remember that parents do not have unlimited power to decide their responsibilities toward their offspring. Consequently, you should assume that if you have children in this relationship, you will be responsible for their support, regardless of any agreement. A written agreement about children can memorialize aspects of your relationship pertinent to the children's welfare, such as a lover's emotional involvement with your children from a previous relationship. You can express your wish, for example, that your lover be allowed continued contact with your children if anything should happen to you. A similar provision could be used by same sex couples where one elects to adopt or bear a child. A court may or may not follow your agreement, but it will at least have made clear your intentions.

If your ex-spouse is still alive, it is probably unlikely that your significant other will want (or be able) to adopt the children. If he or she does not adopt your children, he or she may have very few legal rights to continued contact with the children if you die or if the relationship ends.

Normally, with rare exceptions, in the event of your death, custody of the children will be awarded to your ex-spouse, unless he or she consents to another arrangement. If your ex-spouse is not available, custody will likely be given to another relative if one is willing.

Even if your ex-spouse does not want the children, or is unable to care for them, it is more likely that custody will be given to another blood relative, such as a grandparent, rather than to a lover, although if your lover can prove that he or she has had a warm, stable relationship with the children, he or she may be able to get custody. It is possible to indicate your wishes in a document, such as a will, but a court is not bound by those wishes

Taking care of each other legally

The legal status of cohabitation agreements is, technically, unsettled but it is likely that courts will honor them if the agreement is reasonably fair, the parties made honest disclosures to each other, and the agreement doesn't violate any major social policy or morality. Greenstein says, for example,

> *Colorado courts have not specifically decided whether such agreements can be enforced. However, assuming such an agreement is in writing and is signed by all cohabitants after adequate disclosure to each other regarding financial matters (if the agreement relates to finances), it should be enforceable.*[1]

Regardless of the legal technicalities, you have little or no protection for your financial expectations if you don't have a written agreement, so putting those expectations in writing is a good idea. Drafting a cohabitation agreement can be a difficult business. That's why lawyers get paid. First, talking about money and commitment is hard emotional work and probably next to impossible to do objectively if you are one-half of the couple involved. Second, thinking about the various contingencies in our complex modern lives is intellectually challenging and emotionally painful.

To intelligently draft a cohabitation or prenuptial agreement, you need to agree on the financial aspects of your relationships, as well as the other facets. Then you need to write down those terms in a legally enforceable, clear document.

Sample agreements are in the Workbook. It cannot be emphasized too strongly, however, that you must think through the terms of your relationship for yourself and understand the effect of those terms on your life, now and in the future.

More guidance on writing a cohabitation agreement is in Chapter Nine, starting at page 349 and sample agreements are in the Workbook.

QUESTION: *"How can I ensure that my significant other receives assets that I want her to have?"*

ANSWER: *Transfer titles in some form now, i.e. give it to him or her.*

QUESTION: *"What's wrong with that?"*

ANSWER: *Nothing, unless you ever want to undo your action.*

The law does not favor undoing completed transactions unless there has been a fraud or some other significant unfairness or deception. A gift represented by a formal change in title, such as a deed showing the transfer, is a completed gift, i.e. all the legal formalities have occurred and it is basically a done deal.

Financial arrangements between couples range from the very insecure to the more certain. Basically, the more flexibility that the person making the promise retains, the less secure the recipient is. In other words, the more clear and permanent that the arrangement is, the less able one partner is to back out. Here's a rough list ranging from those arrangements that afford the greatest freedom and least security to those providing the least freedom and most security.

✓ *Vague oral assurances such as "don't worry"–provide little or no security because the person giving the assurance can simply not perform and the "promise" would be hard to prove.*

✓ *More specific oral promises such as "I'll put aside enough to take care of you" – hard to enforce but some possibility of receiving whatever you thought you would get. The person making the promise still has considerable freedom to change his or her mind.*

✓ *Marriage laws – some financial security because most laws provide for some asset sharing between spouses, but the exact result is difficult to predict because individual circumstances vary so much. The couple can change the impact of marriage laws by how they handle their finances.*

✓ *Wills and insurance policies – reasonably certain results (i.e. the named beneficiary will receive what is specified unless someone manages to challenge the validity of the document) but these arrangements can be changed without notice to the beneficiary. In other words, the person writing the will, for example, can easily change his or her mind.*

✓ *Written financial agreements (prenuptial or cohabitation) – can be clearer than marriage laws and more binding than oral promises but can also be affected by changed circumstances and may not be followed by the couple. If the money is simply not there to make the promised payments, for example, the agreement does not provide much security, no matter how clear it is.*

✓ *Shared accounts – reasonably secure if both parties must sign to withdraw funds. If one can act unilaterally, these accounts still afford some protection (e.g. from other family members) but the result is not ensured.*

✓ *Outright transfers – a gift of property or a change in title documents is a (more or less) irrevocable action. The new owner is simply that – the owner. The transaction can only be undone if the recipient agrees to give it back or if the person making the gift can prove that he or she was cheated or coerced.*

Other legal documents

Every couple in a committed long-term relationship (married or not) needs to have other legal documents prepared. These include appropriate wills, medical powers of attorney, advance directives (living wills), designations of guardian, and changes to other appropriate documents such as deeds.

Wills and trusts

Every couple needs to prepare for the possibility of one of them dying. If you intend for your partner to inherit from you, then you must have a valid will that says what you want. If you are relying on inheriting from your lover (and he/she is relying on inheriting from you), then you both need to have wills prepared. You may also need more complex arrangements, which usually involve the legal entity called a "trust."

Wills

A will is a document that specifies what happens to your assets when you die. You can leave your money and other possessions to any legal person, i.e. to a human being or a corporate organization, such as a charity. (You cannot leave property to a pet; to provide for a pet, you need to leave the property in trust with a human being.)

A deceased person who has a will is referred to as dying "testate" and one without a will as "intestate." If a person dies without a valid will, then state law sets out who gets what.

The provisions of the will are carried out in a court proceeding called "probate." Most states have simplified proceedings where the situation is straightforward so fears of excessive probate costs are often exaggerated.

More information about wills can be found in Chapter Seven at page 250 and in the Workbook at page 601. Some of the information here repeats those discussions.

A valid will is one that is written and signed under various specific conditions. Normally, a valid will has to be signed by the person making the will (the "testator") and by two independent witnesses. Some state laws provide that the witnesses must see the testator sign and hear him or her state that "this is my will." Often, the witnesses and testator execute affidavits that all the conditions for the will's validity have been satisfied.

The document itself does not have to contain any particular language except that it must state that it is a will, i.e. it must be clear that this document is not a deed or a statement of vague intentions or whatever.

Despite the fact that particular language is not required, the formalities are critical for valid wills. Lack of a witness or signing the will without complying with the rules can invalidate the will.

Any change to a will usually revokes it. A will cannot be changed by crossing out one part, for example.

In contrast to the formalities of making a will, a will can be revoked by signing a new one, destroying the old one, or writing "revoked" on it. A will is revoked by any action that indicates an intention to revoke the will.

Usually, it is hard to completely disinherit a spouse. Spouses normally have some entitlements to the assets owned by the spouse.

There are several popular programs and websites that write wills and trusts. You can also buy a form at a stationery store or find one in a book at the library. If your financial situation is simple, you can probably use one of these forms if you are scrupulous about complying with the formal requirements. If you want to leave your modest assets to one person, a simple will form will suffice.

Despite all the foregoing, a handwritten will is often valid. A handwritten will is one that is entirely (every word) in handwriting (not computer printed or typed), is signed by the testator, and is clearly a will.

It is important to remember that some important life events changes inheritance rights. For example, marriage, divorce, or birth of a child may change the terms of a will. To be safe, a person needs to make a new will when one of these events occurs.

Sometimes, people agree to make certain wills with particular terms. It is important to see that these agreements are carried out; the agreement itself is not a will. In other words, if your significant other promises to leave you a lot of money, you need to be sure that he or she actually signs a valid will and does not later change it.

Trusts

In more complicated situations, as where a couple has sufficient assets to be concerned about inheritance taxes or where both of them are in frail health, a trust can be used. A trust is a legal arrangement that puts various assets (such as stocks and money) in the hands of another person to manage.

The person who puts the assets in the trust is the "trustor" (or the "settlor"), the person managing and distributing the assets of the trust the trust is called the "trustee," and the person benefiting from the trust is the "beneficiary." Legally, the trustee is obligated to manage the assets (and use them) solely for the benefit of the beneficiaries. Sometimes, the trustor and the trustee may be the same person; for example, parents can set up a trust for a child and also be the trustees of that trust. The child is the beneficiary.

For another example, a wealthy lover could put enough money in a trust to take care of his significant other for some set period of time or for the rest of her life; the trust documents could provide that when she died, or if she married, the money would be paid to other beneficiaries or would revert to the wealthy lover. Similarly, partners with children from previous relationships can agree that each will leave his or her money in trust for the other partner for his or her lifetime and then to their respective children.

The law of wills and trusts, particularly with the complications of inheritance taxes, is a complex field of its own. In addition, the practical aspects of setting up and managing a trust can be daunting.

In addition to a cohabitation agreement, trusts can be used to reflect and protect the financial relationship of the parties. Some experts recommend using trusts to accomplish a couple's sharing of assets through a long-term relationship. For example, the couple can agree that the wealthier person will set up a trust for the poorer one and will add a certain amount to the trust each year that the relationship endures.

Specifically, some experts recommend revocable living trusts for a couple who want to protect and share their assets. A revocable living trust is a legal entity with special rules. The term "revocable" means that it can be undone by the person who sets it up. The term "living" refers to the fact that it is established during the lifetime of those creating it, as opposed to a testamentary trust that takes effect when the founder (called the "trustor") dies.

A trust can also be irrevocable which means, obviously, that the person who sets it up cannot obliterate it nor (usually) withdraw assets from it. The advantage of an irrevocable trust is that, in most circumstances, the beneficiary can count on receiving the benefits of the trust.

So, if a wealthy lover wants to provide for his or her significant other and he or she wants to be assured that has been done, an irrevocable trust can be a great solution.

The obvious problem is that if you set up an irrevocable trust in the heat of passion, you cannot normally undo it later when you may be thinking differently. The obvious advantage is the same – a person who is counting on the trust is protected to a greater degree. The other advantages of trusts, revocable and irrevocable, is that it is harder for disgruntled family members to challenge a trust established for a lover. The trust can be set up and funded while the couple are still alive and together. The transfers have been made to the trust, which now owns the assets. The couple can continue to receive the benefits and may serve as trustees to keep some control over the investments and so on. It's a done deal and harder for disgruntled children to challenge.

Trusts also can be the beneficiaries of estates, i.e. the trust can inherit from a person. Many people leave their assets to a trust for their children, especially if a child or grandchild is imprudent or disabled. Also, the trust assets don't belong to the beneficiary; the trust can provide that the assets will be used to support a beneficiary during his or her life, for example, and then be used for some other purpose, such as a charity or to take care of someone else.

Lawyers and financial planners have differing opinions about the value of using living trusts to embody family financial arrangements. These legal arrangements require attention to detail and consistent management. In other words, if you want the trust to embody a particular financial structure, you have to follow through on the mechanics. If the trust owns property, for example, you will need separate bank accounts and records for the management of that property.

One of the advantages is that a trust can control the beneficiary's access to the money. If a person is imprudent or incapacitated, a trustee can handle investments and so on for the trust. The terms of the trust can also control when a person receives the money. Some sample provisions in trusts for children often provide that the child will receive a certain amount per year or that you may have to file a separate tax return for a trust.

Special rules govern trusts because these entities rest on, literally, a relationship of trust. Trusts are one of the few legal relationships in which the law expressly requires people to behave with loyalty, honesty, and fairness to each other. A trustee cannot legally take the trust assets for himself or herself. He or she cannot benefit at the expense of the trust.

Finally, the trustee must handle trust assets with the same prudence as a reasonable person in the care of his or her own property. That means that the trustee cannot legally invest in highly speculative ventures or gamble with the assets. A fiduciary must also account to the beneficiary for the assets, i.e. provide a statement of what assets were in the trust and what has become of them. This package of duties creates a high standard of care called "fiduciary duty."

Sometimes, of course, the trustee fails to live up to this high standard of care. The temptation to treat money in a trust as one's own is great. If the trustee misbehaves – foolishly or dishonestly – the only remedy is to sue him or her. The exception would be where the trustee posted a bond to guarantee his or her honesty; the bond in this case is like a bond of insurance.

There are several advantages of using a trust in an interpersonal relationship.

First, courts understand fiduciary duties; these standards are, relatively, clear. Second, assets are actually transferred to the trust. That means that your significant other is somewhat less able to rip you off without legal consequences. Therefore, there is less room for disagreement about whether you actually relied on your significant other or not. Third, title to assets, such as a stock fund, can be taken in the name of the trust as a legal entity which may sometimes simplify implementing provisions for children, for example. Finally, assets that are in a living trust, revocable or irrevocable, do not go through the probate process.

What that means is that if you and your lover establish and fund (put money in) an inter vivos trust for each other and one of you dies, the other should receive the benefit of the trust without waiting for the legal handling of the deceased person's estate.

The disadvantages are several.

First, a trust is a taxable entity, which can complicate your life and potentially increase your tax bill. Second, trusts impose additional record keeping and legal maintenance requirements. Third, the fact that someone has the legal duty of a fiduciary does not guarantee that he or she will abide by that responsibility; many a trustee has robbed a trust. Fourth, there is the thorny question of whether a trust should be revocable or irrevocable.

A revocable trust has the advantage that if the relationship ends, then the trust structure can be unwound. If, however, you are relying on the establishment of that trust for your financial future, a revocable trust is a shaky foundation unless the terms under which it can be revoked are clear. In other words, a revocable trust does not confer financial security if your lover can unilaterally revoke the trust.

An irrevocable trust, however, can lock you into a connection with your lover long after you want one. Irrevocable trusts, however, have some legal advantages in that the transfer of assets is a completed gift and the assets no longer belong to the person who set up the trust.

A good example of the appropriate use of an irrevocable trust would be a relationship between a very wealthy person and a person who works for a living. Suppose, for example, that a young man with a promising legal career falls in love with a wealthy older woman. She wants to travel and enjoy life. He's happy to do this too, but he worries about abandoning his career. Where will he be if and when the relationship ends? One option would be for her to establish a trust for his benefit and to agree in writing that she will add a certain amount to it for each year that they are together, up to a given figure. That way, if the relationship lasts, neither of them is harmed and when the relationship ends, each will, we hope, have what he or she counted on.

A word of caution is in order about the use of trusts to impose values or standards of conduct on people. There is a temptation to add a clause such as "provided [the beneficiary] remains faithful to me."

The use of money to control children and spouses has a long and tangled history. Fathers and grandfathers have used trusts or similar legal devices to try to keep their children on the straight and narrow path of virtue by conditioning the child's receipt of benefits from the trust on his or her not smoking, or not drinking intoxicating beverages, or not gambling. Trusts have also been conditioned on the child's not marrying without the consent of the parent or grandparent. Similarly, spouses (usually husbands) or other relatives (usually in-laws) have tried to use the terms of a trust to control a widow or daughter-in-law. For example, the benefits of a trust might be conditional on a daughter's marrying and having children.

These clauses may be legal, at least if they don't conflict with general societal norms. Clauses that require a young woman to finish college or to become a teetotaler or to not have a child out of wedlock in order to benefit from a trust would be valid. However, such clauses may or may not produce the desired behavior and may well produce bitter litigation over whether or not the beneficiary complied with the term in question. At best, they may ensure that one's money does not go to someone of whose conduct one disapproves. At worst, they lead to bitter family divisions. Clauses that require a person to do something immoral to earn the money will not be upheld by the courts.

Trusts are frequently used to provide for a person who is not capable of prudently handling money, such as a child or an imprudent individual, while keeping control of the money in other, more responsible, hands. The terms of the trust provide for the conditions under which the beneficiary gets the money. For example, a typical trust provision would be that the assets would be used to pay for a child's education or to "support my friend, George Smith, in the same style and manner in which we lived when we were together, so long as said George Smith remains single and does not cohabit with a person of the opposite sex." Neither George nor the child own the trust assets, but both have certain rights to funds from the trust.

Many people believe that they should name a banker or lawyer as a trustee, and in fact, many banks, lawyers, and other financial experts will perform this service. However, they charge a fee for doing so; they may well charge a sizable percentage of all the assets in the trust to manage it, even if there is very little to do.

Moreover, they may or may not manage the trust well; banks notoriously leave trust assets in accounts that pay little or no interest, which is profitable for the bank because the bank gets the use of the money for free plus its fees for "managing" the trust. Other "professional money managers" may have an incentive to trade the stocks in the trust frequently (or sell real estate in the trust) because they (or their buddies) can earn a commission on the sales. These managers may charge several thousand dollars to write a few checks a year. Most of these practices are legal or quasi-legal.

Finally, remember that choosing a bank or other institution as trustee is different than naming a particular banker as trustee; the individual person in whom you have confidence may quit or move to another firm. The institution will then name some other employee (whom you have never met) to handle your trust.

On the other hand, banks and professional firms can do an excellent, responsible job, and they usually have insurance to reimburse the trust if there is outright thievery. For these reasons, you may wish to name a close friend or trusted relative (pun intended) as your trustee. Nothing in life is guaranteed. A foolish person, no matter how sincere, can fritter away all the money in the trust that you set aside for your children. Nevertheless, good faith and loyalty, even if the friend is not a financial genius, may be preferable to financial sophistication and the ruthless greed that often characterizes institutional trustees.

A trust can take effect after you die or while you are still alive. A testamentary trust takes effect when you die.

A living trust (also called in Latin an *inter vivos* trust because it is "between the living") is one that is set up while the people are alive. Living trusts are often touted as a way to avoid probate and to take care of another person financially. The idea is that a trust is a sort of legal entity, somewhat analogous to a partnership or corporation.

Assets are transferred to the living trust, which then owns the assets, and the trustee manages things. Usually the trustee is the person who contributed the assets. The enticing theory is that the trustee keeps control of his or her money while he or she is alive but when he or she dies, the assets automatically go to the beneficiary.

A living trust can be a perfectly useful legal device for setting property aside for someone without completely losing control of it. It is well to beware of salesmen peddling living trusts, however, as they have an incentive to persuade you to use one particular structure, which is the one that they are selling. There are many other aspects of this transaction that require careful thought.

Here are some questions that one should ask about trusts:

- ✓ *What if I change my mind later? (i.e. is this trust revocable or irrevocable?)*
- ✓ *What if we split up?*
- ✓ *Does the trustee have fiduciary duties to the beneficiaries? In other words, does he or she have to handle the assets in a fair, honest way?*
- ✓ *What if the trustee wants to sell some of the assets?*
- ✓ *What if the trustee needs some of the assets for him or herself?*
- ✓ *Are there any tax consequences to having a trust?*
- ✓ *What rights does my beneficiary have to get information about the trust now or after I'm gone?*
- ✓ *Can we change the trustee? The terms of the trust?*

Many of these questions can be answered by careful drafting of the trust agreement.

Wills and other documents

A will, as everyone knows, is the document that determines who gets what when you die. These documents can be simple or complex, depending on your family situation and finances.

There are two central legal facts about wills. First, if you don't have one, the law will decide which of your relatives gets what part of your assets. Second, a document is a valid will only if it is signed with the requisite formalities. Usually, a will must either be entirely handwritten or else it must be notarized and witnessed according to the law of your state. A technical error can invalidate the whole thing. There's more guidance on wills in the Workbook at page 601.

You can buy inexpensive software to write wills, durable powers of attorney, living wills and so on. You can also buy form kits at office supply stores. There are also online sites that will prepare these sorts of documents for you; these sites tend to be more expensive than buying a simple program. If your affairs are not complicated, these programs may produce adequate and enforceable documents much more cheaply than an attorney would charge. Some of the software have wizards that walk you through a series of questions and then generate the document for you. Beware of any program or kit that does not provide for state variations. In my opinion, however, these documents are so important that it is worth taking your draft to an attorney for review.

There are other documents that take effect on your death. For example, in Arizona, you can record a beneficiary deed in the public records to indicate who will receive a piece of property. You can records deeds that give someone an interest in real estate for their lifetime, after which it goes to someone else, or you can give away your property and retain the right to use it until you die. The variations are considerable and helpful, especially for unmarried couples. However, the key is that these documents must be carefully and correctly written and recorded in the public records in order to have the effect that you intend.

Durable powers of attorney and advance directives

A durable power of attorney gives another person the legal authority to make decisions for us if we are unable to make them for ourselves. The word "durable" means that the power continues even when you are legally incompetent, such as after an accident. The person named in a power of attorney is not your lawyer and doesn't need to be an attorney.

A durable power of attorney is usually used to give someone else the authority to make medical decisions for you if you are unable to express your wishes. These are called "durable powers of attorney for health care." They are intended to take effect, for example, when a person is in a serious accident or has a stroke. Obviously, the person chosen should be someone who is familiar with your values and who will, to the best of his or her ability, try to make the decision that you would. The document can also contain specific provisions that express your wishes, such as "I do not wish to be sustained on a respirator if it is unlikely that I will ever recover sufficiently to breathe on my own." If you have strong feelings about end of life care, then you should set it out in this document.

Durable powers of attorney for health care are essential if you would prefer that your lover make medical decisions for you, rather than your relatives. In the absence of such a document, If your parents are alive, the doctors and hospital will probably be inclined to follow their wishes, instead of those of your significant other, who has no legal relationship to you. A durable power of attorney should expressly give the person who will decide for you (your "attorney in fact") (1) permission to visit you in the hospital and (2) permission to receive your medical records. Federal privacy laws may make it difficult for a hospital or physician to legally share information with a non-relative. Moreover, if there is an objection by family members, hospitals sometimes try to exclude the decision-maker from the incapacitated person's hospital room. This is particularly likely if the couple is a same sex couple.

A general durable power of attorney gives another person the legal authority to handle your financial affairs if you are incapacitated. For example, a durable power like this would give your significant other the legal power to pay your bills, etc. The authority conveyed can be quite broad however; your lover might also have the power to sell your house and empty your bank account. Again, careful drafting is required for each of these documents.

A simpler document is that called an "advance directive," which was previously called a "living will." It tells doctors and hospital staff what your values are about the end of life. For example, if you strongly feel that you would prefer to be allowed to die naturally, rather than have "everything done that can possibly be done," then you can execute one of these. Also, many people execute organ donor cards to indicate that they would like to donate any usable parts of their body when they die.

Many people find discussing the possibility of having a terrible disease or injury unpleasant and morbid. On other hand, many people commonly say, when they hear of a person being maintained on life support for months, "Oh, I wouldn't want to live like that." If you make that kind of remark, then you need to have a durable power that expresses your actual wishes.

One of the most important decisions that a health care proxy makes is how long treatment should be continued. Most people want to avoid suffering but the amount that they are willing to tolerate for a chance of survival varies greatly. You can see that if your attorney in fact is also your heir, he or she may have a considerable conflict of interest, because he or she will inherit your money if you die. If you are in a nursing home and the cost is devouring your assets, your attorney in fact may have an incentive to decide that you really wouldn't want to live like that.

You should also keep in mind that people's values change when an imagined situation becomes a real one. Many people who believed that they wouldn't want to live if they couldn't enjoy their favorite sports have found that life is good even if some aspects change. The gallant life of actor Christopher Reeve is a good example of a man who found ways to continue a life of creativity, service, and love after a devastating injury.

In addition, some people have undue fears about particular procedures. Being on a respirator, for example, is miserable but tolerable if its only for a few days and afterwards you will make a full recovery. Many medical procedures can be made less painful or distressing with appropriate medication. If you have specific fears, talk to your doctor or another advisor about your concern.

On the other hand, people have fears of someone pulling the plug too early. Sometimes, for example, patients are kept alive by being given water and food intravenously, called "artificial nutrition and hydration." Withdrawal of this support from a comatose person causes death over a period of days, and many doctors believe that this death is relatively painless especially if appropriate medication is given. However, many people are appalled at the thought that someone might let them die of hunger and thirst.

Some of the questions that are commonly asked are the following:

- ✓ *Do you want the doctors to do everything to keep you alive if the chance of your recovery is slim?*
- ✓ *What quality of life matters to you? Would you want to be aggressively treated only to survive with severe mental or physical limitations?*
- ✓ *Are there any medical procedures that you strongly object to? Being on a respirator (i.e. having a machine breathe for you)? Being subjected to agonizing procedures such as treatment for extensive burns?*
- ✓ *Do you want to be treated to sustain your life even if you are unaware of your surroundings or severely mentally impaired?*

✓ *If assisted suicide were legal, would you want that option to be available to you? If so, add appropriate language to the document. (Obviously, of course, your health care proxy cannot legally kill you.)*

✓ *Are there end of life events that are particularly important to you, such as last rites or specific death rituals of your religion? Be sure to provide for these in your durable power and be sure that your health care proxy understands them. Many hospital personnel and physicians are unfamiliar with, and unsympathetic to spiritual concerns, and your health care proxy can help defend your right to your own spiritual comfort.*

You should be aware that if the person who will be your health care proxy is also your heir, then he or she may have a conflict of interest; if you die sooner, there might be more for him or her to inherit. This conflict exists in families, not just in less formal relationships. The well-known ethicist Dr. Baruch Brody has argued that financial considerations are a relevant issue in end of life decisions because, for example, an elderly person might not want the family to dissipate assets in desperate, futile medical interventions if those assets could be better used to send a grandchild to college.

In addition, in families especially, there can be profound psychological conflicts that can lead a family member to make unfortunate decisions for a suffering relative, including extending life because of an inability to let go or because of an unacknowledged a grim satisfaction in the suffering.

A child who feels poorly treated by a parent has ample chance for revenge in these circumstances and may be paralyzed by his or her feelings of anger and guilt. As one angry young man said of his father, "He can do what he wants to me now but I get to pick his nursing home later."

You should also consider who would handle your financial affairs in the event of your being incapacitated. This can be a more difficult decision because the person has to be honest, concerned with your best interests, and have the necessary level of skill in managing business matters. Naming this person is done by a general durable power of attorney, which is like the health care power but covers financial questions.

People who are seriously ill often sign a document called a "do not resuscitate order." This is a special instruction to the hospital that if the person's heart begins to fail or stop, then the staff should not use CPR or other methods to keep the heart going. In other words, this instruction permits a person to die from the heart failure instead of having a lot of painful efforts made to restart the heart when the person is approaching death anyway from other causes. Forms for this instruction need to be obtained from your hospital or doctor.

All of these documents need to be witnessed. The witnesses must be people who do not have an interest in the document; for example, the person that you name as your primary heir can't witness your will or your directive to physicians. The witnesses can be friends or members of your attorney's staff or employees of the notary to whom you take the document to be witnessed. This requirement seems like one more legalistic device but it is designed to help ensure that these documents genuinely express the wishes of the person signing them; if there are independent witnesses, then the person signing at least has a chance to say that he or she is being coerced or doesn't want to sign after all.

You should remember that any special wishes that you have about your funeral should be in a separate, easily accessible, document and not in your will. These wishes might include cremation or earth burial, location of your grave or where you would like your ashes scattered, special hymns, poems, or people that you wish to be invited or excluded.

In all of these matters, it is advisable to reveal your wishes orally to your family and closest friends, if they can bear the conversation. That way, your wishes do not come as a painful surprise to anyone.

Finally, if you break up with your lover, then you may wish to revoke all of these documents. The directive to physicians may not require change because it does not name anyone in particular to decide for you, but the designation of guardian and the two durable powers should be revoked and rewritten. Remember, documents like these can be in effect even if the person named is no longer your lover or, for example, even if you named your spouse and were subsequently divorced. These documents can be revoked in three ways: (1) by executing a new one that cancels the old; (2) by destroying the old original document and all copies, if possible; and (3) by executing a revocation document. If there is family disharmony, then it is safest to execute a new document and to destroy the old ones (or write "revoked" across the front of the document and sign underneath). Obviously, you need to let important people, like your doctor and your grown children and, possibly, your best friends, know that you have changed these documents.

Designation of guardian

Many lawyers recommend naming someone as your guardian in addition to the two durable powers mentioned above (i.e. for health care decisions and for financial management). A guardian is a person appointed by a court to make decisions for an incompetent or incapacitated person. Guardians are appointed to elderly people who have become senile, for mentally handicapped persons, and for persons with intractable drug or alcohol addictions.

Judges tend to appoint family members as guardians. While this is natural and often appropriate, it can lead to mismanagement and abuse, depending on the quality of the family relationships. Other times, the court appoints a lawyer who is a friend of the judge. This also can be appropriate and can relieve the family of these responsibilities. The lawyer posts a bond with the court to protect the incapacitated person's estate. However, obviously, this arrangement can also give ample opportunity for an unscrupulous lawyer to plunder the impaired person's assets for his or her own gain.

You can also execute a document that specifies who you would like to have as your guardian if you are incapacitated or who you would like to have as the guardian of your children. A guardian for an adult takes care of decision-making and financial management for a person who cannot care for himself or herself. The person who is taken care of is called the "ward." Guardians can be appointed for adults who are mentally handicapped or so mentally ill that they cannot make rational decisions. A guardian of a child is like a parent to the child, except that he or she is not financially responsible for supporting the child.

Sometimes courts divide the responsibility for different aspects of a ward's life. A judge may appoint one person to have responsibility for the ward's care and day to day life and another to manage the finances. In that case, the former is called a "guardian of the person" and the latter is called a "guardian of the estate" or sometimes the "conservator."

All guardians are fiduciaries who are legally responsible for taking care of the dependent person in a responsible, honest way. Often, they are required to post a bond to ensure that if they misappropriate money, there is a form of insurance. A designation of guardian, whether in a separate document or in a will, may or may not be completely effective, depending on the laws of your particular state. However, they at least have the merit of making your wishes known.

Designations of guardian are especially important for same sex and unmarried couples because it helps to keep family members from interfering in the life partner's becoming a guardian. Family members who object to the relationship may use a guardianship proceeding to trump durable powers of attorney and other documents; the guardian, once appointed, becomes the decision-maker.

Taking care of each other legally – relationships with other people

Both married and unmarried couples need to pay careful attention to the important documents relating to couples if they truly want to take care of each other. Being married does not obviate all of the potential legal hassles in a family

These documents include durable powers of attorney for health care, durable powers of attorney in case of in capacity, advance directives (living wills), and wills. In addition, an unmarried couple should have a cohabitation agreement and should be sure that all relevant papers, such as bank account documents, deeds, etc. are consistent with their agreement. A married couple may decide not to have a prenuptial agreement but they should also be sure that the title documents relating to their assets are in accordance with their mutual expectations. If those expectations are different from state law, then they need a written agreement setting out their desires and the relevant papers need to match that agreement.

Except where you have designated your lover (or spouse) as your agent, you cannot legally sign his or her name to legal documents (such as loan agreements or mortgages or deeds) and he or she cannot legally sign for you.

Therefore, if you are going to authorize your significant other to sign on your checking account, or take other legal actions on your behalf, the two of you need a written agency agreement, whether you are married or not. Orally authorizing your lover to sign your name to checks or other documents is usually a bad idea; you can't expect the bank to suddenly start scrutinizing your signature on checks when you and your lover split up, and it's a hassle to change accounts. Conversely, if your lover lets you sign his or her name on checks, get the permission in writing. You don't want to be facing an accusation of forgery on top of the general misery of a breakup.

Special circumstances on shared finances or a shared business include those where one of you is authorized to act as the other's agent or where you are partners in a business. Agency can be represented by a formal power of attorney or other, less formal arrangement. A partnership can be represented in a formal, written document or can be an oral understanding, although banks and so on are notoriously (and rightly) reluctant to accept signatures based on oral agreements. Business agreements should always be in writing.

Moreover, there are legal limitations on what you can do for your lover in terms of financial benefits. Federal law, which governs pension plans and other employment benefits, does not generally permit a person to enroll their lover for these and other benefits. You will need to check with your plan administrator to see if you can legally include your partner in such plans. Domestic partner laws and company policy may or may not permit you to include a heterosexual partner.

Here is a basic checklist of establishing a committed cohabitation arrangement. Sample documents are in the Workbook.

- ✓ *Write and sign a cohabitation agreement. Make a note in your calendar to review it on a yearly basis or when any dramatic change happens in your life or relationship, like starting a business. Comply with the terms of the agreement, especially in terms of joint accounts and payments. Be sure to modify the agreement if you change the way that you live.*

- ✓ *If appropriate, change all the needed legal documents involved to reflect those promises. If you have been promised any financial goodies, make sure your lover follows through with the paperwork. These documents include:*
    - ◆ *Bank account records,*
    - ◆ *Credit card records,*
    - ◆ *Life insurance beneficiary designations,*
    - ◆ *Leases,*
    - ◆ *Deeds,*
    - ◆ *Loan agreements,*
    - ◆ *Bank accounts, either new joint accounts or providing, if possible and appropriate, for your significant other as the survivor on bank or brokerage accounts.*

- ✓ *Check with your employer if you have health insurance or pension benefits and change those records if possible.*

- ✓ *If you want your significant other to have the power to make medical decisions for you, if you are unable to decide for yourself (e.g. if you are unconscious or incoherent), execute a durable medical power of attorney.*

- ✓ *If you want your significant other to have the power to make financial decisions for you, if you are unable to decide for yourself (e.g. if you are unconscious or incoherent), execute a durable general power of attorney.*

- ✓ *If you want your significant other to be your guardian if you are incapacitated, execute a designation of guardian. Not all states recognize these, but it is a useful expression of your preferences.*

- ✓ *If you want your lover to inherit from you, change your will and other relevant documents, including trusts and so forth.*

- ✓ *Make sure all liabilities are clearly documented with the creditors as to who owes what to whom.*

- ✓ *Make sure that your insurance covers your changed circumstances. For example, does your car insurance cover your lover driving your car? This needs to be checked carefully; many policies distinguish between occasionally loaning someone your car and allowing them to have regular access to it. The latter is often not covered unless the person is named in the policy as a driver. Homeowner's insurance may also need to be changed.*

- ✓ *Document any business relationships, including forming partnerships or transferring stock to represent corporate ownership.*

- ✓ *Arrange for formal acknowledgement of any children born of the relationship.*

- ✓ *Change the beneficiary designation on IRA's, 401k accounts, and so on.*

- ✓ *Write up any needed permissions about children, pets, and so on. For example, you may want to document that your child can be picked up from school by your significant other or that he or she can consent to medical care for the child. Copies of these papers should be kept handy, such as in the glove compartment of the car. You may also wish to make more formal arrangements for any children, such as adoption or a guardianship of them by your significant other.*

Conclusions and Advice

The amount of effort that you put into crafting the legal side of a relationship depends on your view of yourself and your future. If you don't expect to ever own anything of value or have any meaningful responsibility for another person and you can't stand thinking about your own mortality, you may decide to blunder along as best you can. And, in fact, that may work out more or less OK for you.

On the other hand, if you have thought about your future and if your plans include saving money for retirement or your children's education or owning a house, then you need to plan for the legal structure of your relationship. That structure needs to match your financial expectations. It's part of the work of accumulating more wealth than you started life with.

Similarly, if you truly care about your significant other, you will gather the courage to contemplate your own mortality and the possibility of the bad things that can happen to people, such as illness and disability. You and your significant other can then make loving provision for your joint future and for financially caring for each other.

Legal documents are an important part of taking care of someone we love in this society, whether the couple is married or unmarried. Paperwork doesn't solve every legal problem but it can sure help and it is far better than leaving the decision to be made according to rules of law that may not reflect any of one's wishes or commitments.

(Endnotes)

[1] Greg A. Greenstein, "Relationships Made Easy by Marital and Cohabitation Agreements," downloaded from the internet site of Franconia, Joiner, Goodman, and Greenstein, PC, September, 2001.

Chapter Thirteen

LIVING TOGETHER AND LOVING EACH OTHER – OLDER COUPLES

This chapter is for couples who have already had their families and now seek companionship and a shared life with someone their own age. Many older couples come together after the end of earlier marriages, either by death or divorce.

The advice given in earlier chapters applies to older couples, generally, but some matters differ. First, older couples may be facing an increase in leisure time and, likely, a decrease in income, by virtue of retirement, in the relatively near future.

Second, mature couples should be thinking ahead to the possibility of their own serious illness or their possible need for on-going care; anyone of any age can suffer a disabling accident or illness but the sad fact is that these events are more likely to occur as one grows older.

Third, older couples may have grown children for whom they wish to provide – during the parent's lifetime or after his or her death – or who expect to be provided for. These children may not require the day to day nurturing of young children but they may have expectations of sharing in a parent's accumulated wealth that can lead to bitterness and litigation if those expectations are either not met or not addressed in a timely fashion.

Fourth, age is no guarantee of the stability of a relationship or the trustworthiness of a partner, nor does it mean that both parties automatically want a lifelong commitment. It is no longer unheard of for couples of advanced age to go through a divorce. Likewise, it is common for a couple well along in years to form an informal attachment in which each of them preserves substantial independence.

Here are some important concerns relevant to mature couples.

- ✓ *Older couples must consider the question of marriage vs. cohabitation in the context of governmental and employment benefits.*
- ✓ *Mature persons cannot afford to dilly dally about addressing the financial aspects of their relationship.*

✓ *Issues relating to children are usually more about inheritance than about child rearing.*

✓ *For persons with significant assets, the legal status of marriage has important estate tax and inheritance consequences.*

Financial matters

One of the most important aspects of an older couple's relationship is that they do not have as much time to recover financially from a bad deal as a younger couple does. A deceitful or improvident lover is probably a temporary setback, financially speaking, to a 23 year old but can be ruinous to a 60 year old, especially if the latter has already retired. On the other hand, a couple of modest means can substantially improve their standard of living by pooling their resources and living, for example, in one's home while renting or selling the other's house. Moreover, an older couple may own various assets, such as a house, car, or boat, outright, having paid off mortgages, college loans, etc.

Unless both parties are financially independent, it is vital for a mature couple either to be clear about the economic aspects of their relationship or to refrain from making financial decisions based on the relationship. In other words, if you plan to take early retirement in order to travel the world in an RV with your already retired significant other, it behooves you to be certain you understand what the monetary situation is, to say nothing of who's going to make the payments on the RV. Or the condo in Key West. Or the doublewide in Apache Junction.

Governmental benefits

A painful but necessary question in the minds of older couples needs to be that of the impact of marriage on the availability of various benefits, including Social Security, Medicare, and Medicaid. Although efforts are periodically made by Congress to alter these inequities, it remains true that entitlements to these benefits are affected by marriage, usually but not always to the detriment of the older person.

If you are relying, for example, on a deceased spouse's pension benefits or on Social Security (or any other program, such as veteran's benefits), be sure to check with the appropriate administrator or Social Security office to see whether your particular benefit will be adversely affected by your remarriage. Usually, in fact, a new marriage will end these benefits.

The most tragic impact of an older couple's marriage may be on one spouse's entitlement to Medicaid benefits for nursing home care. Medicare pays part of the medical care costs for persons over 65 but does not cover much of the cost of long-term care. Medicaid is a government program for health care for poor people. After a certain number of days in a nursing home, paid for by Medicare, the older patient must either pay for the nursing care himself or herself or qualify for Medicaid.

Qualification for Medicaid, for a couple who have substantial savings, means "spending down" part of those assets, which can, in effect, mean that the healthier spouse must partially impoverish him or herself to qualify for benefits. For a married couple, or a couple with substantial joint assets, this can be interpreted to mean that a large percentage of their joint savings have to be spent on health care for one of them.

There are some protections for spouses in this circumstance, such as protection for the family home. It may still be advisable, however, either not to marry (if you know that nursing home care may be in your future) or at least to keep all assets carefully labeled as to whose they are.

One solution to this problem is for the couple to decide not to rely on Medicaid, either by having sufficient savings to cover all eventualities or by purchasing long-term care insurance. If such planning is an important consideration to you, then you need to be sure that it is accomplished, both by including it in a cohabitation or prenuptial agreement and by ascertaining for yourself that, for example, the policy has in fact been purchased.

Another solution to the problem may be for the couple to refrain from marrying, including avoiding establishing a common law marriage.

However, to make things more complicated, some government benefits, such as social security survivor's benefits, are only available to spouses (see "Benefit Rights" on page 433 below). Consequently, careful consideration is needed.

QUESTION: *What is a "friendly divorce?"*

ANSWER: *When one of an older couple will need nursing home care in the near future, a lawyer may recommend that the couple divorce, in order to ensure that Medicaid (government health care for poor people) pays more of the cost. In other words, a divorce can protect the family's assets.*

Unfortunately, one of the governmental penalties for marriage is that the rules require that a large part of a married couple's assets be used to pay for nursing home care before governmental assistance programs will help. If the couple divorce and divide up their assets, then the incapacitated person will qualify sooner for federal programs such as Medicaid and the other (now ex) spouse will be able to afford to keep their house and use the money to support a higher standard of living. Obviously, the division is made with this outcome in mind.

Some other strategies are sometimes tried, such as an ill spouse transferring all of his property to the healthy spouse (or to the kids) or having a court legally designate one spouse as the manager of the community property. These strategies often don't work, for several reasons. First, there are legal limits on a couple's ability to do this and still qualify for Medicaid. Second, the legal obligation of one spouse to support the other still applies and nursing home care might be part of that obligation.

Again, one has to be careful. It looks easy to make oneself poor enough to qualify for Medicaid by just giving everything away to other family members. However, an improper transfer by an elderly person in order to try to qualify for Medicaid can result in the person's being denied Medicaid benefits. For example, one lecturer noted that once a parent's assets are transferred to them, the kids may be more inclined to put their parents in a cheap nursing home.[1]

Moreover, any transfers, whether as a gift or to a trust or by a divorce, really do transfer the ownership to the recipient, who can then do what he or she wants with it. This can be especially complicated if the marriage is a second or third one. For example, the healthy spouse who gets all the assets can leave all of them to his or her own children, for example.

Any friendly divorce or transfers of property has to be carefully handled so the result is what the couple is seeking. Insurance, tax, support, pension, and inheritance matters all have to be addressed.

QUESTION: *"Does marriage offer any legal advantages to an older couple who have financial and health problems?"*

ANSWER: *Yes, some, depending on the state.*

The benefits afforded to a widow or widower by law include both rights to various proceeds from government programs and inheritance rights.

Inheritance rights

When someone dies, his or her creditors can seek payment from the assets in the deceased person's estate. When one of a couple dies, however, a surviving spouse often has more protection from creditors than a surviving lover does. The spouse's rights, sometimes, take priority over those of the creditors. In some states, a widow or widower is entitled to remain in the family home until he or she dies, even if there are creditors. He or she may also be entitled to keep some of the deceased's money as a "family allowance" for his or her support.

A lover, even if the will leaves assets to him or her, does not have these protections from creditors. The creditors usually get paid before the heirs (including the lover) get their inheritances.

One of the potentially nastier creditors of an estate is the United States government. In principle, the government can try to recover Medicaid benefits that have been paid to an elderly person from the person's estate when he or she dies. In other words, if a person has been in a nursing home and has had some of the cost paid by government under Medicaid, then when he or she dies, the government can try to get its money back from any assets that were left. (Cold blooded? Yes.) However, the government cannot seize any of the dead person's assets until his or her spouse also dies. In other words, once again, an elderly married person may be able to live in the family home for his or her lifetime even if the government claims a right to be repaid for benefits that were furnished.[2]

Another reason that careful planning is required in the title to family assets is that the title affects whether or not an asset is included in the estate. For example, if a couple own a house jointly with right of survivorship, the title to the house passes automatically to the survivor; the house is not part of the probate estate. Therefore, creditors, including doctors and hospitals, may not be able to claim an interest in the house. On the other hand, the survivor will own the house outright and can leave it to his or her children without considering the other's kids. Find more information on inheritance and survivorship in Chapter Fourteen on page 466

Also, in a community property state, a large portion of their assets do not become part of the probate estate because the surviving spouse already owns one-half of the community property. So a spouse has additional protection, plus any other benefits afforded by state law.

Benefit Rights

Entitlement to some payments, such as from family trusts, pension plans, social security, veterans' benefits, and so on, depends on marital status. A surviving spouse has rights, for example, to a survivor's benefit from a deceased spouse's social security or veteran's benefits. The most common rights that a spouse may have include the following:

✔ *Payments from a retirement account or pension plan;*

✔ *Payments from the veteran's administration;*

✔ *Continuation of health insurance, as for example, where the deceased person had health insurance as a result of his or her employment or retirement program;*

✓ *Social security benefits based on the amount received by the deceased person;*
✓ *Right to be supported by a family trust, if any.*

The important aspect of these rights is not only that they depend on having been married but also often depend on the survivor's not remarrying. Veteran's benefits, for example, cease when the widow or widower remarries. If one of you is receiving alimony, of course, it is likely that it will stop if you remarry or possibly even if you enter into a "marriage-like" relationship.

If a mature person is considering marriage and has not retired, he or she needs to carefully analyze what elections to make under any available pensions. Often such plans provide for an election between greater benefits to the retiree with lesser (or no) benefits to a surviving spouse. Similarly, if you are receiving benefits as the result of an earlier marriage, you need to know whether your remarriage will affect those benefits.

It is essential to consider what election each of you has made under any retirement plan that you have. If you are counting on receiving part of your new spouse's pension, be sure that he or she has not made an election to the contrary and that you will in fact be entitled to some portion of his or her retirement if he or she dies before you do.

Whatever information you receive from the human resources department or plan administrator, be sure that the advice is documented in writing. You should ask to see the written plan provision on which the advice is based and at a minimum you should write a polite letter to the appropriate person stating exactly what you understood that they said and exactly what you are doing in reliance on that advice. Casual advice from someone in the personnel department does not establish your rights.

A lover does not usually have these entitlements, except in the (still relatively rare) cases where a private employer may include domestic partners as beneficiaries of corporate pension plans.

Kids and grandkids

Older couples also have to face the impact of their relationship on children and grandchildren of the relationship. This is particularly so if a grown child is living with one of the parties or if the grown children have been considering Grandma as a lifelong free babysitter.

Here is where candid discussion between the two of you (the new couple) can avert disaster. You will need to distinguish between those outcomes that are likely or imminent from those that are merely hypothetical. There's a big difference between saying "If anything happened to my daughter, I'd feel obligated to raise my grandchildren" and "My daughter has serious drug problems and I expect the grandkids to land on my doorstep any minute now." Similarly, there's a difference between a general feeling that if your son lost his job, he might someday need a place to stay for a couple of months and knowing that the moving van is on its way.

Here are some of the questions one might wish to discuss on the kid issues:

- ✓ *What financial obligations do you have to your grown children? Do you feel obligated to offer a place in your home for them to live? Do they feel that you are obligated to support them if they don't have a job?*

- ✓ *Have you promised your children any particular inheritance? The lake house? Heirlooms?*

- ✓ *What financial obligations do you feel to your grandchildren? Do you feel obligated to have them stay with you for the summer? To pay their college tuition?*

- ✓ *Do you anticipate needing to raise your grandchildren because their parents are too busy or have serious substance abuse problems?*

- ✓ *What financial obligations do your children feel to you? Were you planning on going to live with them?*

Oddly enough, children's feelings can be more bitter over the loss of a (financially) insignificant family heirloom than over the loss of a substantial sum of money. One possibility is to give the kids the heirlooms now and be done with it.

It is often difficult for grown children to accept the fact that their father or mother has formed a new relationship. The reasons for this discomfort range from loyalty to a deceased parent to unconscious psychological issues about a parent's sexuality (usually expressed as "ick!") to loving concern that a parent might be hurt or cheated to sheer greed.

Children's interference can range from mere nastiness and rudeness to a new companion to legal attempts to gain control of a parent's finances. Some of these actions can be selfish and cruel while others may be well-intentioned but mistaken or well-founded and necessary. Remember the story of Beulah and Norbert? (see page 288). Norbert's children were perfectly willing to spirit him off to a lonely existence in a distant nursing home because they disapproved of his friendship with his caring housekeeper.

For more information on these disputes, including comments from a child's perspective, see page 289 in Chapter Seven and page 654 in the Workbook. The basic rule is that an adult child does not have the legal right to interfere in a parent's life unless the parent is incompetent in a legal sense, meaning that a medical or psychological problem has impaired the parent's ability to make sensible decisions in his or her best interest.

Unless an irrevocable trust or other legal mechanism gives the child specific rights, a child is not entitled to his or her parents' wealth. Rights of inheritance only apply when someone is dead; they don't entitle a child, no matter how much he or she has counted on inheriting Grandma's silver or Mom's Intel stock, to control what Grandma or Mom do while they are alive.

QUESTION: *"My children hate my new companion. What are they likely to do if something happens to me?"*

ANSWER: *If you make any financial provision for your companion, your children will probably claim that your companion exerted undue influence over you and that your arrangement should be set aside by a court so that the kids can inherit.*

QUESTION: *"I am an 80 year old widow with considerable savings. I have been lonely for many years and have recently met and married a charming younger man who makes me very happy. If I want to provide for my new spouse, whom my children despise, what should I do?"*

ANSWER: *You should take the following actions (1) make a valid, new, will; (2) if you have sufficient funds, set up a trust to take of your lover; (3) be examined by a good doctor to establish a record that you are mentally competent; (4) avoid taking any irrevocable action in case your new spouse turns out in fact to be a parasite who is planning to exploit your loneliness; and (5) maintain your other social contacts and outlets, as well as any new ones that you and your husband together develop.*

In my personal opinion, a fair arrangement would be to set up a trust to provide for your new companion after you die, for so long as he or she remains alone (i.e. doesn't remarry or cohabit). The assets in the trust can go to your children or a charity when your companion dies or remarries. In that way, you can take care of someone you love without permanently depriving your children of an inheritance that they may have counted on. Practically speaking, the needs of your companion may exhaust the assets in trust but maybe not, depending on your respective ages and the amount involved.

You could also make modest gifts to your companion but be careful not to impoverish yourself in a fit of love or lust. Seek other social outlets so that your new companion is not the sole source of company in your life. Also, turn to a trusted advisor, such as a clergyperson, for guidance in considering your situation.

QUESTION: *"My mother had been severely depressed for many years. She became convinced that her children all hated her and cut off any contact with us. Mom left everything to her nurse. Is her will valid?"*

ANSWER: *Probably, unless the nurse improperly took advantage of your mother.*

Old wills often began with the words like these — "Being of sound and disposing mind, conscious of the uncertainty of life and the certainty of death, and confident in the resurrection of the body, I hereby give, devise, and bequeath my worldly goods ..."

Despite the "sound mind" phrase, a person does not have to be completely sane in order to make a valid will. He or she can be deluded or mistaken so long as he or she understands that the document being signed is a will and what its basic terms are.

However, a will is not valid if the person makes it under duress or undue influence. Duress is threats, and undue influence is excessive pressure or exploitation. For example, a person is unduly influencing another if he or she keeps the other person isolated and puts excessive emotional pressure on him or her. It is hard to tell when whining and nagging amount to undue influence.

A bequest can also be invalid if one heir deliberately misled the person making the will.

For example, a vigorous and independent elderly person marries a younger companion, and the new couple continues to live an ordinary life in their hometown, it is unlikely that a court would later decide that the new spouse exercised undue influence over the elder person. After all, their old friends and relatives would see them at their usual social functions, whether bowling or church, and could see that the older person appeared normal and hopefully, happy. It would seem natural, if a little disappointing to any grown children, for the older person to leave his or her fortune to the new spouse. On the other hand, if the couple marries, and the new spouse immediately demands that they move many thousands of miles away from the elder person's children and cuts off all communication with old friends and relatives, then a claim that the elder person was under undue influence may be more plausible. Exploitative or not, remember that a spouse usually acquires certain inheritance rights, even if a will is set aside by a court.

Unfortunately, many single older people are very lonely in our society. Some come even to enjoy sales calls, just for the conversation. Their friends may have died and their children moved away. A caregiver or nurse may become a treasured companion. Each case needs to be evaluated independently to decide if the caregiver lovingly provided the companionship and care that self-absorbed kids didn't have time to give or whether he or she ruthlessly took advantage of a lonely, defenseless person.

In one case, a lonely but active widow enjoyed taking ballroom dancing classes. She and other ladies in similar circumstances went on cruises with their young and handsome instructors. Gradually, however, her eyesight and health failed, although she continued to live alone in her apartment. One less scrupulous instructor told her that he wanted to open a hair dressing salon but couldn't qualify for a loan. He took her to the bank where she signed a guarantee on the loan and turned over her stock certificates as collateral. The banker later testified that she seemed quite competent, although he admitted that she asked him carefully whether her stocks would be safe with him. Clearly, she didn't fully understand that she was pledging her stocks to the bank, not just placing them there for safekeeping. The stocks weren't safe at all, because the salon quickly failed and the bank foreclosed on her securities. The loan officer was less willing to admit that the lady had been nearly blind at the time and couldn't have read the fine print in the loan agreement with a microscope. Her children eventually stepped in and sued to get her stock back. The bank had to return the stock certificates and pay damages because it had, in effect, colluded with the dance instructor to take advantage of an elderly person.

On the other hand, many grown children have counted on an inheritance to solve their financial woes or put grandchildren through college or whatever. The children may object to a parent's spending money on a new love interest because they are looking forward to inheriting all of it. Sometimes the parents have made promises about future financial help. Only the family members involved can decide whether children's' expectations were legitimate and should be honored or simply an excuse for the younger generation to be improvident and lazy.

Taking care of each other legally

Assuming that an older couple wishes to take care of each other financially, perhaps the most important decisions are to consider whether to transfer certain assets to each other or to change their respective wills or both.

If you want your new partner to inherit certain assets, then whether or not you marry, you should execute a new will.

Many married couples traditionally executed parallel wills that provided for all the family assets to go to the surviving spouse and if one spouse did not outlive the other (i.e. both died at the same time), then to the children. If an older person remarries, he or she needs a new will, but the old parallel format may no longer be appropriate in the new marriage. It may or may not be the best or fairest way to provide for the new spouse, or perhaps the new spouse doesn't need the prospective inheritance. Remember that divorce and marriage revoke a preexisting will and that spouses may have inheritance rights. Prenuptial agreements, trusts, and title documents all need to be considered, especially in light of Medicare and Medicaid and social security issues.

Provision for a significant other should be both by will and by appropriate title documents. For example, if an older couple decides to buy a $200,000 RV to travel in and if both of them are relying on having the RV to live in, then the title to it should probably be in both names, plus putting a provision in their respective wills that the other's interest passes to the survivor.

Bank accounts that contain pooled funds should be joint accounts with right of survivorship. An acceptable variation is to have an account in one person's name with the other designated as survivor on the account, meaning that he or she receives it when the owner dies. It may be prudent to have separate accounts containing enough money for living expenses for a period of time to avoid the money's being tied up in the probate estate, especially if there are hostile children.

In addition, an older couple needs to pay special attention to living wills, advance directives, and powers of attorney. They should be realistic about who is named in these documents. For example, it is usual for a couple to name each other to make health care decisions, if needed. If both of you are over 75, it is possible that it might be better to name a younger person, since both of you could be ill at the same time. That contingency can be covered in the documents by providing that the first choice is the significant other and by carefully naming alternate persons to serve if the first choice person is not available.

It is worth considering whether the person named in your power of attorney is also going to inherit from you. Some people fear that greed or desire to be free of the burden of caring for an aged relative might lead an heir to "pull the plug" sooner rather than later. Older couples can also consider registering as domestic partners, which are discussed further in Chapter Four above.

QUESTION: *"What about these living trusts that are offered at seminars and online?"*

ANSWER: *Any trust needs to be carefully drafted, and any "one size fits all" form can cause more problems than it solves.*

Trusts can serve several useful purposes. Trusts are called either "inter vivos" (among the living) or "testamentary" (after death). Inter vivos trusts are sometimes called "living trusts" and are funded during the lifetime of the person setting it up, although additional money may be added from the estate after his or her death. Testamentary trusts are set up under a will and are funded from the estate.

A family limited partnership is a business-type legal device that is sometimes used for similar purposes.

Sometimes trusts are used to protect assets from creditors. This strategy can be successful if the trust is not a fraud on the creditors.

Sometimes they are used to provide for management of money and property by a younger, responsible person as a couple ages. Assets in a trust can be arranged so as to ensure that both of a couple are taken care of in their old age. They can be protected from making unwise decisions if they become mentally less acute or more vulnerable to exploitation.

One option for reconciling the possibly conflicting interests of children and the new partner can be the establishment of a trust, If enough assets are available, one of you could establish a trust for the benefit of the other, so that the other would have sufficient funds to live on for the rest of his or her life and the remainder would go to your heirs after his or her death. A trust arrangement keeps your partner from having the untrammeled right to dissipate your children's inheritance while providing for your partner's welfare during his or her declining years. Perhaps the two of you might wish to pool some of your assets and establish a trust from which both would benefit. Obviously, this assumes that you expect to stay together. The trust would provide funds to care for both of you; when both have passed on, the assets can be divided among your children. The advantage is that the terms of an irrevocable trust can't be changed.

Sometimes trusts or family partnerships are used to keep assets from being included in a deceased person's estate. That means that the assets are not dealt with by a probate court (court that handles will questions). This has some advantages in terms of privacy but it may or may not lessen the amount of estate tax paid.

However, the trust has to be very carefully designed in order to take care of future problems. Trusts are often not flexible, especially if the trust is irrevocable. If the couple puts everything they own in the trust, then the trustee has almost complete control over their property. He or she is supposed to be loyal to the beneficiaries of the trust but he or she can have a lot of discretion over how to spend the money. For example, suppose a trust is set up to provide for the support of an elderly couple -- what life style does "support" cover? A condo in Acapulco? Keeping up the country club membership? Eating out every day? Cruises to Europe? Or residing in a cramped garage apartment and living on peanut butter? Does the trustee get paid? How much? Obviously, if the trustee will later receive whatever is left in the trust after the beneficiaries' deaths, he or she may be irresistibly tempted to be unduly frugal with the money that was supposed to be used to support the beneficiaries.

Other temptations to trustee misconduct include the urge to speculate with the trust money, to "borrow" from the trust, and to charge unreasonable fees. All of these are supposed to be illegal but it would take a lawsuit to straighten things out, and lawsuits take time and money.

At a recent bar association seminar, one speaker predicted that he and his fellow lawyers were going to make a lot of money in the future trying to solve the problems caused by people who tried to set up a "do it yourself" trust. Some of the potential problems include the trustee's becoming incapacitated, the family finances changing so that a different arrangement is needed, and the couple failing to follow through on transferring title to their assets to the trust.[3] Getting out from under an irrevocable trust can be difficult, if not legally impossible, and there may be serious tax consequences.

QUESTION: *"So once again, you're telling me that I need a lawyer?"*

ANSWER: *Yep. Sorry.*

Not only are the regulations of government and private programs such as Medicaid, long term care insurance, and pensions extraordinarily complicated, but the procedures for claiming those benefits (and fighting off the government's efforts to get its money back) are a legal maze.

If you have any doubt about the complexity of these areas of law, take a look at the endnotes to this chapter; lawyers who already practice in these fields spend days in continuing education classes to keep up with the technical points. The lectures are hours long, and the written materials for the course (on elder law alone) run to a couple of hundred pages.

Not only do you need a good lawyer but you need to be clear about who the lawyer represents. Family members usually have different interests. For example, an elderly parent may want to be sure that he or she stays in his or her home even if home care is more expensive than going into a cheap nursing home. The children, who want to inherit, may want to save money – money that they will then get later.

Mature couples, however, need an attorney with experience in the fields of law that affect older people, including both inheritance and the maze of government and private benefit programs. Attorneys call that field "elder law," and your local bar association may have a list of lawyers specializing in such work. Elder law differs from the field of estate planning, which primarily has to do with the reduction of taxes on the inheritance that you leave your heirs, although the same attorney may work in both areas.

Conclusions and advice

For older couples, some things just have to be taken care of to avoid making the rest of your life financially miserable. Documentation, good advice, and frank discussion are the keys to avoiding tragic errors.

(Endnotes)

[1] "Keeping the Focus on Quality of Care" State Bar of Texas 29th Annual Advanced Estate Planning and Probate Course, Chapter 30, presented June, 2005.

[2] "Medicaid Estate Recovery Update" State Bar of Texas 29th Annual Advanced Estate Planning and Probate Course, Chapter 30, presented June, 2005.

[3] "Elder Law Considerations in Family Law," State Bar of Texas Advanced Elder Law Course, presented, April, 2005.

Chapter Fourteen

BREAKING UP A LONG-TERM RELATIONSHIP

OK, so the honeymoon is over. The two of you have had one too many screaming arguments and you want out.

When a long-term relationship fails, the parties must often face not only the emotional loss and distress, but also financial and legal hassles.   This is certainly true if one of the couple has turned out to be dishonest or completely self-centered. But, even if the relationship was a balanced and loving one, it is remarkable how selfish and unfair former lovers can become during a split. When jealousy and broken hearts are involved, the most greedy, not to say vicious, conduct can be rationalized as acceptable. If nothing else, when the sense of obligation to an ongoing relationship is gone, self-interest and greed can take its place.

Obviously, the process is going to vary depending on the terms of the split. If division is between two amicable adults who have decided to live on different coasts, fine. If you have discovered that your lover is a scum-sucking leech, the process is likely to be different. In any relationship, though, it is better to make love, not war, or at least to make reasonably nice, not notably nasty. It's morally preferable, better for your self-respect, and often, but not always, cheaper.

Also, of course, the process varies if the relationship is ended by the death of one person, instead of by the couple's deciding to part company.

This chapter discusses how legal rights can be worked out when a couple split up. Necessarily, there is some repetition of the rules discussed in earlier chapters.

There are three basic approaches to splitting the blanket (and everything else) when a long, involved, relationship ends. These are:

- ✔ *Reach as fair an agreement as amicably as possible and walk away with some amount that is reasonably satisfactory to both of you.*
- ✔ *Fight for your rights, if any.*
- ✔ *Gather what you can get reasonably easily, leave, and start over as best you can.*

These outcomes can occur whether the ending takes place in the courthouse or over a cup of coffee. From a lawyer's point of view, no one can make an intelligent decision about their best course of conduct unless they know what their rights are. That's not completely true; you can decide what you believe to be equitable, i.e. morally right, regardless of the legal rights involved. A decision based on your view of a fair outcome may be quite satisfactory to the people involved, even if one of them does not insist on his or her every legal entitlement. However, legal ignorance is seldom financial bliss, and since this book is about legal rights, it seems only sensible to start with the likely legal positions of the parties.

One of the bitterest and most unsolvable problems is that of pets. There is no way to divide the cat; one of you will need to suffer the heartache of parting unless you can agree on visitation.

Legal rights and realities at the end

As you already know from Chapter Five and Chapter Six, the respective rights of a couple depend primarily on three factors: (1) whether or not they are married; (2) whether or not they have a prenuptial or cohabitation agreement; and (3)what other documents they have signed (or failed to sign). It also depends on whether the relationship is ended by death or just parting company.

As discussed in Chapter Five, one of the differences between marriage and living together is that a marriage is only ended by a court decision or by death. A cohabitation relationship ends when either one of the couple ends it. The ending may be as informal, but unmistakable, as one lover moving out of the formerly shared apartment (especially if he or she moves in with a new lover) or as formal as the lovers giving each other the 30 days written notice required by their agreement. The fact that you stop living together does not terminate your obligations under your cohabitation agreement; you may no longer be together but your legal obligations to each other don't end until the agreement says they do.

QUESTION: *"If we are living together and we split up, who gets what?"*

ANSWER: *Each of you gets the stuff that each of you have title to unless you and your lover had an agreement about the ownership of your respective assets. Proving who owns what can be difficult if you've been together for a while, especially for things that don't have title documents, like entertainment systems.*

QUESTION: *"If we are married and we divorce, who gets what?"*

ANSWER: *That depends on several factors, including (1) what state you live in; (2) whose name is on the deed or title to the property; (3) when you acquired the property; and (4) whether it was purchased or inherited. Plus, of course, the predispositions of the judge who decides your case.*

In most marriages that last for more than a year or two, the spouses acquire some rights to the assets that accumulated during the marriage. In most cohabitation arrangements, unless the couple had a fairly clear agreement, they do not have any such rights.

Regardless of the form that your parting takes – ending a marriage by divorce or annulment or ending a cohabitation relationship peacefully or in court, your intertwined financial affairs must be disentangled, including dividing assets and paying bills.

Division of assets when a cohabiting couple part company

If you did not marry (and you did not change your respective rights by a legally effective action such as opening a joint account), your rights to the assets that your lover acquired during the relationship are probably very limited, or non-existent. In other words, the legal starting point is that cohabitation does not create any economic partnership, just as the legal starting point with a marriage is that it automatically does create some degree of economic partnership.

Usually, splits between informal couples are relatively easy. They both move out and take their respective things with them. Sometimes, these partings are a legal mess as the couple fight over whether or not they had an agreement and whether or not they complied with it or modified it or whatever.

Some people regard the lack of financial entanglement as one of the primary benefits of living together as opposed to marrying. If the couple has been careful not to create any other legal relationship and have kept their respective financial affairs completely separate, they can leave the relationship without further ado. The risk that a judge will divide their hard-earned savings with someone they now hate is virtually eliminated, as is the risk of having to pay expensive lawyers to assist in dividing everything up.

Couples who kept everything separate and did not have a cohabitation agreement

The simplest situation is where a couple kept all of their significant assets completely separate and where neither claims that they had some form of sharing agreement. No joint accounts, no expensive gifts of antiques or coin collections, no co-signed notes. If each party is reasonably honest, each one takes his or her stuff and leaves. If the couple disagree about what item belongs to whom or if one takes more than his or her things, then the matter is more difficult.

For assets that have legal title documents, such as real estate, bank accounts, and cars, each former significant other gets the assets in his or her name. The formal title to property governs who gets what. Fortunately, it is difficult for a dishonest lover to steal a bank account or stocks in a brokerage account.

For assets that don't have any formal records of ownership, however, things can be ambiguous and there is considerable vulnerability. Some things are relatively clear; presumably, each partner is entitled to his or her clothes, regardless of who paid for what, although there could be serious dispute over whether the sable coat leaves with the departing mistress or stays in the closet for her replacement.

Similarly, it may be reasonably clear that a particular item, like a pearl necklace or an expensive shotgun, was a gift from one of the couple to the other. Here again, recollections can change and circumstances can be ambiguous; did she buy the new shotgun so her companion could use it when they went hunting together or did she mean to give to him as a gift?

There is no clear way to prove ownership of many of the things that we buy in this life unless we have some written evidence of an agreement. Washing machines, sofas, stereos, bicycles, and dining room tables don't have recorded ownership. As a general rule, the person who paid for the item has a good claim to ownership of it, but the other could always claim that he or she paid part of the purchase price or that it was a gift or whatever.

In real life, therefore, the first one to haul household things away (like the stereo or TV) usually ends up with the stuff. The police are reluctant to get involved in a dispute like this, i.e. they are unlikely to chase down your lover and retrieve your loveseat. After all, they are in no position to decide whose claim is better, and since the two of you did live together, your ex-lover's claim that the loveseat is really his has some plausibility. If you really believe that the loveseat is yours, you will probably have to sue to get it back.

You have the right to enter any place that you have legal access to, such an apartment where your name is on the lease, and to peacefully remove your things, including things to which you have a valid claim.

Usually, the name on the deed or the lease determines whose home it is. So, unless you have been ordered by a court to stay away, you have the right to return to property that you own or rent, even if your lover has changed the locks. You can demand that the landlord open the door for you or you can, probably, break in.

However, it is almost always a bad idea to force your way in when your lover is on the premises, even if your ownership of the property is absolutely clear. Even if you have a clear right to be there; your lover may call the police and claim that you attacked him or her; a shattered door or broken window will lend plausibility to his or her claims. If you are absolutely certain that the house is yours, it is still more prudent to wait until your lover is at work, for example, to go in and get your stuff.

You do not have the right to break into someone else's home to retrieve your property nor do you have the right to take it back by force. If your lover's name is on the lease, but you have a key, the situation is ambiguous. Probably, you still have the right to go in and get your property. However, if he or she has changed the locks, you probably do not have a right to demand that the landlord open the door and you do not have the right to break in, even to get your things. You could be arrested for burglary.

If there is a disturbance, whether or not you have a technical right to be on the premises, either of your may be arrested for causing a breach of the peace or assault or assorted other minor crimes. The sofa is not worth it.

If your lover has taken some of your things or if he or she will not allow you to remove them, your only recourse may be to file suit in small claims court, since (unless we talking about valuable antiques), it is unlikely to be worth hiring a lawyer to get your stuff back.

If your ex-lover took things to which he or she is clearly not entitled, such as your family photographs or your clothes, you may receive damages for the loss, even if it is too late to get the items back. In principle, you may be entitled to damages for emotional distress if his or her conduct was outrageously malicious.

Remember that there is no duty for unmarried couples to support each other, unless they agreed to; without a written agreement, it is very unlikely that your significant other will owe you "palimony."

Couples who did not keep everything separate

A couple can end up sharing assets by agreement or by the way the title documents are written.

As discussed earlier, a cohabitation agreement can be written, oral, or implied by a court.

The couple may have signed a formal agreement, in which case that agreement should control the division of their assets when they split up, unless it has been modified. The agreement may not necessarily be in a formal writing but may have been expressed in letters or other informal documents.

In some states, a couple may have reached a valid oral agreement. The ability to enforce an oral agreement depends on one's ability to convince one's ex or a court about what the terms of the agreement were. Once the existence of a valid agreement is proven, then that agreement controls, just as if it were in writing. Remember that oral agreements based on cohabitation are not valid in many states, although a court may still honor an oral business partnership between lovers.

If the relationship has been a long one in which both parties contributed to the welfare of their shared home, a court may imply an agreement between them, such as an agreement by one to compensate the other for his or her help. In other words, the court may decide that, whether or not the couple expressly agreed on any particular sharing, fairness and justice require that some equitable division be made. In that situation, the division will rest in the discretion of the particular judge, based on his or her view of the specific facts. Again, remember that many states do not permit a judge to do this.

Independently of whether they have a valid cohabitation agreement, if a couple has put valuable assets in both their names, then they own those assets jointly. (The technical legality may be that they own it jointly or as tenants in common, depending on state law.) Similarly, if they had an agreement about ownership of an asset and they both paid part of the purchase price, each may own a share, depending on state law, just as if they were any other two people who made a joint investment.

"Joint" or "common" do not necessarily mean "equal," however. The percentage that each can claim depends on their agreement or contribution. In some situations, as with bank accounts, each may own the portion that he or she contributed to the account.

When the couple splits up, therefore, any shared assets have to be split up also. It is possible for a no-longer-romantically-involved couple to stay in business together.

Sometimes even divorced couples continue to operate a joint business amicably but these situations are the exceptions.

Remember also that ownership is not the same thing as control. Each party to a joint bank account has a right, vis a vis the bank, to withdraw all the funds. Consequently, you may be entitled to one-half of the bank account but you may have to chase your lover down and sue him or her to get your share. Similarly, your cohabitation agreement may provide that each of you gets to keep whatever household item he or she paid for, but if your lover packs up the twelve place settings of Limoges china that you bought together, you will probably have to go to court to get it back.

If you are treating each other fairly, or if you have a clear agreement, liquid assets such as money, stocks, bonds and so on, can be divided between the two of you according to your respective shares.

DVD or CD collections, furniture, and other household items can also be divided, with each of you taking an agreed portion, although the process is a little more cumbersome. It's hard to balance the value of a new refrigerator against a slightly older plasma TV screen.

One way to do this is for you to agree to take turns choosing an item. Here's a simple method if the two of you are speaking to each other. First the two of you make up a list of everything that belongs to each of you separately and everything that you need to divide. When you've agreed on the lists, then you flip a coin. The winner gets first choice of one item from the stuff to be divided. The loser gets second pick. You continue each taking one item until everything has been chosen by one or the other.

An alternative is a variation on the childhood method of dividing a candy bar. One person divides the jointly owned items into two groups and the other chooses which pile he or she wants. This method is subject to manipulation if one lover is cynical enough to play on the other's attachment to a particular item.

Even a sufficiently large tract of land can be partitioned into two parts with each of you taking your respective portions.

If, however, you own items like a house or a car jointly, and the relationship has ended, the only workable solution usually is to sell the asset and divide the proceeds.

An alternative is for one of the couple to buy the other's share. However, it is usually not a good idea to be involved in a long-term financial arrangement with someone that you now hate. Moreover, a romance may end at a time when it is economically disadvantageous to sell assets or close a business. Usually, it is cheaper to work out your disagreements and compromise, even if you walk away with less than you are entitled to, unless a major asset in your life is involved. A major asset would be, for example, your share in a booming business that you helped to built or your interest in a piece of real estate that has appreciated in value.

Debts and cohabiting couples

One of the messiest aspects of ending a relationship can be disentangling your financial obligations to other people. Cohabiting couples are not liable for each other's debts unless they agreed to be.

Remember that if you buy a car together, both of you own the car and both of you are liable to the finance company. In other words, you are responsible for the payments even if your lover took the car with him when he left Atlanta for Alaska.

Any dissolution of a cohabitation relationship must deal with obligations as well as assets. In other words, it is prudent to be sure that all the joint credit card accounts are paid before you sign over your share in the house to your lover.

Undoing formal entanglements with other people

Remember that other people are not governed by your arrangement with your significant other, regardless of whether you divide things up amiably or in court. If you split up and rearrange your financial obligations between the two of you, the changes may not affect your obligations to other people, unless they also agree to the change or are officially made part of the court proceeding.

If your name is on the apartment lease, for example, you are still legally obligated to pay rent, even if you and your lover part company. If he or she agrees to take over the rent payments, fine, but if the payments aren't made, then you are on the hook, even if you have moved out. Even if the landlord doesn't sue you and collect a judgment, your credit history can be ruined. It will probably be difficult for you to rent an apartment or buy a house if your credit report shows that you defaulted on a lease.

Therefore, to be safe, you have two choices to try to protect your credit rating. One is to make sure you keep up any payments yourself. If you rented an apartment with your lover, then if it is financially possible, you can keep the apartment and pay the rent. If your significant other will continue to pay his or her half while you look for a new roommate, fine (but fat chance).

The second option is to let your lover keep the apartment and pay the rent without any help from you. If he or she agrees, your arrangement should be in writing.

Regardless, you both then have to deal with the landlord. Remember that you still owe the rent even if you are not living there unless the landlord releases you from your obligation. If you are not released (in writing), then you have to arrange to make sure that the rental payments are being made. You can ask the landlord to let you know if there is a default, for example.

The best outcome is to for the person to whom the money is owed (landlord, bank, etc.) to change the loan or lease in writing. If your lover is going to assume the whole debt, then ideally, the lender can release you from your obligation in writing. Sometimes they will, sometimes they will not. It never hurts to ask. An oral promise by the rental agent not to come after you for the rent is better than nothing, but not by much because it can so easily be denied later.

Again, paperwork is important. At least, be sure that any creditor has your new address and sends you a copy of the statements. That way, if your lover stops paying, you can try to salvage your credit rating by making a payment.

Terminating a cohabitation agreement

If you have a written cohabitation agreement, be sure to check for any provisions regarding terminating of the agreement. You need to follow the requirements about notice etc. Even if the agreement doesn't require it, it is prudent to give your lover written notice that the relationship is over. The notice can set out your understanding of the terms on which you are leaving it. You should set out specifically what assets are covered by the agreement and how you believe that they should be owned after the split.

Undoing the previous agreement may require a new agreement, or at least a mutually agreeable memorandum of what has been done to untangle your financial involvement. For example, you may need to write down who received what, who still owes what to whom, and so on.

If you are giving up an obligation that your lover had to you, that is called a release. Any such release should be in writing. For example, if your significant other promised to pay your tuition, and you agree that he or she doesn't have to make any more payments, then you should release that obligation in writing.

Terminating moral obligations

If you have promised your lover to meet a certain obligation, such as to pay his or her tuition, or if you have informally allowed him or her to use your credit card for a particularly purpose, then you need to consider whether you are morally, if not legally, obligated to continue those payments. Abruptly cutting off access to a credit card on which your lover relies for a necessary expense, such as completing a course of dental treatment, may be mean and unfair.

Acting morally in a break up requires at least three steps. The first is to acknowledge any obligation you have undertaken toward your significant other, whether or not it is legally enforceable. The second is to honestly evaluate both the other's conduct and your own. However angry you may be, you owe it to your own integrity and to someone you once (we hope) loved to try to objectively evaluate fault and fairness. Third, you need to consider whether continuing to honor that obligation will be unfairly burdensome on you in the changed circumstances or simply imprudent. If your lover is relying on your credit card to pay his or her college tuition, and you promised that he or she could do so, and you can afford the charges, then the fairest option may be to permit the continued use for a period of time, such as a semester, perhaps with a new credit limit on that card.

Remember, however, you are morally responsible for obligations that you have undertaken; you are not morally responsible for another competent adult's lifestyle or care.

Division of property when a marriage ends by divorce or annulment

Leaving aside death, for the moment, a marriage ends only when a court enters an order ending it. That order may be a decree of divorce or an annulment.

The legal consequences of the ending are different. A divorce ends a marriage, and the court order sets out who gets what and who owes what to whom. The division of the assets and liabilities of the couple follows state law and any agreement that the couple made.

An annulment is a court determination that no marriage existed. If there was no marriage, then the couple never acquired the rights of married people. On the other hand, they were not merely cohabiting either; they were living together, at least to some extent as if they were married. In these situations, a court will try to reach an equitable result, taking into account whether one of the spouses was deceived, whether the apparent marriage lasted for a long time, and so on. See Chapter Six.

If you are common law married and want to split up legally, you must get a legal divorce. The laws governing marital property, plus any prenuptial or marital agreement, will determine who gets what if the two of you cannot agree. The ex-spouses' assets will be divided according to the law of the state where they married or where the property was acquired.

The title to property that is acquired during a relationship depends on what state the couple lived in when they acquired that asset. The specific rules are discussed in the succeeding sections.

Remember, again the states have different rules about who gets what when a marriage ends. The basic difference is between community property states such as Texas, Arizona, and California, and common-law states such as Illinois. However, the net result when a couple splits up often comes out much the same, regardless of the names of the rules that the court uses. In community property states, each spouse gets more or less one-half of what they acquired during the marriage and in common-law states, each gets an equitable share, often one-half.

In all states, the divorce decree may provide that one spouse will pay the other a sum of money over a period of time. Sometimes the couple's assets are not easily divisible, such as where they have an ongoing business. Some assets, like an apartment house, could be sold (and the proceeds divided) but the real estate market might not be advantageous at the time of the divorce. In other words, for example, if one spouse is awarded a valuable asset, such as a business or a rental property, he or she may be ordered to make payments to the other over time.

The basic process is the same is all states. The court begins by determining who owns what, i.e. what property was inherited, what was acquired during the marriage, whose name is on the deed, etc. Then the judge applies the rules of his or her state to divide the assets between the couple. Very few of the rules are absolutely rigid; there is almost always some way for a judge to adjust the division at least somewhat.

Community property states

In a community property state, the starting assumption is that each spouse gets one-half of the property owned during the marriage. Each spouse gets to keep the property that he or she had before marriage and each also gets to keep any property that he or she inherited.

The process begins with the judge determining what assets are community property and which are separate property. As a general rule, by law, the court can only divide community property between the spouses; separate property is not part of the divorce process.

Some states give the judge more leeway in this respect, however, and permit the judge to give part of a spouse's separate property to the other in certain circumstances. Hawaii, for example, permits the judge to give part of one spouse's separate property to the other if that division is necessary to reach a fair result. Texas prohibits a judge from altering the title to real estate that is separate property.

Consequently, the decision that an asset is separate or community sometimes determines the amount that each spouse receives and always influences it.

The presumption is that all property owned during the marriage is community property. Remember that a presumption is a legal rule that determines the result unless it is refuted by other evidence; in other words, all property that a couple owns during a marriage is community property which will be divided when they divorce unless one of them can prove that a particular asset was separate property. (Separate property is that which was an inheritance, a gift, or acquired before the marriage.) The spouse who claims that property is separate has the burden of proving that claim by clear evidence.

Several matters complicate the process. These include the title that assets are in, whether the couple mingled separate and community property, whether they made contributions toward the other's assets, and whether they have a pension or profit-sharing plan. Finally, the judge has discretion in how he or she actually divides the community property, considering various factors.

There is also a complication if the asset to be divided is the family home. In some states, the law recognizes special rights in the family home, which is often called a "homestead." This doesn't refer to pioneer days but to a residence that is owned and lived in by a person. Homestead rights are different from concepts of separate or community property. In a married couple, a spouse may be given the right to live in the family home for the rest of his or her life, even if it belongs to the other spouse.

Title to assets

The title that an asset is in, whether it is real estate or a car, complicates the question of community property. Title is not determinative of whether an asset is community or separate, but it does influence the decision and may control it.

The question is what the couple intended. If they put the property is both names, then presumably they intended it to be community property. But what if there is only one name on the title?

It might be that one spouse intended to give his or her share to the other. It might be that one spouse cheated the other or bought the property secretly in his or her name alone. It might be just a clerical oversight. It might be that the couple agreed that the particular asset properly belonged entirely to one of them.

In general, the law presumes that if a married couple buys property and puts the title in the name of only one of them, the other intended to give his or her share to the other. Traditionally, this rule especially applied to property that the husband bought and put in his wife's name, both because he was legally obligated to provide for her and because the law recognized that women had fewer economic opportunities than men. However, this presumption can be rebutted.

The case of *Peterson v. Peterson* presents a variation on this theme. Viola Peterson sued her husband Richard for divorce and claimed their house was community property. Viola and Richard were in their fifties when they married. They shopped for a house together and Richard made the down payment before they were married. The sale was completed soon after the marriage. Richard paid the entire purchase price from his separate bank account, but Viola refused to move in unless he put her name on the deed too. He reluctantly agreed because "I really didn't want to stir up any trouble at that early (stage) of a marriage."[1] The court ruled that Richard owned the house as his separate property.

He had paid for it from his separate money, and he proved clearly that he never intended to give Viola half of it. Viola didn't have any evidence that Richard wanted to give her a share in the house, but only evidence of her demands, so she wasn't entitled to a share.

Mingled assets and contributions by one spouse to the other

Assets tend to get mingled together during a marriage, but *the law assumes that property acquired during a marriage is community property*. Sometimes a piece of property may have been sold and another bought with the proceeds, perhaps with some community funds added in.

Intermingled property usually ends up being considered community property because it is not possible to trace what is separate and what is community.

One court set out the rules in these clear words (clear for lawyers, that is):

Property possessed by either spouse during or on dissolution of marriage is presumed to be community property, and a spouse must present clear and convincing evidence to establish that such property is separate property. …Clear and convincing evidence is the degree of proof that will produce in the mind of the trier of fact a firm belief or conviction. …The spouse claiming certain property as separate property must trace and clearly identify the property claimed to be separate. …Tracing involves establishing the separate origin of the property through evidence showing the time and means by which the spouse originally obtained possession of the property.

Therefore, the court begins with the assumption that everything that is not clearly separate property is community property. In other words, if the couple blended their assets together, each is presumptively entitled to one-half of the total unless the other can conclusively prove that an asset is his or her separate property. One way to prove this is to trace an asset from its beginning as separate property (as, for example, from an inheritance) into its present form (as, for example, in a certificate of deposit).

One way that assets can be mingled is when one spouse uses his or her separate property to improve the community property or when the couple uses community property to improve separate property. In these situations, the court may reallocate the assets so as to compensate for the contribution. Part of the community property might be given to the spouse who used his or her separate property for the improvement or vice versa.

One difficult question is who owns an increase in value of separate property. In some community property states, income from separate property becomes community property, but an increase in value remains separate. In others, the income stays separate.

The court's discretion in community property states

However, in all but three states, the judge has discretion in how he or she divides the community property. In other words, although the divorce proceeding begins with the proposition that each spouse owns one-half of the community property, the court can change the percentage actually given to each spouse.

The judge can factor in the spouses' respective earning capacities, their needs, and other factors. These considerations can lead to results that outrage one of the couple at the time. For example, consider the case of Betsy and Horace. Betsy was a dynamic and clever businesswoman. She married Horace primarily because he was handsome and fun to be with. She and Horace started a successful Internet business, but she was the motive force. Horace was a relatively ineffectual fellow with less education than Betsy. He also had some chronic health problems. When they divorced, the couple agreed that Horace would have primary custody of the children. The court awarded the Internet business to Horace because he had less earning capacity than Betsy; the judge felt that Betsy could easily replicate her success with the first business. He ordered Horace to pay part of the profits to Betsy for a few years. So, Betsy saw all the fruits of her work go to Horace, whom she knew would mismanage the business. Her right to part of the profits was worthless because Horace wasn't capable of keeping the business going. On the other hand, it didn't do Horace much good to get the business because, although it produced a lot of money for a few years, it gradually died away under his inept handling. Obviously, Betsy regretted not having a marital agreement that provided that she would get the business in the event of any divorce.

One additional factor is whether the couple has young children. In that situation, the court may rule that the spouse with primary custody should keep the family house so that the children can stay in familiar surroundings.

California, New Mexico, and Louisiana require that community property be divided equally between the spouses. That means that in those states, the designation of property as separate or community greatly affects the outcome of any divorce.

Equitable distribution states (non community property states)

In the 43 states that have an equitable distribution theory of marital property states, the court also begins with differentiating between marital property and separate property. The title to property is still important; the traditional common law rule had been that the title to property determined who owned it. The idea of marital property is a more recent one.

Once the court has decided which property is marital property and which is separate, the judge then divides the marital property equitably between the spouses. Most states begin with a presumption that an equal division will be fair. If the marriage only lasted a short time, the court is likely to let each spouse keep the assets that are in his or her name. At least, the judge is unlikely to determine that one should get much more than the other of the marital property.

Under the Uniform Marriage and Divorce Act, which is fairly typical of most states' laws, the factors that are: (1) what each spouse contributed to the financial side of the marriage, including the value of a homemaker's services; (2) the value of the property that has been set aside to each; (3) how long the marriage lasted, and the economic situation, including earning power, of each spouse when the divorce takes place. The court can also consider whether one spouse supported the other during his or her education. In many states, the judge can consider any factor that he or she finds relevant and fair. Finally, in some states, the court can also divide the couple's separate assets if necessary to reach a fair result.

In a divorce, the court should try to adjust the division of property, the payment of spousal support and the amount of child support, to address the changes in the former spouses' finances in a fair way. For example, a struggling young opera singer married a man who was a singer and also a voice teacher. He traveled with her, critiqued her performances to help her improve, and photographed her for albums and magazine

Chapter 14
Breaking Up a Long-term Relationship

articles. Her name was Frederica von Stade and she became a famous opera star. He, however, didn't become a star. When they divorced, he argued that his share of the marital estate should include something for the value of her career and celebrity status, since he had helped her achieve the pinnacle of success that she now occupied. She responded that her career and her status in the musical world were not the kind of thing that could be owned and therefore he should not be compensated with a share. The court held that the nature of the husband's contribution made the wife's career part of the marital property and therefore that he was entitled to share in her success.

The effect of mingling marital and separate assets varies among the states. Usually, the commingled property is held to be entirely marital property and is divided equally between the spouses if they divorce.

Some states however look to the source of the money used to acquire the asset; to the extent that separate funds were used, for example, the spouse who owned the separate funds may claim that part of the asset is his or her separate property.

The question usually turns on the couple's intentions. If they treat an asset as marital property, then the court will probably decide that it is. If, on the other hand, they mingle funds for a short time in an account and then later treat the account as belonging to only one of them, the court may decide that the account belongs to that spouse alone.

Common Issues in all states

Some issues come up in all states, regardless of the particular property system in that state's laws. These are spousal support, pensions, professional degrees, debts, spousal misconduct, and the effect of prenuptial agreements.

Spousal misconduct

Generally, judges no longer give much, if any, weight to the bad behavior that caused the divorce. The betrayed spouse may be outraged by the other's flagrant adultery, but judges see so many cases of marital infidelity that it does not count for much any more.

Some state law prohibit a court from considering such issues as adultery as factors in dividing the couple's assets. Some states, however, still permit a court to take misconduct into account in dividing the property if the misconduct would have been grounds for a divorce under the traditional rules. In other words, adultery, cruelty, and so on can affect how the judge divides the property. Another exception is where there has been physical or emotional abuse. The judge can alter the division of community property to provide therapy for the injured spouse, for example.

The courts normally count financial misconduct as a relevant factor, however. If one spouse has hidden assets, for example, or wasted community assets by giving them away to his or her friends and relatives, the court can compensate the other spouse, at least if the misconduct amounts to a fraud on the marriage. These actions may be called "fraud on the community" or dissipation.

Dissipation occurs where one spouse wasted money or spent money solely on himself or herself. In other words, if one spouse has tried to glom more than a fair share by buying a lot of things during the last days of the marriage, the court can redress that by giving the other spouse a larger share of the remaining assets or otherwise redistributing the couple's possessions.

The person who spent the money (or gave it away) has the burden of proving clearly that the expenditures were a legitimate marital expense. Usually, this means showing that the money was spent for some reasonable part of the expenses of the marriage or a plausible investment. So, paying for repairs to the furnace in the family home is probably not dissipating assets, but buying a new bass boat solely for the husband's fishing expeditions might be.

An Illinois court stated the rule well:

Where a party has dissipated marital assets, the court may charge the amount dissipated against his or her share of the marital property so as to compensate the other party.[2]

Fraud on the community usually refers to an outright attempt by a spouse to cheat the other spouse. This is often accomplished by gifts to relatives. These cases are difficult ones because, after all, spouses do have some rights to manage the community property and to make gifts. Often the relevant considerations are the intention of the giver and whether the gift, in the circumstances, is a fair and normal one. In other words, giving a car to a child may be regarded as an ordinary thing to do while giving him or her all of one's possessions is probably not, especially if the effect is to impoverish a soon-to-be-ex spouse.

Pensions and other benefits

One major complexity is that federal laws govern employee benefits and pensions. This area of law is quite complicated, particularly where the spouses have different forms of retirement savings, such as IRA's, corporate pension plans, veterans' benefits, 401(k)'s etc.

During the marriage, the employed spouse has control over his or her retirement benefits. He or she can make various choices about investment, contributions, and so on. Some of these assets belong to the employee immediately. Other pension rights only become legal entitlements over a period of time, which is called "vesting."

Dividing these assets in a divorce is very difficult. Community property states and equitable distribution (common law property) states all regard a pension as being some form of marital or community property.

If the pension rights have not vested, then in one sense they are not the spouse's property yet at all. If he or she quits the employment that provides that pension, he or she may never be entitled to anything.

On the other hand, if a couple has been married for many years, both spouses may be counting on a future retirement benefit for their old age. In some sense, that future benefit has been earned and both of them have been working toward the day when a military pension, for example, will support both of them. They may have designed their savings plans around expecting there to be a pension when both are old; now, if the pension is not divided, one spouse may face a bleak future.

Basically, the courts have found ways to divide these assets. If a payment is to be received in the future, the court may order the recipient to pay part of it to the ex-spouse when it is received. If some of the benefits have vested, or if they are in an account like an IRA, the court may divide them between the spouses. The divorce may limit the choices that the employed spouse can make in the future about his or her pension plan.

Alimony and spousal support

Alimony is periodic payments awarded by a court to a spouse. It is also called "maintenance" or "spousal support" in some states. In this book, I use the terms interchangeably.

You can be required to pay maintenance whether the marriage was a common-law one or a ceremonial one. Remember that husband and wife were legally obligated to provide each other with the necessities of life – for life. It is uncommon now, however, for a court to require lifelong payments unless the marriage lasted for many years and the recipient cannot reasonably be expected to support himself or herself in a sufficient style.

Spousal support payments are not usually based on a rigid formula, although the law often puts a ceiling on the amount. That ceiling may be as much as one-third of the person making the payment's income. That's a hefty amount to be paying an ex for many years.

Like child support, alimony payments are set out in a court order. The court can modify the order to increase, decrease, or stop the payments if the parties' circumstances change. The law varies on how much leeway a judge has to change an order that the parties agreed on; remember that it's not part of a judge's job to get you out of a bad bargain.

Also keep in mind that a property division may be effected by having one ex-spouse make payments to the other over time, as where one ex-spouse buys the other's interest in their house. These payments are not alimony and are not usually modified later, except perhaps in bankruptcy court.

The Uniform Marriage and Divorce Act sets out criteria for spousal support that are fairly typical. The factors are the following:

(1) the financial resources of the person seeking support;

(2) the time needed for that person to obtain an education or skills that he or she could use to support himself or herself;

(3) the standard of living to which the couple was accustomed during the marriage;

(4) the length of time that the couple were married;

(5) the health (mental and physical) of the person seeking support; and

(6) the ability of the other spouse to support both of them.[3]

Basically, alimony is intended to provide for an ex-spouse who does not have sufficient assets or skills to provide a reasonable lifestyle for himself or herself, given the length of the marriage, the resources of each spouse, and the lifestyle that the couple enjoyed while they were married.

Many states still consider marital fault, such as adultery, as one of the factors in awarding alimony. Some consider it as just one factor among many while others continue the older rule that a culpable spouse does not deserve to be supported. In those states, a spouse who commits adultery, abuses the other, or abandons the marriage may be barred from receiving alimony. Even if a state provides for "no fault" divorce, adultery or other marital misconduct may still affect the judge's decision about alimony.

The Uniform Marriage and Divorce Act, which is perhaps the more modern trend, however, provides that fault is not a factor. That model statute actually says "the court is expressly admonished not to consider the misconduct of a spouse during the marriage."[4] Many states follow this rule.

Spousal support falls into two basic categories; permanent and rehabilitative. Rehabilitative support consists in payments made for a period of time to enable a less-educated spouse to get an education. Often this form of alimony is used to compensate a spouse who worked while the other went to school.

Permanent alimony is intended to last for the recipient's life or until he or she remarries. When a person remarries, the new spouse assumes the obligation to support him or her.

Modern court orders about spousal support usually provide that it also stops if one spouse cohabits with a person of the opposite sex. This is partly a moral judgment and partly a pragmatic realization that a cohabiting couple can support each other. The provision keeps an ex-spouse from using alimony to support a lover.

Many prenuptial agreements expressly waive the parties' rights to spousal support. In fact, avoiding being obligated to pay support is one of the primary motivations for couples to sign these agreements.

Prenuptial agreements, divorce agreements, and married couples

A valid prenuptial agreement should control the division of any property between the spouses, regardless of whether they live in a community property or common law property state. In other words, each spouse owns whatever the agreement provides that they own, rather than the share that state law would give them. See Chapter Six.

Usually, a prenuptial agreement (or a marital agreement made during the marriage) provides that the couple waives any rights that they each might have under state law. That means that the couple gives up any right to alimony, inheritance, or a share in property earned acquired during the marriage. In place of those rights, each is entitled to whatever the agreement provides.

However, in many states, the judges have the right to examine the terms of a prenuptial or marital agreement and the circumstances under which it was entered to see whether the agreement is substantively fair and to ascertain whether one party was deceived or browbeaten into signing it.

Similarly, courts usually follow an agreement reached by a married couple in their divorce, but the judge is not required to do so. He or she still has a duty to keep in mind the marriage laws and should not honor an agreement that was obtained by fraud, threats, or undue influence or that is so unfair as to be unconscionable. As one court put it, the agreement should not be a hardship on either spouse and should be "just, fair, and proper," in light of state law, particularly where one spouse did not have a lawyer and the other did. [5]

However, mere misjudgment is not grounds for setting aside the agreement. For example, Mr. and Mrs. Manzo signed a separation agreement before their divorce. Mr. Manzo earned more than twice what Mrs. Manzo did. They agreed that Mrs. Manzo would not get alimony and that they would sell their house. Mrs. would get $60,000 from the sale and Mr. Manzo would get the rest. Unfortunately for Mr. Manzo, the net amount they received from the sale was only $70,000. Mrs. Manzo got her $60,000 which left $10,000 for Mr. Manzo. Mr. Manzo asked the court to set aside the agreement because the difference was unfair to him and he had made a mistake about what the house was worth. Mrs. Manzo had not lied to Mr. Manzo about the house; there was no evidence that she had engaged in some kind of sharp dealing that would be inappropriate in a marriage. Mr. Manzo was stuck.

Remember, the courts are not here to get you out of bad decisions.

Debts and divorce

When a married couple divorces, the judge should apportion the responsibility for their debts between them as part of the property settlement. See Chapter Five and Chapter Six.

The existence and amounts of debts are part of the factors that the judge can use in dividing the property. For example, the judge can, if he or she deems it more equitable, give one spouse the house and the other the mortgage payments.

However, just as with cohabiting couples, the divorce decree changes the obligations of the ex-spouses to each other but does not change their obligations to their creditors. In other words, even if the judge orders the husband to pay all of the couple's joint credit card bills, the wife can still be liable to the creditors. She has the right to go back to court to compel her ex-husband to make the payments but the creditors may still hound her. After all, the credit card company is not involved in the lawsuit.

The chief and nastiest creditor is the IRS; provision for the payment of income taxes, especially past due taxes, can one of the most important aspects of the divorce decree.

For these reasons, some lawyers advise their clients to have family assets sold as part of the divorce and proceeds used to pay the debts. It is better to have fewer assets, and be sure that the taxes are paid, for example, that to find out later that your deadbeat ex never made the payments.

Remember too that a division of property, including the allocation of debts, can be changed by a subsequent bankruptcy proceeding.
See page 498.

After a divorce, one ex spouse may file for bankruptcy. In bankruptcy, his or her obligations to make payments are changed. He or she may get out of paying the debts that he or she was ordered to pay in the divorce. Similarly, he or she may be relieved of his or her property division obligation to the ex-spouse under the divorce decree. That can mean (1) that the ex is now completely liable for debts that the divorce judge told the other spouse to pay and (2) that the ex doesn't get his or her share of the marital estate.

Alimony and child support, remember, are not usually subject to change in bankruptcy. Therefore, obviously, the terms of the divorce decree can be critically important. Payments called "property division" may be cancelled while those labeled "alimony" probably won't be.

For this reason, if you are divorcing a deadbeat spouse, again, it is better to get what you can now than to count on him or her making payments to you (or anyone else) in the future. In other words, again, don't agree to a division of the property that requires him or her to pay you over time. Also, make sure that all the debts on which you are also liable are paid, even if it means that all or most of the marital property has to be sold to pay those debts.

If it looks like the only sensible outcome of a divorce is for your deadbeat spouse to make payments to you over time, be sure that those payments are labeled "support" and not "division of property."

Finality – getting it all over with

By the time a relationship ends in divorce, a couple usually wants nothing more than for the wrangling to end, although there are some pathologically hateful couples who prolong the battles for years, scarring their children and enriching their lawyers and psychiatrists.

QUESTION: "My husband and I worked out all the terms of our divorce. Doesn't the judge have to go along with our decision?"

ANSWER: Courts almost always are willing to allow the couple to decide for themselves. However, the judge is not required to do so.

QUESTION: "Once the judge signs the order, we're done, right?"

ANSWER: Sort of. If there is no alimony, no child support, and no on-going payments owed by one spouse to another or to a creditor, the order ends the couple's dispute. However, judges have ongoing power to change orders about alimony and child support and may have some power to change other terms of the decree, such as payment plans.

Busy judges are usually quite happy to see a couple agree on the division of property, child support, and alimony. The normal result is that the judge signs an order, which has been prepared by the parties or their attorneys, that contains the terms of the couple's agreement.

However, remember that the court is not actually required to go along with such an arrangement, especially with regard to child custody and support. For example, a couple might agree that the custodial parent doesn't want or need child support, but the judge might believe that the child deserves and would benefit from receiving child support from the non-custodial parent.

In addition, in family law matters, the court has the continuing power to modify his or her earlier orders. In other words, unless certain legal technicalities have been observed, the court can change some parts of the order later. This is particularly true of orders that set the amounts of alimony and child support. Generally, a denial of alimony and a division of property are final and can't be changed later. Any ongoing payment, however, might be subject to modification if the circumstances have changed.

This is one more difference between married couples and cohabiting couples. In a lawsuit over a contract, the court's decision becomes final after a period of time, usually 30 days. Cohabitation agreement disputes over property are more like ordinary contract cases and the court's decision ends the issue. In all family matters, whether in a divorce or a dispute between an unmarried couple, the court has continuing jurisdiction over child custody and support.

One of the most difficult questions for a court is when it is proper for a judge to modify child support or alimony that was reached by agreement. Nonetheless, the fact is that a court can change the amounts later. The party who wants the order changed has to show that a significant and unforeseen change in circumstances has occurred. The change may be that the person making the payments has a substantially increased income or that the person receiving the support has substantially increased needs.

As with prenuptial agreements, the mere fact that a person made a bad deal in his or her divorce settlement is not sufficient grounds to change the order later.[6]

Division of property when one of you dies

Some of the bitterest family disputes arise when one member of the family dies. Families sometimes fight over who is responsible for the death ("If you hadn't let him keep drinking, the accident wouldn't have happened.") Usually, though, the battle takes place over the dead person's assets, even if not very much is involved.

The rights of various family members depend on whether or not the couple was married and what legal documents they have (or have not) prepared.

In one case, mentioned earlier, Tom and Fred lived together for a number of years. Both had contracted AIDS. This case happened early in the epidemic when little was known about the virus and few effective treatments were available. Tom helped Fred buy a car; Tom signed the financing agreement but Fred made the payments. When Tom died, Tom's family took the car and hid it from Fred, even though Fred was terminally ill. Fred's lawyer persuaded the court to give the car back to Fred. Fred was very lucky that he could convince the judge that he and Tom intended for the car to be his; on paper, the car belonged to Tom and Tom's family controlled his estate, including the car.

To shed another light on human nature, Fred formed a new relationship with George who was also HIV positive. By the time Fred passed away, George was also very ill and unable to make decisions for himself. Their respective families met at the couple's apartment in a big city to divide up their things. One family was Baptist from a small town in the Midwest; the other Catholic from a rural parish in the South.

I had the honor of watching these two families treat each other with the utmost courtesy and honesty. They shared their grief over the loss of their beloved sons, regardless of the sons' lifestyle and their own conservative religious backgrounds. For example, Fred's parents told George's folks to be sure to take plenty of sweaters for him, regardless of who owned them, because they knew that AIDS patients could be sensitive to cold.

Together, they cleaned the apartment and boxed up everything from bicycles to microwaves. They discussed each item of any value, as to who might have owned it, which family could use it, and so on. In addition, the families jointly decided to donate many of the couple's things to a charity for AIDS patients.

Inheritance

When someone dies, his worldly goods are divided among those who are still living. Those worldly goods are called his or her "estate" or "probate estate." Four sets of rules govern the distribution of the deceased's assets:

(1) ownership documents such as deeds;
(2) the terms of a valid will or trust;
(3) the state's laws about marital property; and
(4) the state's laws of inheritance.

Once again, remember that the rules are different for lovers and spouses. First, if there is no valid will, the surviving spouse or a grown child is usually appointed as the personal representative. It is somewhat unlikely that a lover would be. Second, spouses have inheritance rights that lovers do not. Third, in community property states, each spouse already owns one-half of community property so the surviving spouse's half does not become part of the deceased's estate.

The laws govern married couples apply to informal marriages the same as to ceremonial marriages, provided of course, that the common law marriage can be proved. This can be difficult once one of the spouses is dead.

Remember, too, that if a person has been killed by another person's negligence, the estate of the deceased person can bring a lawsuit for his or her injuries. The estate receives any damages awarded and these funds are distributed to the deceased's heirs, along with the rest of his or her assets.

The surviving spouse has three kinds of rights in this situation. First, he or she is normally the executor of the estate and therefore controls the lawsuit. Secondly, he or she is usually an heir. Third, he or she can sue for his or her own losses. See page 178

Again, lovers don't have these rights unless they are named in the will as an exector or as an heir. Even then, a lover does not usually have the right to bring a lawsuit for the loss of his or her significant other.

Legal Mechanics

Usually, there is a court proceeding called "probate" to handle the legal mechanics of memorializing the change in ownership. As with divorce, many states now have simplified procedures for handling these legal mechanics, so that an attorney may not be needed if the heirs are on good terms and the title to assets is not too complicated.

In a probate proceeding, someone is appointed to administer the changes in title and distribution of stuff. That person is called a "personal representative" or an "executor" (feminine form -- "executrix."). In some states, the term is "administratrix" (masculine form – "administrator.") He or she files an inventory of the deceased's assets, sees that any debts are paid, and deeds any real estate to the heirs, and so on. The personal representative is also responsible for seeing that any estate tax return, state or federal, gets filed.

A personal representative is a fiduciary for the heirs, meaning that he or she is supposed to treat everyone with scrupulous honesty and fairness. However, it not uncommon for the personal representative to steal the bulk of the estate, even from his or her relatives.   For example, a dishonest personal representative may buy other heirs' share of the estate for a low price by overstating the deceased's debts and understating the value of the assets.

State laws differ in how much control is exercised by the court over the personal representative, but usually the judge and his or her staff do not have the responsibility of ensuring that everything is done honestly and fairly. The heirs have a right to an accounting of the estate and a right, of course, to challenge the inventory.   Unless the will excuses the personal representative from this responsibility, he or she must post a bond to protect the heirs from outright theft.

The personal representative is entitled to be paid for his or her services, unless the will provides otherwise. He or she may charge by the hour, if he or she is an accountant or lawyer. State laws often set a percentage of the estate as compensation, such as five per cent. If the personal representative dislikes his or her fellow heirs, he or she can siphon off quite a bit of money in fees and still take his or her share of whatever is left.

An important caveat is that some assets never become part of the probate estate and hence are not within the control of the court or the personal representative. These are assets that are owned jointly with right of survivorship and assets that are governed by an inter vivos ("among the living") trust. Remember, an inter vivos trust is one that is set up while people are still alive. The person setting up the trust transfers ownership of various assets to the trust. When he or she dies, the trust continues to exist and to peacefully own its assets. He or she may also leave various assets to the trust by will but those assets go through the probate system.

There are many people who advocate using a living trust to avoid the probate system. It ensures greater privacy and some feel that it saves money. More importantly, a trust may be a way of avoiding a family fight over inheritance; the transfers have already taken place. A trust can be a way of providing for a lover or second spouse of whom grown children disapprove, for example, because it is somewhat harder for them to challenge a trust that is already functioning than to launch a fight in the probate court. For example, one lover might leave assets in trust for his or her partner's lifetime and stipulate that after the partner's death (or remarriage), the assets pass to others, such as children or grandchildren or a charity.

Regardless of the legal structure of an estate, a couple should make sure that each of them has some money that is clearly separate. Otherwise, he or she may have no funds available for many weeks, even if he or she eventually inherits, because everything may be tied up in the probate process.

As discussed in Chapter Four (same sex couples) and Chapter Thirteen, family members may contest the inheritance rights of significant others if the family disapproved of the relationship. The family may claim that one partner unduly influenced or coerced the other; the family may also challenge the legality of the couple's arrangements.

Charles Dickens wrote a masterpiece novel called *Bleak House* about the family machinations surrounding a disputed inheritance. At the end of the protracted litigation, nothing was left for the heirs who had been obsessed about their shares because the entire estate was exhausted in attorneys' fees. It's worth reading if you are thinking about questions of inheritance and don't think that you need a will.

Will or no will

When a person dies without a will, his or her assets are apportioned in the following order.

First, those who own property jointly with right of survivorship now own the asset automatically. (Trusts go on functioning as before). People who own property in common with the deceased, including business partners and significant others, continue to own their share, and in community property states, each spouse continues to own his or her community interest.

Second, the rest of his or her assets pass into the probate estate. These are then divided among his creditors and heirs.

State laws set out who gets what if there is no will.

Married Couples

Here are the basic rules governing married couples.

QUESTION: *"If my husband dies without making a will, will I inherit from him?"*

ANSWER: *Yes. If it is an informal marriage, you will need to prove that you were married.*

QUESTION: *"If my common-law wife makes a will that says 'everything to my husband,' will I inherit from her?"*

ANSWER: *Yes, if you can prove that you were married.*

QUESTION: *"If my spouse cuts me out of his will, do I inherit anything from his estate?"*

ANSWER: *You are probably entitled to a share of his estate. The amount will depend on the terms of the will and the laws of your particular state.*

Spouses have some inheritance rights from each other. These rights can be changed to some extent by a valid will or by agreement between the spouses, such as a prenuptial agreement.

The right to inherit, whether by a will or under state law if the dead person didn't have a will, only applies to property that is in the probate estate.

Remember that some assets do not become part of the deceased spouse's probate estate. Joint property owned with right of survivorship does not become part of the estate. In a community property state, the surviving spouse already owns one-half of any community property so that half also does not become part of the probate estate. Similarly, if the couple own property jointly, only the portion that the deceased owns becomes part of his or her estate. The share that the survivor already owns does not become part of the deceased's estate; the survivor already owns it. Finally, insurance policy proceeds are not part of the probate estate unless the deceased specifically made his or her estate the beneficiary, i.e. if the policy is payable to "my estate."

If the deceased dies without a will (intestate), the surviving spouse receives a share of the estate. This is true both in community property states and common law states. The estate is divided between the spouse, any children of the deceased, and other relatives. The exact proportions depend on state law, whether there are children, and so on. Usually, the surviving spouse gets one-third or one-half of all of the assets in the estate.

In a community property state, that means that the surviving spouse receives a share of the deceased's one-half of the community property as well as a share of the dead person's separate property. In other words, if there is no valid will, the surviving spouse may end up with three-fourths of the community property.

If the deceased has made a valid will, then the surviving spouse receives whatever amount is provided for him or her in the will.

In most states, and under the Uniform Probate Code, however, a spouse cannot completely cut the other spouse out of his or her estate, regardless of what his or her will says. These modern laws are called "elective share statutes," and they replace the ancient doctrines of dower and courtesy which also guaranteed a surviving spouse some share in the family estate.[7]

Under these statutes, the surviving spouse can accept whatever amount is left to him or her in the will or can elect to take the share provided by statute.

The Uniform Probate Code approach incorporates the modern idea of marriage as an economic partnership. Under that approach, the surviving spouse's share of the deceased spouse's estate depends on the length of the marriage and the surviving spouse's separate assets.

Under these elective share statutes, neither spouse has a legal interest in the other's property while they are both alive. They only affect legal interests after one spouse has died. When one dies, the other is entitled to receive a share of the deceased's property, usually one-third to one-half, depending again on whether there are children.

Some states also give the surviving spouse a share in property that the deceased had tried to give away during his or her lifetime, so that these gifts do not defeat the spouse's "partnership" interest in the property of the marriage.

In addition, both community property and common law property states usually allow the surviving spouse some share of the estate as a family allowance and a share of the deceased's personal property as a personal property allotment. Finally, in some states, the surviving spouse has the right to live in the marital home until he or she dies, regardless of who is to inherit the house.

Prenuptial agreements often provide that the couple waives these inheritance rights. If a couple intends to marry and have already made plans for their property after their death, such as providing for a handicapped child or endowing a charity, then it is important that the prenuptial agreement make clear that the new spouse gives up his or her right to inherit.

Unmarried Couples

Here are the basic rules governing unmarried couples. Basically, an unmarried couple does not have a right to inherit from each other unless there is a valid will.

Therefore, when one of them dies without a will (intestate), the other lover is entitled to the following, if any:

(1) his or her share of any joint accounts;
(2) all of any asset owned jointly with right of survivorship;
(3) any insurance proceeds from a policy in which he or she is the named beneficiary;
(4) any other asset that he or she can prove some entitlement to; but
(5) no share in the probate estate.

A lover might be able to prove, for example, that he or she was entitled to a share in a business because the lovers had been business partners as well as lovers. Or, he or she might have rights under a cohabitation agreement.

In most states, litigation over these questions would take place in the probate court system, and the lover's claim would take the form of a claim against the estate. As you can imagine, this pits the lover against the deceased person's family, which is a recipe for bitterness and large legal bills.

When a lover dies with a valid will, the surviving lover has the same right to inherit as any other heir. He or she will receive the share provided for in the will, plus any of the property described above, such as jointly owned accounts.

A lover's inheritance may engender great rage in the deceased's relatives, who may feel that as family, they had first right to inherit his or her money. A relative may believe that the deceased was taken advantage of or even coerced by his or her lover.

QUESTION: *"If my lover dies without making a will naming me, will I inherit from him?"*

ANSWER: *No, you will not get anything, except where your name is on some property, such as a joint account with right of survivorship at the bank.*

QUESTION: *"If my lover's will leaves everything to his wife, will I inherit from him if we have lived together for a long time?"*

ANSWER: *No. The estate will go to his wife, if he is married, even if they aren't living together. If he does not have a legal wife, because he has been divorced, for example, the validity of the will depends on when it was made. Unless you are named in a valid will, you do not inherit.*

QUESTION: *"If my lover's will leaves everything to me by name, will I inherit from him even if we aren't married?"*

ANSWER: *Yes. However, if he is lawfully married to someone else, his wife may be entitled to a share in his estate regardless of the will.*

QUESTION: *"If my lover cuts me out of his will, can I inherit anything from his estate?"*

ANSWER: *No, but you are entitled to (1) any assets that are owned jointly with right of survivorship and (2) your proportionate share of other jointly owned property. You may have a claim to other assets but it depends on what you can prove you both agreed to.*

The point is that lovers have no inheritance rights under the law, except those created by the couple, through ownership documents, contracts, and valid wills. Wives and other relatives have inheritance rights by statute.

In other words, assets stay in the family, and lovers, even long-term ones, are not family in the eyes of the law. The statutes provide for a deceased person's assets to be distributed among members of his family that are alive after he or she dies;: first his or her spouse and children, if any; second his or her parents; third, any living siblings, and fourth, other relatives, such as grandparents, aunts, uncles, and cousins in whatever order of priority the state law sets out. Whether or not you are married, having a proper will and keeping title to property clear are important ways of caring for those you love. Otherwise, your death may not only grieve your significant other, but also leave him or her only a giant hassle.

If you're not married, however, it is critical to have a valid will and to make sure that all legal documents reflect the right ownership. Otherwise, your significant other stands to get nothing.

A dead person's debts

When a person dies, his or her assets and his liabilities become part of a probate estate. Those who hope to inherit from him or her may have disputes about what he or she owned or what debts should be paid. This section only talks about debts.

QUESTION: *"My lover had big credit card bills. He also owed money on his car. He left everything to me in his will. Then, he died. What do I get? What do his creditors get?*

ANSWER: *Usually, the creditors are paid out of the deceased person's assets before the heirs get their share.*

When a person dies, his assets pass to his estate. His or her creditors are entitled to be paid out of those assets before the heirs get their share. However, the creditors have a limited time period in which to make their claim. The rules are different for creditors who have a lien, such as the company that financed a car, and those that don't have a lien, such as credit card companies.

The result can also be different in a community property state. In those states, remember, the spouse owns one-half of the community assets, so only half goes into the deceased spouse's estate.

MYTH—*When a person dies, his heirs have to pay all of his debts.*

FACT—*The creditors are only entitled to be paid by those who owe the money. No one inherits debts.*

Many people believe that a person's family has to pay his debts when he dies. This is not true.

The only people who are liable on a debt are those who have promised to pay it. Usually, these promises have to be in writing.

However, a deceased person's creditors are entitled to be paid first out of his or her estate. In other words, in effect, the family seems to be paying the debts because all of their inheritance goes to the deceased person's creditors.

Also, liens on property follow the property. In other words, suppose that a man owns a house that has a mortgage on it. When he dies, he leaves the house to his son. The son gets title to the house but the finance company still has a valid mortgage on it. The son has to pay the mortgage in order to keep the house.

Life insurance, trusts, and joint accounts with right of survivorship can be used to try to ensure that a surviving partner receives something, even if the other partner has lots of debts or greedy expectant children. The reason is that trusts, joint accounts, and life insurance don't become part of the probate estate, and consequently, creditors and other heirs have a harder time asserting a claim against those assets.

QUESTION: *"What happens if a single person dies without a will (intestate) and doesn't have any close relatives?"*

ANSWER: *Usually, his or her estate goes to distant relatives or, in some states, the state government.*

Some state laws provide an elaborate scheme for dividing up a a person's assets if the person dies unmarried and childless. Usually, the person's assets go to his or her parents, if they are alive, and if they are not, then to siblings, and if there are no siblings, then to grandparents, and so on until the exercise resembles an elaborate genealogy chart. Under some laws, the state governments. Some state laws provide an elaborate scheme for dividing up a a person's assets if the person dies unmarried and childless. Usually, the person's assets go to his or her parents, if they are alive, and if they are not, then to siblings, and if there are no siblings, then to grandparents, and so on until the exercise resembles an elaborate genealogy chart. Under some laws, the state governments could be called the "default heirs." If a person dies without any ascertainable relatives in those states, his or her assets can default (called "escheat" by lawyers) to the state government. Most people have some reasonably close relative, such as a cousin, somewhere. If that person is known and can be located, then he or she might inherit.

There are services that try to locate such lost heirs. Some of these services are legitimate but some are scams. The scams try to collect a fee from a supposedly lost heir on the promise of revealing where an inheritance is, except of course that there isn't any inheritance.

This is another reason to have a valid will, whether you leave all your money to your second cousin twice removed or your high school sweetheart or whomever. Surely, it is better to leave your property to a decent charity or someone you know than to have it go to the state government.

For the same reason, every will should have a default provision that if all the heirs have died before they inherit, then the estate goes to some worthy cause.

By the way, a person cannot leave his or her estate to a pet, no matter how much worthier your cat may be compared to your relatives. The only safe way to provide for a pet after your death is to leave money in trust for the care of the animal. The trustee should be, obviously, someone whom you believe will actually use the money to care for your beloved furry (or feathered or finned) friends.

Some people have put clauses in their will that require their dog or cat to be euthanized when the owner dies. Some judges refuse to enforce these clauses and cooperate with animal rescue organizations to find a good home for the animal.

QUESTION: *"I lived with Harry for ten years. He had a will that left everything to his ex-wife. He crossed out her name and wrote mine in. Don't I inherit?"*

ANSWER: *Probably not. The key to inheritance is a valid will. Changing terms in a will by hand usually simply invalidates the whole thing.*

QUESTION: *"My husband and I both made valid wills with our lawyer. Then, when he died, I found out that he had burned his will. What happens now?"*

ANSWER: *His action revoked his will. Therefore, either an earlier, valid will becomes effective again or, if there isn't such a will, he dies without any will. Remember that people are usually free to revoke or change their will.*

When a person revokes a will, any earlier will comes back into force unless it also has been formally revoked, such as where the testator has destroyed it. If there is no valid will, then the person dies intestate, i.e. without a will, and his or her assets are distributed according to the law.

A will is revoked if the testator destroys it deliberately or if he or she does something else that indicates his or her intention to revoke the will such as writing "revoked" on it or tearing it in half.

A new will replaces any earlier will, and most wills contain a clause that says "this will revokes any other wills that I may have made."

Making any change by hand in a typed or printed will is usually considered a revocation of the will. The reason is that the formalities of making a will, such as witnesses and notaries, are to ensure that the typed document really does reflect the testator's intentions. Handwritten changes nullify all those protections.

In other words, you cannot change a will except by making a new one or by making a codicil. A codicil is an amendment to a will and it has to be done with all the same formalities as a will. Even if there is a contract to make certain provisions in a will, people are usually free to change their wills. The disappointed would-be beneficiary can sue the estate for the benefits that he or she expected, but he or she will have to prove that the contract was legally valid.

QUESTION: *"My husband and I wrote wills (with our lawyer's help and all the formalities) that left everything to the other. In other words, if I died, everything went to him and vice versa. When he died, his sister showed up with a handwritten letter from my husband, dated after our wills, which said, 'When I die, I want you to have everything.' She says that she inherits. Is that true?"*

ANSWER: *In many states, his letter may be a valid will.*

Here is one of those troublesome little quirks in the law. In most states, a handwritten will is a valid will, provided that it is entirely in the handwriting of the testator (person making the will.) An entirely handwritten will is valid without all the formalities of a typed or printed will; in other words, without witnesses and so on.

The handwriting must be that of the testator, the document must be signed, and it must indicate that the testator intended to dispose of his property after his death. In other words, it doesn't have to say "This is my will" but it does have to make clear that the person writing it is talking about what happens to his or her property after death.

So, the husband's letter might be a valid will which would revoke the will that he made with his wife in the lawyer's office.

Usually, a person has the right to change his will without notifying any of the beneficiaries under the earlier will.

Life insurance

Insurance is governed by the terms of the policy. Policies have standard language built in that controls who gets the proceeds. The standard language provides that the beneficiary of the policy is the surviving spouse or children of the deceased, unless some other specification is made. In other words, once again, an unmarried lover is out of luck.

QUESTION: *"If my husband dies, do I get his life insurance?"*

ANSWER: *If you are married, you get the life insurance proceeds provided that either you are the named beneficiary of the policy or the beneficiary is the spouse. If the beneficiary is someone else, you are probably out of luck.*

QUESTION: *"If my lover dies, do I get his life insurance?"*

ANSWER: *No, unless he named you as the beneficiary.*[8]

As a practical matter, life insurance policies come in two basic varieties: those that you purchase from an agent and those that you can get in more nonchalant ways, like signing up for life insurance through an advertisement that came with your credit card bill.

When you fill out a policy, you are asked to put down the beneficiary's name or relationship. If George Traditional fills in the blank with his wife's name -- "Mary Traditional" -- as the beneficiary, then Mary must get the policy proceeds when George dies, if she survives him, whether or not they are still married and even if George and she are divorced and George married someone else. If George changes his mind or is divorced from Mary, then he needs to change the beneficiary on the policy. Some states have laws that change the beneficiary designation on divorce, and the divorce decree might also do this, but it is not safe to count on such provisions.

If, on the other hand, George fills in the blank for beneficiary with "my wife," then the policy proceeds are paid to whoever is married to him at the time of his death. This can be a problem if George gets divorced from Mary and later lives with Jane. When George dies, the insurance policy will not go to either woman, because George has no wife at the time of his death. Instead, the policy will be paid to the secondary beneficiary. That will be either someone George named or some relative specified in the policy.

Obviously, things get complicated when George provides that the beneficiary is "my wife, Mary Traditional" and then divorces Mary and marries Ellen. Should the proceeds go to Mary because her name is there or to Ellen because she is now the wife?

Most typical policies automatically provide that the proceeds are paid to the spouse, unless the insured changes the beneficiary. If the insured is married, common-law or ceremonially, then the benefits go to the spouse, unless the owner of the policy has named another beneficiary.

Insurance policies provide for secondary beneficiaries, i.e. people who will receive the proceeds if the first person named (primary beneficiary) dies before the insured person does.

If the insured person is not married when he or she dies, then the policy contains default provisions providing for who gets the money. Usually these provide that the insurance is paid to the insured person's children; if the insured person is not married and does not have children, the money goes to his or her nearest relatives – parents or brothers and sisters.

However, the purchaser of the insurance may have chosen someone else as the primary or secondary beneficiary. The purchaser (usually the one whose life is insured) can direct the payment of the insurance proceeds to whomever he or she wants. If

George is living with Jane, and puts Jane's name on the insurance form as the beneficiary, then Jane gets the money when George dies, even if they split up years ago and even if they were never married.

Insurance is one place where common law marriage can become financially important. A common law spouse is a legal spouse for life insurance purposes.

In one case, a nice man, Ned, was involved with two women. His ex wife Judy still loved him and carried him on her company's health insurance policy as her husband. He spent some time at her house and she was on good terms with his family. He also, however, lived with another woman, Elaine. She demanded that he pay "rent" and sometimes threw him out when he was broke. On the other hand, he sometimes referred to himself and Elaine as being married. Elaine took out insurance on his life through her credit card company; the form policy provided that the spouse was the beneficiary. Ned died in an accident before Elaine had to pay even one premium. Both Elaine and Judy claimed to be common law married to him. The jury found for Elaine and she received the life insurance.

In other words, the surviving spouse receives the life insurance proceeds under two conditions. Either the policy names the spouse as beneficiary by name or it doesn't. If he or she is not specifically named but the policy specifies that the proceeds go to the spouse, then he or she will get the money *if a valid marriage can be proved*. Consequently, the issue of the validity of a marriage, especially a common law marriage, can determine who gets a lot of money.

There is one more technicality. Usually a person buys insurance on his or her own life, meaning that when the purchaser dies, someone else gets money. In that situation, the insured person and the owner of the policy are the same person.

However, one can buy a policy on someone else's life. So, a husband can buy a policy on his wife's life, meaning that if she dies, he gets the proceeds. A parent can buy a policy on the life of a child, meaning that if the child dies the parent profits. In that situation, the person who bought the policy owns it but the insured is someone else.

A person can buy insurance on another's life only if they have an "insurable interest," meaning a sufficient legal relationship. You can't buy insurance on the life of a stranger or someone that you don't know. A fan cannot buy a policy on a movie star's life.

There was a notorious poisoning case in Houston in which several children became ill after eating tainted Halloween candy. It turned out that the father of one child has poisoned the candy in order to collect the life insurance on his own son's life.

A lover often cannot buy insurance on the life of his or her companion. So, for example, let's assume that George and Fred are long-time companions. If each of them wants to use life insurance to provide for the other, then each must buy a policy on his own life. In other words, George buys life insurance and names Fred as the person to receive the proceeds (the beneficiary) when George dies. George owns that policy and is the insured; Fred is the beneficiary. Fred buys a policy and names George as the person to receive the proceeds when Fred dies. Fred owns that policy and is the insured; George is the beneficiary.

The key here is that the owner of the policy can change the beneficiary without any notice to the previous beneficiary. Consequently, lovers (married or not) cannot rely completely on life insurance because the owner of the policy may change the beneficiary without telling his or her significant other. The owner can also cancel the policy or fail to pay the premiums, which will lead to the policy being canceled or at least reduced in value.

In the above example, George might secretly name his cousin Elfrida as the beneficiary without telling Fred. Although Fred might be able to try to claim that George and he had a contract about the insurance, Elfrida has a good chance of getting the money.

QUESTION: *"My husband and I divorced. I was listed as an heir in his will and as the beneficiary of his life insurance policy. He never changed these before he died. Do I inherit?"*

ANSWER: *You don't inherit under the will but you probably get the insurance proceeds.*

Divorce and marriage both revoke preexisting wills but neither changes an insurance policy.

The law assumes that someone would not want his or her ex to inherit so wills are automatically revoked when there is a divorce. Similarly, it assumes that one would want his or her spouse to inherit so marriage also automatically revokes a prior will. State laws differ as to the exact effect of this revocation, so for example, sometimes children who have been named in a will still inherit. Also, if the will makes clear that the testator wanted his or her ex to inherit, then the ex is a legal heir.

Insurance policies, however, are normally a matter of contract. In almost all states, the terms stay the same until the owner changes them. They are not automatically changed by marriage or divorce, although sometimes insurance policies can be part of the marital property.

A divorce may also automatically revoke some trusts and other financial arrangements that were made for the ex-spouse. However, the final result turns on intricacies of state law.

Children

If there have been children involved in the relationship, then there are many more issues to resolve. It is certainly to the children's benefit for the adults in their lives to resolve things as amicably as possible.

From the standpoint of rights, remember that the best interests of the child govern most decisions about children but that the child's biological parents also have important rights. The courts are not entirely free to rearrange families as they see fit.

It is the responsibility of the adults involved to structure the new situation in the best possible way for the children.

Children who were not born in this relationship

If the children are not the biological offspring of the two of you, then you need to decide what role the unrelated adult (i.e. the ex-significant other) will have in the children's lives in the future, whether the couple was married or not. Ex stepparents don't have much more legal protection for their relationship with the child than ex lovers do, although courts are somewhat more inclined to find their relationship valuable to the child.

Ordinarily, a stepparent who has not adopted a child has no obligation to support the child after the marriage ends and neither does an ex lover. An agreement to pay support, however, can be a binding contract, regardless of the biological facts.

If a responsible ex significant other wants to stay in contact with his or her ex's children and they also want the contact, then in most cases, the biological parent should go along with an informal arrangement permitting them to see each other.

A different question is presented as to whether to put such an arrangement in writing. A written agreement from the mother that makes clear that she has agreed to the children visiting her ex-lover will protect him from charges of kidnapping the children and will clarify the situation for teachers and other people who deal with the kids. If appropriate, the agreement should contain clauses that authorize him to consent to emergency medical care for the children, to pick them up after school, and so on.

On the other hand, a written agreement, especially one that extends over a long period of time, might give a former significant other ongoing rights. For example, if you decide to move to another city, your ex could claim that he or she had a legal right to visit with the children and that you were in breach of contract.

Any arrangement that involves more than a simple permission to visit with the children for a brief, specific time, such as a weekend trip to Disneyworld, requires careful thought and drafting.

A parent who leaves his or her children with someone else for a long period may later be accused of having abandoned them, even if the arrangement was good for the children. For example, a mother who is temporarily unable to care for her children because of mental illness or unemployment might agree to let her significant other (or a relative) take care of the children while she gets her life back together. The significant other or relative may later allege that the parent simply abandoned the children with him or her. If the absent parent shows no interest in or care for the children for an extended period of time, the allegation of abandonment is more plausible. A parent who "abandons" his or her children may lose custody of those children.

This sort of long-term arrangement can lead to grandparents, the biological parent, or an ex-spouse making an effort to get custody or guardianship of the children. Where one parent has abandoned the children, the other would likely be awarded custody, in preference to an unrelated ex or grandparents, while relatives would probably be given preference over the former significant other. If, however, the grandparent or other caregiver can show that the children have been with him her so long that it would be in the best interests of the child to stay there, he or she may be awarded custody or at least a temporary guardianship. This is more likely where the other biological parent has not offered to care for the children or been involved in their lives.

QUESTION: *"I have been married twice. My first husband was an abusive bum, but I had two children with him. My second husband is a great guy and became very close to the kids. He and I can't get along, so we are getting divorced. He wants to continue to be a father to my children and I know that would be best for them. What should we do?"*

ANSWER: *If you are certain about your decision, you and your second husband should sign a careful agreement giving him permission to visit the children. The agreement should detail how important he is to them. You and he should also consider going to court and trying to have his rights legally recognized. You should also write a will naming him as the preferred guardian of your children if you should die.*

A person who is not a parent, but has been involved in the children's lives, has almost no legal rights unless he or she has at least a written agreement with one of the children's parents, and ideally, a court order giving him or her specific legal rights. These rights could be in the form of custody, visitation rights, or being appointed as the child's guardian.

Custody or guardianship is difficult for a biological "stranger" to obtain if the children's other biological parent is still alive, even if the "unrelated" adult is the only father or mother that the children have known. The exception is where the other biological parent has had little contact with the children, and the adult in a parental role has formed a close, loving connection with the child or children over a long time.

If this is the situation, you and your ex-significant other need to consider carefully what legal strategy would be best. Legal recognition of the ex's rights can be desirable, for example, if the mother is certain that she wants her ex-lover involved in the children's lives on a permanent basis and the man is certain that he wants an ongoing relationship.

In many cases, it may be better to leave the unrelated adult's relationship with the children based on an agreement by the mother than to go to court prematurely. If the biological father, for example, continues to show disinterest in the children, particularly, if he is not paying child support, the "unrelated" adult's parental relationship with the children will become ever more apparent. The longer and deeper the relationship between a caring adult and a child, particularly in the absence of meaningful involvement by one of the biological parents, the more likely a court is to recognize legal rights on the part of the adult.

It is possible for an "unrelated" adult to seek custody of children to whom he or she is very close, even if the biological parent objects. Similarly, other relatives such as grandparents sometimes ask a court to give them custody of their grandchildren. However, there are legal limits on a court's power to interfere with the biological parents' rights unless they (or one of them) have legally abandoned the child or are unfit to be the child's parent. Showing unfitness will usually require extreme circumstances such as serious neglect, physical abuse, drug problems, a lengthy prison sentence, or severe mental illness. The mere fact that the other adult might be a better parent is not determinative.

Sometimes, however, a court will award an involved adult some rights in regard to the child, such as a right to spend time with the child. These decisions can lead to years of bitterness and squabbling. It is not possible to give good advice in these complicated circumstances, if the adults cannot work the situation out. Tragically, the children suffer the consequences. An adult may be able to leave one long-term relationship and go on with his or her life, but the children have lost an adult who has been an important presence for most of their lives. If an unrelated adult seeks custody of a child and loses, he or she may be excluded from the child's life; if custody is not sought, he or she may still be excluded.

Children flourish best with the care of loving, responsible adults. Your children will benefit if you and your ex-significant other can work out a reasonable schedule for shared custody, visitation, and so on.

Children born of this relationship

Custody and support issues for children born of a couple must be resolved whether the parents were married or not.

No man should acknowledge paternity of a child unless either he is absolutely convinced that the child is his biological offspring or loves the child regardless of the biology. In our current society, DNA testing may be desirable whether the couple was married or not; if the husband does not raise any doubt about his fatherhood of the children, he will be conclusively presumed to be their legal father. Almost all divorce orders contain a finding that the husband is the father of the children, explicitly or implicitly, and it may be impossible to challenge this finding later.

Children born out of wedlock

If the paternity of the children has never been officially settled, then you should definitely do that when you and your ex part. An official determination of paternity makes clear that if one parent should die, the other would be entitled to custody of the children.

If child support is an issue, it is probably to the parties' advantage to reach a written agreement when the relationship ends. Even if you don't need or want support now, your children may benefit from his or her financial contribution in the future. You may wish to accept support payments and save them for the children's private school or college tuition.

The two of you should agree on the financial arrangement in writing. In addition, any such obligation should be guaranteed by your ex buying a life insurance policy on his or her life, payable to you while the children are small and payable to them when they reach 21. Otherwise, if your ex died, particularly if he or she married someone else in the meantime, you might have to sue to protect your children's needs.

Any agreement to pay child support should be conditioned on the father having such visitation rights as he and the mother agree on.

If the mother has any doubt about whether the father of the child will pay the child support agreed on, she should bring a paternity suit and obtain a court order. A court order for child support can be enforced much more easily than a mere contract between the two of you.

If the father has any doubt about whether the mother will respect his rights to visit with the children and play a role in their lives, he should bring a court action to establish his rights and obligations.

If there is no court order about custody, then both parents have equal rights to possession of the children. Consequently, it is usually a good idea to protect yourself from later disagreements by obtaining a formal court order about custody.

If, however, you are the father of the children and your ex-girlfriend is willing to let you have custody of the children informally, then you may wish to think twice about going to court. Unless the mother is found to have abandoned the children, a mother is still likely to be given custody of small children. If she leaves the children with you over an extended period of time, you may have the basis to claim that she has abandoned them, which will increase your chance of being awarded custody.

Children born in a marriage

If the couple were married at the time of the child's birth, the husband is presumed to be the legal father. If there is any question, then the paternity of the child should be legally established in the divorce action.

Custody and support of children are a necessary part of every divorce proceeding. If the parties do not address it, the court will; in fact, most court procedures include an inquiry as to whether there are any children born or expected from the marriage.

Child Custody – the legal mechanics

When the parents of a child cease living together, whether they are married or not, someone has to decide who will have primary charge of the child and who will pay the expenses of raising the child. If the parents agree about these matters, then a court is quite likely to follow their decision, provided there is no clear reason to think that it is not in the best interests of the child. Where there is no agreement, however, courts and their attendant bureaucracies come into play. If the parents are married, the court that decides the property questions in their divorce will also decide child custody and support issues. If the parents are unmarried, the issues are usually raised in a paternity suit.

Sadly, the question in any custody case is effectively how to divide the child between two parents, which can't be done. That said, there are two basic questions in any custody case. The first is which parent becomes the primary parent in terms of time with the child and authority to make decisions about the child. The second is which parent receives less time with the child, less authority to make decisions about the child, and the responsibility of making payments toward the child's support.

The standard in all states for these decisions is the best interest of the child. In fact, of course, the judge's social values, preconceptions about families, and impression of the parents before him or her influence the decision.

Different states use different terms for the division of responsibility and support. Some refer to "managing conservatorship," some to "primary physical custody," and so on. Nearly all refer to "visitation" and "support." Some have abandoned these terms in favor of terms such as "parenting time."

It is vitally important that you acquire the vocabulary of your state in any custody question. Many of these terms do not have the meaning that they appear to have. In particular, "joint custody" does not usually refer to the parents' having equal say in the child's life or equal time with the child. Usually, "joint custody" means that both parents remain involved in the child's life but that one parent has primary custody.

In this book, I use the term "primary custody" to mean that the parent with whom the child spends most of his or her time and who has the authority to make decisions about the child's life, including where they will live, what school the child will attend, and what medical care the child will receive.

In the absence of unusual circumstances, the result in a custody case is likely to be that the mother gets primary custody of the children, and the father pays child support and gets to have the children visit him for a certain number of days each week.

It is possible, but still difficult, for a father to obtain primary custody of the children; to win such a case, the father must usually show not only that he is the better parent but that the mother is unable, or unwilling, to take proper care of the children. For example, a father may try to prove that the mother uses cocaine or that her boyfriends behave inappropriately around the children.

In one case, a father proved that the mother left her two-year-old son alone in the house while she went to meet her lover at a local hotel. The mother claimed that a teenaged baby-sitter was with the child when she left for her rendezvous and that the baby-sitter had gone home without the mother's knowledge. The judge did not believe her. He awarded primary custody of all six children to the father.

In another case, the father proved that the mother was addicted to crack cocaine and that extensive inpatient treatment had been ineffective. He eventually was awarded primary custody. Sadly, although the mother had visitation rights, she seldom exercised them, probably due to her drug problems. That father spent over $200,000 on legal and medical bills to get custody of his young daughter.

Courtroom procedures

In many states, the case will be tried in court like an ordinary civil trial, although the decision will probably be made by a judge, not a jury. The parents and other witnesses will testify under oath. The judge may talk to the children apart from the parents in his office.

The judge may appoint an independent person as an advocate for the children to help guide the court in deciding what arrangement is in the child's best interests.

Some courts have a staff that includes social workers or volunteers to help ascertain the facts in custody disputes.

Prior to the trial, various mental health professionals may be involved. They will interview both the parents and the children. They may demand to observe the children with the parents. They may inspect each parent's home. Under the rules set out by the American Psychological Association, a psychologist who is evaluating the parents should seek independent confirmation of his or her conclusions, which means that the psychologist may want to talk to employers, neighbors, relatives, and teachers.

Most parents find the litigation process intrusive, frightening, and demeaning, as well as appallingly expensive.

These experts, after all, are judging your qualities as a parent, and you don't know what the expert's values or theories about child raising are. A conservative Christian parent may believe that a spanking with a belt is appropriate in raising a child; a liberal psychoanalyst may believe that such "violence" amounts to child abuse.

Some parents have claimed that consultants asked trick questions, such as pressuring a mother to ignore her crying infant "because we have to fill out this form right now" and then later reporting that the mother failed to respond appropriately to the child's obvious distress. Some parents claim that the supposed expert was corrupt or incompetent. These anecdotes should alert you to the need to be well-prepared and careful in any interview or child study that takes place in a custody case. Chapter Fifteen and the Workbook have additional specific suggestions on custody litigation.

Moreover, your friends and relatives may be drawn into the fray. Hearing a (former) good friend testify that you neglect your children and are a slob is painful.

Factors considered

Within the framework of biological and legal relationships, the basic standard for all custody decisions is the best interests of the child. State statutes set out the factors to be considered in deciding which parent should have custody, or primary control, of the child.

These factors include the ability to provide a stable home with appropriate moral values, supervision, love, and care. In some states, courts are permitted to consider whether one parent will provide a more religious environment.

In most cases, the judge will be influenced by traditional middle class values, including a tidy house, clean and neat clothes, a parent who is home enough of the time to provide appropriate attention to the child, nearness to previous school and friends, etc.

If a parent is cohabiting with another person, then the court may consider whether the environment is an appropriate one for the child. In particular, judges may seek to shelter a child from being exposed to immorality, which may mean anything from Mom's alcoholic boyfriend occasionally sleeping over to Mom having a lesbian lover. It is less common now, but still legally possible, for a judge to award custody to the parent whose life is conducted more in accordance with traditional values instead of to the parent who is involved in a non-marital relationship.

The prevailing (more) liberal standard was set out in the case of *Feldman v. Feldman.*[9] In that case, the father discovered that his ex-wife (who had custody) and her boyfriend participated in group sexual encounters and advertised for others to join them in those activities. Their correspondence on the subject, including photographs, was kept in the house. The father asked the court to change custody to him on the ground that the mother was morally unfit. The court said:

> *Immorality, sexual deviation, and what we conveniently consider aberrant sexual practices do not ipso facto constitute unfitness for custody."* In other words, unless the conduct actually harmed or involved the children, the mother's sexual conduct was her own business. The fact that the mother's conduct might set a standard for the child that some people would disapprove of was irrelevant. In other words, the fact that (on some views) the mother would be conveying immoral values to her child was irrelevant.

That standard is a clear change from the conservative view that part of being a decent parent was providing a conventionally moral home life and that the immorality of the parents harmed the children by its mere presence in their lives. Many people still hold the more conservative viewpoint, especially where gay or lesbian parents are concerned.

In 1985, for example, the Virginia Supreme Court held that "the father's continuous exposure of the child to his immoral and illicit relationship renders him an unfit and improper custodian as a manner of law."[10] The term "as a matter of law" means that the father's open homosexuality made him unfit to have custody of his child regardless of whether he was a good father in any other respect. As one law review put it, some judges believe or fear that "if gay parents have custody, they will molest the children; if gay parents have custody, they will turn the children into homosexuals; if gay parents have custody, they will perform sex acts in front of the children; if gay parents have custody, the children will be harmed because of the immoral environment."[11]

It is not clear how many people still have these beliefs about homosexual people. There is no factual evidence for any of them. Objective studies of children raised by a gay parent do not show any evidence of harm to the children; their grades, social development, and so on are as good as or better than an average child raised by heterosexual parents. Some of the outdated fears have been dispelled by these studies.

However, there are some studies that suggest that a child raised by a homosexual parent is more likely to be homosexual or to suffer other problems. Sometimes, the same data is cited on both sides of the issue. To those who regard homosexuality as a perversion or a sin, these studies support the view that permitting a gay parent to have custody will likely harm the child.

Moral values, however, do not always turn on matters of fact. Theoretically, a judge should not base his or her decision on his or her personal religion but on the law. That said, an openly gay parent is probably far more likely to be awarded custody in a more sophisticated urban court than in a smaller town in the Bible belt. The judge's perception of the parent's conduct may not openly influence his or her decision but it may covertly affect the weight that he or she gives to other factors.

If the morality of the parents were really taken seriously by the court, relatively few salespeople, stockbrokers, or businesspeople would ever get custody.

Division of the child

Courts have considerable leeway in how the control of the child's life is apportioned between the various parties. The options range from precluding one parent from having any role in the child's life, or any contact with the child, to a more or less equal division of the parenting responsibilities.

If the parents, whether in a divorce or the resolution of a cohabitation arrangement, draw up their own agreement about custody, they must use legal terminology with great care, as some of the legal terms do not mean what they appear to mean. Some states use confusing terminology such as "managing conservator" and "possessory conservator." The most misleading term is "joint custody."

A good example of this is the phrase "reasonable visitation." Many divorce lawyers encourage their clients to accept a court order that provides for specific support payments but only "reasonable visitation."[12] In other words, the financial obligation is clear but the emotional rights are vague.

Most couples going through the misery of divorce are in no mood to be reasonable. Moreover, "reasonable" is impossible for a court to enforce because what's reasonable to one person is burdensome to another. "Reasonable visitation" can be a code word for the non-custodial parent's being at the mercy of the custodial parent's convenience, generosity, or spite.

A sensible order provides for clear visitation rights which the parents are at liberty to alter by agreement. Specific, clear, terms do not depend on what one angry ex-spouse thinks is "reasonable." If you are denied the specified visitation, the judge can see exactly what was ordered and, with some luck, you can persuade him or her to make your ex follow its terms.

MYTH—"I don't have to worry about custody. My girlfriend promised that we could have joint custody of the kid, so I'll get him half the time and she gets him the other half of the time."

FACT—Joint custody does not mean an equal division of time with the child nor does it mean equal involvement in the child's life. Moreover, the mother's promise does not necessarily control what a court does.

Custody agreements and court orders

Courts can, but relatively seldom do, endorse arrangements where the child truly does have two homes and two parents equally involved in his or her life. This arrangement is often called "joint physical and legal custody." The reason for its rarity is that the mechanics of the child actually dividing his or her time between two different homes and having two parents, who don't live together, with equal legal shares in his or her life are just too daunting. Really conscientious parents can make this work but it takes true cooperation over many years.

More often, the court may award an unequal form of joint custody. In that situation, one parent has primary responsibility for the child. The child spends most of his or her time in that parent's home and that parent has the legal authority to make the important decisions about the child's life, such as decisions about medical care, schools attended, summer camps, etc. The other parent has the right to have the child visit him or her on a set schedule, often for one week night and every other weekend, and has the obligation to pay child support.

The moral of this story is that any agreement or court order about custody or child support should say exactly what you mean. If you intend that each of you will have the right to make medical decisions for the child or take the child to church or whatever, the agreement should say so. If you mean that child support payments can be made in part by paying for the child's expenses, such as dental care or private school tuition or counseling, say so.

Even if you use an attorney to draft such an agreement (and obviously you should), here are some guidelines for your own conduct in a custody dispute:

- ✓ *Be absolutely certain that your attorney or the court does not use any legal terminology that has not been thoroughly explained to you. Remember that legal terms in custody matters do not always have their ordinary meaning. If you don't understand something that is said to you in court or in mediation, say so right then and make clear what you mean.*

- ✓ *Before you begin negotiating, be clear in your own mind and with your attorney about the arrangement that you believe is best for you and your child.*

- ✓ *Many lawyers press their clients to accept an arrangement that is standard in that court. However, what is commonplace and usual to a jaded attorney may not be at all what you want for your family. Insist that your lawyer do his or her job in advocating your position; his or her busy schedule is not a good reason to accept a bad deal for you and your children.*

- ✓ *To protect yourself, insist that your understanding of the terms be spelled out in ordinary language as well as in legalese, even if the attorney assures you that the legalese means the same thing. Remember, it's not the attorney's kid whose life will be affected.*

- ✓ *Be sure that every important aspect of the agreement is written down in the order; oral promises from your ex will be legally worthless.*

- ✓ *Be wary of any assurance that the order can be "changed later if things don't work out." Judges don't like to revisit cases that they have already decided and the odds are against having an order modified, especially if you agreed to it.*

✔ *You need to have a detailed grasp of the reality of your finances, your time commitments (such as business travel), the children's needs, and your spouse's real situation and intentions. You can't make a rational decision based on suspicion or guesses.*

✔ *Remember that child support is calculated based on formulas set out in the law and unless your spouse agrees to less, he or she is likely to be awarded that amount, regardless of how impossible it seems to you. Check that the formula is properly applied (and that the arithmetic is right). Be sure that all factors are taken into account. Do the computations yourself.*

✔ *Try to compromise in the best interests of your children and keep your personal bitterness toward your ex out of your children's lives.*

✔ *Try to deal with any foreseeable changes in your situation now. If you know that your job is shaky or if you are planning to make a career change, try to make sure that those eventualities are dealt with in the order, if at all possible. Otherwise, you may find that you are effectively stuck in your present job.*

✔ *If at all possible (and if you really want meaningful involvement in your child's day to day life), insist that the parent with primary custody will not move the child more than 25 miles from his or her present residence without permission of the court and that such a move will constitute a material change in circumstances entitling you to ask the court to reconsider the custody question.*

✔ *Similarly, ask that the order provide for both parents' being involved in such decisions as where the child will attend school, medical procedures, and so on. Ask that the order include express provision for both parents to receive medical records and information, school records, and so on.*

✔ *Make sure that open communication is expressly provided for in the order, including your rights to telephone your child (and his or hers to call you), email, correspondence, etc. Email has made efforts of one parent to deprive the other of communication with the children much more difficult.*

✔ *Finally, ask for any limitations that are important to you, such as that cohabiting with a person of the opposite sex will be a material change in circumstances or that the child will attend parochial school or church.*

Judges are busy and most believe that children do better when matters are settled once and for all. Therefore, judges do not like to reopen questions of custody. Moreover, the proposed uniform statutes on child custody provide that the original order should not be changed unless there is a material change in the circumstances.

That provision was designed to keep disgruntled and vindictive parents from endlessly re-litigating custody issues.

Also, judges do not want to be involved in distasteful disputes over the parents' conduct after the divorce. However, if certain conduct is expressly made relevant by the court order, such a prohibition on a homosexual relationship in the child's home, then the judge will be more likely to reconsider custody if the question comes up later.

In other words, a judge may be willing to sign an order that if the living arrangements of the child change in a particular way, the court will consider it as a material change in circumstances, if the parents agree to that provision being in the order. When a material change in circumstance occurs, the question of custody can be reopened. Consequently, if the order specified conduct that will be a material change in circumstances, the parent who does not have primary custody may have more control over the situation.

You need to be realistic about your situation, including your past conduct. If you are a sales representative whose job takes you out of town three days a week, the judge may understandably believe that you are not in a position to have primary custody of the children. You either need to acknowledge the problem and negotiate for more visitation or explain how you will compensate for being gone, such as showing that you live with your parents who are devoted caregivers for their grandchildren.

Jeffrey Leving counsels "The strategy for divorcing dads seems obvious. If you have been hovering at the edges of your children's lives, it's time to get down on the floor or out in the park with them."[13] He advises divorcing fathers to "Prepare for single fatherhood well in advance of the separation" by learning how to take care of a household and by making arrangements for childcare.

 MYTH—*"The court order says that my children will visit me on Wednesday nights, every other weekend, and two weeks in the summer. That means that my ex can't move away because my visitation would be impossible."*

FACT—*Wrong. Most courts now recognize that parents move around, and most do not regard moving to a distant state as a material change in circumstances.*

If the parent who wants to move away can convince the judge that he or she has a good reason to do so, then the judge will probably not change the custody order, except to reduce the amount of time that the other parent has with the child. In other words, the moving parent achieves exactly what he or she often wants which is to deprive the other parent of meaningful contact with the children.

A parent who sees his or her child for a month in the summer has a much more distant and uninvolved role than one who sees the child every Wednesday and many weekends. Moreover, the summer month may interfere with the child's desired plans for the summer, such as going to the same camp as his or her friends. The non-custodial parent may be faced with the fact that visiting him or her is a major disappointment to the child.

Child support

One of the most bitter hangovers of divorce is the payment of child support. A parent, usually a father, may find a third to a half of his income owed every month to a woman that he now may dislike, even after she has remarried a wealthier man.

Each state calculates child support differently. Traditionally, the judges considered a variety of factors, including income and the standard of living that the child would have had if the parents had not divorced and set an amount based on their own prejudices. In some states, such as Arizona, if the parents spend essentially equal time with the children, then each parent is paying for an equal share of the expenses and neither should have to pay child support to the other parent.

Today, almost all support decisions involve a statutory formula. Usually, a statute or court rule sets out an exact formula. These formulas involve primarily the number of children, the non-custodial parent's income, the custodial parent's income, and other factors. These other factors may include child care and medical expenses; while the formulas are relatively rigid, these additional considerations may give the judge some leeway in setting the exact amount.

Some of these formulas are quite complicated. It is worth your while to familiarize yourself with your state's formula before any mediation or hearing on the issue of child support. For example, the amount may be based on the "combined adjusted gross annual income." It is vital to understand each component of that factor. What adjustments count? What counts as income? Often other components of the child's actual expenses may be added to or subtracted from the basic amount of child support that was calculated based simply on income and number of children. You need to make a list of everything that you are paying for that benefits your child, including especially things like health insurance. Your busy lawyer may overlook a factor that entitles you to a reduction in the amount to be paid or an increase. Remember he or she may be quite conscientious but he or she is not going to be writing those monthly checks.

Child support is one area where many states offer excellent online information, including programs to calculate how much the support payment is likely to be. There are ten pages of tables to establish a starting point for calculation of the child support obligation. For example, the Arizona Supreme Court has published the Arizona Child Support Guidelines "to give parents and courts guidance in establishing child support orders and to promote settlements [of child support disputes]."[13]

According to Jeffrey Leving, author of *Father's Rights*, "Census Bureau data indicate that more than 90 percent of fathers with joint custody pay child support on time and in full."[15] Leving and other advocates for the parental rights of fathers argue that figures about nonpayment of child support are exaggerated. The fact remains, however, that the child support part of divorce orders is rigorously enforced from those able to pay and that the child visitation part is seldom enforced and then not vigorously.

Many non-custodial parents are unpleasantly surprised to find what percentage of their income will have to be paid in child support. Typical baselines are around 15 to 20 percent for one child, 20 to 30 percent for two, and so on.

Sometimes, the statutes provide for a ceiling, i.e. a limit on the dollar amount that a court can require to be paid, so that a wealthy parent will not be paying an exorbitant amount.

The exact amount can be varied depending on the parents' income, although the judges' discretion must be based on the facts. A professional ball player with a multimillion dollar yearly income is not going to be required to pay 20 percent of those millions for support of his illegitimate child. On the other hand, a wealthy person may be required to pay more than the maximum amount because it seems reasonable for the child of a rich person to have a lifestyle that appropriately reflects his or her parent's financial status.

Child support awards can be modified if circumstances change. In most cases, remember that child support obligations end when the child reaches age 18, unless the child is disabled or the parent has been ordered to pay for a college education.

MYTH—*"If I have to pay child support, my ex has to use the money solely for my child's benefit."*

FACT—*The person paying child support has little or no right to control how the money is spent. Most courts regard the mother's use of the money for ordinary household expenses, including clothing for herself or a car, as acceptable.*

Paying child support does not give that parent any right to determine how the money is spent or even if it is spent directly on the child's needs. There are many instances in which the father believes the mother is spending his child support payments on her own needs or even on luxuries for her new boyfriend. If the child is not being neglected, the courts will not intervene to compel the mother to use the money in a prudent or even appropriate way. The reasoning is that the parents in an intact family have the right to spend their money as they see fit, and a single parent has a similar right even if she is spending money provided by her ex. (This discussion is primarily in terms of the father's making support payments and the mother's having custody because that is still the usual arrangement.)

MYTH—"If I buy something for my son or pay some of his expenses, I can deduct those amounts from my child support payments."

FACT—No. Child support payments must be made in money (and not in kind), usually to a state agency, unless the court's order expressly provides otherwise.

This dangerous myth has gotten many conscientious fathers in deep trouble. Angry at what they see as their ex-wife's misuse of the child support payment (or eager to win the child's affection with presents), the ex-husband will pay some expense directly, such as buying the child's back-to-school clothes or paying private school tuition directly to the school. Then, he deducts the amount from the monthly support check.

Regardless of how much he spends, his child support obligation remains exactly the same and cannot legally be reduced by these payments unless the court order says exactly that. The spouse with custody can invoke all the remedies of the law against the "non-paying" spouse. The fact that the money was actually spent for the child's benefit is no defense, unless the original court order granting custody expressly says that the payments can be made in this way.

Moreover, the ex-wife's consent to these substitute payments is also no defense. She can quite cheerfully agree to let the father spend money on the child and then demand the child support payments in full; he will be required to pay the full amount regardless of whether his ex-wife agreed to a different arrangement.

QUESTION: *"My ex-wife knows that I have been planning for several years to quit practicing neurosurgery and become a potter. If I close my medical office and open a pottery studio, with the court reduce the child support payments to what I can afford in my new job?"*

ANSWER: *No. Judges are markedly unsympathetic to parents who make career decisions that will reduce a child's standard of living.*

Remember the basic principle – once the legal system is involved in your life, you are no longer free to make the same decisions that you could before. A parent who is not divorced is free to live his or her life as he or she chooses, subject to providing the essentials to his or her children. A parent who is under a court order to pay child support does not have the same liberty.

Some angry ex-husbands, outraged at paying a large percentage of their income to a an ex-wife that they now hate, have quit their jobs or announced a sudden intention to enter a new, much lower paying, career. Some judges have put them in jail for contempt of court.

Many of the penalties for nonsupport are now automatic, such as suspension of driver's licenses and professional licenses. Because the collection of child support is now often through a state agency, even the wife's consent to her ex-husband's career change, won't immunize him from these and other penalties. The judge can still find him in contempt of court and send him to jail until he pays or makes arrangements to pay.

(This intolerance of career changes is, in my opinion, inconsistent with the courts' tolerance of a custodial parent's decision to move to a distant state on a whim. If a mother with custody can decide to effectively negate her ex-husband's visitation rights by moving across the country to go to school, why can't he negate the support payments by making the same decision? But, philosophical consistency is not necessarily a hallmark of the judicial system. Or, to be fairer, you could say that the system is more concerned about money than love.)

A judge should not sentence a non-custodial father to jail who genuinely cannot pay the child support, such as where he has lost his job through no fault of his own. However, the judges hear so many sob stories from fathers who want to escape their obligations that the courts tend not to believe any of them. A remarkable number of fathers who tearfully plead their poverty as an excuse not to pay child support, suddenly "find" the money when faced with a long stay in the county jail.

The moral of the story is twofold for parents who are making child support payments. First, if a change is imminent in your life at the time that you get divorced, such as that you are planning to go back to school or your employer is about to go out of business, try to have that eventuality provided for in the court order.

If you can see that your marriage is ending, you may wish to make any contemplated lifestyle change before divorce proceedings begin. That way, you may have a better chance of persuading the judge that the change is permanent and not a mere spiteful effort to deprive your ex and children of a decent lifestyle.

Second, if something unexpected happens after the court order has been signed, such as that you lose your job, take action at once to have the order modified.

Here are some things that you should consider doing:

✔ *Inform your ex of the situation in writing.*

✔ *Contact the agency to which you make your child support payments and find out what you should do. Inform that agency in writing, and in detail how your financial circumstances have changed. Sometimes these agencies can guide you through the steps to avoid the worst consequences of nonpayment.*

✔ *Immediately file a motion to have the court order changed to reduce your obligations.*

✔ *Gather all the records that you can to show what you can pay, when you might reasonably hope to get another job, and how long it will be to your next paycheck. You will need these to convince the judge that you are not a deadbeat.*

MYTH—"If the judge orders me to pay too much to my ex, I'll just file for bankruptcy."

FACT—Most family obligations are not dischargeable in bankruptcy.

Bankruptcy is a complicated field of its own. However, in 1994, Congress reformed the Bankruptcy Code to keep spouses from escaping family obligations in the bankruptcy court.

Specifically, child support and alimony obligations are not discharged in bankruptcy. That means that those debts continue to be valid, unlike, for example, ordinary loans. Here's where the legalese can change your life, for better or worse. For purposes of the bankruptcy laws, "alimony" means support payments for a former spouse, not periodic payments as part of a property settlement.

Obligations based on property settlements, however, may be ended in a bankruptcy[16] the court will look to see if the debtor has the ability to make the property settlement payment and if the harm to the spouse who is owed the payment outweighs the burden on the debtor spouse.

Consider this hypothetical case. George and Jane get divorced. George owns his own small business. They have one daughter, Georgette, who is 12. George agrees to pay Jane $150,000 over five years for her community interest in his business. The court orders him to pay $1000 per month in child support until Georgette is 18. After two years, the business fails and George files for bankruptcy. George has $10,000 in the bank, but he tells the court he needs the money to reorganize his business. Result: George still has to make the remaining child support payments, but his payments to Jane may end. His debt to her is canceled, just as some of his other personal and business debts may be.

MYTH—*"If I have more kids with somebody else, the judge has to reduce my support payments to my first family."*

FACT—*Maybe, if you don't have enough money for both families. The court can reduce the support payments but it is not required to. If your income is sufficient for both families, the court need not reduce the child support payments.*

Judges can modify child support payments to meet a variety of changed circumstances. If a parent gets a better job after the divorce, his or her payments can be increased. If he or she loses a job or becomes disabled, the payments can be decreased. If a child develops a medical problem and needs more care, the payments can be increased.

However, these are matters of the court's discretion. If a parent has sufficient resources to pay the child support as ordered and to support his or her new family, then the judge need not order a reduction. If the parent cannot pay the support ordered and also meet his or her obligations to the new family, then the judge may reduce the payments.

For example, in case of *Gilley v. McCarthy*, Renee and Paul had an affair when both were married to others.[17] Renee and her husband later got a divorce but Paul stayed married to his wife. Renee had a child fathered by Paul, who also had two children at home. She brought a paternity action and asked for child support. Paul admitted that he was the child's father. He asked the court to compute the child support based the state formula which involved his income and the fact that he had three children – two in his home and one living with Renee. The court applied the guidelines for non-custodial parents with one child. The court reasoned that the guidelines applied to the number of children living in the single parent's household. Only one of Paul's children (which was Renee's child) didn't live with him. Paul could use his obligations to his other children to argue that he couldn't afford to make the payments, but the original amount was calculated as if he had only one child to support.

The difference may sound trivial but it can mean a lot of money to Paul and Renee. If Paul makes enough money to support his first family and to pay the full amount of child support ordered to be paid to Renee, then he will be paying that amount. If Paul and his wife had divorced, then he would have been paying more total in child support but less to Renee because the court would have allowed for the fact that Paul had to support three children of whom he did not have custody.

Moreover, courts are reluctant to reduce child support payments where the decrease in the parent's income was voluntary. For example, if a person reaches retirement age and his or her company requires him to retire, then the reduced income can be grounds for reducing child support. If he or she voluntarily takes early retirement, however, the court may refuse to reduce the child support payments.

MYTH—*"My ex-husband makes it impossible for me to use my visitation rights, so I don't have to make my support payments. He always has some excuse when it's my turn to have the kids."*

FACT—*Wrong. The obligation to pay support for children and the right to time with those children are independent legal facts.*

It may be unfair but the right to see one's children and the duty to support them are legally separate. Court-ordered support payments continue to be obligatory, regardless of the other spouse's conduct. A parent is not entitled to cut off support payments to punish the other spouse for some supposed misconduct.

The only solution to use when a custodial parent interferes with the non-custodial parent's visitation rights is to go back to the court and ask the judge to enforce the order or to change the custody arrangement. The judge can hold a parent who repeatedly thwarts the court's orders in contempt. Some judges will go so far as to put the stubborn parent in jail until he or she complies. [18] If the conduct is extreme, such as moving away without letting the other parent know where the children are, the judge may change custody to the more innocent parent.

Regrettably, judges see so many bitter wrangles between divorced parents that many are reluctant to take any meaningful action to enforce the non-custodial parent's rights. Again, in the legal system, money can be more important than love.

QUESTION: *"My kids refuse to come and stay with me on the weekends when I have visitation rights. My ex is telling them that I'm too strict and they don't have to put up with me. Do I still have to pay support?"*

ANSWER: *Yes, you still have to make the support payments. However, you may have grounds to have the support payments or custody modified.*

The duty to pay support continues even if the child refuses to visit you. If your child truly does not want to visit you, then most courts will not order the child to do so, at least if the child is old enough to make a reasonable decision.

However, the custodial parent had an affirmative duty to see that the court-ordered visitation is carried out. As one judge put it, a mother with custody "must do more than merely encourage the minor children to visit" their father. Until the children could make a true independent and affirmative decision not to visit him, their mother had to obey the court order to deliver the children to him.

Some judges now take seriously the concept of "parental alienation syndrome." That syndrome exists when one parent, often with the help of a new spouse, systematically "brainwashes" the child to dislike or fear the non-custodial parent.[19] Malicious conduct to that degree can result in the court changing custody to the other parent.

Enforcement of support orders

Society has come to believe that the nonpayment of support is a national problem. Some advocates for father's rights dispute the magnitude of this problem and point out that fathers who actually have adequate visitation with their children usually pay their child support.

A variety of new legal mechanisms enforce the payment of support orders. None of them work perfectly, but the burden of collecting the support has to some extent shifted from the custodial parent to the government. The theory is that children receive more support and parents have less opportunity to use nonpayment as part of their ongoing bickering.

Perhaps the most important change is that support payments are made to the state agency, not directly to the custodial parent. In principle, this means that enforcement procedures can begin more or less automatically if the parent doesn't pay. These agencies are not inclined to listen to whining and complaints from the parent obligated to pay child support. The custodial parent is no longer in the position of having to call and complain that the support check is late or less than ordered. He or she, in theory, does not have to call the lawyer to start enforcement proceedings.

In some states, an employer must deduct support payments from the parent's paycheck. In the past, this taking, which is called "garnishment," only occurred after court proceedings; now it is more or less automatic.

Moreover, other mechanisms help to enforce the support obligation. Any income tax refund can be applied to past due support. Professional licenses, such as medical, law, and electrician's licenses, can be suspended for nonpayment of support. In some states, a parent who is behind in his or her support payments cannot get hunting or fishing licenses.

A parent who is sufficiently angry and determined not to support his or her children can still escape his or her obligations. However, it requires greater sacrifice, including frequently changing jobs or working "off the books" so that the garnishment does not work.

Remember, however, that these mechanisms, however, are only in effect to enforce court orders. If the support payments are being made pursuant to an agreement between the parents, these legal mechanisms don't apply. Consequently, the mother of a child born out of wedlock should seriously consider bringing a formal paternity action so that any promised support payments can be enforced effectively.

Custody struggles – when disagreement becomes crime

When a person who loves a child loses a custody battle to another person, whom he or she often now hates, it is tempting to take the child to another state and start over.

That is a really bad idea, even if the parent is willing to live a secretive existence for the rest of his or her life. Most states now make violating a custody order a felony. Being in jail is a more permanent separation from the child than any loss of custody.

Under the federal Parental Kidnapping Prevention Act, the FBI investigates cases where one parent takes his or her child away from the custodial parent. A parent's taking the child, however, is not the federal crime of kidnapping. (Kidnapping is taking a child for "reward or ransom." An unrelated person who is tempted to snatch a beloved child should be aware that his or her conduct may be prosecuted as kidnapping and that he or she may have a difficult time establishing that it was not for "reward or ransom.")

In other words, a parent who snatches his or her child away from the other parent, in violation of a custody order, commits a state felony and the FBI will investigate the crime.

There is a parallel structure for parents who flee to other countries or who bring their children to this country in violation of a custody order entered in another country.

Under the Hague Convention on the Civil Aspects of International Child Abduction, the child's home country has jurisdiction to decide custody questions under its laws. A United States court will honor the other country's jurisdiction by ordering that the child be returned to that country, and a foreign country should do the same.

Moving the child to this country does not automatically change the child's home country which is the country where the child has had his or her primary residence.

In the United States, the International Parental Kidnapping Crime Act makes violating child custody orders a crime, even if the order was entered by a court in a foreign country, although there are some limits on this law.

Persons who marry someone from a different country should remember that other countries have different traditions and laws from the United States and that those laws will probably apply if the couple lives in the other country. In particular, some countries still strongly favor the father's right to custody of his children.

Moreover, not every country is a party to the Hague Convention. Even if another country has signed that treaty, once a child is in a foreign country, it may be pragmatically impossible to secure enforcement of a custody order that is inconsistent with the mores and laws of that country. The United States is not going to invade another country to retrieve a child from a parent who has violated an international treaty.

Disputes over child custody

Custody and support fights are among the ugliest possible forms of litigation, damaging to both parents and children. There is more information about these battles in Chapter Fifteen and in the Workbook.

However, assuming that you are a legal parent of the child, the chief question is whether to keep possession of the child or leave the child with the other parent. Many experts believe that the person who has possession of the children when the disputes begin will probably end up with custody.

It is, however, customary for the man to move out of the family home and leave the mother and children in the house. Some advisers strongly recommend against this because the person who is willing to leave the children may be seen as having less interest in being with them. What the father may have seen as a temporary solution to an intolerable living situation often sets the pattern for the eventual court decision.

Consequently, no matter how awful your home situation is, think long and hard before you move out without your children if you want custody of those children.

If you do leave the children with the other parent, make every effort to stay in regular touch and to be a responsible parent. Remember that until a court order is entered, you have an equal right to be with your child.

On an analogous point, most lawyers believe that the person who gets to the courthouse first will probably win; hence, if you want custody, you should keep possession of the children, assuming that you are able to care for them, and file for divorce. Then, you can seek an interim order that confirms your rights.

Remember that this advice does not apply if you are not legally a child's parent. You do not have any right to take a child that is not yours without the legal parent's permission. If a beloved child is being abused or neglected, you need to involve the appropriate social service agency.

Mechanics of splitting up

This section discusses some of the actions that you need to take to formalize the end of your relationship. The first sections below cover some of the business aspects of splitting, whether the relationship is a marriage or not.

Couples who can foresee that there is going to be a major dispute will also need to get ready to present their respective cases. See Chapter Fifteen as well as the Section "Breaking Up" on page 617 of the Workbook which cover that process. The legal aspects of divorce and litigation are discussed later in this chapter as well.

Whether or not you have a written agreement, here are some items that almost always have to be decided:

- ✔ *What happens to the lease or mortgage payments? Who's going to stay in the apartment/house? Who's going to move and when?*
- ✔ *Who gets the furniture/TV/boat/RV?*
- ✔ *Are there financial things that need to be split or the titles changed? Bank accounts? Stocks? Bonds? IRA's? What happens to them?*
- ✔ *Anything else?*
- ✔ *Any debts? Credit card bills? Loans to each other?*
- ✔ *What will be best for the children?*

Peaceable splits

This section offers guidance to couples who remain on reasonably amicable terms, even if the relationship is ending. The amount of work that needs to be done depends on how entangled your financial affairs are with those of your significant other.

If you have a cohabitation or prenuptial agreement, the first step is to find the signed copy of it. (You **did** keep a copy of the signed document in a safe place that you could remember, didn't you?) When you find the agreement, review it. You may be surprised at how much you have forgotten about its terms, and some of those surprises may not be pleasant ones.) Like, you forgot that if you put the new Jaguar in her name alone, then it belonged to her. Oops. Or, you forgot that the agreement that seemed like such a good idea 10 years ago when his business wasn't worth anything now means that you don't get a share of that business.

Now that you know what the terms are, you can start splitting the blanket (or not, depending on what the document actually says). You will need to make a list of any significant items that you think need to be taken care of or divided of. It might be a good idea to make a copy of it for your former significant other. If you are on civilized terms, then you can sit down together and work through your list of stuff to be done/divided.

If you have any significant assets in common, you need to change the title on them to reflect current realities. If they are in both your names, then you both own an interest in them and you will both have to concur in the title change. The bank or title company or motor vehicle department will not take the word of one of you alone.

Remember that what you have done to memorialize the relationship, needs to be undone. Have you made a will naming your beloved as an heir? Then you need to revoke it. A will is revoked by destroying it (although your lover might later claim that the original was lost and his or her photocopy is still a valid will), by writing "revoked" across the pages, or by making a new will that expressly revokes the old one. It is safest to make a new will. If you have executed powers of attorney, again these need to be revoked or new ones written, naming someone else to act for you.

If you don't have a written agreement with your ex, then you need to work out what financial arrangements seem fair to both of you, in light of your respective needs, any understanding that you had, and your respective contributions to the relationship, as well as any other factors that the two of you think are relevant.

Specific checklists of matters to be dealt with are in the Workbook.

When things are not (entirely) amicable?

Everyone has heard of vicious, mutually exploitative divorces. Relatively few non-marital arrangements become quite that legally nasty when they come apart, although some palimony suits come pretty close. Disgruntled ex-lovers and ex-spouses may stalk, harass, or even assault the former partner.

Prudent salvage — the paperwork

Here are some strategies for maximizing your chances of coming out of the relationship whole, assuming that you have not been completely careful all along. Be honest, now. Detailed suggestions are in the Section "Breaking Up" in Workbook.

The first step is to secure everything that belongs to you alone. Be sure to change the PIN on any of your accounts to which your significant other has access. Take out your share of any joint accounts. Move your possessions (or those of your ex) out of the shared home.

Until a court order controlling the situation is signed by a judge, you have the legal right to peacefully enter any place that you have legal access to and peacefully retrieve your belongings. You do not have the right to break into you ex's house or apartment, for example, but you usually have the right to go into a house that you own part of or an apartment where you are on the lease.

Few circumstances legally justify physical violence; you should avoid heated confrontations. Your washing machine is not worth being arrested for, whether you are trying to take it or trying to keep your ex from taking it.

Second, make sure that no more debt is added by your significant other. If you are the primary party on a credit card account, you can (and probably should) cancel your lover's card. If possible, you should cancel all joint credit card accounts.

Third, you need to get copies of every record that concerns anything that you can make a plausible claim to and put them out of your lover's reach. This includes bank account statements, -- titles, deeds, and brokerage account statements. It is prudent to get copies of all applicable documents as soon as you sense that the relationship is troubled. Otherwise, some of these may disappear or be harder to get when you have moved out.

Fourth, you need to notify banks, mortgage companies, credit card companies, etc. of any claim that you have or action that you want them to take. For example, if you and your lover have bought a house together and both of you are on the mortgage, you should request the company to send duplicate statements, one to each of you.

That's so you can pay the mortgage if your lover doesn't. If your cohabitation agreement provides that you are entitled to a share in a brokerage account, for example, send the brokerage firm a certified letter notifying them of your claim and enclose a copy of the cohabitation agreement. Ask them not to disburse any funds until you receive your share.

You should send these notices unless you completely trust your lover and you are on extremely friendly terms.

Obviously, you don't need to do this with regard to accounts that are in your name alone, which is another reason to have separate accounts.

Financial institutions may or may not honor your requests, depending on the nature of the account and your claim, but at least you'll have tried and they'll be on notice of your claims. Sometimes, if an institution is on notice of a claim to an asset, they will freeze the account and not allow anyone access to it; sometimes, they rely entirely on the names on the account. If the account is in your lover's name alone, however, no responsible institution is going to give you the funds until you have a court order telling them to or until your lover voluntarily transfers your share to you.

Part of the process of prudently separating from an angry ex is to gather the information that will help you to evaluate and support your position later, if things get more heated. You can use your document copies to make your points in informal negotiations with your ex-lover. You can also use them to support your case in mediation and to help your lawyer evaluate your case. More detailed information is in Chapter Fifteen and in the Section "Breaking Up" in the Workbook.

More steps to protect yourself – joint assets

Joint accounts and shared living accommodations (with shared furniture and appliances) present special problems.

Here is the honorable (in my view) way to split from a significant other whom you now intensely dislike but whom you still regard as a reasonably civilized human being. What I mean by honorable is that you take reasonable steps to protect yourself without taking vicious or underhanded actions that really demean your own integrity.

✔ *If there is a joint bank account that was intended to pay household bills, use the funds to pay off any joint debts such as credit card bills that the two of you (be honest now) ran up for joint expenses. Don't use so much of the money that you strip your significant other of money that he or she needs to make it to the end of the month or to make other expected payments.*

✔ *Also take sufficient money out of that joint account to cover your expenses until your next payday unless you have sufficient separate funds to cover them.*

✔ *After you have done the above, then take out your ownership share of any joint account.*

✔ *Take enough furniture, dishes, appliances, and so on, from the joint household (in addition to your own separate possessions) to set up a new household. Again, don't deprive your significant other of enough to live with, unless you paid for everything and believe yourself entitled to it.*

✔ *If there is an asset from the relationship that you absolutely need and that is in both your names, like a car that you use to go to work, make sure that you have access to it. Park it in the garage where you work (if you have the pass card to the garage or other control over removal of it) or park it someplace else that is safe.*

✔ *Don't take anything that clearly belongs to your ex or that is in his or her name alone.*

In other words, first pay the joint bills, then provide for your immediate future needs (and your significant other's), then take your share.

Remember, however, that if the car is in your lover's name alone, in the eyes of the police, he or she owns it until and unless the title is changed or you get a court order giving you possession. Don't take the chance of being arrested for auto theft. The legal hassle will cost you a lot more than the hassle of not having a car. Leave the car with your lover unless he or she gives you written permission to drive it. Buses and even cabs are cheaper than lawyers.

✔ *Make plans to move someplace else if you know that your significant other needs the apartment or house where the two of you lived, as for example if he has custody of his children and they are used to the house.*

When things are really ugly.

Sometimes, relationships not only dissolve in a blaze of hurt feelings but in a flurry of financial recriminations or even physical violence as well.

Some additional steps can be taken to prepare for a split where you have reason to believe that a bitter financial dispute is inevitable or that you are at risk for serious harm. These range from the prudent to the despicable and dishonest. Obviously, more extreme measures for your self-protection are justified if you ex has threatened you with physical violence or other harm, or if you reasonably suspect that your significant other is planning to cheat or exploit you.

Here are some steps to consider, based on your values and the situation:

- ✓ *find a new place to live, in advance, and furnish it. Prepare for the change, such as by moving, unobtrusively, enough dishes, appliances, etc. there to set up a new, separate, existence or by hiring a moving company for a day when your soon to be ex will be at work.*

- ✓ *alternatively, if you own the house or are on the lease alone, pick a day when your significant other will be away and prepare to exclude him or her from the formerly shared living quarters. You could, for example, move all of his or her stuff to a storage unit or other safe place and have the locks changed on the doors.*

- ✓ *use joint funds (or any other legally available money) to pay off any bills that you might later be stuck with, including income taxes, credit cards, etc.*

- ✓ *use any credit card or account on which your significant other is liable to prepare for your new life. This can be particularly relevant in a prospective divorce; the debts will probably be divided equally, so your ex may end up having to pay some of the cost of the furniture for your new apartment.*

- ✓ *use joint funds (or any legally available money) to pay your attorney's retainer and a hefty advance on any likely legal expenses.*

- ✓ *take appropriate steps to secure your possession of the children.*

- ✓ *use great discretion in discussing your plans with anyone.*

It is unwise to go overboard in these maneuvers. If you are excessively greedy, the court may require you to pay your ex back or may otherwise penalize you in any property division. Also, of course, if you take money that you are not entitled to, you will be required to reimburse your ex. Similarly, if you cause financial harm to your ex, such as by putting his or her furniture out in the rain or on the sidewalk where it can be stolen, you could be liable for the damage you have caused.

Extra care needs to be taken with money from business accounts. It is theoretically possible that taking money out of those accounts could be the crime of embezzlement, just as taking money from your significant other to which you are clearly not entitled could be theft. Even if you manage corporate finances, the money is not yours.

The steps for preparing for a divorce are basically the same as for a split between an unmarried couple.

If you are a parent to a child, you can legally take the child with you to a new abode, provided that there has not been a court order entered. Moving the child hundreds of miles away, however, will probably not change the jurisdiction of the court where you lived before and may create an unfavorable opinion of you in the judge's minds. In other words, your ex can probably still go to a local court to file for divorce and custody of the children. If you can prove that your ex poses a serious threat to you or your child, however, more drastic measures may be justifiable. The question is not whether you are simply afraid or vindictive; the question is whether your fears are well-founded and you can prove it.

Anyone who is leaving a troubled relationship needs to be very careful about the person to whom they confide their plans. The best course is usually to keep your plans to yourself, except for discussing them as needed with your therapist or lawyer.

The lack of loyalty or good sense in a trusted confidant can come as a painful surprise. Your best friend, your mother, or your sister may blab to your significant other about your plans. Sometimes, these indiscretions are motivated by a sense of obligation to your soon to be ex. Sometimes, the indiscrete person may believe that he or she is helping to "save" the relationship. Sometimes, the blabbermouth just can't keep a secret or "forgets" that the information was confidential. Regardless of the other person's motives, you may lose whatever advantage or safety you were seeking.

Once litigation begins, try to remain calm in court and outside the courtroom. Ranting and raving may be natural but are unhelpful. If you cannot control your temper around your ex, avoid him or her. Sit in a different part of the courtroom and avoid any chance meeting in the hall or elsewhere. Decline any invitations to meet with your ex unless your attorneys are present.

Whether you fear your own temper or that of your ex, you can take refuge in a restroom until your ex has left, assuming of course that you are of opposite sexes. Avoid lingering in hallways or parking lots.

If you fear violence from your ex, you are safest in the courtroom itself. Most judges have a peace officer who is called a "bailiff" and whose job is to keep order. He or she will probably restrain your ex from causing a disturbance or assaulting you. If you have been assaulted in the past by your ex, your lawyer may with to alert the bailiff that there may be a problem.

Most courthouses now have metal detectors and other security measures. These offer some protection from guns and other weapons in the courthouse itself but will not protect you in a parking lot or elsewhere. You may wish to consider riding to the courthouse with your lawyer or, if you are going alone, in a cab so that you do not have walk to your car after any hearing.

QUESTION: *"I want to really ruin my lover. He broke my heart. What can I do to really wreck havoc?"*

ANSWER: *Ex-lovers do astonishingly mean things to one another, ranging from witty inflictions of poetic justice to vicious, heartbreaking harms. Few of the latter are acceptable actions by a decent human being.*

The ancient proverb that "hell hath no fury like a woman scorned" is truthful, if sexist.

The leading literary example of amatory vindictiveness is probably Medea. In ancient Greek legend, she and the hero Jason were lovers, and they made sacred promises to each other. When he left her to marry a princess, she killed their children and served their bodies to Jason in a farewell dinner.

Injury to children in order to punish a spouse is sufficiently common that it has a name – "the Medea complex." Both men and women are guilty of these appalling actions.[20]

Mean-spirited destructiveness is unworthy of a moral person. Think about whether you would want the next person whom you love to know what you have done. Do you want to reveal what a despicable lowlife you really are? How will your children regard you if they become aware of your spitefulness toward their father or mother? Would you want to be treated as you propose to treat your significant other? Would you want your children to take comparably cynical actions toward you, when you are old and dependent on them?

On the other hand, sometimes retribution is justified and satisfying, provided at least that it does not involve harm to the innocent.

Remember that if you exceed your rights and gratuitously injure your lover, including his or her finances, you may be liable to him or her in damages. In other words, if you maliciously keep him or her from selling a stock in a timely way when you really didn't have any rights to the stock, then you might be liable for the loss that he or she suffered. If you really provoke a battle, he or she may retaliate by charging you with a crime, such as theft or malicious destruction of property (vandalism). In particular, it is prudent to steer away from taking any action to inflict harm on computerized information as you may be violating new laws designed to protect such information.

Frankly, I decline to advise you on how to lie, cheat, and steal your way out of a relationship. Even giving examples might provide a road map for the slimy. There is, however, one urban legend that I cannot resist.

Legend has it that a young woman in Philadelphia was unceremoniously dumped by her boyfriend. He told her that he was going on a long business trip to Japan and she should have her things out of his apartment when he returned. When she finished packing, she used his phone to call the automated time number – in Tokyo – and left the phone off the hook, thereby running up one of the world's largest toll calls, on his bill. She later claimed that she just wanted to check the time so she could call him and say goodbye; leaving the phone off the hook, she explained tearfully, was a pure accident, caused by her being too upset to think clearly.

QUESTION: *"I found a canceled check to a divorce lawyer in our checking account statement. We've had a few arguments but I thought that things were pretty much OK. What should I do?"*

ANSWER: *Assume the worst. Immediately secure your share of any assets, including transferring a reasonable amount of money to a separate account, and seek legal advice.*

If your significant other has sought legal counsel, he or she is not only contemplating leaving but is likely planning to leave on less than friendly terms.

Some father's rights advocates believe that husbands are typically clueless about a wife's unhappiness and divorce plans. Some women's advocates believe that wives tend to be taken completely by surprise by a husband's announcement that he is leaving for another woman. (Usually, of course, there have been signs of discontent in the relationship that one spouse has chosen to ignore or has denied the significance of.) There are books that advise husbands and wives, respectively, how to cynically prepare for divorce without regard to honesty, fairness, or the best interests of their children.

Some divorce lawyers are experts at designing strategies to cause as much mental pain and financial distress as possible, all in the name of protecting their client's rights. They make a lot of money implementing other people's anger and viciousness. Usually, the battles that these lawyers foment result in misery to both spouses, regardless of who eventually "wins."

It pays, therefore, to exercise some prudence to make sure that you are not about to become the victim of a vindictive or dishonorable lover. For the sake of the relationship, you should try to address any problems before they reach the stage of irreconcilable hatred. However, regardless of your view of the relationship – good, bad, or indifferent -- if you have any indication that your significant other is thinking about leaving, you should act to protect your own assets, including being sure that you have sufficient funds in a separate account to live on and to hire a lawyer, if necessary. In particular, if anything in the family's checking account records, calendars, phone messages, etc. indicates a meeting between your spouse and an attorney, you should prepare yourself for a legal battle.

In one case, a socially ambitious woman had long wanted to be the chairman of a high society charity ball. To reach her goal, she needed the backing and money of her eminent husband, whom she no longer cared about. Therefore, she maintained a pretense of being reasonably content in their marriage. Smiling, she sat next to her husband at the elegant banquet and waltzed around the dance floor with him. The following Monday morning, as her husband was leaving for his office, she handed him a sheaf of legal papers. Her lawyer had been working behind the scenes, and a judge had signed a preemptive order excluding the husband from access to the house, the children, the credit cards, the cars, and the bank accounts, all without any advance notice to him. The wife (who had hung on her husband's tuxedoed arm at her party) had secretly claimed to the court that her husband was emotionally abusive and would probably hide "her" assets if not strictly prohibited from touching them. Deprived of cash and credit cards, and without access to anything in the family home, the prominent victim couldn't buy a meal or put on a clean shirt and ended up sleeping for some days on a friend's couch. He had trouble getting the order reversed because initially he didn't have any money to hire an attorney. Eventually, after the two of them spent a fortune on expert witnesses, lawyers, and therapists for their children, the couple ended up with approximately the shares that they would have gotten without the wife's malicious conduct.

Fortunately, these ploys do not succeed as often as they once did. However, the first person to the courthouse often does gain a substantial strategic advantage. Remember judges often are disinclined to alter the initial arrangements for custody, child support, and occupancy of the family home. At the very least, if one spouse gets a court order, the other has the difficult task of persuading a judge to change his or her mind.

The most vicious strategy in a divorce is to falsely accuse a spouse of abusing a child, especially sexual abuse. These accusations became so common at one time, however, that sophisticated judges now tend to be suspicious of them. A false claim can, and should, lead to the court denying the liar custody of the children and awarding the bulk of the family's assets to the innocent spouse. Even sleazy divorce lawyers hesitate to encourage their clients to make these claims unless there is good evidence to support them.

QUESTION: *"My husband secretly hired a lawyer and filed for divorce. I got served with an interim court order that kept me from seeing the kids, using our credit cards, etc. Do I have to obey it?"*

ANSWER: *Yes. Unfortunately, even an unlawful court order is binding until the court changes it.*

Sometimes, people are so outraged by receiving an unfair court order that they ignore it. That's a bad idea. No matter how unjust you think the order is, a court's decision is normally controlling until a court changes it.

In other words, if you defy, for example, a restraining order that tells you to keep away from the family home, you will quite likely be arrested when you show up on the doorstep. If you show up in a screaming rage, you will add support to your ex's claim that you are dangerous.

Moreover, you can be held in contempt if you take an action forbidden by the court order, such as taking money out of a joint account. Being held in contempt can result in a fine or even a stay in jail, neither of which will help your situation.

In all likelihood, you will damage your case if you defy the judge's decision. He or she may have acted perfectly properly, regardless of how unreasonable the outcome seems to you. A judge is not inclined to look favorably on someone who flagrantly disobeys a clear instruction from the court.

If you are truly broke, and literally cannot live without using your credit cards, for example, do so as judiciously as possible and be sure that any use is clearly for necessities, such as groceries, and not for expensive restaurant meals with a date.

The only safe solution is to promptly hire an attorney to challenge the order, even if you have to borrow money to do so.

Usually these interim orders provide for a hearing in a relatively short period of time. Your first order of business is to locate an attorney to appear for you. However, it is critical that you attend that hearing even if you have not had time to hire an attorney.

You must make the effort immediately to get your act together, regardless of how dismayed or shocked you are. Showing up in court without having organized yourself will suggest that you don't need much consideration. The judge's allocated time for preliminary hearings is usually limited and often the court will not hear live testimony from witnesses.

Here are some of the basic things to do:

✓ *make a concise list for yourself of the key problems that the order presents for you and why it is not fair;*

✓ *go to the courtroom early and watch how things are handled in that court so you have some idea what the procedures are;*

✓ *be prepared to explain to the judge concretely the realities of your situation. Have the relevant facts and figures clearly organized. Assure him or her that you will hire an attorney and explain why you haven't yet;*

✓ *gather as much evidence pertinent to the order as possible before the hearing.*

For example, if you need the family car to get to work, bring your pay stub to show where you work and explain that there isn't any bus service to your place of employment. For another example, if all of your money is in a joint account with your spouse, show the judge a copy of an account statement and ask that you be given access to enough money to find a place to live and so on. Point out that the statement shows that you deposited your paycheck in that account.

Even if your spouse has all the records, a bank, for example, will usually be able to give you a duplicate copy of an account statement or similar record. Remember that you may be able to get the relevant information on line if your ex has not changed the password on the account.

At the very least, ask that the judge apply the terms of the order to your spouse on the same basis; if you can't use the credit cards, then neither should he or she. Unless your ex has good evidence that you are dishonest or that he or she has special needs, an equal order is a reasonable request; if the judge grants it, your ex may suddenly realize that he or she can't live with those restrictions either. With luck, the result may be a fair modification of the initial order.

QUESTION: *"My significant other turned out to be a compulsive gambler. He has lied to me about everything. What should I do?"*

ANSWER: *Gather up everything that you have a claim to and get out of the relationship.*

In my view, if you discover that your significant other is dishonest, for whatever reason, and has been cheating you (financially), you should take everything to which you have any plausible claim. This is especially true if you discover that his or her dishonesty stems from substance abuse or compulsive gambling. In that situation, you must act immediately to salvage what you can.

Even if you decide to stick with the person and support him or her through treatment, you need to protect yourself (and your children, if any) financially. If nothing else, your significant other will need money for treatment and, if necessary, lawyers. Your children still need a college education.

Therefore, immediately after you discover the sad facts, do the following:

✓ *take all of the money out of joint accounts and put it in new accounts in your name alone.*

✓ *cancel joint credit cards and change the PIN number on any account that your significant other has access to. Check any and all records, including county deed records, if necessary to make sure that there are not debts and mortgages that you don't know about.*

✓ *take all valuable assets (jewelry, antiques, cameras, big screen TV's, boats) that you own jointly or have a legitimate claim to (such as things that were given to you both or that you bought during your marriage) and put these assets someplace safe, such as a storage unit.*

You have to use good sense here. Don't put your valuable stuff in your mother's garage if you know that your husband has a key or that your mother wouldn't call the cops if he broke in.

Again, however, don't take anything that clearly belongs to your significant other unless you have a good claim to it, such as that it was bought during your marriage or both your names are on the finance agreement.

From a psychological perspective, sometimes staying in a relationship can be a matter of an unhealthy codependence or even enabling destructive behavior, rather than pure love and loyalty. You may be saying to yourself that you are staying out of love or loyalty and that may be partly true. However, your conduct may be helping your spouse or companion to continue his or her behavior. For example, you may be the one who makes excuses, such as "Sorry we can't come to your anniversary party, Mom. Fred has the flu" when in fact Fred is passed out on the couch.

Your leaving may be the clear message that your significant other and you both need to hear, i.e. "I will not stay here and help you continue your destructive/illegal behavior." A substance abuse counselor or group such as those affiliated with Alcoholics Anonymous can help you sort out the emotional components of your behavior as well that of your significant other.

QUESTION: *"My significant other is an accountant. She has been charged with securities fraud. What should I do? Her firm is paying for a lawyer to defend her."*

ANSWER: *Get your own lawyer immediately.*

QUESTION: *"I found a coffee can full of cocaine in our attic. I knew my husband was using but he promised not to keep it in the house. What should I do?"*

ANSWER: *Take the children and leave, immediately, and get a good lawyer, also immediately. Alternatively, exclude your husband from the house and get a good lawyer.*

If your spouse or lover has been charged with a financial crime, such as securities fraud, or a serious drug offense, such as possession with intent to sell, there is a great risk that you will be investigated and possibly indicted also. In these situations, you immediately need good legal advice from a lawyer who specializes in criminal defense work.

Unless you are completely convinced of your significant other's innocence, the prudent thing may be for you to leave the relationship, or at least your shared home, at once.

You need to consider the depth of your relationship, the degree of commitment that you have to each other, and the effect of this conduct on your children. Among other things, will you stay connected with this person if it turns out that he or she is convicted of a crime and goes to prison? Some wives and husbands loyally stand by an erring spouse, even when it puts their own professional career in jeopardy. Others feel so betrayed and endangered that they head directly to the divorce courts.

One major factor needs to be the fact that your significant other has put you in harm's way without, we trust, telling you about the situation.

If dealing in controlled substances or high dollar illegal gambling is involved, you absolutely need to leave the house, at once, that moment. Anything that you do can be construed by the police as aiding in the offense. Not only that but your significant other is possibly involved with some dangerous people who could harm you as part of a disagreement with your lover.

Anyone who is involved with a person who has a substance abuse problem involving illegal substances or unlawfully obtained prescription drugs should keep in clear focus the fact that his or her significant other is engaged in illegal conduct by possession of the drugs, even if he or she is not dealing. Trivial, but true and sometimes over-looked. The tendency is to focus on the dependent person's need for treatment and so on. But, their actions involve crimes, and their addiction may lead them to endanger those they love.

First of all, your significant other's drugs may appear to be in your possession. The coffee can in the attic could belong to anyone in the house. A prosecutor may believe that you must have been involved, especially if you are using drugs too.

With or without realizing it, you may have fostered a crime that is under investigation, such as by running an errand or taking a phone message. If the FBI videotapes you driving a car that has a kilo of cocaine in the trunk, it is going to be difficult, if not impossible, to prove that you were just going out for cigarettes, especially if you test positive for cocaine use.

Second, as everyone knows, some users get involved in dealing drugs, either to support their own habit or simply because they are moving in that milieu. A person who abuses prescription drugs can be led to forge prescriptions or, in the case of a professional such as a dentist, physician, or veterinarian, to write improper prescriptions for himself or herself or for a relative. You don't want to be involved in these crimes, even to the extent of, for example, picking up a forged prescription at the pharmacy.

In the Enron and Dynergy corporate scandals, at least one lover and one wife ended up with criminal charges arising from their involvement in their significant other's activities. When easy money is pouring in, it is very tempting to help hold the bucket.

Third, financial crimes often lead to tax evasion charges. A spouse who signed the erroneous tax return may well also be charged with criminal tax evasion; he or she will need to show that he or she was completely unaware of the criminal activity and believed the return to be accurate. For married couples, this may be a good reason to file separately; if you have filed jointly, consult a good tax accountant/attorney. He or she may recommend filing amended returns.

Fourth, the money that your lover put in your joint accounts may have been earned by his or her criminal activity. Sometimes, the government has the right to seize property of any kind that the investigators reasonably believe is either the fruit of a crime or being used for criminal purposes. Assets that you and your significant other own jointly may be seized by the government, regardless of your claim to part of them. Boats, cars, money, and even houses can be taken on this basis.

The owner of a seized asset has to prove both their innocence and their ownership before they get their property back. Proving this can cost more than the asset is worth. Your new car, for example, could be tied up in court until its value has declined markedly, and you still have to make the payments.

Usually, if the government has not seized a joint account, you can and should take your share out of the account and put it in a separate account, provided that your share is money that you separately earned. You will need money to pay your own attorney.

Ideally, however, you should get legal advice before you do anything because, once you are aware of your significant other's problems, any action that you take could involve you further. For example, if you discover that your significant other is dealing drugs, your taking some of the cash from his desk might be considered to be sharing in the proceeds of illegal conduct. In particular, destroying records can be a separate criminal offense, as is lying to an investigator or otherwise hindering the investigation. It is entirely possible to be convicted of an incidental offense, such as obstructing justice, even when the prosecutor cannot prove that you committed the larger, more substantive offense.

Think style guru Martha Stewart here – she was being investigated for securities law violations that she and friends allegedly committed by profiting from insider information about a company. She was never convicted on any of those substantive offenses; in fact, some of those charges were dismissed. She still went to jail, however, basically for obstructing the investigation into the securities fraud issues by lying to investigators.

Your significant other's lawyer represents him or her; usually, it is not a good idea for two people to have the same lawyer. However, sometimes it is beneficial for both parties to coordinate their defenses.

Where the prospect of prison and a criminal record are involved, you should raise the money for a good lawyer, even if you have to sell your house, your car, or your jewelry. Borrow from friends, max your credit cards, get a second job, whatever. You can reassemble your financial life much more easily without a criminal record.

Moreover, if you cannot pay his or her fees for a lengthy trial, your lawyer may well pressure you to plead guilty. Many prosecutors are indifferent to whether they send an innocent person or a guilty one to jail (or even to the death chamber), partly because they have convinced themselves that anyone who is investigated must be guilty and partly because, in terms of their own careers, a conviction is a success, whether the person in jail is innocent or guilty.

Justice in the United States is very expensive, especially for the innocent.

Dealing with an abusive significant other

If your lover is physically or emotionally abusive, provide for your physical and emotional health immediately. **Leave**. If you have time to plan ahead, gather what money you can and arrange for an alternate place to live. But in any event, go! Seek a battered persons' shelter. Do whatever you have to do to be safe. If you cannot think of anything else, go to a social service agency like the Salvation Army, explain your situation, and see if they can provide you with temporary shelter or refer you to an appropriate shelter. Then, get counseling. Seek counseling or psychotherapy that helps you move on with your life and, ideally, helps you avoid finding another abusive lover in your future.

If you have been assaulted, and the damage is visible, have someone take a picture immediately of your injuries. Do not wait until the black eye fades or the bone mends. You may need to show the pictures to the police if you want to prosecute, to a court to get a restraining order, or to yourself when you start thinking that he or she was not so bad.

Get whatever legal protection is available to put a stop to abuse, stalking, or harassment.

If you are emotionally battered, write down an account of what happened—what does he or she say? How do you react? How does this make you feel? If your lover's conduct regularly makes you feel worthless or helpless or full of rage, leave. The relationship is an unhealthy one and you need to be elsewhere. Painful as it is to remember these events, you may need a diary to refresh your recollection later if you need to go to court.

Enforcing a cohabitation agreement

If your lover is a complete rat fink and totally violates your agreement, then you have basically two options. The first is to salvage what you can immediately and write the rest off so that you can get on with your life. The second is to try to enforce the cohabitation agreement.

If you put an arbitration clause in the agreement, then you can invoke that. If your lover obeys the agreement and a date is set for arbitration, then you need to prepare your case and present it to the arbitrator. Although arbitration proceedings are supposed to be informal, you will need to be well organized and have the documents to support your claims, if at all possible. It is wise to get an attorney at this point if the money really matters. If your lover hires an attorney, you should definitely hire one. Arbitrators are often former lawyers or influenced by legalistic maneuvers.

If you lover ignores the agreement, you may have to file suit to force him or her or to go to arbitration.

If you did not put an arbitration clause in your agreement, or if you don't have a written agreement, then you will need to file suit to recover whatever you can from your ex. Good luck. Litigation between former lovers is a miserable and often humiliating business. Oral agreements are hard to prove and may not be valid. You may really believe that she lovingly promised that if you put her through medical school, she'd give you half of the profits from her practice for five years, but in court she may well portray you as an abusive parasite whom she has finally seen her way clear to getting rid of. If you are a woman, you may be portrayed as a gold-digging whore.

Conclusions and Advice

In disassembly of a relationship, the party who acts most promptly and diligently has the best chance of preserving his or her legitimate rights. In the worst case, sitting on your hands only gives your soon-to-be ex an opportunity to plunder the bank account, run up the charge cards, and generally make your life a mess. Under the best of circumstances, he or she has the opportunity to improve his or her chances of coming out better than you.

The best course is to get clear, accurate information about your rights and take prompt, reasonable, and fair action to protect them.

(Endnotes)

1   *Peterson v. Peterson*, 595 S.W.2d 889 (Tex. Civ. App. – Austin, 1980), writ dismissed), cited in Pamela George, *Texas Marital Property Cases* (Imprimatur Press, Dallas, 2004), at 191.

2   In *re marriage of Partyka*, 511 N.E.2d 676 (ill. App. Ct. 1987), quoted in *Understanding Family Law*, at 416.

3   Uniform Marriage and Divorce Act, § 308; discussed in *Family Law; Examples and Explanations*, infra, at 203.

4   Commentary to Uniform Marriage and Divorce Act, § 308; quoted in *Family Law; Examples and Explanations*, infra, at 203.

5   *Weber v. Weber* 589 N.W.2d 358 (N.D., 1999)

6   Robert E. Oliphant and Nancy Ver Steegh *Family Law; Examples and Explanations*. Aspen Publishers, New York, 2004, at 214 – 215.

7   Uniform Probate Code § 2-202. See *Understanding Family Law*, supra, at 71.

8   There are some rare cases involving a promise to buy life insurance that are too complicated to set out here.

9   *Feldman v. Feldman*, 358 NYS 2d 507 (App. Div. 1974).

10 *Roe v. Roe*, 324 S.E. 691 (Va. 1985)

11 See Leving, *Father's Rights*, infra, for details on what can and should be considered in a custody order.

12 Leving, infra, at 77.

13 Jeffrey Leving with Kenneth A. Dachman, Ph.D., *Father's Rights* (Basic Books, New York, 1997), p 49.

14 *Arizona Child Support Guidelines*, adopted by the Arizona Supreme Court, January 1, 2005.

15 11 U. Dayton L. Rev. 275, 324 (1986).

16 United States Bankruptcy Code, 11 U.S.C.A. §§523(a)(5) and 523(a)(15)(b)

17 *Gilley v. McCarthy*, 469 N.W. 2d 666 (Iowa, 1991)

18 See *Smith v. Smith* 434 N.E.2d 749 (Ct.App. Ohio 1980), cited in Hill and Emanuel, at p. 139.

19 See Richard A. Warshak, *Divorce Poison: Protecting the Parent-Child Bond from a Vindictive Ex* (Regan Books, New York, 2003)

20 L.A. McClosky, "The "Medea complex" among men: the instrumental abuse of children to injure wives" in *Violence Vict.* 2001 Feb; 16(1):19-37; Steward Flory "Medea's Right Hand: Promises and Revenge" *Transactions of the American Philological Association* (1974 -) Vol. 108, 1978, pp. 69 – 74

Chapter Fifteen

TRUTH, PROOF, AND EVIDENCE — LOVERS AND LAWYERS

This chapter deals with disputes that are likely to go to court. In any family dispute, the interaction of the law and the relevant facts is complicated. Small bits of evidence, coherently organized, can create a convincing picture that wins or loses the case.

In this chapter, by the way, the word "court" is used to refer to any formal decision process; it includes an arbitrator or mediator if the parties have agreed to one of those processes. In every dispute, the best prepared and most aggressive party tends to come out with the best deal.

This chapter assumes that there is a significant amount of money involved (or that there are children involved) and that either you and your significant other cannot agree on the division of that property or you want to see what the evidence might look like before making an agreement.

Since you now feel that your case might not be amicably resolved, you will need an attorney. Even if you and your lover work out your differences, you should consult a lawyer. If you don't, you may relinquish rights that you didn't know you had.

This chapter and the relevant sections in the Workbook will help you organize the documents and information that your attorney will need to give you good advice. Gathering this information in advance may also save you some money in attorney's fees, since your discussions can be better organized and more focused. You may be able to bring key documents to the initial meeting, for example. See Chapter One for guidance in dealing with attorneys.

As an attorney, I was often surprised by how nonchalantly some clients took their cases. Sometimes, their version of the facts seemed so transparently, obviously, true to them that they couldn't imagine that any fair person wouldn't agree with them. Sometimes, they had not been honest with themselves about the adverse evidence (the facts that didn't support their story). These clients often refused to do the work they needed to do to help me prepare their cases for trial.

Summary of lawsuits and mediations

The mechanics of lawsuits and mediations are way beyond the scope of this book. However, you need a basic understanding of the mechanics to intelligently follow what's happening.

All lawsuits have four basic parts. The first is the commencement of the legal proceedings by filing a complaint with a court. Second, there are the various legal maneuvers by each side, including the exchange of information. Third, the case is decided, either by a court or someone else. Last the court's decision is embodied in a written order that governs the parties' relationship from then on. (Of course, there can also be appeals and other proceedings later).

After the lawsuit is filed, the parties can try to work out a compromise of any disagreements they have. Often, the court will encourage (or require) the parties to work with a mediator to see if the case can be settled.

Many mediations and arbitrations have much the same outline. One party starts the process, usually by a letter requesting it. Each side presents his or her position to the mediator or arbitrator. There is a decision which should be made in writing.

One difference is that agreements made in mediation are just more contracts. These aren't court orders. Similarly, an arbitrator's decision isn't a court order either, especially if it is an informal decision by, say, your minister. To enforce a mediated agreement, you have to go to court.

Mediation and litigation are often mixed together. Many family disputes, even if there is a court proceeding, are resolved by a mediator. In that situation, the parties' agreement is set out in a court order, just as if there had been a trial.

Sometimes parties to a contract have agreed to mediation or arbitration but refuse to go through with it when there is a dispute. In that case, there has to be an abbreviated lawsuit to force that person to the informal process. Similarly, sometimes a disappointed party refuses to accept the results of the mediation or arbitration. In that case, there has to be litigation also to finally straighten things out.

MYTH—*"Judges and juries often make ridiculous decisions that any sensible person can see are nuts."*

FACT—*Court cases are, by their nature, disputes where both sides have evidence to support their story. Most jurors and judges are as sensible as the rest of us – they are us, after all.*

Everyone has heard stories of court decisions that seem patently absurd. Sometimes, as Dickens said, "the law is an ass." Sometimes, witnesses lie convincingly and the jury believes the wrong side. Sometimes, judges are dumb or prejudiced. Frequently, however, the person telling his or her tale of woe is not recounting all the facts. Anyone who has lost a court case is naturally feeling bitter, angry, and wrongly treated.

Sometimes, the jury may have attached great importance to a bit of evidence that seemed irrelevant to the person telling the story of the case. Facts that seem trivial and commonplace become important in a trial.

These facts can be seen in common law marriage cases. Judge Russell Austin, who has presided over many such cases, observes that juries have been persuaded by "a letter addressed to 'My darling wife;' a holiday card embossed with the words 'For my wife'; a card accompanying flowers stating 'to the best wife a man could have'; and a note written on the back of a grocery receipt stating 'damn it wife, leave me alone.'" A simple greeting card may not seem important in daily life, but it can provide the crucial proof that a man regarded the woman in his life as his wife.

(Most) judges and juries try to make the right decision. They look at the evidence from both sides, using their own common sense, the law, and more or less common social customs and values.

Going to court

There are three cardinal rules to remember if you are involved in a personal dispute that might possibly go to court:

- ✔ *There really are two sides to every dispute.*
- ✔ *A bad settlement is often preferable to a good case.*
- ✔ *Assuming that the law and facts are not flat out against you, the best-prepared party usually wins.*

Truth, justice, and reality – both sides now

Most of us have strong opinions about a variety of things, ranging from questions of religion to which football team is best to whether vitamin C will keep you from getting a cold. Most of the time, we can concede that other rational people may disagree with us.

When our deepest feelings are involved, however, conceding that we do not have unique access to the truth is almost impossible. In a family dispute, even the most even-tempered person may become angry and fanatical, utterly unable to see that the person opposing him or her has anything plausible to say. Family disputes not only involve our present emotional issues but also issues from our childhood and previous relationships. The ex-spouse or ex-lover comes to appear as a completely selfish, dishonest, and exploitative liar.

Sometimes, it is true that one party to a relationship is a completely self-centered, immoral, dishonest, drug-addicted bum. Far more often, however, the other person is more or less like the rest of the world – somewhat selfish, not always completely honest, and dealing with his or her problems as best as he or she can.

The fact is that in any trial, evidence will be presented on both sides and it is at least possible that the jury will believe the other side. You may be completely unable to imagine that anyone could fail to see that your opponent's witnesses are lying, but, whether they are truthful or not, the jury may believe them. The inability to acknowledge this fact of life is the main reason that people who have lost a case are quick to say, "The judge was paid off," or "The psychologist was a crook" or "The jurors were all unemployed idiots."

Therefore, it pays to assume that your ex-significant other will have a reasonably plausible case and to prepare to meet that case. If he or she really is a complete liar, then you will be prepared to prove that. If it turns out, however, that he or she does have a claim, then you will be better prepared to win or to reach a reasonable settlement.

Here is the difference between truth and proof and evidence. No human being has access to the absolute truth about a complicated human situation. Evidence is that accumulation of people's testimony and documents that tends to illuminate your relationship. You may not like the other side's evidence and you may not think that anyone should believe it. Regardless of your conviction, the judge and jury have to be convinced – that's proof.

Settlement – the art of compromise

Good lawyers often encourage their clients to settle their disputes. There are three good reasons for this practice. First, the client then has some control over the outcome. Disputes over money are often decided in court on a winner-take-all basis, and therefore, it is sometimes better to take less than you are entitled to and be certain of getting at least that amount. Second, the attorney may understand that there are unsettled legal issues or that the opposing side has some good evidence. Third, a compromise without a trial can save the clients hundreds or thousands of dollars in legal fees and expenses. For example, a child psychologist who is hired to testify about what a good parent you are may charge $300 an hour and expect to be paid for every moment that he or she is in the courthouse, including the time that he or she spends waiting around to testify. The money that you don't spend in court may be money in your pocket, especially since sometimes one party ends up having to pay the other side's attorney's fees and expenses.

Child custody cases present different reasons for settlement. First, the mere fact of a protracted and bitter battle between the parents is damaging to the child. Second, the child needs both parents and, except in the most extreme cases, both parents are probably going to continue to be involved in their children's lives. Hence, the parents might as well start to work now on trying to get along.

QUESTION: *"My lawyer says that we might lose on a point of law. Does that mean that she doesn't know what the law is?"*

ANSWER: *Yes and no. Contrary to the popular image that law is like the Ten Commandments, written down clearly on tablets somewhere, it is often unclear how the law applies to a particular human situation in all its complexities and ambiguities.*

QUESTION: *"My lawyer won't tell me whether we will win or not. I think that he just wants more money."*

ANSWER: *Maybe, but the lawyer who could consistently predict the outcome of a case would never lose one.*

A trial is like a live play with no script. The outcome depends on how 12 people from the community see the evidence on a particular day. Maybe a witness, who told a very convincing story in the lawyer's office, changes his or her testimony on the stand. Maybe a key document is legally flawed as evidence.

Also, as you now know, the law of family relationships is in flux.

Be prepared

From the moment that you first sense that you and your significant other may disagree radically about the legal consequences of your relationship, you need to give some thought to how a case might eventually be presented.

MYTH—"I don't have to go through all this hoopla because we are going to mediation (or arbitration)."

FACT—In both mediation and arbitration, the more aggressively prepared party usually does better.

Arbitration is essentially a trial to a private judge. You still have to present your case in a coherent, persuasive way. The arbitrator may be an attorney and should apply the same rules of law as a judge would.

Mediation is supposed to be settlement discussions that are guided by a skilled and neutral third party. Many mediators, however, psychologically pressure the parties to reach a final settlement on the day of the mediation. In the face of that pressure, often abetted by your lawyer, you will have a hard time making a rational decision if you are not well prepared ahead of time. How can you decide what rights to give up if you don't know what your rights are?

Often, the mediator will encourage the parties to settle by pointing out the risks of losing in court. You can only evaluate that risk by having your evidence and legal points ready and accessible in advance of the mediation.

Therefore, do not allow your attorney, or any one else, to hurry you into mediation or arbitration. If there really is a deadline, such as a contract provision or a court order, then work hard to get your case together. The primary responsibility falls on you; your lawyer doesn't have to live with the outcome of your case.

Being prepared has three facets:

✓ *having a basic understanding of the applicable law.*

✓ *adjusting your behavior to maximize your chance of winning.*

✓ *gathering and preserving evidence*

Understanding the law

You can gain some understanding of the law by reading this book and by doing your own research on the internet or in a law library. That said, your best source of information on your legal position is an experienced, careful lawyer.

As discussed in Chapter One starting at page 25, you can use your research to organize your understanding of the law and then use that work as a checklist to talk to an attorney. For example, if your research suggests that common law marriage might be an issue in the case, then you can intelligently ask the attorney what the rule of law is in your state in your situation. For example, the law might have changed since this book was written.

Taking action on your own based on your understanding of the law can have disastrous consequences for your case. Suppose, for example, that you believe that you are the father of your girlfriend's child in Delaware. You read in this book that unwed fathers have equal rights to custody. An internet site tells you that unwed fathers can take the child any time they want and have a better chance of getting custody that way. So, you tell the mother that you will pick up the kid at daycare and drop him at her house later, but you grab the kid and move to New Mexico.

Unfortunately, your conduct can land you in jail. If you are not in fact the father of the child, you may have just kidnapped someone else's child, which could get the FBI involved.

Even if you are the biological father, you have shown the judge that you are impulsive and untrustworthy.

It is important to realize that being mistaken, about the facts or about the law, is not usually a defense for wrongful actions. In other words, if your action is illegal, then you may be convicted of a crime, whether or not you thought that you had a right to take that action. Your good intentions, if anyone believes them, may lessen your sentence, or move the district attorney to drop the charges (if you are very lucky), but may be considered irrelevant.

Suppose, for example, that you believe that your lover promised to give you the car. One night, he drops by your apartment and drives the car to his new place. You retaliate by driving the car back to your place. He reports the car stolen. If the title is in his name, you could be arrested. Yes, you may later have a good lawsuit for breach of his promise to give you the car. Nevertheless, you may also have to defend yourself from the criminal charges, post bail, and so on.

Adjusting your conduct

One of the hardest things to do if you are entangled in a bitter relationship dispute is to try to imagine how your conduct "now" will be viewed by strangers "later." Your emotions are in turmoil. You are hurt, angry, or betrayed. You are excited or terrified at the prospect of the birth of a child or the ending of a marriage. You are overwhelmed. You want revenge.

It's hard to keep in mind that smashing your ex's home theatre system to smithereens may be enormously satisfying now but make you look like a violent and unstable person to a jury later. If you were on the jury, would you give custody of a sweet little girl to a man who kicked in the door of his ex wife's house while brandishing a pistol? Well, maybe, if he was trying to rescue his daughter from a bear that happened to be in the house with her, but otherwise, you might well feel that he was dangerously out of control.

To the extent possible, you must strive to act rationally now. Take out your rage at the gym or deal with it in your therapist's office.

Obviously, you need to refrain from any criminal activity, such as physical violence toward your significant other or anyone else. You won't get custody of your children if you're in jail and you won't be able to enjoy your share of the property either.

You will usually improve your chances of winning in court by behaving as a decent human being who deserves to win his or her case. A general guideline is this — act like the person whom you would like the jury to see you as in court, keeping in mind the possible prejudices of a judge or jury. A little revenge might seem like a sweet idea now, but you should take the longer view.

There are relatively few lawsuits for slander or libel, but they do occur. Slander is saying something false and damaging about a person while libel is saying it in print. Accusing a professional, such as an attorney, doctor, or psychologist, of unethical or dishonest conduct can damage his or her practice and get you sued. Therefore, any notice letters that you send should stick to your claim and not characterize your lover's conduct.

Here are three suggestions that may help you adjust your conduct:

✓ *If you are seeking to enforce a cohabitation agreement against your former lover, for example, do not rush into a new cohabitation relationship. It may be difficult for a jury to believe that you were really relying on your previous lover's promises of support if you have already fallen into the arms of a new lover. (More bluntly, to a conservative jury, you may look like a whore or a gigolo.)*

✓ *If you are planning to seek custody of your children, then be a responsible parent now.*

✓ *If you believe that you are entitled to a share in your lover's business, where you previously worked, then act like a person who owns a share of the business. Offer in writing to continue to do your job there, for example. If you have a project for the business under way, then make a reasonable effort to complete it on time and properly.*

✓ *Try to refrain from irrevocable actions until you are in a calm frame of mind and have gotten advice.*

This advice does not mean be completely passive, however. You also need to think about what legal, appropriate actions you can take before trial to protect your own interests. The previous chapter and the Workbook sections on common law marriage, splitting up, cohabitation agreements, and child custody contain suggestions as to actions you can take to protect your own interests.

Robert Seidenberg, a bitter father who has fought hard for custody of his children, argues passionately that a father should never move out of the family home nor give up physical custody of the house or the children. He claims, based on his own experience and that of other men in various support groups, that moving out peacefully simply convinces a judge that you don't really feel entitled to anything. He does caution men to avoid any physical confrontation, however.[1]

The key to success may be to get to court first; hence, if things are deteriorating badly, go to a good lawyer and get to work on your case yourself immediately. Don't wait to be served with papers. Don't waste your time griping to your buddies. Get your case together and get to court. Judges hate to change their minds; the first party who gets an order entered in his or her favor stands a much greater chance of winning.

What counts as evidence and proof

Evidence consists primarily in people's testimony and documents. That testimony can come from the couple themselves or from other witnesses, such as their families and their acquaintances. Independent experts may also be called to testify.

A witness is a person with personal knowledge of the facts who is competent to testify. Very small children are often considered as not competent to testify. People have "personal knowledge" when they have seen something "with their own eyes" that is relevant to the case.

Tangible evidence comprises documents or other things that show the facts. For example, if you are suing for custody on the ground that your ex-girlfriend is neglecting your child, then the child's school and medical records can be relevant. School records may show that the child seldom went to school and medical records may show that he or she didn't receive proper vaccinations.

The rules that govern what evidence may be considered by a judge or jury are different from the considerations that make a document useful in understanding what is going on. For example, an affidavit is often not admissible in court because the rules of evidence may require that the person testify live. However, the affidavit can show what the witness is likely to testify to later. It can be persuasive in negotiations. Similarly, the rules of evidence might exclude some document as being hearsay or not admissible for some technical reason. Again, however, the document may contain important information that will influence negotiations, mediation, or arbitration.

A mediator is not bound by the rules of evidence at all. An arbitrator need not observe them as strictly as a judge and may ignore them. Consequently, don't worry about technical rules of evidence now.

Relevant evidence is testimony or tangible evidence, such as a piece of paper or a photograph, which tends to show that a given claim is true or false. A greeting card sent by a man to a little girl and addressed "to my darling daughter" could be relevant evidence in a paternity case because it shows that he considered her his child. It might establish that he acknowledged her as his child.

Don't forget that the law includes factual assumptions called presumptions. These are a kind of evidence; the fact is considered proven unless it is clearly disproved. The strongest presumption is that the most recent marriage is presumed to be valid. So, the courts will assume that the last in a series of marriages, common law or otherwise, is the valid one.

Finally, the standard of proof required in a courtroom varies depending on the issue at stake. In criminal law, a person can only be convicted by proof beyond a reasonable doubt. In civil law, which includes marriage laws, the standard of proof is usually by a "preponderance of the evidence." That is a much lower standard of proof than beyond a reasonable doubt. Many judges explain the preponderance of the evidence standard by analogy to a pair of scales; "preponderance" means that there is just enough relevant evidence, as the jury sees it, to tip the scales one way or the other.

Sometimes, however, the law requires a standard of proof that is midway between "beyond a reasonable doubt" and "preponderance of the evidence." That standard is by "clear and convincing" evidence. Under that standard, the evidence has to make the matter plain. That standard is applied in some cases where a parent's rights are being involuntarily terminated.

The rules of evidence and the standards of proof are the province of lawyers. If you gather all the evidence that you can, you can begin to make an informed decision about your legal situation; whether you can prove it or not is up to a judge and jury.

Documents

Here are some guidelines for gathering tangible evidence. There is more detailed information in the Workbook about what documents might be useful, starting at page 645.

- ✓ *You should try to get original documents whenever possible. With some legal or official documents such as deeds, decrees, or birth certificates, the original may be recorded in county or court records, but you can obtain a certified copy from the records office. A certified copy is a sort of "virtual original" and as good for most legal purposes as the original. If you cannot get originals, then make copies at a good quality copying machine.*
- ✓ *There are some documents such as your significant other's driver's license that may be difficult to get copies of, if the relationship has become strained or adversarial. Therefore, if you think that the question of your relationship may come up, you may wish to try to assemble a set of such documents in advance, before things get nasty.*
- ✓ *Last but not least, if you are gathering this evidence because your relationship is already troubled or because a dispute has arisen, have the good sense to keep the critical stuff in a safe place, where your significant other and his family cannot get at them.*

Remember that you should not break into an apartment or business to get records. In particular, you absolutely should not tamper with a person's mailbox or otherwise intercept their mail, because doing so can be a federal felony.

Witnesses' statements

Preserving a statement from a witness can be very helpful, even if the statement is not a sworn affidavit or deposition. Therefore, you may wish to consider getting people who know the facts to provide a written statement of their information. Relatives, friends, neighbors, and business people may have relevant information. For example, perhaps your lover told your banker that the two of you were planning to share everything equally. See the Workbook for more detailed guidance, starting at page 642.

One strategy for obtaining these statements is to write down what you believe is the truth and to ask the possible witness to sign the statement. You can do this in advance of talking to them or in the course of the conversation. For example, if you discuss the situation with your sister and she says that your lover told her that he had promised to put the house in your name, you can make a note of that and ask her to sign it.

It is unnecessary at this stage to make fine determinations about whether a statement is "only hearsay" or not. The admissibility of evidence may never be a major factor in resolving the situation anyway, and even if there is litigation later, the final ruling on a piece of evidence depends on many factors that you may not have in mind now. A mediator or arbitrator, for example, may not care that a statement is technically inadmissible hearsay if it is highly relevant to the issues.

QUESTION: *"Should I tape record my conversations with possible witnesses?"*

ANSWER: *Probably not, but maybe.*

It is hard to evaluate the desirability of secretly taping conversations.

The legality of recording conversations varies from state to state. Wiretapping a phone line is illegal in all states. In some states, it is legal to tape record a conversation that you are a party to, i.e. if you are one of the people talking. In some, this is only legal if you disclose in advance that you are taping the conversation.

It **might** be legal to secretly record events that take place **in your own home**, provided that the recording is not unduly invasive of another person's privacy. Don't put a video camera in the bathroom, for example. It is sometimes legal to videotape a person in public or record a conversation that you participate in and that takes place in public. On the other hand, some forms of hidden recorders and cameras are against the law.

Illegally recording a conversation or electronically eavesdropping can cause you far more grief than good. There are serious criminal penalties for doing so. The FBI will sometimes investigate allegations of illegal wiretapping or bugging a home or office. Therefore, the only safe course is to refrain from spying on someone by means of a wiretap, hidden microphone, or other device.

The law in this area is subject to change as the legislatures consider advancing technology.

If you really want this sort of information in a legally usable form, you should hire a licensed private detective who may be able to obtain the evidence by lawful means and who should know the circumstances in which a recording or photograph is legal or illegal.

Lawyers disagree about whether it is good strategy to make a secret recording or not, even if it is legal. On the one hand, you may obtain persuasive evidence that your lover is cheating you. On the other hand, you may look like a sneaky, conniving person yourself. Juries differ in their evaluation of secret recordings. Also, there is growing suspicion of electronic evidence because it can be altered so easily with a home computer. Some courts limit the use of photographs, recordings, or videotapes as evidence for that reason.

Truth, proof, and evidence—common law marriage

On of the most important questions to consider is whether you and your significant other have entered into a common law marriage. To evaluate that possibility, you need to read the section on common law marriage in Chapter Six starting on page 211 and work through the questions in the Workbook on page 611. One of the legal advantages of being married is that in the event of a split, it will be harder for one spouse to sell real estate, such as the family house, at least if the buyer or mortgage company knows that the seller is married and the property might be community property (also refer to "Documents to gather" on page 645 of the Workbook).

Remember that the elements of common law marriage are agreeing to be married, living together as husband and wife, and holding oneself out to the world as married. Relevant evidence to prove that a common law marriage existed is evidence that tends to show that *each* of those facts existed. Relevant evidence to disprove a common law marriage would be evidence that tended to show that *at least one* of those facts did not exist.

For example, suppose that your employer offers health insurance. An employment form that lists your significant other as your husband would tend to show that you held yourselves out as married; leaving that part of the form blank tends to show that you did not.

Similarly, a person who has visited in your home when you were living with your spouse could testify that the two of you acted like a married couple or that you clearly referred to each other as "friends" or "companions," rather than as "husband" or "wife."

Truth, proof, and evidence — paternity, maternity, and child custody

Gathering evidence in paternity cases is relatively easy. It is basically a matter of genetic testing. In child custody cases, it can be expensive and require substantial effort on your part because more factors than parentage are involved. Detailed discussion of the mechanics of these disputes is in the Workbook, see "You want an active role in a child's life, but baby is not yet born" on page 622 and "Preparation for a child custody dispute" on page 634.

Paternity

If you wish to establish the paternity of a child, then DNA testing is the only answer. Blood tests used to be the standard test, and are still sometimes used, but DNA testing is more reliable.

A DNA test involves comparing the genetic structure of the child with that of its mother and alleged father. The test can be done with a small tissue sample, such as swab of the inside of a person's mouth.

There are home kits available on the Internet, although you probably will also want to have a reputable, certified laboratory do a second test as well. There's no point in relying on only one test for something so important; even the best laboratories can make an error.

DNA testing can be done by the parties voluntarily or as part of a court proceeding.

Unwed mothers

As discussed earlier in Chapter Fourteen, a mother has some *de facto* control over whether a man ever learns that he is a father. Assuming that the mother does not want to deprive her child of contact with the other biological parent, and assuming that she intends to carry the child to term, then the mother should take action to establish the paternity of the child legally, as well as get a formal custody order.

Many unwed mothers do not tell the father about his child because they don't want his "interference" in their lives. Some want to place the child secretly for adoption. To me, these actions are usually ill-advised and selfish, if not spiteful. First, they deprive the man of involvement with a child that is, after all, his. Second, they deprive the child of contact with his or her father.

The woman chose this man to be the father of her child by having sex with him. If that choice was misguided or unintentional, in my view, too bad. That man is the biological father of the child and will be so for the rest of their lives. The fact that the mother now has a new lover or has decided that she's angry at the father or whatever does not normally justify her in depriving father and child of their relationship.

On the other hand, in extreme cases, where the man is a career criminal, abusive, or otherwise patently unfit to be around the child, deceitful or at least evasive actions may be justified.

Some mothers hesitate to file a paternity suit because they are afraid it will make the father angry or because they don't want him to "have any rights." The problem is that the father does have rights; without a court determination of custody, he could theoretically take possession of the child. In that case, the mother would have to go to court anyway and try to get the child back.

If the father signs an agreement to support the child, the agreement is only a contract, and if the father defaults, then the mother must file a lawsuit to enforce the contract. That proceeding can take months, and in the meantime, she will probably need to file a lawsuit to determine paternity also. A court decision in the paternity case, however, will set out the father's obligations and the resulting court order will be enforced more quickly.

Unwed fathers.

A man who believes that he may have fathered a child or that he may be accused of having fathered a baby needs to balance his moral obligations, emotional commitments, and legal conduct.

If you believe you may be the father of a child and you want to be involved in your child's life, then you should notify everyone involved, including any registry in your state for expectant fathers, that you believe that you are the father of this particular woman's child and that *if DNA testing confirms your paternity*, you will fulfill your responsibilities as a parent.

Equally important, however, you should not sign anything that legally establishes you as the father until your biological relationship is confirmed. In some states, a father who is identified, for example, on a birth certificate must take legal action to disavow his responsibility for the child if he is not biologically the father.

An agreement to support the child might be binding on the man, even if the child is not biologically his, unless he can show that he was defrauded by the mother. Proving this can be difficult, and the switch will be devastating to a child who has regarded this man as his father. Often, if sufficient time has passed, the law does not permit a man to repudiate an acknowledgement of paternity.

Sometimes the mother makes a mistaken claim about the paternity of her child. Some advocates in child custody wars have claimed that the man identified by the mother as the father turns out not to be the father in 20 to 40 per cent of the cases. She may be uncertain of the facts, mistaken, or just have chosen a hard-working guy with a steady income to support her and her baby.

Since child support payments can amount to half of a man's income for 20 years or more, you should not do not do anything to undertake such an obligation without scientific proof that you are the father. Do not acknowledge the child as yours, take him or her into your home, or allow your name to be put on the birth certificate unless you are certain that you want to support this child regardless of the genetics.

Courts follow a rule called *res judicata* in Latin, which translates roughly as "decided matter," and means that once a decision is made (after all the appeals are over), it is final. The rationale for this rule is that all litigation has to end sometime, regardless of whether the original decision was correct or not. However sensible that sounds, the rule has been applied to the detriment of some alleged fathers. Unjust cases exist in which a man has been told by an unscrupulous woman that he is the father of her child. In reliance on her claim, the man has admitted in court that he is the father and has paid court-ordered child support. Then, some years later, the woman reveals that some other man is actually the father. Unfortunately, some courts have held that the legal basis for the child support order (i.e. the court ruling that a particular man is the father) had been decided long ago and cannot be reopened.

A few men have succeeded in persuading courts to abandon the ancient rule of finality (*res judicata*) by proving that the mother consciously lied to them and to the court. Sometimes, an outraged court has required the mother to pay back the money she has wrongly received. These cases are few and far between, however, and normally courts do not reopen a case "just because" new evidence has come to light. In other words, if the mother reasonably thought that a particular man was the father and he did not bother to have the matter scientifically evaluated when the baby was born, then he can be stuck continuing to pay child support, regardless of what he later discovers about the biological facts.

Some generous and loving men voluntarily undertake to raise a child who is not biologically theirs, which is admirable and a great boon to the child. Any written agreement to that effect, however, should be carefully drafted to fit the situation; at a minimum, in my view, it should set out expressly that the man is not the child's biological father, should state that he has had the role of a father in the child's life, to the benefit of the child, and should provide that his paying support is conditional on his receiving visitation or other time with the child. Otherwise, the man may find himself paying support for a child whose mother has moved the kid half a continent away. If the commitment is truly meant to be a life-long one, then if possible, the man should adopt the child or obtain a court order giving him some legal status, whether as guardian or having joint custody. Absent a court order, all the man has is a contract, which is better than nothing but probably not determinative. Remember, however, that a court will probably not be willing to award formal rights to a man who is not the biological father unless there is substantial evidence that the biological father has shown no interest in the child.

Child custody cases

Paternity cases and child custody cases merge into one another because once biological parentage is established, someone must apportion the access to and financial responsibility for the child that each of them will have.

In a child custody case, the court's standard is the best interests of the child. To establish that you should have sole custody or primary custody (or whatever it is called in your state), you need to show that the child is better off with you. That means showing that you are able to provide the best home for the child and that your home is preferable to that of the other parent. If necessary, where the other parent has a substance abuse or other major problem, you may need to show that he or she is an unfit parent.

The question of when a dispute escalates into a familial war is impossible to determine on a general basis. It is hard to know when to act as if you are fighting for your emotional and financial future against a selfish and implacable adversary and when you can still work things out with a miffed, but basically decent former spouse or lover.

The most important point for any parent is that to maintain your rights to be involved with your child, you must act on them. If you don't visit the kid or take any role in his or her education, then you cannot reasonably expect a court to give your interests a lot of consideration. If you need to go to court to defend your right to the child, then you will have to show that you tried to act like a responsible parent.

Moreover, you must not only act on your rights as a parent, but be able to prove that you have done so. Therefore, you must assemble evidence of what you have done. It is much less plausible to say, "I kept trying to get hold of my girlfriend," than to say, "I called her 23 times. I kept a diary of every time I called." Basically, you need to keep careful records, including copies of documents and a diary of events, including phone calls and conversations. A more detailed list is in the Workbook starting on page 634.

All custody cases, involving a social service agency or the police should always be done with circumspection. Remember that their involvement may spiral out of your control. If you call the cops when you are in a heated argument with your significant other, you cannot predict who will be arrested or, in some states, shot. A criminal conviction for resisting arrest will not help your custody case. Don't invite the police into your home if you are in possession of illegal substances, firearms, or drug paraphernalia. Their interest may shift from the domestic disagreement to much graver charges against you.

Similarly, if you call your state's Children's Protective Services agency to your home to show the caseworker that your child has bruises inflicted by your ex, be sure that your own house will stand inspection. Don't invite a social worker into your life if your apartment is filthy, there's no food in the refrigerator, and your drug addict cousin is passed out on your sofa. Use a little sense.

If your child is genuinely in danger from neglect, or from reckless conduct of the other parent (such as driving with the child while intoxicated), you should consider calling the police or the local child protection agency at that moment. If you do nothing, then you may appear not to be very concerned about the child's safety either. For example, if your ex drives away from your house with your child in the car and he/she has obviously been drinking, then call the police right then and report a drunken driver. Tell the operator the circumstances honestly and make sure that they can reach you, if necessary to take possession of the child if your ex is arrested. If possible in a peaceable manner, go to the place where you have sent the police and be available to retrieve your child. Check with the police station to make sure that there has not been a miscommunication about your availability to care for your child.

And, of course, be sure that you are sober yourself when you meet with the police. It won't make a good impression if you report your ex for DWI and show up at the station to claim your child with liquor on your breath. The police may be obligated to turn your child over to a social services agency for foster care if you are also unfit to care for him or her.

Here are some of the factors that courts can consider in awarding custody:

- ✓ *which parent has had the most involvement in the child's daily care to date, including contact with teachers, doctors, and so on;*
- ✓ *which parent can provide the most stable and healthful home environment for the child;*
- ✓ *which parent can provide the best educational and moral upbringing for the child; and*
- ✓ *whether true shared custody is workable.*

Documents that may be relevant in these disputes include school and medical records and especially family photographs. Work records, for example, may show that one parent consistently works 60 hour weeks and doesn't have time to be with the children.

Witnesses include those people who have had an opportunity to see the family in action, so to speak. Teachers, clergymen, and psychologists are often called as witnesses, as are the couple's relatives and friends. For more detail, check the Workbook sections, starting at "Considerations in getting evidence from witnesses" on page 642.

Child support cases

Most child support decisions are made based on a formula set out by state law. The computations can be complex and rest on many factors, including assets, income, and obligations to other children. To make them accurately, you need detailed financial information about your own resources and those of your ex. Since the computation is mostly arithmetic, documents are usually more important than witnesses. It is vital to know what your state law is, since some states take into account both parents' resources in setting the support payment, while others provide for a fixed percentage from the income of the parent who does not have primary custody.

If you know that you are likely to be required to pay support, you should write down each element of the computation neatly and precisely before any hearing or mediation. It's always a good idea to check your lawyer's math.

If you are going to mediation, remember that you and your ex can probably agree on whatever you want, provided that both of you and the mediator see the wisdom of a particular arrangement. So, it's a good idea to gather any evidence that might convince your ex to take less than the statutory amount, such as evidence of any future medical bills that you are likely to have or evidence of additional income that he or she is likely to receive soon, such as a large bonus at work or an inheritance. Remember the mediator doesn't decide the case but he or she can influence the outcome substantially.

Before going to any mediation or court hearing, you need to understand the permutations that changes in custody arrangements can make in required support payments, as well as the other statutory factors. If you can, prepare a spreadsheet for yourself so that you will understand the financial consequences of a change in custody. Check that spreadsheet carefully with an experienced accountant or lawyer.

For example, if both parents have equal custody rights, then neither may be obligated to make a support payment to the other because each is bearing one-half of the cost of raising the child. Each may be ordered to cover some particular expense, as where one pays for private school tuition and the other pays for health insurance. However, if one parent has primary custody (whatever that is called in your state) and the other has visitation (or "parental time" or whatever it is called), then the one with visitation will probably be paying child support to the other.

If you want your child to have some particular advantage, such as private school or summer camp, try to ensure that your payments for those items are counted as meeting your child support obligation or that your ex is required to send the child to a particular school or whatever.

Truth, proof, and evidence — cohabitation and prenuptial agreements

QUESTION: *"What do courts do in lawsuits about contracts?"*

ANSWER: *Courts determine if there is a valid contract and require the parties to fulfill their (financial) promises.*

In ordinary, straightforward circumstances, if one of the parties to a contract hasn't lived up to its terms, a court will either make the defaulting person do what he or she promised or require him or her to compensate the other one for whatever loss was suffered.

However, there are sharp limits on what a court can force a person to do, because judges don't want to be in the business of monitoring people's activities outside the courtroom. As a general rule, it is tidier for a judge to require one person to pay another money than for the court to get involved in an ongoing struggle over whether a person is carrying out a complicated task. Similarly, it is neater to order a person to refrain from doing something than to compel them to do something. For example, a judge is not going to order Bill to be nice to Jane but the same judge may be quite willing to order Bill to leave Jane alone. In fact, the latter decision, called a "restraining order," is quite common in domestic disputes.

Sometimes a court will order a person to take a particular action if it is short-term and easily enforced. A court, for example, can order the owner of a business to transfer stock to another person or can require that the names on a deed be changed. A judge might order a lover to move out of the family home.

The payment of money is called, of course, damages, and these orders (where the court requires compliance with a contract provision) are called specific enforcement or injunctions.

However, a court cannot legally, and will not, order one person to treat another with respect and affection or even to do the dishes every Wednesday night before the PTA meeting.

Let's look further at the kinds of things that come up in contract litigation.

QUESTION: *"How do people avoid their obligations under contracts?"*

ANSWER: *They claim that the contract is invalid or that they shouldn't be required to obey it. Sometimes, they just lie.*

There are two kinds of legal grounds that may persuade a court that a written contract should not be enforced. A person who signed a contract (a "party") may claim that the contract was flawed at the beginning and, hence, is not valid now. Alternatively, he or she may claim that circumstances have changed since the contract was signed. However, generally, only the behavior of the parties can change the effectiveness of the contract.

Only valid contracts will be enforced by a court. Therefore, one party to a contract dispute may claim that the contract is not valid. A contract is unenforceable (meaning that a court should not require the parties to adhere to its terms) if it was entered into under unfair circumstances, such as where one party was deceived or coerced. One party might claim that he or she was deceived into signing the agreement by misrepresentations about finances or intentions.

A court probably would not be much impressed by a claim that "she said that she loved me, the lying bitch." However, a court might well refuse to enforce an agreement about money where, for example, the woman proves that the man told her that he didn't have any significant assets but was in fact very wealthy.

Coercion is called "duress" in legal terms and it exists where one party is forced to sign the agreement against their will. Usually duress is physical in nature, such as threats of bodily harm, but it can also consist of extreme emotional pressure. It is unclear what the legal status of an agreement would be where, for example, the woman claims that she only agreed because her lover threatened to kill himself if she did not; probably the contract would still be valid. However, your financial problems do not constitute duress; if you make a bad deal because you were broke or stupid, the court will probably not let you out of your obligations.

The second group of defenses have to do with whether the parties properly adhered to the terms of the contract after it was signed. One party may claim that the contract should not be enforced because the other party didn't perform his or her half of the bargain. Thus, if two people live together and agree to pool their earnings in a joint savings account and to each will pay half of the expenses, a court might not divide the savings account equally unlike cases where one party ended up paying all the household expenses.

This legal rule follows the common sense doctrine that you can't have your cake and eat it too. If you didn't live up to your obligations, it is unreasonable to expect a court to make your lover live up to his or hers. Again, however, your lover may have an excuse for not performing, as where you made it impossible for him or her to do so. A closely related situation is where contract obligations are reciprocal, i.e. where one person's responsibility is dependent on the other performing his or her obligations.

Two more analogous defenses are those of waiver and estoppel. A party to a contract may have waived his or her right to insist on the other person performing his or her obligations. Waiver occurs, for example, when a repeated breach of the agreement is simply tolerated, especially if words like "Oh, ok, don't worry about it," have been said.

The concept of estoppel comes up when one party to the contract fails to perform, the other tolerates the failure, and the situation changes to make it unfair later to require the performance.

For example, suppose John and Mary both raise and train horses. They decide to move in together and pool their respective businesses. John agrees that Mary will show his jumper because she is a better rider. They agree to split any winnings from the competition. John agrees to breed the horse to Mary's mares. Mary, however, finds that the horse is too difficult to handle and she stops competing with it. John grumbles but eventually says something like, "Well, ok, that horse is pretty difficult," and stops complaining. In reliance on not having John's horse to show, Mary goes out and buys another show horse. The court may not be sympathetic to John's complaint months later that Mary didn't show his horse.

The court may find that one provision of a contract was conditional on another. If Mary agreed to put a new roof on John's stable if John fixed her horse trailer, then John's failure to fix the trailer might excuse Mary from her obligation.

Finally, one party might claim that the contract was modified later or that there was a separate agreement that wasn't written down or even that the whole agreement was revoked. A written agreement usually cannot be orally modified, but there are exceptions

The sample contracts in this book contain "boilerplate" clauses that are standard provisions that say that the written agreement contains the whole agreement and that it can't be validly modified except in writing. Like everything legalistic, those clauses don't always work. The danger is that sometimes they are effective and sometimes not, depending on the circumstances and sometimes on the unfairness of the outcome.

Perhaps the most common legal/financial dispute in relationship litigation, whether the couple were married or not, is whether they consistently followed whatever terms they agreed on and whether they appropriately modified their agreement when their circumstances changed. Most people don't. From a practical point of view, it is important to remember that the starting point in a dispute is always the way things are when you break up. For example, if all of the money owned by the two of you is in bank accounts in your lover's name, then from a legal standpoint, it all belongs to him/her at that moment. Until he/she either voluntarily puts some of it in your name or a court intervenes, the money legally appears to be his/hers and he/she can withdraw it, spend it, etc. In other words, it is much harder to unwind a tangle than it is to keep things straight.

A cohabitation or prenuptial agreement will not enforce itself automatically. There is less range for disputes and connivance if other documents, such as deeds and bank account records, reflect the terms of the cohabitation agreement. If you have kept these records carefully and in accord with the promises that you made to each other, then it is much harder for your lover (or you) to take more than his or her share.

In other words, if the documents, such as signature cards at the bank, deeds, etc. don't reflect your interests, then your rights will not be fully realized until the documents are changed. For example, remember the hypothetical John and Mary who live together and raise horses? Suppose that one of the foals born on their ranch is Olive Branch, a valuable bay filly. When Olive Branch is born, John and Mary agree that she belongs to Mary. Over time, however, all of the papers about that horse – registration papers, veterinary records, microchip implantation, and other identification papers – have been put in John's name. Until John changes those papers, either voluntarily or because of a court decision, he effectively owns Olive Branch. John can sell Olive Branch because on paper he appears to own her. Mary may be able to stop the sale by telling the prospective buyer that the horse is really hers but if she is wrong, then she may be liable to John for the lost profits from the sale. If the sale goes through, Mary may be able to get the horse back on the ground that the animal never really belonged to John. However, the buyer can say that he or she paid for Olive Branch in good faith and relied on the appropriate documents.

If a truly dishonest lover gloms the couple's money, he or she will quite likely have spent it by the time a court decision is reached. If there is a serious risk of this, the other person must take appropriate practical precautions to protect his or her assets and also take necessary legal action. For example, he or she should take his or her share out of any joint accounts. He or she may also want to file suit and ask the court to restrain the other person from dissipating or hiding any of the assets. The latter order is called an injunction or restraining order.

There are a number of possible variations on these themes. These various situations include those in which (1) the situation of the parties has markedly changed since the agreement was signed, (2) one of the parties doesn't want to abide by the agreement; and (3) the parties haven't exactly followed the agreement over the years.

Times have changed

Whether in a marriage or a cohabitation arrangement, the financial status of the two parties sometimes changes over the years, and frequently, those changes are not parallel. In other words, one party may have a much better job than before the relationship and the other may have the same or one with a less remunerative position. In these situations, the cohabitation agreement sometimes fits the changed situation and sometimes does not.

QUESTION: *"My lover and I signed a cohabitation agreement 20 years ago. We agreed that if we split up, we would just go our separate ways. Neither of us would be entitled to anything in the future from the other. He started a business five years ago, and I worked hard at night and on weekends to help get his business going. Now his business is really flourishing; he's making lots of money and I'm still a secretary. He left me for a sales representative from another company. Shouldn't I get some share in his business?"*

ANSWER: *Probably not. You knew when you worked in his business all those years that you had agreed that neither of you would have any ongoing obligation to each other after you split up.*

If the cohabitation agreement in this case contains a clause that prohibits oral changes to the agreement, its terms probably control the situation. When the situation changed, the agreement should have been changed too. It's possible that a jury might be convinced that the couple's conduct shows that they had a clear new agreement that superseded the terms of the old one, but that's not an easy case to prove.

This kind of outcome is the reason that the parties must change their cohabitation agreement to reflect changes in their life. A contract is more or less static; life is various and fluid. It is possible to argue that there was an implied modification of the agreement or at least that a person should be compensated fairly for the contribution that he or she has made to their significant other's business or career, particularly if substantial sacrifice was involved.

There are circumstances that might create greater sympathy for one party or the other, such as a disabling illness suffered by one of them. However, it is important to realize that these tragedies may not be legal grounds for changing the agreement. Although a person may say vehemently that he or she didn't know that the illness would strike, the fact that one person did not adequately provide for unknown contingencies is not necessarily a legal reason for setting aside the agreement.

I don't want to

When a relationship ends, the strong emotions can spill over onto the financial arrangements. When love is in bloom, agreeing to divide the harvest may seem like a wonderful idea; when the frost is on the pumpkin, however, both parties want the whole pie.

When people are in love, they may make generous promises to each other that seem appropriate in the context of deep affection and mutual caring. When the basis of the relationship is overwhelming sexual attraction or love on one party's side, the other person may exploit the other's emotional vulnerability. Regardless of whether the reason is disappointment, rage, regret at having been taken advantage of, or simple greed, one party may be entirely unwilling to honor the agreement later.

The parties then have three alternatives. First, each can accept the situation as it is when they part, salvaging whatever they can. Second, they can work out a compromise. Third, one can try to enforce the agreement, by mediation, arbitration, or court proceedings.

The most sensible option is usually to work out a compromise, which should involve dividing assets as much as possible now and providing for as little contact in the future as possible, which will minimize future hassles. Remember that any such compromise agreement needs to be in writing and to make sure that all debts are paid, preferably right now.

We didn't exactly adhere to the terms of the agreement

In personal relationships and in business, people often disregard, forget, or simply don't get around to following all the terms of a contract. These actions, however, can make enforcing the contract much more difficult later. It is much harder to persuade a bitter ex-lover to change the title on the car than it is to get the title in the right names when you are both getting along. Also, failing to follow the terms of a contract can create legal ambiguities about the contract's status, such as whether the parties intended to modify the contract or to deliberately waive one provision or another.

QUESTION: *"My wife and I signed a prenuptial agreement. She agreed to pay for my tuition. She kept promising to make the payments, but she never got around to it. Now we have split up and I found out that she saved all that money for herself. Can I force her to pay me back? She says that I didn't do my part in repairing her car and building a greenhouse for her orchids."*

ANSWER: *You may have a good case under your cohabitation agreement. But, it is possible that if you didn't fix the car or build the greenhouse, your failure may at least partly excuse her failure to pay your tuition.*

Often, in contract relationships, neither party has exactly fulfilled their obligations or complied with the agreement. These mutual failings can lead to complicated legal charges and countercharges. See the more detailed discussion of contract obligations in Chapter Eight and Chapter Nine. Also see "Basic questions for all relationship disputes" on page 618 in the Workbook.

To enforce a contract, the person suing must have done their part under the agreement. This is referred to in the law as having clean hands. Moreover, many contract provisions are considered dependent on each other. If both parties have some faults, then a court has to sort out what has happened and reach a reasonably legal and hopefully fair result. There is no clear rule as to when one party's misconduct excuses another's actions.

I was robbed

Sometimes, when people repent of an agreement, it is because the agreement is profoundly unfair. Sometimes, they have a good excuse, other than mere stupidity or lust, for signing it. See Chapter Eight, starting at page 338.

Remember that, basically, the legal defenses to a contract are fraud and duress. Duress means that a person's consent was obtained by threats of immediate, serious harm. Fraud means that the person relied on a statement that was a lie.

Remember that special obligations of good faith and honesty may apply to a prenuptial agreement. A spouse who foolishly signed a prenuptial agreement may have a better chance of getting out of it than a lover who signed an imprudent cohabitation agreement.

We never got around to signing an agreement

If there is no written agreement, then the rights of the parties to their assets are quite likely to be governed by the names on the ownership documents or, if the couple is married, by the marital property laws of that state.

As discussed in earlier chapters, some states have laws that agreements arising out of non-marital cohabitation relationships have to be in writing to be enforceable. Sometimes there might be an exception to those laws if the couple had a clearly provable oral agreement and both of them have acted in reliance on that agreement. That possible exception is not, however, something that can be counted on.

An agreement, however, is not always embodied in a formal document titled "agreement." Letters, notes, and memos have all been used to establish that there was a written agreement and what its terms were. In one case, an engineer and a businessman embarked on a business, selling a complicated energy saving device. Neither had any money, but the engineer understood energy devices and the businessman knew how to promote deals. They didn't have a formal agreement, but along the way, the businessman wrote a handwritten note to the engineer referring to their "partnership." Later, when the business was a huge success, the businessman tried to keep it all for himself, claiming that there was no agreement between him and the engineer. That single sentence in one casual letter helped to convince a jury that the engineer deserved to share in the millions of dollars of profits.

Even if your state law permits oral cohabitation agreements, or if you can find enough in writing to satisfy the law, you still have to prove terms of the agreement. It is not easy to prove an oral agreement or one that is only partly written down unless at least a significant part of your conduct has been in compliance with that supposed agreement. In other words, if you want to claim that you and your lover agreed to divide everything equally, but during the relationship, you allowed him/her to put everything is his/her name alone, it may be difficult to convince a court that both of you had something else in mind.

Given the difficulties and expenses of litigation, it is quite likely that the documents will determine who owns what. The person whose name is on the deed to the house probably owns the house.

Truth, proof and evidence – divorce and money

The evidence that a divorcing spouse needs to win his or her case for a share of the family assets is much like that an unmarried person might need to win a cohabitation agreement dispute. Remember that there is no longer litigation over whether a couple will be divorced -- they will if one spouse wants to be and the only question is who gets what.

As discussed in Chapter Fourteen, in a divorce, the court will first determine which assets are part of the community or marital property and which are the spouses' respective separate property. Then the court will divide the marital property between the spouses.

The critical evidence is that which establishes the character of the property and the parties' respective interests in the various assets.

Documents are the most important part of property disputes. The names on the title often are dispositve. Other records can be relevant and useful. A credit card receipt can show who paid for something or when it was acquired. Paycheck stubs can show when retirement fund contributions were made. Bank records can show that funds were commingled or not. Letters to a real estate agent can show that one spouse was buying the property with his or her own separate funds. Gift cards or notes can show that an item was given as a gift by one spouse to the other.

Witnesses can help to establish the origin of property and the intentions of the parties. For example, suppose that a bride's parents gave her a house when she married. The parents could later testify that they intended the gift to be her separate property (or that they intended it to be the couple's marital property). Customers of a couple's business may testify as to whether both worked there or what their respective activities were.

Financial records and witnesses can also establish the parties' respective situations at the time of the divorce, which will govern the court's decision about spousal support. Doctor and medical records can establish that one spouse is in poor health or that he or she has been abused. Payroll stubs can show the difference in earning capacity. Greeting cards about a graduation can establish that one spouse paid for the other's education.

Letters and emails, as well as phone and credit card records, can be used to trace property that one spouse has tried to hide. For example, if a valuable antique armoire has disappeared from the couples' home and the wife's credit card shows a payment to Jones Moving Company, the husband may be able to prove that his wife shipped the armoire to her sister to hide it.

In child custody cases, witnesses tend to be more important than documents. Teachers can testify about the involvement of each parent in the child's education, for example. In these cases, expert psychologists are often employed to consider what would be best for the child.

Documents can also play an important role, however. For example, family snapshots may show that one parent was present (or absent) on key family occasions.

A newly important aspect of evidence is the information kept on a computer. Court now often order parties to turn over the hard drive of their computer to the opposing lawyer or at least to produce copies of all e-mails, files, etc.

Before you rush to your computer and press the "delete" key, you need to think carefully. It is difficult to erase computer records completely, unless you use a sophisticated erase program or destroy the hard drive. Major e-mail providers can be subpoenaed to produce their records, which means that even if you delete an e-mail from your file, it still exists in the megacomputer of the provider. Also sophisticated programs can recover apparently deleted files from your computer.

Efforts to obliterate computer records, or any other document, can rebound against you in court; your opponent may be entitled to tell the jury that the records must have been adverse because you wouldn't have destroyed them otherwise.

The moral of the story is that you need to be prudent when you see a major court dispute looming on the horizon. Basically, don't write down anything in any form that you don't want a judge to read aloud to a packed courtroom later. This includes collecting pornography, typing love letters to your new inamorata, and making notes about how your secret Cayman Islands bank account will enable you to cheat your lover blind.

Conclusions and advice

The end of an intimate relationship is almost always tinged with some bitterness. In all probability, you would not be reading this book if you did not feel that you had been, or might be, taken advantage of by a significant other.

A virtually certain fact, however, is that any formal dispute proceeding, whether a simple mediation or a bitter divorce case, will make you feel worse, rather than better. Even if they don't make you angrier and more hurt, the legal proceedings may postpone the time when you leave this relationship behind and get on with the rest of your life.

Remember, though, that life does go on and that you will probably recover from whatever losses you suffer in this relationship. The integrity and decency that you display will remain with you throughout the rest of your life. The meanness and dishonesty will likewise go forward with you. Try to be the person whom you would like to be in a relationship with – capable of trust, but not foolish; loving but not blind; prudent for your own interests but neither greedy nor exploitive.

(Endnotes)

1   Robert Seidenberg, *The Father's Emergency Guide to Divorce- Custody Battle* (Takoma Park, Maryland: JES, 1997)

2   Robert Seidenberg, *The Father's Emergency Guide to Divorce- Custody Battle* (Takoma Park, Maryland: JES, 1997)

The Laws of Love:

The Workbook

Checklists
Sources of information
Sample documents

THE WORKBOOK

This workbook can help you organize your thoughts on different aspects of your relationship. This section of *The Laws of Love* can lead you through the analysis of your situation in an organized way.

This workbook **must be used** in conjunction with the substantive text. You need to look back and forth between the two to use this information intelligently. The checklists and questions will not be as meaningful if you do not have the substantive explanation in mind.

The first topics in this Workbook deal with managing an existing relationship or starting a new one. There are sample cohabitation agreements, wills, durable powers of attorney, and other documents. The later sections deal with ending relationships, including disputes. The last section is a questionnaire designed to help you conduct an in-depth evaluation of your relationship. If you seriously want to analyze and understand your relationship as it affects your legal decisions, turn to "Questions toward understanding a relationship" on page 658 for a detailed questionnaire to help you understand yourself and your significant other in the context of the relationship. Better yet, see a good therapist.

People can use this material differently. Some will want to work through all the questions and check the sample agreements, and tables of alternate clauses to figure out what they want to say. Others may just want to start modifying a sample agreement to fit their situation.

You should read all of the sample agreements, even though there are boring repetitions, because each of them contains some variations and alternatives. Only you can decide which combination of provisions best reflects your agreement.

These sample agreements do not cover all the topics that some people might find important. The most important missing issue in the cohabitation is whether and when a couple someday intend to revisit the question of marriage. Other absent topics include:

- ✓ *Vacations. How shall we plan our vacations? Together? Separate?*
- ✓ *Counseling. Do we want to agree in advance to go to counseling if we have problems?*
- ✓ *Sexual fidelity. Should there be a financial penalty for infidelity?*
- ✓ *Health insurance? Should we agree that each of us will carry health insurance?*
- ✓ *Powers of attorney. Do we want to have the power to make decisions for each other in case of emergency?*
- ✓ *Joint business endeavors. These need to be covered in appropriate business documents and in the cohabitation agreement.*
- ✓ *What happens if one of us dies or becomes incapacitated?*
- ✓ *What if one of us has a serious health condition?*

You can add any clause that you want to deal with these or other issues that matter to you both.

PLACES TO GO FOR HELP

The following is a list of resources for finding out more about your state law or for getting assistance in other areas.

Places and people

These are place to seek help and advice. There are too many social service agencies to list them all here.

✓ *Your county law library, which is usually located in the county courthouse, is a good place to look for information on legal matters. The library often has lists of organizations offering free or reduced fee legal services, as well as various legal reference books. The librarian, however, is not supposed to give legal advice.*

✓ *At a law library, a good starting point is the legal encyclopedias American Jurisprudence and Corpus Juris Secundum. Both are organized by topic, like the Encyclopedia Britannica that you may have used in school. However, the topics are those that make sense to lawyers so you may have to rummage a bit.*

✓ *The city or county public library can be a rich source of information. There are free computer services available if you want to look up information online and don't have a private computer available, i.e. you don't want your significant other to know what you are checking into. Some librarians will help you locate local social service organizations or help you find additional self-help books, such as do it yourself divorce manuals.*

✓ *Your county bar association, which is usually listed in the telephone directory under the name of the county. Some local bar associations will help you find legal aid or a lawyer will handle matters for a reduced fee or who specializes in a particular area of law.*

✓ *Your county sheriff, if you live outside a large city, or the city police department will often offer help in dealing with domestic violence, ranging from official intervention to helping you get a restraining order. Many such departments have modernized their thinking about the prevalence of domestic violence and have specially trained officers available.*

✓ *Your local Salvation Army or United Way office can be a source of information on the organizations that offer aid to families. Sometimes, the Salvation Army also provides temporary refuge for families and other assistance. The Salvation Army can often also refer you to programs for substance abuse problems.*

✓ *Local hospitals often have a medical help line that will direct you to locate agencies that can assist with issues of spousal abuse, substance abuse, and other quasi-medical matters.*

✓ *Local churches often have information on social services, although of course the information that they offer may be influence by their particular stance on social issues. Obviously, the local Catholic Church is not going to refer you to a clinic that offers abortions. In addition, if you are a member of a church, even if you are not particularly active, the pastor or priest may be willing to offer marriage or couple's counseling.*

The above references may seem obvious but sometimes we forget about their potential. Obviously, your can just start with your telephone directory and look for an agency that offers the assistance that you are seeking, or you can do an Internet search using standard search engines such as Google.

Useful references — books

These books are among those that were referred to during the preparation of *The Laws of Love* and contain useful information. You need to be careful in referring to any printed material on questions of law as the law can change rapidly. Pragmatic guidance, such as how to conduct yourself during a deposition, remains valid much longer.

These are in alphabetical order.

✓ *American Jurisprudence 3rd (This encyclopedia of the law, which is usually available only in college, law school, or courthouse libraries, provides more detailed information and refers to cases from the various states. Be sure to check the pocket parts (supplemental booklets). A law librarian can help you acquire more information about the rules in your state.) There are also encyclopedias for some states, such as Texas Jurisprudence, which can be very helpful. Be sure that you use the latest edition.*

✓ *Anderson, Patricia. Affairs in Order: A Complete Resources Guide to Death and Dying. (Collier Books, New York, 1991). (A useful guide to the legal and practical mechanics of making arrangements for care of terminally ill persons and taking care of wills, etc.)*

✓ *Belli, Melvin and Krantzler, Divorcing, (St. Martin's Press, New York, 1988). (This edition of the book may be somewhat out of date but much of the advice is practical.)*

✓ *Chambers, Carol A. Child Support; How to Get What Your Child Needs and Deserves, (Summit Books, New York, 1991). (This edition of this book may be somewhat out of date but much of the advice is practical.)*

✓ *Corpus Juris Secundum (This encyclopedia of the law, which is usually available only in college, law school, or courthouse libraries, provides more detailed information and refers to cases from the various states. Be sure to check the pocket parts (supplemental booklets). A law librarian can help you acquire more information about the rules in your state.)*

✓ *Doe, John B., Grandparents' Rights, 3d ed. (Reading, MA: Smith Jones, 1996). (A guide to the rights of grandparents to custody of grandchildren. This book has forms to use to try to handle a custody or visitation claim.)*

✓ *Edmund T. Fleming, Estate Planning and Administration; How to Maximize Assets, Minimize Taxes, and Protect Loved Ones. (Allworth Press, New York, 2001). (A useful guide but always get up-to-date tax advice as tax laws change often.}*

✓ *Forge Leslie and Mosconi, Gail, The Third Choice: A Woman's Guide to Placing a Child for Adoption. (Creative Arts Book Company, Berkeley, CA, 1999).*

✓ *Godwin, Raymond and Laura Beauvais Godwin, Complete Adoption Book; Everything You Need to Know to Adopt a Child, (Adams Media Corporation, Massachusetts, 2000). (A helpful guide to the adoption process, including private adoptions.)*

✓ *Leving, Jeffrey M., Fathers' Rights, (Basic Books, New York, 1997). (A practical guide for fathers involved in custody disputes. A remarkably balanced guide to trial preparation, successful mediation, and other essential topics.)*

✓ *Nearing, Ryam. Loving More: The Polyfidelity Primer. (Written by one of the founders of the advocacy organization, Loving More, this manual argues that it is possible to "move beyond monogamy in a responsible, ethical, and loving way.")*

✓ *Ricci, Isolina, Mom's House, Dad's House; Making Two Homes for your Child. (Simon & Schuster, New York, 1997). (A really excellent, sensible, and helpful guide to managing the divided family.)*

✓ *Warshak, Richard A., Divorce Poison (Regan Books, New York, 2001). (A guide to the miserable things that vindictive and selfish parents inflict on children in divorce. This book describes the theory of parental alienation syndrome in which one parent systematically turns the child against the other parent. A useful book if you find your children becoming alienated from you after a bitter divorce.)*

Internet resources

The following internet references may also be useful. The web is, as everyone probably knows, a wonderful source of information and a possible source for finding support and help.

In doing your own internet research, however, it is important to remember, however, that not every web site is, or remains, reliable. You should evaluate each site based on its sponsor, whether it is an advocacy or advertising or informational site, and so on.

In general, legal source material provided by courts, bar associations, and universities tends to be more reliable than those provided by advocacy organizations. On the other hand, you need to learn how to use legal materials which can be daunting.

Sometimes advocacy organizations or commercial sites can contain useful information in an accessible format. Advocacy groups or individuals with an ax to grind may distort information, sometimes innocently, to suit their particular position. Similarly, material furnished on promotional sites varies in accuracy. Some lawyers, for example, offer excellent question and answer material about family law on websites designed to generate business for their firm. Some internet sites offer document-writing services. These are usually in an interview or wizard format where you answer questions and the program prepares a document for you. In theory, the best of these sites are state-specific, as are the better computer programs. If you review the document carefully (and, yes, ideally, have a lawyer review it), these can be useful.

You have to use your own judgment in relying on these types of sites, as the information might become outdated or just be mistaken.

Here are some sites that I have found useful:

- ✓ *www.unmarried.org. The Alternatives To Marriage Project. This site is expressly oriented toward those who wish to cohabit without marriage. It is an advocacy site but contains much useful information. It has some good links for information on commitment ceremonies, the "marriage free" lifestyle, and other topics at www.unmarried.org/ceremonies.html.*

- ✓ *An advocacy site for same sex couples is www.samesexmarriage.ca.*

- ✓ *www.marriage.about.com. This site focuses on supporting the institution of marriage but contains links to information about marriage.*

- ✓ *www.divorcereform.org/cov.html. This site promotes covenant marriage. You can obtain more information and forms to enter into a covenant marriage.*

- ✓ *www.lectriclawlibrary.com, www.findlaw.com, and www.lawguru.com. All these are excellent starting points for legal research. A specific link for family law resources by state is provided in www.findlaw.com. For easy to understand guidance, you can also try www.sls.rutgers.edu.*

- ✓ *www.loc.gov/law/guide/us-ut.html. This site provides links to researching the law of various states. The reference www.loc.gov/law/guide/us-ut.html, for example, is the link to Utah law on line.*

- ✓ *Many states have self help site sponsored by the courts or the bar associations. www.utcourts.gov/ocap/ is the site for Utah forms, for example. The Washington State Bar Association offers helpful information on marriage and divorce at www.wsba.org. California offers an excellent guide from the California Secretary of State on how to document and register your domestic partnership at www.ss.ca.gov/dpregistry/. This site offers the legally recognized forms to create a domestic partnership and to dissolve one, as well as information on the legal benefits of domestic partnership status in California. Another helpful site is www.TexasLawHelp.org.*

✓ *The Human Rights Foundation web page offers information on which companies provide domestic partner benefits, as well as other useful links at www.hrc.org/. This organization focuses on rights for gay, lesbian, and transgender couples. The Alternatives to Marriage Project also offers information on domestic partnerships at www.unmarried.org/dpres.html.*

Looking up the law

Here are some basic steps to learning about the relevant law.

1.   Start with a book that gives you a clear overview of the subject.

This book is one starting place. Another good starting point for more detailed and specific information is the encyclopedias of the law referred to above.

Oddly enough, law textbooks that are used for courses in law school are not particularly helpful because they are designed to provoke legal reasoning, not to lucidly explain the law. (That's the official reason; the unofficial one has to do with the arcane rituals of becoming a lawyer, including lawyers' congenital delight in obscurity.)

There are some law books that law students use to get an overview of the basic rules (because the textbooks are so opaque). Frequently, these books are written by distinguished law professors. These include the *Black Letter Outlines* series, the *Emanuel* series, and the *Nutshell* series, and the *Hornbook* series. Here are some examples: Harry D. Krause and David D. Meyer, *Black letter Outlines -- Family Law* (West Publishing Company, St. Paul, Minn. 2004); Lawrence A. Frolik and Richard L. Kaplan, *Elder Law in a Nutshell* (West Publishing Company, St. Paul, Minn.1995); and Myron G. Hill and Steven Emanuel, *The Professor Series – Family Law* (Aspen Law and Business, New York, 1994).

Some of these references are paperback outlines, while some are hardcover books. You can find these books at the bookstores near law schools; they are not usually in libraries or ordinary bookstores, although occasionally you can find one in a used bookstore or through online sources such as eBay or www.abebooks.com. Be careful to get the most recent edition that you can find.

When law students study for the bar exam, they take a cram course for six or eight weeks. These course materials can be very useful because they outline the current law in a particular state. You'll have to look for these books second hand. They are not sold separately from the course nor are they in libraries.

2. Refine your understanding to your own state's law.

    If there is an encyclopedia of the law for your state, that's the best place to begin. Look for subjects such as "marriage" or "family law" or "divorce" in the index. Remember that parts of the information that you need may be under several topics. Be sure to check the cross references and the pocket parts which are paperback updates tucked in the back cover.

3. Check the statutes and cases.

    It's a good idea to read the statutes and cases as well as the description of them. Statutes are published in large sets for each state. You can find what you need in the index or ask the librarian to show you how they are organized.

    The statues are usually annotated, meaning that after each section, there is a set of summaries of the main cases that interpreted that statute.

    Court decisions are published chronologically as they are decided. Each state has a set of decisions that runs into hundreds of volumes. There is no real index. The cases are referred to by the names of the parties, the volume where the decision is printed, the series that it is printed in, the exact page, and the year. Sometimes the reference includes a specific notation of what court wrote the opinion. So, the reference *Griswold v. Connecticut*, 381 U.S. 479(1965) refers to the case of Griswold against the state of Connecticut that appears in volume 381 of the United States Reports series at page 479 and that was decided in 1965.

    Court decisions can be hard to read because they are their own literary genre. The court's opinion may include a lot of procedural history that may, or may not, apply to your case. The simplest way to work your way through the case is to focus on the description of the facts and the legal reasoning of the various points that the court discusses.

4. Look for the materials that lawyers in your state use.

    Often, the state bar association will publish handbooks for lawyers in a particular state. These are usually large three ring binders that combine articles on the current state of the law and forms. Your county law library or a law school library should have these books. They are expensive.

    Many people who represent themselves learn to use these materials to good advantage because the books include both the forms and directions, more or less, on how to use them.

    Also, there are paperback books for many states that include all the relevant statutes, case summaries, and annotations on a particular subject. Trial lawyers use a book that contains the rules of procedure and evidence for example. If you can find a book like this for your state, it will be helpful (if not essential) to you in handling your own case.

SAMPLE AGREEMENTS

The following roommate agreement is designed to help you make clear that you don't have any ongoing relationship with someone you are living with. It might be worthwhile if you are expecting to be sharing living space for a long while, as it would hopefully avoid later claims of any romantic involvement.

Sample Roommate Agreement

We are Jane Smith and George Jones. We have agreed to live together. We do not intend or agree to be married. We agree to the following:

(1) We do not intend to have any financial responsibility for each other except what is in this Agreement.

(2) We will share household expenses according to this paragraph. Household expenses include rent, electric, water, gas, cable, renters insurance, and the house telephone, but not cell phone bills.

(3) Each Friday, we will sit down together and go through the bills that have come in that week. We will total them up and George will write a check for one-half the total. Jane will put George's check in her account and pay the bills that week.

(4) Jane will buy the groceries each week and George will give her a check for one-half of the bill. Groceries mean regular food that both of us like and cleaning supplies for the house.

(5) Jane will have primary responsibility for cleaning the apartment and George will take care of the laundry, dry cleaning, and car washing and minor car maintenance, except that Jane will pay for any parts that her car needs.

(6) Neither of us will plan a party at the apartment nor have an overnight guest without the other's permission.

(7) Each of us will pay all of his or her own other expenses, including car insurance.

(8) We have no other financial relationship.

(9) We agree to use birth control to avoid the birth of a child from this relationship.

(10) We have both signed the lease on the apartment at Forever Lover's Lane, Dallas, Texas. We agree to try to stay together for the term of the lease. If we split up before the lease is up, we agree that George will move out. Jane will try to find a new roommate, but George will continue to pay his half of the rent for the month that he moves out and for one more month, unless Jane finds a new roommate sooner. When one of us moves out, we will divide the last week's bills, except the rent, and that will be the end of our relationship.

Signed:

Jane Smith _____   *Date:*

George Jones _____   *Date:*

Suggested Clauses for More Complicated Relationships

This section contains some tables of some possible clauses to cover real estate transactions, household expenses, and shared investments. There are almost an infinite number of ways of arranging these matters, so these clauses can only be a starting point for your own thinking.

Provisions for shared ownership of anything are hard to draft because so many different factual scenarios might occur. What if one significant other doesn't make his or her share of the payments? What if he or she doesn't do the repairs? What if one wants to sell and the other doesn't? These uncertainties and complexities are why a lawyer's or accountant's advice (or both) would be desirable. In particular, with real estate, serious attention needs to be paid to the lease or deed to the property involved so that it reflects your private agreement.

The following table *Table of topics for a prenuptial or cohabitation agreement* can be used to organize your notes about what you want. It covers many common issues.

Table of topics for a prenuptial or cohabitation agreement

Topic: What is the nature of our relationship? Why are we signing this agreement?   **Our Notes**:
Topic: Are we planning to marry or do we want to be clear that we are not married?   **Our Notes**:
Topic: What are our primary financial expectations from this relationship?   **Our Notes**:
Topic: What financial disclosure do we want or need?   **Our Notes**:
Topic: How will we pay everyday expenses?   **Our Notes**:
Topic: What future assets do we plan to share?   **Our Notes**:

Table of topics for a prenuptial or cohabitation agreement (continued)

Topic: Will we have any joint accounts?
Our Notes:
Topic: How will we know who owns what if we buy something during this relationship?
Our Notes:
Topic: How long do we expect this relationship to last?
Our Notes:
Topic: How will we end this relationship if necessary?
Our Notes:
Topic: What happens if we split up?
Our Notes:
Topic: What about kids? Yours, mine, ours?
Our Notes:
Topic: Where will we live? Apartment? House? This city?
Our Notes:
Topic: Anything else? Counseling? Mediation? Arbitration? Attorneys' fees if we go to court? Health insurance? Life insurance? Durable powers of attorney?
Our Notes:
Topic: Are we taking on any other obligations to each other? Tuition? Loans?
Our Notes:

The following table *Table of boilerplate or standard clauses* contains clauses that many people would want in any agreement. You need to be clear that you can comply with these arrangements.

Table of boilerplate or standard clauses

Purpose of Clause: To try to ensure that the written agreement is the only agreement, i.e. to try to exclude claims by an angry significant other that the two of your had some other understanding that you orally agreed to.

Clause: This Agreement is the only agreement between us, except for informal arrangements about household matters. We have not made each other any other enforceable promises or representations except those in this Agreement.

Purpose of Clause: To try to ensure that an angry significant other cannot later claim that you changed the Agreement by a later unwritten promise.

Clause: This Agreement reflects all the terms of our relationship. This Agreement, or any other term of our relationship, cannot be modified except in writing,

Purpose of Clause: To try to ensure that you do not become common law married.

Clause: We do not intend to marry. Any conduct on our part that might be interpreted as our intending to be married, such as referring to each other as "husband" or wife" shall not be so interpreted and is purely for social convenience. If we wish to e married, we will do so by a separate written document or by a formal ceremony.

The following tables *Table of possible rental clauses*, and *Table of possible real estate ownership clauses*, cover various business issues. Each offers three alternatives, but there are many more possible variations that a couple might choose or need.

Table of possible rental clauses

Decision: One of the couple rents an apartment, where they plan to live. He or she wants to be sure that the significant other has to leave if the relationship ends.

Possible Clause: [Name of renter] rents the apartment at [address]. [Renter] is the only person on the lease. [Other party] does not acquire any right to remain in the apartment if this relationship ends and resides there solely as the guest of [Renter]. [Other party] agreed to leave within five days of being asked to do so. [Other party] agrees to pay his or her share of the rent for the month in which he or she leaves.

Decision: The couple decides to rent an apartment together and both want to be sure the other doesn't welsh on the lease.

Possible Clause: We agree to rent an apartment together. We agree that both will be on the lease and both of us will be liable for the rent. If this relationship ends, we agree that we will continue to live together as roommates until the end of the lease. If that is impossible, the one who moves out will remain liable for his or her share of the rent until the one who remains finds another roommate or for two months, whichever comes first. The one who remains will try in good faith to find a new roommate as soon as possible and both will ask the landlord to enter into a new lease, releasing the one who moves out from his or her obligation to the landlord.

Table of possible rental clauses (continued)

Decision: The couple decides to rent a place together but one is more financially stable than the other. This clause may offer better protection if the primary tenant can pay the rent alone. It depends on the landlord's agreement.

Possible Clause: We agree to rent an apartment together at 100 Lover's Lane. We will share the rent equally. Jane will be the tenant on the lease, and we will add William as a subtenant to the lease with the landlord's permission. William agrees to move out within 10 days of Jane asking him to and he will pay the rent to the end of the month in which he moves. Jane agrees to find another subtenant or to pay the entire rent herself after William's obligation ends.

Table of possible real estate ownership clauses

Decision: One of the couple owns a house where they plan to live. He or she wants to be sure that the significant other doesn't end up owning part of the house.

Possible Clause: [Name of owner] owns the house at [address]. That property shall remain [owner's] sole property, and [other party] shall not acquire any interest in that property by virtue of any payment, repair, or improvement made by [other party] unless we so agree in a separate writing.

Decision: One of the couple owns a house and the other wants to be sure that his or her payments entitle him or her to an interest in the house.
Note that this clause expressly excludes the value of labor from the percentage owned; if one of you is contributing money and the other "sweat equity," obviously you need to change that clause.
Note also that you need to decide what to do if one wants to sell and the other doesn't after you split up and how you will handle the possible complexities of co-ownership during any interval. What if the primary owner can't buy the other's interest?

Possible Clause: [Name of owner] owns the house at [address]. We intend that [other party] will contribute significantly to the cost, maintenance, and improvement of that property. [Other party] shall therefore acquire partial interest in that property by virtue of any payment, repair, or improvement made by [other party]. That partial interest shall be determined in proportion to the same factors as contributed by [Owner], including the down payment, real estate taxes, costs of repairs before and after this Agreement, and similar factors. The contributions shall not, however, include the value of the parties' labor. [Name of owner] shall have the sole right in his or her complete discretion to determine whether and when the house will be sold and the terms of that sale, if any, and [other party's] ownership interest shall consist solely in a right to a proportionate share of the proceeds if, and when, the house is sold. In the event that this relationship ends, Owner shall have the right to buy [other party's] interest at a price to be fixed on the date the relationship ends based on the then appraised value of the house. Such right must be exercised within sixty days of the end of this relationship, which shall be the date on which one Party moves out of the house.

Table of possible real estate ownership clauses (continued)

Decision: The couple decides to buy a house together. They are on good terms. There are many more possible complexities – what if one contributes more financially? What if one can't pay for a while? What if one damages the house? If you are inexperienced in real estate matters, you should get advice from a more experienced person or a book. Realtors can be useful but are often biased toward sales.

Possible Clause: We plan to buy a house together. We will own the house jointly with right of survivorship and we agree that all documents in connection with the house will reflect our agreement, including all deeds. We agree to treat each other fairly and honestly in connection with the house, with at least the legal obligation of partners toward each other. We intend that our contributions to the house, including money and work, will equal, regardless of the exact form of these contributions. We expressly intend, for example, that the work of decorating a bedroom should be deemed equal to the work of repairing the roof or for another example, that housework and repairs are of equal value. So long as we are both employed, we will each pay half of the expenses associated with the house, including mortgage payments, taxes, and so on. However, unless there is a gross disparity in the amounts at issue, if we informally agree that one of us will pay for a repair while the other pays another expense, and that such contributions shall be deemed to be equal in value. Similarly, we may agree informally as to other equivalent exchanges, such as for example that one of us will repair the roof while the other makes more of the mortgage payments. Those exchanges shall be deemed to be equal. If we end this relationship, we will at that time agree that one of us will remain in the house and buy the other's one-half interest on such terms as we then find acceptable. We agree that no one else can purchase or acquire either's interest in the house, without written agreement of the other. If we cannot agree on the terms of such a sale, we agree that the house will be offered for sale at its then current value plus 20 per cent, as determined by a certified appraiser, and it will be sold for any offer equal to or above its appraised value.

The following table *Table of Possible Shared Business Clauses* contains clauses to be added to prenuptial or cohabitation agreement in addition to business agreement.

Table of possible shared business clauses

Decision: One of the couple has a business that he or she does not want to share.

Possible Clause: [Name of owner] owns the house at [address]. That property shall remain [owner's] sole property, and [other party] shall not acquire any interest in that property by virtue of any payment, repair, or improvement made by [other party] unless we so agree in a separate writing.

Decision: One of the couple has a business and the other wants to be sure that his or her efforts and other contributions entitle him or her to an interest in the business.
Remember that the end of a relationship where the couple shares a business may mean financial ruin to the business or to one of the couple. It can be misery to share a business with an ex-significant other.

Table of possible shared business clauses (continued)

> **Possible Clause**: [Name of owner] owns a business called [name of business]. We intend that we will work together to grow that business and that [other party] will contribute significantly to the operation and growth of that business. [Other party] shall therefore acquire a partial interest in that property by virtue of any payment, work, or other effort made by [other party]. That partial interest shall be determined in proportion to the same factors as contributed by [Owner], except that [other party's] interest shall not exceed 10 per cent per year to a maximum of 30 per cent, no matter how long he or she works in the business. [Name of owner] shall have the sole right in his or her complete discretion to determine whether and when the business will be operated, closed, or sold and the terms of that sale, if any, and [other party's] ownership interest shall consist solely in a right to a proportionate share of the proceeds if, and when, the house is sold. In the event that this relationship ends, Owner shall have the right to buy [other party's] interest at a price to be fixed on the date the relationship ends based on the then appraised value of the business. Such right must be exercised within sixty days of the end of this relationship, which shall be the date on which one Party moves out of our shared residence.

> **Decision**: The couple plan to start a business together. They recognize that each may put in more money but want their respective work to be counted as equal. This arrangement ignores any later inequalities in work contributed but also tries to avoid disputes over who did what and how much it was worth and whether each did his or her part.
> A more detailed agreement could, and possibly should, be decided on; however, it is hard to predict how a new business will go and what its needs will be.
> Partnership obligations mean that the couple must act fairly and honestly toward each other.

> **Possible Clause**: We plan to start a business together, Our Own Website Design Company. We will both work in the business, and we will own it equally. We will both invest money or other assets in the business as we may agree at any time. We recognize that our contributions at any given time may differ, due to other commitments. We agree that both of us will share in the management. William will have primary responsibility for design work and Jane will have primary responsibility for sales. We will take whatever legal steps seem appropriate to form a limited liability company; the provisions of this Agreement shall be recognized and included in any management agreement or other document executed in connection with that business. Regardless of the legal form of the business, we agree to have at least the same obligations to each other as if we were partners. We further agree to treat each other fairly, honestly, and with due respect to each other's interests and not to take advantage of each other. If our cohabitation relationship later ends, we may elect then to continue the business together, to sell it, or for one of us to buy the other's interest. In the latter case, the fair price will include tangible assets contributed but our labor contributed shall be deemed to be of equal value and the purchase price will be paid from the operation of the business or its sale if it is later sold.

Notes on the Sample Cohabitation and Prenuptial Agreements

The immediately following agreement is a relatively fair one for a couple that are relatively uncommitted to the relationship, by my standards. It effectively waives all of the protections that marriage confers on a couple but provides that the man, who in this hypothetical situation, is the wealthier of the two will make some financial provision for his significant other.

Remember that all the agreements contain the boilerplate clauses about completeness and no modification. If you don't understand these, you need to reread the section on standard clauses at page 565.

Special care needs to be taken if you have good reason to distrust your significant other, such as where he or she has a substance abuse or gambling problem. In those situations, you not only need promises about money but mechanisms to keep assets out of the other's reach.

Same sex couples need to be particularly aware of their state's law; some states have effectively made cohabitation agreements invalid for same sex couples. These couples may need to leave out any language that suggests a romantic relationship and focus on an image of friendship or mutual responsibility, rather than anything like a marriage. In addition, these couples may wish to use other legal devices, such as wills, business partnerships, and joint accounts.

Sample Agreement — Separate but With Some Sharing (cohabitation or prenuptial)

The parties to this Agreement are Jane Jones and Max Smith. The consideration for this Agreement consists in our mutual promises to each other set out herein. Sexual matters form no part of the consideration for this Agreement.

We agree as follows:

(1) We are not presently married and we do not intend to be married at this time, although we are considering marriage. We agree that any reference, now or in the future, to each other as husband or wife or any other such language is a matter of social convenience only and does not indicate an intention to marry. If we later marry, we shall do so in a formal ceremony and not by common law marriage.

(2) The Agreement is intended as a cohabitation agreement. If we marry, this Agreement shall serve as a prenuptial or marital agreement. If we marry, this agreement shall continue to govern our financial relationship, except as set out below. The rights and duties herein are expressly intended by us to replace any rights that we might otherwise have under the laws of any state in which marry, including rights to community property or spousal support.

(3) We agree to treat each us fairly, honestly, and in good faith. Except as set out below, we are not fiduciaries or partners but we intend to be good to each other. Neither of us intends to profit from this relationship at the expense of the other, but each of intends to manage his or her affairs as he or she sees fit.

(4) Both of us are entering this agreement freely, as self-sufficient adults. Neither of us has coerced or imposed on the other, and each of us has had ample time to reflect on the terms of this Agreement and to get such advice as he or she felt was appropriate.

(5) We love each other and intend to be sexually faithful to each other. We recognize that emotional commitments can change and we agree that a change in our feelings shall not be grounds for a claim of one of us against the other.

(6) Neither of us is carrying a sexually transmitted disease. Each of us has had tests for such diseases within the last three months and such tests were negative.

(7) We have made such disclosure of our finances to each other as we mutually consider appropriate and we are satisfied with those disclosures. Jane is employed at _____ and her annual income is presently $_____. Max is employed at _____ and his annual income is presently $_____. Financial disclosure forms for each of us are attached to this Agreement. We represent to each other that our respective disclosures are honest and fairly reflect our respective finances. We agree to inform each other of any significant change in our financial status, including changing employment. Unless one of us has outright lied to the other, we agree that a discrepancy in such disclosure shall not be grounds for challenging this Agreement.

(8) Max has leased the apartment at 105 Lover's Lane, Heartbreak Hotel, Georgia, alone. Jane agrees that lease belongs to Max alone and Max agrees that, if this relationship ends, Jane has no responsibility for the rental payments. Jane agrees that she is not a tenant within the meaning of any applicable law providing for the rights of tenants but is a guest of Max, and that this is a personal cohabitation agreement and not a lease. Jane agrees to move out of the apartment within seven days of being asked to do so by Max.

(9) We are not engaged in a partnership or other business undertaking. If we enter into such a business relationship in the future, we will indicate our new arrangement by some form of written agreement; if there is no written memorial of that new arrangement, then we promise each other that we will not seek to enforce that relationship will indicate that either by written agreement between us or by the names we put on the title.

(10) If we loan each other any amount of money over $_____, we will memorialize that loan by some form of writing, even if it is only a check marked loan. Any loan between us that is not indicated by some writing is not intended by us to be an enforceable obligation, and we agree not to sue to collect it in the future. Unless we agree in writing to other terms, any loans between us shall be free of interest and shall be repayable on demand. Any such loan will be repaid immediately if one of us moves out.

(11) We agree that expenses will be shared as follows: both of us will pay for our own cars, health insurance, and other personal expenses. Max will pay all household expenses. Max will maintain a lifestyle for both of us that are appropriate for his income level and approximately like he lived before we reached this agreement.

(12) We agree to the following additional financial provisions. (i) Max will pay all of Jane's educational expenses so long as we live together. Max will not have any right to be repaid for those payments nor will he have any interest in Jane's career. (ii) If this relationship ends, Jane agrees that she will not assert any right to any support or other payment after the date of ending of this relationship, which shall be the date of any final divorce decree (if we marry) or the date on which we separate as set out above, whichever comes first. (iii) Any money earned by Jane will be for her sole use and any savings that she may accumulate belong to her alone. (iv) Max will also put $50,000 in a brokerage account for Jane and the income on that account shall belong to Jane.

(13) We further agree that any property not specifically addressed in this agreement, whether owned before our relationship commences or acquired afterward belongs solely to the person in whose name it is owned, whether that name is on a receipt, title documents, or other indicia of ownership.

(14) If we purchase any new tangible property while we are together, that property will belong to the person in whose name it is taken, regardless of who pays for it. If we intend any other form of ownership, we will indicate that either by written agreement between us or by the names we put on the title or receipt.

(15) A transfer of property of any value over $500 shall be deemed to be a gift only if there is clear evidence of intent to make a gift, such as a gift card, change in title, etc. A gift of money or other small personal item, such as jewelry, sporting equipment, and so on may be evidenced by it's being in the other's possession but such possession shall not be conclusive evidence. If only one name is on the title to the property, then it shall be presumed that person is the sole owner and that any financial contribution by the other was a gift. If property is in our joint names, it shall be presumed that each of us has an equal interest in that asset and that any disparity in our contributions was a gift.

(16) As to any property in our joint names, we shall be fiduciaries as to each other.

(17) This is the only Agreement that we have made with each other. We may enter into informal agreements between ourselves with regard to the details of loans, household chores, and expenses. Those agreements will be consider to supplement, not to replace, this Agreement. We have not made each other any other promises or representations inconsistent with this Agreement to induce each other to sign this Agreement. Any personal understandings of love or affection, or agreements about daily household management, are not part of this Agreement, nor are they intended to be legally enforceable.

(18) This Agreement will last so long as we live together, if we do not marry. If either of us moves out of our common household while we are not married and does not intend to return, this Agreement is terminated except that it will govern the resolution of any dispute between us. Otherwise, while we are living together, this Agreement may be terminated at any time by either

of us, for any reason or for no reason, just by giving the other written or oral notice that the Agreement is ended.

(19) If we marry, this Agreement will govern the terms of our finances and of any separation or divorce and the termination of this Agreement will be covered by any divorce decree.

(20) The terms of this Agreement may only be modified in writing, except that (i) if over time we conduct our financial affairs inconsistently with this Agreement, we shall be deemed to have modified it to the extent necessary to avoid serious injustice and (ii) if we marry and one of us becomes so disabled as to be significantly impaired in his or her ability to make a living, then a court may modify the terms of this Agreement to avoid serious injustice.

(21) Each of us agrees that by this agreement, we waive any other property rights that we might have as a result of our cohabitation or marriage, including rights to alimony or support, inheritance, or otherwise.

(22) This Agreement will be governed by the laws of Nebraska and venue for any dispute hereunder will be Lincoln, Nebraska. We may change that venue by mutual agreement if we both move.

(23) If there is any dispute over the terms of our relationship or this Agreement, then we will submit the dispute, within twenty days of our splitting up, for binding arbitration to an arbitrator whom we choose at that time or, if we do not agree on who the arbitrator should be, then to Father Michael Saintly. The arbitration shall take place within 20 days after one of us gives the other written notice that a dispute exists and that he/she desires arbitration. If we have a dispute, each of us will pay his or her own attorney.

Signed:

Jane Doe_____ Date:

Max Smith_____ Date:

Notes on the Sample Prenuptial Agreement

The following agreement is a harsh one. It effectively waives all of the protections that marriage confers on a couple. Almost the only couple for whom this agreement would be appropriate would be one where each was absolutely financially secure and comfortable in his or her ability to stay that way.

This agreement might be suitable for a couple where both were completely paranoid about marriage, perhaps as the result of financially ruinous divorces. In that case, however, one might wonder why they were marrying at all, if there was so little trust in the relationship.

It is worth noting that this agreement is so harsh that it might not be enforced by a court unless the parties were both equally financially solvent and equally well advised by independent lawyers.

A more sensible arrangement would be one in which the couple provided for each other more generously, perhaps by providing that all money earned during the marriage would be divided equally and invested in separate accounts for each of them and that all major assets acquired during the marriage would be owned jointly. That agreement could also contain provisions providing that assets owned before the marriage would remain each other's separate property.

Remember that a court may decline to enforce a prenuptial agreement if one party took advantage of the other, or if the couple didn't fairly and honestly disclose their finances to each other, or if one had legal advice and the other didn't. If you have both consulted lawyers, then you might want to put a statement to that effect in the agreement.

Sample Agreement — Keeping Things Separate (prenuptial)

The parties to this Agreement are Jane Jones and Max Smith. The consideration for this Agreement consists in our mutual promises to each other set out herein. Sexual matters form no part of the consideration for this Agreement.

(1) We agree to marry each other. Both of us are entering this agreement freely, as self-sufficient adults. Neither of us has coerced or imposed on the other, and each of us has had ample time to reflect on the terms of this Agreement and to get such advice as he or she felt was appropriate. Neither of us is carrying a sexually transmitted disease. We agree that each of us will have a test for such diseases before we marry. We further agree as follows:

(2) Financial disclosure forms for each of us are attached to this Agreement. We are relying on each other for financial support during this marriage but not afterward, should the marriage end. We each expressly waive any right to support after the marriage. Each of us is fully able to earn a comfortable standard of living.

(3) Each of us has consulted his or her own attorney. Jane's attorney is Mr. Big Firm and Max's is Ms. Independent.

(4) We further agree that each of us waives any right to a community or marital interest in any property acquired during this marriage. We will indicate our rights, if any, by the form in which title is taken. The assumption will be that all property is separate and not shared.

(5) We are not engaged in a partnership or other business undertaking. If we enter into such a business relationship in the future, we will indicate our new arrangement by some form of written agreement; if there is no written memorial of that new arrangement, then we promise each other that we will not seek to enforce that relationship will indicate that either by written agreement between us or by the names we put on the title.

(6) If we purchase any new tangible property while we are together, that property will belong to the person in whose name it is taken, regardless of who pays for it. If we intend any other form of ownership, we will indicate

that either by written agreement between us or by the names we put on the title or receipt. If only one name is on the title to the property, then it shall be conclusively presumed that person is the sole owner and that any financial contribution by the other was a gift.

(7) If we loan each other any amount of money over $500, we will memorialize that loan by some form of writing, even if it is only a check marked loan. Any loan between us that is not indicated by some writing is not intended by us to be an enforceable obligation, and we agree not to sue to collect it in the future. Unless we agree in writing to other terms, any loans between us shall be free of interest and shall be repayable on demand. Any such loan will be repaid immediately if one of us moves out.

(8) We agree that each of us will pay for one-half of the monthly expenses. We will settle up each payday.

(9) This is the only Agreement that we have made with each other. It may only be modified in writing. The only exception is that we may enter into informal agreements between ourselves with regard to the details of loans, household chores, and expenses. Those agreements will be consider to supplement, not to replace, this Agreement. We have not made each other any other promises or representations inconsistent with this Agreement to induce each other to sign this Agreement. Any personal understandings of love or affection, or agreements about daily household management, are not part of this Agreement, nor are they intended to be legally enforceable.

(10) This Agreement will last so long as we are married and shall govern the terms of any divorce. The financial provisions of this Agreement shall, however, be deemed to be modified if, by mutual agreement, one of us reduces his or her earning capacity, for example, if we move to a new city where only one of us has employment comparable to his or her previous job. Mutual agreement must be shown by clear and convincing evidence and the mere fact that one of us loses, or leaves, his or her employment shall not suffice as such evidence. Such modification shall consist in each of us owning one-half of any assets, earnings, and so on acquired at the date of such change.

(11) If there is any dispute over the terms of our relationship or this Agreement, then we will submit the dispute, within twenty days of our splitting up, for binding arbitration to an arbitrator whom we choose at that time or, if we do not agree on who the arbitrator should be, then to Pastor Middlemarch of First Lutheran Church. The arbitration shall take place within 20 days after one of us gives the other written notice that a dispute exists and that he/she desires arbitration. If we have a dispute, each of us will pay his or her own attorney.

Signed:

Jane Doe_____ Date:

Max Smith_____ Date:

Sample Agreement for a Couple Without Children and Who Want To Keep Financial Matters Separate

The parties to this Agreement are Jane Jones and Max Smith. The consideration for this Agreement consists in our mutual promises to each other set out herein. Sexual matters form no part of the consideration for this Agreement.

We agree and represent as follows:

(1) Both of us are over the age of twenty-one. We are not presently married and we do not intend to be married. We agree that any reference to each other as husband or wife or any other such language is a matter of social convenience only and does not indicate an intention to marry. Neither of us is married to anyone else. If we later marry, then this Agreement is revoked.

(2) Both of us are entering this agreement freely, as self-sufficient adults. Neither of us has coerced or imposed on the other, and each of us has had ample time to reflect on the terms of this Agreement and to get such advice as he or she felt was appropriate.

(3) Neither of us is carrying a sexually transmitted disease. Each of us has had tests for such diseases within the last three months and such tests were negative.

(4) We have made such financial disclosure as seems appropriate to us in the form of the lists of assets attached hereto and the contents of this paragraph. We represent to each other that those disclosures are true and correct on the date we sign this agreement. If any of these facts change we agree to inform each other of the change. Both of us are presently Max works at Blank's Accounting Firm and Jane works at the law firm of Jones, Jones, and Williams. Each of us agrees that income from our work and other benefits are the separate property of the person earning them.

(5) We intend to treat each other courteously and with respect. We expect to share our lives and to have fun together. We intend to be sexually faithful to each other. We understand, however, that promises like the ones in this paragraph are inherently personal and depend on the affections of each of us. Each of us agrees that relationships change over time. None of the undertakings in this paragraph, therefore, shall be grounds for a claim by one of us against the other, whether we keep these promises or break them, unless one of us infects the other with a sexually transmitted disease.

(6) Each person's assets and earnings belong to him or her alone. Unless we change this Agreement in writing, or otherwise indicate in writing that a different arrangement has been agreed upon, neither of us shall acquire any interest in the other's assets or income, present or future, by virtue of our living together. Our respective assets and possessions are set out in the attached Exhibits A and B. Neither of us intends to acquire any share of ownership in the listed assets.

(7) If any of the listed items breaks and is replaced during the term of this agreement, the ownership of the replacement shall belong to the person who owned the original item.

(8) Neither of us will assert any interest in savings accounts, IRAs, pension plans or other financial assets.

(9) The house at 9000 Fragrant Road, Nowheresville, Idaho, belongs to Jane, and Max agrees that he will not acquire any interest in the house by virtue of sharing in household expenses or otherwise. He further agrees that he will move out of the house on seven days notice. He agrees that he is not a tenant within the meaning of any applicable law providing for the rights of tenants and that this is a personal cohabitation agreement and not a lease.

(10) We are not engaged in a partnership or other business undertaking. If we enter into such a business relationship in the future, we will indicate our new arrangement by some form of written agreement; if there is no written memorial of that new arrangement, then we promise each other that we will not seek to enforce that relationship.

(11) If we purchase any tangible property while we are together, that property will belong to the person in whose name it is taken, regardless of who pays for it. If we intend any other form of ownership, we will indicate that either by written agreement between us or by the names we put on the title. If only one name is on the title to the property, then it shall be conclusively presumed that person is the sole owner and that any financial contribution by the other was a gift. If there is any conflict between this paragraph and any other paragraph of this Agreement, then this paragraph governs.

(12) If we loan each other any amount of money over $500. we will memorialize that loan by some form of writing, even if it is only a check marked loan. Any loan between us that is not indicated by some writing is not intended by us to be an enforceable obligation, and we agree not to sue to collect it in the future. Unless we agree in writing to other terms, any loans between us shall be free of interest and shall be repayable on demand. Any such loan will be repaid immediately if one of us moves out.

We agree that the following expenses will be shared as set out below:

(13) Both of us will pay for our own cars, health insurance, and other expenses. Max will pay Jane $1000_as his part of the expenses of living in Jane's house, but Jane will be responsible for the mortgage payments. Each payday each of us will put $750 n a joint checking account out of which Jane will pay for food, utilities, and cable TV. Max may also sing checks on that account for household expenses. Any amount left over will be carried forward to the next month or spent as we agree.

(14) Each of us will do one-half of the household chores. All housecleaning, yard work, etc. will be done on Saturday. Max will take care of the laundry and Jane will take the cars in for service.

(15) We do not intend to have children together and we agree to use some form of birth control on which we both agree. For the present, we agree to

use an IUD as birth control, so long as both of us are comfortable with that form; if any change is made, we will discuss it first. If a child is born from our relationship, this Agreement is rescinded. [OR If a child is conceived from this relationship, we agree to get married before the child is born.]

(16) This is the only Agreement that we have made with each other. It may only be modified in writing. The only exception is that we may enter into informal agreements between ourselves with regard to the details of loans, household chores, and expenses. Those agreements will be consider to supplement, not to replace, this Agreement. We have not made each other any other promises or representations inconsistent with this Agreement to induce each other to sign this Agreement. Any personal understandings of love or affection are not part of this Agreement.

(17) This Agreement will last so long as we live together. If either of us moves out of our common household, this Agreement is terminated, except for a final settling up of common accounts as described herein. Otherwise, this Agreement may be terminated at any time by either of us, for any reason or for no reason, just by giving the other written or oral notice that the Agreement is ended.

(18) If there is any dispute over the terms of our relationship or this Agreement, then we will submit the dispute, within twenty days of our splitting up, for binding arbitration to an arbitrator whom we choose.

Signed:

Jane Doe: _____ *Date:*

Max Smith: _____ *Date:*

Notes on a Sample Agreement for a Couple with Children

The possible variations on a couple moving in together with children are far too complicated to cover more than a few options. The most complicated issue is that of money, including child support. The most difficult issue is how to coordinate different standards of discipline, school work, and so on. The most important issue is that of the children's relationship with your significant other.

The basic consideration, however, should be the well-being of the children. You should carefully consider the moral and emotional lessons that you are teaching your children if you cohabit with someone (or enter into a casual marriage). The moral lessons are that commitment and loyalty, leave alone chastity, are unimportant virtues. The emotional lesson is that relationships are temporary and unreliable.

Remember you may tire of this relationship but your children may have grown to love the person with whom you are living or at least to enjoy, and rely on, his or her companionship and guidance. A young boy, for example, benefits from a mature, decent man's companionship and guidance, as a young girl benefits from that of a mature, decent woman. Your children's emotional growth, including their ability to be in a happy marriage of their own as adults, may be stunted or deformed by your conduct now.

Perhaps you believe that relationships should only last as long as both parties are happy in the relationship, that each person is basically on his or her own and should paddle his or her own canoe. That worldview will be transmitted to your children if you force them to move through a series of temporary living arrangements.

If your child forms a solid relationship with your significant other, whether your spouse or your lover, you should in fairness consider making a formal arrangement permitting them to have an on-going relationship.

Similarly, if you are living with a person with children, you may wish to consider whether you should undertake some financial responsibility for them, such as contributing to a college fund. Such arrangements should probably be expressly limited to the term of the agreement, so that if you split up with the parent, you do not have an ongoing financial obligation to the children. You can always continue such an obligation voluntarily.

Sample Agreement for a Couple With Children Who Plan To Live Together and Who Want To Keep Financial Matters Separate

The parties to this Agreement are Jane Jones and Max Smith. The consideration for this Agreement consists in our mutual promises to each other set out herein. Sexual matters form no part of the consideration for this Agreement.

We represent to each other the following:

(1) Both of us are over the age of twenty-one. We are not presently married and we do not intend to be married. We agree that any reference to each other as husband or wife or any other such language is a matter of social convenience only and does not indicate an intention to marry. Neither of us is married to anyone else.

(2) Both of us are entering this agreement freely, as self-sufficient adults. Neither of us has coerced or imposed on the other, and each of us has had ample time to reflect on the terms of this Agreement and to get such advice as he or she felt was appropriate.

(3) Neither of us is carrying a sexually transmitted disease. We agree that each of us will have a test for such diseases before we move in together.

(4) We have not disclosed our finances to each other because we are not looking to each other for financial support and our relationship would not justify such disclosure. We regard each other's finances as their private business.

(5) We intend to treat each other courteously and with respect. We expect to share our lives and to have fun together. We intend to be sexually faithful to each other. We understand, however, that promises like the ones in this paragraph are inherently personal and depend on the affections of each of us. Each of us agrees that relationships change over time. None of the undertakings in this Agreement except for the financial arrangements,

therefore, shall be grounds for a claim or legal action by one of us against the other, whether we keep these promises or break them, unless one of us infects the other with a sexually transmitted disease.

(6) Each person's assets and earnings belong to him or her alone. Unless we change this Agreement in writing, or otherwise indicate in writing that a different arrangement has been agreed upon, neither of us shall acquire any interest in the other's assets or income, present or future, by virtue of our living together. Jane owns a Honda Civic and Max own a Jaguar on which he is making payments. Both of us are presently employed. Max works at Big Law Firm and Jane works at Little Medical Clinic. Jane also owns the following items that may be in our residence: one plasma TV, one heirloom dining room set, and three original oil paintings by Rothko. Max also owns all the furniture now in the apartment and a Cabin Cruiser boat.

(7) Neither of us intends to acquire any share of ownership in the assets that belong to the other whether or not listed above. If any of the listed items breaks or is replaced, the ownership of the replacement shall belong to the person who owned the original item.

(8) In particular and without limitation, neither of us will assert any interest in savings accounts, IRAs, pension plans, or other financial assets.

(9) The house at our address on Blossom Lane belongs to Jane, and Max agrees that he will not acquire any interest in the house by virtue of sharing in household expenses or otherwise. He further agrees that he will move out of the house on seven days notice. He agrees that he is not a tenant within the meaning of any applicable law providing for the rights of tenants and that this is a personal cohabitation agreement and not a lease.

(10) We are not engaged in a partnership or other business undertaking. If we enter into such a business relationship in the future, we will indicate our new arrangement by some form of written agreement; if there is no written memorial of that new arrangement, then we promise each other that we will not seek to enforce that relationship.

(11) If we purchase any tangible property while we are together, that property will belong to the person in whose name it is taken, regardless of who pays for it. If we intend any other form of ownership, we will indicate that either by written agreement between us or by the names we put on the title. If only one name is on the title to the property, then it shall be conclusively presumed that person is the sole owner and that any financial contribution by the other was a gift. If there is any conflict between this paragraph and any other paragraph of this Agreement, then this paragraph governs. As to any property that is in both our names, we are fiduciaries toward each other; otherwise we are not.

(12) We agree to be fair to each other.

(13) Jane has one daughter, Melanie, who will be living with us. Melanie's father, Jack Jones, pays for Melanie's support. Max has two sons, Mark and Matthew. Max has custody of those children on alternate weekends and they

may be staying with us on those weekends. Behavior standards will be set alike for these children, subject to appropriate age modifications, and questions of discipline will be decided by each child's parent. We hereby agree that each of us has our permission to pick up the children at school, to take them to after school activities, and if necessary to consent to emergency medical treatment.

(14) If a child of one of us breaks something belonging to the other, the child's parent will replace the item. If a child of one of us breaks the other's child's toy or possession, the parent of the child who broke the item will replace it.

(15) We understand that our relationship may affect our children. We intend for this to be a loving and wholesome household that benefits all the children. We further agree that if this relationship ends, we will make suitable arrangements for our children to visit each other, if they wish to, or to spend time with the other adult, if both wish to. In these matters, we agree to act for the best interest of the children, and if we are unable to agree, to consult with a therapist, such as a psychologist or family therapist, and to abide by his or her recommendations.

(16) If we loan each other any amount of money over $100, we will memorialize that loan by some form of writing, even if it is only a check marked loan. Any loan between us that is not indicated by some writing is not intended by us to be an enforceable obligation, and we agree not to sue to collect it in the future. Unless we agree in writing to other terms, any loans between us shall be free of interest and shall be repayable on demand. Any such loan will be repaid immediately if one of us moves out.

We agree that the following expenses will be shared as set out below:

(17) Both of us will pay for our own cars, health insurance, and other expenses. Max will pay Jane $500 per month for his part of the expenses of living in Jane's house, but Jane will be responsible for the mortgage payments. Each payday Max will also put $750 in a joint checking account and Jane will put in $750 out of which Jane will pay for food, utilities, and cable TV. Each of us will pay for the extra costs of his or her children, such as movies, videos, dry-cleaning, etc. Any amount left over will be carried forward to the next month or spent as we agree.

We agree that chores will be shared as set out below:

(18) Each of us will do one-half of the household chores. All housecleaning, yard work, etc. will be done on Saturday. Each of us will do any household chores associated with each other's children.

(19) We agree that Jane's children will live with us. Jane agrees that she will attempt to require Little Janey to treat Max politely. Max understands that Jane and Little Janey will spend some time together apart from Max. Max and Jane agree that Jane will set the rules for Little Janey but that Max may enforce those rules when Jane is absent.

(20) We agree that Max's children will be visiting one night a week and two weekends a month, plus 4 weeks in the summertime. Max agrees that he will attempt to require Little Max to treat Jane politely. Jane understands that Max and Little Max will spend some time together apart from Jane. Max and Jane agree that Max will set the rules for Little Max but that Jane may enforce those rules when Max is absent.

(21) We agree that we will try to work together to establish standards for our children that our consistent so that no child feels that he or she is being unfairly treated. We agree that neither of us will deal with the other's ex-spouse in such a way as to cause undue animosity or confusion.

(22) We do not intend to have children together and we agree to use some form of birth control on which we both agree. If a child is conceived from this relationship, we agree to get married before the child is born.

(23) This is the only Agreement that we have made with each other. It may only be modified in writing. The only exception is that we may enter into informal agreements between ourselves with regard to the details of loans, household chores, and expenses. Those agreements will be consider to supplement, not to replace, this Agreement. We have not made each other any other promises or representations inconsistent with this Agreement to induce each other to sign this Agreement. Any personal understandings of love or affection are not part of this Agreement.

(24) This Agreement will last so long as we live together. If either of us moves out of our common household, this Agreement is terminated, except for a final settling up of common accounts as described herein and except for the provisions governing any child from this relationship. Otherwise, this Agreement may be terminated at any time by either of us, for any reason or for no reason, just by giving the other written or oral notice that the Agreement is ended.

(25) If there is any dispute over the terms of our relationship or this Agreement, then we will submit the dispute, within twenty days of our splitting up, for binding arbitration to an arbitrator whom we choose.

Signed:

Jane Doe _____   *Date:*

Max Smith _____   *Date:*

Cohabitation Agreement for a Couple Without Children Who Want to Take Care of Each Other

The parties to this Agreement are Jane Jones and Max Smith. The consideration for this Agreement consists in our mutual promises to each other set out herein. Sexual matters form no part of the consideration for this Agreement.

We represent to each other and agree as follows:

(1) Both of us are over the age of twenty-one. We are not presently married and we do not intend to be married. We agree that any reference to each other as husband or wife or any other such language is a matter of social convenience only and does not indicate an intention to marry. Neither of us is married to anyone else. If we later marry, this agreement will serve as a prenuptial agreement unless revoked in writing. Both of us are entering this agreement freely, as self-sufficient adults. Neither of us has coerced or imposed on the other, and each of us has had ample time to reflect on the terms of this Agreement and to get such advice as he or she felt was appropriate.

(2) We have decided to design our own relationship and set out its terms in this Agreement, which we intend to be legally binding. We intend to provide for each other and direct this agreement to be interpreted in light of our love and commitment.

(3) Neither of us is carrying a sexually transmitted disease. We intend to be monogamous. Both of us have children from previous relationships. Those children are grown. We agree not to make gifts or loans to any of our respective children from joint funds without the other's consent. If this provision is breached, the other may recover such transfer from one of us or from such child.

(4) We have made such disclosure of our finances to each other as we mutually consider appropriate, and we are satisfied with those disclosures. Financial disclosure forms for each of us are attached to this Agreement as Exhibits A and B. We represent to each other that these forms are substantially accurate. Unless one of us has outright lied to the other, we agree that a minor discrepancy in such disclosure shall not be grounds for challenging this Agreement.

(5) To carry out the terms and intent of this Agreement, we have made and executed the following documents, copies of which are attached hereto. We agree that these documents will not be changed during the term of this Agreement without the consent of the other party in writing.

Jane's will;

Max's will;

Durable powers of attorney for health care and in case of incapacity;

Max's designation of Jane as his beneficiary on his life insurance;

Jane's designation of Max as her domestic partner for purposes of insurance and other benefits at Big Company where she works.

(6) Both of us are presently employed. Max works at Small Garage, which he owns, and Jane works at Big Company. We agree to keep each other informed of our respective financial situations. We agree that neither will take on a significant financial liability without informing the other and that we will keep our insurance policies current. We also agree to provide each other with a credit report once a year and to allow each other (including an accountant) to see our paychecks, checking account records, and other relevant financial records as often as the other asks for the information. We also agree that our finances our private and that the information will not be disclosed to others, such as family and friends, except as necessary to implement this agreement.

(7) Despite our decision not to marry, we are looking to each other for financial support, companionship, and emotional intimacy during the term of this Agreement. We promise to treat each other courteously and with respect. We expect to share our lives and to have fun together. We promise to be sexually and emotionally faithful to each other. We understand, however, that promises of fidelity and lifestyle are inherently personal and depend on the affections of each of us. Each of us agrees that relationships change over time. None of these undertakings in this paragraph, therefore, shall be grounds for a claim by one of us against the other, whether we keep these promises or break them, unless as a result of infidelity one of us infects the other with a sexually transmitted disease.

(8) We agree to be fiduciaries toward each other as to our shared property. We agree not to profit at the other's expense during this relationship and to treat each other fairly, honestly and in good faith. We hope and intend that this relationship will benefit each of us financially equally and that both will contribute equally in work, effort, and money.

(9) We intend that this Agreement be implemented and interpreted in accordance with the above statements.

(10) We do not have any obligation to each other with regard to the management of our separate property or the proceeds of that property, unless one of us undertakes to manage the other's separate property or unless separate property is commingled with shared property.

(11) All assets acquired during this relationship (except for the income or proceeds of separate property) shall belong to us in equal shares unless we expressly provide otherwise. That property shall be called "shared property."

(12) Shared property includes our income during this relationship. Each person's earnings (except for profits or income from separate property) during this Agreement belong to us jointly, except for the investment proceeds of separate property. We agree to put our paychecks into a joint account. If for any reason it is unclear whether property acquired during this

relationship should be considered shared or separate, then it shall be deemed to have become shared property.

(13) Any property or asset that is inherited or acquired by gift from someone other than one of us belongs solely to the person receiving it and the other acquires no interest in it. Any property that each of owns before we move in together shall continue to belong to that person and the other acquires no interest in it. We call that property and its proceeds "separate property."

(14) In particular, and without limitation, we agree that the assets listed on Exhibits A and B are the separate property of their present owner. If any of the listed items breaks or is replaced, the ownership of the replacement shall belong to the person who owned the original item.

(15) Jane owns the house at 111 Elm Street, East Overshoe, Missouri, which is called the house in this Agreement. That house will remain her separate property. Any amount contributed to its upkeep or payments by Max will considered simply as his share of household expenses and will not entitle him to any interest in the house unless we agree otherwise in writing. Max agrees that he is a guest in the house and is not a tenant within the meaning of state law. Jane agrees to give Max thirty days notice before asking him to move out pursuant to the termination provisions below. If Jane sells the house during this relationship, the proceeds belong to her alone.

(16) Max owns and operates Max's Small Garage which will be his separate property Jane will not acquire any ownership interest in Max's Small Garage except that any income from it during this relationship shall belong to both jointly. If Max sells Small Garage during the relationship, the proceeds belong to him alone. Jane does not have any right to control any aspect of Small Garage. If Jane helps Max at the garage, she does so to promote the good of the relationship and not for gain.

(17) We intend the property provisions of this Agreement to be analogous to those governing community and separate property for married couples. We intend that property described as belonging to one of us be his or her separate property. We intend for this term to have the same meaning in this Agreement as it is does in the family laws of Arizona.

(18) If a separate asset is commingled with shared property and we do not otherwise indicate in writing, we agree that, if we terminate this agreement, the party who originally owned the separate property shall be entitled to reimbursement for the amount commingled. The reimbursement shall not include interest or a share in any increase in value. Commingled property shall not be presumed to have been a gift.

(19) We intend for property acquired during this relationship from shared property to be shared property, unless we clearly indicate a different intention. We may consistently with this paragraph acquire assets as joint tenants with right of survivorship. If there is any conflict between this paragraph and any other paragraph of this Agreement, then this paragraph governs.

(20) If we intend any other form of ownership, we will indicate that either by written agreement between us or by the names we put on the title. If only one name is on the title to the property and the other party agreed to that at the time of acquisition of the property, then it shall be presumed that person is the sole owner and that any financial contribution by the other was a gift.

(21) Unless we change this Agreement in writing, or otherwise indicate in writing that a different arrangement has been agreed upon, neither of us shall acquire any interest in the other's assets or income that may be acquired after the termination of this Agreement.

(22) All expenditures over $200 from joint funds will be made with our joint agreement.

(23) Any amount from our joint income that is not needed for household expenses and other payments as agreed upon by both of us will be placed in investment account(s) in both our names as joint owners with right of survivorship. Each of us agrees not to change the investments or to make any withdrawals from such account without the other's consent. We agree that we will save five percent of our joint income.

(24) We have agreed to make the following additional provisions for each other's future: (i) To make each other the beneficiary of any life insurance policies that we now have or make acquire; (ii) To make Max the beneficiary of the health insurance offered by Jane's employer, Big Company, under its domestic partner provisions. (iii) To make wills in each other's favor that carry out the terms of this Agreement. (iv) Each year to make the maximum contribution to our separate IRA accounts, which shall remain our separate property.

(25) We are not engaged in a partnership or other business undertaking but we agree to treat each other fairly, honestly, and in good faith. If we enter into such a business relationship in the future, we will indicate our new arrangement by some form of written agreement; if there is no written memorial of that new arrangement, then we promise each other that we will not seek to enforce any such claimed business relationship.

(26) If we loan each other any amount of money over $500, we will memorialize that loan by some form of writing, even if it is only a check marked loan. Any loan between us that is not indicated by some writing is not intended by us to be an enforceable obligation, but a gift and we agree not to sue to collect it in the future. Unless we agree in writing to other terms, any loans between us shall be free of interest and shall be repayable on demand. Any such loan will be repaid immediately if one of us moves out. We are not liable for each other's debts, whether acquired prior to this Agreement or after, unless we assume that obligation in writing. Any debt incurred during this Agreement will be the separate obligation of the one incurring it unless both of us sign the relevant documents with the lender. Neither of us may obligate the other to any debt or liability. Neither of us may act as agent for the other on financial matters except pursuant to the

durable power of attorney attached hereto. Our joint incomes will be pooled and household expenses will be paid out of that account. Each of us will have $100 per month to spend as he or she sees fit without needing the permission of the other. Each of us will do one-half of the household chores. All housecleaning, yard work, etc. will be done on the weekend. We will plan our major vacations to be together.

(27) Neither of us will invite someone to visit or to stay in the house without the other's consent. Neither of us will plan a party in the house without the other's consent. In particular, neither of us will invite our grown children for a visit, or to reside in the house without the consent of the other.

(28) We do not intend to have children together and we agree to use some form of birth control on which we both agree. If a child is born during this relationship, we agree that we are equally liable for his or her support until the age of 18, provided that the child is biologically that of both of us. We also agree that the best interests of that child will be served by both of us having an equal share in the child's life. Therefore, we agree that it shall be presumed that joint physical custody would be in the child's best interest and we agree that, if this agreement is terminated, we will so provide. If a child is adopted by one of us during this relationship, then the same provisions shall apply, provided that the other party agreed to the adoption. We agree that we will never take any action designed to or likely to deprive the other of a meaningful, ongoing role in the child's life.

(29) This is the only Agreement that we have made with each other. It may only be modified in writing. The only exception is that we may enter into informal agreements between ourselves with regard to the details of small loans, household chores, and expenses. Those agreements will be consider to supplement, not to replace, this Agreement. We have not made each other any other promises or representations inconsistent with this Agreement to induce each other to sign this Agreement. Any personal understandings of love or affection are not part of this Agreement.

(30) This Agreement will last so long as we live together. If either of us moves out of our common household with the intention of not returning, this Agreement is terminated as of the date that he or she moves, except for a final settling of common accounts and except for any ongoing obligations that may persist in order for this Agreement to have its intended effect. If the person who moves out is gone from the household for more than a month, except on business, for illness, or for a vacation, his or her absence shall be presumed to be a termination of this Agreement.

(31) The Agreement may also be terminated by either of us by giving thirty days notice in writing to the other. If we do terminate this Agreement, then we will pay all joint debts incurred under this Agreement and divide all assets acquired under this Agreement (remaining after the payment of debts) equally.

(32) Neither of us may act as the other's agent except as set out in our durable powers of attorney. Neither of us is liable for the other's debts unless we agree to be liable in writing.

(33) If we end this relationship, we agree to divide amicably all property covered by this Agreement, including making such changes to title, names on accounts and so on as are required to accomplish such division. If we elect not to divide such property but to continue joint ownership, our ownership shall be as tenants in common unless we provide otherwise in writing.

(34) Health insurance benefits will be continued until the other party can acquire replacement coverage and in no event for less than six months. No life insurance or other investment will be terminated or changed until all property is divided agreeably.

(35) This Agreement shall be governed by the laws of Arizona and venue for any dispute shall be in Phoenix. We may vary the venue by agreement.

(36) If there is any dispute over the terms of our relationship or this Agreement, then we will submit the dispute, within sixty days of the termination of the Agreement, for binding arbitration to an arbitrator whom we choose at that time, or if we cannot agree on such arbitrator, then to Father Frank Mulcahy of Sacred Heart Church for final decision. If Father Mulcahy is not available, then a court may appoint an arbitrator for us. During that sixty-day period, we agree that neither of us will dispose of, hide, nor change any joint assets or any asset that the other claims as a joint asset. If we use attorneys, then each of us will pay his or her own attorney.

Signed:

Jane Doe_____   Date:

Max Smith_____   Date:

Subscribed to before me this 21st day of August, 2001,

Notary public seal

Taking Care of Each Other — More Documents

This section deals with couples who have decided that their relationship is a long term committed one, which will involve sharing the financial aspects of the relationship.

When you decide that this is a long-term committed relationship, you need to execute the appropriate documents.

You should review these documents and other arrangements at least once a year or when any significant change in the relationship takes place. A significant change would include starting a new business together, going back to school, inheriting money, moving to a new city, or having a child. All of these events may change a couple's expectations of each other. The old agreement may not fit the new facts.

A committed relationship requires more in terms of disclosure to each other.

Finally, remember that business endeavors may require separate documents, such as partnership or corporate agreements.

Don't forget to give copies of these documents to your doctor and family members, as well as close friends if appropriate. Remember — your attorney in fact under a durable power is not your lawyer.

Each state has developed its own forms for advance directives (living wills), and many of the current forms contain a durable power of attorney for health care in the form. This is much simpler than executing two documents. However, it does not make your wishes as clear. The sample in this book is from Texas. All of the verbiage that goes with the actual signed form is part of the document. You can get the proper form for your state from your doctor or a local hospital.

Sample Durable Power of Attorney for Health Care
(taken from a Colorado form)

I, Fred Smith, voluntarily appoint

Mary Jones
0000 Lover's Lane
Heartbreak Hotel, Texas
000-000-0000 (phone number)

To be my attorney-in-fact and health care agent ("Attorney in Fact"). I am an adult person of sound mind and I fully understand the effect of this appointment. I have discussed my values and preferences with Mary Jones and she understands my wishes.

(1) If Mary Jones shall, for any reason, be unavailable or unwilling to serve as my attorney in fact, I name the following as alternate attorneys in fact:

　　A. First Alternate Attorney in Fact -

　　[insert name and address]

　　B. Second Alternate Attorney in Fact -

　　[insert name and address]

(2) My alternates shall become my attorney in fact in the order named. Each shall act alone, although they may consult each other if they so desire. I have informed these alternates of my health care preferences and values and they understand my wishes.

(3) THIS IS A DURABLE POWER OF ATTORNEY AND THE AUTHORITY OF MY ATTORNEY IN FACT SHALL NOT BE AFFECTED IF I BECOME INCAPACITATED. This Medical Durable Power of Attorney shall become effective only in the event that I am incapacitated. The term incapacitated means that in reasonable medical judgment I am unable to make rational medical decisions, or to reliably communicate such decisions, about my own health or medical

care. That incapacity shall be certified by two physicians who have examined me, one of which shall, if reasonably possible, be my personal physician, Dr. Gooddoctor.

(4) Unless revoked by me, this Medical Durable Power of Attorney shall remain in effect until certification by two physicians that I am no longer incapacitated or until my death or until terminated by law. Further, any person may rely on this document unless that person knows or has reason to know that I have revoked this document or am no longer incapacitated.

(5) My Attorney in Fact has the same authority to make any health care decision for me as I would have if I were competent to do so.

(6) It is my intention that my Attorney in Fact will make health care decisions for me consistent with my expressed wishes, whether those have been expressed to her orally or have been as set out in this document. My Attorney in Facts decision as to my wishes shall be final unless there is clear and concrete evidence that I have expressed a contrary wish within thirty days of my incapacity. So far as I can now foresee, I have the following preferences:

> *[here insert a description of any particular wish that you have such as not to be sustained on a respirator for more than 21 days or not to be treated aggressively if it is unlikely that you will survive or if survival will entail great pain or eventual mental or physical disability]*

> *[here insert a description of any other particular wish that you have such as not to be sustained on a respirator for more than 21 days or not to be treated aggressively if it is unlikely that you will survive or if survival will entail great pain or eventual mental or physical disability]*

(7) My Attorney in Facts authority shall include but not be limited to the following:

> *To consent, refuse, or withdraw consent to any health care, being performed to diagnose or treat me.*

> *To make all necessary arrangements for my care at any health care facility including a hospice or psychiatric facility, or my home.*

> *To employ or discharge any health care professional involved in my care, including my physician.*

> *To receive any information about my physical or mental health, including all medical records, and to execute any release that may be requested in order to obtain such information. My attorney in facts rights in this regard shall not be limited in anyway and she shall have access to all of my records, including mental health records.*

> *To move me to any place or facility, including a different state or country, if such move will be for my benefit or assist in the carrying out of my wishes regarding my care, including transporting me to a*

locality where the applicable laws will permit my desires to be carried out.

To visit me in any health care facility on at least the same terms as if my attorney in fact were my next of kin or my attorney.

To execute any document [1] which my attorney in fact reasonably believes to be in my best interest; or [2] which my attorney in fact reasonably believes will assist in the carrying out of my wishes; or [3] which my Attorney in Fact believes I would execute if I were competent to do so. Such documents shall include releases from liability on my behalf.

To take any legal action necessary to the implementation of this document. The expenses of any such legal action shall be reimbursed from my assets or from my estate if I should die. All expenses incurred by my attorney in fact in carrying out my wishes shall likewise be reimbursed.

To contact members of my immediate family, friends, and colleagues, about my medical condition and wishes, to the extent my Attorney in Fact deems it appropriate or desirable to do so.

(8) My attorney in fact may decide to take any given action even if the action taken may hasten my death. In particular, and without limitation, my attorney in fact may demand that I be given such pain relief or other palliative care as will lessen my suffering or that I be cared for in my own home, so that I can die in peace as I have wished.

(9) I waive any conflict of interest that might exist on my attorney in facts part.

(10) My Attorney in Fact may not consent to the following:

[here insert any restrictions that you want on the attorney in facts power such as that the attorney in fact may not have you deprived of nutrition and hydration]

[here insert any restrictions that you want on the attorney in facts power such as that the attorney in fact may not have you deprived of nutrition and hydration]

(11) If there is any chance that I can hear or understand the discussion, my Attorney in Fact must try to discuss treatment decisions with me. However, if I am unable to communicate my wishes, or if the situation is ambiguous, my Attorney in Fact may make all decisions for me. If there is any reasonable doubt about whether I can communicate, or whether I can understand, the opinion of my treating physician shall be conclusive on that issue. My attorney in fact shall also consult with my physician in order to understand my situation. My attorney in fact may also consult such other persons, as she deems appropriate and desirable, and shall try to explain my wishes to my family if asked to do so. The costs of such consultation, if any, shall be borne by my estate if not covered by my health insurance.

(12) I request and direct that my family and friends cooperate with my attorney in fact and treat her with consideration and respect. I have deliberately selected my attorneys in fact because I trust them to follow my wishes. I direct that no litigation be brought in my name or on my behalf to challenge any decision of my attorney in fact unless (1) that decision violates an express wish of mine set out herein; or (2) the person bringing such action reasonably believes, based on clear and concrete evidence, either that I have recently changed my mind about my wishes or that I have revoked this document.

(13) I specifically direct that life sustaining treatment not be terminated before [here insert any specific condition that you desire, such as before my children have a chance to say goodbye or before I have received the last rites according to the Greek Orthodox Church.} [If necessary, add additional language that may be needed, such as I further direct that pain relieving or sedating medication be withdrawn, or other necessary actions be taken, to permit me to see my children or whatever.]

(14) I hereby revoke any Medical Durable Power of Attorney that I have previously executed.

(15) If any term of this Medical Durable Power of Attorney shall be invalid under the law, then all other provisions that are valid shall remain in effect.

IN WITNESS WHEREOF, I hereby voluntarily and intentionally sign and execute this Medical Durable Power of Attorney on the _____ day of _____, _____

[add signature line and notary form]

Directive to Physicians (Texas form)

The following sample document was taken from the form prescribed by statute in Texas. Other states have their own forms.

Texas Directive To Physicians and Family or Surrogates

Instructions for completing this document:

This is an important legal document known as an Advance Directive. It is designed to help you communicate your wishes about medical treatment at some time in the future when you are unable to make your wishes known because of illness or injury. These wishes are usually based on personal values. In particular, you may want to consider what burdens or hardships of treatment you would be willing to accept for a particular amount of benefit obtained if you were seriously ill.

You are encouraged to discuss your values and wishes with your family or chosen spokesperson, as well as your physician. Your physician, other health care provider, or medical institution may provide you with various resources to assist you in completing your advance directive. Brief definitions are listed below and may aid you in your discussions and advance planning. Initial the treatment choices that best reflect your personal preferences. Provide a copy of your directive to your physician, usual hospital, and family or spokesperson. Consider a periodic review of this document. By periodic review, you can best assure that the directive reflects your preferences.

In addition to this advance directive, Texas law provides for two other types of directives that can be important during a serious illness. These are the Medical Power of Attorney and the Out-of-Hospital Do-Not-Resuscitate Order. You may wish to discuss these with your physician, family, hospital representative, or other advisers. You may also wish to complete a directive related to the donation of organs and tissues.

DIRECTIVE

*I, **John Smith**, recognize that the best health care is based upon a partnership of trust and communication with my physician. My physician and I will make health care decisions together as long as I am of sound mind and able to make my wishes known. If there comes a time that I am unable to make medical decisions about myself because of illness or injury, I direct that the following treatment preferences be honored:*

If, in the judgment of my physician, I am suffering with a terminal condition from which I am expected to die within six months, even with available life-sustaining treatment provided in accordance with prevailing standards of medical care:

[Check one]

_____ _____ *I request that all treatments other than those needed to keep me comfortable be discontinued or withheld and my physician allow me to die as gently as possible; OR*

_____ _____ *I request that I be kept alive in this terminal condition using available life-sustaining treatment. (THIS SELECTION DOES NOT APPLY TO HOSPICE CARE.)*

, in the judgment of my physician, I am suffering with an irreversible condition so that I cannot care for myself or make decisions for myself and am expected to die without life-sustaining treatment provided in accordance with prevailing standards of care:

[Check one]

_____ _____ *I request that all treatments other than those needed to keep me comfortable be discontinued or withheld and my physician allow me to die as gently as possible; OR*

_____ _____ *I request that I be kept alive in this irreversible condition using available life-sustaining treatment. (THIS SELECTION DOES NOT APPLY TO HOSPICE CARE.)*

Additional requests: [here insert any specific additional requests that you may have as to treatments that you do, or do not, want].

After signing this directive, if my representative or I elect hospice care, I understand and agree that only those treatments needed to keep me comfortable would be provided and I would not be given available life-sustaining treatments.

If I do not have a Medical Power of Attorney, and I am unable to make my wishes known, I designate the following person(s) to make treatment decisions with my physician compatible with my personal values:

[insert name and address of person to make decisions for you]

(If a Medical Power of Attorney has been executed, then an agent already has been named and you should not list additional names in this document.)

If the above persons are not available, or if I have not designated a spokesperson, I understand that a spokesperson will be chosen for me following standards specified in the laws of Texas. If, in the judgment of my physician, my death is imminent within minutes to hours, even with the use of all available medical treatment provided within the prevailing standard of care, I acknowledge that all treatments may be withheld or removed except those needed to maintain my comfort. I understand that under Texas law this directive has no effect if I have been diagnosed as pregnant. This directive will remain in effect until I revoke it. No other person may do so.

Signed:

John Smith
0000 Lovers Lane
Heartbreak Hotel, TX

Two competent adult witnesses must sign below, acknowledging the signature of the declarant. The witness designated as Witness I may not be a person designated to make a treatment decision for the patient and may not be related to the patient by blood or marriage. This witness may not be entitled to any part of the estate and may not have a claim against the estate of the patient. This witness may not be the attending physician or an employee of the attending physician. If this witness is an employee of a health care facility in which the patient is being cared for, this witness may not be involved in providing direct patient care to the patient. This witness may not be an officer, director, partner, or business office employee of a health care facility in which the patient is being cared for or of any parent organization of the health care facility.

Witness I

(signature)

[insert name and address of Witness I]

Witness II

(signature)

[insert name and address of Witness II]

Definitions:

"Artificial nutrition and hydration" means the provision of nutrients or fluids by a tube inserted in a vein, under the skin in the subcutaneous tissues, or in the stomach (gastrointestinal tract).

"Irreversible condition" means a condition, injury, or illness:

[1] that may be treated, but is never cured or eliminated;

[2] that leaves a person unable to care for or make decisions for the person's own self; and

[3] that, without life-sustaining treatment provided in accordance with the prevailing standard of medical care, is fatal.

Explanation: Many serious illnesses such as cancer, failure of major organs (kidney, heart, liver, or lung), and serious brain disease such as Alzheimer's dementia may be considered irreversible early on. There is no cure, but the patient may be kept alive for prolonged periods of time if the patient receives life-sustaining treatments. Late in the course of the same illness, the disease may be considered terminal when, even with treatment, the patient is expected to die. You may wish to consider which burdens of treatment you would be willing to accept in an effort to achieve a particular outcome. This is a very personal decision that you may wish to discuss with your physician, family, or other important persons in your life.

"Life-sustaining treatment" means treatment that, based on reasonable medical judgment, sustains the life of a patient and without which the patient will die. The term includes both life-sustaining medications and artificial life support such as mechanical breathing machines, kidney dialysis treatment, and artificial hydration and nutrition. The term does not include the administration of pain management medication, the performance of a medical procedure necessary to provide comfort care, or any other medical care provided to alleviate a patient's pain.

"Terminal condition" means an incurable condition caused by injury, disease, or illness that according to reasonable medical judgment will produce death within six months, even with available life-sustaining treatment provided in accordance with the prevailing standard of medical care.

Explanation: Many serious illnesses may be considered irreversible early in the course of the illness, but they may not be considered terminal until the disease is fairly advanced. In thinking about terminal illness and its treatment, you again may wish to consider the relative benefits and burdens of treatment and discuss your wishes with your physician, family, or other important persons in your life.

Designation of Guardian

I, Fred Jones [insert address], being of sound mind, do hereby designate Mary Smith [insert address] as the guardian of my person and my estate, should it be determined that I am in need of such a person.

I hereby state for the guidance of my family and any court before which this document may come that:

Mary Smith is my long time companion and is familiar with my wishes in regard to my care and the management of my affairs.

I have previously executed durable powers of attorney, in general and for health care, naming Mary Smith as my attorney in fact.

It is my voluntary and free decision and wish that, in the event that a court determines that I am in need of a guardian, said guardian be Mary Smith. I have carefully considered other possible candidates for this position, including members of my family, and have determined that, based on our long companionship, I prefer Mary Smith to undertake that role.

[add signature line and notary form]

Powers of Attorney — Points to Consider

The point of a durable general power of attorney is to avoid the hassle and expense of your friends or relatives having to go to court and get legal authority to handle your affairs if you are disabled. Remember again -- your attorney in fact is not your lawyer and doesn't need to be a lawyer.

Attorneys in fact serve largely without court supervision so you need to choose someone whom you absolutely trust and whom you reasonably expect to outlive you. The person also needs to be reasonably competent at business matters. Remember, too, that an attorney in fact's position is revoked if a court appoints a guardian for you. Some families file a court proceeding asking for a guardian in order to get rid of an attorney in fact whom they dislike or distrust. This is a particular risk for gay persons whose parents disapprove of their lifestyle. For these reasons, signing a designation of guardian is an important step, even if you have a durable power of attorney. You may also wish to make a notarized statement about your reasons for choosing a particular person as your attorney in fact, including any reasons why you don't want your family members handling your affairs. You might consider videotaping this statement as well as having it in writing, if you anticipate a family fight.

The question is how he or she should manage your assets. Sell the house to pay your medical bills or keep it for your lover and your children to live in? Cash in your stocks to be more conservative or pursue the investment program that you set up?

It is difficult to foresee every possible outcome or need. You can try to think of the options that matter to you.

✓ *Do you want your representative to keep you in the nicest nursing home possible or to preserve your estate for your significant other or your children?*

✓ *If you run out of insurance, should your attorney in fact spend your money or give everything you own away to relatives so that you become poor enough to qualify for Medicaid even if you spend your last months in a crummy facility?*

✓ *Do you have assets, such as a family farm or an heirloom, which you would not want sold for your benefit but want to stay in the family?*

✓ *Do you have specific wishes for your business, such as that a partner run it or the partner have a right to buy your interest?*

✓ *How much do you trust your attorney in fact? Who should have the right to check up on him or her?*

✓ *Is your lover sufficiently experienced in business matters to manage your assets? Perhaps he or she should have someone else's advice or should be jointly responsible with another, more sophisticated, person.*

✓ *Do you have such extensive assets that your attorney in fact should be paid for his or her work?*

As part of preparing a durable power of attorney, you should let your lover know where your assets are and who has information about them. If you don't trust him or her to know this stuff, how can you trust him or her to handle your affairs in the event of an emergency?

Remember, however, that people do make mistakes and that no document can protect you entirely from another person's greed or foolishness. The sample below attempts to give maximum freedom to the attorney in fact while relieving her of any responsibility for errors in judgment, mistakes, etc. In other words, if she sells all your high tech stocks because she thinks that they are too risky, you cannot sue her later. The only liability that your attorney in fact has under this document is for dishonest actions.

Sample General Durable Power of Attorney in the Event of Incapacity

KNOW YE ALL MEN TO WHOM THESE DOCUMENT MAY BY THESE PRESENTS, that I Fred Smith of 0000 Lover's Lane, Fort Collins, Colorado hereby appoint Mary Jones, of 0000 Lovers Lane, Fort Collins, Colorado as my attorney in fact to act for me if I am unable to act for myself due to any incapacity.

(1) This durable power of attorney shall govern my affairs if it appears that I may be incapacitated, as where I am injured or ill. The authority of my attorney in fact shall come into force upon the conditions set forth herein and the question of whether those conditions have or have not been satisfied shall be determined according to the terms of this document.

(2) Her authority shall include, but not be limited to, the following:

To perform any lawful action that I might perform on my own behalf, including the exercise of any legal right that I presently have or later acquire.

This authority includes the authority to deal with any person, transaction, or property, real or personal, tangible or intangible, in which I may have an interest. This authority shall extend to claims and lawsuits. My attorney in fact shall have the same rights to manage all of my assets as I have and may take all such actions in regard to them as I might take, including compromising or abandoning any disputed claim.

To handle all my financial affairs, including my money and similar assets. I intend this to be a general power to deal with my financial affairs, including collecting money and paying bills. This authority shall include holding money spending it for my benefit, and investing it and it includes money owed to me in any form, including but not limited to checks, accounts, deposits, bequests, notes, bonds, and dividends.

To take any action in regard to all property that I now own or later acquire that I myself could take in regard thereto, including but not limited to leasing, selling, or repairing such property,

To conduct any lawful business of whatever kind for me, on my behalf and in my name.

To receive, hold, or cash all payments that I receive from Social Security, Medicare, or any other government program, annuities, pension and retirement benefits, insurance benefits and proceeds.

To make any claim for any such payments or entitlements on my behalf.

To take all lawful actions as she may deem necessary or proper to exercise the authority herein granted, including defending her right to act hereunder.

To enter any safe deposit box, vault or other storage area leased by me alone or in conjunction with any other person, to sign such documents as may be necessary to gain access to same, and to examine, remove and keep the contents as I could if I were present.

To prepare, or cause to be prepared, and filed federal, state and local tax returns, to make such payments as needful, in my name; and to respond to notices and audit inquiries and to settle tax disputes.

To take all actions with regard to pension plans, insurance and retirement savings accounts, and all similar accounts, as I myself could legally take when I was competent.

To make such gifts of my property as are for my benefit or are such as I intended while I was competent.

To pay my lawful debts and obligations and to take any action in regard to claims against me as I might take.

To retain such advisors, accountants, and attorneys as she deems necessary or desirable and to pay same out of my assets.

(3) I ratify and confirm all that attorney in fact shall lawfully do or cause to be done under this power of attorney.

(4) The sole limitations on my attorney in fact's powers are the following:

During the first thirty days after the date of the letter from my physician referred to below, my attorney in fact shall not sell any real estate, compromise any lawsuit, or dispose of any securities, unless such action shall be necessary in the discretion of my attorney in fact to conclude a transaction that I had begun before my incapacity, to protect my interest, or to pay my medical bills.

During the first year after the date of that letter, my attorney in fact shall not sell, rent, or otherwise dispose of my house, my art collection, or my animals, unless such action is necessary in the sole discretion of my attorney in fact to conclude a transaction that I had begun or, in the case of the animals, for humane reasons.

(5) My attorney in fact shall make every reasonable effort to preserve my house, my animals and my art collection in such a way that I may take such enjoyment from them as my condition may permit. For example, and without limitation, she may care for my dogs herself and bring them to visit me.

(6) I direct that, if in the opinion of my doctors, my incapacity is deemed to be likely to persist less than 90 days, my attorney in fact shall try to conserve my assets in their present form, subject to the exceptions set out above. If in the opinion of my doctors, my incapacity is likely to be permanent or to last longer than six months, then I direct my attorney in fact to act as she deems best, subject to the exceptions set out above.

(7) It is my preference that if I am incapacitated, I live the remainder of my life at my home in Fort Collins and be cared for there if reasonably possible. My attorney in fact shall use all reasonable efforts to secure this outcome even if it exposes me to health risks or shortens my life.

(8) If my attorney in fact undertakes to care for me herself, she may compensate herself in addition to other amounts provided for herein up to such amount as would be paid to an independent caregiver.

(9) I expressly direct and authorize my attorney in fact to use my assets to provide for my animals, including my dog Homer and my horse Excalibur.

(10) No person shall be obligated to inquire as to the disposition of any funds paid to or received by my attorney in fact. No person shall have the right to in quire as to any monies received by her or expended by her, except as set out below.

(11) This document shall be binding on my heirs and assigns and no one shall have the right to demand any information from my attorney in fact based on an expectation of inheritance or other benefit from me except as set out below.

(12) I direct and request that my family and friends cooperate with and respect my attorney in fact.

(13) I further direct that no litigation be brought to challenge any action by my attorney in fact, whether such litigation is commenced by any member

of my family on my behalf or for their own interest, or by anyone else acting on my behalf, unless such person reasonably believes based on concrete and clear evidence that my attorney in fact is acting in breach of her fiduciary duty and dissipating my estate for her own advantage. If such action is brought without such concrete and clear basis, I direct that my attorney in fact contest it and that the person bringing such action be required to compensate my attorney in fact and my estate for any loss and expense incurred as a result.

(14) My parents or my brother _____ may, however, request an accounting from my attorney in fact, which she shall furnish within thirty days of the request, but no accounting may be requested until I have been incapacitated for six months and thereafter no more than once a year. Only one such accounting total per year need be furnished by my attorney in fact to any family member or any one else acting on my behalf.

(15) Such accounting shall be limited to a reasonably detailed description of my assets at the time of my incapacity, monies received by and disbursed by my attorney in fact, any amounts paid to my attorney in fact in compensation hereunder, and any other material transaction,. Such accounting shall also set out any changes in my investments or assets made by my attorney in fact.

(16) The cost of preparation of such accounting shall be borne by the person requesting it. If a certified public accountant prepares and signs such accounting, it shall conclusively be deemed sufficient for all purposes including this paragraph and to be correct, unless there is clear evidence of collusion or dishonesty on his or her part.

(17) My attorney in fact shall not be required to furnish any receipts, proof, or justification of her actions to my family or to any one acting on my behalf except pursuant to the paragraphs above.

(18) I release my attorney in fact from any liability for any action taken by her under this power, except for actions taken in clear bad faith or for her own personal advantage.

(19) I have named her as my attorney in fact knowing her strengths and weaknesses in matters of finance and money and intending that she use her own judgment to make decisions about my affairs. In particular, therefore, I release her from any responsibility for errors that she may make or losses that I may suffer, except as set out above.

(20) Further, I direct that the usual standards applicable to professional fiduciaries, such as to diversify assets, shall not be applied to my attorney in fact, except for the duties of loyalty and good faith.

(21) This is a durable power of attorney and shall not terminate on my disability or incapacity. The authority of my attorney in fact shall commence and be in full force and effect only upon my subsequent incapacity. The authority granted herein shall remain in full force and effect thereafter until my death or my recovery from my incapacity

(22) "Incapacity" means that my mental ability to receive and evaluate information effectively is sufficiently impaired so that I lack my normal capacity to manage my financial resources prudently and in my own best interest.

(23) My incapacity shall be decided by my personal physician _____, MD unless he is not available as described below.

(24) If Dr. _____ determines that I am incapacitated, my incapacity shall be conclusively evidenced by a letter from him stating that I am so incapacitated

(25) If Dr. _____ is unavailable to examine me, then such incapacity may be indicated by letters so indicating from three physicians in Fort Collins, Colorado who have examined me. These physicians shall be selected as follows: one by my friend Mary Jones, one by the administrator of any hospital where I may be receiving treatment, and one by my family. The cost of such examination shall be paid from my assets. "Unavailable" means that Dr. ____ is no longer in practice or is absent from the city for a prolonged period or declines to perform such an examination.

(26) If Dr. _____ declines to give such a letter and states that he believes me competent to manage my affairs, then no further examination shall take place and this durable power shall not take further effect.

(27) If my personal physician is unavailable or unwilling to examine me, then my disability may be evidenced by letters so stating from two physicians,

(28) If my personal physician signs such a letter, or if the two other physicians do so, then that letter and this document may be conclusively relied on by anyone who does so in good faith unaware of any dishonesty or collusion in connection therewith.

(29) I waive any physician-client privilege for the purpose of that certification and all matters connected with it, and I authorize the disclosure of such certification by my attorney in fact as necessary.

(30) The effectiveness of this durable power may be relied on until the person so relying knows or should have known that I have recovered from my incapacity or died, provided that the person doing so acts in good faith. If this Durable Power of Attorney in fact is terminated by operation of law, any person acting in reliance upon it in good faith without notice of such termination shall be held harmless.

(31) My attorney in fact shall not be compensated for services performed or activities carried out on my behalf pursuant to this Durable Power of Attorney unless my incapacity extends longer than 30 days. After thirty-day period, my attorney in fact may be draw such compensation as she deems reasonable, which shall not exceed $_____ per month.

(32) My attorney in fact may reimburse her reasonable expenses in carrying out this durable power from my assets, including the cost of obtaining advice and counsel.

(33) A list of my assets, my attorney, and my accountant is attached hereto as Exhibit A. Exhibit A may be changed or updated by me without affecting the validity of this document.

(34) Enumeration of specific items is not intended to limit powers granted herein.

(35) The use of any gender herein includes both gender and the singular includes the plural.

IN WITNESS WHEREOF, Fred Smith has executed this Durable Power of Attorney on _____ at _____.

[insert signature line and notary public form]

Last Will and Testament

Each of a couple should have a will and each should have a copy of the other's will.

If you trust your children, or other heirs, you could provide them with a copy, too. Most people don't want their children to know what, or whether, they will inherit, but some families are comfortable with greater openness.

Writing wills – the details

Making a valid will is a technical business. The formalities of witnesses and so on are rather rigid.

The most common requirements are (1) witnessed by two witnesses; (2) signed by the testator; (3) all signatures notarized; and (4) a sufficient indication that the document is a will, as opposed to some other legal document. The witnesses must see the testator (person making the will) sign it and they must hear him or her say, "This is my will." In other words, the witnesses and the testator usually must all be in the same room at the same time and sign the document right then. It is not sufficient for the witnesses to sign at a different time without the person making the will there. The purpose of the witnesses is to prove that the will was not a forgery and that the testator was not under any obvious duress.

In addition to these requirements, some states provide for specific clauses that make probating the will easier.

A mistake in the technicalities can invalidate the will, in which case either a previous will becomes effective or the estate passes according to the law as if there were no will. Under the law, a person's property passes to their spouse and children, or other relatives, when they die without a will, although the proportions vary among the states. Consequently, children may try to challenge a will naming a new lover as the heir.

Oral wills are rarely valid, although there are exceptions for soldiers in time of battle, people who are on the verge of death, and similar unusual situations.

In many states, a handwritten will is valid without the additional formalities of witnesses and notaries if the document clearly says that it is intended as a will, i.e. that the writer intends that the document govern what happens to his or her assets after death. The catch is that a handwritten will must be entirely in handwriting; a typed document with a handwritten signature is usually not a valid will.

For example, in the days when people wrote their correspondence by hand, a letter of the form "Dear Sis, If I should die, please make sure that Mother gets the ranch. Your loving brother, Fred" could be a valid will.

Like many legal documents, it is possible to write a perfectly nice will without using an attorney, if you are careful to check the requirements in your particular state. Some inexpensive legal software programs and online services have will forms for different states. Remember, though, that by the time you find out that there's a problem, it's usually too late to do anything about it. To be certain, an attorney should supervise the signing of the will.

Complicated wills usually need the assistance of an attorney, particularly if the person has enough money to be subject to inheritance taxes or if there are young children involved.

Every will should provide for all meaningful contingencies. For example, there is a provision in this sample will that if everyone named in the will (the old lady's lover, her children, and her grandchildren) should die before her, then her estate goes to a charity, the Nature Conservancy of Texas. One reason that many people do not like writing wills is that they have to contemplate the possible deaths of people whom they love. The possibility is a sad one but sometimes occurs.

If you do not specify what happens in a particular circumstance, the law will often fill in the gaps. For example, if you don't name a trustee to take care of the assets that you leave to your young children, then the court will appoint someone, sometimes a bank or a crony of the judge. That may not be the best result for the kids, since a greedy bank or lawyer can (more or less legally) dissipate the assets in fees and charges.

Where a family disagrees over money and relationships, as where grown children object to Mom or Dad's new spouse, some lawyers take extra precautions against a will contest, at least if significant money is involved. For example, they may have the testator (person making the will) examined by a psychiatrist who can then testify that he or she was of sound mind when the will was signed. Similarly, if everyone that you wanted to inherit from you dies before you do, your assets will go to some other relative whom you may not have thought of in years. They may videotape the signing of the will including, perhaps, a filmed statement of the testator explaining why he or she made this particular will.

The safest and most convenient place for your will to be kept is in the office of your lawyer, if you remember to let your family or friends know who that is. This safeguards the will from being lost (or destroyed by a family member who might like its terms). The plain fact is that your children will probably not be thrilled if you leave anything to your lover and may feel entitled to do whatever it takes to secure what they feel entitled to.

Most experts recommend against putting the will in a safe deposit box, unless there is a joint tenant on the box, because the bank is not supposed to permit it to be opened after your death without a court order. If you have a safe or fireproof strongbox, that can be a reasonable substitute provided that you prudently limit who has the keys.

If you wish to change part of your will, you must destroy the original or write "Revoked" across it and make a new will. You cannot write in new terms or cross out one name and substitute another. Under the law, these changes nullify the will. Another method is to execute a codicil, which is a small modification of a will, but that must be done with all the formalities of a will.

Other preparations for death or incapacity – funerals, pets, etc.

Another grim fact is that if you have specific wishes about your funeral, you need to write those down in another document, not your will. Most families don't consult a will, even if they can find it, before the funeral. Consequently, the best place for your final wishes is in a letter to those whom you leave behind. You can tell your friends and family before you die and leave a letter to be opened by them after your death.

Really well organized people keep all the relevant documents in one place. That includes the following:

- ✓ *List of assets, including real estate, bank and brokerage accounts, and insurance policies. Don't forget safety deposit boxes, storage units, and so on.*
- ✓ *Durable powers of attorney.*
- ✓ *Directive to physician.*
- ✓ *Designation of guardian.*
- ✓ *Letter explaining health care values, including organ donation, and funeral arrangements.*
- ✓ *Letter expressing love and forgiveness to family members and friends.*
- ✓ *Copy of last will.*
- ✓ *Names of attorneys, accountants, and other people with knowledge.*
- ✓ *Spare set of keys to everything.*
- ✓ *Other instructions, such as arrangements for pets, etc. You may wish to have a separate power of attorney for the animals if they are very dear to you. (Some care needs to be taken in writing this as it may modify a will especially if it is handwritten.)*

You have to use your own judgment about where to keep these materials. If you don't trust your companion or family, a desk drawer may not be safe enough. On the other hand, putting them in a safety deposit box may be a bad idea. The bank will not allow anyone who is not a signatory on the box to have access to it. Consequently, these records will not be available when they are needed. By the time an executor is appointed by a court, many of these documents won't be needed anymore, and the very event that you wanted to prevent may have already happened.

Basically, you have to trust someone. If you are incapacitated, people will frequently find a way to get access to whatever it is that they want. The key is to keep out those that you don't trust and allow in someone whom you do.

If necessary, you can place these documents in different places. For example, you can leave copies of the relevant health care documents with your primary physician, the original of your will with your attorney, and financial information with your accountant. You could leave a spare set of car keys, a letter about your funeral, and so on in a desk drawer.

Don't forget to make arrangements for your pets. A helpful neighbor or friend can take them in temporarily or, if necessary, they can be boarded. Be sure to select the boarding facility carefully; some, including some veterinarians, will destroy the animals after a short period of time if the bill is not paid or if there is no contact from the owner.

Sample will — notes

In the following sample will, an older woman leaves her companion Peter Peterson their RV, a couple of condominiums, and their joint accounts. The rest of her assets will go to her children on her death, except for her jewelry, which will go to her granddaughter.

During her lifetime, she effectively controls how much her lover has by how much she puts in the joint accounts. She can control how much actually goes to her lover or her children by spending her money or giving it away.

Notice that her children each get one-half of everything that doesn't go elsewhere. The left over part is called the "residue" of the estate and it is often the largest portion of a person's assets.

If one of her children should die, that child's children split one-half among themselves and the surviving child gets the other half. These proportions are set out by the Latin phrase "per stirpes."

Notice also that the lady's estate does not go to any nieces or nephews but only to her significant other, her children, and grandchildren, if they outlive her. If none of those specified people outlive the lady making the will, then her property goes to charity. If you want another proportion, you need to set it out clearly.

A will affects the future of your family; be sure it says exactly what you want to happen in the future.

Sample Will

I, Amanda Williams of Resume Speed, Iowa, declare this to be my Will and revoke all other Wills.

(1) My Personal Representative shall pay for my funeral, including the acquisition of any burial site and any markers, regardless of any limitation fixed by statute or rule of court and without order of court, provided only that my funeral is conducted in accordance with my wishes.

(2) For the guidance of all to whom this will may come, I hereby state that Peter Peterson is my cherished friend and companion. By agreement between us, and in token of our love and affection, I wish to leave him the recreational vehicle and condominiums described in this will, together with all the furniture and other items in those places, and together with any joint accounts and insurance policies as we may have established, so that he may continue to enjoy the benefits thereof. I have provided elsewhere and in such fashion as I deem appropriate for my children, other relatives, and friends.

(3) My Personal Representative shall distribute my estate as follows:

(i) to my friend Peter Peterson, if he survives me, my share in the recreational vehicle Fair Wind, VIN 000-000-0000; my interests in the time share communities Island Breeze and Desert Palms; my interests in any joint accounts that Peter Peterson and I may have established; and all of my personal property in the above listed recreational vehicle and condominiums on the day of my death, except for my jewelry.

(ii) to my granddaughter Winnie Williams, if she survives me, all of my jewelry and the Winslow Homer painting entitled "Seascape."

(4) If any bequest under the foregoing paragraphs shall fail for any reason, then that bequest shall become part of the residue of my estate. In particular, if my friend Peter Peterson shall not survive me, then any bequest to him shall be distributed as part of the residue. My Personal Representative shall distribute all of the rest and residue of my tangible personal property as set forth in the following paragraphs.

(5) I give the rest and residue of my property to the following beneficiaries in the following proportions:

(i) To my son William Williams and to my daughter Wilhelmina Williams, one-half each.

(ii) If either of them shall not survive me, then that child's share shall pass to their issue, per stirpes. If either of them shall not survive me and dies without issue, his or her share shall pass to the surviving child.

(iii) If both my children fail to survive to me and die without issue, then the rest and residue of my estate shall pass to my brother, George Smith, if he survives me.

(iv) If my brother does not survive me, then the residue of my estate shall pass to the Nature Conservancy so long as that organization is in existence and appropriately pursuing the goal of preserving areas of ecological importance or natural beauty. Should that organization cease to exist or cease to pursue such goal appropriately, in the sole judgment of my Personal Representative, then the residue of my estate shall be paid to such other charitable organization(s) for the alleviation of the suffering of animals or the protection of the natural environment, as may be selected by my personal representative in his or her discretion.

(6) A beneficiary shall be deemed to have died before me (and not to have survived me) if the beneficiary is not living on the fifth day after the date of my death.

(7) The term "issue" shall include an adopted child and such child's descendants, provided that the adopted child is less than twelve years old on the date of the court order granting such adoption. The term "issue" shall not include any child born out of wedlock.

(8) I have only the following children who are now living: Wilhelmina Williams and William Williams. I intentionally do not include in this will any other person who may for any reason believe that he or she has come claim to be my heir or to share in my estate.

(9) The provisions in this Will for the distribution of my estate shall be subject to the following:

(i) My Personal Representative shall pay all taxes (including inheritance taxes) owed because of my death (including any interest and penalties) out of the residue of my estate. The payment of the taxes shall be made regardless of whether the taxes are owed on property passing under this Will or outside of this Will and regardless of whether the taxes are owed by my estate or by any beneficiary; provided, however, that my Personal Representative shall be entitled to reimbursement from each beneficiary for the payment of the taxes in proportion to the amount of tax generated by the property received by each beneficiary.

(ii) If any beneficiary of my estate is under a legal disability or, in the judgment of my Personal Representative, is for any reason unlikely to use the distribution wisely, my Personal Representative may elect in his discretion to make the distribution directly to the beneficiary or to the conservator of the beneficiary's property or to a person with whom the beneficiary resides at the time of the distribution in whatever manner my Personal Representative shall deem best. In the alternative and if the beneficiary is under twenty one years of age, my Personal Representative may, in the discretion of my Personal Representative, distribute the property to a custodian for the beneficiary under a Uniform Transfer or Gift to Minors Act. The receipt by the beneficiary, conservator, custodian, or other person of any distribution so made shall be a complete discharge to my Personal Representative regarding the distribution.

(10) In addition to the existing authority of my Personal Representative, my Personal Representative may as he or she deems advisable:

(i) Take any action in regard to the management of my estate as he or deems best in his discretion, including the sale, lease or other disposition of any of my property and including maintaining such property.

(ii) Make any division or distribution of my residuary estate in money or in kind as he deems best in his sole discretion, provided only that such shares be equal or approximately equal in value. He may also decide any dispute as to the value of the residuary estate, or any portion of it, as he sees fit, provided only that such decision be reasonably in accord with the available evidence as to value.

(iii) Permit any beneficiaries of my estate to make personal use of any property during the administration of my estate, without paying any rent or other charge, without giving any security, and without liability for loss or damage, except as provided herein. This provision shall not apply to cash, negotiable instruments, stocks, or bonds, all of which shall remain in the custody of my Personal Representative during the administration of this estate. My Personal Representative shall not be liable or responsible for any loss or reduction in value of any property so used except as provided herein. (a) However, if such beneficiary, other than Peter Peterson, use such property for profit or if his or her use prevents such property from yielding income to the estate, then my personal representative may require that beneficiary to pay rent or make such other payment as he deems fair given the terms of this will. (b) Moreover, such beneficiary shall secure appropriate insurance for the value of such property. Should such property be lost or consumed by that beneficiary during the administration of this estate, then the value thereof, in excess of any insurance proceeds, shall reduce that beneficiary's share of my estate. If such beneficiary shall be shown to have acted in bad faith, then he or she shall compensate the estate for the loss. (c) In no event, however, shall Peter Peterson be required to pay rent on or compensation for the recreational vehicle and real estate left expressly to him.

(iv) The expenses of the administration of the estate, including actions relating to the above paragraph, shall be expenses of the estate. Any income from my property during the administration of this estate shall be income of the estate to be divided as part of my residuary estate.

(v) Make advances in his sole discretion of an heir's interest to that heir during the administration of my estate provided that such advance does not diminish the share of any other heir.

(11) However, my personal representative shall endeavor to close my estate as soon as reasonably possible, taking into account any substantial tax consequences of his actions.

(12) I appoint my friend Peter Peterson, as Personal Representative of my estate. If Peter Peterson shall fail to qualify or cease to act as Personal Representative, then I appoint my daughter Wilhelmina as alternate or

successor Personal Representative. If my daughter Wilhelmina shall fail to qualify or cease to act as Personal Representative, then my son William shall serve as Personal Representative.

(13) To the extent permitted by law, and except as provided below, my Personal Representative shall, in his or her discretion, have my estate administered without any order, oversight, or direction of the court having jurisdiction over my estate. My personal representative shall serve without bond or surety and without any court order other than his appointment.

(14) It is my wish that my estate be peacefully administered without dispute. If any court proceeding is brought to challenge any provision of this will or any aspect the administration of my estate, and such challenge is pursued in bad faith or without reasonable justification, I hereby direct that the court may in his or her discretion award the payment of attorneys' fees and costs to the successful party and that such award may be paid from the unsuccessful party's share in my estate, if any. This paragraph shall not apply to the rights of any heir, or potential heir, to request an accounting of my estate as provided by law.

(15) Throughout this Will the use of the male gender shall include the female, and the use of the singular the plural, and vice versa.

I_____, the Testator, sign my name to this instrument this _____ day of _____, and being duly sworn, I declare that I execute this instrument as my last will and testament, that I sign it willingly, as my free and voluntary act, and that I am eighteen years of age or older, of sound mind, and not under any duress or undue influence.

[signature]

[typed name]

We, the witnesses, at the Testator's request, sign our names to this instrument, being first duly sworn, and do hereby declare to the undersigned authority that the Testator indicated in our presence that she signs and executes this instrument as her will and that she signs it willingly, and that each of us, in the presence and hearing of the Testator, hereby signs this will as witness to the Testator's signing, and that to the best of our knowledge the Testator is eighteen years of age or older, of sound mind, and under no constraint or undue influence.

[print or type name and address and phone number of each witness beneath the name]

Witness

_____

(insert printed name and address)

Witness

_____

(insert printed name and address)

Witness

_____

(insert printed name and address)

State of_____

County _____

We, the Testator and the witnesses, respectively, whose names are signed to the attached or foregoing instrument, being first duly sworn, do hereby declare to the undersigned authority that the Testator signed and executed the instrument as the Testator's will and that the Testator had signed willingly (or willingly directed another to sign for the Testator), and that the Testator executed it as the Testator's free and voluntary act for the purposes expressed in the will, and that each of the witnesses, in the presence and hearing of the Testator, and at the request of the Testator, signed the will as witness and that to the best of the witnesses' knowledge the Testator was at that time eighteen years of age or older, of sound mind, and under no constraint or undue influence.

[signatures of everyone]

Subscribed, sworn to and acknowledged before me by Amanda Williams, Testator, and subscribed and sworn to before me by _____, _____, and _____, witnesses, this _____ day of _____.

[notary public's signature and seal]

Sample Letter to Family and Friends

Dear Loved Ones,

I am writing this letter for you to read in the event of my death. I want you to know that I love each of you and that I forgive all of you for any role that you have played in the disputes that have plagued us over the years.

Please take care of my dog Muffin. I ask that one of you take her into your home and give her a good home until she dies. When she dies, I'd like her to be buried near me.

I would like to be buried in Bethel Road Cemetery, where I own a plot. Please ask Reverend Goodpastor to officiate at my funeral. I would like the service to include the 23rd Psalm and the old hymn, "Bringing in the Sheaves." Please put a bouquet of daisies in the coffin with me.

I enclose a list of my friends and relations with this letter. Please let these people know that I have passed on.

Sincerely,

Revocation of Documents

A will is revoked if it is physically destroyed. In this age of copiers, it is hard to be sure that all copies are destroyed, so the safest way to revoke a will is to make a new one. If a will cannot be found, the law presumes that it was destroyed and revoked.

If you have executed several documents benefiting an ex-significant other, you might want to execute something like the following:

Sample Revocation of Documents

I, Mary Smith, hereby revoke the durable power of attorney for health care, the general durable power of attorney, the directive to physicians, and any other document that I have previously executed naming John Jones to make decisions for me or giving him any interest in any of my assets. I also revoke the will that I executed naming him as my personal representative and as one of my heirs.

Mary Jones

On this _____, before me personally appeared Mary Jones, known to me, who executed the foregoing instrument and acknowledged to me that she executed document as her voluntary act and that it expressed her wishes.

Notary Public

INFORMAL MARRIAGE

This section deals with whether a person is common law married or not. If you think you may be common law married, you should also assemble the documents listed on page 645.

These questions (starting on the next page) can help determine whether there is any likelihood that you are common law married or not.

Try to answer them as honestly as you can. The space is left so that you can fill in details to the yes or no type questions. Remember this is not a school test; it is a way of gathering information so you should try to be as complete as you can.

Remember too that it may be prudent not to keep this questionnaire at home if you are still living with your significant other but the relationship is troubled.

Common law marriage questions

1. What is your name? What is your significant other's name? If your last names are different, why is that so?

2. Have you ever told anyone that you were married to your significant other? Yes _____ No _____ Whom did you tell?

3. Has your significant other ever told anyone that you were married? Yes _____ No _____ Whom did he tell?

4. Have you ever had sexual relations with your significant other? Yes _____ No _____

5. Have you ever lived with your significant other as husband and wife? Yes _____ No _____

6. Have you ever agreed to be married to your significant other? Yes _____ No _____ Has he or she ever agreed to be married to you? Yes _____ No _____ How do you know that?

7. Have you ever lived together as husband and wife in one of the following states or visited there? Describe the circumstances.

a	Alabama?	Yes _____	No _____
b	Colorado?	Yes _____	No _____
c	District of Columbia?	Yes _____	No _____
d	Idaho?	Yes _____	No _____
e	Iowa?	Yes _____	No _____

f	*Kansas?*	Yes _____	No _____
g	*Montana?*	Yes _____	No _____
h	*Ohio?*	Yes _____	No _____
i	*Oklahoma?*	Yes _____	No _____
j	*Pennsylvania?*	Yes _____	No _____
k	*Rhode Island?*	Yes _____	No _____
l	*South Carolina?*	Yes _____	No _____
m	*Texas?*	Yes _____	No _____

8. If you have you been married before and your former spouse is still alive, have you been divorced legally? Yes _____ No _____ (If your former spouse is deceased, fill in the date of death and other facts here).

9. If your significant has been married before and that spouse is still alive, have they been divorced in court? Yes _____ No _____ Set out what details you know about that relationship.

10. How long did you live together? Where did you live?

11. How do the two of you refer to your living arrangements when you are describing them to other people? Are you "shacking up?" "Living together?" "Married?" "Cohabiting?"

12. Have you and your significant other lived together continuously since you got together or have you sometimes split up?

13. If you sometimes split up, how many times did that happen? When you were split, where did each of you live?

14. Did either of you live with someone else while you were apart? Yes _____ No _____ Sometimes _____

15. Did either of you get married while you were apart from each other? Yes _____ No _____

16. If you did, how did that marriage end?

17. Have you and your significant other ever referred to each other as being my fiancé? Yes _____ No _____ Sometimes _____

18. Have you ever told anyone that you were engaged or planning to get married to your significant other? Yes _____ No _____ Sometimes _____ Who did you tell?

19. Have you ever announced that you were now married or had a party to celebrate being married? If so, when?

20. Do you wear a wedding ring? Yes _____ No _____ Sometimes _____

21. Does your significant other wear a wedding ring? Yes _____ No _____ Sometimes _____

22. Do either of you have children (from a previous relationship) who live with you and your significant other? Yes _____ No _____ Sometimes _____ What do they call each of you?

23. Do your children believe that you are married to your significant other?

24. Have you had children with your significant other? If so, what does the birth certificate say about their parents? What are their names?

25. How do you divide up household expenses?

26. Who pays the bills and from what account? Mortgage? Groceries? Car payments? Other significant, regular bills such as insurance, cable television, and so on?

27. Do you own a car or more than one car? What name or names are on the title?

28. Do you have a checking account? If so, is it joint or separate?

29. Does your significant other have a checking account? If so, is it joint or separate?

30. Do you have joint credit card accounts? If you do, what are the names on that account?

31. Do you own a house or other real estate? If you do, what are the names on the deed?

32. Do you and your significant other have an on-going sexual relationship?

33. Have you ever told anyone that you were married to your significant other? Yes _____ No _____ Sometimes _____ Whom did you tell?

34. What do you tell your parents about your relationship with your significant other? Do you tell them that you are married? Engaged?

35. What do you tell your boss or co-workers?

36. What do people whom you know call you and your significant other? Do they call you "Mr. and Mrs."?

37. What do you and your significant other call each other in public when you are introducing each other? "My husband?" "My wife?" "My girlfriend?" "My roommate?" "My fiancée?"

38. Has your significant other ever told anyone that you were married? Yes _____ No _____ Sometimes _____ Whom did he tell?

39. Have you ever called your significant other your husband (or wife) in front of other people? Yes _____ No _____ Sometimes _____ Did he or she object or correct you? Yes _____ No _____ Sometimes _____

40. Has either of you ever identified the other as their husband or wife on any of the following papers? If you answer yes to any of these questions, fill in as many details as you can remember, including where you can get copies of these documents.

    a   *Employment forms, such as job applications or emergency notification forms?*

    b   *Public benefit (welfare) forms?*

    c   *Hotel and motel registrations?*

    d   *Social invitations or greeting cards that you have sent out?*

    e   *School papers for kids?*

    f   *Club or church membership rolls?*

    g   *Loan applications?*

    h   *Mortgage applications?*

    i   *Other formal papers?*

    j   *Passports?*

    k   *Children's birth certificates?*

    l   *Horse or dog registrations?*

    m   *Greeting cards or Christmas cards? (Especially those that say "To be my dear hubby" or something comparable.)*

    n   *Union papers?*

    o   *Military documents?*

    p   *Fraternal group (Elks, Moose, Lions, etc.) or other club papers (Rotary, Toastmasters, etc.)?*

    q   *Social invitations or greeting cards addressed to both of you?*

Here's How To Understand Your Answers

Remember the elements of common law marriage – living together as husband and wife in a state that recognizes common law marriage, agreeing to be married, and holding oneself out as married.

The first 11 questions cover most of these elements. The significance of questions about where you live has to do with whether you and your significant other have ever lived together in (or had some significant contact with) a state that recognizes common-law marriage. If you didn't answer "yes" to one of the states listed, then you haven't lived together as husband and wife in a state that recognizes informal marriage. If you haven't lived there or at least visited for some significant time, then you are not common-law married.

The significance of questions about your lifestyle is whether you and your lover act like married people, as for example, taking names that identify you as married. The traditional form is, of course, for the woman to take the man's last name, but it is also significant if you, for example, have hyphenated your names. It is unlikely that you can be considered common-law married if you have not had sexual relations.

To be common law married, a couple must hold themselves out as married. Basically, this means telling the public that you are married; obviously, denying that you are married tends to contradict this requirement. Sometimes documents such as greeting cards To my lovely wife on Mothers Day show that the couple thought of each other as husband and wife. Similarly, if a man lists a woman as his wife on an application for health insurance, then he has indicated more or less publicly that they are married.

The questions about what you told other people relate to whether you held yourselves out as married. If one of you has that you are married and the other one not, then situation is complicated. If you answered "no" to these questions, then you are probably not common-law married.

You cannot be common law married if you didn't agree to be married. If you answered "no," to questions about agreement, then you are probably not common-law married. Sometimes, an agreement to be married can be deduced from other actions, like living together and telling people one was married. In Texas and some other states, however, the agreement has to be proven affirmatively, i.e. there has to be more or less express evidence of intent to marry.

To be common law married, both of you must have been legally free to marry during at least part of the time that you were together. If either you or your significant other has been married before, and has not been legally divorced, (so that you answered "no" to the question about divorce) then you cannot be common-law married. If, however, the spouse who was still married to someone else gets divorced from the previous spouse, then you might have entered into a common-law marriage if the two of you continue to live together after that divorce.

So, the bottom line is that if you answered "yes" to all of the first 11 questions, then you might well be common-law married. If you answered "no" to the questions on divorce (i.e. if one of you is still legally married to someone else), then you are clearly not common-law married to each other right now. If you answered "yes" to some of the other questions and "no" to others, then you might be married but a court will probably have to decide.

Remember also that there may be legal time limits within which a claim of marriage must be made. Act promptly if the question is important to you.

The remaining questions simply flesh out the facts that may be relevant and perhaps help you assemble evidence.

If your answers consistently describe a separate existence, then those answers tend to describe a living together arrangement rather than a marriage, although a marriage can still exist. If, for example, you keep everything separate and lead a relatively separate life from your lover, but you identify yourself as married on every formal document, have told your friends that you are married, and live in the same house together, then you may well be informally married.

Some of these questions relate to the change from just living together to considering yourselves married. For example, if a couple who have been just living together, announce that they are now married, they may have entered into a valid common-law marriage.

Some of these questions relate to the common outward signs of marriage in American society, which include wearing wedding rings and the woman changing her last name to that of her spouse. These are symbols of marriage; they are not part of the legal requirements. However, if a jury has to decide the question, they will have to look for objective evidence that the couple considered themselves married. If both the woman and the man wear wedding rings, a jury may well conclude that both of them intended to be married.

An important question is whether you refer to your significant other as your "fiancé." That term refers to a person whom one intends to marry someday, not to one's spouse. When people get married, they stop calling their significant other their "fiancé" and start using the words that refer to spouses. In other words, calling your significant other your "fiancée" is a statement that you are not married.

Some of the questions have to do with the ordinary American concept of marriage and family. For example, most people probably consider that some form of sharing of living expenses and supporting each other to be a sign of marriage; completely separate finances except for household expenses can be maintained by a married couple but it probably would seem unusual to most married people. Although having children out of wedlock is no longer so uncommon, many people still take having children together as a sign of intending to be married, especially if the children believe that their parents are married.

Remember – you may need to take prompt action to prove any claims that you have as a person's spouse. Some states have time limits within which you must act. You might have to file for divorce, for example, or make a claim in your significant other's estate or whatever.

616

BREAKING UP

This section gives you information and reminders about things that you need to do if you split up with your significant other after some time together and perhaps some financial entanglements. These steps should be in writing.

Basic steps to take when you break up with a significant other

Here is a checklist of some basic steps to take for ending a relationship. These steps recapitulate those in the main volume in Chapter Fourteen.

- ✓ *Officially end the relationship (following the terms in your agreement if there is one).*
- ✓ *Divide joint accounts and close accounts. Provide an accounting of what you have taken or what you claim.*
- ✓ *Terminate joint credit cards.*
- ✓ *Divide assets and make appropriate changes in title documents. These include boats, cars, houses and other real estate, horses, dogs, and cats, trailers, campers, etc.*
- ✓ *Divide other assets, such as furniture and appliances.*
- ✓ *Return personal possessions. Some couples duplicate snapshots and videos so each can have a copy.*
- ✓ *Change the beneficiary designations in life insurance, 401k, IRA, and pensions as needed.*
- ✓ *Have a new will drawn or at least mark old one as "revoked." If you have been divorced from your significant other, then the provisions in the will for him or her will be automatically revoked. However, you need a new will.*
- ✓ *Deal with your landlord if you live in a rental property and if you are on the lease. Even if you are not on the lease, it is probably a good idea to let him or her know that you are moving out.*
- ✓ *Notify creditors and service providers of change and arrange to have only one name on the bill or account These include the cable company, Internet service provider, utilities, cell phone company (if you share an account), car finance company or bank, mortgage company, etc.*
- ✓ *Change password or PIN as needed on all accounts unless you're sure that your lover doesn't know your password or PIN. Remember to cancel or change as needed all credit and debit cards, financial accounts (including online trading arrangements), email accounts, and so on.*
- ✓ *Don't forget to change or cancel shared eBay and other online accounts.*
- ✓ *If your lover has something that you believe you are entitled to, make a written claim to the item, and notify any third parties involved.*

✓ *Resolve child custody, visitation, and support issues. Consider whether paternity has been established under state law.*

✓ *Make sure that all debts are resolved and it is clear who is going to pay what.*

✓ *Try not to be a complete jerk.*

Remember that you need to be careful and meticulous in winding up a relationship. You must follow through to make sure that any obligation undertaken by your ex is fulfilled. If he or she agreed (or has been ordered by the court) to pay a credit card bill, you need to check to make sure that this is done.

Remember you may still be liable on debts from the marriage or relationship even if your ex is supposed to pay them. It is up to you to see that these debts are paid. Try to arrange for them to be paid in full now if at all possible or to have the lender release you from any liability.

What to do if things are acrimonious and may wind up in court

This section deals with the aftermath of a relationship that is in the process of ending. It will help you assemble the evidence that you might need to prove that you are informally married to your partner or that you are entitled to some asset from the relationship.

Organizing your case

To assemble evidence, though, it is helpful to have some clear organized information about the relationship. If you don't understand what your own version of events it, it is hard to gather relevant evidence. Remember, however, that if a lawsuit is pending, it is best to consult a lawyer to help you decide what is important and what not. Therefore, a good place to begin is by writing down your version of events and your rights. You can use the sections on gathering evidence to suggest topics that you will want to have in mind and you can answer the questions below at page 666, as a starting point.

Basic questions for all relationship disputes

1. Where did you meet?

2. How long have you known each other?

3. How long have you lived together?

4. Do you believe that you are married to your significant other? (If so, why?)

5. Describe the circumstances under which the two of you decided to live together. (Did he move in with you? Did things just sort of evolve or did the two of you explicitly decide to live together?)

6. Did you and your significant other make promises to each other? If so, what?

7. If the two of you have lived together in more than one place, list of all them here.

8. Has there been any physical or emotional abuse in the relationship?

9. Are there any children involved in the relationship? Describe their situation and what you want for them.

10. Do you have (or have you ever had) a substance abuse or alcohol problem?

11. Does your significant other have (or has he/she ever had) a substance abuse or alcohol problem?

12. Have either or both of you seen a therapist during this relationship? If so, who?

13. Do you or your significant other suffer from a serious mental illness? (Schizophrenia, suicidal depression, bipolar disorder?)

14. Would you be willing to seek couple's therapy to restore this relationship?

15. How did the relationship end?

16. Does he/she have anything that belongs to you that you want to get back? If so, what?

17. Did you and your significant other sign any formal documents together? These formal documents might include leases, mortgages, car notes, wills, powers of attorney, and insurance documents. You might also consider registration papers for purebred animals, club memberships, and so on.

18. What do you want or need from your significant other now that the relationship is apparently over? Support? Payment of joint debts?

19. Were you and your significant other in business together?

20. Does your significant other owe you for anything that you contributed to the relationship, such as paying for his or her education, working in his or her business, etc.? If so, describe.

21. Has your significant other hired an attorney? Give details, including name, address, and phone number.

22. Do you and your significant other have any legal relationship that needs to be unwound, such as joint debts, joint leases etc.? If so, describe them.

If you believe that you had a cohabitation agreement or any significant financial relationship, you should also answer the questions in the section "These cohabitation agreement questions should help you assemble your thoughts if you believe that your significant other made promises to you that should be enforced." on page 633

Child Custody and Visitation Questions

Here are questions that you need the answers to if a child is involved in your relationship with your significant other.

1. Did you and your significant other have a child together? If so, set out the names, ages, and addresses of the child(ren) here.

2. Is another child expected from the relationship?

3. For men, are you certain that this child (or these children) is biologically yours?

4. For women has your lover acknowledged the child is his? Be specific.

5. Whose name is on the birth certificate as the father of this child?

6. Has there been any formal legal acknowledgement of the child by the father?

7. What relationship do you want to have with this child in the future?

8. What relationship does your significant other want with this child?

9. Has any effort been made to place this child for adoption or, if the baby hasn't been born yet, is adoption being contemplated?

10. Are you financially able and emotionally willing to provide food, clothing, shelter, and medical care for this child? Give details.

11. Are you able to provide a stable home environment, love, guidance, education, and religious upbringing for this child? Give details.

12. Are you currently employed? If so, where and for how long.

13. Is your significant other financially able and emotionally willing to provide food, clothing, shelter, and medical care for this child? Give details.

14. Is your significant other able to provide a stable home environment, love, guidance, education, and religious upbringing for this child? Give details.

15. Is your significant other a fit parent to have custody of this child? Why or why not?

16. Has there been any emotional, physical, or sexual abuse of the child? Give details.

17. What evidence is there of the abuse?

18. Do you have children from a previous relationship? Give names, ages, and addresses.

19. What is your present relationship with those children?

20. What are your present legal obligations/rights in terms of support and visitation?

21. Are you current on those obligations?

22. Have the grandparents of the child shown any interest in having visitation or custody rights?

23. Are there other children (besides your biological children) in this relationship with whom you would like to continue to have a relationship? In other words, do you want to continue your relationship with your significant other's children?

24. What relationship have you had with your significant other's children?

25. What relationship would you like to have in the future with your significant other's children?

26. Is he/she agreeable to that continuing relationship?

27. Who would have significant information about your relationship with the child? (i.e. who has witnessed your interaction with the child, your significant other, etc.?) Consider pediatricians, teachers, coaches, relatives, etc. Give names, addresses, and phone numbers.

28. What would these people say?

29. Has your significant other (or any one else involved) hired an attorney? Give details, including name, address, and phone number.

Please note if your lover or spouse has hired a lawyer, then you need to do so also, as soon as reasonably possible. If you have received any official paper from a court or other government agency, you should consult an attorney immediately. There are deadlines for responding to these matters and failing to comply with them could cost you your case.

Information for Fathers of Children Born Out of Wedlock

This section is to help fathers protect their rights. The first parts cover basic steps that should be taken by a father who wishes to remain involved in his child's life. A subsequent section contains steps to be taken by a man who believes that he is not the child's father and wishes to avoid parental responsibility for the child.

A man who sires a child owes it to the child to act as the child's father, unless he is wholly incapable of doing so (as for example due to severe mental illness). The presence of another man who is willing to act as the father benefits the child but does not relieve the father of his basic responsibility. I decline to offer advice to a man who has fathered a child and wishes to avoid his responsibility. If you have sired a child and wish to limit your responsibility to minimal financial obligations, you may be able to do so legally and you may be able to deduce from the forms in this book how to do so but there are no forms included for that purpose.

The relevant steps should be taken as soon as you become aware that you are going to become a father. Do not leave any of them out except on an attorney's advice.

Some of the steps may seem stupid, such as informing the mother in writing that you are the father of her child after all; she ought to know, right? Wrong. The point of your letter is not that she doesn't know who the father is, but that you can prove later that you believed that you were the father and that she knew that you were the father and where you could be located. These steps are intended to help you protect your rights to be involved in the child's life, e.g. to make it more difficult for the mother to give up the child for adoption without your consent.

If you are living with the mother, and are on good terms with her, then some of these steps may not be essential. It could be risky to leave any of them out, however, because they will help to document your position if you and the mother later separate.

To preserve your rights to a role in your child's life, you must not only act on your rights as a father, but be able to prove that you have done so. Therefore, you must assemble evidence of what you have done. It is much less plausible to say "I kept trying to get hold of my girlfriend" than to say "I called her 23 times. I kept a diary of every time I called."

You want an active role in a child's life, but baby is not yet born

Here is a checklist for expectant fathers who want an active role in their child's life.

✓ *Inform the mother in writing (preferably by certified mail, Federal Express, etc. so that you have a record of the notice being given) of the following:*

- *that you believe that you are the father of her child,*
- *that if you are the father, then you want to be involved in your child's life and to support your child and help pay the mothers medical expenses;*
- *and where you can be located.*

Give her your address and phone number. If possible, especially if you are likely to be hard to reach (as where you are in the military or have to go back to school), give her an alternate address where she can contact you, such as the address of your parents, a trusted friend or relative, or your clergyman.

✓ *Tell everyone else involved that you believe that you are (or might be) the father of this child, etc. This includes the expectant mother's parents, her doctor (if you know who that is), the hospital administration (if you know where the baby is likely to be born or if the mother has already gone to the hospital), and any adoption agency that you believe the mother may have contacted (or may decide to contact), and any other person necessary to protect your rights.*

✓ *In appropriate cases, you may also want to notify her closest friends, her pastor, etc. In this delicate matter, you must use your own judgment. If the mother is keeping her pregnancy a secret, then your position is a difficult one. You may not wish to embarrass her unnecessarily but you also need to protect your own interests; her desire for secrecy may indicate that she intends to relinquish the baby for adoption, in which case you should let more people know. In particular, if you learn that the mother has contacted an attorney about a private adoption (or has been in touch with prospective adoptive parents), then you should inform these people in writing as well.*

In addition to telling her in general that you want to be an active father to the child, your letter should include the following:

✓ *Tell her that you want to support your baby and to help pay her medical bills.*

✓ *Tell her that you want to be notified of the birth (and, if true, that you would like to be present at the delivery.)*

✓ *Tell her that you have registered with the putative fathers' registry in your state.*

If this is what you want, and if you really want to provide a stable home for your child, offer to marry her.

A hospital will not permit you to be present at the delivery if the mother objects; in this regard, she is the hospital's patient and her right to make her own medical decisions, including her privacy interests, trumps your interest in your child's birth. In addition, the hospital will probably not inform you of the child's birth.

In addition to notifying people of your possible interest in this child, you should:

✓ *Follow all state law requirements to be recognized as the father of the child once it is clear that you are the father. Check with the county clerk's office, welfare, or social services agencies, or on line to see what the requirements are in your state.*

✓ *Register with the putative fathers' registry in your state. You can find out how to do this by doing a little Internet research, by visiting the county clerk's office (usually in the courthouse). If the mother lives in another state, or might go to another state to have the baby, register there as well. Recording your interest in the state where the baby is likely to be born is the goal.*

✓ *Make financial arrangements to be able to pay part of the mother's medical expenses for prenatal care and delivery.*

✓ *Check with your health insurance carrier to see if care for the mother of your child is covered. If so, inform the mother in writing of what benefits are available and give her the information as to how to contact the insurance company.*

✓ *If you do not have health insurance coverage, make every effort to have enough money to pay for some portion of the costs.*

Here again, some caution may be needed. If the mother is on welfare, or if Medicaid benefits are available to pay for prenatal care, etc., you may not want to take financial burden yourself. Moreover, if you tell the hospital that you can pay the whole bill, this may complicate the mothers claim for welfare benefits and increase your financial responsibility more than necessary.

On the other hand, you are responsible for this birth and offering to pay a portion of the expenses clearly demonstrates your awareness of this fact. Therefore, if you are not sure what to do, you can make an offer to "pay as much as I can" or to "pay $_____ toward your expenses or whatever."

You may wish to consider borrowing the money for these expenses. However, you should also consider what expenses you will have in the future in regard to the child, such as support, possible attorneys' fees, etc. It would be unwise to beggar yourself to pay medical bills now when you may need the money in the near future for something else.

Remember, however, that the final decision as to whether you have any rights to this child will turn on DNA testing to establish paternity. If some other man is the father, then you probably do not have any legal rights, at least to a newborn baby. You can perhaps, for example, later adopt the child or become his or her guardian, if an agreement can be reached with the child's biological parents or if their rights are terminated by a court.

Checklist — what to do after the child is born

Here is a list of proposed steps to take if you believe that you are the father of a child that has already been born.

✓ *If you have not already done so, give the notices described above.*

✓ *Make clear your willingness to support the child to the extent that you can. This offer should be as concrete as possible so, for example, you can offer to provide $_____ per month support and enclose a check for that amount. Do not offer more as a monthly amount than you can actually afford to pay on a regular basis. It is prudent to avoid committing yourself to an obligation that you may not be able to keep in the future so you should condition any amount that you send as what I can afford right now or for the time being.*

✓ *Visit the child.*

624

✓ *Offer to take care of the child for a time, such as baby sitting while the mother is in school or at work.*

✓ *If you can get help from your parents or a reliable relative in caring for the child, make these arrangements.*

To maintain your rights to be involved with your child, you must act on them. If you don't visit the kid or take any role in his or her care, then you cannot reasonably expect a court to give your interests a lot of consideration. If you need to go to court to defend your right to the child, then you will need to convince the court that you tried to act like a responsible father. If you are "too busy" to visit the child or to fill out all the paperwork or whatever, the court will likely find that you are too busy to have custody of your child or significant visitation. A judge may even find that you have waived your rights or abandoned the child.

If the mother says will not allow you to have access to the child, make peaceful efforts to do. Unless she has instructed you not to, show up at her house and ask to see the kid. Call her and ask to be allowed to visit. Write her notes (and keep copies) asking to see the child, be allowed to care for him or her, etc.

If you want to raise the child and the mother wants to give the child up for adoption, inform her in writing of your desire to raise the child. Also notify any agency, attorney, or prospective parents that she may contact.

If you want to raise your child, begin arranging to be able to do so. Check into child care, take a parenting class, find out what benefits you have at work as a new parent, etc. These steps will benefit your child if you do get custody and will help you prove your case in getting custody.

It is prudent to keep in touch with everyone to whom you have given the notices.

A person who has acted as a parent to an older child for a time may, in some circumstances, acquire some rights to the child. If you are in that position, consult the following checklist and get a good attorney. If you want an ongoing role in the child's life, it is prudent to make every effort to continue your connection with the child; even if the mother refuses to let you see the child, it may be important to a court that you politely asked to be allowed to continue your relationship with the child. You cannot, of course, harass the mother or kidnap the child. As an unrelated adult, until a court determines otherwise, you do not have any right to contact the child or to take possession of him or her. To do so will probably violate a variety of criminal laws, including kidnapping, stalking, etc.

The following are some sample letters that an expectant father might want to send.

Sample Notice Letter for Father to Send (who wants to be involved with his child) Before the Baby Is Born

As always, a sample needs to be modified to fit the facts of your actual situation. This is a sample for the situation where the parents are no longer together but are not on hostile terms with each other.

Dear Mary,

I have learned that you are pregnant. I believe that I am the father of this child because you and I were living together when you became pregnant. If you don't think that I am the father, please tell me why you think that someone else is the father. Under the circumstances, I want the child's paternity confirmed by DNA testing after the baby is born. I have registered with the putative fathers registry in our state.

If I am the father, I very much want to be involved in my child's life. I want to have an ongoing role in raising the baby and to fulfill my responsibilities in supporting him or her.

Please let me know when the baby will be born. I want to be present at the birth and would like to be your labor coach if you decide to take a Lamaze course.

If I am the father, please put my name on the birth certificate. If you need help with medical expenses, please let me know. I have checked with my health insurance carrier at work, and the costs of prenatal care and delivery for my child would be covered under my policy. You can get more information by calling Sarah in the Human Resources department at My Employer, Inc., telephone 000-000-0000. I want our baby and you to have good care during your pregnancy and delivery.

Id really like to visit you and see how you are doing. If you need a ride to the doctor or anything like that, let me know.

I can also help pay for maternity clothes and so on. We could go shopping together if you like or you could let me know what you need. I am sending you a check for $300 with this letter to help out.

Sincerely,

Sample Notice Letter for Father to Send (who wants to be involved with his child) After the Baby Is Born

As always, this letter needs to be modified to fit the facts of your actual situation. If the mother is nursing the baby, an overnight visit will require more cooperation and preparation from everyone involved. A mother can, however, use a breast pump to gather enough breast milk to permit the baby to stay with the father for some time. It is also possible for the father to feed the baby formula for the visit. Many children adapt to different feeding arrangements.

Dear Mary,

I have just learned that you had a baby. I believe that I am the father of this child because you and I were living together when you became pregnant... If you don't think that I am the father, please tell me why. Under; under the circumstances, however, I want the child's paternity confirmed by DNA testing

If I am the father, I very much want to be involved in my child's life.

I want to have an ongoing role in raising the baby and to fulfill my responsibilities in supporting him. I have checked with my health insurance carrier at work, and my child is covered under my policy. You can get more information by calling Sarah in the Human Resources department at My Employer, Inc., telephone 000-000-0000. I know that children need vaccinations and so on, so lets get this set up.

Id really like to visit the baby as soon as possible. Would Saturday afternoon at 3 be OK with you? I'd plan to come by for a couple of hours. If you want to go out, I can take care of him until you get back.

My mother will help me care for him if I keep him overnight, so I'd like to have my son for a weekend visit soon. The weekend of the 23rd would be convenient for us; you and I can work out the details when I see you.

I can also help pay for baby clothes for my child and so on. We could go shopping together if you like or you can let me know what you need. I am sending you a check for $300 with this letter to help out for now. We need to get together on what support he needs and what I can pay.

Sincerely,

Sample Notice Letter for Person Who Has Been In a Parental Role to Send to the Biological Parent

This is a sample letter for a person to send who has become emotionally involved with a significant other's child but has no biological connection with the child and no official legal status.

Dear George,

Although we are no longer living together, I want to continue to be involved in little Georgiana's life. I feel that I became a mother to her since you and I lived together for five years. Among other things, I went with you to parent teacher meetings and helped her with her English homework. I very much hope that I can continue to be a meaningful part of her life.

If you agree, Georgiana could stay with me on alternate weekends. I'd be happy to have her next weekend from Friday night through Sunday night about 7. She and I could go to the zoo to see the new baby elephant.

I can also help pay for her tuition at Saint Anne's School, since we agreed that she was getting a better education there than in public school and you probably can't afford the tuition on your salary alone.

If Georgiana stays with me, you probably ought to give me written permission to have her and authority to consent to emergency medical care, just in case anything happens.

Sincerely,

Mary

Here is a simple letter giving Mary permission to have Georgiana with her and to consent to medical care for her. Be careful not to create ongoing rights unless you really intend to do so.

To Whom It May Concern:

I am Georgiana Smith's father and I have legal custody of her. I hereby consent to Georgiana's visiting with my friend Mary for such periods of time as we agree on. We have agreed that Georgiana will visit Mary for some weekends. I authorize Mary to pick up Georgiana from school or other places. I also authorize Mary to consent to medical treatment of Georgiana in an emergency or if I am unavailable.

Sincerely,

George Smith

Checklist for men (wrongfully) named as a child's father

This checklist is to help men protect their rights if a woman says that he is the father of her child and he believes that he is not. This list covers the basic steps that should be taken, but other actions may be necessary.

These steps should be taken as soon as you become aware of the claim. Do not leave any of them out except on an attorney's advice.

Again, the point of writing a letter is not that the mother doesn't know who the father is, but that you can prove later that you made clear from the beginning that this child was not yours.

✓ *Inform the mother in writing (preferably by certified mail, Federal Express, etc. so that you have a record of the notice being given) that you are not the father of her child.*

✓ *If there is a significant chance that the child is yours and if you want to be involved in the child's life, then say so, and tell her where you can be located. Give her your address and phone number.*

✓ *Tell everyone else involved that you believe that you are not the father of this child, etc. This includes the expectant mother's parents, her doctor (if you know who that is), the hospital administration (if you know where the baby is likely to be born or if the mother has already gone to the hospital), and any adoption agency that you believe the mother may have contacted (or may decide to contact), and any other person necessary to protect your rights. If necessary, tell them why you believe that you are not the father. Do not allow your name to be placed on any official document, including the birth certificate, as the father. If you find out that the mother has named you as the father, take prompt steps to have the record corrected.*

It would probably be prudent for you not to pay for the expenses of pregnancy or contribute to the support of the child. This may sound harsh but, even if the child is not yours, you might be held to have agreed to support him or her. If you want to help the mother, then you should say, in writing, something like "I am not the father of this baby but I know that you are having problems so I'd like to give you $200 to help out."

There are legal steps that can be taken to correct public records. These vary from state to state. If necessary, a man who has been identified as the child's father can bring a paternity action to establish that he is not the biological parent.

A man who fails to keep the official record correct may later be held to have acknowledged the child as his. Also, if the man does not correct records, the child may believe that he is the father and may not have the chance to find out who his or her real father is.

If a man who does not believe that he is the father is asked to consent to an adoption or is notified of a pending adoption, it may be prudent to notify the court or agency that he believes that he is not the father but that, if he is, he consents. In that way, the adoption can go forward, so far as this man is concerned, but the man has not admitted to a court that he is the child's father.

Agreement for support and custody of a child — considerations

Here is a sample agreement relating to the support and custody of a child. This agreement assumes that the couple was living together before the child was born and that the man is the father of the child.

It is important to remember that such a court may decide not to enforce such an agreement if there is a dispute about custody, because the court should look to the best interests of the child.

An agreement like this could obligate a man to support a child, even if it is not his. It can also be evidence that he is the father.

Therefore, you should not sign such an agreement unless you are certain that you want to make payments to this woman for support of this child, regardless of the child's parentage.

Sample Agreement for the Support and Custody of a Child

John Smith and Mary Jones agree as follows:

(1) John Smith and Mary Jones had a baby girl, Christine, on March 33rd, 2200. At that time, Mary and John were living together and John is the father of that child. As of June 1, 2200, John and Mary are no longer living together.

(2) John will take appropriate steps to establish his legal paternity of Christine and will provide Mary with copies of the appropriate documents. He will pay the costs of these actions.

(3) Mary will pay her own medical bills associated with the birth.

(4) Every provision in this Agreement is believed by them to be in the best interests of Christine's happiness.

(5) Both of them are fit parents of Christine. Christine's best interests will be served if both her father and mother are equally involved in her life.

(6) Subject to the terms of this Agreement, they will have joint physical custody of Christine.

(7) Therefore, John and Mary agree that they will both continue to live in the Wilmington area within reasonable driving distance of each other. Neither will move his or her residence without informing the other. Neither will take Christine out of the state of Delaware without informing the other.

(8) Christine will spend alternate weeks with each parent, one with John and then one with Mary. A week means the period from 6 pm Sunday to 6 pm the following Sunday.

(9) Both parents will have the right to consent to medical and dental care for Christine. Each will enroll Christine under his or her health insurance if possible.

(10) They will alternate years in taking the tax deduction for a dependent child and other tax benefits unless advised by a tax accountant that this is not proper.

(11) John will have sole possession of Christine during his two-week vacation in the summer and Mary will have sole possession of Christine during her two-week vacation in the summer.

(12) Major holidays such as Christmas and Thanksgiving will be spent with alternate parents in alternate years. One year, Christine will spend Thanksgiving with John and Christmas with Mary and the next year vice versa.

(13) If either parent is incapacitated or unable to care for Christine for all or part of his or her time, Christine will stay with the other parent if possible. The parties agree that it is in Christine's best interests if Christine is not habitually left in the care of baby-sitters or nannies alone for a 24-hour period. In other words, Christine may be left in the care of a responsible nanny or baby-sitter or other child care person for an occasional evening or the workday, while the parent is out or at work, but shall not ordinarily be left in such care for an entire 24-hour period.

(14) If one parent must be gone for longer than an ordinary evening out or workday, he or she may either arrange for Christine to stay with the other parent or with one of her grandparents or aunts.

(15) After she is six months old, Christine will be in child care and preschool at the Greek Orthodox Annunciation parochial child care center and preschool. John and Mary will each pay one-half of these costs. The payments will be made directly to the school.

(16) John and Mary intend that Christine will attend a private parochial school of the best quality that they can afford. Each of them will pay half of the tuition and other costs.

(17) John and Mary will both set up a college savings fund for Christine and shall each contribute $2000 to that fund each year. These funds shall be in such form as each parent shall decide but shall be in such form as will assure that the money is safe for Christine and cannot be seized by their respective creditors.

(18) John and Mary will both immediately purchase a life insurance policy on their respective lives in the amount of $100,000 and provide that the proceeds of that policy will be paid to the survivor of them for the benefit of Christine.

(19) So long as Christine spends approximately half of her time with each parent, neither will owe the other child support because each will be paying one-half of the expenses.

(20) If any provision in this Agreement needs to be changed in the future, due to changed circumstances, John and Mary will try in good faith to work out an amicable resolution. If they cannot agree, they will seek mediation from an agreed upon person. If they have to go to court, each will pay his or her own legal bills.

(21) If either parent wants to move to such a distance that this Agreement is no longer workable, then they agree that it would be better for Christine to remain with the parent who stays in Wilmington so that she can be close to her grandparents and other relatives and so that she can continue in the good schools of the area. Therefore, John and Mary agree that Christine will live with the parent who stays in Wilmington and visitation with the other parent will be arranged.

(22) If a court order is ever sought in regard to custody of Christine, John and Mary agree to ask the court to incorporate the terms of this Agreement in that order.

(23) They further agree that if support payments are ever ordered by a court in regard to Christine that such payments shall be expressly conditioned on the other parents using the funds for Christine's benefit and on the other parents complying in good faith with any visitation provided in that order.

(24) They further agree that if child support payments are ever ordered by a court on any terms significantly different from those in this Agreement, then any other payments, including college savings, specified herein shall no longer be required.

(25) At present John and Mary make approximately equal salaries.

(26) If the financial situation of either John or Mary changes, then changes may be made in this Agreement, except that neither shall be asked to reduce their time with Christine in exchange for a reduction in his or her support obligation.

(27) The financial situation of John and Mary shall never be a reason for changing the amount of time Christine spends with the other parent or the terms of custody even if one parent could provide Christine with a more materially comfortable existence. The parties agree that having the love and guidance of both parents is far more important than material advantages.

[add signatures of both parties and dates.

Both parties should sign and date this agreement. It might be a good idea to have it witnessed and notarized as well so that the statements have some force as being under oath.

Cohabitation dispute information

This section concerns gathering evidence to support your case if you think that you might have to go to court about a cohabitation dispute. It includes information on cohabitation agreement disputes, custody disputes, and others.

These cohabitation agreement questions should help you assemble your thoughts if you believe that your significant other made promises to you that should be enforced.

If the relationship is over, these questions should help you remember whether you need to get anything tangible back from your lover. The items may range from your CD collection to your share in a brokerage account. Remember that the longer that you wait to take action, the harder it may be to establish your rights.

- ✓ *Are the terms of a cohabitation agreement at issue in the split between you and your significant other? Explain.*
- ✓ *Does your significant other owe you money? Give details.*
- ✓ *Does your significant other have property or other assets that belong to you or that you are entitled to share in? Give details what, where, etc.)*
- ✓ *Did you and your significant other have a written cohabitation agreement?*
- ✓ *Did you and your significant other have an express oral agreement? If so, write down all the terms that you believe to have been agreed upon.*
- ✓ *Do you believe that you would be entitled to some tangible asset because of the relationship? (i.e. did you think that you would own half the house or half the stocks or a share in a business?)*
- ✓ *Did you work in your significant other's business? If so, do you feel that you are entitled to a share of the business or other compensation for that work?*
- ✓ *Does your significant other believe that he/she would be entitled to some tangible asset because of the relationship? (i.e. does he/she think that he would own half the house or half the stocks or a share in a business?)*
- ✓ *Did your significant other work in your business? If so, does he/she feel that he/she is entitled to a share of the business or other compensation for that work?*
- ✓ *Have you made a claim in writing for what you are entitled to?*
- ✓ *What was your significant other's response?*
- ✓ *Has your significant other made a claim in writing for what he/she thinks that he/she is entitled to?*
- ✓ *How did you respond?*
- ✓ *What do you sincerely believe the merits of your lover's claim to be?*

✓ *Who would have significant information about your financial relationship with your ex? Consider friends, bankers, realtors, landlords, business associates, colleagues, lawyers, relatives, etc. Gather names, addresses, and phone numbers.*

✓ *What would these people say?*

✓ *Has your significant other hired an attorney? Gather all the details that you can, including name, address, and phone number.*

Preparation for a child custody dispute

These guidelines may be helpful whether the child custody dispute arises when a marriage dissolves or when a parent seeks to protect their rights to a child born in an informal relationship.

Basic preparation

To prepare for a child custody dispute, you need to take the following actions.

✓ *Set up a file folder or at least a file box where you can keep copies of all of your correspondence etc.*

✓ *Keep a record of every time you call anyone involved and what they tell you. The handiest way to do this is on a pocket calendar.*

✓ *Comply completely and in every detail with any court order or agreement that is entered, whether or not you agree with it or think it is fair.*

✓ *In particular, pay any support payments on time and in full. If you really cannot make a payment for a good reason, such as that you have lost your job; have your attorney file an immediate motion to modify the support order.*

✓ *If you have custody of the child, be sure that he or she is ready for your ex's visits (or is dropped off at the agreed upon location), on time.*

✓ *Keep a diary of the time that you are with your child, if you do not have primary custody of the child, whether or not there is a court order.*

✓ *If you are denied visitation by your ex, then keep a diary of every time that you tried to visit the child.*

✓ *Keep a diary of the times that your ex is with the child. If your ex rarely visits or calls, make a note of the times that he or she does (or doesn't). For example, if your ex is supposed to pick up the child at 6 pm and doesn't show up until 8:30, make a note of that fact.*

✓ *Take pictures or videos of the child.*

- ◆ *If you believe that the other parent is not keeping the child clean or in proper clothing, or is otherwise not taking proper care of the child, take pictures that show this. For example if you ex drops the child off without a jacket on a snowy day, then take a picture of the kid as he or she arrived.*

- ◆ *Take pictures of yourself (and, for example, your parents, or other relatives) with the child. Pictures of the two of you at the zoo or with your brother at your family's lake house show that you are taking an active role in your child's life.*

✓ *If your child is bruised or injured (or if you suspect sexual abuse) after being with your ex, take the child to a doctor promptly. Also, take pictures of the bruises.*

✓ *If the child is injured or ill while he or she is with you, take the child to the doctor. Otherwise, you may be accused of neglecting the child.*

✓ *If you believe that your child is neglected by the other parent (or his or her new lover), make sure that other people see and note the injuries or neglect. If the child doesn't have a jacket in winter, for example, get a statement from a teacher that the child arrives at day care or school without proper clothing.*

✓ *If you believe that your ex has a substance abuse problem, then you must seek to document this. Try to find out who has seen him or her using drugs or under the influence of liquor. If he/she drives under the influence with your child in the car, then document this. At least make a diary note that you suspected that your ex had been using drugs or drinking, because e.g. you smelled marijuana on her clothes or beer on his or her breath. Your lawyer can formally request that he or she take a drug test.*

Remember that if your child is genuinely in danger, you need to take appropriate official action, such as calling the police or your local child protective services agency. However, keep in mind that you should not involve the police or a social service agency unless you sincerely believe that it is warranted and you have some evidence of your belief.

Preparation for an interview with a psychologist or social worker

Having your qualifications as a parent evaluated by a stranger can be one of life's least pleasant experiences. You may feel like you are being judged – and you are. You may feel that the evaluator is asking intrusive questions that are none of his or her business. Unfortunately, in a court case over family matters, your personal family life is now the business of judges, psychologists, and others.

Preparation is the key to making a favorable impression in these evaluations.

If there are issues of abuse in the case, you need to be especially well-prepared to answer questions about those allegations.

If you have an attorney, you should insist that he or she prepare you thoroughly for any interview (or deposition). Many lawyers have been through so many of these cases that they give the client little or no meaningful advance preparation. If your lawyer tells you to "Just relax" or "Just tell the truth. You'll do fine," you are not getting good representation. He or she should help you organize your thoughts and prepare emotionally for the expected questions. He or she should also help you be aware of the factors that may be most important to the judge in your case. However, a responsible attorney will not coach you in lying.

The key point of an interview with a psychologist who will testify in your case is that it is not therapy. The psychologist may be a friendly, helpful person – most psychologists are. But, he or she is not there to help you "vent" or to help you work through your feelings. A psychological expert, whether a child psychologist, psychiatrist, or other professional, is not your therapist. He or she is a special witness called to help the court make an informed decision. Remember, too, that the expert has no obligation of confidentiality to you; he or she may (and indeed often must) disclose anything that you say to all of the attorneys and to the judge.

This is particularly so if the expert is a professional hired by your ex. In that situation, you need to assume that he or she is your adversary, no matter how pleasant or engaging his or her manner is.

✓ *Keep in mind that your goal is to win your case, not to express your political opinions of the court system or your ex or psychologists or anything else.*

✓ *Get a grip on your temper. Dress appropriately but comfortably, which means in a manner that shows how important this is to you. Wearing dirty jeans and a ragged tank top may suggest that you are a disorganized slob who doesn't consider this case very important. Fancy clothes are not required; a good guide is to dress as you would to go to church or to a nice dinner with friends.*

✓ *This does not mean that you should try to be a robot.*

It is natural for a parent in a custody dispute to express anger and disappointment at his or her ex. Threats or statements like "I could kill that bitch" may be taken more literally than you mean. Shouting and cursing during the interview, no matter how provoked you are, may convince the psychologist that you are an unstable person with a violent temper. You should try to keep statements of anger and pain on a reasonable level and describe how you deal with these reactions in some appropriate way. Here's an example of what a furiously angry father might say to a court custody evaluator:

Of course it makes me angry that my ex wife lets her new boyfriend swim in the nude with my son. I think that it puts my boy in a sick situation. That's why I'm going to court. When I feel really angry about it, I go for a run or workout at the gym until I calm down.

The father makes clear that he is angry and concerned about his son and that he is taking appropriate action to deal with his anger. This sounds more responsible than candidly stating his real intention which may be "to kick the boyfriend's ass the next time I see him."

Denigrating the profession of psychology will not make a good impression either. (Remarking that "you candy assed faggots think you know more about being a parent than real people do" is not calculated to help your case. Neither is noting that "Judge Blankety Blank is the crookedest judge in the state. Everyone knows that if you paid him enough, he'd give custody to a madam in a brothel."

It doesn't matter if you are right or wrong in your views; what matters is that the judge will rely on the opinion of the person whom you are insulting. The psychologist may interpret your smart remarks or insults in psychological terms, as "aggression" or "instability" or even as evidences of some mental pathology. He or she may weigh these factors in recommending against you. Moreover, the expert is quite likely to repeat your remarks to the court, which won't help either. Remember if the judge thought that the expert was a moron, he or she would probably have chosen someone else. Also, remember that very few smart remarks sound amusing when repeated later by someone else; what you thought was a witty remark may sound offensive or insensitive to someone else.

✓ *Know the essential facts about caring for your child or be prepared to explain why you don't know.*

> An involved parent should know common facts about his or her child, including the names of the child's friends, his or her teacher, and his or her pediatrician. A father who has left all of these "details" to his wife will have a hard time convincing anyone that he now ought to be the child's primary caretaker.

✓ *Think about your strengths as a parent and the best parts of your relationship with your child and be prepared to tell the evaluator about them.*

> For example, if you and your child spend time hunting or fishing together and those times give you a chance to talk to your child about values and life, then have some of these trips in mind when you go to the interview.

✓ *If you have a serious objection to the other parent's raising of your child, be prepared to express that objection concretely and in a non-malicious tone.*

✓ *If there are flaws in your behavior, be prepared to explain them and what you are doing to correct the situation.*

For example, here is a persuasive hypothetical dialogue between a mother whose soon to be ex husband has a new girlfriend and a psychologist appointed by the court:

Psychologist: Mrs. Jones, do you have a problem with Janey visiting your husband?

Mrs. Jones: I want Janey to have a good relationship with her Daddy. She loves him very much. But, I am worried about my daughter being in my husband's home the way things are now. My daughter Janey told me that when his girlfriend Mary comes over, he and Mary go into the bedroom for hours and leave Janey alone.

Psychologist: How do you feel when Janey tells you that?

Mrs. Jones: Of course, it makes me jealous and angry. But, also, I am worried that Janey is too young to be alone in the house. She could get hurt or not get her homework done. She says that she makes herself a jelly sandwich if Daddy is "busy." That's not a good dinner. Also, she is asking me what Daddy and Mary are doing in the bedroom and why they are making those noises. I don't want her exposed to that sort of behavior because I think that it's immoral. I think it is not good for her to have those questions in her mind when she is only six.

Psychologist: Don't you have a new boyfriend too?

Mrs. Jones: Yes, I'm dating George Smith, who's a teacher at Janey's school. We try to schedule our evenings out for when Janey is with her father. George does not stay overnight at my house when Janey is there.

Psychologist: Have you ever left Janey for an entire night with a baby-sitter

Mrs. Jones: Well, not exactly. My baby-sitter is a lady who lives in the neighborhood. Mrs. Figg. She's in her sixties and Janey likes her. One night a man and I went out on date. He was driving and he had three or four glasses of wine with dinner. I didn't want to ride home with him so I called a cab. It took a long time to come because it was raining, and I didn't get home until almost four in the morning. I called Mrs. Figg to let her know and she agreed to stay with Janey until I got home. When I got home, I fell asleep so Mrs. Figg got Janey dressed and off to school.

Psychologist: I'll bet you had a hell of a headache the next morning.

Mrs. Jones: No, I felt OK. I think that you are asking me if I was drunk. Obviously, I'd been drinking. I felt so sad then. It was right after my husband moved out. I talked to my doctor about it and he said that he didn't think that I had a problem with alcohol. However, he did prescribe antidepressant medication for me. Obviously, I haven't gone out with that man again.

Mrs. Jones' statement is persuasive because it is detailed, concrete, and addresses concerns that most reasonable parents would understand.

The focus is on Janey's needs. Mrs. Jones acknowledges that she is upset but makes clear that she has substantive reasons for being worried about her husband's conduct beyond her own hurt feelings.

Clearly, also, Mrs. Jones is well aware that her husband is claiming that she is as neglectful of Janey as he is. She is prepared to respond to his charge that she goes out on dates and stays out all night. She also knows that Mrs. Figg might be a witness so she doesn't furiously deny that she dates or shout that she's not an immoral hussy. She responds reasonably calmly and has the facts in mind.

Moreover, Mrs. Jones is prepared to not blurt out more than she needs to. It might be tempting for her to confess that she got blind drunk, she spent a passionate two hours in her date's car, came home, and passed out. It might be equally tempting for her to deny angrily that she drinks too much. Or to demand that she has a right to her own life too.

Instead, she recognizes the psychologist's maneuver to see what she will say about her conduct. She is prepared to show how she addressed any issue about her drinking. She is prepared not to be too defensive about her own behavior and to point out her responsible behavior in seeing her doctor and not dating an unsuitable man.

✓ *Be prepared to state concisely and clearly why you should have custody of your child. This may be your most important opportunity to state your case yourself.*

An interview with a court investigator or psychologist in your child custody case may be the best opportunity that a parent has to state his or her position informally and persuasively. It is no time to stumble around making vague claims of "just being a better parent, that's all."

✓ *Do not be entirely passive in the interview. Try to politely bring up your important points.*

Some evaluators will have a mental checklist of questions to ask. Others prefer a more unstructured format. An invitation to "Tell me why you don't think that your wife should have unsupervised visitation with the children" merits a carefully considered response from you, not a rant. On the other hand, if the evaluator doesn't ask a question that brings up your primary concerns, you should politely ask for time to express yourself.

The point of all this is that many loving, conscientious parents are not in the habit of describing their parenting skills and conduct to others. If you have a great relationship with your child and want the primary role in his or her future care, practice describing why you are the better parent.

On the other hand, try to keep any responses brief and to the point. Be careful not to panic and blurt out information about yourself that may not be at issue in the case. If for example, you've been drinking too much now that you are alone and no one has mentioned it, don't volunteer that unhappy fact now.

✓ *Do not take any medication before the interview that you do not normally take and do not have an alcoholic drink before the interview.*

Tranquilizers, alcohol, and other drugs can loosen inhibitions and impair your ability to be rational during the interview. Showing up with liquor on your breath or appearing stoned are not signs of being a responsible parent.

Checklist of steps to take in a cohabitation agreement dispute

Here are some additional, more detailed, suggestions as to possible actions that you can take to protect your interests. Remember that you also need to take the steps set out in the suggestions for splitting up as well as these actions. See Chapter Fourteen and Chapter Fifteen as well as earlier sections of this Workbook.

Obviously, a certain amount of common sense is required. It would be foolish to carefully make all of the payments that you owe to your ex under a cohabitation agreement if it is apparent that your lover can't or won't do his or her part. In that situation, you should instead offer, in writing, to do your part when he or she does.

✓ *All notices, requests, etc. should be in writing. All of these documents should be clear, specific, and polite. Stick to the facts of your claim and refrain from calling names or making accusations.*

✓ *Reread your cohabitation agreement. Make a note for yourself of any changes that you believe have been made.*

✓ *Tell your lover what you believe your responsibilities are and fulfill them.*

✓ *If one of your responsibilities is conditioned on your lover doing something, then request him or her to do so and offer to perform your part. In other words, if he was supposed to pay for the new roof on the house and you were supposed to pay for painting the living room, then offer to have the room painted as soon as the new roof is on.*

✓ *Be sure that any obligation that you are fulfilling after the relationship ends really is one that continues after the two of you split up. In other words, if you agreed to pay for his dog's obedience training so long as you lived together, you don't need to pay for additional training after you split up, although you should pay for any training that took place during the relationship.*

✓ *If you need to make a payment to protect your own credit rating, then make the payment and notify your lover that you have done so and that you expect to be repaid by him or her.*

✓ *Tell your lover what you believe his or her obligations to be and clearly ask him her to fulfill them. Be as specific as possible and send a copy of the agreement.*

✓ *If your lover is not performing his or her obligations, notify him or her of that fact in writing. In the same letter, state what you believe your obligations are and make clear that you will perform your obligations when he or she does.*

✓ *Ask your lover to keep you informed of any payments made by him or her and to give you all pertinent information, including statements, relating to any jointly owned property.*

✓ *Withdraw your legal share of any joint accounts.*

✓ *Pay all proper bills from any joint funds, such as the rent on a shared apartment, the utilities, any joint credit cards, etc.*

✓ *If you believe that your lover promised to support you for some period, then ask him or her in writing to do so.*

✓ *Your request should include at least an itemized list of your expenses and a clear request that he or she pay the bills associated with those expenses.*

✓ *You should also send copies of any credit card bills, phone bills, etc. that you expect him or her to pay.*

✓ *If you believe that your lover promised you a share in some asset, such as a brokerage account, then you need to notify him and any holder of the account, such as the bank or brokerage firm,*

✓ *Ask him or her in writing to provide you with a recent statement from that account and a check for your interest. If you want your share in some other form, such as half of the securities that are in the account, then state that request.*

✓ *Sent a notice letter to the firm involved stating your rights and requesting that no withdrawals be permitted from the account until the matter is clarified.*

✓ *If you believe that your lover promised to provide you with some employment benefit, such as health insurance, then request in writing that he or she do so. You may wish to consider notifying the human resources department at his or her employer of your rights but the effect of that action depends on the situation.*

✓ *If your lover has excluded you from your residence, as by changing the locks, you need to get access to retrieve your things. Only a court can give you legal access, if your lover owns the property or refuses to allow you in a peaceful way.*

◆ *If you are on the lease, you can go to the landlord and demand to be let into the apartment. Be sure to make this demand in writing; if you can't retrieve your property and your lover steals or destroys it, you want to be able to claim that the landlord caused your loss.*

◆ *If the landlord refuses, you can try going to court to get immediate access to your apartment. Be sure that you have a copy of your lease with you.*

◆ *If the landlord refuses you access to the apartment, be sure to notify him or her that you have been wrongfully evicted and that you will no longer be responsible for the rent.*

✓ *If you believe that your lover promised you a job, then show up for work. Don't quit; make him or her fire you.*

✓ *If you believe that your lover promised you a share in a business, then notify his partners or business associates of your claim.*

Considerations in getting evidence from witnesses

Evidence includes the testimony of people who know both of you. Testimony can be preserved by depositions, which are a series of questions asked by a lawyer, or by an affidavit, which is a written statement of what the witness knows. Forms for affidavits are included here. You will need to retype them and fill in the facts to match your own situation.

An affidavit is a sworn statement by a witness. Therefore, the affidavit must be signed in front of the notary, so you will need to take your witness to a notary at the bank or wherever. If that is not feasible, a witness can sign a statement, which then becomes evidence of what he or she said to you.

It is vitally important, however, that you carefully modify these affidavits to reflect the facts of your situation. It is worse than useless to persuade an important witness to sign something that really doesn't match their recollection because they will be contradicted in court by the erroneous affidavit. The jury will not be as likely to believe someone who has lied before.

This book assumes that you and your witnesses are going to be truthful; remember there are penalties for perjury and a false affidavit is perjury.

There are two basic ways to get a statement from a witness. One is to talk to the witness and then write up an accurate account of what he/she told you. Be aware that the witness may not be willing to sign something as strong as he or she was willing to say to your privately. The other method is to sit down with the witness and write up a draft affidavit together. This can be conveniently done on a laptop or by hand. Then, you and the witness can arrive at an agreeable version together, and he or she can sign it on the spot.

Be as specific as possible. Leave out name-calling and absurdly exaggerated statements, as these weaken rather than strengthen the witness' account. A persuasive statement is one like this: "I am Timmy Smiths kindergarten teacher. At the parent/teacher meeting in November, Mr. Smith kept looking at his watch and saying that he had to go back to the office. He did not seem interested in Timmy's problems at school and he seemed unaware of the information that I had emailed to him about Timmy's difficulties. He left before the other parents did and Timmy cried because Mr. Smith did not get to see his finger paintings." A statement such as "Mr. Smith has absolutely no interest in Timmy's welfare" is so extreme that the witness may back down later or be shown as exaggerating.

Hearsay is a complicated branch of the law of evidence, with a number of exceptions. Basically, hearsay is the witness repeating what someone else told him or her. Try to have a witness focus on what he or she has seen or knows directly, but don't be paranoid about trying to keep all hearsay out. The judge will need to decide anyway, and you might leave out something important. For example, if Mary testifies that Fred told her that he was having an affair with Alice, the testimony might not be hearsay because Fred is admitting to doing something wrong. Therefore, if one of your witnesses has something important to say, go ahead and include it. It probably won't hurt, although it might result in part or all of the affidavit or testimony being excluded later.

The information from the United States Coast Guard is a useful template for remembering what facts establish a common law marriage. It also lists some of the documents that are considered good evidence of a common law marriage.

Considerations in your own testimony

You should approach being deposed as seriously as testifying in court. The lawyers will be allowed to read your remarks to the jury or show them a videotape. Jokes, rage, or smart remarks will usually hurt your case.

The key to giving persuasive testimony is being prepared and telling the truth. With the exception of pathologically narcissistic or sociopathic people, most people are more convincing when they are telling the truth. Moreover, the advantage of the truth is that you are less likely to be tripped up by an adverse bit of evidence.

Being prepared means having the facts clearly in mind. You need to get clear in your own mind on dates, numbers, events, and other facts.

You may not be able to pinpoint exactly when something happened. Only people in detective movies can do that. But, you should be able to narrow the time down to a month (or at least a season) and year. One way to help your memory is to think about other things that were happening at the same time.

Here are some additional things to do:

✓ *Be sure that you understand your case.*

   Again, your lawyer needs to help you prepare by explaining what questions that the other lawyer is likely to ask and why they are important or not.

✓ *Review all the pertinent papers.*

   You should read over the documents that are part of the evidence in your case.

✓ *Have a reasonably clear chronology in mind of the key events.*

   Some lawyers will advise their clients not to make notes before a deposition because the opposing lawyer may be entitled to see them, especially if you want to refer to them during your testimony. You should get advice on this point from your attorney.

✓ *Keep your answers short and to the point. Most attorneys advise their clients not to volunteer information that has not been asked for.*

Considerations in other people's testimony

Unfortunately, when you are involved in a lawsuit, your friends and relatives may get involved too.

You should consider exercising some care about what you tell them. If you confess to your best friend that you've been doing a lot of cocaine or tell your mother that you and your lover never really had an agreement about money, then you can expect that those remarks will come up in court.

You may also find that your friends do not have the rosy view of you that you do. Some may be willing to support your claims. Some, however, will not, especially if it means lying for you. Even if they don't take sides in the dispute, some of your friends and relations may end up giving testimony that hurts your case.

Your therapist is another person who may be called to testify. Confidentiality may not protect what you have told him or her if your mental health is an issue in the case. For example, if your fitness as a parent is in question, then your therapist may be a witness, as may your child's therapist.

Documents in disputes and common law marriage questions

Actually, the concept is tangible evidence, which includes physical things, such as photographs or other objects, as well as computer records (including email), accounting records, letters, and formal documents such as deeds. So, if your significant other hung a banner over the driveway announcing your marriage, then the banner would be evidence that you were married.

Photographs that show the two of you at work, for example, might tend to support a claim that you thought of the business as a joint enterprise.

Remember that legal relevance is an elastic concept. A tender photo of the two of you together at your parents 50th anniversary party may be technically irrelevant to a dispute about a cohabitation agreement but it may be very relevant to the jury's opinion.

Think expansively. For example, horse show entry forms may show that the horse was identified as belonging to both of you. Or, for another example, if you and your ex traveled to Vegas for a business convention and he deducted your travel expenses as business expenses, it might support your claim to have worked in his business.

Gather all of these documents, even if you don't see the point right now, and put them in a safe place out of reach of your ex or soon to be ex lover (and his/her friends, family, etc.). A safety deposit box would be best but your office (if your desk locks) or a storage unit (to which only you have the key) or, as a last resort, a trusted friend, or relative. Your lawyer's office is a possibility also but it is prudent to keep copies for yourself.

Documents to gather

Here is a list of suggested documents that may be useful to your case:

- ✓ *Photographs, such as vacation pictures, family gatherings, etc.*
- ✓ *Health insurance papers (either forms at work or on a claim form).*
- ✓ *Life insurance policies or applications.*
- ✓ *Pension benefit forms.*
- ✓ *Apartment rental application or the lease.*
- ✓ *Hotel or motel registration.*

    Hint: look at those vacation snapshots and see if they remind you of someplace that you stayed.

- ✓ *Job applications or other employment forms.*
- ✓ *Unemployment compensation or other public benefit applications.*

- ✓ *Club or church membership rolls or other papers. (An invitation to the annual tennis club awards dinner? A directory of church members?)*
- ✓ *Loan applications.*
- ✓ *Mortgage applications.*
- ✓ *Drivers' licenses.*
- ✓ *Greeting cards, whether sent to other people or given to each other, including Christmas or Hanukkah cards.*

    Hint: think about how you and your significant other signed the cards that you sent out as well as those that you received.

- ✓ *Divorce and marriage certificates.*

    Hint: If your significant other tells you that he or she was divorced, and you have some doubt about the truth of that statement (i.e. you think that the miserable twit is lying to you), check the court records in the county where he or she lived at the time.

- ✓ *Cohabitation agreement or drafts of one.*
- ✓ *Financial records (yours, his, both of yours), including:*
    - *Bank account statements*
    - *Brokerage account statements*
    - *Mortgage or lease agreements*
    - *Deeds*
    - *IRA or 401k or other pension documents*
    - *Title to cars and car notes*
    - *Credit card statements*
    - *Horse, dog or cat registration papers*
    - *Any other document relating to financial matters, including bills, receipts, etc. (Utility bills can prove that both of you signed up for service together, canceled checks and receipts can show who paid for what, etc.)*
- ✓ *Medical bills.*
- ✓ *Letters, greeting cards, printouts of emails, etc.*
- ✓ *Photos or videos of the two of you.*
- ✓ *Family photos (children, parties etc.).*
- ✓ *Union documents.*
- ✓ *Competition entries (tennis matches, golf matches, horse shows).*
- ✓ *Any business contracts, financial records, etc.*

✓ *School and medical records for children.*

✓ *Photographs of family groups, including you with the children.*

Coast Guard Requirements to Prove Common-law Marriage

The United States Coast Guard has published a guide to information required by it to establish an informal marriage as a basis for claiming government benefits. These guidelines can be useful in gathering information for other agencies also.

Here is the information required as set out by the Coast Guard.

"Consideration may be given to common law (mutual consent) marriage only if it existed in a State that recognizes such a marriage. Proof of a common law marriage may consist of:

Affidavits from at least two persons who know the facts concerning the common law relationship.

The persons making the affidavits should state: The length of time you lived together; The address or addresses at which you resided while you lived together; Whether there was any public announcement in connection with your common law marriage; and Whether you were regarded among your neighbors, friends, and relatives as being husband and wife during the time you lived together.

In addition to the affidavits mentioned above, your own affidavit is required. In your affidavit you should state: The date when and the State in which you mutually agreed to become husband and wife; Whether you were ever married, ceremonially or under common law, to anyone else before entering into the common law relationship. If so, state in your affidavit, all the facts of each previous marriage, including the date it took place and the date of the death or divorce that ended it. Any other facts that you believe will help prove you are husband and wife.

Also, if you have any of the following documents which will show a husband and wife relationships, send them in together with the affidavits required in 1 and 2 above: Excerpts from a naturalization certificate, deeds, immigration record, insurance policies, passports, child's birth certificate, original business, employment, fraternal, school, labor organization, church, or other records, bank books made out in the joint names of husband and wife.

(AFFIDAVITS MUST BE SWORN TO OR AFFIRMED BEFORE A NOTARY PUBLIC OR OTHER OFFICER WHO IS AUTHORIZED BY LAW TO ADMINISTER OATHS.)

WARNING

AFFIDAVITS AND OTHER EVIDENCE ARE SUBJECT TO VERIFICATION BY PERSONAL INVESTIGATION. ANY INTENTIONAL FALSE STATEMENT, WILLFUL CONCEALMENT OF A MATERIAL FACT, OR USE OF A WRITING OR DOCUMENT KNOWING THE SAME TO CONTAIN A FALSE, FICTITIOUS, OR FRAUDULENT STATEMENT OR ENTRY, IS A VIOLATION OF THE LAW PUNISHABLE BY A FINE OF NOT MORE THAN $10,000 OR IMPRISONMENT OF NOT MORE THAN 5 YEARS, OR BOTH. (18 U.S.C. 1001)."

Sample Affidavits

Sample Affidavit in a Common Law Marriage Dispute

On this the _____ day of _____, 200_, personally came before me_____ [insert name of witness] and on his/her oath did swear and affirm as follows:

I, _____, make this affidavit of my own personal knowledge. The facts stated herein are true and correct.

I am married to _____. From _____ to _____, we lived together as husband and wife in the state of _____. We agreed to be married and we held ourselves out as married.

[Insert specifics e.g. "We signed an apartment lease as husband and wife." A true copy of that lease is attached.]

FURTHER AFFIANT SAYETH NAUGHT.

So sworn.

[Signature]

Sworn to before me this __ day of ___, 200_

Notary's signature.

My commission expires on _____, 200__.

[Notary forms vary from state to state so check for the usual form in your state.]

[add signature line and notary form]

Sample Affidavit from Friend or Neighbor in a Common law Marriage Dispute

On this the _____ day of _____, 200_, personally came before me_____ [insert name of witness] and on his/her oath did swear and affirm as follows:

I,_____, make this affidavit of my own personal knowledge. The facts stated herein are true and correct.

I am acquainted with _____ [name of husband] and _____ [name of wife]. I have known them for _____ years. I have been their neighbor/friend/co-worker.

During the time that I have known _____ and _____, I have believed them to be married. They behaved like a married couple toward each other and, in my presence; they referred to each other as husband and wife. They lived at the same address and it is my belief, based on having been in their home for social occasions, that they shared the same bedroom.

[Insert other specific facts e.g. "On ___ date, _____ told me that they had gotten married."]

FURTHER AFFIANT SAYETH NAUGHT.

So sworn.

[add signature line and notary form]

Sample Affidavit from a Relative in a Common law Marriage Dispute

On this the _____ day of _____, 200_, came before me _____ [insert name of witness] and on his/her oath did swear and affirm as follows:

I,_____, make this affidavit of my own personal knowledge. The facts stated herein are true and correct.

I am acquainted with _____ [name of husband] and _____ [name of wife.] I am _____s mother. [Insert correct relationship.]

They have lived together for ___ years and I have believed them to be married since _____. [Insert details of belief, such as "They told me they were married."]

They behaved like a married couple toward each other and, in my presence; they referred to each other as husband and wife. They attended family gatherings as a married couple. Attached are true copies of family pictures that show both of them as part of our family.

FURTHER AFFIANT SAYETH NAUGHT.

So sworn.
[add signature line and notary form]

Sample Affidavit of Minister in a Common Law Marriage Dispute

On this the _____ day of _____, 200_, came before me
_____ [insert name of witness] and on his/her oath did
swear and affirm as follows:

I, _____, make this affidavit of my own personal knowledge. The
facts stated herein are true and correct.

I am acquainted with _____ [name of husband] and
_____ [name of wife]. I have known them for _____years. I am
an ordained minister/rabbi of the _____ [insert name of church
or temple].

_____ and _____ attended my church/temple, _____
[insert name and address of church etc.], for _____ years. During this
time, I believed them to be married.

They behaved like a married couple toward each other and, in my presence;
they referred to each other as husband and wife. They attended services as
a married couple.

The church register identifies them as a husband and wife. A true and correct
copy of that register, which is a business record of the church and is kept in
the ordinary course of the church's business, is attached to this affidavit.

FURTHER AFFIANT SAYETH NAUGHT.

So sworn.

[add signature line and notary form]

Sample Affidavit about an Oral Cohabitation Agreement

This affidavit might be used to support a claim about an investment agreement based on trust in the significant other).

On this the 22nd day of January, 2003, came before me Fred A. Foghorn and
on his/her oath did swear and affirm as follows:

I, _____, make this affidavit of my own personal knowledge. The facts stated
herein are true and correct to the best of my recollection and belief.

George Smith and I decided to live together in about _____, 200__. We lived
together for ___ years.

While we were together, we agreed that we needed to save money. I worked
at Super Department Store and Mr. Smith worked at Smith, Smith & Jones,
LLC, which is an accounting firm.

Mr. Smith knew more about investments than I did, so we agreed that he would handle the investments. He promised to take care of the account for both of us and he told me that the account was in both of our names. I trusted him to do so. I gave him a check each month for my contribution. He told me that each of us was putting in an equal amount every month; he said that the account was at Union Bank.

Attached is a statement from Union Bank that I found in our apartment while I was packing Mr. Smiths belongings. It refers to an account in Mr. Smiths name but the amount is about what should be in our joint account. Mr. Smith and I are no longer living together. He has refused to account for the money that I gave him or tell me where our investments are.

FURTHER AFFIANT SAYETH NAUGHT.

So sworn.

[add signature line and notary form]

Sample Affidavit of Relative in a Cohabitation Dispute

This affidavit might to used to prove that Jeffrey promised to divide his brokerage account with his lover Jane.

On this the 24ᵗʰ day of February 2010, came before me Eleanor McGuire and on her oath did swear and affirm as follows:

I, Eleanor. McGuire, make this affidavit of my own personal knowledge. The facts stated herein are true and correct.

I am acquainted with Jeffrey Robertson and Jane Glenn. I am Jane's mother. Jane and Jeffrey lived together for about five years. I saw them socially many times. Among other times, they came to my house every year for Thanksgiving and they took me out to dinner for my birthday. Last October, when they were at my house for dinner one night, I told Jeffrey that I was worried about Jane's future because she had turned down a promotion at work so she could stay here in Tulsa with Jeffrey. He told me that I didn't have to worry and that he was going to make up the financial loss to Jane. He said that he had set up a joint account at Extravagant Investing for himself and Jane so that Jane would get half of his stocks and bonds if they ever split up.

FURTHER AFFIANT SAYETH NAUGHT.

So sworn.

[add signature line and notary form]

Sample Affidavit from Business Associate in a Cohabitation Dispute

This affidavit might be used to disprove Mary's claim that she worked in George's business.

On this the 22nd day of January, 2003, came before me Fred A. Foghorn and on his/her oath did swear and affirm as follows:

I, Fred A. Foghorn, make this affidavit of my own personal knowledge. The facts stated herein are true and correct to the best of my recollection and belief.

I am acquainted with George Smith and Mary Jones. I work for Yellow Auto Parts, which is an auto parts supply company that supplies parts to George's garage, Smiths Smiling Repairs. I have been supplying parts to George's garage for about eight years. On the average, George orders parts from me two or three times a week. I have met Mary Jones at George's annual Fourth of July barbecue.

I have never seen Mary Jones working at Smiths Smiling Repairs. Neither George nor Mary ever told me that she was working there. When I telephone the garage, she doesn't answer the telephone, and she has never come to Yellow Auto Parts to pick up a part. Once in while, when I make deliveries to the garage, she has been sitting in the office, but she did not seem to be working. I remember that one time I saw her in the office but she was doing her nails.

FURTHER AFFIANT SAYETH NAUGHT.

So sworn.

[add signature line and notary form]

Sample Affidavit of Teacher in a Child Custody Dispute

On this the 19th day of November 2019, came before me Mrs. Jane Doe and on his/her oath did swear and affirm as follows:

I, Jane Doe, make this affidavit of my own personal knowledge. The facts stated herein are true and correct.

I am acquainted with George Smith and Mary Jones. I am a teacher at Green Valley Elementary School. I have been a teacher for twenty years. Fred Smith, the son of George Smith and Mary Jones, is in my third grade class at that school.

Mary Jones usually brings Fred to school and picks him up afterwards. She attends all of the parent/teacher conferences. George Smith has never attended one of these conferences.

Last October, Fred Smith had to stay after school because he damaged a schoolbook. He was crying when he left school and he told me that he was afraid of his father. Mr. Smith came to pick up Fred that day and he appeared very angry. His face was red and he spoke roughly to Fred. The next day Fred told me that his father whipped him with a belt.

In my opinion, the best interests of Fred would be served by Ms. Jones having custody of the child.

FURTHER AFFIANT SAYETH NAUGHT.

So sworn.

[add signature line and notary form]

Sample Affidavit of Minister in a Child Custody Dispute

On this the 19th day of November 2019, came before me Reverend Elbert Pompous and on his/her oath did swear and affirm as follows:

I, Reverend Elbert Pompous, make this affidavit of my own personal knowledge. The facts stated herein are true and correct.

I am acquainted with George and Mary Smith. I have known them for five years. I am an ordained minister of the Pleasant Valley Christian church.

Mary Smith has attended my church for the past five years on a regular basis. She brings her children James and Janie to Sunday school. She has brought them to holiday parties at the church, such as our annual Halloween festival. The children are clean and well cared for. I believe that Mary Smith is a good mother to James and Janie and that she is raising them with sound moral values.

George Smith does not attend my church regularly, although he does come sometimes. I have never seen him bring the children to Sunday school or to any church function.

In my opinion, the best interests of the children would be served by Ms. Smith having custody of the children.

FURTHER AFFIANT SAYETH NAUGHT.

So sworn.

[add signature line and notary form]

Other family disputes – parents and adult children

Family disputes can include issues having to do with older parents, including elder abuse. These are too diverse to cover in this book. The shift from being the child in a relationship to being the caregiver is daunting and painful. If you believe that your parent is no longer able to care for himself or herself, here are some questions to ask:

1. What is my current relationship with my parent? Cordial? Troubled? Close?

2. How often do I see him or her? Talk on the phone?

3. What is the basis for my concern? Change in manner? Disappearing assets?

4. Is there a new companion in my parent's life? Why am I concerned? Am I jealous? Upset over my other parent's being replaced?

5. Has my mother or father executed a durable power of attorney or other documents?

6. Who would have more information about this situation? My parent's doctor? Other relatives? Old friends?

7. Where can I turn for guidance? Family lawyer? Family doctor? Social workers at the hospital?

8. Do I have financial expectations that are clouding my judgment? Am I really entitled to those expectations?

To get more information, you can talk to people who know your parent, such as doctors, clergymen, relatives, and family friends. Sometimes you will find that your parent's physician has noticed changes also. However, in today's medical world, many physicians no longer have sufficient long-term contact with their patients to notice significant changes. You may have to persuade your parent to have a check up with a competent psychiatrist or gerontologist who are more expert in detecting subtle changes in functioning.

In these situations, a good social worker (especially one who spent time with your parent while he or she was in the hospital) can be an invaluable resource. These people often not only have psychological insight but also a good grasp of the social resources available.

The only way to care for your parents is to spend time with them. The only way to know what is going on is to be there. Yes, it can be burdensome and interfere with your vacation. On the other hand, it is your responsibility.

If you feel entitled to inherit from your parents, keep an eye on things now. Will contests are always ugly and expensive.

Remember that the mere fact that you resent your parents' spending all their money does not mean that they are incompetent. A person has a right to be foolish. Being in love does not necessarily mean that a person is being cheated.

Remember also that you do not have the right to put your parent in a nursing home or mental hospital without his or her consent or appropriate legal procedures. Many older people are confined to nursing homes without legal formalities when the need is obvious. However, technically, this should not be done if the older person objects or wants to go home. Restraining a person against his or her will is kidnapping or assault unless a court has authorized it.

If your parents have executed the appropriate documents, such as a durable power of attorney, you may be able to assume some control over the situation without going to court. If they have not, or if they object to your claiming that they are unable to manage their own affairs, then the only way to gain any control over their spending or other imprudent actions is to go to court and have a guardian appointed. This requires the testimony of a physician and other witnesses to establish that your parent is no longer able to make prudent decisions for himself or herself. See Chapter Thirteen on considerations concerning older couples for additional information.

Obviously, if your parent believes that he or she is quite capable of making his or her own decisions, a formal, legal challenge may be a bitter and miserable process. You may wish to seek careful guidance from a physician and other relatives before undertaking this unpleasant mission. If at all possible, enlist the support of your siblings or other relatives in this effort.

UNDERSTANDING YOUR RELATIONSHIP

Philosophers tell us that the unexamined life is not worth living; psychology suggests that the unexamined relationship is unlikely to be a lasting and satisfying one. However, many people get through life without reflecting on their life or their relationships.

This section is for those who want to work toward an in-depth understanding of their needs and desires in a relationship. It begins, however, with a consideration of the character of the persons involved. Answering these questions can be a fairly long undertaking, especially if you give some thought to your answers. If you find these questions too burdensome, you can turn directly to a simpler version in Chapter Ten.

Being unwilling to answer these questions, however, may convey information about you (or your significant other) in relationships. Talking things to death and obsessing over details about how you see your future can be unhelpful traits, but a refusal to think about a relationship may mean that the relationship has no mutual structure. If you cannot bear to answer these questions, it may be that you cannot face important aspects of your own conduct. The importance of being able to reflect in detail on ones life and relationships depends on the particular human context. Two people who both dislike reflecting on their lives may still share an unspoken and harmonious concept of how to live together. Two people who both devote great energy to analyzing every detail of their existence may be unable to reach mutually acceptable compromises on any important issue.

This Workbook contains questionnaires to bring out the facts about your present relationship and offers some guidelines on how to deal with those facts. The questionnaire is not intended as a quick fix list of questions where you can total up a score that will tell all about you. Rather these questions are intended to elicit information that will help you understand yourself and your current relationship better. These are not questions that are designed to enable you to fill in the blanks in a cohabitation agreement. These questions, however, can help you decide on the reality of your current relationship and therefore on the basic structure of an agreement. If, for example, you discover that you have difficult remaining in any relationship for more than six months, you may conclude that there is no point in working out a cohabitation agreement that involves a thirty-year mortgage.

The information that these questions can elicit can be about a persons conduct and about their emotional life. Sometimes, as the old proverb says, actions speak louder than words if a person has never been able to keep a job or maintain a friendship, the odds are against him or her being able to sustain a marriage, regardless of the reasons that he or she gives for the lost jobs and lack of friends.

These questions also involve another premise, which is that values and conduct are more important shared tastes in music or food. Many relationship questionnaires focus on ascertaining whether a couple share tastes in food or music or movies. These things can be important but, for most people, are subject to some compromise. For example, if you like Thai food but your lover prefers Italian, the two of you can probably work out some reasonable accommodation, such as alternating between the two cuisines when you eat out.

(If, however, you enjoy trying the foods of different countries and your lover will only eat all-American food, such as hamburgers and fries, and denigrates all other cuisines as weird or what other people eat because they aren't as well off as us, then your problem is not that you don't like the same food your problem is that your lover is, at best, a limited person and, at worst, a narrow-minded bigot who feels the need to impose his or her preferences on other people.) The important question is not whether the two of you agree on everything; the important question is whether the two of you have enough common ground to work through your inevitable disagreements.

Moreover, these questions emphasize both ideas and actual conduct. Many people pay lip service to being willing to compromise or being willing to talk things out but in fact behave in just the opposite ways. The question is not whether you and your lover say that, for example, fidelity is vital to a serious relationship; the question is whether you and your actually are faithful. A lover who has never had a monogamous relationship is unlikely to have one with you.

There are two ways to use this questionnaire.

[1] You can answer the entire set of questions by yourself. Then you can use the question and answer format as a springboard to help you reflect on yourself in the context of your current relationship. In particular, some of the questions may help you make decisions about prudent actions in the present relationship; for example, if your significant other has a criminal record for embezzlement, it probably is not a good idea to open a joint bank account with him.

[2] Better yet, you and your lover can each answer the entire set of questions separately. Then you can sit down together and compare your answers. You may be surprised how differently the two of you see things and how much you didn't know about the other person and the relationship. This course of conduct may bring you much closer together or it may reveal (or cause) fatal splits in the relationship.

There are two sets of questions. The first set is about your view of yourself (the person filling out the form). The second is about your view of your significant other.

Here are some directions to help in answering the questions:

✓ *First, try to answer the questions as honestly as you can.*

✓ *Second, answer each question in writing so that you have a record of your thought to look back at later.*

✓ *Write your answers on a separate sheet of paper or photocopy the pages. This enables you to share your answers or not with your significant other, to answer the questions at a different time when you may be in a different mood or place in the relationship, and to let your significant other have a turn too.*

Questions toward understanding a relationship

1. Describe the circumstances under which you are answering these questions. Are you alone? With someone? Trying to understand a present relationship?

2. How do you feel about your answers in relationship to your lover? Do you plan to share them with him/her? Do you feel comfortable in doing so? Afraid that he/she might find out?

3. Will your present lover be answering the questions for himself/herself? Would he or she be interested in doing so? Why or why not?

4. How many persons have you lived with since you moved away from home? Include roommates, friends, family members etc. but not lovers or spouses.

5. Describe how and why those living arrangements ended, if they have. Happily? By mutual consent? Bitterly? When you got a job? Were thrown out?

6. Have you had boyfriends/girlfriends with whom you did not have sexual relations? Describe those relationships — were they happy, unhappy, warm, cold, loving?

7. Have you had lovers with whom you did not cohabit? Were these ongoing relationships or one-night stands? How many of each?

8. Have you cohabited with a spouse or lover? If so, describe the relationship. If not, why not?

9. Describe how those relationships ended, if they have. Happily? By mutual consent? Bitterly?

10. Have you ever had a happy marriage/cohabitation relationship? If so, describe it. If not, why haven't you?

11. If this is not your first relationship, describe the character of your past lovers/spouses/boyfriends/girlfriends. Have they generally been good people, bums or bitches, loving or cold, etc.?

12. How do you feel you were treated in previous relationships? Mistreated? Cheated? Physically abused? Lied to? Well? Lovingly? Coldly?

13. Looking at your most serious past relationship, what was the biggest problem in the relationship? Too much/little sex? Nothing in common? He/she drank too much?

14. Looking at your most serious past relationship, what was the best part of that relationship? Common interests? Great sex? Good fun? Love?

15. On the average, how long were your previous serious relationships? Less than a week? More than two years?

16. Where did you usually meet your previous significant others, if any.

17. Describe your parents' marriage or living arrangement, if any.

18. If your parents are divorced or no longer together, describe the break-up.

19. Describe your current relationship with your parents.

20. What do you think of your father?

21. What do you think of your mother?

22. If you are in a relationship now, describe it in as much detail as you can, in terms of happiness, common interests, sex, shared values etc.

23. Do you have a pet? Describe your relationship with the pet and what you expect from your significant other concerning the pet.

24. Do you have or have you had a pet? What became of them?

25. Describe the perfect relationship. Lifelong marriage? Cohabitation?

26. What moral or ethical or religious values are most important in a relationship?

27. If you want to have children, describe the best environment for them. If you don't want to have children, describe your feelings on the subject.

28. Do you have deep religious beliefs? If so, what does your religion teach about relationships?

29. Describe your present financial situation in general. Are you in debt? Saving money? Barely able to pay the bills? Comfortable?

30. Describe the way that you handle money. Are you careful and well organized? Stingy? Spendthrift?

31. What are your financial goals? Wealth? Comfort? Security?

32. Specifically, describe how you feel about the following: Health insurance, Retirement savings and pensions, Savings for college (for yourself and for your children), Job security. Owning a house., Owning a luxury car., Owning an expensive recreational item, such as a boat, country club membership, horse, etc.,

33. Describe where you would like to be financially when you are ten years older than you are now.

34. Describe what kind of house you would like to be living in ten years from now.

35. What are your hobbies/interests? Do you prefer to pursue these alone or in company?

36. How do you want your significant other to participate in your hobbies, sports, etc.?

37. Describe your ideal vacation.

38. Describe a perfect evening after work.

39. Describe a perfect weekend.

40. What role would you like your significant other to play in the perfect vacation, evening, weekend?

41. Do you have a professional or personal goal such as further education, building a business, getting promoted, achieving a sport triumph, etc.? If so, describe it here.

42. How important is that goal to you?

43. How do you want your significant other to help with that goal? What impact will it have on the relationship?

44. Do you use illegal drugs? Do you ever abuse prescription medications for purposes other than as prescribed? Describe your use of these substances. Often? Only with friends?

45. Do you smoke? How much?

46. Do you drink alcoholic beverages? How often and when?

47. What are your feelings about sex? What positions do you like? How often? Only when you love the other person?

48. How many close friends do you have?

49. What activities do you share with your friends?

50. What relationship would you like your lover to have with your friends?

51. Do you have a job? Go to school? Why or why not?

52. How many jobs/schools have you had in the last five years?

53. Why do you usually leave a job or get fired?

54. Where did you meet your significant other?

55. Have you introduced your significant other to your friends? Parents? If not, why not?

56. What do your friends, parents, etc. think about your significant other? Are they right or wrong?

57. How does your significant other relate to your friends?

58. What is the nicest thing that you ever did for another person? Why did you do it?

59. Are you involved in any volunteer activities?

60. What part have you played in the ending of any previous serious relationship?

61. Why did those relationships end?

62. What does your former significant other say about your role in the ending of the relationship? (i.e. what does your former spouse say about the divorce?)

63. Do you understand other peoples feelings easily?

64. If another person is upset or angry, how do you feel?

65. What have you done that hurt the feelings of a significant person in your life? Why did you do it?

66. Do you have any serious health issues? HIV positive? Multiple Sclerosis? Serious allergies? Back pain? Herpes? Depression?

67. How do you deal with those problems?

68. Do you have a substance abuse problem?

69. Do you have any close friends of the opposite sex?

70. Do you have any close friends of your same sex?

71. Do you have any emotional problems such as depression or anxiety that interfere with your daily life?

72. Are you in therapy? What do you think about your therapist and your work together?

73. Do you have any character traits that cause you problems in relationships? Hot temper? Jealousy?

74. Do you have a criminal record or a record of any other wrongdoing, such as being fired for dishonesty? Describe it.

75. Have you ever been sexually unfaithful to a significant other? Describe the circumstances.

76. What do you think that significant other felt about your conduct?

77. What is the best way to resolve a disagreement in a relationship? Talk it over? Abandon your preferences to keep the peace?

78. How do you characteristically resolve disagreements or misunderstandings in your relationships?

79. Have any friends ever felt cheated or betrayed by you? Describe the circumstances and what you did, both to cause the feelings and to repair them, if anything.

80. Have you ever shoplifted? Have you ever stolen anything? Describe the circumstances and how you feel about the event.

81. Describe your view of the moral character and integrity of most people that you know? E.g., are most of them honest? Dishonest? Out for their own self interests?

82. If you hear a story of someone who did a really clever business deal, how do you feel? Jealous of how clever they are? Wondering whether the deal was really fair to the other person? Thinking that you have to be clever to get ahead in this world?

Consequences of your answers

The above questions have three purposes, which are intermingled. The first is to gather facts about how you deal with relationships. The second is to learn about your moral character. The third is to assemble information about your goals and desires.

The fact is that most people tend to repeat patterns of behavior. As discussed above, their expressed values may or may not be consistent with their behavior.

Moreover, people tend to carry the same set of values and actions into different contexts. For example, a person who is suspicious of his co-workers and who often feels that he is treated unfairly in the work group will probably carry that same suspicious attitude and feeling of being abused into his intimate relationships.

With that in mind, review your answers to the questions about relationships. These questions include those about people (including friends, lovers, and your therapist), family, and jobs. Try to see if there is any pattern to your answers, even if the questions seem to be about different things. Look for common facts, such as the length of relationships, the role of sex in relationships, and so on. Try to focus on the facts, not your explanation for them. In other words, the important thing now might be that all your past relationships have been short-lived, not that you believe that was because you moved around a lot.

Here are some of the patterns that people might see:

Facts: My father was an alcoholic and two of my boyfriends have had substance abuse problems. My best friend smokes a lot of dope

Pattern: I seek out relationships with people who have substance abuse problems. Perhaps I am most comfortable with the behavior of impaired people.

Facts: My parents fought a lot about my mother having an affair. Three of my girlfriends broke up with me because I flirted with their friends. My best friend in college stopped speaking to me because I asked his girlfriend for a date. I have never had a relationship with a woman that didn't include sex. I had a dog but he got run over when I forgot to keep the gate closed.

Pattern: Like my mother, I do not behave loyally in relationships. I act selfishly regardless of the effect of my behavior on my friends.

Facts: My parents have both been divorced twice. None of my relationships lasts very long. I don't have any friends from high school and most of the people I hang out with are people I work with. I don't know why other people get so upset. I had a cat for a while but she scratched my sofa so I had to have her put to sleep.

Pattern: Like my parents, I have trouble forming lasting relationships. My action with my cat suggests that I put material possessions ahead of relationships.

Facts: I have had a number of sexual relationships, mostly one night stands. I didn't finish my degree. I have had ten jobs in the last five years. Sometimes I get fired and sometimes I just leave. I have been divorced twice. My ex-wife number 1 says that I don't care about other people.

Pattern: I behave in an unstable manner. I do not form lasting attachments to other people.

Facts: My parents were married for twenty years. I still keep in touch with my best friend from high school. I have dated a lot, but I've only slept with the two men that I was in love with. My best friend now is a woman that I met at the skating rink, but I'm really close to a guy that works at my office. I have a dog that I found when he was lost in the woods.

Pattern: I form solid relationships. I am capable of empathy and affection.

Obviously, all of these patterns, except the last one, suggest that you could benefit from therapy. None of those patterns reflect a capacity for a fulfilling, happy relationship or life. In particular, if you are often involved with people who drink too much or abuse drugs, you could benefit from one of the groups associated with AA.

Now, think about why you believe that pattern exists and write your answer on a separate sheet of paper. Some reasons that people might give include:

I have really bad luck in falling in love with guys who are bums.

All women are conniving bitches.

My father was in the Army and we moved around a lot. I never really learned to make and keep friends and I tended to avoid making friends because then it hurt when we moved away again.

Most people are pretty nice if you try to treat them fairly.

Now, look at the questions about actions that you have taken, including your criminal record, if any, your ability to be faithful in a relationship, your friends feeling that you betrayed them, and your conduct at work.

Once again, look for consistency or inconsistency in those answers and summarize your conclusion.

Some conclusions that people find about themselves are the following:

I try to get my own back before someone takes advantage of me. I stole some money from the cash register at work and I shoplift at ritzy stores. If someone has something I want, I think that it is unfair. I have been unfaithful to a couple of boyfriends but they never found out.

I have never stolen anything in my life. I don't think anyone believes that I have betrayed them. The nicest thing that I ever did for someone was to stop at an accident scene and hold an injured persons hand until the ambulance got there. I did it because we are supposed to help people.

None of my relationships have lasted very long. Once a friend gave me the money to pay the rent on his storage unit and I forgot to do it. He thought I cheated him. I was really sorry. The same thing happened at work; the boss told me to file some papers at the courthouse and I forgot to do it. I was really sorry but I don't know why people get so angry at me. I'm just absent minded is all.

Each of those paragraphs shows the writer's values and view of himself or herself in a consistent way in different contexts. If your significant other sees cheating — at work, on his or her taxes, in relationships — as just the way the world is, then the odds are that he or she will cheat on you, whether sexually, financially, or emotionally. If he or she believes that the world is a dog-eat-dog place where everyone is entitled to look out for himself/herself first, then he or she will quite likely feel no scruples about taking advantage of your trust or laxity in financial matters. The sad fact is that people behave consistently more of ten than not.

Moreover, if your partner consistently says things like "Who cares if I cheat on my expense statements at work? They can afford it," you should take those statements as a quite literal statement of his or her real values and take appropriate precautions with the financial side of your relationship.

Values and morals are beliefs that we consciously hold about the worth of various things and actions. Because these are more or less conscious, we can talk about them more openly. Therefore, the conclusions about these questions can be more direct. These questions mainly gather information that you can compare with those of your partner.

For example, if your passionate dream is to ride on the United States Olympic equestrian team and you want your partner to help finance your riding lessons and to groom your horse at competitions, these questions should elicit his or her willingness to be part of that enterprise.

In other words, you have two separate tasks with regard to your significant other. The first is to find out his or her answers to the same questions that you answered, assuming of course that he or she will cooperate. The second is to explore how you see him or her. He or she may say that honesty is the best policy or that a quiet evening at home is the best way to spend one's time but behave completely differently, i.e. by lying whenever it is convenient or spending six nights a week at the local bar.

Seeing your partner clearly

The point of this section is to elicit the same information about your partner as seen by you. The important thing here is less what the truth is than what you believe. If you don't have the information asked about, you might want to consider how much intimate information that you and your significant other have shared.

1. How many close friends does he/she have?

2. How many persons (other than lovers) has he/she lived with since he/she moved away from home? Include roommates, friends, family members etc. but not lovers or spouses.

3. Describe how and why those living arrangements ended, if they have ended. Happily? By mutual consent? Bitterly? When he/she got a job? Was thrown out?

4. Has he/she had boyfriends/girlfriends with whom he/she did not have sexual relations? Describe those relationships — were they happy, unhappy, warm, cold, loving?

5. Has he/she had lovers with whom he/she did not cohabit? Were these ongoing relationships or one-night stands? How many of each?

6. Has he/she cohabited with a spouse or lover? If so, describe the relationship. If not, why not?

7. Describe how those relationships ended, if they have. Happily? By mutual consent? Bitterly?

8. Have he/she ever had a happy marriage/cohabitation relationship? If so, describe it. If not, why hasn't he/she?

9. If this is not his/her first relationship, describe the character of his/her past lovers/spouses/boyfriends/girlfriends. Have they generally been good people, bums or bitches, loving or cold, etc.?

10. How does he/she feel he/she were treated in previous relationships? Mistreated? Cheated? Physically abused? Lied to? Well? Lovingly? Coldly?

11. Looking at his/her most serious past relationship, what was the biggest problem in the relationship? Too much/little sex? Nothing in common? He/she drank too much?

12. Looking at his/her most serious past relationship, what was the best part of that relationship? Common interests? Great sex? Good fun? Love?

13. On the average, how long were his/her previous serious relationships? Less than a week? More than two years?

14. Where did he/she usually meet his/her previous significant others, if any.

15. Describe his/her parents' marriage or living arrangement, if any.

16. If his/her parents are divorced or no longer together, describe the break-up.

17. Describe his/her current relationship with his/her parents.

18. What does he/she think of his/her father?

19. What does he/she think of his/her mother?

20. If he/she is in a relationship now, describe it in as much detail as you can, in terms of happiness, common interests, sex, shared values etc.

21. Does he/she have a criminal record or a record of any other wrongdoing, such as being fired for dishonesty? Describe it.

22. Describe the perfect intimate relationship as he/she sees it. Lifelong marriage? Cohabitation?

23. What moral or ethical or religious values are most important to him or her in a relationship?

24. If he/she wants to have children, describe the best environment for them. If he/she doesn't want to have children, describe his/her feelings on the subject.

25. Does he/she have deep religious beliefs? If so, what do they tell you about relationships?

26. Describe his/her present financial situation.

27. Describe the way that he/she handles money. Is he/she careful and well organized? Stingy? Spendthrift?

28. What are his/her financial goals? Wealth? Comfort? Security? Describe concretely what accomplishing each of those goals would be like, i.e. what is wealth as compared to comfort?

29. Specifically, describe how he/she feels about the following:
    - Health insurance
    - Retirement savings and pensions,
    - Savings for college (for his/herself and for his/her children)
    - Job security,
    - Owning a house.
    - Owning a luxury car.
    - Owning an expensive recreational item, such as a boat, country club membership, horse, etc.

30. Describe where he or she would like to be financially when you are ten years older than you are now.

31. What are his/her hobbies/interests? Does he/she prefer to pursue these alone or in company? With buddies? With you?

32. Describe his/her ideal vacation.

33. Does he/she have a professional or personal goal such as further education, sports achievement, etc.? If so, describe it here.

34. How important is that goal to him/her?

35. Does he/she use illegal drugs? Does he/she ever abuse prescription medications for purposes other than as prescribed? Describe his/her use of these substances.

36. Does he/she smoke? How much?

37. Does he/she drink alcoholic beverages? How often and when?

38. What do you feel about his/her drug use, smoking, and drinking, if any?

39. What does he or she think about your drug use, smoking, and drinking, if any?

40. Describe a perfect evening after work for him or her.

41. Does he/she have a job or go to school? If not, why not?

42. How many jobs/schools has he had in the last five years?

43. What part has he/she played in the ending of any previous serious relationship? Why did those relationships end?

44. Does he/she have any serious health issues? HIV positive? Multiple Sclerosis? Serious allergies? Back pain? Herpes? Depression? How does he or she deal with these problems? How do you plan to cope with them?

45. Does he/she have a substance abuse problem?

46. Does he/she have any close friends of the opposite sex?

47. Does he/she have any friends of the same sex?

48. Does he/she have any emotional problems such as depression or anxiety that interfere with his/her daily life?

49. Is he/she in therapy? What does he/she think about his/her therapist and his/her work together?

50. Does he/she have any character traits that cause problems in relationships? Hot temper? Jealousy?

51. Is he/she trustworthy? In sexual matters? With money?

52. Has he/she ever physically or emotionally abused you?

53. Has he/she made you cry by the things that he or she said? How many times?

What to do with this information alone

It would be nice to be able to draw up a complicated table that would predict, accurately, whether a particular combination of traits would work in a relationship. Unfortunately, such a prediction is seldom achievable. The possible variations are too great. Sometimes, opposites attract and balance one another in unexpected ways. Sometimes, people modify their behavior and their beliefs over time. More often, perhaps, a couple can achieve a stable equilibrium despite their differences and even despite the misery that they periodically cause one another.

There, however, some guidelines, or at least precautions for relationships that can be drawn from this information. Remember—if you or your lover displays a consistent pattern of short-term relationships, then you probably should assume that the present relationship will not last either. That assumption is particularly well founded if the reason for the short duration of previous relationships is always described as being the fault of the other person.

People find it immensely difficult to change. A tremendous effort of will and commitment, as well as therapy, is usually needed to effect any significant change in a fixed pattern of behavior, although sometimes people do change in order to preserve a relationship. Therefore, you may assume that the way you or your significant other acted in the past is the way you or he/she will continue to act in the present relationship.

In other words, you may assume that your partner will act as he or she has acted in the past toward others. You should consider whether you would feel well treated if your partner behaves to you as he or she has behaved to others. In other words, you may reasonably ask yourself, "If he treated me like he treated his ex-wife, would I feel good about the relationship?" Or, "Will it make me happy if she is unfaithful to me the way she was to her former husband?"

You can assume that he or she will evaluate actions according to his or her most cynical values. If, for example, your partner believes that everyone is out for himself or herself, he or she will likely examine all of your actions in that light. More importantly, he or she will likely seek to advance his or her own interests in the relationship at your expense. Such a person cannot be relied upon to be fair or honest.

However, you cannot count on a person acting in accordance with his or her expressed values or moral beliefs. People are skilled at rationalizing away their own inconsistencies. That is why you should look at a person's actions rather than what he or she says about those actions.

People often act in accordance with the experiences that they had in childhood. Sometimes, of course, they consciously change their own behavior in order to avoid being like their mother or father. Sometimes, they repeat large or small aspects of that experience. Regardless of the form it takes, however, the experiences of childhood typically shape our adult relationships to a large degree.

A person who consistently blames other people (or the world at large) for his or her problems is unlikely to make any change in himself or herself. In other words, if your partner says that he lost his three previous jobs because his boss was unreasonable or stupid, he probably isn't going to respond well to the demands that your relationship makes on him. Moreover, he is probably going to tell his next lover that you were unreasonable or a nag.

People who recognize that they might have played some role in the way their life turns out usually have the best chance of being able to develop some insight into their actions and to act differently in the future.

If, therefore, your significant other has behaved dishonestly or unfaithfully in other contexts or other relationships, then you should not trust him or her with any of your money or possessions. A better bit of advice would be that you should skip this relationship and look for a person with more integrity.

If your and your partner's values differ markedly, the relationship is unlikely to succeed. It may be possible to compromise on some things but many values cannot and should not be compromised. If, for example, your partner's ideal vacation is sailing in Aruba and you prefer scuba diving in Belize, some compromise can be reached. If, however, your perfect vacation is visiting gothic cathedrals in rural France and his is drinking piña coladas by the pool at the country club, compromise may be hard, if not impossible, to reach. While it is possible that you could, for example, alternate vacation destinations (or go on separate trips), it is more likely that the difference in dreams reflects a profound and more irreconcilable difference in interests and values. You'll be bored by his description of getting plastered by the pool and hell yawn through your slide show of gothic arches. You may secretly despise his indolence and he may secretly resent your intellectual pretensions.

If your and your partner's values about money differ markedly, the relationship is likely to be troubled, if not doomed. The view one takes of money influences a multitude of actions and decisions. Someone, for example, who strongly believes that financial success is the only kind that matters will not be uncomfortable with a spouse who believes that family life and love are the most important things. When she wants to work overtime or travel six days a week on business, he will feel deprived of her company and support at his family reunion. If honesty, kindness, and environmental soundness are more important to you than money, you will not likely prosper in a relationship with someone who values financial success more highly.

What to do with this information together

If you can bring yourself to sit down with your partner and exchange these questionnaires (both the answers that you gave about yourself and those about the other), then you have a wonderful opportunity to work through any differences.

The great Scottish poet Robert Burns wrote more or less as follows: "Oh, what some gift the good Lord give us/ to see ourselves as others see us." You may be surprised (and hurt or pleased) to learn what your partner believes your values to be.

The process provides you an opportunity to correct any misunderstanding that your lover may have. Perhaps you are not as focused on getting ahead at the firm as he thought. On the other hand, the process affords you an opportunity to look hard at yourself from another's point of view. You may not like what you see and decide to change it.

Every therapist knows that therapy, including especially in depth therapies such as psychoanalysis, often means the end of the patient's marriage. Sometimes the increased self-knowledge leads the patient to recognize that he or she is unhappy in the present arrangement. Sometimes, the spouse cannot tolerate the healthier person that the patient has become.

It follows that any process of exploration and change can bring about the end of a relationship. When you look clearly at your present relationship, whether or not your significant other participates, you may well be confronted by a relationship that you do not want. If you look past the excuses and rationalizations, you may see a person whose actions are simply not acceptable.

Consequences and conclusions—myself

Here are some basic questions that you can try to answer from the questionnaires above:

1. The pattern that I see in my relationships (job, friends, family, significant others) is:

2. That pattern exists because:

3. My actions toward other people have the following characteristics:

4. My character can be described as:

5. The most important thing in life to me is:

Consequences and conclusions about my significant other

Now you can answer the same consequence questions about your partner as you did about yourself. Remember to try to stick to factual events and to rely less on conclusions and explanations.

1. The pattern that I see in my significant other's relationships (job, friends, family, significant others) is

2. In my opinion, that pattern exists because:

3. His/Her actions toward other people have the following characteristics:

4. His/Her character can be described as

5. The most important thing in life to him/her is

Using this information

The above information can be useful in beginning the process of sorting out the relationship. From the perspective of this book, it can help you make more informed decisions about legal matters. If your lover, for example, has consistently been in short term relationships, then it may be unwise to count on this one lasting.

Some of the questions may lead you to think about whether the relationship can be saved or not. For example, it may be worthwhile to try couples therapy, if you have not yet done so.

You may want to explore, in your own mind or with your partner or both, whether these consideration mean that the relationship is not one that you want to continue.

At the very least, whether or not your partner will participate in this exercise with you, you should act on your view of his or her character and behavior, as best you can understand it. Try to bring yourself to face facts; if he or she has never been in a relationship for more than two years, he or she is not likely to be with you longer. If he or she has consistently lived with people but not had sexual intimacy with them, then he or she probably is not going to be an ardent lover with you. If he thinks all women, including his mother, are cold-hearted bitches, he probably won't regard you as an exception. If she hates her father for not paying child support when she was a little girl, she probably will be concerned to get "her share" from you and resent any limits that you set on your financial contribution to her welfare.

GLOSSARY

Adoption: The legal process by which the parental rights of the biological parents are ended and new persons become the legal parents of a child.

Advance directive: Instructions to physicians as to the care that a person wants, or doesn't want, if he or she is unable to communicate and is terminally ill. Also called "living will."

Alimony or spousal support payments: Payments made by one spouse to another after a divorce, pursuant to court order. Spousal support payments are sometimes made during a separation of the spouses or pending a divorce. Also called "maintenance."

Annulment: A legal declaration that an apparent marriage was not in fact a legal marriage, as where one of the parties was under the legal age to get married.

As husband and wife: Cohabitation of a man and a woman, usually considered as including sexual relations. Living together in the manner our society considers that of married people

Bastard: A person born out of wedlock

Bigamy: A crime. A person commits bigamy when, while legally married to one person, he or she goes through a marriage ceremony with another.

Biological father: A man whose sperm created the child (contributed ½ of the child's DNA).

Biological mother: Usually, the woman who gave birth to the child, at least if she conceived the child in the ordinary way. Sometimes also used to refer to a woman whose egg created the child (contributed ½ of the child's DNA).

Birth mother: Woman who carried the child in her womb and gave birth to the child. Usually, but not always, also the biological mother.

Ceremonial marriage: In this book, a marriage formally celebrated according to the law. Usually requires obtaining a license and going through some form of ritual. In many contexts, the term "marriage" denotes a formalized relationship, as opposed to all others.

Child support: Payments made by a parent for the support of a minor child. Child support can be collected whether the child is legitimate or illegitimate.

Civil union: A marriage-like relationship sometimes afforded to same sex couples or to unmarried couples. Some state laws prohibit recognition of this status.

Cohabitation/Living together: Literally, this term applies to roommates, lovers, gay couples, and married people. In this book, it refers to lovers who are living in the same residence on a long term basis.

Common-law marriage: A marriage entered into without the formalities required by the law, such as a license, or where there is some legal defect in the formal requisites of a marriage. Generally, a marriage established by the couple living together as husband and wife, holding themselves out as married, and intending to be married. See "Common law marriage " on page 211.

Community property: Property that is earned by a married couple while living in a community property state. Generally, each spouse owns one-half of such property. See "Marital property in community property states" on page 151.

Divorce: The legal dissolution of a legal marriage.

DNA: (For purposes of this book) Genetic material in human cells that is tested to determine the parentage of a child.

Domestic partner: One of an unmarried couple that are living together on a more or less committed or long-term basis. In legal terminology, domestic partners may include persons of the same sex, and the term is sometimes limited to same sex couples.

Durable power of attorney: A document authorizing one person to act for another if the former is incapacitated. Often used to authorize someone to make medical decisions for another and referred to as a "health care power of attorney" or "health care proxy."

Equitable distribution system: The laws applicable to marital property in 43 states. This system has replaced the old separate property system. It provides that marriage is an economic partnership in which each spouse is entitled to share in the assets of the marriage.

Executor (feminine "executrix": A person who administers a deceased person's estate pursuant to a will. Also called "administrator" and "administratrix."

Fiduciary: One who is obligated to care for another's assets with the utmost loyalty. A fiduciary cannot legally advance his or her own interest at the expense of the other person.

Fornication: Sexual relations between a man and a woman who are not married. In law, sometimes a crime, which was defined as sexual conduct between unmarried persons where the conduct was "open and notorious."

Gay, lesbian, homosexual: These terms refer to persons whose primary sexual attraction is to those of the same sex. It is generally accepted by most mental health professionals that this sexual preference is innate (i.e. is not acquired by one's life experiences and is not a conscious choice), but the issue is debated. "Gay" and "homosexual" are sometimes used to refer to male homosexuals with the term "lesbian" used for females.

Guardian: A person who is appointed by a court to take care of another person who is unable to do so. For example, a child is not able to manage complex financial affairs or make decisions about his or her living arrangements. Similarly, an adult who is incapacitated due to mental illness or other infirmity may not be able to make sensible decisions in their own best interests.

Guardianship: A legal status created by a court order in which one person has the right and obligation to care for another. A guardian may be appointed for a child or for an incapacitated adult.

Husband: Legally, a man who is married to a woman. Also used now by some gay couples to denote one partner, but marriages between persons of the same sex are not currently recognized by the law, except in one state.

Illegitimate child: A child whose biological parents were not married at the time of his or her birth and did not get married later.

Informal marriage: Legal term with the same meaning as common-law marriage.

Inter vivos: Latin for "among the living." A term used to refer to legal arrangements, such as trusts, set up while all the interested persons are still alive, as opposed to testamentary (will) arrangements that take effect on death.

Legitimate child: A child whose parents were married at the time of his or her birth or who married each other later.

Marriage: The legal status of being married, created by a couple's fulfilling the requirements of state law. Also, defined in some laws as a relationship between one man and one woman.

Marvin **case:** A lawsuit seeking palimony. Named after a famous lawsuit against an actor by his live-in girlfriend.

Meretricious relationship: A sexual relationship outside of marriage. In legal terminology, an immoral relationship or, specifically, one where the parties have no intention of being married.

Palimony: A more or less slang term referring to claims that one person is entitled to be supported by another because they lived together. A claim for palimony is, logically, inconsistent with a claim of common-law marriage. "Palimony" is not a legal term.

Polyamorous: A recently coined term used by persons in multiple-party consensual relationships. Somewhat like the recognized sociological terms polyandrous and polygamous but without the connotation of legal marriage.

Polyandrous: A type of marriage in which one woman has more than one husband. Almost unknown in the western world.

Polygamous: A type of marriage in which one man has more than one wife. Approved by some religions, such as Islam and the original Church of Jesus Christ of Latter Day Saints (Mormons).

Putative spouse: One of a couple that believed that he or she was married to his or her partner but where there is some legal impediment to the marriage. A person to whom the law extends some of the protections of marriage.

Separate property: (1) Under earlier law, in non-community property states, including money, which is earned by a spouse. (2) Property that is inherited by a spouse or owned by a spouse before marriage in a community property state. See "Ownership " on page 148.

Significant other, lover: One of a couple. Terms used in this book to denote people who form a couple, "significant other" and "lover" are intended to refer to a person who is in a relationship where the legal status of the relationship is not specified, as opposed to terms like "husband" and "wife." Lover is the gender-neutral equivalent of "boyfriend" or "girlfriend." Socially, however, some people use "significant other" to refer, somewhat facetiously, to their spouse.

Sodomy: Usually, anal intercourse (penetration of the anus of one person by the penis of another) but sometimes also used to refer to oral intercourse (contact between the genitals of one person and the mouth of another).

Spousal equivalent: A term used by some people to designate one member of a couple who are living together as husband and wife, but who are not married. Sometimes also used by gay couples.

Stepparent: A person who is married to a child's biological parent. Marriage to a child's biological parent does not usually create the legal relationship of parent to the child. A stepparent becomes a child's legal parent through an official proceeding, such as adoption,

Surrogate mother: A woman who agrees to carry a child in her womb where the child is not biologically (genetically) her own. Usually, the embryo is created in the laboratory by fertilizing an egg from another woman with the sperm from a man. It is then implanted in the surrogate mother's womb and she carries the baby to term.

Wife: Legally, a woman who is married to a man. Some gay couples now use this term to refer to one partner, but marriages between persons of the same sex are not currently recognized by the law, except in one state. See "Husband" above.

INDEX

Abortion

    Contract and 248–249, 324–325

    History of 51–64, 67–68

    In documents 246, 316

    Information about 115, 241–245, 271–275

Abuse (of a partner – See also Child abuse and neglect, Elder abuse) 100, 140, 185–187

Adoption

    Information about 75–77, 120, 128, 196, 232, 262–263, 266–268, 280, 296, 305–314

    Putative or equitable 284–285

Advance directive (living will)

    In documents and checklists 591

    Information about 411, 419–421, 439, 588

Adultery 47, 73–76, 97, 100, 115, 124, 129, 186, 210–211, 227, 294, 325, 458–459, 461

Alimony (See Spousal support)

Annulment 71, 101, 130, 194, 206, 212–213, 220, 222–227

Arbitration and medication 30, 197, 359–362, 491, 494, 507, 524, 528, 532, 541, 547, 551, 564, 632,

Artificial insemination (See also Assisted reproduction) 294–298, 303

Assisted reproduction 293–304

Attorneys

    Dealing with and acting as your own 24–34, 129, 137, 184, 197, 286, 291–292, 309–312, 337, 345, 350, 442, 469, 491, 509, 510, 514, 520, 523, 526–528, 602–604, 621–622–629, 634, 636, 644

    In documents and other documents 572, 573, 574, 587, 597, 608

Bank accounts

    Criminal conduct and 518–519

    In divorces and other breakups 445–446, 448–449, 455, 458, 472, 474, 504–509, 512–516, 539, 543–545

    In documents and checklists 556–558, 562 et seq, 569 et seq, 597 et seq, 603–607, 613–617, 634 et seq, .641, 646, 651 et seq

    Information about 140, 145, 152–153, 159, 161–165, 166, 172, 176, 199–200, 218, 289, 324, 332, 335, 350, 355, 387, 396, 399, 407, 411, 414, 417, 420, 424 - 427, 439

    Offshore 343–345, 551

Bigamy 66–67, 387, 389–390,

Birth control

    History 37, 44, 51–58, 61, 64–65, 109, 115–117, 119,

    Information about 15, 125, 244, 269–271, 353, 357

    In documents 562 et seq, 576 et seq. 586 et seq.

Child abuse and neglect 21, 33, 44, 48, 183, 197, 206, 210, 232–238, 240–242, 251–260, 266–268

Child custody (See also Assisted reproduction, Paternity)

    Criminal law and 502–505, 529

    Contracts about 326, 357–358, 481–483, 490–494, 630–633

    Disputes over 503, 510, 513, 527, 530–532, 536–540, 551, 620–634

    Gay parents and 260–261

    In documents and checklists 578, 586, 618–629, 630–632, 634–653

    Information about 5, 11, 19–22, 53, 97, 113, 123, 132, 184, 193, 219, 225, 260, 268, 276–285, 298, 304, 308, 324, 326, 391, 395–396, 409, 456, 465, 485–494, 558

Child support

    Bankruptcy and 464

    Contracts about 246–248, 297, 326, 357–358, 481–483

    Disputes about 541–542

    In documents and checklists 571 et seq, 625,

    Information about 230–234, 243–246, 385–386, 389, 396, 451, 458 - 459, 477–498

Cohabitation (See also Cohabitation agreement, Inheritance, Retirement benefits)

    Adoption and 309

    Children and 91–93, 197, 261–262, 280, 294–295, 357, 395

    Criminal law and significant others 517–520

    Debts and 170–173, 176, 450–451

Different from marriage 136–138, 168–188, 197–201

Ending 146, 192–194. 498–506

Information about 35–37, 87–92, 136–146, 167–177

Inheritance and 466–470

Law and 17–18, 23, 66, 93–94, 188–189

Older couples and 423–426

Property and 138–144, 159–168, 439–444

Sociological facts 35–36, 67–68, 87–91

Well being and 98–101, 197

Cohabitation agreement

At the end of the relationship 449, 498–507, 520–521

Children and 284, 481–483

Enforcing 520, 640

Evidence about (See also Evidence) 542–548

Forms and checklists 556–581, 627–628, 634–636, 640–645

Gay couples and 125–128

Information about 4, 6–10, 145–146, 188–191, 317–366, 409–410

Jurisdiction over 19–20, 195–197

Representing yourself 30–31

Terminating 451

Common law marriage

Evidence of 213–214, 218, 535

In documents and checklists 611–615

Information about 69- 72, 147, 211–220, 388–389

Community property (See also Divorce, Inheritance, Real estate) 394, 396, 432, 453–456, 460, 462, 467, 469, 470–474, 535, 569

Covenant marriage 101–102, 194, 209–210, 559

Criminal conduct (in a relationship) 511–514

Debts 169–174, 473–477

Divorce (See also Assisted reproduction, Child support, Child custody, Spousal support)

Agreements about 8, 48–50, 73, 101, 139, 149, 324–326, 362, 456, 462–463, 465–466

Bigamy and 206–208, 389–390

Common law marriage and 211–213, 219–220, 386–387, 615–616, 647

Constitutional issues and 14

Court jurisdiction over 11–12, 19–24

Court procedures in 27–29, 193–194, 232, 344, 465–466, 484, 504–520, 531, 556, 561

Covenant marriage and 209–210

Debts and 169–171, 176, 463–464

Division of assets in 22–23, 71–73, 78, 141–142, 146, 148–154, 156, 168–169, 175, 199, 319–320 332–333, 337–338, 341, 445–460,

Domestic partnerships and 111–112

Evidence in (See also Evidence) 132, 550–551

"Friendly" 431–432

Grounds for 97, 122, 124, 269, 294–295, 332

History 36, 46–47, 48–50, 70, 72–74, 76–78, 82, 96–98

In documents and checklists 533, 571–574, 617–620, 634–640, 646

Information about 14, 19, 36, 96–98, 122, 194–196, 220–229, 199, 227–229, 234, 319–321, 377, 382, 393–394, 429

Prenuptial agreements and 137–139, 147, 316

Religion and (See also Covenant marriage) 100–101, 227–229, 394

Sexual conduct and 122, 124, 134, 186, 332, 462

Statistics about 35–36, 87–88, 90–91, 96, 99, 195

Wellbeing and 98–99, 197

Wills and 412–413, 423, 439, 480–481

Domestic partner 11, 23, 110–113, 135, 168–169, 178, 181, 188–190, 386, 425, 434, 439, 559–560, 583, 585

Duress 127, 224–226, 311, 437–438, 543, 548, 601, 608

Elder abuse 51, 287–289, 654

Embryos (See also Assisted reproduction) 300–301

Emotional abuse 187, 251, 459, 619

Equitable division of property 457–458, 462

Evidence 525–529, 636–646

Family legal disputes (See also Divorce, Child custody, Child support) 434–437, 654–655

Financial disclosure
    In documents and checklists 364, 365, 563, 570–578, 582, 587
    Information about 176, 188, 330–331, 339, 356, 395, 401–405, 409,

Fraud 154–157, 222–225, 327–333, 431–432

Grandparents 279–280, 284, 308, 428–430, 558

Guardianship 127, 179–180, 208–209, 270, 285–286, 290–291, 298, 411, 423–424, 426–427, 482–485, 539, 595, 603, 624, 655

Homosexuality
    Criminal law and 114–119
    Marriage and 106–109, 120–124,
    Rights of partners 110, 119–121, 124–128

Illegitimate children 76, 88–89, 236, 248–250, 267–268, 276–277, 281–282

Infertility (See Assisted reproduction) 122, 269–271, 303, 332, 376,

Inheritance (See Parents, Trusts, Wills) 5, 38, 77, 79, 108, 111, 122, 140, 150, 154, 169, 199, 206, 218, 249–251, 287, 294, 402, 412, 430, 432–433, 435–436, 438–439, 454, 462, 467–477, 598

Individual retirement accounts (See Bank accounts, Retirement benefits)

Impotence 332

Lesbians (See Homosexuality)

Living together (See Cohabitation)

Living will (See Advance directive)

Marriage (See also Bigamy, Common law marriage, Covenant marriage, Divorce)
    Current role in society 96–103
    Different from living together 137–199
    History of 35–83
    Same sex couples and 106–110

Wellbeing and 197

Marital agreements (See Prenuptial agreements, Cohabitation agreements)

Medicare and Medicaid 291, 430–432, 439, 597

Out of wedlock children (See Illegitimate children)

Palimony 143, 146, 190, 327–328, 384–385, 447, 506

Parents (See also Adoption, Assisted reproduction, Child abuse, Child custody, Child support, Inheritance, Paternity)
  Birth parents, identity of 29, 305, 307
  Children's obligations to 287–293, 432, 655
  Inheritance and 216, 287, 436, 473, 475
  Insurance and 478
  Legal status 5, 265–276
  Marriage of children and 38, 42, 81, 109, 204, 215, 223
  Obligations 10, 231–247
  Rights of 14–15, 179, 234–243, 263–284, 421, 481
  Same sex couples as 120–121, 129, 130, 134, 262, 283
  Termination of parental status 261–263
  Welfare of children and 42–45, 99, 198, 395, 408

Paternity (See also Assisted reproduction, Adoption, Child custody, Child support)
  In documents and checklists 614–624
  Information about 273–279, 285, 289

Pensions (See Retirement benefits)

Polyamory (See Polygamy)

Polygamy 64–66, 191–194

Powers of attorney
  In documents and checklists 587–600
  Information about 413–417, 420, 433

Prenuptial agreements (See also Cohabitation agreements) 316–340, 341–359, 456–457

Privacy